MOON HANDBOOKS

NEVADA

SCOTT SMITH

D0104818

Here's what people are saying about Moon:

MOON HANDBOOKS

". . . well-written and exceptionally
informative guides."

–THE NEW YORK TIMES

MOON METRO

". . . a sleek two-in-one blend of advice and
street maps."

–U.S. NEWS & WORLD REPORT

MOON OUTDOORS

". . . thoroughly researched, and packed full
of useful information and advice. These
guides really do get you into the outdoors."

–GORP.COM

MOON LIVING ABROAD

". . . provides well-rounded insight into the country and
its culture, and then gives you the real scoop on how to
make the best move."

–TRANSITIONS ABROAD

We want to hear from you, too.
Tell us what you have to say: feedback@moon.com

 HANDBOOKS | METRO | OUTDOORS | LIVING ABROAD

MOON HANDBOOKS

MAY 0 0 2011

NEVADA

SCOTT SMITH

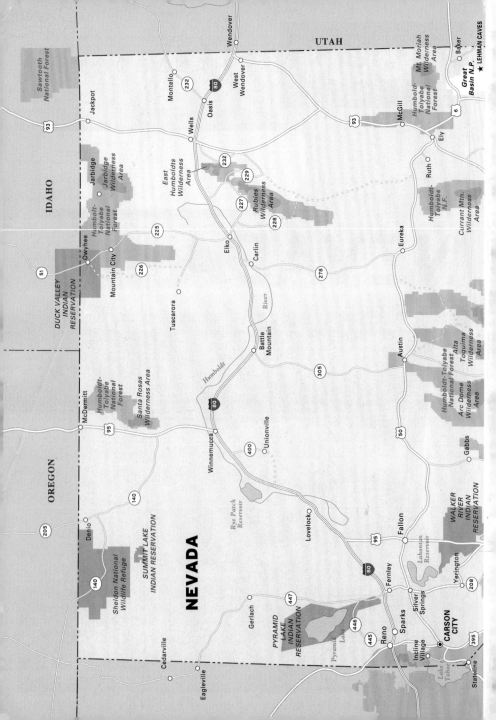

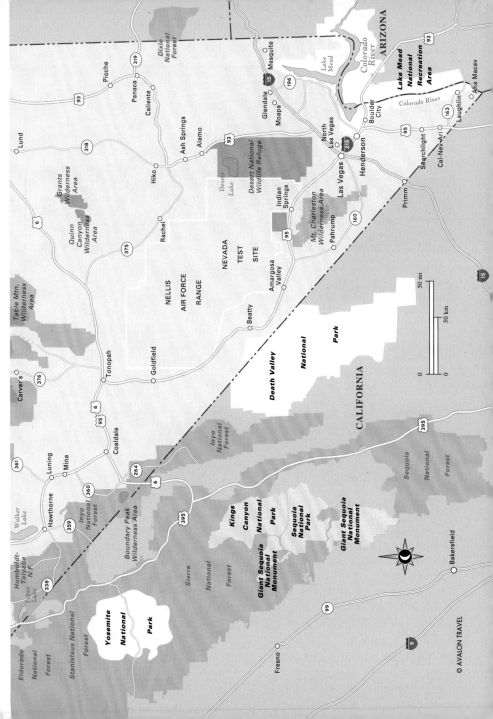

Contents

Discover Nevada

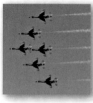

In 1855 prospectors in what would become Nevada scrabbled through the ubiquitous heavy blue-black sand to pluck a few scattered precious yellow nuggets at Gold Canyon. Only a few of those miners gave that troublesome sand a second look. Assays proved it to be rich silver ore, the harbinger of the great Comstock Lode. Those miners struck it rich.

You too will be rewarded for digging a little deeper into Nevada.

Hike in the cool pine forests of the Sierra Nevada. But also consider a more surreal landscape and wander amid the shadows of the sorrel shale slot canyons of Cathedral Gorge.

Soak in a therapeutic après-ski spa treatment in an ultramodern Lake Tahoe ski chalet. But dig a little deeper and you'll discover entrepreneurs have been exploiting the healing powers of these waters for 150 years. Mark Twain wrote about the baths at Steamboat Springs in 1863, where "the devil boils the water." Even earlier, the Washoe people journeyed to Tahoe for a welcome respite from the summer heat.

Enjoy trout almandine in a rustic-chic restaurant. But also explore hundreds of Carson and Truckee River tributaries in the backcountry, where you can cast a line and battle for your own cutthroat, rainbow, or brookie. The hard-won meal will be all the more satisfying.

Lose your inhibitions in Las Vegas, a microcosm where you can experience New York, Paris, the South Pacific, or ancient Rome, depending on which casino is offering the best deal for the weekend. In Sin City, a single hotel may house more restaurants and movie screens than your hometown. But there's more to it than bright lights and unchecked hedonism: Vegas has a burgeoning art scene and cuisine to rival any of the world's top cities. Nearby you can marvel at the engineering genius behind the design and construction of Hoover Dam, and venturing a little farther downriver, you'll find raining caves, surefooted bighorn sheep, and eagles enjoying the long dry winter.

For sin on a smaller scale, head to Reno, "The Biggest Little City in the World," but stay long enough to see beyond the poker tables and showgirls. Enjoy the small town that it really is – a town of studious coeds and industrious warehouse workers, a community like any other that enjoys homespun pleasures like balloon festivals and farmers markets.

Like tumbling dice, Nevada is multifaceted, an astonishing collection of contrasts, complexities, and challenges to conventional wisdom. Don't just scratch the surface; dig deeper. You'll realize that Nevada's true riches aren't hard to find.

Planning Your Trip

▶ WHERE TO GO

Las Vegas

Some 36 million visitors a year can't be wrong. Gambling is Nevada's lifeblood, and Vegas is the heart, pumping millions of dollars into the state's economy thanks to its irresistible lure. Las Vegas has a way of winning people over. Even nongamblers horrified at the thought of throwing away their hard-earned money often break down and slide $20 into a slot machine—hey, you never know, right? Even strict dieters simply *must* sample a seafood buffet. Wallflowers gyrate themselves into a lather under pulsing strobes. Dine, drink, dance, and double down, then do it all again tomorrow.

Reno

We know showgirls and Elvis impersonators live here too, but somehow Reno seems like a real town. Where Las Vegas is a gambling city, Reno is a city that has gambling. The Truckee River flows right through town, giving Reno a meandering, almost pastoral feel just a few blocks from the casinos. Still, upscale boutiques, more fine dining than you can experience in a month of Mother's Day celebrations, and yes, plenty of opportunities to venture a few dollars ensure that you never forget this is a real city—and this is Nevada.

Lake Tahoe and Vicinity

Aspen and Innsbruck have nothing on the Sierra Nevada resorts. Plentiful runs, from bunny slopes to the blackest of black diamonds, challenge all alpine skill levels. For all intents and purposes, Nevada began in nearby Virginia City, the state's first boomtown; here you can relive the 1850s, when the Comstock Lode created overnight silver millionaires. The pristine waters of Lake Tahoe and its rugged, tree-lined shoreline bear testament to nature's

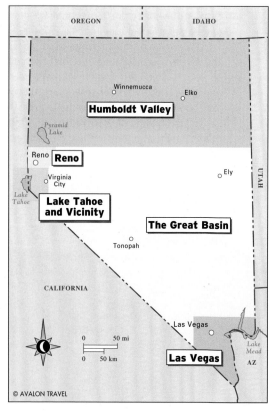

© AVALON TRAVEL

Towering trees and powder-perfect slopes entice skiers of all ability levels to Mount Rose, Reno's closest ski and snowboard resort.

ability to bounce back from humankind's exploitation.

Humboldt Valley

Northern Nevada's Humboldt River Valley is your high school geography and history lessons come to life—only more interesting. Sheer-faced Ruby Dome reigns from 11,000 feet, while Pyramid Lake, with its perfect triangular rock jutting through the placid surface, is one of the most beautiful desert waterways in the world. The Black Rock Desert, an expanse of playa at turns spiritually calm and eerily still, comes alive for a couple of weeks each year during the annual Burning Man festival to celebrate individuality, freedom of spirit, and whatever else the eclectic gatherers decide is important.

The Great Basin

Whereas much of Nevada panders to visitors'

Rail fans can ride the Virginia & Truckee Railroad's mine-to-mill route from Virginia City.

IF YOU HAVE . . .

- **ONE DAY:** Visit the Las Vegas Strip and Downtown.
- **THREE DAYS:** Add Red Rock Canyon and Mesquite.
- **ONE WEEK:** Add Great Basin National Park.
- **TWO WEEKS:** Add Reno, Lake Tahoe, and Virginia City.
- **THREE WEEKS:** Add Elko and Winnemucca.

transports visitors to a different world and a different age. This region is home to quintessential icons of the American West. Native American petroglyphs and boomtown relics shed light on the lives of our ancestors; sulfurous hot springs and the hauntingly beautiful formations at Lehman Caves take travelers even further back to primordial times when great ichthyosaurs patrolled the warm shallow seas and Columbian mammoths trod the desert sands. Perhaps it's this rich past that, if you believe the believers, drives restless spirits to haunt the historic landmarks of Ely, Austin, and Tonopah. Maybe it's this otherworldly landscape or the supersecret military tests at Area 51 that draw, depending on your point of view, extraterrestrial visitors or tinfoil hat–wearing conspiracy theorists.

desire to live fully in the moment, Nevada's Great Basin beckons those who want to step into the past. A visit to central Nevada

▶ WHEN TO GO

Ironically, the Lake Tahoe region's fabulous winter recreation makes the other three seasons a perfect time to visit. Similarly, the brutal (but dry) heat of southern Nevada is no reason to ignore Las Vegas when making summer vacation plans: The rooms are cheap, the blackjack odds never change, and the swimming pool is always open. Nevada in winter gives you the chance to shred the manicured slopes of the north or escape the bitter wind, with January daytime temperatures routinely reaching 60°F in the south.

Spring showers bring out Mojave Desert wildflowers, and the shad hatch entices hungry striped bass close to the shoreline at Lake Mead, while the crisp morning air invites hikers to explore the higher elevations. Summer means celebrations of ethnic traditions and history. Fall sees the baking heat in the south abate in time for family picnics, outdoor

concerts, and football, while northern Nevada sneaks in one more camping trip to the Ruby Mountains, a final bargain-hunting expedition among boutiques and antiques shops, and perhaps a dig through a few more bucketfuls of mud in search of the elusive fire opal.

If you're heading to Las Vegas and have some flexibility in your travel dates, keep in mind that the last two weeks in July, the first two weeks in August, and the period from after Thanksgiving to just before Christmas are the relatively slow seasons in Las Vegas. Hotel rooms are often so available that the hotels nearly bribe you to stay in them. Generally, it's a good idea to make a few calls to Las Vegas hotels or to the Las Vegas Convention and Visitors Authority (702/892-0711) *before* you make a final determination on the dates of your vacation to find out if there's a convention, event, or holiday then that will cause room rates to skyrocket.

The beauty of Lake Mead is revealed in this shot from a helicopter.

▶ BEFORE YOU GO

Las Vegas's McCarran International Airport is one of the busiest in the country, and Reno-Tahoe International knows a little something about handling visitors as well. Most air visitors will make use of one of these state-of-the-art facilities. However, the resort cities receive huge percentages of their clientele from California. Starting on Thursday nights, the eastbound traffic on I-80 and I-15 can be murder; it's more of the same in the other direction beginning on Sunday afternoon. Those visitors at least have the advantage of having their cars with them, a must for exploring beyond the resort corridors. However, the big cities are well provided with rental-car companies, and public transportation and taxis are easy to find.

You'll need copious amounts of sunscreen and water, but you can stock up when you get here. Summer nights in all but the highest elevations are mild. But in late fall, even when daytime highs flirt with 90°F, you'll often need a sweater when the sun goes down.

Nevada has a bit of a split personality when it comes to attire. Most restaurants are casual, but some—even in the most out-of-the-way places in the state—may require jackets. On the other hand, men often attend southern Nevada church services in shirt sleeves and even shorts. The trendy clubs usually enforce dress codes, most disallowing jeans, tank tops, and tennis shoes.

Explore Nevada

▶ LOST VEGAS WEEKEND

If you only have a few days to spend, don't mind a little sleep deprivation, and your bankroll and liver are up for a challenge, Vegas calls!

Day 1

Pay your bills, gather up what money's left, and fly into McCarran International Airport. Even if you arrive in the morning, you'll be itching to hit the tables right away. Get your gambling fix, then relax by the pool and regain your strength. Wear sunscreen, and go easy on the margaritas. Schedule a tour of Lake Mead, nestled startlingly on the desert floor, and Hoover Dam, the engineering marvel that created it, for the afternoon. Then it's time for a late dinner at Paris's Mon Ami Gabi, if you came with your sweetie, or Excalibur's Carnegie Deli if it's just you and the boys. There is only time for one headliner show on this trip, so make it Blue Man Group at the Venetian.

Day 2

Time for a slice of vintage Vegas, baby. Head downtown, stopping at Bonanza Gifts to stock up on Elvis sideburns and Sammy Davis Jr. sunglasses before fueling up with the Gamblers Special breakfast at the Binion's Café counter. Walk over to the Neon Boneyard, the final resting place of some of Las Vegas's iconic signage. And while you're in the neighborhood, witness

the Neon Boneyard

SKIING IN TAHOE

The first dusting of snow in late October sends Lake Tahoe residents scurrying for the ski wax and the mountain resorts fielding reservations calls. Most resorts open around Thanksgiving, but you can bet they'll be open any time an early cold front dumps a foot or so of the white stuff. But natural snow isn't a prerequisite for these resorts; when the temperature dips, they can make their own. Heavenly ski resort operates the most extensive snowmaking operation at Lake Tahoe, capable of layering two-thirds of its runs in the artificial stuff. Its machines can make enough snow in an hour to cover an acre 42 inches deep. The season lasts until temperatures rise so high the mountain can't sustain snow, around mid-April.

All the resorts in the region cater to all ski and snowboard skill levels, but each features slight differences that make them unique.

- **Mount Rose** is the closest ski area to Reno, and considering cost and variety of runs, it is perhaps the best overall resort on the Nevada side. With a base elevation of 8,260 feet, it's positively arctic at the top and chilly enough along the runs to keep the snow in optimal shape even when the sun beats down. Families will find something for everyone, with 43 runs evenly divided among beginner, intermediate, and expert. The 16 chutes — all black diamond or double diamond — are favorites for advanced snowboarders.

- **Diamond Peak** is more overtly family-oriented, with special touches for children such as private and group lessons, indoor and outdoor play areas, and all-day ski and day care packages.

- **Heavenly** is for the hard-core downhiller. More than one-third of the trails are rated for experts, and the more than 40 intermediate runs will challenge even the most proficient of alpine aficionados. The undulating, swaying blue runs are long and wide, perfect for snowboarders.

skiing at Lake Tahoe

the rise and fall of the Mafia in Las Vegas at the Museum of Organized Crime and Law Enforcement, aka the Mob Museum. Order the linguini and clams for dinner at Carluccio's Tivoli Gardens, which once belonged to piano maestro Liberace. Back at the hotel, change into your tux and beat it down to the Sahara. Order up a neat bourbon and watch Sinatra try to make it through "Luck Be a Lady" while Dino, Joey, and Sammy heckle and cut up from the wings in Sandy Hackett's Rat Pack Show.

Day 3

It's your last day in Vegas, so live like a high roller. After breakfast, go for a swim or a workout in the hotel's gym—you'll want to do justice to that silk shirt or micromini

at the club later tonight. Body rejuvenated, it's time to put a dent in the casino's quarterly profit statement. Use the basic optimal blackjack strategy. It's the best way to extend your bankroll, and you might double up if the cards fall your way. Bankroll rejuvenated, you won't feel bad about dropping a few bills at Caesars Palace's Forum Shops on a hot outfit for your night on the town. Never fear if it's a Tuesday: Celebrity knows no weeknights at Pure at Caesars Palace; its Tuesday parties are frequented by national and local stars (be prepared for a long line). Locals seem partial to Blush at Wynn and its themed Tuesday parties. Moon, high above the Palms, has plenty to look at, whether you're into cityscape, cheesecake, or beefcake.

▶ GREAT NEVADA ROAD TRIP

Nevada is too tall, wide, and diverse to fully experience it in one visit. But five days will give you a good feel for what makes the state special. If you have more time, consider

adding a few days in Las Vegas at the beginning of your trip. Even if Las Vegas glitz holds little charm for you, it boasts one of the world's most efficient airports, endless

the Las Vegas Strip: the most exciting skyline in the world

hotel rooms, and easy egress from the city, so consider it the starting point for your road trip.

Day 1

Heading out early from Las Vegas, drive 4.5 hours up I-93, the Great Basin Highway, to Great Basin National Park. Stop in Baker for picnic fixings, and eat at the idyllic area adjacent to the Lehman Caves visitors center. Spend the afternoon and evening exploring Nevada's only national park. The ranger-guided caves tour is a must. Drive the 12-mile scenic road around Wheeler Peak, then stretch your legs on the 0.3-mile Sky Island Forest Trail, which meanders through an isolated conifer forest. Have dinner and spend the night at the Silver Jack Inn. Relax under starry skies, burnished sunsets, and dramatic canyon vistas. If you have a day to spare, go on a snowshoe or cross-country ski photo safari in search of elk and antelope.

Day 2

Heading west on U.S. 50, "The Loneliest Road in America," for an hour brings you to Ely, the biggest city in east-central Nevada and home to the Nevada Northern Railway. Spend an hour in the museum and a couple more riding the 1905-vintage railcars powered by a steam locomotive. Lunch at the Red Apple, and save room for pie. Pick up I-93 north and drive two hours to I-80; turn west and go another hour to Elko, a town settled by Basques and buckaroos. Have a look at the Northeastern Nevada Museum, home to a mastodon and an extensive collection of Western art. Take an evening horseback ride and bunk down at the Pine Lodge, 20 miles southeast of Elko in Lamoille. A hearty breakfast fit for the cowpokes at this working cattle ranch is included.

The enamored can demonstrate their unbreakable commitment at Lovelock's Lovers Lock Plaza, dedicated on Valentine's Day 2006.

Day 3

Back on I-80 westbound for Reno, you'll enter Lovelock in about three hours. If you're traveling with your significant other, buy a decorative lock and attach it to the chain at Lovers Lock Plaza near the round courthouse. Throw away the key to show your love can never be undone. Back on the road, it's another 3.5 hours to Reno. After spending most of the day in the car, your legs will appreciate a stroll through the Riverwalk District along the fabled Truckee River. Browse the art galleries and dine at one of the riverside restaurants. Check into the Peppermill and find out if the tables are any more generous than they were back in Vegas.

Day 4

Take U.S. 395 south to Highway 341 and follow the signs to Virginia City and the heart of the Comstock Lode silver rush. Take a guided tour of Piper's Opera House, where

After sweating a bucket of blood in Comstock mines, many a miner retired here for a refreshing beverage.

Ulysses S. Grant, Mark Twain, Al Jolson, and other luminaries once graced the stage. Visit the *Territorial Enterprise* Museum and see the desk where Twain launched his writing career. Your nose will lead you to Virginia City Jerky & Smokehouse for a bodacious pulled pork sandwich with all the fixings. If there's time, see how miners worked with a tour of Chollar Mine. Then see how they diverted themselves with a cocktail and honky-tonk piano at the Bucket of Blood Saloon, dating to 1876. Dine at the Cider Factory; the main dining room was built in 1863 to manufacture cider and vinegar. Check into one of the 19 individually decorated rooms and lodges at the Gold Hill Hotel, the oldest in Nevada.

Day 5

Take Highways 341 and 431 to Incline Village on the shores of Lake Tahoe. If you're here in summer, mosey along the Tahoe Meadows Interpretive Trail, an easy 1.2-mile loop through imposing pines and gurgling creeks. Signs point out the abundant wildlife and plant life you might encounter. If you've come in winter, drive straight to Diamond Peak Ski Resort with 30 runs—half geared toward the intermediate skier and about one-third for advanced. After your last run of the day, stow your skis and walk across the parking lot at the bottom of the hill for perfectly smoked pork chops at Big Water Grille. Check into the Hyatt Regency Lake Tahoe, have the grilled buffalo tenderloin at Lone Eagle Grille, and let the hotel's Stillwater Spa ease you back into the 9-to-5 routine waiting at the end of your flight from Reno-Tahoe International Airport.

BURNING MAN

What started 25 years ago when Larry Harvey expressed himself by burning a human effigy in San Francisco as a dozen of his neo-hippie friends watched has evolved into a $10 million annual festival of individualism for 50,000 free spirits. Burning Man, the weeklong celebration in **Black Rock Desert,** is part avant-garde art show, part rebellion against commercialism and societal mores, part self-actualization, and whatever else each participant wants it to be.

The climax comes at the end of the week with the burning of the Man, a towering sculpture of a person. His immolation also represents something different for everyone in attendance. Perhaps it's a statement about the precariousness of life, or the futility of clinging to material possessions, or rebirth after destruction; or maybe it's just a really cool bonfire.

Whatever Burning Man is, it certainly has grown. In 1998 the gathering attracted an estimated 15,000 participants, and by 2010 there were 51,000. In recent years the community known as **Black Rock City** that springs up on the playa outside **Gerlach** is temporarily one of the 10 largest towns in Nevada. Huge art installations, bizarre art cars, ornate costumes, all-night music parties, lights everywhere and, of course, lots and lots of fire are the hallmarks of the party in the playa. So too are nudity, alcohol, and drugs.

Since no commerce is allowed except at the café and ice station, "burners" have to haul everything they need in and out with them, although everyone is encouraged to share with others. And there is a lot of infrastructure. The city is mapped out on arcs of streets in which theme camps and individual participants set up elaborately decorated sites. Black Rock City also has its own constabulary (the Black Rock Rangers), radio stations, daily newspapers, and village lamplighters as well as fire, emergency, and sanitation departments. Bicycles are the primary mode of transportation.

Still, taking the leap at Burning Man provides a lesson in survival: Scenes from the parched playa often resemble the film *Mad Max Beyond Thunderdome*. Everything and everyone is constantly covered in a thin brown coat of alkaline dust. Most participants carry dust masks and goggles with them at all times; dust storms blow through the city, knocking over tents and installations, without warning. Daytime temperatures can soar to over 100°F, and it has been known to freeze at night.

The event takes place on federal Bureau of Land Management land. There's a **hefty admission fee** ($220-360 in 2010), part of which goes to the Bureau of Land Management. Ticket prices increase throughout the year, so it pays to buy tickets well in advance.

Organizers promote the festival as an experiment in temporary community, where participants can shed the fetters of society and stretch the ordinary limits of life. They put a lot of effort into trying to make Burning Man a peaceful and safe experience; although police are present, citations are rare. Participants are required to take away everything they brought in, and volunteers stay for weeks to return the Black Rock Desert to its pristine condition. After a while, it's as though the event never took place... until next year.

Burning Man happens the week around Labor Day (late August-early September) outside Gerlach; check out **www.burningman.com.**

the playa in Black Rock Desert

▶ TIME TRAVEL

History almost back to the dawn of time is visible in Nevada. Dinosaurs dating back millions of years, primordial reptiles, and ancient mammals roamed and swam throughout the state during the Triassic and glacial Pleistocene eras. Several Nevada sites preserve their remains, and a few Nevada locations provide homes for the prehistoric creatures' descendants. People came to the area about 12,000 years ago, and relics from these civilizations provide striking insight into the lives of our ancestors. Travel the state and discover another side—and another time— of Nevada.

Day 1

Start your exploration of Nevada's ancient history at Las Vegas's Nevada State Museum & Historical Society, southern Nevada's only nationally accredited museum. See the remains of an ichthyosaur, a marine reptile that prowled Nevada's shallow sea 200 million years ago and the official state fossil. The ichthyosaur shares its home with the eons-younger woolly Columbian mammoth.

Not far away is the Marjorie Barrick Museum at the University of Nevada, Las Vegas. Its collections introduce visitors to pre-Columbian civilizations in Nevada, the Southwestern United States, and Mesoamerica. Adults as well as children will be enthralled by the museum's "archaeology dig" in the lobby. Kids can unearth buried relics and make artifact rubbings.

Continue your dig into Nevada's past at the Las Vegas Natural History Museum, where kids can dig for fossils and see a paleontology laboratory. Beasts from the area are featured, and the museum has a collection of

Valley of Fire State Park is one of dozens of petroglyph sites throughout Nevada.

dinosaurs from around the world, including a 35-foot-long roaring animatronic *T. rex.*

Days 2-3

A paddle down the Colorado River cures museum burnout while keeping the education coming. During your float down the river, stop for hot spring soaks, slot canyon hikes, and cave explorations, coming across Anasazi petroglyphs at Boy Scout Canyon on the Nevada side and Petroglyph Wash on the Arizona bank. Fully exploring the 13-mile stretch of river to Willow Beach, 2,500 years ago a Native American trading post, will take at least two days. Pack a tent, sleeping bags, and food in your canoe, and camp along the tranquil riverbank.

Day 4

Anasazi ("Ancient Ones") Indians lived in southern Nevada about 300 B.C.–A.D. 1150, farming the valley and leaving their mark through petroglyphs. Though the arid region around Valley of Fire State Park precluded the Anasazi living or farming there, the Indians considered the place sacred. They came here not only to hold religious rites and marvel at the valley's iron-stained rock walls but also probably to hunt and gather native food-bearing plants. Mouse's Tank and Atlatl Rock have particularly stunning examples of petroglyphs.

A half-day visit to Valley of Fire will reignite your interest in Nevada's ancient people and leave enough time to get to Overton, 45 minutes via I-15. Spend the rest of the day at the Lost City Museum, with its Pueblo artifacts that include an entire ancient village. Why the Anasazi abandoned the city a thousand years ago is unclear; there are no signs of war, natural disaster, or disease among the ruins. Continue to Mesquite to dine and overnight at the Casablanca Casino.

Day 5

Nevada's vastness and sparseness are evident today on a 6.5-hour drive through central Nevada. You'll skirt the Nellis Air Force Base bombing and gunnery range, home to the infamous Area 51. Keep your eyes peeled for experimental (and alien) aircraft. Stop for lunch and pick up some out-of-this-world souvenirs at the Little A-Le-Inn in Rachel. Take a room at the El Capitan Resort & Casino in Hawthorne, a town founded on explosives. The Hawthorne Ordnance Museum and Mineral County Museum celebrate the town's U.S. Navy Ammunition Depot and its role in the country's history.

Day 6

Drive to Berlin-Ichthyosaur State Park in Ione and take the tour of ichthyosaur excavation sites. More than 40 huge sea serpent fossils have been uncovered here. Interpretive

Ichthyosaurs were king of the warm, shallow sea that covered Nevada during the Mesozoic Age.

Pyramid Lake's namesake outcropping rises serenely from the cornflower blue water.

displays tell of the creatures' habitat, food sources, and more. After a half-day at the park, continue west to Carson City and get a room at the Carson Nugget before savoring wonton shrimp at Garibaldi's.

Day 7

Belly up to the counter for old fashioned bacon and eggs at the Crackerbox before hitting the Carson City version of the Nevada State Museum. Its specialty is prehistory; the Changing Earth exhibit shows how the world changed during the period from 1.7 billion to 40 million years ago, and the museum also shows the biggest Columbian mammoth you'll ever see. Spend the rest of your last day at Pyramid Lake, what remains of a vast glacial lake that covered northern Nevada 20,000 years ago. There's not much evidence of it now, but back then, at the end of the Pleistocene period, mammoths, giant sloths, cheetahs, and even camels lived here. The cui-ui fish, whose ancestors date to this last ice age, lives only in Pyramid Lake.

▶ THE LONELIEST ROAD

Twenty-five years ago central Nevada was a vacuum, as dark and mysterious as outer space—at least according to *Life* magazine and its source from AAA. Only those "confident of their survival skills"—the Chuck Yeagers and Buck Rogers of the vacation universe—should attempt to traverse the void between Ely and Fernley. Today's road-trippers prove the magazine was wrong. U.S. 50, which *Life* called "The Loneliest Road in America," remains a road to discovery for the mind and a path to freedom for the spirit.

Great Basin National Park

At 13,000 feet above sea level, Wheeler Peak greets visitors entering Nevada from the east. The snow-dusted behemoth in Great Basin National Park convincingly rebuts arguments

Wheeler Peak, Great Basin National Park

SMALL-TOWN CHARM

With just four metropolitan areas with populations over 200,000, Nevada is virtually all small towns. For visitors, that means neighborly hospitality, home-style cooking, fenceless wilderness, and live-and-let-live sensibilities. So kick your shoes off at the state line and take a load off your mind in small-town Nevada:

- **Elko** invites visitors to enjoy the view at the end of a hike in the Ruby Mountains, a lunker pulled from a Lamoille Canyon stream, or a well-turned phrase at the National Cowboy Poetry Gathering.

- **Hawthorne** has been supporting our troops since long before yellow-ribbon bumper stickers, with a patriotism rooted in the townsfolk's appreciation of their sacrifices.

- **Pioche** offers a community park as unassuming as the town's residents. It includes a target-shooting range, a motorcycle course, a lassoing field, and a nine-hole golf course built and maintained by volunteers.

- **Winnemucca** was there at the birth of Nevada's hospitality industry in the 1850s,

when entrepreneurs established trading posts, ferries, and other businesses to cater to travelers along the Humboldt Trail. Today visitors still come here in search of fiery opals, messes of crappie, and peace of mind.

- **Ely** is a microcosm of Nevada history, from ancient Native American populations to the Pony Express and the mining and railroad days. It's a great base for exploring Great Basin National Park.

farmland and desert in the town of Elko

that Nevada is one vast desert with intermittent outposts of neon.

Ely (70 miles)

Seventy miles west of Great Basin National Park on the Loneliest Road, Ely rewards intrepid souls with myriad treasures: semiprecious trinkets from Garnet Hill, monstrous brown trout lurking in Cave Lake, and the romance of the railroad, the gold mine, and the Pony Express.

Eureka (78 miles)

Another hour (78 miles) west, you'll reach Eureka. The town's Opera House and courthouse, both built in 1880, are still in use, a testament to Nevadans' heartiness, resilience, and frugality.

Austin (70 miles)

Back on the westward trail, Austin looms 70 miles ahead through ranchland, abandoned mines, and narrow mountain passes. Tucked into a valley in the northern Toiyabe Range, Austin is to mountain biking what Lake Tahoe is to skiing. Get your tires wet on the Castle Loop Trail, a 4.5-mile tasting menu of climbs, descents, and curves beginning and ending at the town park. As you gain experience, the trails around Austin and the Toiyabe, Shoshone, and Toquima Ranges toss up longer, tougher, and more exhilarating challenges.

Diversion to Berlin-Ichthyosaur State Park (91 miles)

Here's a good place to venture off the highway,

south through Smith Creek Valley. If U.S. 50 is lonely, Highway 722 and National Forest Road 060 are positively solitary, but the views are worth it. And the destination—Berlin-Ichthyosaur State Park—will reward your determination. Berlin sits only 60 miles from Austin, but the teeth-rattling terrain makes the travel time nearly two hours. Make sure you veer left onto Forest Road 060 at Peterson Station. The old mining town appears to have been well preserved, requiring only another silver strike nearby to pick up right where it left off in the 1870s. Head back to the main drag, a tedious hour (31 miles) northward on Snakebite Road, portions of which are unpaved, via Ione. You'll hit U.S. 50 at Eastgate.

Fallon (55 miles)

It's 55 miles west to Fallon, home to migratory birds and war birds, all-terrain vehicles, and ancient art. Hawks, loons, pelicans, egrets, and 140 other species stop at the waters around Fallon in the spring, while F-18 and F-14 pilots can be spotted on the wing year-round.

Dayton (50 miles)

Dayton, 50 miles ahead, is as picturesque as its location near Gold Canyon Creek amid the Pine Nut Mountains and the Flowery Range would suggest. Dayton is a county fair every day, inviting visitors to slow down, enjoy a camel- or horse-drawn carriage ride, and play a leisurely round of golf. It's also the gateway to the much less lonely destinations of Virginia City, Reno, Carson City, and Lake Tahoe, where hot tubs and massage tables await your weary muscles.

► ON THE TREASURE TRAIL

Many of Nevada's treasures are aesthetic and historical, but more than a few are tangible—and convertible to cold hard cash. Nevada is the Silver State, and since silver is found almost exclusively in ore form, it can only be obtained through hard-rock mining—not an option for the amateur treasure hunter or rock hound. But Nevada is generous with her valuables, from turquoise, garnet, and other semiprecious stones to the stuff from which wealth fantasies are made: fire opals and gold nuggets as rare and rewarding as a royal flush.

Gold

The glint at the bottom of the pan and the sparkling vein on the shaft wall have lured argonauts to northern Nevada for more than 150 years. Today, only South Africa and Australia disgorge more gold than Nevada. Almost all Nevada's gold is in lode form, extracted from deep underground using massive hard-rock

a gold nugget

mining equipment. But with a good metal detector, you can literally pick up a valuable memento of Nevada. And with gold selling for $1,400 per ounce, "nugget shooting" can be a very lucrative hobby.

Mountain runoff and ancient glaciers

deposited placer nuggets in Nevada's dry washes and fast-running streams. To get your hands on some, venture 50 miles north of Lovelock past the Rye Patch Reservoir dam to the Rye Patch or Majuba placer district, which is dotted with mining claims. Like their 19th-century counterparts, modern-day prospectors and law enforcement do not look kindly on claim jumpers, even if the trespassing is unintentional. Respect all claims.

Large-scale gold mining is big business in Nevada, and Newmont Gold Company is one of the largest private-sector employers in the state. It owns mines throughout the world, and its operations along the Carlin Trend in Eureka County have found more than 50 million ounces of gold. Newmont offers public tours on the second Tuesday of each month April–October. You can see how the company extracts gold ore from its open-pit mines and then processes and refines it. Visitors are bused to the mine from the Northeastern Nevada Museum in Elko. Space is limited; reserve at 775/778-4068.

Opals

The miraculous primordial forces of heat, pressure, and volcanic eruption transformed common silica in what is today Nevada's Virgin Valley into brilliant fire opals. Millions of years of geologic upheaval pushed these ebony, blue, green, and peach gems near the surface, just waiting for someone to free them from their clay prisons. Commercial mines and hundreds of claims continue to uncover them. To get in on the action, visit the Peacock or Bonanza Mines in Denio, just south of the Oregon state line in north-western Nevada. For a daily fee of about $60, they'll set you up at the diggings and turn you loose—and you can keep what you find.

Meteorites

Not nearly as beautiful as gold nuggets or

a large specimen of uncut opal

light-capturing fire opals, meteorites nevertheless are quite valuable, commanding $30–100 per ounce. Meteorites fall all over Nevada—indeed, all over the world—but are often overlooked. Nevada is an ideal location to metal-detect for meteorites (gold detectors have the sensitivity required for productive hunts). Its arid climate means the otherworldly treasures don't deteriorate rapidly; the state's vast expanses—especially its big dry lake beds with little or no vegetation—make for happy hunting grounds. Roach Dry Lake near Jean and several other sites in southern Nevada are good places to start as they're near a known "strewn field" where meteorite fragments rained down in the last century. Weather forces and continual cosmic pelting constantly replenish the spots for searchers.

Novices may not recognize a meteorite when they find one. They're often dark brown or black—like a lot of the rocks found in the Nevada desert. You may have a meteorite if it feels heavy for its size, attracts a magnet, and seems to have "crust" formed by friction as it entered the earth's atmosphere. Also check out any rock that looks out of place among its neighbors.

Other Gems

Variety, accessibility, and quantity of specimens makes Nevada a rock hound's paradise. Nevada's turquoise regions are all mined aggressively, leaving only crumbs for collector hobbyists. Still, you might be able to scoop up a few aqua chips 20 miles north of Tonopah at the old Crow Springs stagecoach stop. Look below the mines in the washes and arroyos. Even if you don't find turquoise, you're sure to locate some clear, glassy, and poignantly named Apache tears.

Find different but just as distinctive shades of blue and green in the copper ore deposits near the Cold Springs Valley exit off U.S. 395 north of Reno. Malachite, brochantite, and chrysocolla all make appearances.

Seven miles west of Ely, Garnet Hill yields its namesake gemstones with colors ranging from rose to maple. Break apart clumps of rhyolite to discover the garnets, often encrusted in chunks of quartz, making for interesting specimens.

For an exhaustive listing and directions to Nevada's other gemstone sites, consult James R. Mitchell's *Gem Trails of Nevada.*

LAS VEGAS

Pack your dancing shoes, your hiking boots, and your flip flops, but leave your sensible shoes at home. Las Vegas is where New Year's resolutions come to die. From the first glimpse of neon glowing in the middle of the empty desert, Las Vegas seduces the senses and indulges your appetites. An oasis of flashing marquees, endless buffets, feathered showgirls, chiming slot machines, and grand re-creations, the city surrounds visitors—all 35 million of them each year—as a monument to fantasy. Here, you can stroll the streets of Paris, float down a Venetian canal, lie on a tropical beach, soak up Rat Pack swank, and most of all dream that tremendous riches are a slot pull away.

After a brief attempt to pawn itself off as a family destination, the Neon Jungle has stepped into its sequins, ordered a Jäger Bomb, and hollered, "Hit me, baby!" But no one back home has to know you've succumbed to Vegas's siren song. After all, "What happens in Vegas . . . "

With odds overwhelmingly favoring the house, jackpot dreams may be just that—dreams. The slim chance at fortune is powerful enough to have lured vacationers into the southern Nevada desert for more than 75 years, ever since the Silver State legalized gambling in 1931. At first, the cowboy casinos that dotted downtown's Fremont Street were the center of the action, but they soon faced competition from a resort corridor blooming to the south on Highway 91. Los Angeles nightclub owner Billy Wilkerson dubbed it "The Strip" after his city's Sunset Strip, and together with Bugsy Siegel built the Flamingo, the first upscale alternative

RYAN JERZ

HIGHLIGHTS

LOOK FOR (TO FIND RECOMMENDED
SIGHTS, ACTIVITIES, DINING, AND LODGING.

(**Caesars Palace:** Las Vegas is an apt heir to the regality and decadence of ancient Rome, and Caesars Palace carries on the empire's excesses with over-the-top statuary, testosterone-dripping centurions, toga-clad cocktail servers, gluttony-inducing restaurants, endless jugs of wine, and dancing till dawn (page 44).

(**Fremont Street Experience:** Part music video, part history lesson, the six-minute shows presented in "Viva Vision" – a four-block-long, 12-million-diode, 550,000-watt sensory overload – are the star of this downtown Las Vegas promenade. Caricature artists and strolling musicians add to the street fair atmosphere (page 57).

(**Gondola Rides:** Just like the real Grand Canal, only cleaner, the Venetian's waterway meanders beside quaint shops, under intricate frescoes, and along the Las Vegas Strip. Gondoliers singing Italian ballads provide the soundtrack (page 60).

(**Secret Garden and Dolphin Habitat:** Trainers and caretakers don't put on shows with the big cats and marine mammals at the Mirage's twin habitats, but the tigers, lions, and leopards can often be seen playing impromptu games, wrestling, and cavorting in the water, and the bottlenose dolphins can never seem to resist the spotlight (page 61).

(**Las Vegas Springs Preserve:** Natural springs attracted early Native Americans and inspired visiting Mormons to establish a settlement here. Las Vegas's birthplace now displays the area's geological, anthropological, and cultural history along with what very well might be its future: water-conserving landscaping, solar and wind energy, and other "green" initiatives (page 63).

(**Atomic Testing Museum:** Commemorating Las Vegas's unique position as the almost literal ground zero of the atomic age, the museum celebrates the science and technology of nuclear power while also taking a sobering look at its sometimes dreadful consequences (page 63).

(**Jubilee!** The showgirl has outlived the mob, the Rat Pack, and the Stardust. This show at Bally's pays tribute to one of Las Vegas's most enduring icons in all her sequined statuesque grandeur. Dozens of feathered femmes fatales strut their way through intricate production numbers amid juggling, contortionist, and aerial acts (page 66).

to frontier gambling halls. Their vision left a legacy that came to define Las Vegas hotel-casinos. This shift to "carpet joints," as opposed to the sawdust-covered gambling floors of frontier Las Vegas, was only one of the many reinventions Las Vegas has gone through—from city of sleaze to Mafia haven, family destination, and finally upscale resort town—each leaving its mark even as the next change takes hold.

Today each megaresort offers more to do than many a small town. Under one roof you can indulge in a five-star dinner, attend spectacular productions, dance until dawn with the beautiful people, and browse in designer boutiques. If there's still time you can get a massage and ride a roller coaster too. The buffet, a fitting metaphor for this city with an abundance of everything, still rules in the hearts of many regulars and visitors, but an influx of celebrity chefs is turning the town into a one-stop marketplace of the world's top names in dining. Similarly, cutting-edge performers such as Blue Man Group and Cirque du Soleil have taken up residence alongside such beloved showroom fixtures as Elvis impersonators and *Jubilee!* These hip offerings are drawing a younger, more stylish crowd that harks back to the swinging '60s, when Las Vegas was a pure adult recreation and celebrity magnet.

Some say Old Vegas is as hard to find as a game of single-deck blackjack. It's true that you can no longer have your picture taken in front of Binion's million-dollar display, but the King and the Rat Pack can still be found in

❨ Red Rock Canyon: Every bit as vibrant as the Strip's neon, the canyon's coral, amber, maroon, and eggshell sandstone beckons visitors to this outdoor paradise. Scramble up the rusty rock faces and strewn boulders, or enjoy a restful stroll through a verdant canyon (page 75).

❨ River Tours: Motorized rafts give riders a trout's-eye view of the Colorado River as it rolls through Black Canyon downstream from Hoover Dam. Guides lead rafters through slot canyons to hot springs and bracing wading

pools. On the other side of the dam, the Desert Princess plies the waters of Lake Mead, coming within a few dozen feet of the dam wall and exploring peaceful coves (page 120).

❨ Lost City Museum: The ancient Anasazi people inexplicably abandoned this settlement in Overton, leaving behind a pit house and pueblo dwellings. The museum building houses Native American artifacts excavated from various sites in southern Nevada, many of which are now under the waters of Lake Mead (page 123).

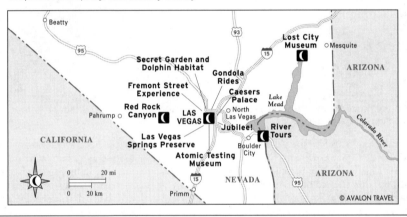

impersonators and tribute shows, torch singers still croon in low-lit lounges, and showgirls still prance in sequined headdresses (and little else).

That's not to say the city wholeheartedly relishes its reputation as Sin City. Downtown's art district, Broadway productions, gourmet restaurants, and a few top-notch kids' attractions balance sin with sophistication and sanity. And despite the go-go reputation, Las Vegas really is a small city surrounded by idyllic retreats and world-class recreational activities.

Lounge beside a gurgling snowmelt stream on Mount Charleston and feel last night's hangover wash away. Skim across Lake Mead on a rented Jet Ski, and soon you'll forget all about that bad beat at the hold 'em table.

Gaze at mesmerizing Red Rock Canyon long enough, and your swivel-hipped karaoke rendition of "Viva Las Vegas" seems almost résumé-worthy.

HISTORY

Hearths, arrow points, tools, and scarred and charred animal bones found near Tule Springs suggest nomadic peoples traveled through the Las Vegas Valley up to 11,000 years ago. A dearth of water made the area uninhabitable from about 7000 B.C. to 3000 B.C., but after 2500 B.C. the climate changed to nearly what it is today: cool and damp enough, relatively speaking, to support an Anasazi civilization throughout the Archaic or Desert period. Humans have been here ever since.

The Las Vegas Springs Preserve recreates the townsite auction that created the future gambling capital of the world.

Franciscan friars Silvestre Vélez de Escalante and Francisco Garcés were the first Europeans to visit what would later become the Las Vegas area, but they showed little interest in exploring the region. It took another 50 years before fur trader Jedediah Smith and his party came through, and 20 more years before legendary surveyor and cartographer for the Army Topographical Corps, John C. Frémont, passed through the Las Vegas Valley. By then Las Vegas already was an established camping spot along the Old Spanish Trail. By 1854 this section of the Old Spanish Trail from central Utah to Los Angeles had been tamed by Mormon guides and wagon trains.

A contingent of Latter Day Saints established the first Las Vegas town site in 1855, building a fort, irrigation canals, and farms. Though hardships, lack of supplies, and conflicts with area miners drove the Mormons to abandon the settlement within a few years, Las Vegas wasn't empty for long. Even before transcontinental railroad travel made the town easily accessible, it boasted 1,500 residents and a

thriving economy. In April 1905, with the start of regular through service, the San Pedro, Los Angeles, and Salt Lake Railroad organized the Las Vegas Land and Water Company and platted and built a 40-block downtown. Demand exploded, and a hasty two-day auction sold all the lots. Brothels and gambling dens, along with more "mainstream" businesses, went up virtually overnight, and Las Vegas was on its way. Floods, fires, social upheaval, labor unrest, and political conflict slowed but could not stop the little railroad city.

When the Union Pacific closed its Las Vegas repair shops—a major employer—and the Great Depression hammered the state a few years later, Las Vegas's future seemed to be in limbo. Victorian values lost the battle with economic reality, and the city found itself perfectly positioned to lure libertine thrill-seekers with money to spend. Booze ran freely, divorce laws were liberalized, prizefights were staged, prostitution was more or less accepted, and, of course, gambling became legal.

The Boulder Dam project in Las Vegas's

backyard created an instant middle class and helped pull the city out of the Great Depression. World War II stimulated local industry and ensured prosperity for the next 25 years.

Organized crime's hammerlock on the Las Vegas casino industry in the postwar years is well documented. While old-timers still speak wistfully of those days, the Mafia's blatant flaunting of its control of the city tarnished Las Vegas and the gambling industry. Federal government pressure and a few influential muckrakers brought a renewed effort to break Las Vegas free of the mob's clutches. The organized crime era began to wane with the arrival of Howard Hughes. The quirky billionaire bought up a huge segment of the casino industry, transforming it from the seedy domain of guys named Lefty, Bugsy, and Lucky into a legitimate—even glamorous—business.

Since then, for better or for worse, entrepreneurs and accountants rather than gamblers and mobsters, have run Las Vegas. Sophistication, opulence, and indulgence are now the watchwords in the city's casinos.

PLANNING YOUR TIME

Southern Californians have weekend visits to Las Vegas down to a science. If you only have a few days to spend, follow in their footsteps. Head straight to **The Strip**—a moderately priced resort is a fine option, as long as it makes up in location for what it may lack in dining, nightlife, and fancy-shmancy amenities. Soak up the Vegas vibe with intense gambling sessions, lavish shows, and soul-thumping clubs by night, followed by rejuvenating spa treatments and poolside lounging by day.

If you have more than a couple of days, mix in a little exercise: biking through **Red Rock Canyon,** hiking an alpine trail at **Mount Charleston,** or paddling through **Black Canyon** on the Colorado River. Better yet, rent a houseboat at **Lake Mead** and see the basin's sheer walls and colorful mineral-stained boulders in style. The lake's deep, wide bays and inlets offer boaters access to slot canyons, backcountry camping sites, and secret fishing holes. Marinas within the Lake Mead National

Recreation Area and the stores in Boulder City and Overton have all the supplies you'll need.

If you've chosen the Overton Arm of Lake Mead, don't miss the **Lost City Museum,** where you'll learn about the Anasazi people, the valley's first residents. Or continue on to **Virgin Canyon** near Mesquite. The Virgin is Nevada's last wild river, and the gorge carved by its raging waters abounds in recreational activities.

If you opted for the Boulder Basin, of course you'll visit **Hoover Dam.** The best view is from the recently completed bypass bridge, just downstream. Park at the bridge and stroll across (there's a protected pedestrian walkway), learning about the arch bridge's fascinating construction process and taking full advantage of its dam photo ops. A tour of the dam and visitors center make for an afternoon well spent.

Choosing Accommodations

The most important considerations when planning your visit to Vegas are when to go and where to stay. Las Vegas boasts more than 100 hotels and 200 motels, but sometimes that makes it harder, not easier, to choose the perfect place to stay. Also keep in mind that accommodations either sell out or nearly sell out every weekend of the year. Long weekends and holidays, especially New Year's Eve, Valentine's Day, Memorial Day, Fourth of July, Labor Day, and Thanksgiving, along with international holidays such as Cinco de Mayo, Mexican Independence Day, and Chinese New Year, are sold out weeks in advance. Special events such as concerts, title fights, the Super Bowl, the Final Four, NASCAR Weekend, and the National Finals Rodeo are sold out months in advance. Reservations are made for the biggest conventions (Consumer Electronics, Men's Apparel, and so on) a year ahead of time.

Those 125,000 rooms fill up fast—especially the top hotels, the best-value hotels, and the cheapest motels. What's more, the crowds are relentless; Las Vegas rarely gets a break to catch its breath. There are some minor quiet times, such as the three weeks before Christmas and a noticeable downward blip in July–August when the mercury doesn't see fit to drop below 90°F.

Also, Sunday–Thursday—when there aren't any large conventions or sporting events—are a little less crazy than usual; almost all the room packages and deep discounts are only available on these days.

If you're just coming for the weekend, keep in mind that most of the major hotels don't even let you check in on a Saturday night. You can stay Friday and Saturday, but not Saturday alone.

No two people pay the same amount for a seat on the same airline, and no two people pay the same amount for a hotel room in Las Vegas. If you have to call the hotel reservations desk for your room, you'll pay top dollar, if you can even get a room. That's because the hotel reservations departments are set up to charge the rack rate, one of the most expensive room rates used. Probably the most expensive rate is the convention rate—never tell a hotel reservations agent that you're coming for a convention.

Shop around. Casino profits continue to subsidize the other revenue-producing departments, so Las Vegas hotels can afford to discount their rooms up to a whopping 80 percent at times. Also, most Las Vegas hotels have a variety of rooms at different rates. At the older places, two classes of rooms are typical: low-rise motel-style rooms, and the more expensive "tower" rooms in newer high-rises. Some offer mini suites and suites for higher prices. It never hurts to ask for better rates.

When making reservations, it's time well spent to scour the Internet for bargains and call around—not only to compare prices but to find out if something is going on in town during the time you're planning your trip; special events can make room rates skyrocket. Las Vegas hotel room rates change minute to minute, and the range of rates can be spectacular. A standard room that goes for $300 per night during huge conventions might be available for $40 per night on some midweek dates starting a week later. You might also try an online reservations service, such as www.vegas.com.

Discounts on rooms can often be obtained by finding a good "package," either one that the hotel itself is offering, one that a tour-and-travel packager has put together, or one that a travel wholesaler is advertising. Look for package deals, often airfare plus a room but sometimes a room only, advertised in the Sunday travel supplement of big-city newspapers. Travel clubs, such as the Entertainment Book, often contain 50-percent-off coupons for Las Vegas hotel rooms. Other discounts might be offered by the hotel for corporate affiliations, AAA, members of the military, or seniors.

Once you're ready to make a reservation, you have several options. There are four or five different departments within the hotel as well as a number of outside agents that are allocated rooms to sell (or give away); depending on whom you book your room through, your rate can range from free-room comps issued by the casino to top dollar for last-minute reservations through the front desk.

In Las Vegas, the best way to get deep discounts is to stay where you play. If you play table games with an average bet of at least $25, you should be able to get the "casino rate," a 40–50 percent discount off the rack rate for the room (except for the high-roller casinos, such as Caesars, Mirage, the Venetian, Bellagio, and MGM Grand, where an average bet of $50–100 is often required). If you play slots or video poker, it behooves you to join the slot club at the casino that sees most of your action. The more slot-club points you accumulate in your account, the more free rooms and other free stuff you get.

Of course, your room is where you'll spend the least amount of time during your stay in Las Vegas, so remember the old travelers' axiom: Eat sweet, pay for play, but sleep cheap. Otherwise, as always, it's best to make your room reservations far in advance to ensure the appropriate type, price, and location.

ORIENTATION

The most famous and flamboyant resort city in the world spreads out over a small, harsh low-desert valley in an unlikely corner of the U.S. Southwest. It's hard to imagine a less welcoming climate and terrain for a resort, yet 3 million visitors each month and another 2 million locals wouldn't have it any other way. Sitting as it does in the middle of the minor Mojave Desert, with

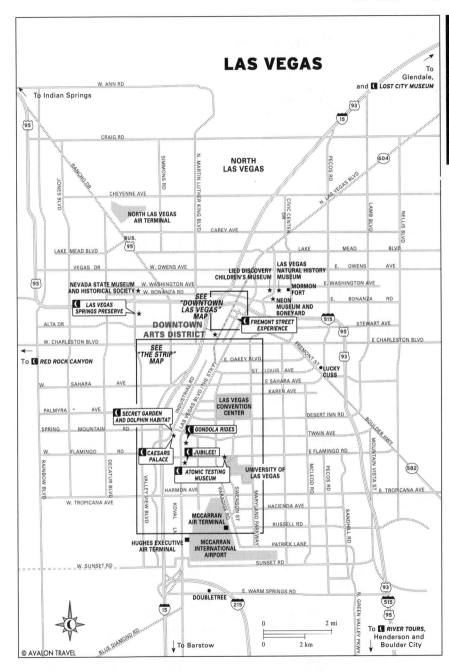

LAS VEGAS

To Glendale, and ☾ *LOST CITY MUSEUM*

To Indian Springs

W. ANN RD

95

CRAIG RD

NORTH LAS VEGAS

RANCHO DR

JONES BLVD

SIMMONS RD

N. MARTIN LUTHER KING BLVD

PECOS RD

N. LAS VEGAS BLVD

LAMB BLVD

NELLIS BLVD

604

CHEYENNE AVE

NORTH LAS VEGAS AIR TERMINAL

CIVIC CENTER DR

CAREY AVE

BUS. 95

LAKE MEAD BLVD

LAKE   MEAD   BLVD

VEGAS DR

W. OWENS AVE

E.   OWENS   AVE

95

NEVADA STATE MUSEUM AND HISTORICAL SOCIETY ★

W. WASHINGTON AVE

W. BONANZA RD

LIED DISCOVERY CHILDREN'S MUSEUM

LAS VEGAS NATURAL HISTORY MUSEUM

E. WASHINGTON AVE

★ ★★

MORMON FORT

E.   BONANZA   RD

☾ *LAS VEGAS SPRINGS PRESERVE*

★ ★ **NEON MUSEUM AND BONEYARD**

ALTA DR

DOWNTOWN ARTS DISTRICT

SEE "DOWNTOWN LAS VEGAS" MAP

★ **FREMONT STREET EXPERIENCE**

515

STEWART AVE

95

W. CHARLESTON BLVD

★

FREMONT ST

E CHARLESTON BLVD

SEE "THE STRIP" MAP

E. OAKEY BLVD

93

To ☾ *RED ROCK CANYON*

W.   SAHARA   AVE

ST. LOUIS. AVE

E SAHARA AVE

LUCKY CUSS

INDUSTRIAL RD

LAS VEGAS BLVD THE STRIP

KAREN AVE

BOULDER HWY

PALMYRA * AVE

LAS VEGAS CONVENTION CENTER

DESERT INN RD.

MOUNTAIN VISTA ST

SPRING   MOUNTAIN   RD

☾ **SECRET GARDEN AND DOLPHIN HABITAT**

★ **GONDOLA RIDES**

TWAIN AVE

582

W.   FLAMINGO   RD

★

RAINBOW BLVD

DECATUR BLVD

☾ **CAESARS PALACE**

★ **JUBILEE!**

E FLAMINGO RD

MCLEOD RD

PECOS RD

SANDHILL RD

E. TROPICANA AVE

★ **ATOMIC TESTING MUSEUM**

UNIVERSITY OF LAS VEGAS

VALLEY VIEW BLVD

KOVAL   LN

PARADISE RD

SWENSON ST

MARYLAND PARKWAY

HARMON AVE

W. TROPICANA AVE

HACIENDA AVE

RUSSELL RD

MCCARRAN AIR TERMINAL ■

PATRICK LANE

HUGHES EXECUTIVE AIR TERMINAL

MCCARRAN INTERNATIONAL AIRPORT

W. SUNSET RD

SUNSET RD

93

515 95

E. WARM SPRINGS RD

DOUBLETREE ●

15

215

N. GREEN VALLEY PKWY

To ☾ *RIVER TOURS,* Henderson and Boulder City

BLUE DIAMOND RD

↓ To Barstow

0   2 mi

0   2 km

© AVALON TRAVEL

WELCOME TO FABULOUS LAS VEGAS, NEVADA

When someone says "Las Vegas," what image pops into your mind? If you're like many, there's one landmark that encapsulates everything the city represents. Watch any movie or television show set in Las Vegas and you're sure to see it; drive past it at any time of day or night and somebody – road-tripping buddies from Los Angeles or a bachelorette party from Lexington – will be having their pictures taken in front of it.

"It" is The Sign, a beacon that has guided thrill seekers to the Strip for more than 50 years. Its message is simple: "Welcome to Fabulous Las Vegas, Nevada." But the design, imagery, colors, and vocabulary of Betty Willis's creation at 5100 Las Vegas Boulevard South epitomize a trip to the most exciting city in the world. Silver dollars, harking back to a time when slot players actually plunked coins into the machines, pay homage to the precious metal that put Nevada on the map and appear behind the "welcome" letters. The message's only adjective, *fabulous*, is a distinctly Vegas word: LA may be hip, New York is cosmopolitan, Miami is trendy, but Vegas is "fabulous" – spoken with jazz hands and Liberace enunciation. Bold primary colors and neon flash hint at the visual explosion lying just behind the sign. "Las Vegas" is bold and unapologetic, like the city itself. The sign's diamond shape is a subtle reminder that riches can be yours if Lady Luck smiles. The red-and-gold star promises fun at all hours in a city that never sleeps.

The 25-foot-tall sign even performs double duty: The back reminds motorists to "Drive Carefully; Come Back Soon."

Willis, whose parents were among the first settlers in Las Vegas, considered the sign's design her gift to the city; as a result, she never copyrighted it, so it's in the public domain. You'll see the sign appropriated for souvenirs and event announcements – especially when out-of-towners hold conventions, trade shows, and other happenings in Las Vegas.

---

the northern edge of the great Sonoran Desert and the southern edge of the even larger Great Basin Desert hemming it in on all sides, Las Vegas is one of the hottest and driest urban areas in the United States. It's also one of the country's most remote cities, but looking at a map of the Southwest it is obvious that Las Vegas is a perfectly situated playground. Located almost precisely in the geographical middle of the population centers of California, Nevada, Arizona, and Utah, Las Vegas is only a five-hour drive from Los Angeles (272 miles) and less than a two-hour flight from Phoenix (285 miles), Reno (446 miles), San Francisco (570 miles), and Salt Lake City (419 miles).

The heart of the Las Vegas Valley is a relatively flat 18- by 26-mile strip cutting diagonally northeast to southwest across Clark County. The Spring Mountain Range to the west, which includes Mount Charleston, eighth highest in the state at 11,910 feet, and Sunrise and Frenchman's peaks to the east rise sharply from the smooth, gently sloping valley floor. Ten miles southeast of town is the lowest point, the Vegas Wash, which drains the valley's meager surface water into Lake Mead. Other nearby topographical features of note include Valley of Fire State Park, Red Rock Canyon, Mount Charleston, and the interminable desert.

The city of Las Vegas clings to and branches out from the intersection of the three main highways through southern Nevada: I-15, which runs from northeast (Mesquite) to southwest (the California state line), U.S. 95, from northwest (Beatty) to south (Laughlin), and U.S. 93, from northeast (Caliente) to southeast (Boulder City). Together they define central Las Vegas like the X on a treasure map.

Main Street, Las Vegas Boulevard, and I-15 run roughly parallel through the downtown casino district. Main Street juts due south at Charleston Boulevard and joins Las Vegas Boulevard at the Stratosphere. The Strip and I-15 continue parallel southeast and south out of town.

The corner of Main and Fremont Streets, in the heart of downtown at the Plaza Hotel, is ground zero: All street numbers and directions originate here. Fremont Street, which is technically East Fremont Street because it dead-ends at Main Street, separates north from south until it intersects Charleston Boulevard, which continues east; Fremont Street then cuts south. East of Fremont Street, Charleston Boulevard then separates north from south.

The west side is even vaguer. Here the Las Vegas Expressway (also known as Oran K. Gragson Expressway and U.S. 95) defines north and south, even though it is not a street itself. To further complicate matters, U.S. 95 is a major highway that runs north–south from Canada to Mexico, but in Las Vegas cuts due east (labeled "South") and west ("North").

This may become clearer if you look at the map of the area, but if not, many visitors never venture more than half a block from the Strip: Las Vegas Boulevard South between East Sahara Avenue and East Tropicana Avenue. For that matter, some never even step out of Caesars Palace, Circus Circus, the MGM Grand, or wherever they're staying. The casinos like it that way, and they strive to provide everything their target guests could want under one roof.

Most visitors, however, do manage to find their way between the Strip and downtown. One good reason to know your way around a little is that rush hour in Las Vegas runs about 6–10 A.M. and 3–7 P.M. and is particularly brutal on Las Vegas Boulevard. Use Paradise and Swenson Roads (a long block or two to the east) and Industrial Road and the freeway (a block west) as alternatives.

Watch for speed bumps, installed in most parking lots and some side streets: A few, like those at the airport, are so wide that they're painted yellow and used for crosswalks. Also, slow down for flashing yellow lights and speed-limit signs at school zones. The police and courts rightly take these 15-mph limits quite seriously. Also, be sure to turn on your headlights at night, especially downtown and on the Strip. These areas can be so bright that even though your lights won't help you see, they will ensure you are seen.

Finally, take extra care driving around Las Vegas. So many drivers are visitors in rental cars, locals in a daze from the casinos, or visitors and locals full of free booze that the city has some of the highest accident and car-insurance rates in the country. Jaywalking is rampant on the Strip, and one or two people are killed every year.

Casinos

UPPER STRIP
Stratosphere Casino, Hotel, and Tower

- **Restaurants:** Top of the World, The Buffet, Roxy's Diner, Fellini's Ristorante Italiano, Mamma Ilardo's, El Nopal Mexican Grill, Tower Pizzeria

- **Entertainment:** American Superstars, *Bite*

- **Attractions:** Top of the Tower thrill rides

- **Nightlife:** The Back Alley Bar, C Bar, Airbar, Images Dueling Pianos

It's altitude with attitude at this 1,149-foot-

tall exclamation point on the north end of the Strip. Depending on how nitpicky you want to be, the Stratosphere Tower (200 Las Vegas Blvd. S., 702/380-7777 or 800/99-TOWER—800/998-6937, $69–200 d) is either the largest *building* west of Chicago or the largest *tower* west of St. Louis. Entrepreneur, politician, and professional poker player Bob Stupak opened the Stratosphere in 1996 as a marked improvement over his dark and dive-y Vegas World Casino. Daredevils will delight in the vertigo-inducing thrill rides on the tower's observation deck. The more faint-of-heart may want to steer clear not only of the rides

LAS VEGAS

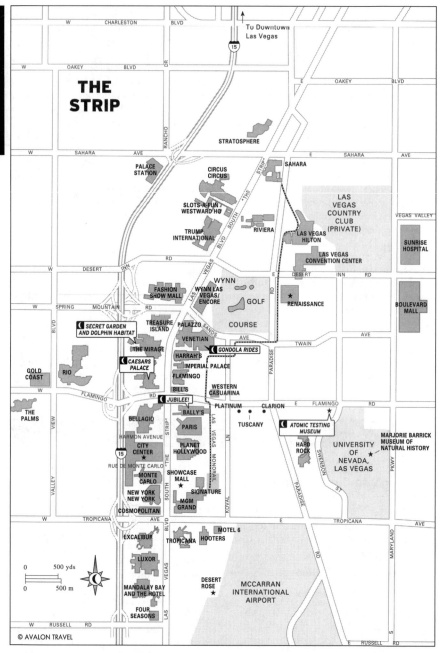

THE STRIP

© RYAN JERZ

White-knuckle rides at 900 feet lure thrillseekers to the Stratosphere Tower.

rock, dancing, and aerial acts. It's a little kitschy, perhaps, but definitely something different.

Roxy's Diner (11 A.M.–11 P.M. Sun.–Thurs., 11 A.M.–midnight Fri.–Sat., $12–20) is a trip back to the malt shop for comfort food and singing waitresses.

Circus Circus

• **Restaurants:** Circus the Garden Grill, Circus Buffet, Casino Café, Pizzeria, Mexitalia X-press, The Steak House, Westside Deli, Rock & Rita's

• **Entertainment:** Circus acts

• **Attractions:** Adventuredome theme park

but also the resort's double-decker elevators that launch guests to the top of the tower at 1,400 feet per minute. But even agoraphobes should conquer their fears long enough to enjoy the views from the restaurant and bars more than 100 floors up, and the **Chapel in the Clouds** can ensure a heavenly beginning to married life.

If the thrill rides on the observation deck aren't your style, perhaps you'll find the rush of gambling action on the nearly 100,000-square-foot ground-floor casino, two swimming pools (one where you can go topless), and a dozen bars and restaurants more your speed.

Theater of the Stars is home to **American Superstars** (6:30 and 8:30 P.M. Tues.–Wed. and Fri., 7 P.M. Sat.–Sun., $40, $45 including buffet), a song-and-dance tribute show heavy on impressions of recent pop idols and old standbys. It's good, but not as good as Legends in Concert at the Imperial Palace. The showroom also hosts *Bite* (10:30 P.M. Fri.–Wed., $49), a fantasy mix of sexy vampires, hard

Quite a contrast to its upscale sister properties in the MGM Mirage family, Circus Circus (2880 Las Vegas Blvd. S., 702/734-0410, $79–200 d) is perhaps the "themiest" of the theme casinos in Las Vegas. While the city briefly flirted with selling itself as a family destination in the 1990s, Circus Circus has always courted young families with limited gambling budgets. High above the casino floor, aerialists, clowns, and jugglers regularly entertain children and gambling-weary adults. A carnival-style midway lets teenagers test their luck and skill at whacking moles and tossing Ping-Pong balls while their parents test theirs at splitting aces and rolling sevens downstairs. In keeping with its budget-conscious target market, most of the restaurant and bar selections are cheap and predictable. Circus Circus began life as a casino without a hotel and still hasn't embraced the Vegas-style self-contained vacation experience. Apparently figuring its target customers have traded party time for story time, it eschews Vegas-style shows and nightclubs.

Families with picky eaters will find something for everyone's palate at the **Garden Grill** (2 P.M.–2 A.M. daily, $15–25). In addition to Mexican, Italian, Asian, and American food, a $12 all-you-can-eat prime rib dinner is a good option.

LAS VEGAS CASINO CHRONOLOGY

- 1906: Hotel Nevada (now **Golden Gate**)

- 1931: Meadows Club, Railroad Pass

- 1932: Apache Hotel

- 1935: Sal Sagev (now the **Golden Gate**)

- 1938: Pair-O-Dice

- 1941: El Rancho Vegas, El Cortez

- 1942: Last Frontier, Pioneer Club

- 1946: **Flamingo, Golden Nugget**

- 1948: Thunderbird

- 1950: Desert Inn, Royal Nevada

- 1951: **Horseshoe**

- 1952: **Sahara,** Sands

- 1954: Showboat

- 1955: Royal Nevada, Last Frontier, Stardust, **Riviera,** Moulin Rouge, **Four Queens,** Dunes, Hacienda

- 1956: **Fremont**

- 1957: **Tropicana,** Mint

- 1961: **Las Vegas Club**

- 1963: Castaways, Tally Ho (now **Planet Hollywood**)

- 1964: Lady Luck, Casino Royale

- 1965: Western

- 1966: **Caesars Palace**

- 1968: **Circus Circus,** Boardwalk

- 1969: Landmark, International (now **Las Vegas Hilton**)

- 1970: Paddlewheel

- 1971: Plaza (now **Union Plaza**)

- 1972: Holiday

- 1973: MGM Grand (the original; now **Bally's**), Holiday

- 1975: **California,** Marina, Continental, Rendezvous (now **Gold Spike**)

Las Vegas Hilton

- **Restaurants:** Garden of the Dragon, TJ's Steakhouse, The Buffet, Teru Sushi, Casa Nicola, Paradise Café, Benihana, 888 Noodle Bar, Hacienda Margarita, Fortuna

- **Entertainment:** *Sin City Bad Girls, Voices,* Steve Dacri, Andrew Dice Clay, *The King One Night with You* starring Trent Carlini

- **Attractions:** Sports Zone video arcade

- **Nightlife:** Tempo lounge

The **C Hilton** (3000 Paradise Rd., 702/732-5111 or 888/732-7117, $89–300 d) began life as the International in 1969 and has the distinction of being the final stage home to the jumpsuit-and-sideburns Elvis of the 1970s. Today, the Hilton takes advantage of its location adjacent to the Las Vegas Convention Center and its own 220,000 square feet of exhibit and meeting space to cater to the expense-account crowd. The Hilton is gadget-geek central when the Consumer Electronics Show rolls into town, but bargains can be had when no major conventions reserve blocks of rooms, and local horse racing fans brave the convention crowds to soak up the atmosphere of the 30,000-square-foot race and sports book (nearly one-third of the total casino space) and its 30 large-screen television monitors. The most loyal patrons enjoy reserved parking outside the book, where a larger-than-life statue of Man o' War greets punters. The Hilton's 2008 renovations saw the removal of Star Trek: The Experience, a virtual reality fantasy, and the **Hilton Theater** hosts delightfully eclectic performers. Recent shows have included glam rockers Twisted Sister's Christmas concert,

- 1976: Bingo Palace
- 1977: Maxim (now **Westin Casuarina**)
- 1979: **Sam's Town,** Barbary Coast (now **Bill's Gamblin' Hall**), Vegas World
- 1980: **Imperial Palace,** Sundance
- 1983: Westward Ho, **Slots O'Fun**
- 1985: Bourbon Street
- 1986: **Gold Coast**
- 1988: **Arizona Charlie's West**
- 1989: **Mirage**
- 1990: **Rio, Excalibur,** Vacation Village, **Santa Fe**
- 1992: **Main Street Station**
- 1993: **Luxor, Treasure Island, MGM Grand**
- 1994: Boomtown (now **Silverton**), **Fiesta Rancho**

- 1995: **Hard Rock, Boulder Station, Texas Station**
- 1996: Monte Carlo, Reserve (now **Fiesta Henderson**), **Orleans**
- 1997: **New York New York, Sunset Station**
- 1998: **Bellagio**
- 1999: **Venetian, Paris, Mandalay Bay**
- 2000: Aladdin (now **Planet Hollywood**), **Suncoast**
- 2001: **Green Valley Ranch, The Palms**
- 2003: Tuscany, Westin Casuarina
- 2005: **Wynn**
- 2006: **Red Rock Resort, South Coast**
- 2007: **Palazzo**
- 2008: **Encore, Aliante Station**
- 2010: **City Center**

Properties listed in boldface remain open.

Carol Burnett Show alum Tim Conway, and swing-era scion Louis Prima Jr. Lounge acts such as topless rock-and-roll revues, magicians, and comedians frequent the **Shimmer Showroom.**

Teru Sushi (5:30 P.M.–10:30 P.M. Tues.–Sat., $30–40) inside Benihana Village is popular with locals and conventioneers.

CENTER STRIP
Wynn Las Vegas/Encore

- **Restaurants:** Alex, Bartolotta Ristorante di Mare, Stratta, The Country Club, Daniel Boulud Brasserie, Okada, Red 8 Asian Bistro, Pizza Place, SW Steakhouse, Tableau, Terrace Pointe Café, The Buffet, The Café, Wing Lei, Zoozacrackers

- **Entertainment:** *Le Rêve*

- **Attractions:** Penske Wynn Ferrari Maserati, Wynn Country Club

- **Nightlife:** Blush, Tryst

An eponymous monument to indulgence, **☾ Wynn** (3131 Las Vegas Blvd. S., 702/770-7000 or 888/320-9966, $200–400 d) marked the $2.5 billion return of Steve Wynn, "the man who made Las Vegas," to the Strip in 2005. Wynn invites fellow multimillionaires to wallow in the good life and the hoi polloi to sample a taste of how the other half lives: Gaze at Wynn's art, one of the best and most valuable private collections in the world, or drool over the horsepower at the **Ferrari-Maserati dealership** Wynn partly owns. If you're not in the market for an $800,000 ride, logo T-shirts, coffee mugs, and key chains are available.

Never one to rest on his laurels, Wynn opened

© RYAN JERZ

The beautiful and the rich find a home away from home at Steve Wynn's trendy twins.

the appropriately named Encore Tower next door in 2008. Red must be his favorite color, because the casino area is awash in it. The twins' opulence is matched by the resort's Tom Fazio–designed golf course, open to hotel guests only, of course. Although guests come to explore the privileges of wealth, they also can experience the wonders of nature without the inconvenience of bugs and dirt. Lush plants, waterfalls, lakes, and mountains dominate the pristine landscape.

In addition to the gourmet offerings, don't miss the dim sum at **Red 8 Asian Bistro** (11:30 A.M.–11 P.M. Sun.–Thurs., 11:30 A.M.–1 P.M. Fri.–Sat., $30–45). **Bartolotta** (5:30–10 P.M. daily, $40–55) works as hard on creating a sense of the Mediterranean seaside as it does on its cuisine. The à la carte menu and especially the tasting menus are quite dear, but the appetizers will give you a sense of Italy for about $25.

Wynn-Encore's formal sophistication belies its location on the site of the old Desert Inn with the unself-conscious swagger Frank, Dino, and Sammy brought to the joint. Both towers boast some of the biggest rooms and suites on the Strip, with the usual although better-quality amenities

and a few extra touches, like remote-controlled drapes, lights, and air-conditioning. Wynn's rooms are appointed in wheat, honey, and other creatively named shades of beige. Encore is a bit more colorful, with the color scheme running toward dark chocolate and cream.

Treasure Island

- **Restaurants:** Isla Mexican Kitchen, Phil's Italian Steak House, Kahunaville, The Buffet at TI, Canter's Deli, Gilley's Saloon, Dance Hall & BBQ, The Coffee Shop, Khotan, Pho, Pizzeria Francesco's, Starbucks, Ben & Jerry's

- **Entertainment:** Treasure Island Theatre, Cirque du Soleil's *Mystère*

- **Attractions:** Sirens of TI

- **Nightlife:** Christian Audigier; Gilley's Saloon, Dance Hall & BBQ; Kahunaville Party Bar; Isla Tequila Bar; Breeze Bar

Much of Treasure Island's (3300 Las Vegas Blvd. S., 702/894-7111 or 800/288-7206, $90–250 d) pirate theme walked the plank when the MGM Mirage property helped Las Vegas shed its family-friendly facade and reclaim its adult playground status. The resort replaced its pirate-skull sign with a more subdued TI logo in a further attempt to distance it from the buccaneer brand that is no longer part of MGM Mirage (Phil Ruffin, owner of the New Frontier, bought it in 2009). The Battle of Buccaneer Bay show out front has been transformed into the sultry **Sirens of TI** (5:30 P.M., 7 P.M., 8:30 P.M., and 10 P.M. daily, free), trading cutlasses for stilettos and swashbuckling for sensuality. Arrive early if you want a good vantage point. Cross Las Vegas Boulevard if you want to get past the hotel during showtime.

Canter's Deli (11 A.M.–midnight Sun.–Thurs., 9 A.M.–midnight Fri.–Sat., $10–20) brings traditional Jewish fare and tradition to Las Vegas from its home base in Los Angles.

The 2,885 standard rooms and suites, modernized in 2008, meet Las Vegas resort standards, but nothing more. They're only average in size, but upper floors often sport unforgettable views.

Venetian

- **Restaurants:** AquaKnox, B&B Ristorante, Bouchon, Canaletto, Canyon Ranch Café, Delmonico Steakhouse, Enoteca San Marco, Grand Lux Café Venetian, Noodle Asia, Pinot Brasserie, Postrio, Tao Asian Bistro, Taqueria Cañonita, The Grill at Valentino, Timpano Tavern, Tintoretto's, Trattoria Reggiano, Valentino, Riva Poolside, Zeffirino

- **Entertainment:** Blue Man Group, *Phantom—the Las Vegas Spectacular*

- **Attractions:** Madame Tussauds Las Vegas, Gondola Rides, Streetmosphere

- **Nightlife:** Tao, V Bar, La Scena Lounge

While Caesars Palace bears little resemblance to the realities of ancient Rome and Luxor doesn't really replicate the land of the pharaohs, the ◖ Venetian (3355 Las Vegas Blvd. S., 702/414-1000 or 866/659-9643, $200–400 d) comes pretty close to capturing the elegance of Venice. An elaborate faux-Renaissance ceiling fresco greets visitors in the hotel lobby, and

the sensual treats just keep coming. A life-size streetscape with replicas of the Bridge of Sighs, Doge's Palace, the Grand Canal, and other treasures give the impression that the best of the Queen of the Adriatic has been transplanted in toto. Tranquil rides in authentic gondolas with serenading pilots are perfect for relaxing after a hectic session in the 120,000-square-foot casino. Canal-side, buskers entertain the guests in the **Streetmosphere** (various times and locations daily, free), and the **Grand Canal Shoppes** (10 A.M.–11 P.M. Sun.–Thurs., 10 A.M.–midnight Fri.–Sat.) entice strollers, window shoppers, and serious spenders along winding streetscapes. Don't miss the Fabergé eggs at Regis Galerie and blown-glass figurines at St. Mark's Square.

After you've shopped till you're ready to drop, **Madame Tussauds Interactive Wax Museum** (10 A.M.–10 P.M. daily, $25 adults, $18 over age 59, $15 ages 7–12, free under age 7) invites stargazers for hands-on experiences with their favorite entertainers and sports stars. Then you can dance the night away at **Tao** (10 P.M.–late, lounge 5 P.M.–late Thurs.–Sat.).

Fine dining options abound, but for a change, **Trattorio Reggiano** (11 A.M.–11 P.M. Sun.–Thurs., 11 A.M.–midnight Fri.–Sat.) offers pizza and pasta dishes in a bistro setting for about $20. **Canyon Ranch Café** (7 A.M.–3 P.M. daily, $15–25) is a good bet for a light breakfast.

The Venetian spares no expense in the hotel department. Its 4,027 suites are tastefully appointed with Italian (of course) marble, and they're big at 700 square feet. They include roomy bedrooms with two queen beds and comfy sitting rooms.

Palazzo

- **Restaurants:** Carnevino, Cut, Lavo, Morels French Steakhouse & Bistro, Table 10, SushiSamba, Zine Noodles Dim Sum, Canyon Ranch Grill, Dal Toro Ristorante, Dos Caminos, Espressamente Illy, First Food & Bar, Grand Lux, Lagasse's Stadium, Solaro, Sweet Surrender

- **Entertainment:** *Jersey Boys,* Palazzo Showroom

OUT WITH THE OLD

Las Vegas gets a bad rap as a city with no sense of history. Part of that reputation undoubtedly comes from its willingness to consign its slightly shabby, outdated casinos to the scrap heap. But remember, Las Vegas Strip real estate is some of the most valuable in the world, and only establishments with the grandeur to compete with the striking neighborhood architecture can generate a satisfactory return on investments. This in no way should be considered a lack of respect for the venerable old gals that gave Las Vegas such character throughout the mobbed-up '50s, the swinging '60s, and the booming '80s. Like the head, heart, and hooves of champion race horses, the facades and neon signs of the Sands, Dunes, Desert Inn, Silver Slipper, and other Vegas landmarks (including The Landmark) are preserved at the Neon Boneyard downtown.

And like their thoroughbred brethren, the disposal of the rest of a hotel-casino's carcass is a sign of respect. The Bellagio, Venetian, and Wynn stand on the shoulders of giants.

The Dunes was the first ancestor to give its life so that its progeny could prosper. The *Arabian Nights*-themed resort heralded the now-iconic topless showgirl review shortly after it opened in 1955. Steve Wynn, who bought the

casino just for the land, arranged the now-iconic hotel implosion in 1993, making a media event out of strategically placed dynamite. The Dunes's second tower went down with much less fanfare a year later. The Bellagio now occupies this hallowed ground.

Plenty of the Dunes's sisters have met the same fate over the last 17 years, though not all can claim they gave their lives for such a noble cause as the Bellagio. The Landmark's sci-fi architecture — it looked like a cross between the Stratosphere and a flashlight — certainly made it a landmark on the Las Vegas skyline when it went up in 1963. During its life, the Landmark hosted Elvis and Sinatra and starred in the movies *Casino* and *Diamonds Are Forever*. Its death in 1995 is captured in another classic film, *Mars Attacks!* But while other stars get a star on the pavement, the Landmark *became* the pavement. The site is now part of the Las Vegas Convention Center parking lot.

The Chairman of the Board and his cronies made the Sands Rat Pack Central. Gathered for the filming of *Ocean's 11*, Frank, Sammy, Peter, Dean, and Joey developed the concept for their musical-comedy shows that set the standard for Las Vegas entertainment for decades to come. Opened in 1952 after a succession of owners,

- **Attractions:** Lamborghini dealership and showroom
- **Nightlife:** Lavo Nightclub, The Lounge at Dos Caminos, Salute Lounge, Fusion Mixology Bar, Laguna Champagne Bar, Double Helix Wine Bar

In 2007 the colorful Sheldon Adelson, chairman of Las Vegas Sands Corporation, unveiled the Venetian's sister property, The Palazzo (3325 Las Vegas Blvd. S., 702/607-7777 or 866/263-3001, $200–400 d), next door. In the latest broadside in Adelson's rivalry with Steve Wynn, Adelson expanded his vision during construction to ensure the Palazzo towers more than 100 feet over Wynn Las Vegas. In another swipe at Wynn and his Ferrari showroom,

the Palazzo houses Las Vegas's Lamborghini dealership.

The hotel lobby is bathed in natural light from an 80-foot dome, and half of the 100,000-square-foot casino is smoke-free, part of the Palazzo's efforts in achieving Leadership in Energy and Environmental Design status.

The smell of Corinthian leather emanates from the high-end boutiques at **The Shoppes at the Palazzo** (10 A.M.–11 P.M. Sun.–Thurs., 10 A.M.–midnight Fri.–Sat.). Prada, Manolo Blahnik, and Barneys New York draw in the fashionistas, and aesthetes of all stripes will find something, from collectible books to haute and hot accessories.

Sugarcane (7 P.M.–2 A.M. Fri.–Sat.) is a mash-up of Brazilian and Asian cultures with a the Sands slipped through the hourglass when it became evident that the new Bellagio and the expanding Caesars Palace were taking resort hotels to a level the Sands could never recapture. Sands corporate chairman Sheldon Adelson kept the grand dame's name for his company even after ordering it imploded in 1996. The Venetian and Palazzo are the mountains Adelson created out of the sand hill.

Owner Doc Bailey's innovations made the Hacienda Hotel a success in the 1960s and 1970s despite its isolated location way down at the end of Las Vegas Boulevard. Bailey bought a fleet of airplanes so he could ferry guests to his resort, making him the first to offer gambling junkets. He also installed a miniature golf course on the property so the little ones would have something to do while Mom and Dad gambled away their college funds. The sprawling casino on 48 acres was close to the airport and was the first major hotel motorists from Southern California encountered after their long drive. Circus Circus came along in the early 1990s and stole some of the Hacienda's south-Strip mojo. The Hacienda was sold to Circus Circus, who bid it adios with a fiery 1996 New Year's Eve send-off; Mandalay Bay stands on the ruins.

The Aladdin was imploded in 1997 and was replaced three years later by...The Aladdin. It weathered financial and other difficulties before Aladdin II gave way (through a major renovation, not an implosion) to Planet Hollywood in 2007.

The Desert Inn was 50 – old by Las Vegas standards – when Steve Wynn bought it in 2000, but it retained the grandeur and aura it had developed through its life. Still, Wynn's vision did not include the centerpiece tower, and he had it imploded later that year to make room for Wynn's namesake casino. The DI's other towers went down in 2004 after someone asked Wynn, "What will you do for an Encore?"

Implosions have claimed the lives of several other Las Vegas resorts. The El Rancho went down in a cloud of dust in 2000. The financially troubled and stalled Fontainebleau now graces the site. The Castaways, which began life and gained a bit of fame among bowlers and Roller Derby fans as the Showboat, sank in early 2006. Bourbon Street on the Strip went down in the wee hours of February 14, 2006. The Boardwalk bit it a couple of months later; it's the foundation for City Center. The Stardust and New Frontier shuffled off their mortal coils in 2007.

dance floor and eclectic entertainers. The North African bathhouse-themed Lavo (10 P.M.–late Tues.–Sun.) will attend to your late-night dining, dancing, and drinking (but not bathing) desires. Lavo's restaurant (702/791-1818) offers patio dining with a view of Sirens of TI across the way.

The Palazzo is a gourmand's dream, with a handful of four-star establishments. The refreshing take on traditional Mexican fare at **Dos Caminos** (11 A.M.–11 P.M. Mon.–Fri., 10 A.M.–4 P.M. Sat.–Sun., $15–25) is highlighted by made-to-order guacamole and tequila tastings.

Accommodations are all suites, with sunken living rooms and sumptuous beds that would make it tough to leave the room if not for the lure of the Strip.

Harrah's

- **Restaurants:** Café at Harrah's, Carnaval Court Bar & Grill, Flavors Buffet, KGB, Ming's Table, Oyster Bar at Harrah's, Starbucks, The Range Steakhouse, Toby Keith's I Love This Bar

- **Entertainment:** Rita Rudner, Improv Comedy Club, Mac King Comedy Magic Show, *Legends in Concert*

- **Nightlife:** Carnival Court

Once the world's largest Holiday Inn, then an antebellum riverboat, Harrah's (3475 Las Vegas Blvd. S., 800/898-8651, $60–400 d) reinvented itself in 1996 with a Mardi Gras theme. **Carnaval Court,** outside on the Strip's sidewalk,

WORLD SERIES OF POKER

In 1970, after a week of high-stakes poker in Reno, a few dozen gamblers decided Johnny Moss was the best among them and crowned him the poker world champion.

Thirty-three years later, a regular guy, appropriately named Chris Moneymaker, won a no-limit hold 'em poker tournament in Las Vegas and became the newest world champion. These events, separated by a generation and half a state, mark the watershed events in one of the most astonishing gambling revolutions in history. Both brought unprecedented attention to a game of skill and chance that had been played at kitchen tables around the world but had never been seen as a serious casino endeavor. When "Amarillo Slim" Preston won the second World Series of Poker, he bested 11 other players. Fortunately for the "sport," Preston is engaging, intelligent, and likes the sound of his own voice. He relished the role as poker champion and poker promoter, talking up the game and the World Series with Johnny Carson and appearing as himself in several films.

Moneymaker, a Nashville accountant and pretty good Thursday night poker player with the boys, got into the main event by winning a "satellite tournament" with a $40 entry fee. His winner's share was $2.5 million. Moneymaker's everyman status, his victory over seasoned poker pros, the tournament being televised by ESPN, and the fortune he won spurred other quarter-ante players to try to match his success. The World Series of Poker exploded, as did the World Poker Tour, a series of televised no-limit events, often with million-dollar payouts.

In 2006 the also appropriately named Jamie Gold (we're thinking of changing our name to "Cash" and entering the tournament this year) topped 8,772 other players who ponied up $10,000 each to play in the World Series main event. Gold took home $12 million. That marked the largest field to date, as soon after many online poker sites began barring U.S. players from their satellite tournaments and other real-money games to comply with federal law.

Harrah's Entertainment owns the World Series of Poker, the only asset it kept after buying, then selling, Binion's Horseshoe in 2004.

---

capitalizes on the street party atmosphere with live bands and juggling bartenders. Just inside, the **Piano Bar** invites aspiring comedians and singers to the karaoke stage weekend evenings, and dueling keyboardists take over at 9 P.M. each night.

The rotating acts at **The Improv Comedy Club** (8:30 P.M. and 10:30 P.M. Tues.–Sun.) offer witty, sometimes gritty, observations on life and relationships.

The country superstar lends his name and unapologetic patriotism to **Toby Keith's I Love This Bar & Grill** (11:30 A.M.–2 A.M. Sun.–Thurs., 11:30 A.M.–3 A.M. Fri.–Sat., $12–20). Try the freedom fries. **Ming's Table** (11:30 A.M.–11 P.M. Sun.–Thurs., 11:30 A.M.–midnight Fri.–Sat., $15–30) features pan-Asian specialties.

For a while it seemed Harrah's was unwilling to engage in the one-upmanship of its colleagues, content instead to carve out a niche as a middle-of-the-action, middle-of-the-road, middle-of-the-price-scale option. But now it's exploring plans to build a pedestrian thoroughfare with bars and shops behind its property—Harrah's own private urban renewal investment. Called Project Linq, it would be highlighted by a 550-foot Ferris wheel, giving riders unimpeded views of the Strip.

The Mirage

- **Restaurants:** B. B. King Blues Club, Blizz Frozen Yogurt, BLT Burger, Stack, Fin, Kokomo's, Samba Brazilian Steakhouse, Onda, Cravings, California Pizza Kitchen, Coconuts Ice Cream Shop, Japonais, Roasted Bean, Roasted Bean Express, Paradise Café, Carnegie Deli, Starbucks

- **Entertainment:** *LOVE,* Terry Fator

© RYAN JERZ

It's no illusion; Steve Wynn's masterpiece helped return Las Vegas to its grown-up sensibilities.

- **Attractions:** Secret Garden, Dolphin Habitat, Mirage volcano

- **Nightlife:** JET, Revolution Lounge, Rhumbar, King Ink Tattoo Studio and Bar

Steve Wynn reinvented Las Vegas and ushered in a building boom on Las Vegas Boulevard with the opening of his first major Strip property in 1989. While grand and attention-grabbing, the Mirage (3400 Las Vegas Blvd. S., 702/791-7111 or 800/627-6667, $150–300 d) was the first understated megaresort, starting a trend that signifies Las Vegas's return to mature pursuits. This Bali-Hai–themed paradise lets guests bask in the wonders of nature alongside the sophistication and pampering of resort life. More an oasis than a mirage, the hotel greets visitors with exotic bamboo, orchids, banana trees, secluded grottoes, and peaceful lagoons. Dolphins, white tigers, stingrays, sharks, and a volcano provide livelier sights.

Jet (10:30 A.M.–4 A.M. Mon. and Thurs.–Sat.) has three rooms with three different kinds of music and crowded dance floors. **King Ink Tattoo Studio and Bar** (11 A.M.–4 A.M. daily) doesn't really mix alcohol and needles—Mario Barth's parlor is completely separate from the tattoo art–inspired barroom.

Headliners and a Beatles production show are the high-end entertainment options, but **B. B. King's Blues Club** (6:30 A.M.–2 A.M. Sun.–Thurs., 6:30 A.M.–4 A.M. Fri.–Sat.) dishes out delta blues and other genres nightly, with Cajun and creole fare. **Stack** (5–10 P.M. Sun., Tues., and Thurs., 5 P.M.–midnight Mon. and Fri.–Sat., $35–50) serves variations of what Mom used to make (pigs in a blanket, Shake 'n Bake chicken, a grown-up version of Tater Tots) and what she never would have attempted (sashimi, calamari).

Since a 2008 renovation, the Mirage's rooms have jettisoned the South Pacific theme in favor of tasteful appointments and some of the most comfortable beds in town. The facelift gave Mirage rooms a modern and relaxing feel in browns, blacks, and splashes of tangerine and ruby.

Imperial Palace

- **Restaurants:** Emperor's Buffet, Pizza Palace, Hash House a Go Go, Embers, Burger Palace, Quesadilla, Ginseng Barbecue, Betty's Diner
- **Entertainment:** *Human Nature, Matsuri, Divas Las Vegas*
- **Attractions:** Automobile Collection, King's Ransom Museum
- **Nightlife:** Karaoke Club, Rockhouse Bar and Nightclub

Built by the intriguing Ralph Englestad, one of the last holdouts among independent casino owners on the Strip, the Imperial Palace (3535 Las Vegas Blvd. S., 702/731-3311 or 800/351-7400, $74–300 d) was added to the Harrah's family in 2006.

The IP started the trend of entertainment at the tables. Its celebrity look-alikes deal blackjack in the **Dealertainers Pit.** The Imperial Theater is home to *Matsuri* (4 P.M. Sat.–Wed., 7 P.M. and 9:30 P.M. Fri.), a celebration of Japanese athleticism and acrobatics.

Embers (5–10 P.M. Thurs.–Mon., $15–30) is the choice for the meat-and-potatoes crowd, and **Hash House a Go Go** (7 A.M.–11 P.M. Sun.–Thurs., 7 A.M.–2 A.M. Fri.–Sat., $20–35) is the IP's take on comfort food.

Like Harrah's, the Imperial Palace is a low-cost alternative surrounded by upscale neighbors. An unassuming pagoda facade hints at the interior's unassuming Oriental decor but gives little clue that it's one of the largest hotels in the world, with 2,640 guest rooms.

◖ Caesars Palace

- **Restaurants:** Augustus Café, Beijing Noodle #9, Bradley Ogden, Cafe Lago, Cypress Street Marketplace, Guy Savoy, Hyakumi Japanese Restaurant & Sushi Bar, Mesa Grill, Munch, Neros, Payard Pâtisserie & Bistro, Rao's, Sea Harbour, Serendipity 3, Trevi, La Salsa, Max Brenner, Chocolate by a Bald Man, The Palm, Planet Hollywood, Spago, The Cheesecake Factory, BOA Steakhouse, Il Mulino, Joe's Seafood, Prime Steak & Stone Crab, Sushi Roku, Cafe Della Spiga

- **Entertainment:** Celine Dion, Matt Goss
- **Attractions:** Fall of Atlantis and Festival Fountain shows, Aquarium
- **Nightlife:** Pure, Cleopatra's Barge

It's not hard to imagine that Rome would look a lot like Las Vegas had it survived this long. But since the empire doesn't exist, Jay Sarno had to invent Caesars Palace (3570 Las Vegas Blvd. S., 866/227-5938, $200–600 d), incorporating all the ancient civilization's decadence and overindulgence and adding a few thousand slot machines. Sarno's palace—there's no apostrophe in the name because Sarno wanted to treat all his guests like Caesars—opened with great fanfare in 1966. It has ruled the Strip ever since. And like the empire, it continues to expand, now boasting 3,348 guest rooms in six towers and 140,000 square feet of gaming space accented with marble, fountains, gilding, and royal reds. Wander the grounds searching for reproductions of some of the world's most famous statuary. The eagle-eyed might spy Michelangelo's *David* and Giovanni da Bologna's *Rape of the Sabines* as well as the Brahma Shrine.

The casino is so big that the website includes a "slot finder" application so gamblers can navigate to their favorite machines.

Cleopatra's Barge (6 P.M.–3 A.M. daily), a floating lounge, attracts the full spectrum of the 21-and-over crowd for late-night bacchanalias, while **Pure** (10 P.M.–4 A.M. Tues. and Thurs.–Sun.) accommodates a mostly younger crowd of up to 2,400 at a time and keeps them all happy by spinning different dance music in different areas of the club.

All roads lead to the **Forum Shops** (10 A.M.–11 P.M. Sun.–Thurs., 10 A.M.–midnight Fri.–Sat.), a collection of famous designer stores, specialty boutiques, and restaurants. Not all the shops are as froufrou as you might expect, but an hour here can do some serious damage to your bankroll. You'll also find the **Fall of Atlantis and Festival Fountain Show** (hourly 10 A.M.–11 P.M. Sun.–Thurs., 10 A.M.–midnight Fri.–Sat., free), a multisensory, multimedia depiction of the gods' wrath. The saltwater **aquarium** is also nearby. Feeding times (1:15 P.M. and 5:15 P.M. daily, tours 3:15 P.M. daily) offer the best views of the sharks and other denizens of the deep.

If you (or your wallet) tire of Caesars's high-on-the-hog dining, nosh on a burger or salad at the **Cypress Street Marketplace** (11 A.M.– 11 P.M. daily) alfresco, agora-style.

With so many guest rooms in six towers, it seems Caesars is always renovating somewhere. The sixth tower, Octavius, opened in 2010, and the Palace Tower was overhauled in 2009. Most newer rooms are done in tan, wood, and marble. Older rooms still feature Roman niceties like plaster busts and columns.

Flamingo

- **Restaurants:** Tropical Breeze, Paradise Garden Buffet, Jimmy Buffet's Margaritaville, Steakhouse46, Hamada of Japan, Java Coast, food court, Pink Bean, Beach Club, The Burger Joint

- **Entertainment:** George Wallace, Nathan Burton Comedy Magic, Donny and Marie, Vinnie Favorito, *X Burlesque*

- **Attractions:** Wildlife Habitat

- **Nightlife:** Sin City Brewing Co.

Named for Virginia Hill, the long-legged girlfriend of Benjamin "don't call me Bugsy" Siegel, the Flamingo (3555 Las Vegas Blvd. S., 702/733-3111 or 800/732-2111, $50–200 d) has at turns embraced and shunned its gangster ties, which stretch back to the 1960s. After Bugsy's (sorry, Mr. Siegel) Flamingo business practices ran afoul of the Cosa Nostra and led to his untimely end, Meyer Lansky took over. Mob ties continued to dog the property even after Kirk Kerkorian bought it to use as a training ground for his pride and joy, the International (now the Las Vegas Hilton). Hilton Hotels bought the Flamingo in 1970, giving the joint the legitimacy it needed. Today, its art deco architecture and pink-and-orange neon beckon pedestrians and conjure images of aging mafiosi lounging by the pool, their tropical shirts half unbuttoned to reveal hairy chests and gold ropes. And that image seems just fine with the current owner, Caesars Entertainment, in a Vegas where the mob era is remembered almost fondly. Siegel's penthouse suite, behind the current hotel, has been replaced by the **Flamingo Wildlife Habitat** (8 A.M.–dusk daily, free), where pheasants, a crane, ibis, swans, and, of course, Chilean flamingos luxuriate amid riparian plants and verdant streams.

Vinnie Favorito (8 P.M. daily, $60–71) channels Don Rickles in Bugsy's Cabaret, followed by the naughty nymphs of *X Burlesque* in the same venue (10 P.M. daily, $54–66). The all-ages crowd will enjoy **Nathan Burton Comedy Magic** (4 P.M. Tues. and Fri.–Sun., $22–49) in the Flamingo Showroom.

Guests can search for their lost shaker of salt in paradise at **Jimmy Buffett's Margaritaville** (8 A.M.–2 A.M. Sun.–Thurs., 8 A.M.–2 A.M. Fri., 8 A.M.–3 A.M. Sat., $20–30) while people-watching on the Strip and noshing on jambalaya and cheeseburgers.

The Flamingo recently completed the transformation of many of its guest rooms into "GO rooms," dressed in swanky mahogany and white with bold swatches of hot pink. The rooms are swank and savvy with high-end entertainment systems. Suite options are just as colorful and include 42-inch TVs, wet bars, and all the other Vegas-sational accoutrements.

Rio

- **Restaurants:** All-American Bar & Grille, Búzios, Café Martorano, Carnival World Buffet, Gaylord, Hamada Asian, Mah Jong, Sao Paulo Cafe, Sports Kitchen, The Village Seafood Buffet, VooDoo Steak & Lounge, McFadden's Irish Pub, Starbucks, Wetzel's Pretzels

- **Entertainment:** Penn & Teller, Chippendales

- **Attractions:** Show in the Sky

- **Nightlife:** I-Bar, Flirt Lounge, VooDoo Lounge

A hit from the beginning, this carnival just off

the Strip started expanding almost before its first 400-suite tower was complete in 1990. Three towers and 2,100 more suites later, the party's still raging with terrific buffets, beautiful-people magnet bars, and steamy shows. "Bevertainers" at the Rio (3700 W. Flamingo Rd., 866/746-7671, $80–200 d) push the stereotype of the starving artist as waitress to the hilt, taking turns on mini stages scattered throughout the casino to belt out tunes or gyrate to the music. Dancers and other performers may materialize at your slot machine to take your mind off your losses.

The South American vibe comes to life with the **Show in the Sky** (hourly 7 P.M.–midnight Thurs.–Sun., free). Formerly a pseudo-family-friendly parade of bead tossing and floats, the show has morphed into a naughty, scantily clad writhe fest. For $12.95, guests can get into costume and become part of the show. Three unique productions keep the show fresh. **Flirt Lounge** (6:30 P.M.–late Thurs.–Tues.) and its all-male waitstaff keep the Rio's Ultimate Girls Night Out churning. **VooDoo Lounge** (9 P.M.–late daily), 51 stories up, is just as hip.

Búzio's (5–11 P.M. Wed.–Sun., $30–50) has great crab-shack appetizers and buttery lobster and steak entrées.

All of the Rio's guest rooms are suites—two small sofas and a coffee table replace the uncomfortable easy chair found in most standard rooms. Rio suites measure about 650 square feet. The hotel's center-Strip location and room-tall windows make for exciting views. The his-and-hers dressing and vanity areas are a nice touch.

LOWER STRIP
The Palms

- **Restaurants:** Alizé, Blue Agave Oyster & Chile Bar, Garduños, Little Buddha, N9NE, Nove Italiano, 24/Seven, Bistro Buffet, food court
- **Entertainment:** Playboy Comedy Club
- **Nightlife:** Rain, Ghostbar, Moon, Playboy Club

The expression "party like a rock star" could have been invented for The Palms (4321 W. Flamingo Rd., 702/942-7777, $120–400 d). Penthouse views, Playboy bunnies, and starring roles in MTV's *The Real World: Las Vegas* and Bravo's *Celebrity Poker Showdown* have brought notoriety and stars to the property's fantasy suites and recording studio. **The Pearl** regularly hosts rock concerts, and Playmate appearances at the **Playboy Comedy Club** (9 P.M. Thurs.–Fri., 8 P.M. and 10 P.M. Sat., $40–60) add some sex appeal to the stand-up. The **Moon** nightclub (11 P.M.–late Tues., Thurs., and Sat.) is three floors up from the Playboy Club in the same tower, giving it a commanding view of the stars. **Ghostbar** (8 P.M.–late daily) is small, with a capacity of 300, and has vistas of the Strip and a bird's-eye perspective on the pool area through a section of transparent floor. For a more down-to-earth party experience, you can't go wrong with **Rain** (11 P.M.–late Fri.–Sat.) and its light shows and fireballs over the dance floor.

The Palms has plenty of gourmet restaurant choices, but to give your wallet a bit of a break, try the dark, intimate **Little Buddha** (5:30–11 P.M. Sun.–Thurs., 5:30 P.M.–midnight Fri.–Sat., $25–45). The cuisine is French-Chinese fusion.

The Fantasy Tower houses the Playboy section and the fantasy suites, while the original tower offers large guest rooms. They're nothing special to look at, but the feathery beds and luxurious comforters make it easy to roll over and go back to sleep, even if you're not nursing a hangover. The newest tower, Palms Place, is part of the Las Vegas "condotel" trend. Its 599 studios and one-bedrooms are highly recommended.

Bellagio

- **Restaurants:** Café Bellagio, Café Gelato, Circo, FIX, Jasmine, Jean-Philippe Pâtisserie, Le Cirque, Michael Mina, Noodles, Todd English's Olives, Palio, Palio Pronto, Petrossian Bar, Picasso, Pool Café, Prime, Snacks, The Buffet, Sensi, Yellowtail Sushi Restaurant & Bar
- **Entertainment:** Cirque du Soleil's *O*

- **Attractions:** The Fountains at Bellagio, The Conservatory, Bellagio Gallery of Fine Art, Tuscany Kitchen

- **Nightlife:** The Bank, Caramel

With nearly 4,000 rooms and suites, Bellagio (3600 Las Vegas Blvd. S., 702/693-7444 or 888/987-6667, $180–500 d) boasts a population larger than the village perched on Lake Como from which it borrows its name. And to keep pace with its Italian namesake, Bellagio created an 8.5-acre lake between the hotel and Las Vegas Boulevard. The view of the lake and its **Fountains at Bellagio** (3 P.M.–midnight Mon.–Fri., noon–midnight Sat.–Sun.) are free, as is the aromatic fantasy that is **Bellagio Conservatory** (24 hours daily). And the **Bellagio Gallery of Fine Art** (10 A.M.–6 P.M. Sun.–Tues. and Thurs., 10 A.M.–7 P.M. Wed. and Fri.–Sat., $10–15) would be a bargain at twice the price—you can spend an edifying day at one of the world's priciest resorts (including a cocktail and lunch) for less than $50. Even if you don't spring for gallery admission, art demands your attention throughout

the hotel and casino. The glass flower petals in Dale Chihuly's *Fiori di Como* sculpture bloom from the lobby ceiling, foreshadowing the opulent experiences to come.

The display of artistry continues but the bargains end at **Via Bellagio** (10 A.M.–midnight daily), the resort's shopping district, including heavyweight retailers Armani, Prada, Chanel, Tiffany, and their ilk.

Would you like not only to eat like an Italian but to cook like one too? **The Tuscany Kitchen** (by reservation only, 15-person minimum, $75–150) is your own private Food Network special. World-class chefs demonstrate the preparation of Tuscan delights, and generous samples are included.

Befitting Bellagio's world-class status, intriguing and expensive restaurants abound. **Sensi** (5–10 P.M. Mon.–Thurs., 5–10:30 P.M. Fri.–Sun.) offers a worldwide menu heavy on Italian and seafood for moderate prices. Authentic Asian dishes are the specialty at **Noodles** (11 A.M.–2 A.M. daily), another affordable option.

© RYAN JERZ

The Bellagio perches on a lagoon on the Las Vegas Strip.

CITY WITHIN A CITY

True to its reputation for doing things on a grand scale, Las Vegas recently celebrated the completion of the largest private construction project in U.S. history. Project City Center, a 67-acre complex for hotel, casino, residential, retail, dining, art, and entertainment uses built between Bellagio and Monte Carlo, would have been serious overkill in any other city. In Las Vegas it's impressive, but it's also a natural progression in the city's continuing love affair with grandeur.

City Center employs 12,000 permanent workers, making it the country's largest single hiring effort when it came online in 2009. Its key elements include **Aria,** a more-or-less "traditional" Las Vegas hotel casino: 4,000 guest rooms, 16 restaurants, a spa, nearly a dozen nightclubs and bars, convention space, a pool, 150,000 square feet of slots, table games, and race and sports betting, and *Viva Elvis,* a Cirque du Soleil show.

Vdara is a Euro-chic boutique hotel (no gaming, no smoking, exclusive amenities). The well-heeled can luxuriate in the hotel's health,

beauty, and fitness salons, sip martinis at Bar Vdara, bask in private pool cabanas, and dine in style.

If you have to ask the price, maybe **Crystals** isn't for you. The 500,000-square-foot mall lets you splurge among hanging gardens. Restaurants fronted by Eva Longoria, Wolfgang Puck, and Todd English take the place of Sbarro's and Cinnabon.

Veer Towers and **Mandarin Oriental** are the megaresort's residential spaces. Both come with exclusive pool and spa areas, large condo-style rooms and suites, and a feeling of superiority.

City Center brings another bit of culture to Las Vegas, with its public-area Fine Art Collection. Presented with little fanfare, the art is accessible by anyone strolling the corridors. You can see innovative works by Maya Lin, Jenny Holzer, and Richard Long, among others.

City Center's developers exhibit a concern for the environment, earning six Leadership In Energy and Environmental Design gold designations.

The Bank (10:30 P.M.–4 A.M. Thurs.–Sun.) is a busy upscale nightclub, with most partiers opting for bottle service and the table space and legroom it buys. **Caramel** (5 P.M.–4 A.M. daily) is a bit more laid-back but no less sophisticated. Primarily a wine and martini bar, it caters to the before- and after-show crowd.

Bellagio's tower rooms are the epitome of luxury, with Italian marble, oversize bathtubs, remote-controlled drapes, Egyptian-cotton sheets, and 510 square feet in which to spread out. The hunter green and mauve decor is a refreshing change from the goes-with-everything beige and the camouflages-all-stains paisley often found on the Strip.

Paris

- **Restaurants:** Café Belle Madeleine, Eiffel Tower Restaurant, Les Artistes Steakhouse, Mon Ami Gabi, Le Provençal, Le Village Buffet, du Parc, Le Café Île St. Louis, JJ's

Boulangerie, La Creperie, Sugar Factory, Le Burger Brasserie Sports Grille

- **Entertainment:** Barry Manilow, Anthony Cools

- **Attractions:** Eiffel Tower

- **Nightlife:** Napoleon's Dueling Piano Bar, Gustav's Casino Bar, Le Cabaret, Le Central Lobby Bar, Le Bar du Sport

Designers used Gustav Eiffel's original drawings to ensure that the half-size version that anchors Paris Las Vegas (3655 Las Vegas Blvd. S., 877/242-6753, $120–300 d) conformed—down to the last cosmetic rivet—to the original. That attention to detail prevails throughout this property, which works hard to evoke the City of Light, from large-scale reproductions of the Arc de Triomphe, Champs Élysées, and Louvre to more than half a dozen French restaurants. The tower is perhaps the most romantic spot in town to view the Strip; you'll catch your breath as the elevator whisks you to the observation deck 460 feet up, then have it taken away again by the lights of the resorts up and down one of the most famous skylines in the world. Back at street level, the cobblestone lanes and brass streetlights of **Le Boulevard** (10 A.M.–11 P.M. daily) invite shoppers into quaint shops and "sidewalk" patisseries. The casino offers its own attractions, not the least of which is the view of the Eiffel Tower's base jutting through the ceiling.

The **Paris Theatre** hosts headliners. With the showroom named after him, **Anthony Cools–The Uncensored Hypnotist** (9 P.M. Tues. and Thurs.–Sun., $54–75) appears destined for a long run, cajoling his mesmerized subjects through very adult simulations.

Waiters at **Le Provencal** (5–10:30 P.M. daily, $15–30) serenade diners with traditional French and Italian songs between the caprese salad and the bouillabaisse.

Standard guest rooms in the 33-story tower are decorated in a rich earth-tone palate and have marble bathrooms. There's nothing Left Bank bohemian about them, however. The rooms exude little flair and little personality, but the simple, quality furnishings make Paris a moderately priced option in the midst of a top-dollar neighborhood.

Hard Rock

- **Restaurants:** Ago, Johnny Smalls, Mr. Lucky's 24/7, Nobu, Rare 120, Pink Taco, Starbucks, Espumoso

- **Entertainment:** The Rogue Joint

- **Nightlife:** Wasted Space, Vanity

The Palms and a few others have stolen a bit of the Hard Rock's (4455 Paradise Rd., 800/473-7625, $200–500 d) mojo, but young stars and the media-savvy 20-somethings who idolize them contribute to the frat party in the casino and the spring-break atmosphere poolside. The casino is shaped like a record (although if your music collection dates back to records, this probably isn't the place for you), with the gaming tables and machines in the "record label" and the shops and restaurants in the "grooves."

Contemporary and classic rockers regularly grace the stage at the **Rogue Joint** and party with their fans at **Wasted Space** (9 P.M.–4 A.M. Wed.–Sun.). **Vanity** (10 P.M.–4 A.M. Thurs.–Sun.) is a little more refined, with a 20,000-crystal chandelier that showers sparkles on the sunken dance floor.

The provocatively named **Pink Taco** (11 A.M.–10 P.M. Sun.–Thurs., 11 A.M.–midnight Fri.–Sat.) dishes up Mexican and Caribbean specialties.

Undersized and always in demand, the Hard Rock Hotel has undergone major expansion and renovation in the last few years, including construction of HRH Towers, an effort to attract more mature visitors. The resort's 1,500 guest rooms are decorated in warm hues and include Bose CD sound systems and plasma TVs.

Monte Carlo

- **Restaurants:** Andre's, Buffet, BRAND Steakhouse, d.vino, Diablo's Cantina, Dragon Noodle Co., Café, Monaco Garden Food Court, The Pub

- **Entertainment:** Frank Caliendo

- **Nightlife:** BRAND Lounge, Diablo's Lounge

As evidenced by all the marble and chandeliers we've come to expect from a European-themed Vegas resort, Monte Carlo (3770 Las Vegas Blvd. S., 702/730-7777 or 800/311-8999, $100–300 d) doesn't compromise on quality. But its location, entertainment, dining, and prices make it a good choice for families seeking a happy medium. Parents will appreciate the continental theme, and its flair is understated in comparison to Bellagio and Paris. Kids and teens especially will enjoy the pool, **Easy River,** and the wave pool. The magic and comedy impersonator shows are tame by Vegas standards.

Diablo's Cantina (11 A.M.–1 A.M. daily)

opens onto the Strip for terrific people-watching. Margaritas, sangrias, and Mexican-tiled floors carry through the south-of-the-border party atmosphere.

High-end shops dot **Street of Dreams** (10 A.M.–11 P.M. daily), tempting big winners with jewelry and motorcycles and enticing the rest to smother their losses in decadent designer cupcakes.

With 3,000 rooms, Monte Carlo provides the casino-resort feel, but room rates are reasonable, especially for families not willing to settle for the bare-bones kitsch of Circus Circus. Standard guest rooms include dark wood furniture, overstuffed chairs, and brass bathroom fixtures. The layout allows you to reach your room without a detour through the casino, so you can more easily resist the urge to drunkenly throw down a Benjamin on the hard four as you stumble through after a night of revelry.

New York New York

- **Restaurants:** America, Chin Chin Café, Coney Island Pavilion, Gallagher's Steakhouse, Gonzalez y Gonzalez, Greenberg's Deli, Il Fornaio, Nine Fine Irishmen, Schrafft's Ice Cream, Village Eateries

- **Entertainment:** Cirque du Soleil's *Zumanity,* Dueling Pianos

- **Attractions:** The Roller Coaster

- **Nightlife:** Rok Vegas, Coyote Ugly

One look at this loving tribute to the city that never sleeps and you won't be able to fuhgedaboutit. From the city skyline outside (the skyscrapers contain the resort's hotel rooms) to laundry hanging between crowded faux brownstones indoors, New York New York (3790 Las Vegas Blvd. S., 866/815-4365, $200–500 d) will have even grizzled Gothamites feeling like they've come home again. Window air conditioners in the Greenwich Village apartments evoke the city's gritty heat. A more poignant sight, the fence surrounding the replica Statue of Liberty contains tributes to the victims of the World Trade Center attack.

The **Roller Coaster at New York New York** (11 A.M.–11 P.M. Sun.–Thurs., 10:30 A.M.–midnight Fri.–Sat., $14) winds its way around the resort, an experience almost as hair-raising as a ride in a New York City cab, which the coaster cars are painted to resemble. **Coney Island Emporium** (hours vary, daily) has games of skill and luck, motion simulators, and rides.

Dueling pianists keep **The Bar at Times Square** (8 A.M.–2 P.M. daily) rocking into the wee hours, and the sexy bar staff at **Coyote Ugly** (9 P.M.–2 A.M. Sun.–Thurs., 9 P.M.–3 A.M., Fri.–Sat.) defy its name.

New York New York's 2,023 guest rooms are standard size, 350–500 square feet. The roller coaster zooms around the towers, so you might want to ask for a room out of earshot.

MGM Grand

- **Restaurants:** Joël Robuchon, L'Atelier de Joël Robuchon, Seablue, Tom Colicchio's Craftsteak, Pearl, Diego, Fiamma Trattoria, Emeril's New Orleans Fish House, Nobhill Tavern, Rainforest Cafe, Wolfgang Puck Bar & Grill, Grand Wok and Sushi Bar, Shibuya, Studio Café, Stage Deli, Grand Buffet, 'Wichcraft, Cabana Grille, Starbucks, food court

- **Entertainment:** Cirque du Soleil's *Kà,* Crazy Horse Paris

- **Attractions:** Lion Habitat, CBS Television City Research Center, CSI: The Experience

- **Nightlife:** Studio 54, Tabú

When the MGM Grand (3799 Las Vegas Blvd. S., 888/646-1203, $150–400 d) opened in 1993, guests entered through the gaping maw of the MGM lion. This literal and figurative ingress to the belly of the beast didn't sit well with the superstitious Asian high rollers that the megaresort sought. After renovation, gamblers now enter through portals guarded by the 45-foot-tall king of the jungle. The uninitiated may feel like a gazelle on the savanna, swallowed by the 171,000-square-foot casino floor, the largest in Las Vegas. But the watering hole, MGM's 6.5-acre pool complex, is relatively predator-free.

MGM capitalizes on the movie studio's greatest hits. Even the hotel's emerald facade evokes the magical city in *The Wizard of Oz*.

Boob tube fans can volunteer for studies at the **CBS Television City Research Center** (10 A.M.–8:30 P.M. daily), where they can screen pilots for shows under consideration by the network. And if your favorite show happens to revolve around solving crimes, don some rubber gloves and search for clues at **CSI: The Experience** (9 A.M.–9 P.M. daily, $30 age 12 and up, not recommended for children under 12). Three crime scenes keep the experience fresh. Patterned on the French classic, **Crazy Horse Paris** (8 P.M. and 10:30 P.M. Wed.–Mon., $61) bills itself as "artistry of the nude." Enough said.

MGM Grand houses enough top restaurants for a week of gourmet dinners. Winning selections include **Diego** (4–10 P.M. Sun.–Fri., 5–10 P.M. Sat., $35–55), for tangy rib eyes in a vibrant setting, and **Pearl** (5:30–10 P.M. daily), for crispy Peking duck in a subtle Asian-Pacific atmosphere.

Standard guest rooms in the Grand Tower are filled with the quality furnishings you'd expect in Las Vegas's posh hotels. The West Tower guest rooms are a bit smaller but exude the swinging style of a posh Hollywood studio apartment crammed with a CD and DVD player and other high-tech gizmos; those in the Grand Tower are more traditional. All 5,000-plus guest rooms and suites measure more than 440 square feet.

Tropicana

- **Restaurants:** Bacio Pasta & Vino, Legends Steak & Seafood, Havana Go Go Café, South Beach Café & Deli

- **Entertainment:** Hypnosis Unleashed, Brad Garrett's Comedy Club

- **Attractions:** Las Vegas Mob Experience

- **Nightlife:** Nikki Beach, Celebration Lounge

When it opened at Tropicana Avenue and Las Vegas Boulevard in 1959, the Tropicana (801 Las Vegas Blvd. S., 888/381-8767, $75–175 d) was the most luxurious, most expensive, and southernmost resort on the Strip. It has survived several boom-and-bust cycles since then, and its decor reflects the willy-nilly expansion and refurbishment efforts through the years. Another $125 million renovation was completed in 2010, renovating every guest room and the casino while incorporating a new sports book and poker room. Standard guest rooms now reflect the beach theme, with plantation shutters and art deco colors, 42-inch plasma TVs, and iPod docks.

The South Beach–inspired changes in 2011 will see transformation of the Trop's historic four-acre pool area into **Nikki Beach Club** and **Club Nikki,** which will capture the sultry vibe à la South Beach and Saint-Tropez with fruity cocktails, cocoa butter–scented bikini babes, and cool, fresh cuisine.

The renovation will go a long way toward the Tropicana shedding its image as the ugly stepsister to the Luxor, Monte Carlo, MGM Grand, and even Excalibur, which share its intersection. That's good, we suppose, but there was an undeniable charm to the old joint's laid-back atmosphere and commitment to treating low rollers with deference (the casino even offers free gambling lessons to help guests mitigate their losses). We hope the facelift doesn't give the Trop airs.

Touting "interactive entertainment technology," the **Las Vegas Mob Experience** uses artifacts, photos, and videos to provide a multisensory immersion into the seedy underworld of Las Vegas past and the law enforcement efforts that cleaned up the city. Details were sketchy at press time, but promoters promised visitors "an authentic reach and real perspective into the personal lives and property of the fascinating individuals" who helped create one of Las Vegas's enduring legacies.

The Trop is not big on entertainment, but it did open **Brad Garrett's Comedy Club** (800/829-9034, 8 P.M. Sun.–Thurs., 8 P.M. and 10 P.M. Fri.–Sat., $43–65), and **Hypnosis**

Unleashed (800/829-9034, 9 P.M. nightly, $44–66) is performed in The Cellar. It's only a short walk to world-class entertainers at nearby resorts.

Excalibur

- **Restaurants:** The Steakhouse at Camelot, Regale, Dick's Last Resort, Sherwood Forest Cafe, Roundtable Buffet, Krispy Kreme, Starbucks, food court

- **Entertainment:** *Tournament of Kings, Thunder from Down Under, Defending the Caveman*

- **Attractions:** Fantasy Faire Midway, simulated motion rides

- **Nightlife:** Octane Lounge

This bright white castle with vibrant parapets was one of the more interesting designs when it opened on the Strip in 1990, and despite some design changes—a robotic Merlin no longer slays the dragon in a nightly battle—it still clings to the Arthurian legend throughout. It's difficult to shed the whole "quest for the Holy Grail" image when your hotel is a depiction of Camelot. Shops and restaurants are named for the trappings of medieval Europe; minstrels and strolling entertainers transport guests into the realm of fantasy role-play. Sitting between the Luxor and New York New York, Excalibur (3580 Las Vegas Blvd. S., 877/750-5464, $50–200 d) provides a logical (for Las Vegas) progression along the timeline of world civilization. Like the rest of Las Vegas, the resort has grown up, replacing those primary colors with rich burgundies and navies, updating the casino decor and filling the rooms with modern conveniences. The clientele is still of the nickel-slot and $5 blackjack ilk, but not every casino can attract the whales. And to its credit, Excalibur doesn't try to be all things for all people. Its entertainment, restaurants, and attractions— the beefcake-y **Thunder from Down Under** (702/597-7600, 9 P.M. Sun.–Thurs., 9 P.M. and 11 P.M. Fri.–Sat., $40–50) notwithstanding— are geared more toward budget-minded families than perk-seeking big spenders.

Little gamers can lose themselves for hours at the **Fantasy Faire Midway** (10 A.M.–midnight Sun.–Thurs., 10 A.M.–1 A.M. Fri.–Sat.), home to carnival games and the Spongebob Squarepants 4-D ride.

Kevin Burke's witty observations bridge the gender gap at **Defending the Caveman** (3 P.M. Sun.–Thurs., 3 P.M. and 7 P.M. Fri.–Sat., $49–72) in the Down Under Showroom.

Restaurant choices are of the nongourmet variety, but the snarky waitstaff at **Dick's Last Resort** (1 P.M.–late Mon.–Thurs., 11:30 A.M.– late Fri.–Sat.) is good for some laughs. Dig in to some fried finger food and leave your manners at the door.

Standard guest rooms feature hardwood furniture and dark accents. An upgrade can get you a "Widescreen Room" with a 42-inch TV, padded headboard, and the Las Vegas standard marble bathroom.

Luxor

- **Restaurants:** Backstage Deli, Company Kitchen and Pub House, TENDER Steak & Seafood, Pyramid Cafe, T&T Tacos & Tequila, Luxor Food Court, Starbucks, MORE the Buffet at the Luxor

- **Entertainment:** *Criss Angel Believe,* Carrot Top, *Fantasy, Menopause the Musical*

- **Attractions:** Bodies…the Exhibition, Titanic: The Artifact Exhibition

- **Nightlife:** CatHouse, LAX, Flight, Noir Bar, Aurora, Liquidity, Flight, High Bar, Playbar

With a pyramid shape and a name like Luxor (3900 Las Vegas Blvd. S., 877/386-4658, $50–175 d), it's difficult to imagine this resort without an Egyptian theme, but that's the strategy MGM Mirage has taken over the last few years. Similar to the company's move away from the pirate theme at Treasure Island, beginning in 2007 the parent company moved the resort away from the archeological-dig theme. Much of the mummy-and-scarab decor from the casino, hotel lobby, and public areas was swept away in a $300 million revamp in 2007. In their place are upscale and decidedly postpharaoh nightclubs, restaurants, and shops. The large (120,000-square-foot) casino received a big part of that makeover budget, as did all 2,500 guest rooms in the pyramid and twin 22-story towers.

What remains are the largest atrium in the world, the intense light beam that is visible from space, and inclinators—elevators that move along the building's oblique angles.

Magic meets magic mushrooms in the surrealistic, psychedelic dream sequences of *Mindfreak* Criss Angel in **Believe** (702/262-4400 or 800/557-7428, 7 P.M. and 9:30 P.M. Tues.–Sat., $65–176). The Atrium Showroom (702/262-4400 or 800/557-7428) is home to **Fantasy** (10:30 P.M. daily, $54–70), a typical jiggle-and-tease topless review; **Menopause the Musical** (5 P.M. and 8:30 P.M. Tues., 5:30 P.M. Wed.–Mon., $60–77), a musical salute to the change; and the comedian and prop jockey **Carrot Top** (8 P.M. Mon. and Wed.–Sun., $55–66).

For late-night noshing or traditional dinner, visit **Company Lounge** (5 P.M.–late Wed. and Fri.–Sat., $15–25) for a rustic yet sophisticated atmosphere. A good spot to end the evening after partying is **LAX** (5 P.M.–late Wed. and Fri.–Sat.).

The hotel's pyramid shape makes for interesting room features, such as a slanted exterior wall, as well as a few challenges. Tower rooms are more traditional in their shape, decor, and amenities.

Mandalay Bay

- **Restaurants:** Aureole; Bay Side Buffet; Beach Bar & Grill; Border Grill; China Grill; Fleur de Lys; House of Blues; Mizuya; Raffles Cafe; Red, White and Blue; Red Square; Rumjungle; Sea Breeze Pizza, Ice Cream, and Juices; Shanghai Lilly; Strip-Steak; Trattoria del Lupo; The Noodle Shop; Turf Club Deli; Hussong's Cantina; Giorgio Caffé & Ristorante; The Burger Bar; Mix; food court

- **Entertainment:** House of Blues, Disney's *The Lion King*

A shimmering gold ingot, Mandalay Bay is the jewel of Las Vegas's lower Strip.

LOCALS' FAVORITE CASINOS

Often, frequent Las Vegas visitors will claim they could never live here because they love to gamble too much. Several casinos cater to that local trade, tailoring their offerings to ensure loyal customer bases with locals-only discounts and generous cash-back programs through frequent-player clubs, free poker, video poker, and slot tournaments. They also offer gaming without the traffic and congestion of the Strip and downtown.

THE CANNERY AND EASTSIDE CANNERY

Decor straight out of an Andrews Sisters song attracts military veterans and active-duty flyboys from nearby Nellis Air Force Base. But most locals go here for the deals. The Can Club players program gives cash back for points earned by playing slots and video poker machines and table games. On special days, players earn extra points, and the Cannery (2121 E. Craig Rd., North Las Vegas, 702/507-5700 or 866/999-4899, $40-100 d) and Eastside Cannery (525 Boulder Hwy., 702/507-5700 or 866/999-4899) give special deals for reaching specific point totals. In addition to cash, points can be redeemed for free slot play, show tickets, restaurant meals, and logo merchandise. These casinos also have developed partnership programs allowing players to receive discounts or gift cards good at local merchants.

RED ROCK

The secret of Red Rock casino (11011 W. Charleston Blvd., 702/797-7777, $85-300 d) is spreading beyond locals to high rollers and celebrities who want a more secluded destination with all the resort amenities. Kanye West and Justin Timberlake have stayed here, preferring the "boutique" feel of the 800-room hotel to the megaresorts of the Strip. Westside residents like the

something-for-everyone amenities. While the adults belly up to the craps table, teens can take in a movie on one of 16 screens or bowl a few frames in the 72-lane bowling center. Younger kids will have fun climbing, crawling, sliding, and bouncing at Kids Quest, an indoor child care center with lots of ways to burn off excess energy.

SAM'S TOWN

Tranquil Mystic Falls, with its animatronic wildlife and real foliage, suddenly turns into a raging flood punctuated by urgent wolf calls, fountains, and lasers. Locals stroll the park just to see first-timers react to the sudden transformation. Many east-siders also prefer the moseying Old West pace of Sam's Town (5111 Boulder Hwy., 702/456-7777 or 800/897-8696, $26-120 d) and its restaurants and shopping opportunities. Other amenities include 56 lanes of bowling, an 18-screen movie theater, and Sam's Town Live!, an entertainment venue that hosts soft rock, country, and rockabilly acts — perfect for boot-scootin' locals and visitors alike.

SILVERTON

Slot-club points at this south-Strip resort (3333 Blue Diamond Rd., 702/263-7777 or 866/722-4608, $50-160 d) are good for meals, rooms, shows, and even merchandise at the huge Bass Pro Shops located right inside the casino. But the best part of membership is the invitations to members-only events like blackjack tournaments, NASCAR races, and UNLV basketball games. **Twin Creeks** (5-9 P.M. Tues.-Thurs., 5-10 P.M. Fri.-Sat., $30-50) evokes alpine luxury with hardwood floors, exposed beams, subtle lighting, smoky scotch, and small-batch bourbon complementing big ol' steaks. The hotel rooms carry on the lodge feel, with rustic but plush decor and subdued lighting but all the conveniences of home.

- **Attractions:** Shark Reef, Lion King Exhibit
- **Nightlife:** Rumjungle, Foundation Room, Eyecandy, Mix Lounge

Enter this South Pacific behemoth at the southern tip of the Las Vegas Strip and try to comprehend its mind-boggling statistics. **⊄ Mandalay Bay** (3950 Las Vegas Blvd. S., 877/632-7800, $120–600 d) has one of the largest casino floors in the world at 135,000 square feet. Wander into Mandalay's beach environment, an 11-acre paradise comprised of three pools, a lazy river, and a 1.6-million-gallon wave pool complete with a real beach made of 5 million pounds of sand. There's also a tops-optional sunbathing pool deck. You could spend your entire vacation in the pool area, gambling at the beach's three-level casino, eating at its restaurant, shopping for pool gear at the poolside stand, and loading up on sandals and bikinis at the nearby Pearl Moon boutique.

When you're ready to check out the rest of the property, don't miss **House of Blues** (hours and days vary by event), with live blues, rock, and acoustic sets as well as DJs spinning dance tunes.

Mandalay Place (10 A.M.–11 P.M. daily) is a bit smaller and less hectic than other casino malls. Unusual shops such as Viva Dogs Vegas, for owners who want to pamper their pooches, share space with eateries and high-concept bars like **Minus 5** (11 A.M.–3 A.M. daily), where barflies don parkas before entering the below-freezing (23°F) establishment. Here the glasses aren't just frosted, they're fashioned completely out of ice. The promenade also houses the **Lion King Exhibit** (10 A.M.–11 P.M. daily), a look into the creative genius behind the Broadway smash that is presented in the Mandalay Bay Theatre.

Sheathed in Indian artifacts and crafts, the **Foundation Room** (11 P.M.–late daily) is just as dark and mysterious as the subcontinent, with private rooms, a dining room, and several bars catering to various musical tastes.

Vegas pays tribute to Paris, Rome, New York, and Venice, so why not Moscow? Round up your comrades for caviar and vodka as well as continental favorites at **Red Square** (5 P.M.–2 A.M. Sun.–Thurs., 4 P.M.–4 A.M. Fri.–Sat., $25–40). Look for the headless Lenin statue at the entrance.

Standard rooms are chic and roomy (550 square feet), with warm fabrics and plush bedding. The rooms are nothing special visually, but the bathrooms are fit for royalty, with huge tubs, glass-walled showers, and king's-and-queen's commodes. To go upscale, check out Thehotel; for ultraposh, book at the Four Seasons—both are part of the same property.

DOWNTOWN
Main Street Station

- **Restaurants:** Garden Court Buffet, Triple 7 BrewPub

As its full name suggests, Main Street Station Casino, Brewery, and Hotel (200 N. Main St., 800/522-4700, $40–100 d) works hard to provide something for everyone. The result is an eclectic blend of interesting curios, themes, and styles. The casino combines a railroad motif—with Pullman cars belonging to Louisa May Alcott, Buffalo Bill Cody, and Theodore Roosevelt—with European Victorian-era decor—artifacts from London's Barclay's Bank, Paris's Figaro Opera House, and Belgium's city streets. A hunk of the Berlin Wall graces the men's restroom, and a chandelier from the El Presidente Hotel in Buenos Aires is thrown in for good measure.

Despite these extras, Main Street Station comes up short on amenities that travelers may want. Restaurant choices are limited, but the **Triple 7 Brewpub** (11 A.M.–7 A.M. daily, $10–20) has the hotel's five signature brews on tap as well as pretty good pizza and bargain breakfasts for early risers and late partiers.

Main Street does not offer room service. It also lacks a swimming pool, not unusual for a downtown hotel; but guests have access to the pool at the California just up the street.

Just steps away from the Fremont Street Experience, the hotel's 400 guest rooms are bright and airy, but they are smallish by Las Vegas standards at 400 square feet.

Binion's

- **Restaurants:** Ranch Steakhouse, Binion's Café, Benny's Bullpen

Before Vegas became a destination resort city, it catered to inveterate gamblers, hard drinkers, and others on the fringes of society. Ah, the good old days! A gambler himself, Benny Binion put his place in the middle of downtown, a magnet for the serious player, offering high limits and few frills. Binion's (128 Fremont St., 702/382-1600) still offers single-deck blackjack and a poker room frequented by grizzled veterans. While Binion's and the rest of Las Vegas have been overtaken by Strip megaresorts, the little den on Fremont Street still retains the flavor of Old Vegas, though the Binion family is no longer involved. Harrah's bought the place in 2004 but kept its popular and profitable World Series of Poker.

The hotel at Binion's closed in 2009, but the casino and restaurants remain open, including the **Ranch Steakhouse** (5:30–10:30 P.M. daily, $25–40), famous for its Fremont Street views and primo cuts.

Golden Nugget

- **Restaurants:** The Buffet, Chart House, Lillie's Noodle House, Vic & Anthony's, Grotto Ristorante, Red Sushi, Carson Street Cafe, Starbucks

- **Entertainment:** Gordie Brown

- **Attractions:** Hand of Faith, The Tank

- **Nightlife:** Rush Lounge, Gold Diggers

Considered by many to be the only Strip-worthy resort downtown, the (**Golden Nugget** (129 E. Fremont St., 800/634-3454, $50–150) has been a fixture for 65 years, beckoning diners and gamblers with gold leaf and a massive gold nugget. Landry's, the restaurant chain and new Nugget owner, has embarked on an ambitious campaign to maintain the hotel's opulence, investing $160 million for casino and guest room upgrades.

If you don't feel like swimming with the sharks in the poker room, you can get up close and personal with their finned namesakes in **The Tank** (10 A.M.–8 P.M. daily, $10–20 nonguests, free for hotel guests), an outdoor pool with a three-story waterslide that takes riders through the hotel's huge aquarium, home to sharks, rays, and other exotic marine life. Bathers can also swim up to the aquarium for a face-to-face with the aquatic predators. Waterfalls and lush landscaping help make this one of the world's best hotel pools.

Gold Diggers nightclub (9 P.M.–late Wed.–Sun.) plays hip-hop, pop, and classic rock for the dancing pleasure of guests and go-go girls.

When checking in, pause to have your picture taken with the **Hand of Faith,** a 62-pound gold nugget. Rooms are appointed in dark wood and chocolate hues.

The Plaza

- **Restaurants:** Firefly, Downtown Grill, Stuffed Buffet, food court

- **Entertainment:** *The Rat Pack Is Back*

- **Nightlife:** Aqua Lounge

The largest hotel in Las Vegas when it opened in 1971 as the Union Plaza—a nod to the Union Pacific rail line out back—the Plaza (1 Main St., 702/386-2110 or 800/634-6575, $40–100 d) has held court over Main Street ever since. The hotel's location was the site of the first Las Vegas land auction in 1905. All street numbers in town originate here—1 Main Street—making it the center of modern Las Vegas. In keeping with the hotel's place in history, the **Rat Pack is Back** (7:30 P.M. daily, $55, $69 with dinner) does a credible job of recreating the heyday of Frank, Dean, and Sammy.

Still one of the larger places downtown, with more than 1,000 guest rooms, the Plaza also offers a variety of suites; expect to get what you pay for.

Sights

DOWNTOWN
(Fremont Street Experience

With land at a premium and more and more tourists flocking to the opulence of the Strip, downtown Las Vegas in the last quarter of the 20th century found its lights beginning to flicker. Enter Fremont Street Experience (702/678-5777), an ambitious plan to transform downtown and its tacky "Glitter Gulch" reputation into a pedestrian-friendly enclave. Highlighted by a four-block-long canopy festooned with 12 million light-emitting diodes 90 feet in the air, Fremont Street Experience is downtown's answer to the Strip's erupting volcanoes and fantastic dancing fountains. The canopy, dubbed Viva Vision, runs atop Fremont Street between North Main Street and North 4th Street.

The casinos were slow to embrace the vision at first, concerned that the productions would cause a mass exodus from their slot machines and table games at show time. Viva

Vision's backers even wanted the properties to dim their marquees, reducing ambient light, to make the shows more vibrant. But with little else to help them compete with the Strip, they acquiesced.

Urban architect Jon Jerde unveiled his $70 million creation in 1995, and it has been drawing millions of people each year ever since, introducing new generations to "Old Vegas," the casinos that birthed the gambling boom, launched legendary careers, and developed Vegas-style service that makes every gambler feel like a high roller.

A $17 million upgrade in 2004 boosted the resolution of the light show, bringing it nearly to video quality to complement its high-fidelity 550,000-watt sound system.

Once an hour, the promenade goes dark and all heads lift toward the canopy, supported by massive concrete pillars. For six minutes, visitors are enthralled by the multimedia shows that chronicle Western history, span the careers of classic rock bands, or transport viewers to fantasy worlds.

Before and after the light shows, strolling buskers sing for their supper, artists create five-minute masterpieces, and caricaturists airbrush souvenir portraits. Fremont Street hosts top musical acts, including some A-listers during big Las Vegas weekends such as National Finals Rodeo, NASCAR races, and New Year. Viva Vision runs several different shows daily at 8:30 P.M., then on the hour 9 P.M.–midnight.

Las Vegas Natural History Museum

Las Vegas boasts a volcano, a pyramid, and even a Roman colosseum, so it's little wonder that an animatronic *Tyrannosaurus rex* calls the valley home too. Dedicated to "global life forms…from the desert to the ocean, from Nevada to Africa, from prehistoric times to the present," the Las Vegas Natural History Museum (900 Las Vegas Blvd. N., 702/384-3466, 9 A.M.–4 P.M. daily, $10 adults, $8 seniors, military, and students, $5 ages 3–11) is filled with rotating exhibits that belie the

notion that Las Vegas culture begins and ends with neon casino signs.

Visitors to the Treasures of Egypt gallery can enter a realistic depiction of King Tut's tomb to study archeological techniques and discover golden treasures of the pharaohs. The Wild Nevada gallery showcases the raw beauty and surprisingly varied life forms of the Mojave Desert. Interactive exhibits also enlighten visitors on subjects such as marine life, geology, African ecosystems, and more.

The 35-foot-long *T. rex* and his friends (rivals? entrées?)—a triceratops, raptor, and ichthyosaur—greet visitors in the Prehistoric Life gallery. And by "greet" we mean a bloodcurdling roar from the *T. rex,* so take precautions with the little ones and the faint of heart.

Neon Museum and Boneyard

The Neon Museum and Boneyard (821 Las Vegas Blvd. N., 702/477-7751), which reopened in late 2010 after construction of Neon Park, is a trip to Las Vegas's more recent past. Housed in the relocated scallop-shaped lobby of the historic La Concha Motel, the museum includes a walking tour north from the Fremont Street Experience. The lamp from the Aladdin Hotel, The Silver Slipper, the Red Barn's martini glass, and the Hacienda's horse and rider, all in glorious twinkling lights, are part of the tour. The self-guided tour is accessible 24 hours a day, but the neighborhood is a bit dubious, so be careful if you go at night.

Neon Park, just behind the clamshell visitors center, is home to some 200 other flashy homages to Old Vegas. Las Vegas doesn't often hold onto its past, so this little walking tour of old signs is an intriguing sight—and it's free.

The small park includes interpretive signage, benches, picnic tables, and a "NEON" sign created from the N's from the Golden Nugget and Desert Inn, the E from Caesar's Palace, and the O from Binion's.

Lied Discovery Children's Museum

Voted Best Museum in Las Vegas by readers of the local newspaper, the Lied Discovery

Children's Museum (833 Las Vegas Blvd. N., 702/382-5437, 9 A.M.–4 P.M. Tues.–Fri., 10 A.M.–5 P.M. Sat., noon–5 P.M. Sun., $8.50 adults, $7.50 seniors and minors) presents more than 100 interactive scientific, artistic, and life-skill activities. Children enjoy themselves so much that they forget they're learning. Among the best permanent exhibits is *It's Your Choice,* which shows kids the importance of eating right and adopting a healthy lifestyle. Exhibits show kids creative ways to explore their world: drama, cooperation, dance, and visual arts. Adult-guided science and arts education programs help open youngsters' imaginations as well, and traveling exhibitions run the gamut from fun and frivolous (a recent special exhibit challenged problem-solvers of all ages to find their way through mazes) to serious and thought-provoking (the museum recently hosted *Torn From Home: My Life as a Refugee*).

Mormon Fort

This tiny museum (500 E. Washington Ave., 702/486-3511, 8 A.M.–4:30 P.M., $1) is the oldest building in Las Vegas. The adobe remnant, constructed by Mormon missionaries in 1855, was part of their original settlement, which they abandoned in 1858. It then served as a store, a barracks, and a shed on the Gass-Stewart Ranch. After that, the railroad leased the old fort to various tenants, including the Bureau of Reclamation, which stabilized and rebuilt the shed to use as a concrete-testing laboratory for Hoover Dam. In 1955 the railroad sold the old fort to the Elks, who in 1963 bulldozed the whole wooden structure (except the little remnant) into the ranch swimming pool and torched it. The shed was bought by the city in 1971.

Since then, a number of preservation societies have helped keep it in place. The museum includes a visitors center, a re-creation of the original fort built around the remnant. A tour guide presents the history orally while display boards provide it visually. Your visit will not go unrewarded—it's immensely refreshing to see some preservation of the past in this city of the ultimate now.

Mob Museum

The Museum of Organized Crime and Law Enforcement (300 Stewart Ave., 702/229-6582) is scheduled to open in 2011—but you didn't hear it from us. Celebrating Las Vegas's Mafia past and the cops and agents who finally ran the mob out of town, the museum is located inside the city's downtown post office and courthouse, appropriately the site of the 1951 Kefauver Hearing investigating organized crime.

Displays include "The Skim," an examination of how casinos funneled unreported income to their unacknowledged underworld owners, and "Mob Mayhem," which shows the violence, ceremony, and hidden meanings behind Mafia "hits," all against a grisly background—the wall from Chicago's St. Valentine's Day Massacre that spelled the end of six members of Bugs Moran's crew and one hanger-on. "Bringing Down the Mob" displays the tools federal agents used—wiretaps, surveillance, and weapons—to clean up the town.

Downtown Arts District

Centered at South Main Street and East Charleston Boulevard, the district gives art lovers a concentration of galleries to suit any taste, plus an eclectic mix of shops, eateries, and other surprises. **The Arts Factory** (107 E. Charleston Blvd., 702/383-3133), a two-story redbrick industrial building, is the district's birthplace. Its ground floor is home to **Contemporary Arts Collective,** where artists meet, share ideas, and find creative support and patrons can explore and learn about artists, their media, and their styles. Contemporary Arts Collective hosts shows monthly; performing arts as well as two- and three-dimensional artworks are included—"as long as it can fit through the door," says local artist and volunteer Mark Diederichsen.

Upstairs at **Damned Ink,** you'll find paintings and ink drawings that explore artist Danny Roberts's sometimes hopeful, sometimes heartbreaking examinations of humankind's conflicted relationship with culture, nature, and responsibility. "Each subject is on the verge of an epiphany and facing a new conflict," Roberts says. "It is a brief moment of either acceptance or rebellion."

Make an appointment to stop by **S2 Editions Atelier** (1 E. Charleston Blvd., 702/868-7880), next to the Arts Factory, to see the painstaking process the master printers use to reproduce fine art lithographs on massive 140-year-old presses. Pick up one of the colorful Tom Everhart "Snoopy" lithos printed at S2, or journey north to the **Arts Village** (1039 N. Main St., 702/249-3200) to see Sharon Gainsburg's realist and abstract stone sculptures and wine-rack art.

Virtually all the galleries and other paeans to urban pop culture participate in Las Vegas's First Friday event (6–10 P.M. first Fri. of every month), but otherwise galleries keep limited hours, so if there's something you don't want to miss, call for an appointment.

From here, you can head south to **Commerce Street Studios** (1551 S. Commerce St., 702/678-6278) to browse out the edgy, often avant-garde displays at **The Fallout** and neighboring **Circadian Gallery,** with its aggressive, brooding expressions and impressionistic nudes by Daniel Pearson. Or you can mosey westward to **Gallery P** (231 W. Charleston Blvd., Suite 160, 702/384-8155), where Joseph Palermo displays his modernist art. Or check out the renovated **Holsum Design Center** (241 W. Charleston Blvd.), a former 1950s bakery recently converted to shops, studios, and artist lofts.

CENTER STRIP
Imperial Palace Auto Collection
The exhibits are always changing at this gem hidden atop the parking garage at the Imperial Palace Hotel (3535 Las Vegas Blvd. S., 702/794-3174, 10 A.M.–6 P.M., $9 adults, $5 children and seniors, free under age 3). That's because most of the classic muscle and luxury cars are for sale, but this is far from your run-of-the-mill used car lot.

Among the beauties recently on display were two dozen Duesenbergs, Elvis Presley's 1976 Cadillac Eldorado, and a 1957 Jaguar XKSS, appraised at about $7 million.

History buffs and celebrity watchers as well as motor-heads will find plenty to pique their interest. The museum recently featured W. C. Fields's custom-made Fleetwood limousine—complete with electric martini mixer—and one of Johnny Carson's first rides, a 1939 Chrysler Royal sedan that ferried him and his date to Carson's senior prom.

In all, more than 250 cars and a few motorcycles fill several galleries. Discount coupons are plentiful, so don't pay full price.

Madame Tussauds
Ever wanted to dunk over Shaq? Marry George Clooney? Leave Simon Cowell speechless? Madame Tussauds (3377 Las Vegas Blvd. S., 702/862-7800, www.madametussauds. com/lasvegas, 10 A.M.–9 P.M. Sun.–Thurs., 10 A.M.–10 P.M. Fri.–Sat., $25 adults, $18 seniors, $15 children) at the Venetian Hotel gives you your chance. Unlike most other museums, Madame Tussauds encourages guests to get up close and "personal" with the world leaders, sports heroes, and screen stars immortalized in wax. Photo ops and interactive activities abound. With "Karaoke Revolution Presents: American Idol" you can take to the stage and then hear Simon Cowell and Ryan Seacrest's thoughts on your burgeoning singing career. The crowd roars as you take it to the rack and sink the game-winner over Shaquille O'Neal's vainly outstretch arm. You'll feel right at home in the "mansion" as you don bunny ears and lounge on the circular bed with Hugh Hefner.

But it's not all fun and games, especially in the Chamber of Horrors, where the inmates have taken over the asylum. Relax and take a deep breath—all the figures are made of wax, after all. Or are they? Discounts are available on the website.

◖ Gondola Rides
We dare you not to sigh at the grandeur of Venice in the desert as you pass beneath quaint bridges and idyllic sidewalk cafés, your gondolier serenading you with the accompaniment of the Grand Canal's gurgling wavelets.

The indoor gondolas skirt the Grand Canal Shoppes inside the Venetian Hotel (3355 Las Vegas Blvd. S., 702/607-3982, 10 A.M.–11 P.M. Sun.–Thurs., 10 A.M.–midnight Fri.–Sat., $16 for a half mile) under the mall's painted-sky ceiling fresco.

Outdoor gondolas skim the Venetian's 31,000-square-foot lagoon for 12 minutes, giving riders a unique perspective on the Las Vegas Strip.

Plying the waters at regular intervals, the realistic-looking gondolas seat four, but couples who don't want to share a boat can pay double.

❮ Secret Garden and Dolphin Habitat

It's no mirage—those really are pure white tigers lounging in their own plush resort on the Mirage casino floor. Legendary Las Vegas magicians Siegfried and Roy, who have dedicated much of their lives to preserving big cats, opened the Secret Garden (Mirage, 3400 Las Vegas Blvd. S., 702/791-7188, 10 A.M.–7 P.M. daily, $15 adults, $10 ages 4–12, free under age 4) in 1990. In addition to the milky-furred tigers, the garden is home to blue-eyed, black-striped white tigers as well as panthers, lions, and leopards. Though caretakers don't "perform" with the animals, if your visit is well-timed, you could see the cats playing, wrestling, and even swimming in their pristine waterfall-fed pools. The cubs in the specially built nursery are sure to register high on the cuteness meter.

While you're here, visit the Atlantic bottlenoses right next door, also in the middle of the Mirage's palm trees and jungle foliage. The aquatic mammals don't perform on cue either, but they're natural hams, and often interact with their visitors, nodding their heads in response to trainer questions, turning aerial somersaults, and "walking" on their tails across the water. An underwater viewing area provides an unusual perspective into the dolphins' world. Feeding times are a hoot.

Budding naturalists (age 13 and over and willing to part with $550) won't want to miss

© RYAN JERZ

Goldoliers serenade families and couples on the canal at the Venetian.

Dolphin Habitat's Trainer for a Day program, which allows them to feed, swim with, and pose for photos with some of the aquatic stars while putting them through their daily regimen.

LOWER STRIP
Showcase Mall

"Mall" is an overly ambitious moniker for the Showcase Mall (3785 Las Vegas Blvd. S.), a mini diversion on the Strip. The centerpiece, the original **M&M's World** (702/736-7611, 9 A.M.–11 P.M. Sun.–Thurs., 9 A.M.–midnight Fri.–Sat., free), underwent a 2010 expansion and now includes a printing station where customers can customize their bite-size treats with words and pictures. The 3,300-square-foot expansion on the third floor of the store, which originally opened in 1997, includes additional opportunities to stock up on all things M: Swarovski crystal candy dishes, an M&M guitar, T-shirts, and purses made from authentic M&M wrappers. The addition brings the chocoholic's paradise to more than 30,000 square feet, offering key chains, coffee mugs, lunch boxes, and the addicting treats in every color imaginable. Start with a viewing of the short 3-D film, *I Lost My M in Las Vegas*. A replica of Kyle Busch's M&M-sponsored No. 18 NASCAR stock car is on the fourth floor.

Everything Coca-Cola really should be named "A Few Things Coca-Cola." The small retail outlet has collectibles, free photo ops, and a soda fountain where you can taste Coke products from around the world, but it's a pale vestige of Coke's ambitious marketing ploy, à la M&M's World, that opened in 1997 and closed in 2000. The giant green Coke bottle facade, however, attracts pedestrians into the mall.

GameWorks (702/432-4263, 10 A.M.–midnight Sun.–Thurs., 10 A.M.–1 A.M. Fri.–Sat., games priced individually), with various all-you-can-play options, gives you the chance to work off your sugar rush as you assume the role of hunter, snowboarder, and race-car driver on the virtual gaming floor. The virtual bowling is a kick. You can even go old-school, showing off the Pac-Man and pinball skills that made you an arcade legend. A bar and restaurant are on-site to keep the energy levels up.

Bodies...the Exhibition and *Titanic* Artifacts

Although they are tastefully and respectfully presented, the dissected humans at Bodies... the Exhibition at Luxor (3900 Las Vegas Blvd. S., 702/262-4400 or 800/557-7428, 10 A.M.–10 P.M. daily, $31 adults, $29 ages 65 and over, $23 ages 4–12, free under age 4) still have a bit of the creepy factor. That uneasiness quickly gives way to wonder and interest as visitors examine 13 full-body specimens, carefully preserved to reveal bone structure and muscular, circulatory, respiratory, and other systems. Other system and organ displays drive home the importance of a healthy lifestyle, with structures showing the damage caused by overeating, alcohol consumption, and sedentary lifestyle. Perhaps the most sobering exhibit is the side-by-side comparisons of healthy and smoke-damaged lungs. A draped-off area

contains fetal specimens, showing prenatal development and birth defects.

Luxor also hosts the 300 less surreal but just as poignant artifacts and reproductions commemorating the 1912 sinking of the *Titanic* (3900 Las Vegas Blvd. S., 702/262-4400 or 800/557-7428, 10 A.M.–10 P.M. daily, $31 adults, $29 age 65 and over, $23 ages 4–12, free under age 4). The 15-ton rusting hunk of the ship's hull is the biggest artifact on display; it not only drives home the *Titanic*'s scale but also helps transport visitors back to that cold April morning a century ago. A section of the *Titanic*'s grand staircase—featured prominently in the 1997 film with Leonardo DiCaprio and Kate Winslet—testifies to the ship's opulence, but it is the passengers' personal effects (a pipe, luggage, an unopened bottle of champagne) and recreated first-class and third-class cabins that provide some of the most heartbreaking discoveries. The individual stories come to life as each patron is given the identity of one of the ship's passengers. At the end of tour they find out the passenger's fate.

Lion Habitat

A descendant of the famed MGM Studios movie lion and a couple of dozen friends cavort in the luxurious **MGM Grand Lion Habitat** (3799 Las Vegas Blvd. S., 11 A.M.–7 P.M. daily, free). It's a palace fit for a king—of the jungle—in the middle of the casino. Big cat expert Keith Evans designed the habitat to educate and protect the majestic beasts. Evans cares for his 26 lions, three tigers, and two snow leopards at his 8.5-acre Las Vegas compound when they're not entertaining casino guests. The habitat invites visitors to get up close and personal with the lions, separated only by a couple of inches of bulletproof glass. Like your teenage son, lions sleep about 19 hours a day. However, they do rouse themselves twice a day for feeding time—again, just like a high schooler—so it's best to arrive well before the dinner bell rings at 11:15 A.M. and 4:15 P.M. daily to get a good viewing spot. If you come at other times, the handlers may be able to entice the cats into a bit of training or roughhousing. But given the lions' adolescent bent, be prepared to watch a whole lot of snoozing and lazy grooming. Still, it's worth a detour, and posters around the exhibit offer insights into the lion lifestyle.

Shark Reef

Just when you thought it was safe to visit Las Vegas…this 1.6-million-gallon habitat proves not all the sharks in town prowl the poker rooms. Shark Reef (Mandalay Bay, 3950 Las Vegas Blvd. S., 702/632-4555, 10 A.M.–8 P.M. Sun.–Thurs., 10 A.M.–10 P.M. Fri.–Sat., $17 adults, $11 ages 5–12, free under age 5) is home to 2,000 animals—almost all predators. The premise, though a bit farfetched, is pretty cool: Patrons traipse through a slowly sinking ancient temple, coming face to face with some of the most fearsome creatures in the world, such as the sand tiger shark, whose mouth is so crammed with razor-sharp teeth that it doesn't fully close. Fifteen shark species call the reef home, along with golden crocodiles, moray eels, piranhas, giant octopuses, the venomous lion fish, stingrays, jellyfish, water monitors, and the fresh-from-your-nightmares eight-foot-long Komodo dragon.

Mandalay Bay guests with dive certification can dive in the 22-foot-deep shipwreck exhibit at the reef. Commune with eight-foot nurse sharks as well as reef sharks, zebra sharks, rays, sawfish, and other denizens of the deep. Scuba excursions (Tues., Thurs., and Sat.–Sun., age 18 and over, $650) include 3–4 hours underwater, a guided aquarium tour, a video, and admission for up to four guests. Chain mail is required.

OFF STRIP
◖ Las Vegas Springs Preserve

The Springs Preserve (333 S. Valley View Blvd., 702/822-7700, 10 A.M.–6 P.M. daily, $19 adults, $17 students and age 65 and over, $11 ages 5–17, free under age 5) is where Las Vegas began, at least from a Eurocentric viewpoint. More than 100 years ago, the first nonnatives in the Las Vegas Valley—Mormon missionaries

from Salt Lake City—stumbled on this clear artesian spring. Of course, the native Paiute and Pueblo people knew about the springs and exploited them millennia before the Mormons arrived. You can see examples of their tools, pottery, and houses at the site, now a 180-acre monument to environmental stewardship, historic preservation, and geographic discovery. The preserve is home to lizards, rabbits, foxes, scorpions, bats, and more. The nature-minded will love the cactus, rose, and herb gardens, and there's even an occasional cooking demonstration using the desert-friendly fruits, vegetables, and herbs grown here.

Las Vegas has become a leader in water conservation, alternative energy, and other environmentally friendly policies. The results of these efforts and tips on how everyone can reduce their carbon footprint are found in the Sustainability Gallery.

Nevada State Museum and Historical Society

Once money can be found in the state budget, the state museum (700 Twin Lakes Dr., 702/486-5205, 9 A.M.–5 P.M. Wed.–Sat., $4 adults, free under age 18) will be moving to the Las Vegas Springs Preserve. In the meantime, the Lorenzi Park location is a comfortable and enjoyable place to spend a hour or two studying Mojave and Spring Mountains ecology, southern Nevada history, and local art. Permanent exhibits describe southern Nevada's role in World War II and include skeletons of the Columbian Mammoth, which roamed the Nevada deserts 20,000 years ago, and the ichthyosaur, a whalelike remnant of the Triassic Period. The Cahlan Research Library houses Clark County naturalization and Civil Defense records, among other treasures.

◖ Atomic Testing Museum

Kids might not think it's da bomb, but if you were part of the "duck and cover" generation, the Atomic Testing Museum (755 E. Flamingo Rd., 702/794-5161, 10 A.M.–5 P.M. Mon.–Sat., noon–5 P.M. Sun., $12 adults, $9 military, age 65 and over, ages 7–17, and students, free under age 7) provides plenty to spark your memories of the Cold War. Las Vegas embraced its position as ground zero in the development of the nation's atomic and nuclear deterrents after World War II. Business leaders welcomed defense contractors to town, and casinos hosted bomb-watching parties as nukes were detonated at the Nevada Test Site, a huge swath of desert 65 miles away. One ingenious marketer promoted the Miss Atomic Bomb beauty pageant in an era when patriotism overcame concerns about radiation.

The museum presents atomic history without bias, walking a fine line between appreciation of the work of nuclear scientists, politicians, and the military and the catastrophic consequences their activities and decisions could have wrought. The museum's best permanent feature is a short video in the Ground Zero Theatre, a multimedia showing of an actual atomic explosion. The theater, a replica of an observation bunker, is rigged for motion, sound, and rushing air.

One gallery helps visitors put atomic energy milestones in historic perspective along with the age's impact on 1950s and 1960s pop culture. The Today and Tomorrow Gallery examines the artifacts associated with explosives, war, and atomic energy, including a section of I-beam from the World Trade Center. Just as relevant today are lectures and traveling exhibits the museum hosts. A recent offering was

Journey through Japan, a look at the postwar culture and development of the only nation to be attacked with atomic weapons.

Computer simulators, high-speed photographs, Geiger counters, and other testing and safety equipment along with first-person accounts add to the museum's visitworthiness.

Marjorie Barrick Museum of Natural History

The museum and the adjacent **Donald H. Baepler Xeric Garden** (4505 S. Maryland Pkwy., 702/895-3381, 8 A.M.–4:45 P.M. Mon.–Fri., 10 A.M.–2 P.M. Sat., donation) on the University of Nevada, Las Vegas (UNLV) campus are good places to bone up on local flora, fauna, and artifacts. First, study the local flora in the arboretum outside the museum entrance, then step inside for the fauna: small rodents, big snakes, lizards, tortoises, Gila monsters, iguanas, chuckwallas, geckos, spiders, beetles, and cockroaches.

Other displays are full of native baskets, kachinas, masks, weaving, pottery, and jewelry from the desert Southwest and Latin America, including Mexican dance masks and traditional Guatemalan textiles.

To find the museum and garden, drive onto the UNLV campus on Harmon Street and follow it around to the right, then turn left into the museum parking lot.

Entertainment

HEADLINERS AND PRODUCTION SHOWS

Production shows are classic Las Vegas–style entertainment, the kind that most people identify with the Entertainment Capital of the World. An American version of French burlesque, the Las Vegas production show has been gracing various stages around town since the late 1950s and usually includes a magic act, acrobats, jugglers, daredevils, and maybe an animal act. The Cirque du Soleil franchise and *Jubilee!*

keep the tradition alive, but other variety shows have given way to more one-dimensional, specialized productions of superstar imitators, sexy song-and-dance reviews, and female impersonators. Most of these are large-budget, skillfully produced and presented extravaganzas, and they are highly entertaining diversions.

As Las Vegas has grown into a sophisticated metropolis, with gourmet restaurants, trendy boutiques, and glittering nightlife, it has also attracted Broadway productions to compete with the superstar singers that helped launch the town's legendary status.

Since they're so expensive to produce, the big shows are fairly reliable, and you can count on them being around for the life of this edition. They do change on occasion; the smaller shows come and go with some frequency, but unless a show bombs and is gone in the first few weeks, it'll usually be around for at least a year. All this big-time entertainment is centered, of course, around Las Vegas's casino resorts, with the occasional concert at the Thomas & Mack Center on the UNLV campus.

Blue Man Group

Bald, blue, and silent (save for homemade PVC musical instruments), Blue Man Group (Venetian, 3355 Las Vegas Blvd. S., 702/414-9000 or 800/258-3626, 7 P.M. and 10 P.M. nightly, $65–149) was one of the hottest things to hit the Strip when it debuted at Luxor in 2000 after successful versions in New York, Boston, and Chicago. It continues to wow audiences with its thought-provoking, quirkily hilarious gags and percussion performances. It is part street performance, part slapstick, and all fun.

Garth Brooks

Steve Wynn lured the country music superstar out of retirement in 2009 for a series of concerts to run through 2015. Garth and his friends in low places put on a dazzling rock concert–worthy stage show (Encore, 3131 Las Vegas Blvd. S., 702/770-9966, $225) while he delivers his lengthy repertoire of hits with gusto. Shows dates and times for the best-selling solo artist in history are announced a few months in advance.

Frank Caliendo

Talk show–circuit veteran and football prognosticator Frank Caliendo (Monte Carlo, 3770 Las Vegas Blvd. S., 702/730-7160 or 844/386-8224, 9:30 P.M. Thurs.–Sat., 7:30 P.M. Sun.–Mon., $49–81) has all the standard voices down pat, including George W. Bush, John Madden, Robin Williams, and Bill Clinton.

But it's more than just the voice, mannerisms, and facial expressions that capture his foils' personae; Caliendo also stars in a few video skits, allowing him to display his wide range of talents.

Celine Dion

Family connections re-established and vocal cords rested, the ultimate diva returns to the Caesars Palace Colosseum (3570 Las Vegas Blvd. S., 877/423-5463—877/4CELINE, 7:30 P.M., days vary, $55–250) after a year out of the limelight. The multi-platinum, multi-Grammy songstress is back to deliver pitch-perfect versions of "My Heart Will Go On" and all of her signature hits.

Chippendales

With all the jiggle-and-tease shows on the Strip, The Chippendales (Rio, 3700 W. Flamingo Rd., 702/777-7776, 8 P.M. Sun.–Thurs., 8 P.M. and 10:30 P.M. Fri.–Sat., $50–97) deliver a little gender equity. Tight jeans and rippled abs bumping and grinding with their female admirers may be the main attraction, but theirs is a fairly strict hands-off policy. The boys dance their way through sultry and playful renditions of "It's Raining Men" and other tunes with similar themes.

Crazy Horse Paris

A faithful reproduction of the original French "celebration of the nude," Crazy Horse Paris (MGM Grand, 3799 Las Vegas Blvd. S., 702/891-7902 or 866/740-7711, 8 P.M. and 10:30 P.M. Wed.–Mon.) is sensual and alluring but not overtly sexual. The premise is a celebration of women of each astrological sign. Though the dancers are topless and nearly nude, lighting effects and their ballet training puts the spotlight on the movement of their bodies rather than on their exposed parts.

Donny and Marie

Donny and Marie Osmond (Flamingo, 3555 Las Vegas Blvd. S., 702/733-3333, 7:30 P.M. Tues.–Sat., $104–285) hurl affectionate put-downs between musical numbers. The most famous members of the talented family perform their solo hits, such as Donny's "Puppy Love" and Marie's "Paper Roses" along with a little bit country, a little bit rock-and-roll duets while their faux sibling rivalry comes through with good-natured ribbing.

Terry Fator

America's Got Talent champion Terry Fator (Mirage, 3400 Las Vegas Blvd. S., 702/792-7777 or 800/963-9634, 7:30 P.M. Tues.–Sat., $59–129) combines two disparate skills—ventriloquism and impersonation—to channel Elvis, Cher, and others. Backed by a live band, Fator sings and trades one-liners with his foam rubber friends. The comedy is fresh, the impressions spot-on, and the ventriloquism accomplished with nary a lip quiver.

Matt Goss

A three-year deal he signed in 2010 means Matt Goss (Caesars Palace, 3570 Las Vegas Blvd. S., 800/745-3000, 10 P.M. Fri.–Sat., $40–95) will be delivering his selections from the great American songbook for some time to come. Backed by a swingin' nine-piece band and the requisite sexy dancers, Goss, in fedora and bowtie, brings his own style to standards like "I've Got the World on a String," "Luck Be a Lady," and other Rat Pack favorites.

Jersey Boys

The rise of Frankie Valli and the Four Seasons from street-corner doo-woppers to superstars gets the full Broadway treatment in *Jersey Boys* (Palazzo, 3325 Las Vegas Blvd. S., 702/411-9000 or 866/641-7469, 7 P.M. Thurs.–Fri. and Sun.–Mon., 6:30 P.M. and 9:30 P.M. Tues. and Sat., $63–200). Unlike, say, *Mamma Mia,* the popular ABBA spectacular, *Jersey Boys* has a true story line, chronicling the lives of the falsetto-warbling Valli and his bandmates. Terrific sets and lighting create the mood, alternating from the grittiness of the Newark streets to the flash of the concert stage. Remember, it's the story of inner-city teens in the 1950s, so be prepared for more than a few F-bombs in the dialogue.

◖ Jubilee!

The last of the old-style variety shows, *Jubilee!* (Bally's, 3645 Las Vegas Blvd. S., 800/237-SHOW—800/237-7469, 7:30 P.M. and 10:30 P.M. Sat.–Thurs., $53–113) is showgirl heaven, with dozens of the statuesque, feathered, rhinestoned, topless beauties escorting audiences through seven revue acts that include acrobats, contortionists, aerialists, jugglers, and other specialty acts. Complicated production numbers with intricate dance steps and nearly 100 performers on the 150-foot stage give the showgirls appropriate backdrops for strutting their stuff (the early show is suitable for families; the late show is topless). The climactic sinking of the *Titanic* is a real show-stopper. A Strip must-see for 30 years, *Jubilee!* is a throwback to the swanky Vegas of old.

Kà

Returning to more "traditional" Cirque du Soleil fare, *Kà* (MGM Grand, 3799 Las Vegas Blvd. S., 702/531-3826 or 866/740-7711, 7 P.M. and 9:30 P.M. daily, $69–150) explores the yin and yang of life through the story of two twins' journey to meet their shared fate. Martial arts, acrobatics, plenty of flashy pyrotechnics, and lavish sets and costumes bring cinematic drama to the variety-show acts. The show's title was inspired by the ancient Egyptian *Ka* belief, in which every human has a spiritual duplicate.

Legends in Concert

The best of the celebrity impersonator shows, *Legends in Concert* (Harrah's, 3475 Las Vegas Blvd. S., 702/369-5111, 7:30 P.M. and 10 P.M. Sun.–Fri., $48–70), emceed by "Jay Leno," relies on the tried-and-true superstars, eschewing the flavor-of-the-day pop idols. Elvis is here, of course, for an extended set, as is Madonna. On any given night, you might hear the Temptations, Garth Brooks, Dolly Parton, or James Brown. A Vegas fixture for 25 years, *Legends* is truly legendary.

Le Rêve

All the spectacle we've come to expect from the creative geniuses behind Cirque du Soleil is present in this stream-of-unconsciousness known as *Le Rêve* (Wynn, 3131 Las Vegas Blvd. S., 702/770-WYNN—702/770-9966 or 888/320-7110, 7 P.M. and 9 P.M. Fri.–Tues., $99–179). The loose concept is a romantically conflicted woman's fevered dream (*rêve* in French). Some 80 perfectly sculpted specimens of human athleticism and beauty cavort, flip, and show off their muscles around a huge aquatic stage. More than 2,000 guests fill the theater in the round, with seats all within 50 feet; those in the first couple of rows are in the "splash zone." Clowns and acrobats complete the package.

The Lion King

The familiar story of Simba's rise from tragedy to his rightful place at the head of his pride comes to life through African beats, glorious costumes, and elaborate choreography in *The Lion King* (Mandalay Bay, 3950 Las Vegas Blvd. S., 877/632-7400, 7:30 P.M. Mon.–Thurs., 4 P.M. and 8 P.M. Sat.–Sun., $77–127). It's based on the Disney animated film, but because it's a resident show, the staging and lighting are tailored for extra appeal.

LOVE

For Beatles fans visiting Las Vegas, all you need is *LOVE* (Mirage, 3400 Las Vegas Blvd. S., 702/792-7777 or 800/963-9634, 7 P.M. and 9:30 P.M. Thurs.–Mon., $94–150). This Cirque du Soleil–produced trip down Penny Lane features dancers, aerial acrobats, and other performers interpreting the Fab Four's lyrics and recordings. With a custom soundscape using the original master tapes from Abbey Road Studios and breathtaking visual artistry, John, Paul, George, and Ringo never sounded so good.

Barry Manilow

Straight men may not appreciate his talent, but Barry Manilow (Paris, 3655 Las Vegas Blvd. S., 800/745-3000, 7:30 P.M. Fri.–Sun., $95–250) sure gives the audience everything he has in every performance. From tear-inducing "Mandy" to the can't-help-but-dance-in-your-

seat "Copacabana," Manilow is the consummate showman, professional yet personal. His stage demeanor during spoken interludes between "Looks Like We Made It" and other radio favorites evinces the gratitude and appreciation of his fans.

Mystère

At first glance, Cirque du Soleil production *Mystère* (Treasure Island, 3300 Las Vegas Blvd. S., 702/894-7722 or 800/392-1999, 7 P.M. and 9:30 P.M. Sat.–Wed., $76–120) is like a circus. But it also plays on other performance archetypes, including classical Greek theater, Kabuki, and surrealism. A mix of theater, sport, and art, this production dazzles audiences with its revelations of life's mysteries.

O

Bellagio likes to do everything bigger, better, and more extravagant, and *O* (Bellagio, 3600 Las Vegas Blvd. S., 702/693-7722 or 888/488-7111, 7:30 P.M. and 10 P.M. Wed.–Sun., $94–150) is no exception. This Vegas Cirque du Soleil incarnation involves a $90 million set, 80 artists, and a 1.5-million-gallon pool of water. The title comes from the French word for water, *eau,* pronounced like the letter O in English. The production involves both terrestrial and aquatic feats of human artistry, athleticism, and comedy. It truly must be seen to be believed.

Penn & Teller

The oddball comedy magicians Penn & Teller (Rio, 3700 W. Flamingo Rd., 702/777-7776, 9 P.M. Sat.–Wed., $83–94) have a way of making audiences feel special. Seemingly breaking the magicians' code, they reveal the preparation and sleight-of-hand involved in performing tricks. The hitch is that even when forewarned, observers often still can't catch on. And once they do, the verbose Penn and silent Teller add a wrinkle no one expects.

Phantom: The Las Vegas Spectacular

From the hauntingly romantic Paris sewers to the famous Paris Opera House above, *Phantom*

(Venetian, 3355 Las Vegas Blvd. S., 702/414-9000 or 888/641-7469, 7 P.M. Wed.–Fri., 7 P.M. and 9:30 P.M. Tues. and Sat., $69–165) captures the epic story of Christine's rise to fame and subsequent escape from the clutches of her obsessed patron. The chandelier scene and the heroine's flight from the Phantom's lair are not to be missed; it's probably the best show in town.

Rita Rudner

Showbiz veteran Rita Rudner (Venetian, 3355 Las Vegas Blvd. S., 702/414-9000 or 866/641-7469, 8:30 P.M. Mon.–Wed., 6 P.M. Sat., $49–69) finds humor in the everyday world of wifehood, motherhood, aging, shopping, the gender gap, and life in Las Vegas. Best of all, she elicits laughs with true observational wit, not relying on blue language, bathroom humor, or insults.

Tony n' Tina's Wedding

Feuding future in-laws, a drunken priest, a libidinous nun, and a whole flock of black sheep can't keep Tony and Tina from finding wedded bliss in *Tony n' Tina's Wedding* (Planet Hollywood, 3667 Las Vegas Blvd. S., 702/949-6450, 7:30 P.M. daily, $70–100). Or can they? You play the role of a wedding guest, sitting among the actors, where you learn where the family skeletons are hidden and the bodies are buried. Will you play the peacemaker, or stir up the jealousies and hidden agendas among the family members? Each show is different, based on the audience reaction. So keep your ears peeled; you just might pick up the juiciest gossip between the lasagna and the cannoli.

Tournament of Kings

Pound on the table with your goblet and let loose a hearty "huzzah!" to cheer your king to victory over the other nation's regents at the *Tournament of Kings* (Excalibur, 3580 Las Vegas Blvd. S., 702/597-7600, 6 P.M. Mon.–Thurs., 6 P.M. and 8:30 P.M. Fri.–Sat., $57). Each section of the equestrian theater rallies under separate banners as their hero participates in jousts, sword fights, and riding

contests at this festival hosted by King Arthur and Merlin. A regal feast, served medieval style (that is, without utensils), starts with a tureen of dragon's blood (tomato soup). But just as the frivolity hits its climax, an evil lord appears to wreak havoc. Can the kings and Merlin's magic save the day? One of the best family shows in Las Vegas.

Viva Elvis

Nothing says "Elvis" like acrobats and roller skaters. It might be a stretch to fit the King's image into the Cirque du Soleil mold, but *Viva Elvis* (Aria, 3730 Las Vegas Blvd S., 702/590-7760 or 877/25-ELVIS—877/253-5847, 7 P.M. and 9:30 P.M. Fri.–Tues., $99–175) comes close. Building on its success with the Beatles' *LOVE,* Cirque du Soleil lets the music do the talking in a retrospective of Elvis's life through live performances, video and photographic montages, and theater. Of course, it wouldn't be Cirque du Soleil without some displays of athletic and dancing prowess. That's where the skaters come in, with graceful choreography to the accompaniment of "Can't Help Falling in Love."

George Wallace

Hailed as the voice of Las Vegas, George Wallace (Flamingo, 3555 Las Vegas Blvd. S., 702/733-3333 or 800/221-7299, 10 P.M. Tues.–Sat., $60–87) has made a career of snappy one-liners and "yo' mama" jokes. A "don't give a spit what people think" attitude and his ability to blend in interactions with the audience make Wallace a crowd favorite. He got his show business start as a writer for *The Redd Foxx Show,* to give you an idea of the type of hilarious ranting diatribes you can expect.

Zumanity

Cirque du Soleil seems to have succumbed to the titillation craze with the strange melding of sexuality, athleticism, and comedy that is *Zumanity* (New York New York, 3790 Las Vegas Blvd. S., 866/606-7111, 7:30 P.M. and 10 P.M. Fri.–Tues., $69–105). The cabaret-style show makes no pretense of storyline, but instead takes audience members through a succession of sexual and topless fantasies—French maids, schoolgirls, and light autoerotic S and M.

SHOWROOM AND LOUNGE ACTS

Showrooms are another Las Vegas institution, with most hotels providing live entertainment—usually magic, comedy, or tributes to the big stars who played or are playing the big rooms and theaters under the same roofs.

The Vegas lounge act is the butt of a few jokes, but they offer some of the best entertainment values in town—a night's entertainment for the price of a few drinks and a small cover charge. Every hotel in Las Vegas worth its salt has a lounge, and the acts change often enough to make them hangouts for locals. These acts are listed in the free entertainment magazines and the *Las Vegas Review-Journal*'s helpful Friday "Neon" section, but unless you're familiar with the performers, it's the luck of the draw: They list only the entertainer's name, venue, and showtimes.

Rat Pack Show

If we needed any proof that cool transcends generations, Sandy Hackett's *Rat Pack Show* (Sahara, 2535 Las Vegas Blvd. S., 702/737-2654 or 866/830-0287, 5 P.M. daily, $50–90) delivers it. The Rat Pack was the epitome of cool when it owned Las Vegas; today, even the ersatz Pack's delivery and singing remains as fresh as ever. And this group plays up Frank, Dean, Sammy, and Joey's camaraderie to the hilt, with the others interrupting Frank's heartfelt renditions of his classics, all the while treating him with the mock deference the Chairman of the Board deserves. And Frank plays right along, pretending to rule his crew with an iron fist. Martin is as self-effacing as the real thing, making the most of his reputation as a boozer. "I'm on the whiskey diet," he tells the crowd. "Last week, I lost four days." Classic.

The Rat Pack Is Back

The Rat Pack Is Back (Plaza, 1 Main St., 702/386-2444, 7:30 P.M. nightly, $57–74) is pretty much the same as the *Rat Pack Show*. In fact, the producers of the two productions are former partners whose messy split in 2009 continues to simmer. The Plaza show offers the option of dinner in the showroom at 6 P.M. for about $15.

Barbra and Frank: The Concert that Never Was

Sinatra and fellow legend Streisand finally share a stage in *The Concert that Never Was* (Riviera, 2901 Las Vegas Blvd. S., 800/634-3420, 7 P.M. Sun.–Thurs., $60–70). At one point in the show the Streisand impersonator, Sharon Owens, sings along with a video of Sinatra, in a Nat–Natalie Cole riff. Owens, especially, and Sebastian Anzaldo both bear striking resemblance to the superstars. The show progresses like you might expect the real thing might have, given the strong personalities of both Sinatra and Streisand. There is little interaction, except in a duet of "Luck Be a Lady," each seemingly content to put on their own separate concerts.

Trent Carlini in The King: One Night With You

Crowned *The Next Big Thing* on the ABC TV contest, Carlini (Las Vegas Hilton, 3000 Paradise Rd., 800/222-5361, 8 P.M. Mon., $39–79) is the best of the 245 registered Elvis impersonators in town, combining a strong resemblance to the King with pitch-perfect singing. His show traces Presley's career from rockabilly sensation to "Jailhouse Rock" to Vegas jumpsuit.

The King Lives

Legends in Concert alum Pete Willcox's *The King Lives* (Hooters, 115 E. Tropicana Ave., 702/739-9000, 7:30 P.M. Wed.–Sun., $25) is a close second to fellow alum Trent Carlini in the Elvis impersonator sweepstakes.

Mac King Comedy Magic

The quality of afternoon shows in Las Vegas is spotty at best, but Mac King Comedy Magic (Harrah's, 3475 Las Vegas Blvd. S., 702/369-5222, 1 P.M. and 3 P.M. Tues.–Sat., $25) fits

MOULIN ROUGE BROKE THE COLOR BARRIER

Tuxedo jackets shed and bow ties untied, Frank Sinatra, Sammy Davis Jr., and Dean Martin swap stories with their friends between sips of bourbon. It's one of the more indelible images of 1950s Las Vegas. But this scene didn't play out in a late-night dinner club at the Sahara or in a dark smoky bar at the Desert Inn. Before 1960, Davis, his nightly performance with his Rat Pack cronies complete, no longer would have been welcome in the swank hotel casinos on the Strip. African Americans could work at the hotels – usually as maids or porters – but not even Sammy Davis Jr. could eat, drink, socialize, or sleep in the whites-only establishments.

Thankfully, the Moulin Rouge, a west-side casino build in 1955, countenanced no such bigotry. Though it was located in the "black"

section of Las Vegas, its doors were open to anyone. To their credit, Sinatra and other white entertainers frequented the club along with African American stars such as Nat "King" Cole and Joe Louis. "After the shows on the Strip were over, they'd all came to the Moulin Rouge," recalled casino employee Bob Bailey.

The hotel survived less than a year, but the attitude of its owners and patrons remain a symbol of the country's progress on racial issues. Placed on the National Register of Historic Places in 1992, the Moulin Rouge was the site of a historic 1960 meeting among Strip casino managers and civil rights leaders, where, under threat of a protest march, the big resorts agreed to desegregate the town's casinos.

---

the bill for talent and affordability. King's routine is clean both technically and content-wise. With a plaid suit, good manners, and a silly grin, he cuts a nerdy figure, but his tricks and banter are skewed enough to make even the most jaded teenager laugh.

Human Nature

Blue-eyed soul gets the Down Under treatment with the exhaustingly titled *Human Nature— The Ultimate Celebration of the Motown Sound Presented by Smokey Robinson* (Imperial Palace, 3535 Las Vegas Blvd. S., 888/777-7664, 7:30 P.M. Sat.–Thurs., $60–71). Four clean-cut, well-dressed Aussies, backed by a small live band, belt out Motown classics with enough verve and coordinated dance moves to make Robinson a fan.

Divas Las Vegas

Female impersonator Frank Marino has been headlining on the Strip for nearly 25 years, and he still looks good—with or without eye shadow and falsies. Marino stars as emcee Joan Rivers, leading fellow impersonators who lip-synch their way through cheeky renditions of tunes by Lady Gaga, Cher, Madonna, and

others in *Divas Las Vegas* (Imperial Palace, 3535 Las Vegas Blvd. S., 888/777-7664, 10 P.M. Sat.–Thurs., $47–91).

Vinnie Favorito

Vinnie Favorito (Flamingo, 3555 Las Vegas Blvd. S., 702/885-1451, 8 P.M. daily, $55–65) is not impressed, and he'll let you know it. Whatever your profession, level of education, athletic achievement, or other worthy attribute, Favorito will turn it into an instrument of shame. Working with no set material, Favorito is reminiscent of Don Rickles, mingling with and interviewing audience members to find fodder for his quick wit.

Amazing Johnathan

Not much seems to go right for the Amazing Johnathan (Planet Hollywood, 3667 Las Vegas Blvd. S., 702/836-0836, 9 P.M. Tues.–Sat., $60–70), and that's the best part of the comedy magician's act. He panics when he plunges scissors into his assistant's head. Johnathan responds with F-bombs and middle fingers when the audience laughs at—not with—his ineptitude during a magic trick. He takes his revenge on the audience and one volunteer in particular.

Gordie Brown

A terrific song stylist in his own right, Gordie Brown (Golden Nugget, 129 E. Fremont St., 866/946-5336, 8 P.M. Fri.–Tues., $48–70) is the thinking person's singing impressionist. Using his targets' peccadilloes as fodder for his song parodies, Brown pokes serious fun with a surgeon's precision. Props, mannerisms, and absurd vignettes incorporating several celebrity voices at once add to the madcap fun.

Comedy

Comedy is still serious business in Las Vegas, and fans of the genre will find both comedy clubs as well as comedians with permanent gigs. For every Rita Rudner and George Wallace playing regularly in their own showrooms, there are dozens of touring headliners and hundreds of talented up-and-coming comics paying their dues in club stops around town. Among the headliners, veteran Louie Anderson ended a four-year run at Excalibur in 2010 and now waxes nostalgic—and hilarious—as the resident headliner at **Bonkerz** (Palace Station, 2411 Sahara Ave., 8:30 P.M. Mon.–Sat., $30–50).

The up-and-coming have a dozen places to land gigs when they're in town. There's **The Improv** at Harrah's (3475 Las Vegas Blvd. S., 702/369-5223, 8:30 P.M. and 10:30 P.M. Tues.–Sun. $29–45), the **Riviera Comedy Club** (2901 Las Vegas Blvd. S., 702/794-9433 or 877/892-7469, 8 P.M. and 10 P.M. daily, $25–35), the **Comedy Stop** (Sahara, 2535 Las Vegas Blvd. S., 702/737-2654 or 866/830-0287, $35–40), and the **Four Queens L.A. Comedy Club** (202 Fremont St., 800/634-6045, 8:30 P.M. Wed.–Thurs. and Sun., 7:30 P.M. and 9:30 P.M. Fri.–Sat., $16–33).

Magic

Magic shows are nearly as ubiquitous as comedy, with the more accomplished, such as Penn & Teller and **Lance Burton** getting stable long-term contracts. Burton ended a 14-year run at the Monte Carlo in 2010; chances are the master of the big illusion and sleight-of-hand will remain in Las Vegas, but his new home had not been determined at press time. Wherever he ends up, Burton's show is recommended. Burton shows true reverence for the craft as he perplexes audiences with close-up trickery before engaging in some alchemy, turning a woman into a gold statue. Talent, rather than distracting special effects, rule Burton's kid-friendly shows. He invariable invites youngsters on stage to be part of the act.

Nathan Burton (Flamingo, 3555 Las Vegas Blvd. S., 702/733-3333, 4 P.M. Tues. and Fri.–Sun., $22–49)—no relation—has parlayed his *America's Got Talent* success into a long-term gig as well, and he may be the next big thing to wield the wand in Las Vegas.

Other magic shows in town include **The Magic & Tigers of Rick Thomas** (Sahara, 2535 Las Vegas Blvd. S., 702/737-2515 or 866/830-0287, 7 P.M. daily, $40 adults, $20 under age 13) and **Steve Dacri** (Las Vegas Hilton, 3000 Paradise Rd., 800/222-5361, 7 P.M. Sun.–Mon., $49–79).

LIVE MUSIC

With all the entertainment that casinos have to offer—and the budgets to bring in the best—there's some surprising talent lurking in the dives, meat markets, and neighborhood pubs around Las Vegas. Locals who don't want to deal with the hassles of a trip to the Strip and visitors whose musical tastes don't match the often-mainstream pop-rock-country genre of the resort lounges might find a gem or two by venturing away from the neon.

Feelgoods (6750 W. Sahara Ave., 702/220-8849), named for the Mötley Crüe song "Dr. Feelgood" and partly owned by lead singer Vince Neil, brings in the sort of bands you'd expect: hard rock and hair. With more than 20,000 square feet of space and a 2,500-square-foot dance floor, **Stoney's Rockin' Country** (9151 Las Vegas Blvd. S., Suite 300, 702/435-2855) could almost *be* its own country. It's honky-tonk on a grand scale, with a mechanical bull and line dancing lessons. Jeff Healy and B. B. King have graced the stage at the **Sand Dollar** (3355 Spring Mountain Rd., 702/485-5401), where blue-collar blues rule. Bands start around 10 P.M. on weekdays, 7:30 P.M.

weekends. The people your mama warned you about hang out at the **Double Down Saloon** (4640 Paradise Rd., 702/791-5775), drinking to excess and thrashing to the punk, ska, and psychobilly bands on stage.

THE ARTS

With so much plastic, neon, and reproduction statuary around town, it's easy to accuse Las Vegas of being a soulless, cultureless wasteland, and many have. But Las Vegans don't live in casino hotels and eat every meal in the buffet. We don't all make our living as dealers and cocktail waitresses. Las Vegas, like most others, is a city built of communities. So why shouldn't Las Vegas enjoy and foster the arts? As home to an urban university and many profitable businesses just itching to prove their corporate citizenry, southern Nevada's arts are as viable as any city of comparable size in the country.

The local art scene will receive a big boost in 2012 with the projected opening of the **Smith Center for the Performing Arts,** a major cog in the revitalization of downtown, along with the development of 61 acres of former Union Pacific Railroad land the city has been working to turn into a pedestrian-friendly showplace. It will become home to the Las Vegas Philharmonic, the Nevada Ballet Theatre, local and school performances and classes, and national touring companies.

Classical Music

The **Las Vegas Philharmonic** (702/258-5438) presents a full schedule of pops, masterworks, holiday, and youth performances at the Artemus Ham Concert Hall on the UNLV campus (4505 S. Maryland Pkwy.). The Phil also works with the local school district to develop music education classes.

Ballet

With a 36,000-square-foot training facility, **Nevada Ballet Theatre** (702/243-2623) trains hundreds of aspiring ballerinas from 18 months to adult and provides practice and performance space for its professional company.

The company performs at the Artemus Ham Concert Hall on the UNLV campus (4505 S. Maryland Pkwy.). The fledgling **Las Vegas Ballet Company** (702/240-3263, www.lasvegasballet.org) was founded by former Nevada Ballet Theatre principal dancers as a performance outlet for students at their ballet and modern dance academy.

Theater

Theater abounds in Las Vegas, with various troupes staging mainstream plays, musical comedy, and experimental productions. **Las Vegas Little Theatre** (3920 Schiff Dr., 702/362-7996, www.lvlt.org), the town's oldest community troupe, performs mostly mainstream shows in its Mainstage series and takes a few more chances on productions in its Black Box theater. **Insurgo's** (702/771-7331, www.insurgotheater.org) repertoire is even more stretched: Its 2010 season included *Macbeth* as well as *Sugar Puppy Comedy Burlesque.*

The highest quality acting and production values can be found at the University of Nevada, Las Vegas, Performing Arts Center (4505 S. Maryland Pkwy., 702/895-ARTS—702/895-2787, http://pac.unlv.edu), comprised of the Artemus Ham Concert Hall, the Judy Bayley Theater, and the Alta Ham Black Box Theater. The **Nevada Conservatory Theatre,** the university's troupe of advanced students and visiting professional actors, perform fall–spring. Shows in the Bayley run from the farcical to the poignant (*Noises Off* and Sam Shepard's *Fool for Love* bookended the 2010–2011 season), while Black Box shows range from Euripides to Lanford Wilson.

Guests become witnesses, sleuths, and even suspects in **Marriage Can Be Murder** (Fitzgeralds, 301 Fremont St., 702/388-2111, 6:30 P.M. daily, $60–77) interactive dinner theater. Soon the bodies start piling up between the one-liners and slapstick. Dig out your deerstalker and magnifying glass and help catch that killer.

Visual Art

Outside the downtown arts district and the fabulous art collections amassed and displayed by Steve Wynn and other casino magnates, the **Donna Beam Fine Art Gallery** at UNLV (4505 S. Maryland Pkwy., 702/895-3893, 9 A.M.–5 P.M. Mon.–Fri., 10 A.M.–2 P.M. Sat., free) hosts exhibitions by nationally and internationally known painters, sculptors, designers, potters, and other visual artists. In addition to helping visitors enhance their critical thinking and aesthetic sensitivity, the exhibits teach UNLV students the skills needed in gallery management.

Sadly, the Las Vegas Art Museum, which shared space with the West Las Vegas Library, closed in 2009, a victim of the economic downturn. Its board hopes to reopen the gallery when good times return.

FESTIVALS AND EVENTS

Las Vegas's event season sidesteps the jarring heat of the summer months. The World Series of Poker, contested in air-conditioned comfort, is the only major southern Nevada event conducted during May–August.

January

Laughlin Desert Challenge: Some 150 racers and 16 classes of vehicles rumble through rugged desert terrain to claim top honors in an early-year tune-up for the famous Baja 1000. Race week also includes the "Laughlin Leap," where steely-nerved drivers hurtle themselves and their cars off a ramp. The rules are simple: The one who flies the farthest and survives collects $3,000.

February-March

Held in late February or early March, the Sam's Town 300 and the Shelby American Sprint Cup events on **NASCAR Weekend** pack in 140,000 race fans for a weekend of paint-swapping action.

April

Native American Arts Festival: Musicians, artisans, dancers, and historians from around the West share and celebrate Native American culture at the Clark County Museum.

The intimate 2,800-seat amphitheater at the Clark County Government Center hosts the **Las Vegas City of Lights Jazz and R&B Festival,** an extravaganza of vocal and instrumental music.

Funnel cakes, fried Twinkies, and the finest specimens of farmyard physique in southern Nevada gather over four days in Logandale for the **Clark County Fair and Rodeo.**

Laughlin River Run: 75,000 Harley jockeys, wannabes, and spectators soak up the history with scenic rides through ghost towns and desert landscape, get rowdy with classic rockers, swap road stories, and ogle biker chicks.

July

Millions of dollars are on the line as the top pros and lucky amateurs bluff, raise, and go all-in for their shot at poker immortality in the **World Series of Poker.** The tournament lasts nearly the whole month, with the final table of the main event played in November.

September

Smith's 350 NASCAR Camping World Truck Series Race: These ain't our daddies' pickups. Trucks speed around the high-banked tri-oval at the Las Vegas Motor Speedway.

October

Held each fall, the **Bikefest** motorcycle gathering is not nearly as wild as Laughlin River Days, but there is the requisite beer drinking, a bikini contest, and a poker run, along with a bike-building contest and trade show.

Tough guys try to stay on 1,500 pounds of meanness for eight seconds and scoop up scads of cash in the culmination of the Professional Bull Riders' schedule, the **Professional Bull Riders World Finals.**

December

National Finals Rodeo is when the whole town polishes its Tony Lamas and slides into Wranglers as the world's best riders and ropers compete for obscene amounts of money over 10 days at the Thomas & Mack Center. Casinos get into the act, rustling up parties, Western trade shows, and country music concerts.

A HAVEN FOR PERSECUTED WRITERS

The free exchange of ideas – especially when those ideas criticize the government or protest social ills – is a concept Americans hold sacred, and it's a freedom protected by the Constitution. Las Vegas is helping protect that freedom, serving as a City of Asylum for writers and other creative types facing censorship or persecution – even the threat of death – for expressing their beliefs. Cities worldwide have been named safe havens for writers, but in 2001 Las Vegas became the first U.S. city to achieve the designation. Pittsburgh and Ithaca, New York, have since joined Las Vegas in harboring threatened writers.

The program operates as "a free space, unfettered by censorship or political repression, in which writers who have undergone such hardship may safely practice their craft." Writers are hosted by a city or region for 1-2 years. The writer receives a $40,000 annual stipend and a place to live.

Like Salman Rushdie, author of *The Satanic Verses* sentenced to death in 1989 by Iran's Ayatollah Khomeini – whose experience spurred the formation of Cities of Asylum – Syl Cheney-Coker's life was in danger when he came to Las Vegas. Cheney-Coker, a novelist and poet, found himself on the wrong end of the political spectrum after a regime change in Sierra Leone following a military coup in 1997. Nigerian writer Wole Soyinka, himself persecuted and imprisoned in his native land for his work, was teaching at the University of Nevada, Las Vegas, and brought Cheney-Coker to town as the first guest of the Las Vegas City of Asylum project. Cheney-Coker returned to Sierra Leone in 2003 after the political situation in his homeland stabilized.

Chinese writer, critic, and painter Er Tai Gao ran afoul of Mainland China's Communist government with the publication of the essay "On Beauty" and spent several years imprisoned and doing hard labor in the Gobi Desert. His work, with its humanistic slant, continued to challenge government policy. Persecution led him to Las Vegas, where he became the second author in the city's asylum program.

Moniru Ravanipor, an Iranian novelist and short story writer, is the program's current writer in residence. Because of her work, highly regarded even in her homeland, where female expression is not always welcomed, she was the victim of censorship and threats before her immigration to the United States in 2007.

Members of the Lake Mead Boat Owners Association and their watercraft get into the holiday spirit with the **Lake Mead Parade of Lights.** All sizes of floats compete for trophies and bragging rights.

Businesses and civic organizations build and decorate intricately beautiful holiday displays for **Magical Forest** on the campus of Opportunity Village, a nonprofit outfit that provides occupational training for people with intellectual disabilities. Proceeds help defray the costs of the training.

Thousands of people run, jog, or walk the Strip and downtown course of the **Las Vegas Marathon,** lined with musicians and other entertainers. Fitness-supply vendors as well as prerace and postrace events draw top athletes from around the world.

Sports and Recreation

All the glitter and glitz of Vegas can lead to sensory overload. Thankfully, there is abundant natural beauty where you can unwind within an hour's drive of the Strip. Wander a wildlife refuge, hike to a mountain's summit, and scramble over red rock, and you'll forget how close you are to the biggest adult playground in the world.

PARKS
◖ Red Rock Canyon

West of Las Vegas, stretching across the horizon and nestled in the middle of the rugged Spring Mountains, Red Rock Canyon National Conservation Area (702/515-5350, $7 cars, $3 motorcycles, bicycles, and pedestrians) features sandstone in shades of umber, crimson, lavender, and rust vibrant enough to rival the brightest neon.

Drive west on Charleston Boulevard 12 miles from the casinos. The last vestiges of city sprawl give way to desert scrub and Joshua trees as the mountains rise ahead. As you round a final bend, Red Rock Canyon's 200,000 acres of stark yet hospitable wilderness comes into view.

An outstanding interactive **visitors center** (8 A.M.–4:30 P.M. daily), completed in 2009, is the place to get your bearings as well as learn about the trails, animals, plants, and recreational activities the park supports and the history and geography of the colorful cliff faces. Take in the big picture on the **scenic drive** (6 A.M.–7 P.M. daily Mar., 6 A.M.–8 P.M. daily Apr.–Sept., 6 A.M.–7 P.M. daily Oct., 6 A.M.–5 P.M. daily Nov.–Feb.) that circumnavigates the park, with pullouts at popular trailheads, picnic areas, and scenic overlooks. On many warm windless days, you can spot rock climbers clinging to many of the rock faces in designated climbing areas.

When you're ready to stretch your legs, find the trail that fits your mood and fitness level. In the park's northwest corner, the La Madre Spring trailhead at the Willow Springs picnic area leads to a moderate walk through a meandering, narrow, steep-walled canyon. Cool, lush gashes between the cliffs lead up to a trickling spring. For a more taxing scramble, catch the Turtlehead Peak trailhead near the sandstone quarry on the park's northeast side. Five miles of arrow grades and enormous rounded boulders lead to a panoramic summit.

Red Rock Canyon clearly reveals the limestone formed when most of Nevada lay under a warm shallow sea as well as the massive sand dunes that later covered this desert. Chemical and thermal reactions petrified the dunes into polychrome sandstone, and erosion sculpted it into strange and wondrous shapes. When the land began faulting and shifting roughly 100 million years ago, the limestone was thrust up and over the younger sandstone, forming a protective layer that inhibited further erosion, known as the Keystone Thrust. The contact between the limestone and the sandstone accounts for the bands of contrasting colors in the cliffs. Except for the spectacular canyons carved from runoff over the past 60 million years, the 15-mile-long, 3,000-foot-high sandstone escarpment today remains relatively untouched by the march of time.

Camping is available year-round at **Red Rock Campground** (W. Charleston Blvd./ Hwy. 159 at Moenkopi Rd., 702/515-5000, $15), two miles east of the visitors center.

Spring Mountain Ranch

Not far from spectacular Red Rock Canyon is Spring Mountain Ranch State Park (6375 W. Charleston Blvd., 702/875-4141, $7), where Paiute Indians and early explorers found refuge from the desert heat in the many springs that crisscross the valley below the Wilson Range. Watch for wild burros along the stretch of Highway 159 between Red Rock Canyon and the state park; some might be very friendly, but don't feed them. Not only is it bad for the burros, it's against the law.

The 530-acre parcel's later use as a working

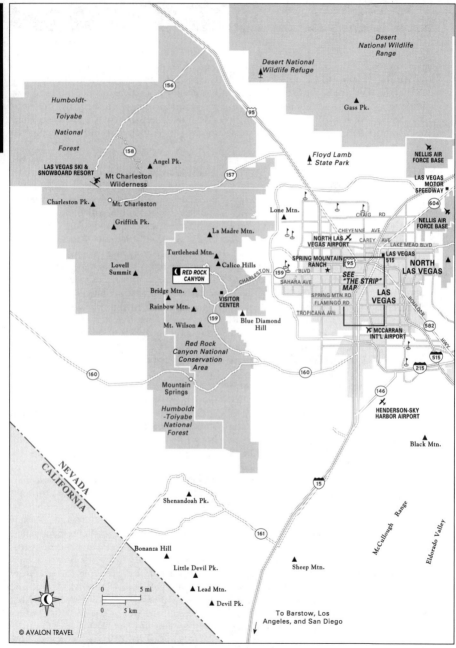

Desert National Wildlife Range

Desert National Wildlife Refuge

Humboldt-Toiyabe National Forest

156

95

Gass Pk.

Floyd Lamb State Park

158

Angel Pk.

157

LAS VEGAS SKI & SNOWBOARD RESORT

Mt Charleston Wilderness

NELLIS AIR FORCE BASE

LAS VEGAS MOTOR SPEEDWAY

Charleston Pk. Mt. Charleston

Lone Mtn.

CRAIG RD

CHEYENNE AVE

604

NELLIS AIR FORCE BASE

Griffith Pk.

La Madre Mtn.

NORTH LAS VEGAS AIRPORT

CAREY AVE

LAKE MEAD BLVD

Turtlehead Mtn.

SPRING MOUNTAIN RANCH

95

LAS VEGAS 515

NORTH LAS VEGAS

Lovell Summit

RED ROCK CANYON

Calico Hills

159

BLVD

CHARLESTON

SAHARA AVE

SEE "THE STRIP" MAP

LAS VEGAS

Bridge Mtn.

VISITOR CENTER

SPRING MTN RD

FLAMINGO RD

Rainbow Mtn.

Blue Diamond Hill

TROPICANA AVE

BOULDER HWY

582

Mt. Wilson

159

MCCARRAN INT'L AIRPORT

215

Red Rock Canyon National Conservation Area

160

160

515

146

Mountain Springs

HENDERSON-SKY HARBOR AIRPORT

Humboldt-Toiyabe National Forest

Black Mtn.

NEVADA
CALIFORNIA

15

Shenandoah Pk.

McCullough Range

Eldorado Valley

Bonanza Hill

161

Little Devil Pk.

Sheep Mtn.

Lead Mtn.

0   5 mi

Devil Pk.

0   5 km

To Barstow, Los Angeles, and San Diego

© AVALON TRAVEL

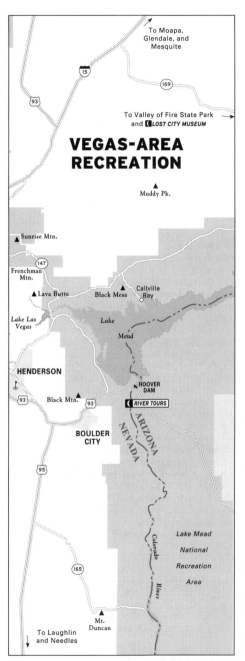

VEGAS-AREA RECREATION

To Moapa, Glendale, and Mesquite

15

169

93

To Valley of Fire State Park and ◖LOST CITY MUSEUM

▲ Muddy Pk.

▲ Sunrise Mtn.

147

Frenchman Mtn.

▲ Lava Butte   Black Mesa   ▲ Callville Bay

Lake Las Vegas

Lake Mead

HENDERSON

93   Black Mtn.▲   93   ■HOOVER DAM

◖ RIVER TOURS

BOULDER CITY

NEVADA   ARIZONA

95

Lake Mead National Recreation Area

Colorado River

165

Mt. Duncan

To Laughlin and Needles

ranch can be seen in the still-standing bunkhouse, blacksmith's shop, barn, cemetery, outhouse (a two-holer), and other structures. The main ranch house serves as the visitors center (10 A.M.–4 P.M.), where you can arrange a guided tour, inquire about picnic and camp sites, and enroll in living history programs.

Three generations of Wilsons owned the land 1876–1948, with subsequent owners including Howard Hughes. The State Parks Division acquired the ranch in 1974 when it was worth more than $3 million.

The long green lawns, bright white picket fences, and New England–style red ranch house make an idyllic setting for picnics, football, Frisbee tossing, daydreaming, and snoozing. And with temperatures 10–15 degrees cooler than in Las Vegas, it's ideal for summer concerts, musicals, and kids events. The well-received **Super Summer Theatre** (702/594-PLAY—702/594-7529, www.supersummertheatre.com, $12–15, free under age 6) takes over the ranch for several weekends during the summer, presenting G-rated theater performances. Families are encouraged to bring lawn chairs, blankets, and picnic dinners to enjoy before the shows begin around dusk.

Floyd Lamb State Park

Roughly 15 miles north of downtown Las Vegas on U.S. 95 is one of the least desertlike places in the Las Vegas desert. Once a haven for prehistoric mammals and later to Native Americans and prospectors, Floyd Lamb State Park (9200 Tule Springs Rd., 702/229-6297, 8 A.M.–8 P.M. daily May–Aug., 9 A.M.–5 P.M. daily Sept.–Apr., $6 per car or $1 pp) remains a favorite place for Las Vegans to picnic and try their luck in the four stocked ponds.

Some of the oldest and most complete archaeological evidence of giant ground sloths, mammoths, prehistoric horses, American camels, and condors was discovered at this watering hole, originally known as Tule Springs, where these animals congregated around the tules 14,000–11,000 B.C. Perhaps as early as 13,000 B.C., but definitely by 11,000 B.C., humans were present and hunting the big game.

MOUNT CHARLESTON

In the middle of spring, when Las Vegas temperatures often already flirt with 90°F, many an urbanite gazes wistfully at the white-frosted summit of Mount Charleston, only 35 miles away. As late as mid-May, snow still clings stubbornly to the 12,000-foot-high peak, the jewel of the Spring Mountain range.

Its elevation, resulting cool temperature, and more than 25 inches of precipitation per year make Mount Charleston a summer oasis for Las Vegans and create diverse, distinctive ecosystems that contrast strikingly with that of the desert floor. The Spring Mountains are home to 30 endemic plant species and support a system of six distinct ecological zones. Ascending from Las Vegas to Mount Charleston in terms of altitude is the equivalent of traveling from Mexico to Alaska in terms of latitude. In the valley, creosote bush and Joshua trees thrive. Higher, piñon pine and sagebrush take over before giving way to aspens and finally the hearty bristlecone pine. But even this grizzled veteran of numerous winter campaigns can't survive at Mount Charleston's summit.

Well-maintained roads allow two-wheel-drive vehicles to ascend to about 8,500 feet, high enough for a day of respite from the July heat or a December afternoon of sledding. Nearly a million Las Vegans and others take advantage of the mountain's recreational opportunities, hiking, camping, picnicking, and skiing among its natural wonders.

A little more than 10 miles from U.S. 95, Highway 157 climbs into the forest. For an alpine lodge honeymoon or just a hot chocolate on your way up or down the mountain, stop at the **Resort on Mount Charleston** (2 Kyle Canyon Rd., 702/872-5500 or 888/559-

1888, $60–180), which has a large chalet-like lobby complete with a roaring fireplace, a bar with big TVs, a pool table, slot machines, and a spacious restaurant. Built in 1984, this romantic hideaway received a multimillion-dollar upgrade in 2010, making it a perfect place to propose (you can then return to Las Vegas and get married an hour or two later and come back to check into the resort's bridal suite).

Beyond the hotel, Highway 157 continues another four miles past **Kyle Canyon Campground** (702/872-5577, year-round, $19–34) at 7,100 feet. This is the lowest of five high-mountain campgrounds in the vicinity, roughly 5,000 feet higher in elevation than downtown Las Vegas (and at least 20 degrees cooler). It's also the closest, a mere 45 minutes from the city. Here you'll find 25 campsites for tents or self-contained motor homes up to 40 feet. Reservations are accepted May–September.

A little farther along is **Mount Charleston village,** with a few residences and a U.S. Forest Service district office. Next to it is **Fletcher View Campground** (877/444-6777), with 12 sites (half can be reserved) for tents and trailers. It is smaller and more compact than the Kyle Canyon Campground, with just one road in and out. Sites are a little closer together and a bit shadier. If both campgrounds are full, **Mount Charleston Lodge** (702/872-5408 or 800/955-1314, $135–270), is the main action on the mountain. It is a funky alpine operation with rustic one-room cabins and a restaurant. The cabins come in two sizes, single (500 square feet with a king bed) and double (900 square feet with two kings). The bar is open till midnight, and the restaurant (8 A.M.–9 P.M. Mon.-Fri.,

8 A.M.–10 P.M. Sat.–Sun., $13–28) serves warming fare.

On Highway 157 just before the hotel, Highway 158 heads off to the left and in six miles connects with Highway 156, the Lee Canyon Road. **Robbers Roost** is a short easy hike to a large rock grotto that, if you believe the legend, once sheltered local horse thieves. A mile north is **Hilltop Campground** (702/515-5400, $19–47), at 8,400 feet. It has asphalt pavement, picnic tables and grills, wide staircases from the parking areas to the uphill tent sites, and clean restrooms and shower facilities.

Corn Creek Springs, with its lush environment, three spring-fed ponds, woodland, and pasture, is a fantastic place to have a picnic, view wildlife, or just stroll in the quiet, clean air and meditate. More than 240 species of birds have been observed at the springs; early mornings and evenings are the best time to spot rabbits, squirrels, and occasionally mule deer, coyotes, badgers, and foxes around the field station.

The nearby **Desert National Wildlife Range** (702/646-3401) was established in 1936 to protect the overhunted desert bighorn sheep. It encompasses approximately 1.5 million acres of the Mojave Desert, making it the largest National Wildlife Refuge in the Lower 48.

About four miles up Mormon Well Road, the surrounding mountains offer the best bighorn habitat in the entire range; they visit this area early and late in the year when it is cooler. Their coats blend well with the rugged terrain, so watch the high crags and pinnacles for movement or their telltale white muzzle.

Just before you get to the parking lot for the Las Vegas Ski and Snowboard Resort, you'll pass two campgrounds. At 8,600 feet, **McWilliams Campground** (877/444-6777, $19–34) is 1,600 feet higher than the ones at Kyle Canyon. The trees are still tall but more sparse, and there's less undergrowth, so there's more space among the 40 campsites. There is piped drinking water, picnic tables, grills, fire rings, and a campground host. Slightly up the hill is **Dolomite Campground** (877/444-6777, early May–early Oct., $19), similar to McWilliams but with 31 sites; the higher ones at the back of the campground are more desirable than those terraced below.

At 6,500 feet, **Las Vegas Ski & Snowboard Resort** (Hwy. 156, 702/385-2754, snow conditions 702/593-9500, 8:30 A.M.–4:30 P.M. daily Thanksgiving–Easter, $45–60 adults, $25–35 under age 12 and over 60) is only 45 miles from sizzling Sin City. The base elevation is 8,500 feet, and the top of the chairlift is another 1,000 feet higher, making for some thin air. But cliff walls towering above the slope protect skiers from biting westerlies. A beginner chairlift and ski school feeds the bunny slope; chairlifts ferry skiers to six intermediate runs and four black diamonds. Get here early on the weekend.

There is also a day lodge with a coffee shop and a lounge, a ski shop (702/645-2754) that rents equipment, and a ski school. Snow machines ensure packed and groomed slopes all winter.

Down the mountain from the ski area are plentiful places for tubing, sledding, snowmobiling, and cross-country skiing. The best Nordic skiing is on north-facing slopes in open meadows above 8,000 feet. Scott Canyon, Mack's Canyon, and the Bristlecone Trail are popular Nordic ski areas.

Tule Springs was purchased by Prosper Goumond, owner of a casino on Fremont Street, in 1941; he turned it into a self-sufficient ranch and dude ranch with big hay barns, a water tower, a pump house and well, a foreman's house, a root cellar, coops, stables, and storage buildings. He also built guesthouses, a bathhouse and pool, and a gazebo. The city bought the property in 1964, and it became a park.

At the front gate you can pick up a brochure that identifies all the buildings in the historic area, including the ruined 1916 adobe hut, now behind a cyclone fence. The lush grounds invite exploration, with ducks, geese, and domesticated peacocks by the foreman's house, the occasional roadrunner scurrying by, and big cottonwoods, oleanders, screwbean mesquites, and tules surrounding the four ponds. The largest, Tule Springs Lake, is stocked with catfish during summer and rainbow trout in winter.

RIDES AND GAMES
Top of the Tower

Daredevils will delight in the vertigo-inducing thrill rides on the observation deck at the Stratosphere Tower (200 Las Vegas Blvd. S., 702/380-7711, 10 A.M.–1 A.M. Sun.–Thurs., 10 A.M.–2 A.M. Fri.–Sat., $12–100). The newest ride, Sky Jump Las Vegas, invites the daring to plunge into space for a 15-second freefall. Angled guide wires keep jumpers on target and ease them to gentle landings. This skydive without a parachute costs $100. The other rides are 100-story-high variations on traditional thrill rides: The Big Shot is a sort of 15-person reverse bungee jump; X-Scream sends riders on a gentle (at first) roll off the edge, leaving them suspended over Las Vegas Boulevard; Insanity's giant arms swing over the edge, tilting to suspend riders nearly horizontally. These attractions are about $13 each, plus a charge just to ride the elevator to the top of the tower ($16 adults, $10 children, $12 seniors, hotel guests, and Nevada residents). Multiple-ride packages and all-day passes are available but don't include the Sky Jump.

Adventuredome

Behind Circus Circus, the Adventuredome Theme Park (2880 Las Vegas Blvd. S., 702/794-3939, 10 A.M.–midnight daily summer, 10 A.M.–9 P.M. daily during the school year, $25 over 48 inches tall, $15 under 48 inches) houses a roller coaster, a log flume, laser tag, and other topsy-turvy and simulated motion machines—all inside a pink plastic shell. The main teen and adult attractions are the Canyon Blaster, the largest indoor coaster in the world with speeds up to 55 mph, which is pretty rough; and the Rim Runner flume ride, a big drop, a big splash, and you walk around wet the rest of the day. The five-acre fun park can host birthday parties. The all-day passes are a definite bargain over individual ride prices, but carnival games, food vendors, and special rides and games not included in the pass give parents extra chances to spend money. It's not the Magic Kingdom, but it has rides to satisfy all ages and bravery levels. Besides, Las Vegas is supposed to be the *adult* Disneyland.

Speed: The Ride

Speed: The Ride (2535 Las Vegas Blvd. S., 702/737-2750, noon–8 P.M. Mon.–Thurs., noon–10 P.M. Fri.–Sun., $10), the Sahara's foray into the roller coaster market, straps you in for a turning, twisting, looping journey at a "mere" 55 mph. Wrapping its way around the hotel, the coaster climbs 200 feet above the Strip. You pause at this vantage point for one breathtaking moment and then hurtle back the way you came, backward.

Las Vegas Cyber Speedway

If Speed: The Ride's 55 mph doesn't get your juices flowing, graduate to the most extensive and sophisticated virtual-reality attraction in town, the Las Vegas Cyber Speedway (Sahara, 2535 Las Vegas Blvd. S., 702/737-2750, noon–10 P.M. daily, $10). The $15 million, 35,000-square-foot Cyber Speedway lets you channel Danica Patrick or Kyle Busch in replicas of Indy and NASCAR cars as you zoom around a simulated track or through the streets of Las Vegas at up to 220 mph. With your choice of automatic or manual transmission and 10 customizable performance metrics, you control whether you beat the seven other drivers to the checkered flag. The cars are mounted on hypersensitive hydraulic platforms, surrounded by 20-foot-wide, 133-degree wrap-around screens of the racecourse and 15 speakers. The screen displays the track whizzing by as you speed around it. The sound effects include the roar of acceleration, the screech of rubber against pavement, even the crunch of metal against metal. If you feel the need for speed, this is the ride for you.

Indy and NASCAR Driving

If, after your virtual driving practice, you're ready to take the wheel of a 600-hp stock car, check out the **Richard Petty Driving Experience** (Las Vegas Motor Speedway, 7000 Las Vegas Blvd. N., 800/BE-PETTY—800/237-3889, days and times vary, $159–1,299). The "Rookie Experience" ($499) lets NASCAR wannabes put the stock car through its paces for eight laps around the 1.5-mile tri-oval after extensive in-car and on-track safety training. Participants also receive a lap-by-lap breakdown of their run, transportation to and from the Strip, and a tour of the Driving Experience Race Shop. Even more intense—and more expensive—experiences, with more laps and more in-depth instruction, are available. To feel the thrill without the responsibility, opt for the three-lap ride-along ($109) in a two-seat stock car with a professional driver at the wheel.

The **Mario Andretti Driving Experience** (Las Vegas Motor Speedway, 7000 Las Vegas Blvd. N., 877/RACE-LAP—877/722-3527) offers similar high-speed driving using Indy cars.

Primm Attractions

The resorts in Primm, 40 miles south of Las Vegas on I-15, attract families with a lineup of several amusement park–quality thrill rides (702/679-RIDE—702/679-7433, call for hours). The best is the **Desperado** (48 inches or taller, $8), one of the highest and fastest roller coasters in the country. The first hill

ferries riders 209 feet almost straight up for an unparalleled view of the flat valley. But look quickly before your car plunges over the precipice on its way to 2.5 minutes of 80-mph twists and turns. There's not much time to catch your breath, because next up is the **Turbo Drop** (48 inches or taller, $6), a 4.5-G plummet from 170 feet up. Riders reach speeds of 45 mph as they hurtle toward earth. Only a bit tamer, **Adventure Canyon Log Flume** (46 inches or taller, $6) challenges riders to shoot not only the rapids but also strategically placed targets using laser light pistols. Waterfall plunges ensure everyone gets wet.

There's plenty of virtual fun in Primm as well. **The Vault** (48–78 inches, $6) lets you choose from eight 3-D thrills: float to Arabia aboard a magic carpet, or careen out of control in an ore cart through an abandoned mine. Another virtual experience awaits in the **Maxflight Cyber Coaster** (48 inches or taller, $5), with motion-simulated rides on roller coasters from around the world. Little thrill seekers get their chance with **Frog Hopper** (36 inches or taller, $3), a tot-size version of Turbo Drop. Cap the evening with a few racing, fighting, and shooting games at **Attraction Zone Arcade.**

GOLF

With its climate, endless sunshine, and vacation destination status, its no wonder that Las Vegas is home to more than 40 golf courses. Virtually all are eminently playable and fair, although the dry heat makes the greens fast and the city's valley location can make for some havoc-wreaking winds in the spring. Las Vegas courses, especially in recent years, have removed extraneous water-loving landscaping, opting for xeriscape and desert landscape, irrigating the fairways and greens with reclaimed water. Greens fees and amenities range from affordable municipal-type courses to some of the most exclusive country clubs anywhere. The following is a selective list in each budget category.

Henderson's **Black Mountain** (500 Greenway Rd., 702/565-7933, $50–75) received a $2 million makeover in 2008. Rolling fairways and strategically placed bunkers challenge all skill levels. Black Mountain features three distinct nine-hole sets; mix and match to play your favorite 18. At **Highland Falls** (10201 Sun City Blvd., 702/254-7010 or 800/803-0758, $35–60) you'll be treated to some stunning mountain and city views. Water hazards are tough but infrequent, and flat greens help make up for the challenging 126 slope rating on the 6,512-yard course.

There's much more water to contend with at **Siena Golf Club** (10575 Siena Monte Ave., 702/341-9200 or 888/689-6469, $99–169). Six small lakes, deep fairway bunkers, and desert scrub provide significant challenges off the tee, but five sets of tee boxes even things out for shorter hitters. The large, fairly flat greens are fair and readable. A perfect example of many courses' move toward more ecofriendly design, **Painted Desert** (5555 Painted Mirage Rd., 702/645-2568, $60–149) uses cacti, mesquites, and other desert plants to separate its links-style fairways. The 6,323-yard, par-72 course isn't especially challenging, especially if you're straight off the tee, making it a good choice for getting back to the fundamentals. Bring plenty of balls when you accept the challenge at **Badlands** (9119 Alta Dr., 702/363-0754, $89–140), as you'll routinely be asked to carry beautiful but intimidating desert gullies and ravines full of lush wildflowers and cacti. This course does not forgive poor tee shots, and even if you do find your ball, hitting from this rough delivers more punishment for golfer and clubface alike.

The only course open to the public on the Strip is **Bali Hai** (5160 Las Vegas Blvd. S., 888/427-6678, $125–295), next to Mandalay Bay on the south end of casino row. The South Pacific theme includes lots of lush green tropical foliage, deep azure ponds, and black volcanic outcroppings. A handful of long par-4s are fully capable of making a disaster of your scorecard even before you reach the sphincter-clinching par-3 16th. Not only does it play to an island green, it comes with a built-in gallery where you can enjoy your discomfort while dining on Bali Hai's restaurant patio.

Reserved only for hotel guests, the **Wynn Golf Club** (3131 Las Vegas Blvd. S., 702/770-3575, $300 and up) transcends indulgences and borders on ostentation. Still, you get what you pay for on the course designed by Tom Fazio with significant input from Steve Wynn. Serenity just steps from the Strip, much of the Wynn sits where the venerable Desert Inn course once resided. It has more than 1,000 mature pine trees salvaged from the previous course, water on 11 holes, a waterfall, and wildly undulating greens and sloping fairways—no small engineering feat on the flat Vegas valley floor and guaranteed to mesmerize and entice players.

SPECTATOR SPORTS

Despite being the 30th most populous metropolitan area in the United States, many still consider Las Vegas a minor-league city. With 1.8 million people, Las Vegas is larger than many cities that host major-league teams in at least one of the four big sports, while minor-league hockey, soccer, basketball, and football teams in Las Vegas have foundered and died. Still, other big-time sports have proven Las Vegas can get behind events that make important contributions to the city's economy and quality of life, and the town's Pacific Coast League baseball team and East Coast Hockey League club each have found loyal followings for their modest ticket prices and professional-quality play.

Las Vegas Motor Speedway

Home to NASCAR's Sprint Cup and Sam's Town 300 Nationwide Series race, the Las Vegas Motor Speedway (7000 Las Vegas Blvd. N., 800/644-4444) is a racing omniplex. In addition to the superspeedway, a 1.5-mile tri-oval for NASCAR races, the site also brings in dragsters to its quarter-mile strip; modifieds, late models, bandoleros, legends, bombers, and more to its paved oval; and off-roaders to its half-mile clay oval.

The speedway underwent a multimillion-dollar renovation project between NASCAR Weekends in 2006 and 2007, resulting in an unprecedented interactive fan experience known as the Neon Garage. Located in the speedway's infield, Neon Garage has unique and gourmet concession stands, live entertainment, and the winner's circle. Fans can get up close or watch drivers and crews from bird's-eye perches.

National Finals Rodeo

The West's quintessential test of frontier skills has held its premier event in Las Vegas since 1984, when city leaders dangled bagfuls of money in front of the Professional Rodeo Cowboys Association and wrested the National Finals Rodeo from Oklahoma City. Every December, 120 of the world's best bull riders, calf ropers, team ropers, bareback riders, steer wrestlers, barrel racers, and bronco busters compete for $5 million in prize money, selling out the Thomas & Mack Center at UNLV (4505 S. Maryland Pkwy., 702/269-3249 or 800/506-3048) every event, every year. Reserve early, and be prepared to pay hundreds of dollars per performance for good seats. The cheaper nosebleed seats go for $95–225, depending on the location and day.

Official rodeo hotels and casinos host Miss Rodeo USA pageant events, trade shows, awards ceremonies, hoedowns, and even a rodeo radio talk show.

When the rodeo's in town, Las Vegas trades its rhinestones for Wranglers and goes cowboy crazy: Hotels book the best country music stars and Western trade shows abound, headed by the rodeo's own Cowboy Christmas, which sprawls over the massive Las Vegas Convention Center floor. 400 vendors from all over North America sell crafts, jewelry, boots, saddles, and official National Finals Rodeo merchandise.

Boxing and Mixed Martial Arts

Even before Sonny Liston floored Floyd Patterson to retain his heavyweight title at the Las Vegas Convention Center in 1963, Las Vegas had begun to knock out New York City's Madison Square Garden as the undisputed champion of the boxing venues. Boxing, more than the Lennon Sisters, Andy Williams, and the other superstars that played

the showroom, established Caesars Palace as the gem of the desert it has become. Ken Norton, Evander Holyfield, Muhammad Ali, and Larry Holmes all fought here. And Sugar Ray Leonard, Thomas Hearns, and Marvin Hagler took turns beating each other up in a classic series of bouts through the 1980s.

The International and its reincarnation as the Las Vegas Hilton jumped into the fight game with both feet, hosting Sonny Liston and George Foreman in separate matches in 1969 and continuing to serve as a major venue until the early 2000s. It was here that Mike Tyson first wrested the heavyweight belt in dominating fashion over Trevor Berbick. Other Las Vegas hotels have been the sites of some of the greatest fights of the century. The fragmenting of the boxing sanctioning bodies, the absence of an engaging heavyweight champion, and the emergence of other venues have taken some of the luster off the fight game in Las Vegas; no longer do the big bouts turn into celebrity fests.

But the sweet science is far from dead in Las Vegas. Nevada's legalized sports betting and the drama surrounding the on-again, off-again Floyd Mayweather Jr.–Manny Pacquiao bout of 2010 rekindled Las Vegas's romance with boxing.

For every Leonard-Hearns or Tyson-Berbick matchup, there are plenty of pugs looking for a payday. Dozens of casinos host occasional or regular fight cards. Cheap tickets, entertaining bouts, occasional former contenders, and lots of punchers working way up the ladder for a shot at a minor alphabet-soup belt make Las Vegas a boxing fan's Shangri-la.

The advent of mixed martial arts has solidified the city's position as the fight capital of the world. Three separate Las Vegas gyms cater to fighters training to become king of the octagon, and some of the biggest pay-per-view events are held in Las Vegas casinos.

Las Vegas 51s

Venerable Cashman Field (850 Las Vegas Blvd. N., 702/798-7825) has served as the home diamond for the Las Vegas Triple-A baseball franchise since 1983. The 51s—named for the secretive government facility that believers say houses aliens and their spacecraft—play in the Pacific Coast League as the Toronto Blue Jays' affiliate. The season runs April–September. Tickets are just $9–15, all the seats are good ones, and the team puts on popular promotions such as fireworks nights, merchandise giveaways, $1 beer nights, and family nights as well as contests and demonstrations between innings.

Las Vegas Wranglers

The winningest (though championship-less) team in the East Coast Hockey League since it joined the league in 2003, the Las Vegas Wranglers are still in search of their first league championship. The club, which competes in the Pacific Division during the October–April season, plays its home games at the Orleans Arena (4500 W. Tropicana Ave., 702/471-7825, $13–38).

UNLV Teams

Members of the Mountain West Conference, the University of Nevada, Las Vegas, has teams in nine women's and seven men's sports. The Runnin' Rebels men's basketball team is a perennial qualifier for the NCAA Tournament and won the title in 1990 under Jerry Tarkanian, who was forced out after it was learned his program violated several NCAA rules, at which point the basketball program fell on hard times. Veteran college coach Lon Kruger has returned the team to prominence after taking the helm in 2004. UNLV plays its home games at the Thomas & Mack Center (4505 S. Maryland Pkwy.) on campus. The Rebels football team has not met with similar success: A 5–7 mark in 2009 spelled the end of Mike Sanford's coaching career at UNLV. The Rebels were a dismal 16–43 in his five seasons. Bobby Hauck was hired in hopes of returning UNLV to its winning ways. On the bright side, UNLV is undefeated in bowl games, winning in 1984, 1994, and 2000, although it later had to vacate the 1985 California Bowl victory.

Accommodations

ORIENTATION

Las Vegas hotels congregate in three locations: downtown, the Strip, and off-Strip. The Fremont Street Experience unifies the majority of downtown hotels into one multifarious attraction. Downtown's guest rooms are uniformly less expensive, the food is cheaper with no loss of quality, the gambling can be more positive if you know what you're looking for, and the cast of characters is far more varied and colorful. Henderson has stepped up to the plate with a couple of expansive and luxurious hotels at Lake Las Vegas and a few others in the Green Valley area.

The Strip has the biggest, newest, most themed, and most crowded hotels. Fifteen of the 20 largest hotels in the world are along a four-mile stretch on Las Vegas Boulevard South between Sahara and Tropicana Avenues. These hotels are self-contained mini cities, and although you never have to leave them, you're also somewhat captive in them: It's often hard to find your way out, the distance from your car to your room can be daunting, the distances between the hotels can be prohibitive, and the lines to do anything—eat, drink, play blackjack, see a show, or catch a cab—can drive you to distraction. But if you want to be right in the thick of the gambling action, the Strip is the ticket.

The off-Strip hotels have the popular casinos, but they often have fewer guest rooms. They're frequented mostly by out-of-towners who specifically like them and by relatives of locals who live nearby. But you can often find good room deals, because even with so few rooms, the locals casinos often have trouble filling them; most visitors want to be in the thick of the neon—on the Strip or downtown.

Note: The casino hotels are covered in the *Casinos* section.

RESERVATIONS

Booking a room at a major Las Vegas hotel can be as simple as calling the 800 reservations number, agreeing to pay the rack rate, and guaranteeing it with a credit card number. In this scenario, all you have to worry about is getting the kind of room you want in the location you desire at the price you're willing to pay. One word to the wise: Whenever possible, make a few calls to Las Vegas hotels *before* you make a final decision on the dates of your vacation to find out if something is going on in town (convention, event, holiday) for which you'll have to pay top dollar for your room. You can also call the Las Vegas Convention and Visitors Authority (702/892-0711) and ask what conventions are scheduled for the dates that you'll be in town.

However, if you like to get the best deal humanly possible on everything and are willing to travel during the low seasons, Sunday–Thursday, and maybe even play a little to see if you can win your room, the booking of Las Vegas hotel rooms will send you straight to bargain-hunter heaven. There's no doubt about it: The supply of Las Vegas hotel rooms is up and going even higher, while the ongoing economic slowdown is sending occupancy rates and gambling down. When demand is low, they're giving 'em away.

SPECIALS

As previously mentioned, the last two weeks in July, the first two weeks in August, and the period after Thanksgiving to just before Christmas are the comparatively slow seasons in Las Vegas. These are the only times of year when hotel rooms are readily available—so available, in fact, that the hotels nearly bribe you to stay in them to keep the casinos busy and the profits flowing. If you can come to Las Vegas the first or second week of December and you do a marginal amount of research, you'll be hard-pressed to spend more than $10 per night for a room.

HOTELS
Center Strip

With a name like **Trump** (2000 Fashion Show

Dr., 702/982-0000 or 866/939-8786, $99–190) you know that no whim will go unfulfilled. Standard studio suites open onto an Italian marble entryway leading to floor-to-ceiling windows with the requisite magnificent views. In-room amenities include a unique "Euro kitchen" will all appliances, including a stocked refrigerator. Dual sinks, plasma TVs embedded in the mirrors, and spa tubs highlight the marble-studded bathrooms. A bigger plasma and a convertible sofa share the living area, and feather comforters and Italian linens make for heavenly restfulness in the bedroom. Dining options include the chic **DJT** steak house and the hip **H2(EAU)** poolside. **The Spa at Trump** offers unique packages such as the "Party Relief Recovery" ($149). The hotel's resort fee includes a $25 spa credit.

One of the newest landmarks on the Las Vegas skyline, **Platinum** (211 E. Flamingo Rd., 702/365-5000 or 877/211-9211, $119–179) treats both guests and the environment with kid gloves. The resort uses the latest technology to reduce its carbon footprint through such measures as low-energy lighting throughout, ecofriendly room thermostats, and motion sensors to turn lights off when restrooms are unoccupied. Suites are an expansive 950 square feet of muted designer furnishings and accents, and they include all modern conveniences, such as high-speed Internet, high-fidelity sound systems, full kitchens, and oversized tubs. **Kilowatt** (6 A.M.–3 P.M. daily, $10–20) with sleek blue and silver decor accented with dark woods, is a feast for the eyes and the palate for breakfast and lunch.

Lower Strip

Offering sophisticated accommodations and amenities without the hubbub of a rowdy casino, the **Renaissance** (3400 Paradise Rd., 702/784-5700 or 800/750-0980, $120–210) has big standard rooms that come complete with triple-sheeted 300-thread-count Egyptian cotton beds with down comforters and duvets, walk-in showers, full tubs, 32-inch flat-panel TVs, a business center, and high-speed Internet. Upper-floor rooms overlook the Wynn golf

THE WORLD'S LARGEST HOTELS

Rank	Name	Location	Size
1. First World Pahang, Malaysia – 6,118 rooms			
2. MGM Grand, Las Vegas – 5,044 rooms			
3. Luxor, Las Vegas – 4,408 rooms			
4. Mandalay Bay, including The Hotel Las Vegas – 4,341 rooms			
5. Ambassador City, Jomtien, Thailand – 4,210 rooms			
6. Venetian, Las Vegas – 4,027 rooms			
7. Caesars Palace, Las Vegas – 4,013 rooms			
8. Excalibur, Las Vegas – 4,008 rooms			
9. Aria, Las Vegas – 4,004 rooms			
10. Bellagio, Las Vegas – 3,993 rooms			
11. Circus Circus, Las Vegas – 3,697 rooms			
12. Planet Hollywood, Tokyo – 3,680 rooms			
13. Shinagawa Prince, Las Vegas – 3,636 rooms			
14. Flamingo, Las Vegas – 3,565 rooms			
15. Palazzo, Las Vegas – 3,443 rooms			
16. Hilton Hawaiian Village, Honolulu – 3,386 rooms			
17. The Mirage, Las Vegas – 3,044 rooms			
18. Monte Carlo, Las Vegas – 3,002 rooms			
19. Venetian Macau, Macau – 3,000 rooms			
20. Las Vegas Hilton, Las Vegas – 2,956 rooms			

course. The pool and whirlpool are outside, and the concierge can score show tickets and tee times. **Envy Steakhouse** (6:30 A.M.–2 P.M. and 5–10 P.M. daily, brunch 11 A.M.–3 P.M. Sun., $30–50) has a few seafood entrées, but the Angus beef gets top billing.

Every room is a suite at the **Signature** (45 E. Harmon Ave., 877/612-2121 or 800/452-4520, $95–170) at MGM Grand. Even the junior suite is a roomy 550 square feet and includes a standard king bed, kitchenette, and spa tub. Most of the 1,728 smoke-free rooms in the gleaming 40-story tower include private balconies with Strip views, and guests have access to the complimentary 24-hour fitness center, three outdoor pools, a business center, and free wireless Internet throughout the hotel. A gourmet deli and acclaimed room service satisfy noshing needs, and **The Lounge** provides a quiet, intimate spot for discussing business or pleasure over drinks.

Located on the top four floors of Mandalay Bay, **Four Seasons** (3960 Las Vegas Blvd. S., 702/632-5000, $225–375) gives guests its own lobby, exclusive elevators, and a semiprivate entrance, insulating them from the madness of the casino atmosphere. The location on floors 36–39 along with the glass curtain walls overlooking the pool, mountains, or bustling Strip ensure that guests truly "rise above it all." The 424 rooms and suites include 42-inch plasma TVs and DVD players, deep bathtubs, glass showers, and granite throughout the bathroom. The Four Seasons takes care of all its guests, not just those paying the bills. Kids will delight in the complimentary chocolate puzzle awaiting them at check-in. Older kids receive their own welcome gift: popcorn and soda. The **Verandah Lounge** (noon–10 P.M. daily, $25–40) gives comfort food a gourmet tweak, such as oxtail sloppy joes and Kobe beef sliders.

The condominium suites at **Desert Rose** (5051 Duke Ellington Way, 702/739-7000 or 888/732-8099, $100–300) are loaded, with new appliances and granite countertops in the kitchen as well as private balconies or patios outside. One-bedroom suites are quite large, at 650 square feet, and sleep four comfortably. Complimentary continental breakfast is included, as is a manager's reception Monday–Friday. Rates vary widely, but depending on your needs and travel dates, you might find a suite deal.

Although it includes a full-service casino and is just steps from the Strip, the draw of the **Tuscany** (255 E. Flamingo Rd., 702/893-8933 or 877/887-2264, $48–88) is the relaxed atmosphere, from its restaurants and lounges to its lagoon pool. The sprawling 27-acre site with footpaths and impeccable landscaping belies its proximity to the rush-rush of the Strip one block west. A cocktail bar poolside assists the Las Vegas sun in taking the edge off. Dining here is more low-key than at many of Tuscany's neighbors. Although there is a semiformal restaurant, **Tuscany Gardens** (5–10 P.M. daily, $20–35), the casual **Cantina** (11 A.M.–10 P.M. daily, $10–20) and **Marilyn's Café** (24 hours daily, $8–15) are more in keeping with the resort's métier. That's not to say Tuscany is strictly the purview of fuddy-duddies; the 50,000-square-foot casino has all the games you expect in Las Vegas, and there's nightly entertainment in the **Piazza Lounge.** All suites, the Tuscany's guest rooms boast more than 625 square feet and come with galley kitchens, wet bars, 25-inch TVs, and mini fridges.

Airport

Near the airport and quite removed from the Strip, **Doubletree** (7250 Pollock Dr., 702/948-4000, $89–129) is perfect for visitors troubled by the smoke that can penetrate the guest rooms at even the most persnickety Las Vegas hotels. Guest rooms here undergo extensive processes that dramatically purify the air and significantly mitigate respiratory irritants. Business travelers will appreciate the airport shuttle. While there's no casino and the Convention Center and the Strip are quite far, the hotel also offers a shuttle to the MGM Grand with connections to the Convention Center and the Strip resorts via monorail.

Also close to the airport, **Club 36** (372 E. Tropicana Ave., 702/856-2900, $89–129) has apartment-style rooms reminiscent of prewar Paris artists studios, complete with velour accents and compact kitchenettes and dinettes. Quiet despite its location directly beneath airline flight paths, the rooms are a comfortable and clean 480 square feet; the indoor pool and workout room complete the on-site amenities. The hotel is located in a retail center, so budget-minded guests can stock up on snacks and drinks and even prepare some meals in their own rooms. There's no casino at Club 36, but the restaurants and shops in the area mean video poker is never more than a block away.

MOTELS

Many travelers prefer motels to hotels. Since you'll be spending very little time in your room, the quality of amenities isn't particularly critical. A bed, shower, TV, heater–air conditioner, and a good lock on the door are the salient features; the rest is luxury. Price is another consideration, since motels are generally 25–50 percent less expensive than hotel rooms. Distance is also a factor: At a motel you can pull your car right up to your door and don't have to navigate large parking lots or garages, crowded casinos, slow elevators, and long hallways.

On the other hand, most Las Vegas motel rooms tend to be older and more run-down than their high-rise counterparts. They're also generally in funkier neighborhoods. They have thinner walls, flimsier beds, smaller bathrooms, and shabbier carpet; you need a little bit of a sense of adventure to stay in them.

As with hotel rooms, motel room rates have more ups and downs than an elevator. During the summer, prices are 10–20 percent higher. Weekend rates can be double those of weekdays; on holidays they can go up by another 25 percent. Conventions? Forget it. Sometimes a reservations clerk will leaf through the Las Vegas Convention and Visitor Authority's schedule of conventions to see if there are any in town at the time of your arrival before quoting a price. Occasionally he or she will ask you if you're coming to town for a convention. Again, deny it with authority. Often, the rate quoted beforehand is for one type of room, but when you arrive, if you haven't made a reservation, only a more expensive room is available. Most motels have refundable key deposits. Always add room tax to the rate you are quoted.

The Strip

Several good-value motels are located on Las Vegas Boulevard South between the Stratosphere and the Sahara; these places are also good to try for weekly rooms with kitchenettes. When the temperature isn't in the triple digits, they're also within walking distance to the Sahara, Riviera, Circus Circus, and the Adventuredome. **Clarion** (325 E. Flamingo Rd., 800/732-7889, $55–100 d) offers clean doubles.

Motels along the lower Strip, between Bally's below Flamingo Avenue all the way out to the Mandalay Bay at the far south end of the Strip, are well placed to visit all the new big-band casino resorts but have prices that match the cheaper places north of downtown. The independent motels here are hit-and-miss. You're better off sticking with established brands like **Travelodge Las Vegas Strip** (3735 S. Las Vegas Blvd., 702/736-3443, $49–129), which gets a top rating for its reasonable prices; location near the MGM Grand, Luxor, and Mandalay Bay; and little extras like free continental breakfast, newspapers, and heated swimming pool. The supersize **Super 8** (4250 Koval Lane, 702/794-0888, $45–89), just east of Bally's and Paris, is the chain's largest in the world. It offers a heated pool but no other resort amenities; on the other hand, it doesn't charge resort fees. There's free Internet access but not much of a budget for decor in the rooms or common areas. If you stay here, order the ribs and a microbrew at the **Ellis Island Casino & Brewery** next door.

Another group of motels clings to the south side of the convention center on Paradise and Desert Inn Roads as well as the west side between Paradise Road and the Strip on Convention Center Drive. If you're attending a convention here and plan well in advance, you can reserve a very reasonable and livable room at any of several motels within a five-minute walk of the convention floor. Most of them have plenty of weekly rooms with kitchenettes, which can save you a bundle. It's a joy to be able to leave the convention floor and walk over to your room and back again if necessary—the shuttle buses to the far-flung hotels are very often crowded, slow, and inconvenient. Even if you're not attending a convention, this is a good part of town to stay in, off the main drag but in the middle of everything. You won't find whirlpool tubs, white-beach pools, or Egyptian cotton at **Rodeway Inn** (220 Convention Center Dr., 702/735-4151, $35–55), but you will find everything the budget traveler could ask for: hot showers, clean beds, and a refreshing pool. You'll also get extras such as a free continental breakfast and Wi-Fi. **Royal Resort** (99 Convention Center Dr., 702/735-6117 or 800/634-6118, $69) is part time-share, part hotel. Its outdoor pool area nestles against tropical landscaping, private cabanas, and a new hot tub. Guests in its 191 rooms receive free newspapers, use of the fitness center, and Internet.

Downtown

Glitter Gulch fills Fremont Street from South Main Street to South 4th Street, but beyond that and on side streets, bargain-basement motels are numerous. Dozens of places are bunched together in three main groupings. It's not the best part of town, but it's certainly not the worst, and security is usually seen to by the management (but check with them to make sure). Generally speaking, the motels along East Fremont Street and Las Vegas Boulevard North are the least expensive. Motels between downtown and the Strip on Las Vegas Boulevard South are slightly more expensive and in a slightly better neighborhood.

East Fremont Street has plenty of motels, sometimes one right next to another or separated by car dealerships and bars. It's a few minutes' drive to the downtown casinos and an excursion to the Strip. This is also RV country, with RV parks lining the highway past motel row and the big parking lots at the casinos. And with so many possibilities out here, it's a good stretch to cruise if you don't have reservations and most "No Vacancy" signs are lit.

Two reliable standards in this neighborhood, with rooms generally under $50, are **Lucky Cuss** (3305 Fremont St., 702/457-1929) and **Downtowner** (129 N. 8th St., 702/384-1441).

Las Vegas Boulevard North from Fremont Street to East Bonanza Road, along with North Main Street and the north-numbered streets from 6th to 13th, are also packed with motels one after the other. Stay on the lighted streets. It might be a little unnerving to deal with the front desk person through bars, but Glitter Gulch is very handy if that's where you want to spend your time, and these rooms can be amazingly reasonable if a room is not where you want to spend your money. The **Bonanza Lodge** (1808 Fremont St., 702/382-3990, from $38) offers the basics with double rooms with two beds. The **Super 8** (700 Fremont St., 866/539-0036, from $62) is nicer, and the rates are a bit higher.

The motels on Las Vegas Boulevard South between downtown and the north end of the Strip at Sahara Avenue have the most convenient location if you like to float between downtown and the Strip or if you're getting married in one of the wedding chapels that line this stretch of the boulevard. It's also brighter and busier, and right on the main bus routes. Most of these motels also offer weekly room rates with or without kitchenettes. The **High Hat** (1300 Las Vegas Blvd. S., 702/382-8080, $35–95 d) has been around for several years.

Hostels

It's hard to beat these places for budget accommodations. Downtown, **USA Hostels Las Vegas** (1322 Fremont St., 702/385-1150 or 800/550-8958, $24–55) has a swimming pool and a hot tub. The rates include a pancake breakfast, coffee and tea, pool and foosball, and wireless Internet connections. The hostel also arranges trips to the Strip and visits to the Grand Canyon and other outdoorsy attractions.

Reserved only for international student travelers (ID required), the dorms at **Sin City Hostel** (1208 Las Vegas Blvd. S., 702/868-0222, from $16–18) fit the starving student's budget and include breakfast. Located on the Strip, the hostel features a barbecue pit, a basketball court, and Wi-Fi.

CAMPING AND RV PARKING
Camping

Camping options near the city include **Red Rock Campground** (W. Charleston Blvd./Hwy. 159 at Moenkopi Rd., 702/515-5000, $15), two miles east of the visitors center. Rigs as well as tents are welcome in any of the 71 sites, but there are no water, electrical, or sewer hookups. Potable water is available and firewood is for sale.

Callville Bay Resort (off Northshore Rd., 702/565-8958 or 800/255-5561, $22), on Lake Mead about 20 miles east of Las Vegas, has five full-hookup sites in its Trailer Village. Campers have access to the resort?s gift shop, boat rentals, and snack bar. Nearby, the National Park Service runs **Callville Bay Campground** (702/293-8990, $10) with 80 tent and RV sites with running water, dump stations, picnic grills and tables.

A half-dozen picturesque campsites dot **Mount Charleston** (Hwy. 157, 800/280-2267), 40 miles north of Las Vegas. Kyle Canyon (elevation 6,900 feet), Dolomite (elevation 8,300 feet), and Hilltop (elevation 8,400 feet) are open May–October. Fletcher View(elevation 7,000 feet) is open year-round. All but Dolomite have vault toilets and potable water, but no hookups.

Casino RV Parking

A number of casinos have attached RV parks. Other casinos allow RVs to park overnight in their parking lots but have no facilities.

Circusland (2800 Las Vegas Blvd. S., 702/794-3757 or 800/562-7270, about $40) is a prime spot for RVers, especially those with kids, who want to be right in the thick of things but also want to take advantage of very good facilities. The big park is all paved, with a few grassy islands here and a shade tree there; the convenience store is open 24 hours. Ten minutes spent learning where the Industrial Road back entrance is will save hours of sitting in traffic on the Strip. The park has 399 spaces operated by KOA. All have full hookups with 20-, 30-, and 50-amp power, and 280 are pull-through. Tent sites (about $8) are also available. Wheelchair-accessible restrooms have flush toilets and hot showers, and there's also a laundry, a game room, a fenced playground, a heated swimming pool, a children's pool, a spa, a sauna, and groceries.

Sam's Town Nellis RV Park (4040 S. Nellis Blvd., 702/456-7777 or 800/634-6371, $21–25) has 500 spaces for motor homes, all with full hookups and 20-, 30-, and 50-amp power. It's mostly a paved parking lot with spacious sites, a heated pool, and a spa; the rec hall has a pool table and kitchen. And, of course, it's near the bowling, dining, and movie theater in the casino.

Arizona Charlie's East (4445 Boulder Hwy., 702/951-5911, $20) has 239 spaces. The **California** (12 E. Ogden Ave., 702/385-1222 or 800/634-6505, $30–35) has 239 spaces, and nearby **Main Street Station** (200 N. Main St., 702/387-1896, $17–22) has 100 sites. Both are essentially parking lots close to the gambling and nothing more.

RV Parks

The best of the RV parks are a bit more expensive than the casino RV parks, but the amenities—especially the atmosphere, views, and landscaping—are generally worth the price.

The **Hitchin' Post** (3640 Las Vegas Blvd. N., 702/644-1043 or 888/433-8402, $29–35) offers free cable TV and Wi-Fi at its 196 spaces. The northern Las Vegas location is perhaps not the most desirable, but security is never a problem at the park. It's clean, and the on-site restaurant-bar rustles up a nice steak.

Oasis RV Park (2711 W. Windmill Lane, 800/566-4707, $30–67) is directly across I-15 from the Silverton Casino. (Take exit 33 for Blue Diamond Rd. 3 miles south of Russell Rd., then go east to Las Vegas Blvd. S. Turn right and drive one block to West Windmill, then turn right into the park.) Opened in 1996, Oasis has 936 spaces, and huge date palms usher you from the park entrance to the cavernous 24,000-square-foot clubhouse. Each space is wide enough for a car and motor home and comes with a picnic table and patio. The foliage is plentiful and flanks an 18-hole putting course along with family and adult swimming pools. The resort features a full calendar of poker tournaments, movies, karaoke, and bar and restaurant specials. Wheelchair-accessible restrooms have flush toilets and hot showers; there is also a laundry, a grocery store, an exercise room, and an arcade.

Food

It wasn't long ago that dining in Las Vegas meant $0.99 shrimp cocktail for lunch, a gorging buffet for dinner, and a late-night steak-and-eggs breakfast for $2.50. The institution that is the Las Vegas buffet was inaugurated in the late 1940s when the El Rancho Vegas put out a big spread called the chuck wagon midnight–4 A.M. to keep patrons in the casino after the late headliner show. A lavish feast for $1—a bargain for players—it was a boon for the casino as it was simple to prepare and didn't keep the restaurants open all night. Soon all the big casinos laid out major midnight smorgasbords.

In the mid-1950s, weekend chuck wagon hours were extended to include breakfast, the precursor to today's champagne brunch. By the late 1960s the chuck wagon was served at most of the major casinos for all three meals. It wasn't until the early 1980s that chuck wagons became buffets, and today Las Vegas is the buffet capital of the world.

Las Vegas buffets have evolved from little better than fast food to lavish spreads of worldwide cuisine complete with fresh salads, comforting soups, and decadent desserts. The exclusive resorts on the Strip have developed their buffets into gourmet presentations, often including delicacies such as crab legs, crème brûlée, and even caviar. Others, especially the locals casinos and those downtown that cater to more down-to-earth tastes, remain low-cost belly-filling options for intense gamblers and budget-conscious families. The typical buffet breakfast presents the usual fruits, juices, croissants, steam-table scrambled eggs, sausages, potatoes, and pastries. Lunch is salads and chicken, pizza, spaghetti, tacos, and more. Dinner is salads, steam-table vegetables, and potatoes with several varieties of meat, including a carving table with prime rib, turkey, and pork.

Buffets are still a big part of the Las Vegas vacation aura, but when the town's swank and swagger came back in the 1990s, it brought sophisticated dining with it. Las Vegas has come a long way from the coffee-and-sandwich shop shoved in a casino corner so players could recharge quickly and rush back to reclaim their slot machine.

As part of Las Vegas's return to "adult Disneyland" status, the city has developed an epicurean reputation. Fueled by a desire to keep their patrons on-site by catering to their every whim—from the time they wake in their 300-thread-count sheets to their final nightcap just before dawn—casino restaurant offerings have evolved into a veritable restaurant row. Some of the best chefs in the world have lent their skills and names to the casinos' gourmet rooms, making many hotel restaurant offerings the equals of any block in San Francisco, New York, or Paris.

That's not to say that coffee shops don't have a place in Las Vegas's casino culture—they're still home to the best deals in town, and there's still room for discovery among ethnic restaurants and comfort-food purveyors.

Most major hotels have a 24-hour coffee shop, a steak house, and a buffet along with a couple of ethnic restaurants. Noncasino restaurants around town are also proliferating quickly. Best of all, menu prices, like room rates, are consistently less expensive in Las Vegas than in any other major city in the country. The reason is that almost all Las Vegas hotel-casino food and beverage departments lose money. Food, like every other hotel amenity, is a loss leader for the casino, where the real profits are made; noncasino restaurants have to compete with the casino restaurants, so they're forced to hold the line on prices.

At first glance, it is easy to believe that the casinos take a loss on their buffets, $7 breakfasts, $10 prime rib, and $15 steaks.

UPPER STRIP
Buffets

Assuming you're not a food snob, the **Garden Court Buffet** (Main Street Station, 200 N. Main St., 702/387-1896 or 800/713-8933, 7 A.M.–3 P.M. and 4–10 P.M. daily, breakfast $7, lunch $8, dinner $11–16, weekend brunch $11) will satisfy your taste buds and your bank account. The weekend brunch is a particular bargain. The fare is standard, with lunch presented in good variety by world region. At **◖ The Buffet** (Golden Nugget, 129 E. Fremont St., 800/634-3454, 7 A.M.–10 P.M. daily, breakfast $10, lunch $11, dinner $18, weekend brunch $18), the food leaves nothing to be desired, with extras like Greek salad, perfectly seasoned pork chops, and a delicate fine banana cake putting it a cut above the ordinary buffet, especially for downtown. Glass and brass accents and colorful wall and window treatments make for peaceful digestion.

Just a notch below these two, but still recommended—especially for fans of Mexican and Southwest staples—**The Feast** (Texas Station, 2101 Texas Star Lane, 702/631-1000, 8 A.M.–9 P.M. daily, breakfast $7, lunch $9, dinner $12, weekend brunch $13) has terrific made-to-order fajitas, great tacos, and barbecue ribs.

Las Vegas Hilton's **The Buffet** (3000 Paradise Rd., 702/732-5111, 7 A.M.–2:30 P.M. and 5–10 P.M. daily, breakfast $14, lunch $15, dinner $20, weekend brunch $19) serves beer and wine at no extra charge during lunch and dinner.

Shrimp Cocktail

The Golden Gate's **Du-Par's** (1 Fremont St., 702/385-1906, 11 A.M.–3 A.M. daily) began serving a San Francisco–style shrimp cocktail in 1955, and more than 30 million have been served since. The price up until a few years ago was only $0.49, but it's still a number-one value at $1.99. In fact, it's the oldest meal deal in Las Vegas—appropriate for the oldest hotel in Las Vegas. It goes great with a draft beer. Du-Par's Restaurant is also famous locally for melt-in-your-mouth pancakes. The version at the **Westside Deli** (Circus Circus, 2880 Las Vegas Blvd. S., 702/734-0410, 6 A.M.–3 P.M. daily, $3) is pretty good too. The deli still sells a meal's worth of hot dog for $2.95 as well.

Breakfast

Brave the downtown neighborhood (it's a little seedy, but not scary during daylight) to visit the White Cross drug store and belly up to the counter at **Tiffany's** (1700 Las Vegas Blvd. S., 702/444-4459, 24 hours daily, $7–15) where you can watch short-order cooks hard at work at the griddle. The eggs and pancakes are fluffy and the gravy is smooth, so load up—you've got a busy day ahead of you. When you've burned off the biscuits, bacon, and fried eggs, come back for a comfort-food lunch.

It's all about hen fruit at ◖ **The Egg and I** (4533 W. Sahara Ave., 702/368-3447, 6 A.M.–3 P.M. daily, $7–15). They serve other breakfast fare as well, of course—the banana muffins and French toast are notable—but if you don't order an omelet, you're just being stubborn. It has huge portions, fair prices, and on-top-of-it service—go.

Steak

Easily the best steak house downtown, and perhaps in all of Las Vegas, **Vic & Anthony's** (Golden Nugget, 129 E. Fremont St., 702/385-7111, 5–11 P.M. daily, $30–50) isn't the most visually arresting restaurant in town, but that just means there's nothing to distract you from the perfectly cooked rib eyes and generous side dishes. What sets Vic & Anthony's apart from most of the other steak places in town is the way the chefs finish the entrée: Mushroom-wine reductions and an unusual red sauce for the pasta make for memorable meals.

The perfectly cooked steaks and attentive service that once attracted Frank Sinatra, Nat "King" Cole, Natalie Wood, and Elvis are still trademarks at **Golden Steer** (308 W. Sahara Ave., 702/384-4470, 5–11 P.M. daily, $30–50). A gold-rush motif and 1960s swankiness still abide here, but the menu now includes more modern variations on prime rib, filet mignon, and New York strip.

French and Continental

Hugo's Cellar (Four Queens, 202 E. Fremont St., 702/385-4011, 5:30–11 P.M. daily, $35–55) is class from the moment each woman in your party receives her red rose until the last complimentary chocolate-covered strawberry is devoured. Probably the best gourmet room for the money, Hugo's is located below the casino floor (it is a cellar, don't forget), shutting it off from the hubbub above. It is pricy, to be sure, but the inclusion of sides, a mini dessert, and salad—prepared table-side with your choice of ingredients—helps ease the sticker shock. Sorbet is served between courses. The house appetizer is the Hot Rock, four meats sizzling on a lava slab; mix and match the meats with the dipping sauces.

The pink accents at **Pamplemousse** (400 E. Sahara Ave., 702/733-2066, 5:30–10 P.M. daily, $30–45) hint at the name's meaning (grapefruit) and set the stage for cuisine so fresh that the menu changes daily. If you eschew the prix fixe menu and order à la carte, be sure to ask about prices to avoid surprises. Specialties include leg and breast of duck in cranberry-raspberry sauce and a terrific escargot appetizer with mushrooms and red wine sauce.

Italian

Decidedly uncave-like with bright lights and an earthen-tile floor, **The Grotto** (Golden Nugget, 2300 S. Casino Dr., 702/385-7111, 11:30 A.M.–11 P.M., $30–45) offers top-quality northern Italian fare with a view of the Golden Nugget's shark tank (ask for a window table). Portions are large, and the wine list is above average.

Wall frescoes put you on an Italian thoroughfare as you dine on authentic cuisine at

Fellini's (Stratosphere, 200 Las Vegas Blvd. S., 702/383-4859, 5–11 P.M. daily, $20–35). Each smallish dining room has a different fresco. The food is more the American idea of classic Italian than authentic, but only food snobs will find anything to complain about.

Chicago Joe's (820 S. 4th St., 702/382-5637, 11 A.M.–10 P.M. Tues.–Fri., 5–10 P.M. Sat., $15–25) screams Italy, with red-and-white checked table cloths and meats prepared picante, Marsala, Angelo, and more. Its setting is in a tiny Tuscan cottage–like building.

Japanese

Enjoy the chefs' spectacle at **Benihana** (Las Vegas Hilton, 3000 Paradise Rd., 702/732-5821, 5:30–10:30 P.M., $25–45). After you walk through Japanese gardens filled with statues and koi ponds, your chef arrives at your table-side hibachi grill to perform deft feats with his knives. You'll be treated to an onion-ring volcano and other food acrobatics.

Seafood

The prime rib gets raves, but the seafood and the prices are the draw at **Second Street Grill** (Fremont, 200 Fremont St., 702/385-3232 or 800/634-6460, 5–10 P.M. Thurs. and Sun.–Mon., 5–11 P.M. Fri.–Sat., $15–25). The Grill bills itself as "American contemporary with Pacific Rim influence," and the menu reflects this Eastern inspiration with steaks and chops—but do yourself a favor and order the crab legs. The restaurant is not easy to find, but that generally means your table is waiting.

Steaks and seafood get equal billing on the menu at **Triple George** (201 N. 3rd St., 702/384-2761, 11 A.M.–10 P.M. Sun.–Thurs., 11 A.M.–11 P.M. Fri.–Sat., $15–35), but again, the San Francisco–style fish and the martinis are what brings the suave crowd back for more.

Vegas Views

The 360-seat, 360-degree **Top of the World** (Stratosphere, 200 Las Vegas Blvd. S., 702/380-7777 or 800/998-6937, 11 A.M.–11 P.M. daily, $40–60), on the 106th floor of Stratosphere Tower more than 800 feet above the Strip, makes a complete revolution once every 80 minutes, giving you the full city panorama during dinner. The view of Vegas defies description, and the food is a recommendable complement. Try the tenderloin carpaccio and seafood fettuccine, and be sure to save room for Chocolate Stratosphere—white and dark chocolate with raspberry mousse.

A glass elevator delivers you to the **Ranch Steakhouse** (Binion's, 128 Fremont St., 702/382-1600, ext. 7255, 5:30–10:30 P.M. daily, $30–45) on the 24th floor. Before Stratosphere opened, this was the best view in Las Vegas, and it's still fine. Steaks are the play here—filet mignon, porterhouse, New York—and the Binion's Cut prime rib is as thick as a Michener novel.

CENTER STRIP
Breakfast

Any meal is a treat at **Tableau** (Wynn, 3131 Las Vegas Blvd. S., 702/248-DINE—702/248-3463 or 800/352-DINE—800/352-3463, 8–10:30 A.M. and 11:30 A.M.–2:30 P.M. Mon.–Fri., 8 A.M.–2:30 P.M. Sat.–Sun., bar service 5–9 P.M. daily, $15–25), but the huckleberry pancakes ($16) or white chocolate French toast ($16) in the garden atrium make breakfast the most important meal of the day at Wynn.

Buffets

The best buffet for under $85 in Las Vegas is, without a doubt, the **Village Seafood Buffet** (Rio, 3700 W. Flamingo Rd., 702/967-4000 or 866/462-5982, 4–10 P.M. Sun.–Thurs., 3:30–10 P.M. Fri.–Sat., $38 adults, $24 children). Extensive remodeling in 2008 added vibrant artwork, a cool sound system, and video screens. You have an incredible choice of seafood preparations: grilled scallops, shrimp, mussels, and calamari with assorted vegetables and sauces, snow crab legs, oysters on the half shell, peel-and-eat shrimp, steamed clams, and lobster tails. There's even hand-carved prime rib for the nonfan of seafood. The Village Buffet also has the highest-quality after-dinner goodies in town. The pies come in chocolate cream, coconut cream, coconut pineapple, lemon meringue, key lime, apple, blueberry, pecan, cherry, peach, and more, and there's also assorted pound cakes, cheesecakes, pastries, tortes, mousses, cookies, and a terrific gelato selection. It's all quality stuff, but at $38 for dinner, you'd better come hungry to get your money's worth.

Many people give the Rio top marks as the best "traditional" buffet near the center Strip, but we think it has been overtaken by **The Buffet at TI** (3300 Las Vegas Blvd. S., 702/894-7111, 7 A.M.–10 P.M. daily, breakfast $15, lunch $18, dinner $23–27, weekend brunch $24). The offerings are mostly standard—barbecue ribs, pizza, Chinese—but the ingredients are the freshest we've found on a buffet, and the few nontraditional buffet selections (especially the sushi and made-to-order pasta) make the higher-than-average price worthwhile.

Steak

Steak houses—even really good ones—are a dime a dozen in Las Vegas. That makes it a buyer's market. You can be extremely discriminating and patronize only the best few around, or you can shop based on price and still be pretty well assured you'll get a decent meal wherever you go. Among the best, you'll relish ❼ **Del Frisco's** (3925 Paradise Rd., 702/796-0063, 5–11 P.M. Mon.–Sat., 5–10 P.M. Sun., $45–75). We always wonder at people who order chicken, pasta, or seafood at a steak house, but lobster fans will be forgiven here: The Australian coldwater lobster tail beats those at all but the premium seafood restaurants. Still, the rib eye is a must-order. The wine list is formidable and just as pricy as the rest of the menu.

The same accolades and price advisory hold true for **Capital Grille** (3200 Las Vegas Blvd. S., 702/932-6631, 11:30 A.M.–10:30 P.M. Mon.–Fri., noon–10:30 P.M. Sat., 4–10 P.M. Sun., $35–45), in the Fashion Show Mall, but lunch—try the grilled Parmesan sourdough club sandwich with homemade potato chips, or the lobster salad—can be had for less than $20.

Stepping down the fanciness and price ladder, the **All-American Bar and Grille** (Rio, 3700 W. Flamingo Rd., 702/967-4000 or 866/462-5982, 11 A.M.–6 A.M. daily, $25–35) offers casual table and bar dining on choice beef or dry-aged black angus. The sides are big enough to share.

French and Continental

Many times, "bistro food" means French comfort food—hearty, hot, and tasty, yes; imaginative and experimental, no. At first glance, **Pinot Brasserie** (Venetian, 3355 Las Vegas Blvd. S., 702/414-8888, 11:30 A.M.–3 P.M. and 5:30–10 P.M. Sun.–Thurs., 11:30 A.M.–10:30 P.M. Fri.–Sat., $25–45) seems to fit the mold: linguini, chicken, lamb, and so on. But on closer inspection, you'll find West Coast–inspired variations that bring a fresh perspective to these old favorites: the prosciutto-potato hash that accompanies the sea bass and the balsamic vinegar, pepper, and vanilla reduction that accompanies the roasted strawberries and goat cheese. Top it all off with the Belgian chocolate soufflé.

The vanilla mousse–colored banquettes and chocolate swirl of the dark wood grain tables at **Payard Patisserie & Bistro** (Caesars Palace, 3570 Las Vegas Blvd. S., 702/967-4000 or 866/462-5982, 6:30 A.M.–3 P.M. daily, $15–25, pastry counter 6:30 A.M.–11 P.M.) evoke the delightful French pastries for which François Payard is famous. Indeed, the bakery takes up most of the restaurant, tantalizing visitors with cakes, tarts, and petits fours. But the restaurant, open only for breakfast and lunch, stands on its own, with the quiches and paninis taking best in show.

Italian

It's no surprise that a casino named after the most romantic of Italian cities would be home to two of the best Italian restaurants around. **Valentino** (Venetian, 3355 Las Vegas Blvd. S., 702/414-3000, 5:30–11 P.M. daily, $25–50) is headed by partner Luciano Pellegrini, recognized as one of the best chefs in the country. The amber and aquamarine interior foreshadows the golden pasta and treasures *de mare* awaiting your order. If you can't wait till dinner, Valentino's grill is open for lunch. The ravioli with blue cheese fondue is a little heavy for lunch, but perhaps you're up to the challenge. **Canalaletto** (11:30 A.M.–11 P.M. Sun.–Thurs., 11:30 A.M.–midnight Fri.–Sat., $15–25) focuses on Venetian cuisine. Chef Gianpaolo Putzu and his crew perform around the grill and rotisserie—a demonstration kitchen—creating sumptuously authentic dishes. The filled pastas—cannelloni filled with chicken and mushrooms, ravioli stuffed with pears—are among the favorites.

You can almost picture Old Blue Eyes himself between shows, twirling linguini and holding court at **Sinatra** (Encore, 3121 Las Vegas Blvd. S., 702/248-DINE—702/248-3463 or 888/352-DINE—888/352-3463, 5:30–10 P.M. daily, $30–50). The Chairman's voice wafts through the speakers, and his photos and awards decorate the walls while you tuck into classic Italian food tinged with Chef Theo Schoenegger's special touches.

Unpretentious and perfectly willing to play into the long-*I* "Italian joint" convention, **◖ Battista's Hole in the Wall** (4041 Audrie St., 702/732-1424, 5–10:30 P.M. daily, $20–35), behind the Flamingo, serves family-style meals with garlic bread, minestrone, all-you-can-eat pasta on the side, and all-you-can-drink wine included. Classic Italian restaurant decor and an accordionist make us long for the old country—and we're not even Italian. From a similar mold is **Maggiano's Little Italy** (3200 Las Vegas Blvd. S., Suite 2144, in the Fashion Show Mall, 702/732-2550, 11 A.M.–11 P.M. daily, $15–30). The shareable "large plates" are more than enough for two. Order the eggplant parmesan even if you don't like eggplant.

It's a completely different vibe at **Piero's** (355 Convention Center Dr., 702/369-2305, 5–10 P.M. daily, $25–40). As enchanting as the exotic animal lithographs on the walls, Piero's has attracted celebrities ranging from Dick Van Dyke to Larry Bird. The decor, colorful owner Freddie Glusman, and low-key sophistication give the place a vaguely speakeasy feel.

Seafood

Submerse yourself in the cool, fluid atmosphere at **AquaKnox** (Venetian, 3355 Las Vegas Blvd. S., 702/414-3772, 5:30–11 P.M. Sun.–Thurs., 5:30–11:30 P.M. Fri.–Sat., $30–70). Its cobalt and cerulean tableware and design elements suggest a sea-sprayed embarcadero. The fish soup is chef Tom Moloney's signature entrée, but the crab dishes are the way to go. If you can't bring yourself to order the $69 crab-stuffed lobster, at least treat yourself to the crab cake appetizer for $18.

Adventurous palates are in for a treat at **Sea Harbour** (Caesars Palace, 3570 Las Vegas Blvd. S., 877/346-4642, 3:30–11 P.M. Wed.–Fri., 11:30 A.M.–11 P.M. Sat.–Sun., $30–45). The Chinese import features sea cucumber, jellyfish, shark fin, and other Andrew Zimmern–worthy delicacies. More traditional tastes will find plenty to like here too: Traditional Chinese fare and the boneless chicken are safe options.

Although it's named for the Brazilian beach paradise, **Buzios** (Rio, 3700 W. Flamingo Rd., 702/777-7923, 5–11 P.M. Wed.–Sun., $25–40) serves its fish American and South American style. Hawaiian ahi, Maine lobster, Alaskan crab, and Chilean sea bass are always fresh and presented in perfect complement with tomato reductions, soy emulsions, and butter sauces.

Asian

The Mirage boasts two top center-Strip offerings in this category. A few critics have panned **Japonais** (3400 Las Vegas Blvd. S., 702/792-7979, 5–10 P.M. Thurs. and Sun.–Mon., 5–11 P.M. Fri.–Sat., $25–40) as overpriced, and while we agree the portions tend to be small by American standards, Japonais has several deals that put it solidly in the mid-range for a Japanese dinner. The early-bird lounge dinner ($45) for two includes a pair of appetizers, an entrée, and dessert. Or you could opt for Japanese dim sum (is there such a thing?) with the $7 appetizers and drinks. Japonais's Chinese counterpart is **Fin** (3400 Las Vegas Blvd. S., 866/339-4566, 5–11 P.M. Thurs.–Mon., $25–45). Again, some contend you pay for the setting as much as for the food, but why not? Sometimes the atmosphere is worth it, especially when you're trying to make an impression on your mate or potential significant other. The metallic-ball curtains evoke a rainstorm in a Chinese garden and set just the right romantic but noncloying mood. Still, we have to agree that while the prices are not outrageous, the food is not gourmet quality either; you can probably find more yum for your yuan elsewhere.

Better value can be had at **◖ Tao** (Venetian, 3355 Las Vegas Blvd. S., 702/388-8338, 5 P.M.–midnight Sun.–Thurs., 5 P.M.–1 A.M. Fri.–Sat., $25–40), where pan-Asian dishes—the roasted Thai Buddha chicken is our pick—and an extensive sake selection are served in decor that is a trip through Asian history, from the Silk Road to Eastern spiritualism, including imperial koi ponds and feng shui aesthetics.

At **Wing Lei** (Wynn, 3131 Las Vegas Blvd. S., 5:30–10:30 P.M. daily, $30–60), French colonialism comes through in chef Ming Yu's Shanghai style.

Vegas Views

Overlooking perfectly manicured fairways and the imposing 18th-green waterfall on Steve Wynn's exclusive course, the view from the glass-partitioned patio at **Country Club** (Wynn, 3131 Las Vegas Blvd. S., 702/248-DINE—702/248-3463, 11:30 A.M.–3 P.M. Mon.–Tues., 11:30 A.M.–10 P.M. Wed.–Fri., 8 A.M.–3 P.M. Sat.–Sun., $30–60) is enough to make us drool even before we see the menu. The food is perfectly prepared standard steak house fare. The fresh Cobb salad is a lunch favorite.

West Coast fixture **Sushi Roku** (Caesars Palace, 3570 Las Vegas Blvd. S., 702/733-7373, noon–10 P.M. Sun.–Thurs., noon–11 P.M. Fri.–Sat., $25–40) has terrific views both inside and out. Within the restaurant are a veritable Zen garden, bamboo, and shadowy table alcoves. Outside are unparalleled views up and down the Strip. The Imperial Palace's lavender-lit pagoda facade across the street adds to the Japanese fantasy feel.

More Strip views await at **Voodoo Steak**

(Rio, 3700 W. Flamingo Rd., 702/777-7923, 5–11 P.M. daily, $30–50) along with steaks with a N'awlins creole and Cajun touch. Getting to the restaurant and the lounge requires a mini thrill ride to the top of the Rio tower in the glass elevator. The Rio contends that the restaurant is on the 51st floor and the lounge is on the 52nd floor, but they're really on the 41st and 42nd floors, respectively—Rio management dropped floors 40–49 as the number 4 has an ominous connotation in Chinese culture. Whatever floors they're on, the Voodoo double-decker provides a great view of the Strip. The food and drink are expensive and a bit tame, but the fun is in the overlook, especially if you eat or drink outside on the decks.

Kokomo's (Mirage, 3400 Las Vegas Blvd. S., 866/339-4566, 5–10:30 P.M. daily, $30–45) sits under hut-like canopies within the rain forest of the Mirage's domed atrium. It's slightly noisy from the casino and the waterfalls, but the hubbub quickly becomes part of the unusual atmosphere. Try the oven-roasted sea bass ($30) and the ahi tartar appetizer ($18).

LOWER STRIP
Breakfast

The **Verandah** (Four Seasons, 3960 Las Vegas Blvd. S., 702/632-5000, $25–40) transforms itself from a light, airy, indoor-outdoor breakfast and lunch nook into a late dinner spot oozing with South Seas ambiance and a check total worthy of a Four Seasons restaurant. As you might expect from the name, dining on the terrace is a favorite among well-to-do locals, especially for brunch on spring and fall weekends.

Buffets

If you think "Las Vegas buffet" means a call to the trough of mediocre cheap prices and get-what-you-pay-for food quality, Bally's would like to invite you and your credit card to the **Sterling Brunch** (702/967-7999, 9:30 A.M.–2:30 P.M. Sun., $85). That's right, $85 for one meal, per person, and you have to fetch your own vittles. But the verdict is almost unanimous: It's worth it, especially if you load up on the grilled lobster, filet mignon, caviar, sushi, Mumm champagne, and other high-dollar offerings. Leave the omelets and salads for IHOP; a plateful of sinful tarts and chocolate indulgence is a must, along with just one more glass of champagne.

On the other hand, for the price of that one brunch at Bally's, you can eat for three days at the **Roundtable Buffet** (Excalibur, 3580 Las Vegas Blvd. S., 7 A.M.–10 P.M. daily, breakfast $15, lunch $16, dinner $20, ages 4–12 get $4 off). The Excalibur started the trend of the all-day-long buffet, and the hotel sells all-day wristbands for $30. If that's not enough gluttony for you, the wristband also serves as a line pass. The **French Market Buffet** (The Orleans, 4500 W. Tropicana Ave., 702/365-7111, 8 A.M.–4 P.M. Mon.–Sat., 8 A.M.–9 P.M. Sun., breakfast $8, lunch $9, dinner $14–19, Sun. brunch $15, ages 4–7 get $3 off) has a similar all-day deal for $24 (Fri. $27).

Steak
The care used by the small farms from which Tom Colicchio's **Craftsteak** (MGM Grand, 3799 Las Vegas Blvd. S., 702/891-7318, 5:30–10 P.M. Tues.–Thurs., 6–10 P.M. Fri.–Mon., $40–60) buys its ingredients is evident in the full flavor of the excellently seasoned steaks and chops. Spacious and bright with red lacquer and light woodwork, Craftsteak's decor is conducive to good times with friends and family and isn't overbearing or intimidating.

The original **Gallagher's Steakhouse** (New York New York, 3790 Las Vegas Blvd. S., 702/740-6450, 4–11 P.M. Sun.–Thurs., 4 P.M.–midnight Fri.–Sat., $30–42) has been an institution in New York City since 1927, and the restaurant here is decorated with memorabilia from the golden age of movies and sports. You'll know why the longevity is deserved after sampling its famed dry-aged beef and notable seafood selection.

Bringing the ultralounge vibe to the restaurant setting is **◖ N9NE** (Palms, 4321 W. Flamingo Rd., 702/933-9900, 5–10 P.M. Sun.–Thurs., 5–11 P.M. Fri.–Sat., $40–75). Sleek furnishings of chrome highlighted by rich colored lighting add accompaniment, but N9NE never loses focus on its raison d'être: flawlessly prepared steak and seafood and impeccable service.

French and Continental
Award-winning chef Andre Rochat lays claim to two top French establishments on this end of the Strip. **Andre's** (Monte Carlo, 3770 Las Vegas Blvd. S., 702/798-7151, 5:30–10 P.M. Tues.–Sun., $35–55) has an up-to-date yet old-country feel, with smoky glass, silver furnishings, and teal-and-cream accents. The menu combines favorites from around the world with French sensibilities to create unique "French fusion" fare, such as lamb with curried risotto and goat cheese or a peppercorn and cognac cream sauce for the delectable fillet of beef. The cellar is befitting one of the best French restaurants in town, and the selection of port, cognac, and other after-dinner drinks is unparalleled. Rochat's **Alizé** (Palms, 4321 W. Flamingo Rd., 702/951-7000, 5:30–10 P.M. daily, $40–60) is similar but includes a sweet Strip view from atop the Palms.

The steaks and seafood at **◖ Mon Ami Gabi** (Paris, 3655 Las Vegas Blvd. S., 702/944-4224, 7 A.M.–11 P.M. Sun.–Fri., 7 A.M.–midnight Sat., $20–35) are comparable to those at any fine Strip establishment—at about half the price. It's a bistro, so you know the crepes and other lunch specials are terrific, but you're better off coming for dinner. Try the trout Grenobloise.

When you name your restaurant after a maestro, you're setting some pretty high standards for your food. Fortunately, **Picasso** (Bellagio, 3600 Las Vegas Blvd. S., 702/693-7223, 6–9:30 P.M. Wed.–Mon., $113–123) is up to the self-inflicted challenge. With limited seating in its Picasso-canvassed dining room and a small dining time window, the restaurant has a couple of prix fixe menus. They're seriously expensive, and if you include Kobe beef, lobster, wine pairings, and a cheese course, you and a mate could easily leave several pounds heavier and $500 lighter.

Italian

Break out the fedora and wingtips and hoof it to the (**Bootlegger Bistro** (7700 S. Las Vegas Blvd., 702/736-4939, 24 hours daily, $15–25), where it's not supper until you slosh red sauce on your tie. Check out open-mike night Mondays at 9 P.M. Order the linguini and clams, sit back in a plush red high-backed booth, and enjoy the song stylings of up-and-coming singers and comedians as well as Strip performers trying out new material. The Bootlegger's owner, Lorraine Hunt-Bono, is not only a former Nevada lieutenant governor but also used to steam up the Vegas lounges with sultry standards. Husband Dennis Bono is a veteran of East Coast and Vegas show-rooms. Black-and-white photos of their industry friends dot the walls, and the couple's political and music industry connections are often in the audience, so if you knock 'em dead with your own rendition of "That's Amore," you might just get discovered.

Seafood

You can go to a lot of restaurants in Las Vegas and get a pretty good shrimp and crab-leg dinner for $30, but when that dinner comes with quality all-you-can-eat sushi, $30 is a bargain. That's just what you get at **Todai** (Planet Hollywood, 3667 Las Vegas Blvd. S., 702/892-0021, 11:30 A.M.–2:30 P.M. and 5:30–9:30 P.M. Sun.–Thurs., 11:30 A.M.–2:30 P.M. and 5:30–10:30 P.M. Fri.–Sat., $30–32, discounts under age 12 and over 65). Go during peak dinner hours—the more people are eating, the fresher the sashimi is.

Rick Moonen is the "it" chef of the moment, making his **RM Seafood** (Mandalay Bay, 3950 Las Vegas Blvd. S., 702/632-9300, 11 A.M.–11 P.M. daily, $35–55) the place to be seen whether you're a seafood junkie or just another pretty face. You can almost hear the tide-rigging whirr and the mahogany creak in the yacht-club restaurant setting. RM Upstairs delivers a tasty and reasonably priced tasting

menu ($75) that recently featured beef tartare, foie gras, and baked salmon. You have to try the rabbit trio; it's available à la carte or on the tasting menu for a supplemental charge.

Asian

Voted one of Zagat's favorite restaurants in Vegas, **China Grill** (Mandalay Bay, 3950 Las Vegas Blvd. S., 702/632-7404, 5–11 P.M. Sun.–Thurs., 5 P.M.–midnight Fri.–Sat., $30–45) is another one of Mandalay Bay's architecturally arresting designer restaurants, using a crystal foot bridge, multiple levels, a light-projected ceiling, and the ubiquitous exhibition kitchen to heighten the dining experience. Signature specialties include exotic twists on traditional Chinese favorites (we suggest the grilled garlic shrimp or lobster pancakes with red curry coconut sauce). More traditional, expensive, and classic is China Grill's next-door neighbor, (**Shanghai Lilly** (3950 Las Vegas Blvd. S., 702/632-7409, 5:30–10:30 P.M. Mon., 5:30–11 P.M. Thurs.–Sun., $32–52), where Cantonese and Szechuan creations reign supreme and the decor is understated and elegant.

Chinese art in a Hong Kong bistro setting with fountain and lake views make **Jasmine** (Bellagio, 3600 Las Vegas Blvd. S., 5:30–10:30 P.M. daily, $40–60) one of the most visually striking Chinese restaurants in town. The food is classic European-influenced Cantonese.

Other high-end options include **Pearl** (MGM Grand, 3799 Las Vegas Blvd. S., 702/891-7380, 5:30–10 P.M. Sun.–Thurs., 5:30–11 P.M. Fri.–Sat., $45–60), which specializes in steamed, baked, and fried Cantonese seafood specialties; and **Little Buddha** (Palms, 4321 W. Flamingo Rd., 702/942-7778, 5:30–10:30 P.M. Sun.–Thurs., 5:30–11:30 P.M. Fri.–Sat., $30–45), offering French-inspired Chinese and other Asian classics in a stunning setting. Make sure you get an eyeful, if not a snoot full, at the suave and colorful bar.

Vegas Views

Paris's (**Eiffel Tower Restaurant** (3655 Las Vegas Blvd. S., 702/948-6937,

11:30 A.M.–2:30 P.M. and 5–10 P.M. Sun.–Thurs., 11:30 A.M.–2:30 P.M. and 5–10:45 P.M. Fri.–Sat., $35–55) hovers 100 feet above the Strip. Your first "show" greets you when the glass elevator opens onto the organized chaos of Chef Jean Joho's kitchen. Order the soufflé, have a glass of wine, and bask in the romantic piano strains as the bilingual culinary staff performs delicate French culinary feats.

The story goes that that Tony Marnell—the "M" in the M Resort—was frustrated at not finding an Italian restaurant to his liking in Las Vegas, so he built his own. We think Tony must not have looked very hard if he couldn't find good Italian in town, but there's no denying his **Panevino** (246 Via Antonio Ave., across Sunset Rd. from McCarran Airport in the Marnell Corporate Center, 702/222-2400, 11 A.M.–3 P.M. and 5–10 P.M. Mon.–Fri., 5–10 P.M. Sat., $20–40) has earned its place at least *among* the top Italian places in town, especially considering the terrific view of the McCarran runway across the road. At night, if you have the right table, you can see planes lined up six deep on their descent.

OFF STRIP

There are plenty of fine restaurants outside the resort corridor. Among our favorites: Not only beatniks (or whatever the young whippersnappers are calling themselves these days) will dig the breakfast vibe at **The Beat** (520 E. Fremont St., in the downtown arts district, 702/686-3164, 7 A.M.–7 P.M. Mon.–Thurs., 7 A.M.–10 P.M. Fri., 9 A.M.–10 P.M. Sat., $5–10). Another plus, especially for locals in the know: The Beat's joe is from Colorado River Coffee Roasters in Boulder City, and the bread is from Bon Breads Baking in Las Vegas.

Carluccio's Tivoli Gardens (1775 E. Tropicana Ave., Suite 29, 702/795-3236, 4:30–10 P.M. Tues.–Sun., $10–20) is Liberace's old restaurant. It reopened a few years after Mr. Showmanship's 1987 death with the same tasteful, understated decor he designed. Who'd a' thunk Liberace would be good at interior decorating? The food is workman-like Italian, with the usual pasta in red or clam sauce along with chicken, veal, and seafood plates. Try the crab-stuffed shrimp. Sadly, the Liberace Museum next door closed in 2010.

Its delicious dim sum is no secret, so parking and seating are at a premium during lunch at **Cathay House** (5300 W. Spring Mountain Ave., in Chinatown, 702/876-3838, 10:30 A.M.–10 P.M. daily, $10–20). Dim sum is available any time, but be a purist and only order it for lunch. For dinner, opt for orange beef or garlic chicken. **Thai Spice** (4433 W. Flamingo Rd., 702/362-5308, 11:30 A.M.–10 P.M. Mon.–Thurs., 11:30 A.M.–10:30 P.M. Fri.–Sat., $10–17) is the best Thai restaurant in town; the soups, noodle dishes, and traditional curries, pad thai, and egg rolls are all well prepared. Tell your waiter how hot you want your food on a scale of 1 to 10. The big numbers peg the needle on the Scoville scale, so macho men beware.

We're sure everything else at **Dona Maria's** (910 Las Vegas Blvd. S., 702/382-6538, 8 A.M.–10 P.M. Mon.–Fri., 8 A.M.–11 P.M. Sat.–Sun., $6–16) is plenty satisfying, but we wouldn't know. We can't bring ourselves to order anything but the enchilada with green chili. Heck, with prices like these, order two or three enchiladas, tacos, and tostadas—carne, chicken, beef, chorizo, or bean—just make sure they're all slathered in that green sauce. Dona Maria's also serves burgers and traditional Mexican breakfasts. Did we mention the green sauce? Among Las Vegas's other good Mexican restaurants are **Viva Mercado's** (3553 S. Rainbow Blvd., 702/871-8826, 11 A.M.–9:30 P.M. Sun.–Thurs., 11 A.M.–10 P.M. Fri.–Sat., $7–20) and **Lindo Michoacán** (2655 E. Desert Inn Rd., 702/735-6828, 11 A.M.–11 P.M. daily, $10–20). Other restaurants in the Michoacán family dot the valley.

Shopping

Whether you're a blackjack widow, a big winner bent on converting some of your winnings into something tangible before Lady Luck turns fickle, or a careless packer stocking up on critical items you omitted from your suitcase, Las Vegas has what you need. Traditional shopping malls, factory outlets, retail streets of dreams in casinos, hip boutiques, and kitschy souvenir stands ensure that you go home with just the right memento of your Las Vegas vacation.

MALLS

The most upscale and most Strip-accessible of the traditional indoor shopping complexes, **Fashion Show** (3200 Las Vegas Blvd. S., across from the Wynn, 702/784-7000, 10 A.M.–9 P.M. Mon.–Sat., 11 A.M.–7 P.M. Sun.) is anchored by Saks Fifth Avenue, Dillard's, Neiman Marcus, Macy's, Nordstrom, and Bloomingdale's. The mall gets its name from the 80-foot retractable runway in the Great Hall, where resident retailers put on weekend fashion shows. Unique stores include Futuretronics, to keep you on the cutting edge of technological gadgetry, and Painted with Oil, with thousands of original artworks minus the intimidating gallery atmosphere. The 17-restaurant food court has something for every taste, or better yet, dine alfresco at a Strip-side café, shaded by "the cloud," a 128-foot-tall canopy that doubles as a projection screen.

Parents can reward their children's patience with rides on cartoon animals, spaceships, and other kiddie favorites at two separate play areas in the **Meadows Mall** (4300 Meadows Lane, 702/878-3331, 10 A.M.–9 P.M. Mon.–Sat., 10 A.M.–6 P.M. Sun.). There are more than 140 stores and restaurants—all the usual mall denizens along with some interesting specialty shops. The **Boulevard Mall** (3528 S. Maryland Pkwy., 702/735-8268, 10 A.M.–9 P.M. Mon.–Sat.) is similar but older and in a less trendy setting.

A visit to **Town Square** (6605 Las Vegas Blvd. S., 702/269-5000, 10 A.M.–9:30 P.M. Mon.–Thurs., 10 A.M.–10 P.M. Fri.–Sat., 11 A.M.–8 P.M. Sun.) is like a stroll through a favorite suburb. "Streets" wind between stores in Spanish, Moorish, and Mediterranean-style buildings. Mall stalwarts like Victoria's Secret and Abercrombie & Fitch are here along with some unusual surprises—Tommy Bahama's includes a café. Just like a real town, the retail outlets surround a central park, 13,000 square feet of mazes, tree houses, and performance stages. Around holiday time, machine-made snowflakes drift down through the trees. Nightlife, from laid-back wine and martini bars to rousing live entertainment, as well as the 18-screen Rave movie theater round out a trip into "town."

Easterners and Westerners alike revel in the wares offered at **Chinatown Plaza** (4255 Spring Mountain Rd., 702/221-8448). Despite the name, Chinatown Las Vegas is a pan-Asian clearinghouse where Asians can celebrate their history and heritage while stocking up on favorite reminders of home. Meanwhile, Westerners can submerge themselves in new cultures by sampling the offerings at authentic Chinese, Thai, Vietnamese, and other Asian restaurants and strolling the plaza reading posters explaining Chinese customs. Tea sets, silk robes, Buddha statuettes, and jade carvings are of particular interest, as is the Diamond Bakery with its elaborate wedding cakes and sublime mango mousse cake.

CASINO PLAZAS

Caesars Palace initiated the concept of Las Vegas as a shopping destination in 1992 when it unveiled the **Forum Shops** (702/893-4800 or 800/CAESARS—800/223-7277, 10 A.M.–11 P.M. Sun.–Fri., 10 A.M.–midnight Fri.–Sat.). Top brand luxury stores coexist with fashionable hipster boutiques amid some of the best people-watching on the Strip. A stained glass–domed pedestrian plaza greets shoppers as they enter the 175,000-square-foot expansion from the Strip. Here you'll find one of only two spiral escalators in the United States. When you're ready for a break, the gods come alive hourly to extract vengeance in the *Fall of Atlantis* and *Festival Fountain*

© RYAN JERZ

A modern-day agora, the Forum Shops at Caesars Palace tempt shoppers with high fashion and indulgent trinkets.

Show; or check out the feeding of the fish in the big saltwater aquarium twice daily.

Part shopping center, part theater in the round, the **Miracle Mile** (Planet Hollywood, 3667 Las Vegas Blvd. S., 702/866-0703 or 888/800-8284, 10 A.M.–11 P.M. Sun.–Thurs., 10 A.M.–midnight Fri.–Sat.) is a delightful (or vicious, depending on your point of view) circle of shops, eateries, bars, and theaters. If your budget doesn't quite stand up to the Forum Shops, Miracle Mile could be just your speed. The offbeat Amazing Johnathan and *Tony n' Tina's Wedding* showrooms are here too.

Las Vegas icon Rita Rudner loves the **Grand Canal Shoppes** (Venetian, 3355 Las Vegas Blvd. S., 702/414-4500, 10 A.M.–11 P.M. Sun.–Thurs., 10 A.M.–midnight Fri.–Sat.) because "Where else in Vegas can you take a gondola to the Gap?" And where else can you be serenaded by opera singers while trying on shoes? The shops line the canal among streetlamps and cobblestones under a frescoed sky. There's not really a Gap here—the Venetian is way too upscale for such a pedestrian store. Instead,

nature gets a digital assist in the photos for sale at Peter Lik gallery, and Mikimoto and Dooney & Bourke compete for your shopping dollar. The "Streetmosphere" includes strolling minstrels and specialty acts, and many of these entertainers find their way to St. Mark's Square for seemingly impromptu performances.

Money attracts money, and Steve Wynn was able to lure Oscar de la Renta and Jean-Paul Gaultier to open their first retail stores in the country at the indulgent **Esplanade** (Wynn, 3131 Las Vegas Blvd. S., 702/770-7000, 10 A.M.–11 P.M. daily). A cursory look at the tenant stores is enough to convince you that the Esplanade caters to the wealthy, the lucky, and the reckless: Hermès, Manolo Blahnik, and even Ferrari are at home under stained-glass skylights. Looking around at all the expensive casino-based shopping venues in town, the developers of **Crystal** (City Center, 3730 Las Vegas Blvd. S., 702/590-9299 or 866/754-2489) opted to go in another direction. Rather than going high-end, "We realized this is a niche the market is missing—a selection of retailers under one roof that are *extremely* high-end," the mall's general manager said. Vuitton, Tiffany, Versace: After viewing the directory, you can't argue with his logic.

The truth is, unless you're looking for a specific item or brand, or you're attracted to the atmosphere, attractions, architecture, or vibe of a particular Strip destination, you can't go wrong simply browsing the one in your hotel. The spots outlined above are our favorites, but you'll find others just as nice at **Le Boulevard** (Paris, 3655 Las Vegas Blvd. S., 702/739-4111, 10 A.M.–11 P.M. daily), **Promenade** (Bally's/Paris, 3645 Las Vegas Blvd. S., 702/739-4111 or 888/266-5687, 10 A.M.–11 P.M. daily), **The Shoppes** (Palazzo, 3325 Las Vegas Blvd. S., 702/414-4525, 10 A.M.–11 P.M. Sun.–Thurs., 10 A.M.–midnight Fri.–Sat.), **Via Bellagio** (Bellagio, 3600 Las Vegas Blvd. S., 702/693-7111 or 888/987-6667, 10 A.M.–midnight daily), or **Mandalay Place** (Mandalay Bay, 3950 Las Vegas Blvd. S., 702/632-7777 or 877/632-7800, 10 A.M.–11 P.M. daily).

FACTORY OUTLETS

Downtown, near the Clark County Government Center, **Las Vegas Premium Outlets** (875 S. Grand Central Pkwy., 702/474-7500, 10 A.M.–9 P.M. Mon.–Sat., 10 A.M.–8 P.M. Sun.) offers the savings you'd expect from the outlets you'd expect, plus a few you wouldn't: Ed Hardy and Juicy Couture have a presence in this outdoor plaza, as do premier sellers Coach and Swarovski. Under the same management, the **Las Vegas Outlet Center** (7400 Las Vegas Blvd. S., 702/896-5599, 10 A.M.–9 P.M. Mon.–Sat., 10 A.M.–8 P.M. Sun.) loses the "premium" in the name but not in the retailers. DKNY, Tommy Hilfiger, and Aéropostale are among the tenants. Taking the 45-minute shuttle ($15 round-trip) from the Strip to the **Fashion Outlets of Las Vegas** (32100 Las Vegas Blvd. S., Primm, 702/874-1400, 10 A.M.–8 P.M. daily) gets you a savings card with $800 in discounts and lets you plan your shopping strategy. Or you could drive and spread your retail safari over two days, with an evening of daredevilry on Primm's thrill rides in between. Either way, you'll need a plan to efficiently cover the 100

shops and restaurants housed in the Urban and South Beach courtyards. Fountains and strolling musicians keep the stress level down.

SOUVENIRS

Boasting a selection of dice clocks to match any decor, **Bonanza Gifts** (2460 Las Vegas Blvd. S., 702/385-7359, 8 A.M.–midnight daily) bills itself as the world's largest gift shop, with more than 40,000 square feet of floor space. Though you'll find intricate Indian jewelry and vintage Rat Pack posters, much of the Bonanza's inventory is pure Vegas schlock: Elvis sideburns, Polly the Insulting Parrot, and, well, dice clocks to match any decor.

The treasures at **Gambler's General Store** (800 S. Main St., 702/382-9903, 9 A.M.–6 P.M. daily) are more practical, especially if you're intent on continuing your gambling junket at home. The store specializes in custom poker chips and cards emblazoned with your logo, initials, or picture. You can also stock up on strategy books on poker, blackjack, horseracing, and more so that your next trip to Vegas will be even more successful. Better yet, buy a regulation craps or poker table, roulette wheel, or replica mini slot machine and practice in your spare time.

BOOKS AND MUSIC

Las Vegas malls have their full allotment of Barnes & Nobles and Borders, but we believe used book stores are the true measure of a community's worth. Fortunately, Las Vegas measures up, supporting a handful of these nook-crammed, slightly musty-smelling delights. **Michael's Used Books** (3430 E. Tropicana Ave., Suite 9, 702/434-1699, 10 A.M.–6 P.M. Mon.–Sat.) is tops, based on its size, knowledgeable staff, and wide variety of genres. It's a history buff's dream, and there's also a small section of used records and CDs. If Michael's is number 1, **Dead Poet** (937 S. Rainbow Blvd., 702/227-4070, 10 A.M.–6 P.M. daily) is next in line. It's cramped and eclectic, like a good used book store should be. It's not large, but the inventory turns over quickly, giving us reason to return often, especially to check out the small selection of leather-bound and gilded-page volumes and first editions.

Book Lovers (3142 N. Rainbow Blvd., 702/658-8583, 10 A.M.–6 P.M. Mon.–Sat., noon–5 P.M. Sun.) is small but so well organized that it seems bigger; it has a nice selection of bargain-bin books you might actually consider reading. **Plaza Books** (7380 S. Eastern Ave., Suite 120, 702/263-2692, 10 A.M.–6 P.M. Mon.–Sat.) is run by a book-savvy family. They offer fair prices and a reasonable store credit policy for trades. **Westgate Book Exchange** (3957 W. Charleston Blvd., 702/877-9501, 10 A.M.–5 P.M. Tues.–Sat.) deals almost exclusively in paperbacks, so their prices are cheap. Genre fiction and a few hobby titles dominate the shelves.

Gambler's Book Shop (5473 S. Eastern Ave., 702/382-7555 or 800/522-1777, 9 A.M.–5 P.M. Mon.–Fri.) moved into its new permanent location in 2010. The parking is sparse, but it's worth searching for a space just for the chance to browse the crowded shelves crammed with books on every form of wagering, from craps to keno, jai alai to horse racing. It also has a large case devoted to Mafia books and biographies, lots of local fiction, history, and travel guides, books on probability theory, casino management, gambling and the law, magic, and a room in the back full of used books.

ANTIQUES

It makes sense that many of Las Vegas's best antiques marts are situated around the downtown arts district at East Charleston Boulevard and South Main Street. Start your quest for the ultimate treasure at **Charleston Antique Mall** (307 W. Charleston Blvd., 702/228-4783, 10 A.M.–6 P.M. Mon.–Sat., 11 A.M.–5 P.M. Sun.), probably the city's biggest. It's well organized and displays uniquely Vegas collectibles along with jewelry and glassware as well as vintage furniture and kitchen items for your swank pad.

One-of-a-kind furnishings are the mainstay at **Not Just Antiques** (1422 Western Ave., 702/384-4922, 10:30 A.M.–5:30 P.M. Mon.–Sat., noon–6 P.M. Sun.). Rooms are grouped by theme in the 12,000-square-foot business, which specializes in estate liquidations and consignments. A quaint tea room serves traditional buttered scones and other goodies. It's perfect for a mother-daughter snack and shopping spree.

Right in the middle of the arts district, pop into the flamingo-pink art deco **Retro Vegas** (1211 S. Main St., 702/384-2700, 11 A.M.–6 P.M. Mon.–Sat.) for furniture in all styles, with heavy emphasis on 1960s modern. There are plenty of other art and antiques outlets here, but don't miss the aptly named **Funk House** (1228 S. Casino Center Blvd., 702/678-6278, 10 A.M.–5 P.M. Mon.–Sat.). Part Grandma's attic, part junk drawer, the Funk House has everything from Persian rugs to an 1880s embalming table.

Information and Services

INFORMATION BUREAUS

The **Las Vegas Convention and Visitors Authority** (LVCVA, 3150 Paradise Rd., 702/892-0711 or 877/VISIT-LV—877/847-4858, www.lvcva.com, 8 A.M.–5 P.M. daily) maintains an online visitors guide at http://guides.weaver-group.com/lv/ovg/2010/ and a website of special hotel deals and other offers at www.visitlasvegas.com. One of LVCVA's priorities is filling hotel rooms—call its reservations service at 877/VISIT-LV—877/847-4858. You can also call the same number for convention schedules and for an entertainment schedule.

The **Las Vegas Chamber of Commerce** (6671 Las Vegas Blvd. S., 702/735-1616, www.lvchamber.com) has a bunch of travel resources and general fact sheets on its website.

VISITORS GUIDES AND MAGAZINES

Nearly a dozen free periodicals for visitors are available in various places around town—racks in motel lobbies and by the bell desks of the

NELLIS AIR FORCE BASE'S BIRDS OF PREY

Headquartered at Nellis Air Force Base in Las Vegas, the U.S. Air Force Weapons School provides the world's most advanced training in weapons and tactical employment. For years, Nellis trained only fighter pilots. It continues to teach air-to-air combat maneuvers to F-15 and F-22 jockeys in the massive annual Operation Red Flag. Responding to the ever-evolving geo-military environment, however, Nellis's role has expanded over the years to train the instructors that will in turn teach air-to-air and air-to-ground combat techniques to tomorrow's pilots.

Every six months, the school produces a new class of graduates who return to their home stations, taking the latest tactics and techniques back to their units. Graduates of the F-22 Raptor Weapons Instructor validation course often return to the combat Air Force to serve as weapons officers on the military's most advanced fighter.

The Air Force turned out its first class of unmanned aircraft systems experts in 2009. These five graduates remain at Nellis to teach successive classes the ins and outs of surveillance, reconnaissance, rescue, and precision strike capabilities of the MQ-1 Raptor and MQ-9 Reaper.

large hotels are the best bet. They all cover basically the same territory—showrooms, lounges, dining, dancing, buffets, gambling, sports, events, coming attractions—and most have numerous ads that will transport coupon clippers to discount heaven.

Anthony Curtis's monthly **Las Vegas Advisor** (www.lasvegasadvisor.com) is a must for serious and curious Las Vegas visitors. The *Advisor* ferrets out and presents objectively (no advertising or comps accepted) the best dining, entertainment, gambling, and hotel room values, reviews shows and restaurants, and doles out gambling strategies. A year's subscription is only $50 ($37 for an electronic subscription) and includes exclusive coupons worth more than $3,000. The *Advisor* is highly recommended; sign up online.

Today in Las Vegas (www.todayinlv.com) is a 64-page weekly mini magazine bursting its staples with listings, coupons, previews, maps, and restaurant overviews. To get an issue before you leave on your trip, visit www.todayinlv.com/send-for-copy.html.

The digital magazine **What's On** (www.whats-on.com) provides comprehensive information along with entertainer profiles, articles, calendars, phone numbers, and lots of ads. Single issues cost $2.95.

The 150-page **Showbiz Weekly** (http://lasvegasmagazine.com) spotlights performers and has listings and ads for shows, lounges, and buffets. Subscribe or buy single digital online.

The annual publication **Las Vegas Perspective** (www.lvperspective.com) Is chock-full of area demographics as well as retail, real estate, and community statistics, updated every year.

LIBRARIES

The **Clark County Library** (702/507-3400) main branch is at 1401 East Flamingo Road, and the **Las Vegas Public Library** (702/507-3500, 9 A.M.–9 P.M. Mon.–Thurs., 10 A.M.–6 P.M. Fri.–Sun.) main branch is at 833 Las Vegas Boulevard North.

The **UNLV Library** (4505 S. Maryland Pkwy., 702/895-2111) is for serious study and research. **Special Collections,** on the third floor of the Lied library, includes hundreds of computer entries under Las Vegas—everything from Last Frontier Hotel promotional material (1949) and mobster biographies to screenplays for locally filmed movies and the latest travel videos. Also in Special Collections is the Gaming Research Center, the largest and most comprehensive gambling research collection in the world. It covers business, economics, history, psychology, sociology, mathematics, police science, and biographies, all contained in books, periodicals, reports, promo materials, photographs, posters, memorabilia, and tapes.

SERVICES
If you need the police, the fire department, or an ambulance in an emergency, dial 911.

The centrally located **University Medical Center** (1800 W. Charleston Blvd. at Shadow Lane, 702/383-2000) has 24-hour emergency service, with outpatient and trauma-care facilities. Hospital emergency rooms throughout the valley are open 24 hours, as are many privately run quick-care centers.

Most hotels will have lists of dentists and doctors, and the **Clark County Medical Society** (2590 E. Russell Rd., 702/739-9989, www.clarkcountymedical.org) website lists members based on specialty. You can also get a physician referral from **Desert Springs Hospital** (702/733-6875 or 800/842-5439).

Getting There and Around

BY AIR
Las Vegas is one of the easiest cities in the world to fly to. The number of airlines keeps fares competitive. A Southwest Airlines plane lands every three minutes, it seems. Package deals can be an especially good value if you're only staying for a week or a long weekend, but you might have to do your own research to get the best deals. A good way to start is to look in the Sunday travel supplement in the largest daily newspaper in your area, where many of the airlines, wholesalers, packagers, and hotel specials are advertised. Also, look in the travel supplements of the Los Angeles, Chicago, Dallas, and New York newspapers if you can; although the advertised tour operators and wholesalers might not serve your area, sometimes you can get in on the airfare-only or room-only part of their packages. You can also check the websites of various government agencies charged with promoting Las Vegas and tourism as well as private publishers of Las Vegas guides.

Given the popularity of Las Vegas, it's best to make your reservations as early as possible; last-minute deals are few and far between, and you'll pay through the nose to fly to Vegas on a whim. Unless your travel agent specializes in Las Vegas, don't count on him or her to help much. Las Vegas prices are so cheap that agents don't make much money selling it, and therefore they don't have much incentive to stay up on the deals, which change with the wind.

McCarran International Airport is one of the 10 busiest in the country. The wide-eyed rubbernecking that this town is famous for kicks in the moment you step into the terminal, with its slots, maze of people movers, monorails, advertisements full of showgirls, and Vegas personalities' video admonitions not to leave your luggage unattended.

Las Vegas City Area Transit buses serve the airport. Route 108 runs up Swenson Street, and the closest it comes to Las Vegas Boulevard is the corner of Paradise Road and West Sahara Avenue, but you can connect with the Las Vegas monorail at several stops. Or, if you're headed downtown, take the bus to the end of the line. Alternately, grab the Route 109 bus, which runs east of the 108 up Maryland Parkway. To get to the Strip, you have to transfer at the large cross streets onto westbound buses that cross the Strip. There are stops at Charleston Boulevard, Sahara Avenue, Desert Inn Road, Flamingo Road, and Tropicana Avenue. Route 109 also ends up at the Downtown Transportation Center. Bus fare is $2, with passes of varying duration available.

You can take a **Gray Line** airport shuttle van to your Strip ($12 round-trip) or downtown ($16 round-trip) hotel. These shuttles run continuously, leaving the airport about every 15 minutes. You'll find the shuttles outside the baggage claim area. You don't need reservations from the airport, but you will need reservations from your hotel to return to the airport. Call 702/739-5700 to reserve a spot on an airport-bound shuttle 24 hours in advance.

BY CAR

Downtown Las Vegas crowds around the junction of I-15, U.S. 95, and U.S. 93. I-15 runs from Los Angeles (272 miles, 4–5 hours' drive) to Salt Lake City (419 miles, 6–8 hours). U.S. 95 meanders from Yuma, Arizona, on the Mexican border, up the western side of Nevada, through Coeur D'Alene, Idaho, all the way up to British Columbia, Canada. U.S. 93 starts in Phoenix and hits Las Vegas 285 miles later, then merges with I-15 for a while only to fork off and shoot straight up the east side of Nevada and continue due north all the way to Alberta, Canada.

If you drive into town or rent a car at the new state-of-the-art facility at the airport, you'll have the opportunity to experience some real thrills while you travel around town. If you're staying at a Strip hotel and don't plan on going off the beaten track, you probably don't need a car: Just ride the Strip buses or monorail, or grab a cab. But if you want to take a day trip or two, a car gives you the freedom you'll need. Check with your insurance agent at home about coverage on rental cars; often your insurance covers rental cars (minus your deductible), and you won't need the rental company's. If you rent a car on most credit cards, you get automatic rental-car insurance coverage.

Rental car rates change even faster than hotel room rates in Las Vegas, and the range can be astounding. When you call around to rent, be sure to ask what the *total* price of your car is going to be. With sales tax, use tax, airport fees, and other miscellaneous charges, you can pay upward of 21 percent over and above the quoted rate.

Generally, the large car-rental companies have desks at the **McCarran Airport Rent-A-Car Center** (702/261-6001). Dedicated McCarran Airport shuttles leave the main terminal from outside Exit Doors 10 and 11 about every five minutes bound for the Rent-A-Car Center. Taxicabs are also available at the center. Companies represented at the center include

Advantage (800/777-9377), **Alamo/National** (800/GO-ALAMO—800/462-5266), **Avis** (800/331-1212), **Budget** (800/922-2899), **Dollar** (800/800-4000), **Enterprise** (800/RENT-A-CAR—800/736-8222), **Hertz** (800/654-3131), **Payless** (800/729-5377), **Sav-Mor** (800/634-6779), and **Thrifty** (800/367-2277).

LAS VEGAS MONORAIL

Since 2004, the Sahara on the north end of the Strip and the MGM Grand near the south end have been connected via the Las Vegas Monorail (702/699-8200, 7 A.M.–2 A.M. Mon.–Thurs., 7 A.M.–3 A.M. Fri.–Sat., $5), with stops at the Las Vegas Hilton, the Convention Center, Harrah's/Imperial Palace, Flamingo/Caesars Palace, and Bally's/Paris. More than 30 major resorts are now within easy reach along the Strip without a car or taxi. Reaching speeds up to 50 mph, the monorail glides above traffic to cover the four-mile route in about 14 minutes. Nine trains with air-conditioned cars carry up to 152 riders along the elevated track running on the east side of the strip, stopping every few minutes at the stations. One-day ($12) and three-day ($28) passes are also available. Tickets are available at vending machines at each station as well as at station properties.

BY BUS

Citizen Area Transit (CAT, 702/228-RIDE—702/228-7433, www.rtcsouthernnevada.com/transit/transitguide), the public bus system, is managed by the Regional Transportation Commission. CAT runs 54 routes all over Las Vegas Valley. Fares are $2–3, half price for seniors, ages 6–17, and people with disabilities. Call or access the ride guide online. Bus service is pretty comprehensive, but even the express routes with fewer stops take a long time to get anywhere.

The **Greyhound depot** (200 S. Main St., 702/383-9792) is on the south side of the Plaza Hotel. Buses arrive and depart frequently throughout the day and night to and from all points in North America, and they are a reasonable alternative to driving or flying.

HIGH-SPEED TRAINS RACE TO VEGAS

Two competing projects are aiming to give 13 million Las Vegas visitors more time to indulge in the city's gambling, dining, and entertainment. More than one-third of Las Vegas's visitors come from Southern California, but the 300-mile one-day journey and the region's notorious traffic congestion cut deeply into fun time – especially for weekend travelers.

Two high-speed train projects hope to eliminate much of the commute time and a lot of the hassle and stress Angelenos deal with on their voyage east. A maglev train is the more ambitious, more expensive, and more futuristic project. The estimated $12 billion train project would whisk visitors between Anaheim, California, and Las Vegas at some 300 mph, cutting the travel time to about 80 minutes. The project lost funding and the support of Nevada senator Harry Reid, who is unhappy with what he sees as the project's lack of progress. Others are concerned that while maglev trains have been successful in Europe and Asia, the technology is untested in the United States. Still, many support the project because of its potential to create jobs, its linking of two major tourist cities, and the speed of bringing more tourists to town.

Desert Xpress is a more traditional wheels-and-rail train project designed to operate between Las Vegas and Victorville, California. It is expected that Southern California visitors to Las Vegas would park at the Victorville station, to be located just off I-15. The $4 billion train project would parallel I-15, potentially alleviating traffic snarls on that major route. While the project would not continue south through California's Cajon Pass to Los Angeles, it could connect to terminals serving the California high-speed rail line, making it accessible from most population centers in Southern California. It promises to make the trip from Victorville to Las Vegas in 81 minutes.

BY TAXI

Except for peak periods, taxis are numerous and quite readily available, and drivers are good sources of information (not always accurate) and entertainment (not always wholesome). Of course, Las Vegas operates at peak loads most of the time, so if you're not in a taxi zone right in front of one of the busiest hotels, it might be tough to get one. The 16 companies plying the streets of Las Vegas charge $3 for the flag drop and $2.40 per mile. A $1.80 surcharge is assessed for pickups from the airport. Waiting time is $0.50 per minute. This means that it's cheaper to take the surface streets from the airport to your destination rather than the freeway, which is several miles longer. A taxi ride should run no more than $25 from the airport to a hotel on the Strip or downtown.

BY LIMO

Offering chauffer-driven domestic and imported sedans, shuttle buses, and SUVs in addition to stretch and superstretch limos,

Las Vegas Limousines (702/736-1419 or 888/696-4400) can transport up to 20 people per vehicle to and from sporting events, corporate meetings, airport connections, bachelor and bachelorette parties, sightseeing tours, and more. Rates are $55 per hour for a six-seat stretch limo, $75 for a 10-seat superstretch. **Presidential Limousine** (702/731-5577 or 800/423-1420) charges $59 per hour for its stretch six-seater, $80 per hour for the superstretch eight-seater; both include TVs and video players, mobile phones, champagne, bottled water, and roses for the women. **Bell Trans** (702/739-7990 or 800/274-7433) has 24- and 29-passenger coaches, a party bus, and a 12-passenger stretch SUV in addition to its fleet of stretch ($52 per hour) and superstretch ($80 per hour) limos.

The distinctive grill and white leather interior will make just the right impression when your chauffer delivers you in the silver Rolls Royce Phantom offered by **CLS Las Vegas** (702/740-4545). CLS has a full fleet, including Hummer limos and buses that seat up to

36. The stretch goes for $68 per hour, the superstretch for $80 per hour.

TOURS

Several companies offer the chance to see the sights of Las Vegas by bus, helicopter, airplane, or off-road vehicle. The ubiquitous **Gray Line** (702/384-1234 or 800/634-6579) offers tours of the city by night as well as tours of Hoover Dam and the Grand Canyon. City tours (6:30 P.M.–midnight, $55) visit the major Vegas free sights: the Mirage volcano, the Bellagio Conservatory, the "Welcome to Las Vegas" sign, the Fremont Street Experience, and some of the more opulent hotels. You can add a helicopter overview of the neon-lit Vegas skyline to cap your experience. The Hoover Dam tour ($60) can include a luncheon cruise on Lake Mead ($92). To book a lake cruise directly, call **Lake Mead Cruises** (702/293-6180, $24 adults, $12 ages 2–11, Sun. brunch cruise $39 adults, $18 ages 2–11, dinner cruise $49 adults, $25 ages 2–11).

Vegas Tours (866/218-6877) has a full slate of outdoor, adventure, and other tours. Some of the more unusual include soaring in a motorized glider ($129–159) and a visit and tour of the Techatticup gold mine ($113–189). Tours of the Grand Canyon and other state and national parks in the area are available as well.

All Vegas Tours (702/233-1627 or 800/455-5868) has all the usual tours plus a high-speed you-drive-it dune buggy adventure over the Nellis Dunes ($150–199, drivers must be over age 15). **Pink Jeep Tours** (888/900-4480) takes visitors in rugged but cute and comfortable 10-passenger ATVs to such sites as the Las Vegas Springs Preserve, Eldorado Canyon, the Valley of Fire, and Mount Charleston.

There are plenty of other tour operators offering similar services. Search the Internet to find tours tailored for your needs, the best prices, and the most competent providers.

For history, nature, and entertainment buffs looking for a more focused adventure, themed tours are on the rise in Las Vegas. **Haunted Vegas Tours** (702/339-8744, $66) takes an interesting if macabre trip to the "Motel of Death," where many pseudo-celebrities have met their untimely ends. Guides dressed as undertakers take you to the spot where Tupac Shakur died and where the spirits of Bugsy Siegel and other famous people are still said to walk the earth. The same company offers the **Las Vegas Mob Tour** (702/339-8744, $66), taking visitors to the sites of Mafia hits. Guides, dressed in black pinstriped suits and fedoras, tell tales of the 1970s, when Anthony "The Ant" Spilotro ran the city, and give the scoop on the fate of casino mogul Lefty Rosenthal.

Hoover Dam and Lake Mead

Hoover Dam began detaining the Colorado and Virgin Rivers in 1935. By 1938, Lake Mead was full of three years' worth of river water braced by the monolithic buttress at Black Canyon. The largest artificial lake in the West, Lake Mead measures 110 miles long and 500 feet deep, has 822 miles of shoreline, and contains 28.5 million acre-feet of water (just over 9 trillion gallons), a little less than half the water stored along the entire Colorado River system. The reservoir irrigates 2.25 million acres of land in the U.S. and Mexico and supplies water for more than 14 million people. Nine million people use Lake

Mead each year as a recreational resource; it's one of the most-visited National Park Service–managed areas in the country.

For all this, Lake Mead is only incidental to the dam's primary purpose: flood and drought control. In addition, Lake Mead is only the centerpiece of the 1.5-million-acre Lake Mead National Recreation Area, which includes Lake Mojave and the surrounding desert from Davis Dam to the south, Grand Canyon National Park to the east, all the way north to Overton—the largest U.S. Department of the Interior recreational acreage in the Lower 48.

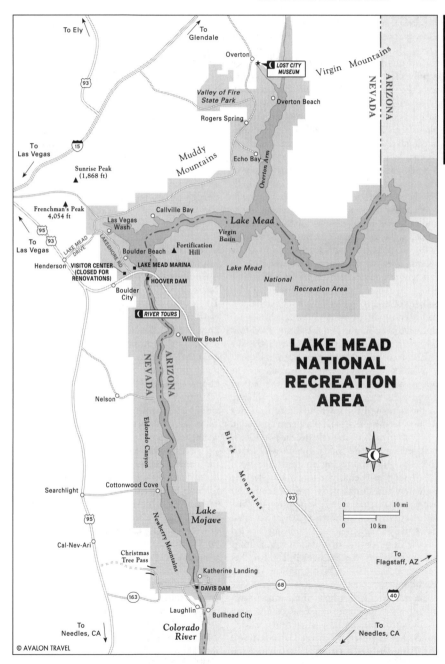

To Ely

To
Glendale

Overton

LOST CITY
MUSEUM

Virgin Mountains

NEVADA

ARIZONA

93

Valley of Fire
State Park

Overton Beach

Rogers Spring

To
Las Vegas

15

Muddy
Mountains

Echo Bay

Overton Arm

Sunrise Peak
(1,868 ft)

Frenchman's Peak
4,054 ft

Callville Bay

Lake Mead

95

93

To
Las Vegas

LAKE MEAD DRIVE

LAKESHORE RD

Las Vegas
Wash

Virgin
Basin

Henderson

Boulder Beach

Fortification
Hill

Lake Mead

VISITOR CENTER
(CLOSED FOR
RENOVATIONS)

LAKE MEAD MARINA

Lake Mead

Boulder
City

HOOVER DAM

National

Recreation Area

RIVER TOURS

Willow Beach

**LAKE MEAD
NATIONAL
RECREATION
AREA**

NEVADA

ARIZONA

Nelson

Eldorado Canyon

Black

Mountains

93

0   10 mi

0   10 km

Searchlight

Cottonwood Cove

Lake
Mojave

95

Newberry Mountains

To
Flagstaff, AZ

Cal-Nev-Ari

Christmas
Tree Pass

Katherine Landing

40

163

DAVIS DAM

68

Laughlin

Bullhead City

To
Needles, CA

Colorado
River

To
Needles, CA

© AVALON TRAVEL

HENDERSON

Only four years after the completion of Hoover Dam, the Germans started dropping terror on England in the form of bombs whose deadly incendiary properties were attributed to magnesium, until then a little-known metal. Lightweight magnesium was also discovered in various components of downed German airplanes. In 1940, Allied scientists and engineers had analyzed the qualities of this metal, and geologists had located huge deposits near Gabbs, Nevada. Since vast amounts of electrical power are required to process magnesium, a site halfway between Hoover Dam and Las Vegas was selected for the magnesium processing plant, and in September 1941 construction started on a massive factory known as Basic Magnesium. More than 10,000 workers spent just a few months erecting the plant, the town, and the transportation systems necessary to aid the war effort. Five thousand people lived in "Basic" by early 1942, and 16 million pounds of magnesium had been produced by 1943. So much magnesium had been shipped from Basic by 1944 that the government had a surplus, and with the war in Europe winding down, the plant was closed.

With the town threatened to become yet another ghost in the Nevada desert, the federal government agreed to turn over the property to the state, and the town, renamed to honor Albert Henderson, a local politician and judge who was pivotal in the takeover negotiations, received a new lease on life. By the early 1950s the huge manufacturing complex had been subdivided to accommodate smaller private industry, and by the early 1980s Henderson accounted for half of the state's non–tourist industry output. The town made the national news in 1988 when a huge explosion leveled Pacific Engineering, manufacturer of ammonia perchlorate, the oxidizer in solid rocket fuel, and the Kidd's Marshmallow factory next door.

Henderson is aesthetically...um...interesting, with its huge industrial complex set off from the residential and commercial districts that sprouted up in the last quarter of the 20th century. In early 1994 Henderson joined the Nevada 100,000 Club, an exclusive group of towns with more than 100,000 residents (it now boasts about 250,000), along with Las Vegas, North Las Vegas, and Reno. Until the 2008–2010 recession, Henderson was one of the fastest-growing cities in the fastest-growing state in the country, and it is consistently named among the nation's most livable communities thanks to its jobs, parks, relatively low crime rate, and the development of several new casinos in the Green Valley subdivision. Its excellent location is undeniable— only 15 minutes from Lake Mead, and close enough to Las Vegas to enjoy that city's benefits while far enough away to outdistance the disadvantages.

Casinos

Just north of Sam's Town on Boulder Highway is **Boulder Station** (4111 N. Boulder Hwy., 702/432-7777); farther south, just north of Tropicana Avenue, is **Eastside Cannery** (5255 N. Boulder Hwy., 702/507-5700) and **The Longhorn** (5288 N. Boulder Hwy., 702/435-9170). They're all small local joints with a tradition of low limits, good cheap grub, and basic hotel rooms. On Sunset Road near Boulder Highway, the **Skyline** (1741 N. Boulder Hwy., 702/565-9116) is home to The Dumkoffs, a wildly entertaining costumed oompah band. They keep the party going Sunday afternoons with their comedy and music. **Joker's Wild** (920 N. Boulder Hwy., 702/564-8100), near the intersection with Water Street, has no hotel but offers blackjack, Caribbean stud, craps, roulette, a coffee shop, a buffet, and a lounge.

Two major casinos and one minor gambling house are the center of entertainment downtown. The **Eldorado** (140 S. Water St., 702/564-1811) is a typical small Boyd Group property like the California, Main Street Station, and Fremont downtown and Sam's Town and Joker's Wild on the Boulder Strip: a large, bright, classy place with a large pit full of blackjack, crap, and roulette tables along with a sports book, keno, bingo, a couple of bars, a 24-hour coffee shop, and Mariana's Mexican restaurant.

Next door, the **Rainbow Club** (122 S. Water St., 702/565-9777) is dark and gaudy by comparison, with a multicolored facade, startling neon borders, signage inside and out, and crowds around the slots and video poker, giving it the unmistakable signature of Reno's Peppermill.

Classing up the accommodations offerings in Henderson is the **Green Valley Ranch** (2300 Paseo Verde Pkwy., 702/871-7777, $110–180), one of the latest and most upscale of the Station Casinos properties. Located on I-215 just west of town, the property offers a lavish spa and attractive rooms packed with amenities such as free newspapers and down comforters. The pool areas offer private cabanas and infinity dipping pools. Guests will also find upscale dining, headliner entertainment, eye-catching bars, and a Regal cinema.

Way west of town, **M Resort** (12300 Las Vegas Blvd. S., 702/797-1000, $150–220) is Henderson's other casino to earn the title "resort." Located far afield from Henderson proper, nearly at Sky Harbor Airport on St. Rose Parkway (take I-215 west to the St. Rose exit and head west to Las Vegas Blvd.), the M is every bit as lavish as Green Valley Ranch, with a strong entertainment schedule and fine dining; the rooms are a spacious 550 square feet with all the electronic entertainment you'd expect, including 42-inch TVs. Getting in on the Food Network craze, M hosts *Martini Time with Chef Tina Martini* (noon and 4 P.M. Thurs.–Sun., $40), a cooking show with a live studio audience.

Food

Henderson is no match for Las Vegas when it comes to haute cuisine, but **Todd's Unique Dining** (4350 E. Sunset Rd., 702/430-7544, 4:30–10 P.M. Mon.–Sat., $30–45) holds its own against any in Sin City. With unpretentious decor and food, the seafood is always fresh, but the short ribs are the way to go. The cellar always has just the right accompaniment. From the kitchen to the waitstaff, you'll always be professionally catered to. Other top gourmet choices include **Hank's Fine Steaks &**

Martinis (Green Valley Ranch, 2300 Paseo Verde Pkwy., 702/617-7515, 5:30–10 P.M. daily, $45–65) for steaks with juices sealed in with a perfect charbroil and a sweet South African lobster tail; start with the crabmeat cocktail. Green Valley also has the perfect spot for a late supper, **China Spice** (2300 Paseo Verde Pkwy., 702/617-7515, 5 P.M.–1 A.M. Sun.–Thurs., 5 P.M.–3 A.M. Fri.–Sat., $20–40). Don't miss the crispy duck.

With dinner covered, turn to M Resort for breakfast and lunch. **Studio B** (12300 Las Vegas Blvd. S., 702/797-1000, 7 A.M.–9 P.M. daily, $16–30) brings gourmet to the lunch buffet. Live cooking demonstrations by culinary experts preparing the buffet's dishes are shown on huge video monitors inside the main buffet room. You'll see dedicated professionals preparing delicate pastries, sushi, and Asian cuisine worthy of the top Chinese rooms in town. The beef on the carving station is tender enough to be cut with a plastic knife. Beer and wine is included at no extra charge. To start the day right, bop on into **Hash House a Go-Go** (12300 S. Las Vegas Blvd., 702/797-1000, 7 A.M.–11 P.M. Sun.–Thurs., 7 A.M.–2 A.M. Fri.–Sat., $10–20). Chicken, turkey, and barbecue along with more traditional breakfast meats figure heavily among the scrambled-egg dishes. For a bargain, try the 6–11 A.M. breakfast at **Images** (122 S. Water St., 702/565-9777, 24 hours daily, $7–15) inside the Rainbow Club; $1.89 gets you two eggs, bacon or sausage, and hash browns, toast, or biscuits and gravy.

Lake Las Vegas

Henderson's latest attempt to shed its image as the grittier, less attractive step-sister of Las Vegas is a new development seven miles east of town. Lake Las Vegas, the ambitious, ultra-luxurious Mediterranean-themed housing and resort development centered on a 320-acre artificial lake, has fallen on hard times. Designed as a playground for the rich and pampered, Lake Las Vegas has had to close two of its three golf courses, its casino, and a hotel; another of the three hotels is in bankruptcy. Montelago Village, a collection of shops on a pedestrian way, is still open—for now—and a strengthening economy has many people optimistic that the area can rebound.

Loews Hotel (101 Montelago Blvd., 702/567-6000, $130–180) maintains a pride of place and a lakeside getaway for the rich and those who want to dream for a weekend or a week. Loews is Lake Las Vegas for many people, its championship golf courses and water activities the upscale area's most memorable features and inviting locales for weddings and corporate events. Just the right size at about 500 guest rooms and suites, Loews tempts guests with a private white-sand beach and cabanas on two pools, children's activities, kayaks, pedal boats, and electric skiffs for exploring the inlets and lagoons as well as a full-service spa and fitness room. Bright and airy, **Marssa** (6–10 P.M. Tues. –Sat., $30–50) carries on the lakeside theme with sushi and Pacific Rim–inspired seafood, while **Rick's Café** (6 A.M.–3 P.M. daily, $15–30) dishes up delicacies with a continental bent.

Clark County Museum

As you continue east on Boulder Highway, the next attraction is the extensive and fascinating Clark County Museum (1830 S. Boulder Hwy., 702/455-7955, 9 A.M.–4:30 P.M. daily, $1.50 adults, $1 seniors and children). The main museum exhibit is housed in the new pueblo building, with fine displays tracing Native American cultures from the prehistoric to the contemporary and chronicling nonnative exploration, settlement, and industry: Mormons, the military, mining, ranching, railroading, riverboating, and gambling up through the construction of Hoover Dam and the subsequent founding of Henderson.

The old depot that houses the railroad station and rolling-stock collection has been restored. Also be sure to stroll down to the Heritage Street historical residential and commercial buildings: the **Townsite House,** built in Henderson in the 1940s; the 1890s print shop; the **Babcock and Wilcox House,** one of 12 original residences built in Boulder City in early 1933; and the pièce de résistance **Beckley**

House, a simple yet stunning example of the still-popular California bungalow style, built for $2,500 in 1912 by Las Vegas pioneer and entrepreneur Will Beckley.

Other displays include a ghost town trail, a nature trail with a simulated Paiute village, a general store, a jailhouse and a blacksmith. The gift shop sells some interesting items such as books, magazines, minerals, jewelry, beads, pottery, textiles, and even Joshua tree seeds.

Henderson Bird Viewing Preserve

Southern Nevada's natural side isn't always easy to find, but when you peel back the neon, the discoveries are often surprisingly rich. The Henderson Bird Viewing Preserve (2400 Moser Dr., near Boulder Hwy. and Sunset Rd., 702/267-4180, 6 A.M.–2 P.M. daily Mar.–May, 6 A.M.–noon daily June–Aug., 6 A.M.–2 P.M. daily Sept.–Nov., 7 A.M.–2 P.M. daily Dec.–Feb., free) is a good example. Situated on 140 acres at the city's water treatment center, the preserve is home to hundreds of hummingbirds, ibis, ducks, eagles, roadrunners, and numerous other migratory species. The park, which is managed by the City of Henderson, offers nine ponds with both paved and dirt paths. Don't feed the wildlife.

Railroad Pass

U.S. 93/95 continues southwest up and over a low gate between the River Mountains and the Black Hills known as Railroad Pass (2,367 feet), named for the Union Pacific route to Boulder City and the dam. With a full-service casino, coffee shop, and buffet, **Railroad Pass Hotel and Casino** (2800 Boulder Hwy., 702/294-5000, $39–59) sits at the top of the pass. Just beyond is the junction where U.S. 95 cuts right, south and west of Laughlin, and U.S. 93 heads east into Boulder City.

Information and Services

Past downtown on Water Street are the convention center, city hall, a library, and a park; Water Street runs around to the left and joins Major Street, which heads right back out to Boulder Highway. The **Chamber of**

Commerce (590 S. Boulder Hwy., 702/565-8951) is right at the corner.

BOULDER CITY

In 1930, when Congress appropriated the first funds for the Boulder Canyon Project, the Great Depression was in full swing, the dam was to be one of the largest single engineering and public works construction tasks ever undertaken, and urban architects were increasingly leaning toward the social progressiveness of the community planning movement. Boulder City was born of these unique factors and remains the most unusual town in Nevada. In 1930 Saco R. DeBoer, a highly regarded 35-year-old landscape architect from Denver, developed the Boulder City master plan. He set the government buildings at the top of the site's hill. The town radiated out like a fan, and parks, plazas, and perimeters enclosed the neighborhoods in pleasant settings. Construction of the town began in March 1931, only a month before work started at the dam site. The increasing influx of workers, most of whom were housed in a cluster of temporary tent cabins known as Ragtown, forced the government to accelerate construction, and most of DeBoer's more grandiose elements (neighborhood greenbelts, large single-family houses) were abandoned in favor of more economical and expedient dormitories and small cottages. Still, Boulder City became a prettified all-American oasis of security and order in the midst of a great desert and the Great Depression. The U.S. Bureau of Reclamation, charged with constructing the dam, controlled the town down to the smallest detail; a city manager, answerable directly to the Commissioner of Reclamation, oversaw operations with complete authority.

After the dam was completed, the town master plan was further dismantled as workers left and company housing was moved or torn down for materials. It seemed Boulder City was in danger of becoming a ghost town, but it gradually became a service center for the recreation area. For 30 years the federal government owned the town and all its buildings, but in 1960 the municipality became independent,

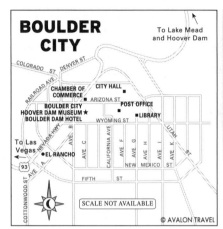

the feds began to sell property to longtime residents, and alcohol sales were allowed for the first time. Gambling, however, remains illegal in the only town in the state with laws against it. Boulder City today is far from it's squeaky-clean government origins, but it retains its own atmosphere—especially in contrast to the rest of southern Nevada.

Sights

Coming into Boulder City on U.S. 93 (Nevada Highway) is more like entering a town in Arizona or New Mexico: The downtown streets are lined with Indian and Mexican gift shops and a number of galleries and shops selling crafts, jewelry, antiques, and collectibles as well as businesses catering to the lake-bound crowd. Boulder City has no casinos.

Stop at the **Boulder Dam Hotel** (1305 Arizona St., 702/293-3510, $69–135) for a glimpse at dam-construction and divorce-era Las Vegas. This darling, built in 1933 to accommodate visitors to the construction site, found new life as divorce tourists booked accommodations to wait out Nevada's residency requirements for ending their marriages, and the lobby is now home to the **Boulder City/Hoover Dam Museum** (702/294-1988, 10 A.M.–5 P.M. Mon.–Sat., noon–5 P.M. Sun., $2 adults, $1 seniors and children). The colonial-style interior looks exactly as it did in 1933 when it was constructed, as you can see in the black-and-white photos that grace the walls. Inside are interesting photos from the 1930s of the Six Companies' rec hall and high scalers working high up on the canyon walls. You can also see the high-scaler chair, and pick up Dennis McBride's excellent book on Boulder City, *In the Beginning*. The restaurant is open for breakfast (included for hotel guests) and lunch. And the hotel is available for tea parties, reunions, and other special events.

Get a walking tour brochure at the hotel and stroll up Arizona Street then down Nevada Highway to get a feel for the history and design significance of downtown. Then continue on the residential and public-building walks to get an intimate glimpse of DeBoer's plan for the town as modified by the practicalities of government work. You can also head back toward Henderson on Nevada Highway to the Frank T. Crowe Memorial Park (named for the chief dam engineer, immortalized in the book *Big Red*) and take a right onto Cherry Street to see the fine row of bungalows from the 1930s built for dam workers, Boulder City's first residents.

At the Boulder City branch of the **Nevada State Railroad Museum** (600 Yucca St., 702/486-5933), railroad buffs can take a train ride on the **Nevada Southern Railway** ($10 adults, $5 ages 4–11, free under age 4); get a discount coupon at www.nevadasouthern.com/PDFs/Dollar Off Coupon.pdf. The renovated historic cars make treks along the old Boulder Branch Line departing at 10 A.M., 11:30 A.M., 1 P.M., and 2:30 P.M. Saturday–Sunday. The Pullman coaches, some of which date back to 1911, take passengers for a seven-mile, 45-minute round-trip journey across the stark Mojave Desert. All the cars and engines have been refurbished, and the enclosed cars have been retrofitted with air-conditioning. The spur used for the excursion was donated to the Nevada State Railroad Museum in 1985, and the train still chugs along the original tracks. The ride goes as far as the Railroad Pass Casino, and along the way passengers can expect to see jackrabbits, the occasional bighorn sheep, a variety of desert plant life, and a few historic sites.

Accommodations

Boulder City has a handful of motels, all strung along Nevada Highway (U.S. 93) as you enter town. Coming from the west, bypass the first several inns you come to; you'll be greeted by the impeccable landscaping and the retro-chic sign of the **El Rancho** (725 Nevada Hwy., 702/293-1085, $60–110). The spotless grounds mirror the accommodations. Sparkling microwaves and refrigerators, spacious rooms, quilts on the beds, and ceiling fans give the El Rancho a homey feel. Save even more with a cookout on barbecue grills outside, but be sure to eat at least one meal at the Southwest Cafe right next door.

If you're looking to save even more on your room, or you crave some nearby gaming action, you could continue even farther, almost to the shore of Lake Mead, to **The Hacienda Hotel & Casino** (Hwy. 93, just east of Lakeshore Rd., 702/293-5000 or 800/245-6380, $48–63). The hotel is pet-friendly, which is a plus for folks looking to hike the Lake Mead area with their dogs, but guests who are finicky about sanitary conditions may want to book elsewhere; The room rates are dirt cheap, and while the beds and guest rooms are perfectly clean, the common areas and carpeting are showing signs of age. A Lake Mead and Hoover Dam helicopter tour company and a river rafting concession operate out of the Hacienda, making it a convenient and inexpensive place to stay for sightseers, and there's a decent buffet, a 24-hour café, a steak house, and a lounge with life entertainment.

Canyon Trail RV Park (1200 Industrial Rd., 702/293-1200, $35) has plenty of overnight spots among its 242 sites. There's no shade and precious little greenery, but craggy sandstone mountains rise from the rear of the place. To get there, from the traffic light in Boulder City, take the truck route one block to Canyon Road. Turn left, drive to the end of Canyon Road, and turn left on Industrial Road. The park is half a block down on the right. Another RV park, **Boulder Oaks** (1010 Industrial Rd., 702/294-4425, $38), is quiet despite its in-town location.

Information and Services

The **Chamber of Commerce** (465 Nevada Way, 702/293-2034) has all the local brochures and can answer questions about the town, the dam, and the lake.

HOOVER DAM

The 1,400-mile Colorado River has been carving and gouging great canyons and valleys with red sediment-laden waters for 10 million years. For 10,000 years Native Americans, the Spanish, and Mormon settlers coexisted with the fitful river, rebuilding after spring floods and withstanding the droughts that often reduced the mighty waterway to a muddy trickle in fall. By the turn of the 20th century, irrigation ditches and canals had diverted some of the river water into California's Imperial Valley, west of its natural channel, but in 1905 a wet winter and abnormal spring rains combined to drown everything in sight: Flash floods deepened the artificial canal and actually changed the course of the river to flow through California's low-lying valley. For nearly two years engineers and farmers wrestled the Colorado back into place. The Salton Sea, a lake that had covered 22 square miles, grew to 500 square miles, and 95 years later it still covers more than 200 square miles. But the message was clear to federal overseers: The Colorado had to be tamed, and over the next 15 years the Bureau of Reclamation began to "reclaim" the West, primarily by building dams and canals. By 1923, equitable water distribution for the Colorado River had been negotiated among the states and Mexico, and six years later Congress passed the Boulder Canyon Project Act, authorizing funds for Boulder Dam to be constructed in Black Canyon; the dam's name was eventually changed to honor Herbert Hoover, then Secretary of Commerce.

The immensity of the undertaking still boggles the mind. The closest settlement was a sleepy railroad town 40 miles west called Las Vegas, and the nearest large power plant was in San Bernardino, more than 200 miles away.

© RYAN JERZ

Hoover Dam is an engineering marvel. The arch under construction in the photo is now complete, alleviating traffic congestion over the dam.

Tracks had to be laid, a town built, workers hired, and equipment shipped in just to prepare for construction. Of course, before dam work could begin, the Colorado had to be diverted. That project began in April 1931. Workers hacked four tunnels, each 56 feet across, through the canyon walls. They moved thousands of tons of rock every day for 16 months. Finally, in November 1932, the river water was rerouted around the dam site. Then came the concrete: 40 million cubic yards of it, eight cubic yards at a time. Over the course of the next two years, 5 million bucketfuls of cement were lowered into the canyon until the dam—660 feet thick at the base, 45 feet thick at the crest, 1,244 feet across, and 726 feet high—was complete.

The top of the dam was built wide enough to accommodate a two-lane highway. Inside this gargantuan wedge were placed 17 massive electricity-generating turbines. The cost of the dam surpassed $175 million. At the peak of construction, more than 5,000 workers toiled day and night to complete the project under extreme conditions of heat, dust, danger from heavy equipment, explosions, falls, and tumbling rocks. An average of 50 injuries per day and a total of 94 deaths were recorded over the 46 months of construction. Contrary to popular legend, none of the dead were entombed in the dam.

The largest construction equipment ever known had to be designed, built, and installed at the site, and miraculously the dam was completed nearly two years ahead of schedule—this was a government project, remember. In February 1935 the diversion tunnels were closed, and Lake Mead began to fill up behind the dam, which was dedicated eight months later by President Franklin Roosevelt. A month later, the first turbine turned, and electricity started flowing.

Today, the Colorado River system has several dams and reservoirs, storing roughly 60 million acre-feet of water. An acre-foot is just under 326,000 gallons, about as much water as an average U.S. household uses in two years. California is allotted 4.4 million acre-feet,

Arizona gets 2.8 million, Nevada 300,000, and Mexico 1.5 million. Hoover Dam, meanwhile, supplies 4 billion kilowatt-hours of electricity annually, enough to power 500,000 homes.

Visitors Center and Tours

In 1977, the Bureau of Reclamation started to build a new and improved **visitors center** (702/494-2517, 9 A.M.–6 P.M. daily summer, 9 A.M.–4:45 P.M. daily winter, $8, free under age 4, parking $7) to accommodate the 700,000 people who visit every year; more than 32 million visitors have taken the tour of the most-visited dam in the country. Construction on the 44,000-square-foot facility lagged through four presidential administrations until it was completed in 1995 for an expected cost of $435 million; the Luxor resort in Las Vegas cost only $375 million. To be fair, the project did include building a five-story, 450-car parking garage wedged into a ravine in the mountain, and as visitors centers go, this one is terrific. It has some exhibits, a movie about the Colorado River, and elevators that take you into the bowels of the dam. You can buy tickets for the 35-minute **dam tour** ($6 adults, $9 over age 61, ages 4–16, and military, free for military in uniform and children under age 4). Get in line as early as possible to shorten the wait time. The 53-story descent into the dam's interior takes more than a minute. Tunnels lead you to a monumental room housing the monolithic turbines. Next, you step outside to look up to the top of the dam and the magnificently arched bypass bridge downstream. The tour ends with a walk through one of the diversion tunnels, a 30-foot-wide water pipe. The guides pack extensive statistics and stories into the short tour.

Getting There

To get to the dam from Boulder City, stay on Nevada Highway through town for eight miles. You enter **Lake Mead National Recreation Area,** and arrive at the junction of U.S. 93 and Highway 166 (Lakeshore Dr.). Taking a left on the state route brings you right to the **Alan Bible Visitor Center** (702/293-8990,

8:30 A.M.–4:30 P.M. daily) and park head-quarters for the recreation area. Named for a popular U.S. senator from Nevada, the center has maps, brochures, knowledgeable rangers, and a 15-minute movie on the lake and its ecosystem.

Across Lakeshore Drive from the visitors center is a parking lot for the trailhead to the **U.S. Government Construction Railroad Trail.** The 2.6-mile one-way route follows an abandoned railroad grade along a ledge overlooking the lake. It passes through four tunnels blasted through the hills and ends at the fifth tunnel, which is sealed. This is an enjoyable level stroll that anyone can do. Mountain bikers can get on the **Bootleg Canyon Mountain Bike Trail,** which has 36 miles of cross-country and downhill runs (the "Elevator Shaft" has a 22 percent grade). Trailhead access is off Yucca or Canyon Streets.

Another trail to consider in Boulder City is the **River Mountain Hiking Trail,** a five-mile round-trip hike originally built by the Civilian Conservation Corps in 1935 and recently restored. It has good views of the lake and the valley. The trailhead is on the truck bypass, just beyond the traffic light in downtown Boulder City, on the left as you're heading toward the dam.

LAKE MEAD NATIONAL RECREATION AREA

Three roads provide access to Lake Mead from the Nevada side. From the north, take Highway 147 (Lake Mead Blvd.) as it runs east from North Las Vegas before turning south to the lake and continuing along the east shore to Lake Mead Marina and Boulder Beach. It connects with Highway 167 (Northshore Rd.), which follows the north shore of Las Vegas Bay past Callville Bay and turns north along the Overton Arm.

From Henderson and points south, you can follow Highway 564 (Lake Mead Dr.) northeast past Lake Las Vegas, where it ends at Highway 147. Turn left to hook up with Northshore Road or right to Lakeshore Road. You can also take U.S. 93 to Boulder City,

© RYAN JERZ

Lake Mead

where it takes on an additional name: Nevada Highway. If you stay on this road, you'll wind through canyons and eventually reach Hoover Dam, but if you turn left in town, you'll be on Lakeshore Road heading north along the eastern shore.

Lakeshore Road

On Lakeshore Road about two miles north of the Nevada Highway ingress to the recreation area is the **Lake Mead RV Village** (288 Lakeshore Rd., 702/293-2540, $45), which has many permanent mobiles and trailers but has 115 spaces dedicated to transient RVers, including many pull-throughs (register at the office near the entrance). A Laundromat and groceries are available. Turn right off Lakeshore Road into the entrance and right into the trailer village. If you take a left at the entrance, you enter **Boulder Beach Campground** ($10), a sprawling and somewhat rustic site with water, grills, a dump station, and plenty of shade under cottonwood and pines, but no hookups. There are 150 campsites for tents or small self-contained motor homes. It's a three-minute walk down to the water, or 0.5 miles' drive north on Lakeshore Drive. They don't call it Boulder Beach for nothing: The bottom is rocky and hard on the feet (bring your sandals), but the water is bathtub warm, around 80°F July–September. Sheltered picnic tables and restrooms are available waterside.

Seven miles beyond Boulder Beach is **Las Vegas Bay Campground** (702/293-8907, $10). Turn right into the Las Vegas Marina, then take your first left; the campground is about one mile down the spur road. The campground sits on a bluff over the lake; it's not quite as shady or as large as Boulder Beach. Also, you have to climb down a pretty steep slope to get to the water, and there's no real beach. There are 86 campsites for tents or self-contained motor homes up to 35 feet. Piped drinking water, flush toilets, picnic tables, grills, and fire pits are provided, and there is a campground host.

Continuing north, follow Lakeshore Road around to the left (northwest), then take a right

onto Northshore Road (Hwy. 167). In another few miles, turn right at the intersection with Lake Mead Boulevard (Hwy. 147). In another seven miles is the turnoff for Callville Bay.

Callville Bay

From the highway, you rock and roll four miles down to the marina, which is green from oleanders, Russian olives, yuccas, palms, and pines. Callville Bay is the site of Callville, founded by Anson Call in 1865 in response to a directive by Mormon leader Brigham Young. Callville flourished briefly in the 1860s as a landing for Colorado River steamboats and an Army garrison, but the post office closed in 1869. Today the stone ruins of Call's warehouse lie under 400 feet of Lake Mead water and 10 feet of Lake Mead silt.

As you come into the marina, the first left is to **Callville Bay Trailer Village** (702/565-8958, $22), most of which is occupied by permanent mobiles and trailers. There are only five spaces for overnight motor homes, all with full hookups and three with pull-throughs. RVs, along with tent campers, can also park without hookups at the campground across the road.

Callville Bay Campground (702/293-8990, $10) is a little farther down the access road. A beautiful grassy area greets you at the entrance, with stone picnic benches under shelters and a restroom. The sites closer to the front have the taller shade-giving oleanders; those toward the rear are more exposed. A 0.5-mile trail climbs from the dump station near the entrance to a sweeping panorama of the whole area. There are 80 campsites with running water, flush toilets, picnic tables, and grills, and there is a campground host.

The marina has a grocery store with a snack bar, and there is a bar-restaurant with a wall of big picture windows overlooking the lake. Down at the boat launch, you can rent houseboats.

Back on Highway 167, continue east; it's rugged country out here, with the Black Mountains between you and the lake, and the dark brooding Muddy Mountains on the left. Eventually the road turns north toward the east edge of the Muddy Mountains. The turnoff to Echo Bay, 24 miles from Callville, is on the right.

Echo Bay

Four bumpy miles down Bitter Spring Valley is **Echo Bay Marina** (702/394-4000, $30). This resort has a similar layout to Callville Bay but is much larger. The trailer village has shaded spots arranged in a horseshoe with the restrooms and laundry facilities in the middle. During summer, a shuttle delivers campers to the marina. The marina rents personal watercraft as well as patio, ski, and fishing boats. Recent low water levels have meant that there are no houseboats for rent. Tents are not allowed, but the upper section a National Park Service campground (702/394-4066, $10) is nearby. The lower section, close to the water, has 20-foot-tall oleander bushes for shade and privacy. The upper camprground is north across the road, just inland from the marina.

As you continue down toward the marina, you'll see the **Echo Bay Hotel** (702/394-4000, $70–125). The restaurant next door is open for breakfast, lunch, and dinner.

The great thing about Echo Bay is the beach, the best and most accessible on the Nevada side of the lake. There's no shade, but it's sandy, unlike the rocks at Boulder Beach, and not crowded. The bay is shallow for a long distance out, so the swimming is safe; there's no lifeguard.

Overton Beach

Back on North Shore Road, continue north, skirting the east edge of the Muddies. In less than a mile is **Rogers Spring,** which bubbles up clear and warm in a wash that runs east from the Muddy Mountains into Roger's Bay in the Overton Arm of Lake Mead. The warm turquoise pool, outlined by towering palms and sturdy old cottonwoods, overflows into a bubbling creek that meanders down a tree-lined course toward Lake Mead. Tropical fish, the descendants of the denizens of a failed hatchery from the 1950s, dart in the shallows and thrive in its warm waters. This spring has long been a favorite camping spot of southern Nevadans; it was originally developed by the Civilian Conservation Corps in the 1930s under the direction of Thomas W. Miller, the colonel who was instrumental in developing the first facilities at nearby Valley of Fire State Park. The National Park Service has plans to develop 250 campsites with water, sewer, and power. For now, there are chemical toilets and picnic shelters. A sign cautions swimmers not to put their heads under the water. The trailhead for a mile-long trail to an overlook is across the bridge.

A mile up the road from Rogers Spring is **Blue Point Spring,** which provides a grand view of Lake Mead on one side and the back of Valley of Fire on the other. In the early 1900s, farmers near St. Thomas (now at the bottom of the lake) worked to divert the waters of Blue Point and Rogers Springs to irrigate their fields. They dug the canal and hand-mixed concrete to line it. Their work eventually delivered water to the fields, but their health deteriorated; apparently, they drank from the springs, whose mineral content acted as a laxative, resulting in weakness and weight loss. Because of their fate, Blue Point Spring became known as "Slim Creek."

The recent decade-long drought has forced the closure of Overton Beach resort, formerly a terrific spot for fishing for striped bass.

Virgin Basin

Just above Overton Beach, the Virgin River to the northeast and the Muddy River to the northwest empty into Lake Mead. The Virgin Basin is a widening of the Virgin River just before it enters the reservoir. It's a primary habitat for numerous species of wildlife, including mammals, waterfowl, birds of prey, fish, reptiles, and amphibians. In the fall and spring, for example, numerous migrating species use the Virgin Basin as a resting place. Some species, including bald eagles, spend the winter in the Virgin Basin. Because it's accessible only by boat or a jolting primitive access road, it is well protected and offers a habitat safe from most human intervention. If you're careful, the basin provides an excellent opportunity to view and photograph wildlife in one of the few river wilderness areas left near the lake. To get there, you have to boat in from the Overton Arm. Most of the time there isn't enough water in the Virgin River below Riverside (just south of Mesquite) to float anything but an inner tube.

◖ River Tours

Tour operators bus rafters to the restricted side of the dam, where they board 35-person craft for a 3.5-hour ride with **Black Canyon River Adventures** (800/455-3490, 9 A.M. and 10 A.M. daily year-round, $86 adults, $83 youth, $53 children). The motorized raft trips end at Willow Beach, 13 miles downstream on the Arizona side of the Colorado River. Ospreys and bighorn sheep are often sighted on these trips, and rafters can wade and swim in the chilly water before enjoying the box lunch provided.

The **Desert Princess** (702/293-6180), a 250-passenger Mississippi-style stern-wheeler, and its little sister, the 149-passenger side-wheeler *Desert Princess Too,* cruise Lake Mead from the Lake Mead Cruises Landing (490 Horsepower Cove Rd., off Lakeshore Rd. near the junction with U.S. 93). Ninety-minute cruises ($24 adults, $12 children) leave at noon and 2 P.M. daily, and there is a two-hour dinner cruise (6:30 P.M. Thurs.–Sun., $49 adults, $25 children) as well as a two-hour brunch cruise (10 A.M. Sun., $39 adults, $18 children).

Recreation

Motorized fun is the most obvious recreation on Lake Mead. **Boating** options on the vast lake range from power boats skipping across the surface to houseboats puttering lazily toward hidden coves and personal watercraft jumping wakes and negotiating hairpin turns. **Las Vegas Boat Harbor** (702/293-1191) and **Lake Mead Marina** (702/293-3484), both at Hemenway Harbor (Hemenway Rd., off Lakeshore Rd. near the junction with U.S. 93, 702/293-1191), rent power boats, pontoons, and WaveRunners for $50–75 per hour, with half-day and daily rates available. **Callville Bay Marina** (off Northshore Rd., 17 miles east of Lake Las Vegas) has all these and houseboat

rentals too. For nonmotorized water fans, sailing and windsurfing are year-round thrills, and there's plenty of shoreline to explore in a canoe or kayak.

For **anglers,** largemouth bass, rainbow trout, catfish, and black crappie have been mainstays for decades. These days, however, striped bass are the most popular sport fish. Fishing supplies and fishing licenses can be obtained at the marinas.

Sixty miles south of Boulder City, recreation is also abundant at **Lake Mojave,** created by Davis Dam in 1953. This lake backs up almost all the way to Hoover Dam like a southern extension of Lake Mead. The two lakes are similar in climate, desert scenery, vertical-walled canyon enclosures, and a shoreline lined with numerous private coves. There is excellent trout fishing at Willow Beach on the Arizona side, where the water, too cold for swimming, is perfect for serious angling. A few rainbows over 55 pounds have been caught, and 20-pounders are not at all rare. **Cottonwood Cove Resort** (10000 Cottonwood Cove Rd., Searchlight, 702/297-1464), 14 miles east of central Searchlight, sits just north of the widest part of the lake. Access is also available on the Arizona side at Katherine Landing, just north of Davis Dam.

Swimming in Lake Mead requires the least equipment—a bathing suit. Boulder Beach (Lakeshore Rd., Boulder City), just 30 miles from Las Vegas and just down the road from the Alan Bible Visitor Center, is the most popular swimming site. For **divers,** visibility in Lake Mead averages 30 feet, and the water is stable. There is a dive park north of the swimming beach at Boulder Beach. It slopes gently to about 70 feet with placed objects and boats to explore, makes it a good introduction to the sport for novice divers. The sights of the deep are more spectacular elsewhere: the yacht *Tortuga* rests at a depth of 50 feet near the Boulder Islands; Hoover Dam's asphalt factory sits on the canyon floor nearby; the old Mormon town of St. Thomas, inundated by the lake in 1938, has many a watery story to tell; and Castle Cliffs at Gypsum Reef has drop-offs and irregular formations caused by erosion.

VALLEY OF FIRE STATE PARK

Working with a palette of red-tinged rock for 150 million years, the sun, wind, and rain created the masterpiece that is Valley of Fire State Park (29450 Valley of Fire Hwy., 702/397-2088). Proving that nature's opus remains a work in progress even after eons, the Dragon, a 40-foot-tall arch that resembled the mythical beast, crumbled and fell in 2009. Like Red Rock Canyon, this valley, six miles long and 3–4 miles wide, gets its distinctive color from the oxidizing metals in its Mesozoic-era sandstone. It is part of the Navajo Formation, a rocky block that stretches from southern Colorado through New Mexico, Arizona, Utah, and Nevada, and its monuments—arches and protruding jagged walls in brilliant vermilion, magenta, and gold—epitomize the Southwest.

The highest and youngest formations in the park are mountains of sand deposited by desert winds 140 million years ago. These dunes petrified, oxidized, and were chiseled into psychedelic shapes and colors. Underneath them is a 5,000-foot-deep layer dating back at least 250 million years, when brown mud was uplifted to displace the inland sea. The gray limestone below represents another 200 million years of deposits from the Paleozoic marine environment 550 million years ago.

This stunning valley was venerated by Native Americans, as seen in numerous petroglyphs in the soft rock, and it was part of the old Arrowhead Trail through southern Nevada. It was originally included in lands set aside by the federal government for construction of Boulder Dam in the 1920s, then donated to the state in 1931 to become a state park. Nevada had little money at the time to spend on development, so the feds sent in the Civilian Conservation Corps, which built the road, campgrounds, and some cabins.

Sights

A turnout near the entrance to the park has a self-service fee station: $6 for cars, $1 for bicycles, $14 for camping. There is also an information

© BETHANY DRYSDALE

Sand, wind, and geologic upheaval created the striking formations at Valley of Fire State Park.

shelter with a description of **Elephant Rock,** one of the best and most photographed examples of eroded sandstone in the park; a short trail leads to it from the sign. Continue west past signs for the Arrowhead Trail and petrified logs to the **cabins,** built for travelers out of sandstone bricks by the Civilian Conservation Corps in 1935. Farther in, the **Seven Sisters** are stunning sentinels along the road.

The **visitors center** (8:30 A.M.–4:30 P.M. daily) has a truly spectacular setting under a mountain of fire. Outside is a demonstration garden, and inside is the finest set of exhibits at any Nevada state park. Signboards by the front window describe the complex geological history of the landscape. You can spend another hour reading all the displays on the history, ecology, archaeology, and recreation of the park as well as browsing the changing exhibit gallery and the bookshelf near the information desk. There is a colorful interpretive signboard describing the most popular features in Valley of Fire. Don't forget to pick up a map of the park here.

From the visitors center, take the spur road to **Petroglyph Canyon Trail** and dig your feet into some red sand. **Mouse's Tank** is a basin that fills with water after a rain. A fugitive Native American named Mouse hid here in the late 1890s. The spur road continues through the towering canyon and peaks at **Rainbow Vista,** which has a parking area and a spectacular overlook.

The road continues four miles to **Silica Dome,** where you can park and gape at the walls, pillars, and peaks of sparkling white rock.

Head back toward the visitors center and take the through road, Highway 169. Driving west, you come to a 0.25-mile loop trail to fenced-in **petrified wood,** the most common local fossil. On the other side of the highway, another spur road leads to the campgrounds and the high staircase up to sheer **Atlatl Rock,** which is inscribed with petroglyphs. This is the tallest outdoor staircase in the state, more than 100 steps up to the face of the rock; you'll wonder how the petroglyphs' creators got up here.

Atlatl Rock is between the two campgrounds. Together they total 51 campsites for tents or self-contained motor homes up to 30 feet. Both have piped drinking water, picnic tables under ramadas, grills, and fire rings.

The loop road continues back to the highway. Take a right and continue west to the **Beehives,** which are worth a look. From here you can turn around, return to the east entrance, and take a left on Highway 169 toward Overton, or you can head to the west end of the park and back to Las Vegas (55 miles).

BITTER SPRINGS TRAIL AND BUFFINGTON POCKETS

The Bitter Springs Back Country Byway Trail to Buffington Pockets and beyond is a worthwhile scenic trip through brightly colored red and tan sandstone bluffs. The 28-mile drive is a challenging adventure, but 4WD is not necessary—a dependable vehicle with decent ground clearance will be up to the task. However, make sure your spare tire and jack are in order and that someone knows where you're headed and when you expect to return. Stay on the main road and avoid side trips into the many canyons unless you have 4WD. The beginning of the Bitter Springs Byway is 4.5 miles east of the Valley of Fire exit on I-15; follow the sign for "Bitter Springs" to the left (south).

The trail starts out cutting through the foothills of the Muddy Mountains, then travels through several dry washes and past numerous abandoned mining operations, before ending up on Northshore Drive. Along the way you have the opportunity to view natural water tanks and geologic formations that are rare in this region. Landforms are colorful, complex, and add to the feeling of isolation. Among the more striking scenes you'll encounter is Bitter Ridge, a sweeping arc that cuts across a rolling valley for eight miles. Geology buffs will appreciate the features of this tilt fault, with its rugged vertical southern face looming several hundred feet off the desert floor.

Moving past rolling red, brown, black, and white landforms, you drop into Bitter Valley, where red buttes stand on the desert floor. Emerging from the canyon, you'll be captivated by the sight of the brilliantly colored sandstone hills of Buffington Pockets and Color Rock Quarry.

The trail continues through a field of sandstone boulders, and you'll soon arrive at the entrance to Hidden Valley, tucked away a short distance from the road up a deep, winding, boulder-choked canyon. Between the valley walls, which soar hundreds of feet into the desert sky, you'll see sandstone windows, arches, and hoodoos. A short hike up into the valley brings you to a scenic overlook, where—judging by the large number of pictographs—prehistoric visitors were inspired by the view.

Abandoned buildings and other relics and remnants from the American Borax mining operation appear next on ground pocked by 30-foot-deep cisterns that once held water. Mine tunnels and passages are also abundant in the area, along with the debris associated with old mining districts. Be careful around the old mines: Cave-ins, rattlesnakes, and other dangers lurk. Obey all signs and fencing that have been installed for your protection.

There are no services along this isolated road, but maps of the area are available from the local Bureau of Land Management office (4701 N. Torrey Pines Dr., Las Vegas, 702/515-5000). Ask for the Nevada Back Country Byway guide for Bitter Springs Trail.

MOAPA VALLEY

Lake Mead terminates at the Muddy River Wash, the outlet of Moapa Valley, along Highway 169 (Northshore Rd.) north of Valley of Fire State Park. A thin strip of rich agricultural green lines the road up the river valley. The Anasazi people successfully farmed this land 1,000 years ago and built the Pueblo Grande de Nevada, or Lost City, on the fertile delta between the Muddy and Virgin Rivers. The Paiute replaced the Pueblo and still lived in the valley when the Mormons began to colonize it in 1864. The Mormons' farming efforts were also successful, and today this well-tended

plot is their legacy. Settlement extends six miles north up the irrigated green Moapa Valley, surrounded on three sides by flattop buttes, to Logandale.

Farther north, seven miles past I-15 exit 90 on Highway 168, is the **Moapa Valley National Wildlife Refuge** (9 A.M.–3 P.M. Fri.–Sun. Labor Day–Memorial Day). The refuge manages habitat for the Moapa White River springfish and the endangered Moapa dace.

Overton

Overton, 50 miles northeast of Las Vegas, is a compact agricultural community whose downtown is strung along several blocks of Highway 169, also known as Moapa Valley Boulevard and Main Street. Surprisingly for such a small town, Overton offers two strong lunch options. **Sugars Home Plate** (309 S. Moapa Valley Blvd., 702/397-8084, $7–15) serves $7.50 bacon and eggs, $8–9 burgers such as the Sugar Burger (a cheeseburger with polish sausage), and homemade pie. There's also a sports bar with bar-top video poker and sports memorabilia. The other food pick is just a block away: **Inside Scoop** (395 S. Moapa Valley Blvd., 702/397-2055, $10–20) has 30-plus ice cream flavors and filling sandwiches. The baked potatoes come with a variety of toppings. The town also has the Red Rooster Bar, a pizza place, and a Chevron station.

Best Western North Shore Inn (520 N. Moapa Valley Blvd., 866/538-0187, $65–130) provides basic guest rooms.

◖ Lost City Museum

A glimpse of the Anasazi legacy is found at the Lost City Museum (721 S. Moapa Valley Blvd., 702/397-2193, 8:30 A.M.–4:30 P.M. daily, $3) just south of Overton. The museum houses an immense collection of Pueblo artifacts, including an actual pueblo foundation, and a fascinating series of black-and-white photos covering the site's excavation in 1924. In a November 1976 article in *Nevada* magazine, David Moore made the insightful point that the Lost City wasn't so much lost as simply overlooked; Jedediah Smith mentioned it during his travels through southern Nevada in the 1820s, and another expedition reported these "ruins of an ancient city" in the *New York Tribune* in 1867, but an official excavation was not initiated until 1924. Some of the Anasazi ruins were drowned by Lake Mead, but in 1975 an entire ancient village was uncovered by workers digging a leach line.

The exterior of the museum, a re-creation of an adobe pueblo like those used by the Anasazi, was constructed by the Civilian Conservation Corps in 1935. It is possible to climb down the log ladder into the authentic pit house in front, and stroll around back for petroglyphs, more pueblos, picnic tables, and a pioneer monument.

MESQUITE

Thirty miles north on I-15 is Mesquite, on the Arizona border. Ten miles west of Mesquite, Highway 170, a 13-mile spur road off I-15, drops into Virgin Valley toward the high Virgin Mountains. The road crosses the Virgin River at Riverside, then continues along the Virgin River Valley, parallel to I-15, through dairy farmland

and past Bunkerville, another Mormon settlement from the 1870s, and finally into Mesquite.

Casino resorts have sprung up in Nevada wherever a major artery enters the state, giving Nevada's neighbors a chance to scratch the gambling itch as soon as they cross the state line. Mesquite is probably the best, although like the rest of the nation it has suffered in the recent economic downturn. The Peppermill Hotel-Casino, the first gambling in Nevada for westbound travelers along I-15, put Mesquite on the map in 1990. Reincarnated in 1993 as the Oasis and bankrupt in 2009, virtually the entire operation is closed and was scheduled for demolition. Still, the city's livability, lush golf resorts, and remaining viable gambling venues keep it going strong. Thanks to the casinos, the town went from a population of 900 in 1980 to about 15,000 today.

The Oasis's demise leaves two major hotel-casinos, and there are six manicured golf courses in town, including a country club and two Arnold Palmer–designed 18-hole championship links.

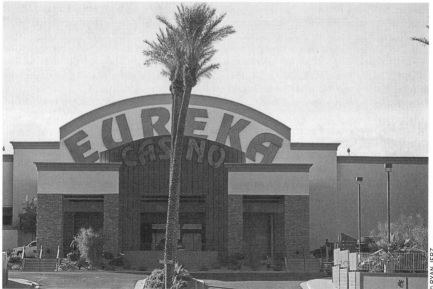

Mesquite's Eureka Casino and Hotel

© RYAN JERZ

Casinos

Virgin River (100 N. Pioneer Blvd., 702/346-7777 or 800/GETAWAY—800/438-2929, $29–49) is on the east side of town. It's smaller and more crowded, with the usual games as well as bingo, a buffet, a coffee shop, a lounge, a bowling alley, golf, a gun club, and 772 guest rooms.

Player's International, Merv Griffin's casino company, opened Player's Island in 1994, but a little more than a year later it had lost so much money that it was put up for sale; in 1997 it was sold to the Black family, owners of the Virgin River across town. The name has been changed to the **CasaBlanca** (950 W. Mesquite Blvd., 702/346-7529 or 877/771-2777, $29–55). It has 500 guest rooms, an RV park, an attractive casino, a lounge, a showroom, a coffee shop, a buffet, a steak house, and a large pool area. The pièce de résistance is an extensive European-style health spa complete with warm and hot pools, a *watsu* pool, Virgin River mud baths, a steam room and sauna, and all kinds of massage and skin therapies.

In 1997 Holiday Inn built a 215-room hotel with a 45,000-square-foot casino called the **Eureka Casino and Hotel** (275 Mesa Blvd., 702/346-4600 or 800/346-4611, $39–75) up the hill from the Virgin River.

Accommodations

Besides the big casinos, several smaller gambling houses offer hotel rooms, including the **Falcon Ridge Resort** (91030 W. Pioneer Blvd., 702/346-2200 or 866/374-6659, $50–75), which has meeting space as well as guest rooms, and the **Best Western Mesquite Inn** (390 N. Sandhill Blvd., 702/346-7444 or 800/931-8376, $75–99).

CasaBlanca (702/346-7529, $22) has 45 spaces for motor homes up to 35 feet, all with full hookups; 30 are pull-throughs. Tents are not allowed. **Desert Skies** (350 E. Hwy. 91, Littlefield, AZ, 928/347-6000, $50) has 340 large sites, free Wi-Fi, clean facilities, and even a library. The brand new **Solstice Motorcoach Resort** (345 Terrace View, 866/762-0664, $49) boasts great views, a putting green, and a boccie ball court.

© RYAN JERZ

The pool area at the CasaBlanca in Mesquite is a tropical paradise.

Food

The Oasis and Virgin River casinos offer several dining options, including fast food, buffets, and gourmet rooms. For fine dining, your best bet is **Katherine's** (CasaBlanca, 950 W. Mesquite Blvd., 702/346-7529 or 800/459-7529, 5–10 P.M. daily, $20–30). It's a traditional steak and Italian spot. For comfort food in a family atmosphere, go to the Virgin River's **Chuckwagon Restaurant** (100 N. Pioneer Blvd., 702/346-7777 or 800/346-7777, 24 hours daily, $10–15). The Virgin River also has the better buffet, the **Sierra** (7 A.M.–2 P.M. and 4–9 P.M. daily, $10–15). **Gregory's** (Eureka, 275 Mesa Blvd., 702/346-4600 or 800/346-4611, 4–9 P.M. daily, $25–50) is another gourmet option, especially if you're in the mood for salmon, although the steak is good too.

Virgin Canyon

The Virgin River is the only wild river left in southern Nevada. It ends in Lake Mead across from Overton, creating a silted marshland where waterfowl prowl for fish, frogs, and mud-turtles. The headwaters of the Virgin River, one of the main tributaries feeding the Colorado River and Lake Mead, are in Utah's Dixie National Forest, where winter ice and snow and summer rainstorms feed the 300-mile-long river. Occasionally, violent deluges flood out the valleys below Dixie, eroding forests and sending enormous walls of water sweeping through narrow canyons in Zion National Park.

By the time the Virgin reaches the Virgin River Canyon, or Virgin Gorge, as it has come to be known (in the far northwest corner of Arizona, I-15 runs through it), its waters are somewhat tamer, but during years with heavy rain, they can still be wild and dangerous. During calmer times of the year, it is possible to explore sections of the Virgin River in canoes, kayaks, inner tubes, and hiking boots.

Among some of the treasures you'll find in the gorge are extensive hikes to places where ancient Native Americans carved petroglyphs into rock walls. When you get tired, you can relax on soft sandy riverbanks under salt cedars and watch the happy birds hunting fat insects, or contemplate what these rock walls have seen during the last 50 million years. Caves abound along the riverbanks; inside some are large tree trunks, pounded into the caves by the force of a raging torrent in times past. In some places the granite walls are polished smooth by water levels dating to thousands of years ago. In other caves, high up on the face of the cliffs, you can see where the campfires of ancient people blackened the ceiling. Deer and other small game abound in the gorge.

BLACK CANYON

Black Canyon, which starts at the base of Hoover Dam and extends downriver to Katherine, is the river nearest to Las Vegas. The discharge from Hoover Dam generally creates a current of about 3 mph, an easily negotiated upstream paddle even for novices.

The dam discharges water from the bottom of Lake Mead, so it comes out at a chilly 53°F all year, warming up as it goes downriver toward Eldorado Canyon, where it widens out and is warm enough for swimming in the summer. Navigational and mile markers are posted on the shores of the river: red triangles with even numbers on the Arizona side, green squares with odd numbers on the Nevada side. These markers indicate the approximate distance, in miles, from Davis Dam at the extreme southern end of Lake Mojave. Also look for bighorn sheep on the cliffs along the river throughout Black Canyon. Sighting them provides the sharp-eyed observer a special opportunity to see these majestic animals in their natural environment. Cormorants, lizards, and small mammals are easier to find as you explore the shoreline.

Remember that the water level in the canyon can fluctuate considerably during the day, sometimes as much as 4–6 vertical feet, depending on releases from Hoover Dam. When stopping to camp, picnic, or explore, small craft should be pulled well up out of the water and tied off; larger craft should be well anchored on shore above any high-water marks to prevent being stranded.

Launching

The launch site is restricted to federal employees and licensed vendors. To put in here, you must make arrangements with one of these contractors to shuttle you and your canoe or kayak to the launch site. The contractor will add the $12 launch fee and $3 park entry fee to its bill. The U.S. Department of the Interior's Bureau of Reclamation places strict limits on the number of people allowed to access the canyon from this location. All popular dates, such as weekends and holidays, are booked far in advance. Weekday launches can usually be acquired with a few weeks' notice. The authorized livery services, such as **Boulder City Outfitters** (702/293-1190), **Desert River Outfitters** (928/754-5320), **Jerkwater Canoe Co.** (928/768-7753), and **Desert Adventures** (702/293-5026) can also rent you the watercraft of your choice and arrange motorized rafting trips through the canyon.

Other put-in and takeout points include Cottonwood Cove and Eldorado Canyon on the Nevada side as well as Willow Beach and Katherine Landing on the Arizona side.

Exploring on the River

Once on the river, there are several exciting places to visit and things to do. At the base of Hoover Dam is the Portal Road launch site; just a few hundred yards downstream on the Nevada side is a long gravel spit with tamarisk bushes. At the end of a lagoon just past the spit are some **rain caves** on the west wall. Some of the drops of water are hot while others are cold. During the construction of Hoover Dam, workers started to drill a tunnel at this site, but they encountered 122°F water and had to abandon the work. The partially drilled **Sauna Cave** remains. As you go deeper into the cave, it becomes darker and

hotter, and you'll encounter a heavy hot mist. Geothermal activity is high all along the canyon, and you'll find more evidence of it as you drift downstream.

Fifty yards below the entrance to the lagoon on the left is a small, very hot spring near **Goldstrike Canyon.** A short walk up the canyon leads to hot pools and a hot waterfall that is about as hot as humanly tolerable—123°F. Algae gives the surrounding rocks a vivid green color. The rock formations are spectacular, and there are many hot pools. The rocks and pebbles in the hot stream are sharp, so wearing shoes is advised. Be aware that *Naegleria fowleri,* an amoeba common in thermal pools, can enter the human body through the nose, causing a rare infection and possible death. Do not allow water from the hot springs or the streams to enter your nose, and never dive into or submerse your head in any thermal water in this recreation area.

Another hot waterfall is located within a few feet of the river about 100 yards below Goldstrike Canyon on the Arizona side. To ensure you don't drift past it, paddle upstream from Goldstrike Canyon to allow enough space to get across the river. This waterfall is larger and not as hot as the one in Goldstrike Canyon. Just past the waterfall is a palm tree, a nonnative species planted around 1970 by G. W. Paulin, who loved these canyons and spent much time exploring the river.

Back on the Nevada side, **Boy Scout Canyon** is about 0.3 miles south of the mile 62 marker. This sandy beach at the mouth of a large canyon leads to hot springs and hot pools about 0.5 miles up the canyon. The hike involves some climbing, and hand lines have been installed to aid the scramble up some boulders. The stream goes underground before it reaches the river.

In the last half of the 19th century, steamboats plied the Colorado River, even this far north. Their engines, however, were insufficient to make the upriver journey without help. Ringbolts were anchored in the riverside boulders, and towropes were threaded through the bolts to assist the boats. You can see one of these bolts on the Arizona side about 50 yards upriver from **Ringbolt Rapids.** The construction of Davis Dam, 60 miles downstream, and the resulting Lake Mojave significantly tamed these rapids, which at one time were some of the most challenging on the Colorado River. The rapids are adjacent to White Rock Canyon and the Arizona Hot Springs on the Arizona side of the river.

An old **Gauging Station** is an interesting remnant of Hoover Dam's construction. It clings to the Nevada canyon wall at mile 54.25. The gauging station was used prior to and during construction of Hoover Dam for monitoring the water level, flow rate, and silt content of the Colorado River. A cable car provided access to the station from the Arizona side. Just across the river on the Arizona side is the trail and catwalk used by the resident engineers, who were responsible for gathering the data at the gauging station, to travel from their residence to the station. The catwalk can be seen high up on the sheer walls above the river; it is unsafe to access. A second cable car across a side canyon enabled the engineers to go from the trail over to the catwalk. The foundations of the engineers' house and garage are located just down the river at about mile 53.

The buildings on the Arizona bank just before mile 52 are the **Willow Beach Fish Hatchery.** The buoys floating on the Arizona shore mark an area that is closed to all watercraft, including canoes and kayaks. The Willow Beach area extends for about 0.5 miles along the Arizona shore. If you're ending your trip at Willow Beach, boat to the south end at the harbor, past the marinas, and bring your vessel to shore at the south end of the parking lot. There is convenient vehicle access to this location, and you will not come into conflict with other boaters as you remove your boat from the water. South of Willow Beach, the river is still narrow and cold; it continues flowing through the deep canyon for about 3.5 miles. Life jackets must still be worn. The hatchery supplies planted

rainbow trout to the river, Lake Mead, and other fishing holes nearby. The just-released fingerlings provide monster striped bass with a buffet, and lunkers lurk during plant time. A few rainbows escape to replenish what the stripers and anglers take.

The point where the river widens is known as **Monkey Hole.** With a bit of imagination, the rock formation high on the Arizona shore kinda sorta resembles a monkey. Just below Monkey Hole and mile 48, the Mead-Liberty power lines cross the river.

The stretch of river between miles 45 and 44A is called **Windy Canyon.** On occasion, upriver winds become quite strong in this area, and the canyon more than earns its name. People in canoes and other small boats are recommended to check the wind currents before venturing below Willow Beach, the last takeout point before Windy Canyon. Below mile 44A, the river spreads out into Copper Basin; several canyons open out in this area, providing good places to camp.

Just below Squaw Peaks on the Nevada side are **Chalk Cliffs.** A navigational light and marker 43, high on the Nevada side, mark the mouth of Black Canyon. Life jackets are not required below this point, but their continued use is strongly recommended, as the river current is still strong.

Eldorado Canyon is on the Nevada side at about mile 39. The takeout point is a 0.25-mile-long uphill portage to the road. The canyon is a prime spot to see birds and other wildlife, and it's home to the **Techatticup Mine,** once the most productive gold, silver, and copper mine in southern Nevada. The new owners operate a general store and give tours of the mine and remnants of a mill, cabins, and a bunkhouse. Scenes from the movie *3000 Miles to Graceland* were filmed here, and the crashed airplane prop is still here.

For intrepid boaters who want to continue south of Eldorado Canyon, be prepared for open water, possible very windy conditions, and extreme temperature ranges. Cottonwood Cove is 17 miles away, and Katherine Landing is 40 miles.

Laughlin

Laughlin is one of the hottest spots in the country, with the second-highest temperatures after Laredo, Texas. In 1994, the official thermometer at Laughlin's Clark County Fire Department station registered a sizzling 125°F, Nevada's highest recorded temperature. In another way, Laughlin is pretty cool: You'll immediately notice how airy and bright the casinos are, thanks to the big picture windows overlooking the river. Their more comfortable and less claustrophobic atmosphere makes you wonder what Las Vegas has against natural light. The hotel rooms can be 50 percent cheaper than comparable ones in Las Vegas. And the food, like the cheap hotel rooms, expansive casinos, cooperative weather, and playful river, is user-friendly.

Don Laughlin went from working as a gaming and amusement machine distributor to city founder and casino magnate before his 35th birthday. In the late 1960s Laughlin had sold his gambling holdings in Las Vegas and plunked down his profits on six acres of real estate in the fierce Sonoran Desert on the Colorado River about as far south as you can go and still be in Nevada. When Southern California Edison built a coal-fired power plant just up the hill from the river, expanding the population base, people began frequenting the homegrown river resort–casino as an alternative to corporate Las Vegas. By 1984, Don Laughlin's Riverside Resort Hotel and Casino was a 14-story, 350-room hotel with half a dozen other casinos lining the river—and little else. In that year Laughlin had a grand total of 95 residents—the temperature was still higher than the population, and there was one casino for every 16 townspeople. The rest of the 3,000 employees lived on the Arizona side of the river in Bullhead City, commuting across the river on the Davis Dam bridge or the casino ferries. Don Laughlin proceeded to spend more than $1 million of his own money in road improvements, $3 million to build the new

bridge from Bullhead City to his hotel (he then had a little trouble getting Nevada to take it over), and $6 million to expand the airport across the river. Today the Aquarius is Laughlin's largest hotel, with 1,912 rooms; Harrah's is second, having expanded to 1,616. Ramada Express has a total of 1,500 rooms, and Don Laughlin's own Riverside has a total of 1,440.

More competition arrived as the Fort Mojave Tribe opened the Avi Hotel-Casino 10 miles south of Laughlin, right at the point where Nevada, Arizona, and California meet.

CASINOS

From the Nevada side of the Laughlin bridge it's exactly a mile to the traffic light at the Ramada Express, then another mile exactly to Harrah's. March–November, unless you're a camel, it's a long sweaty walk from one end to the other, even if you take the fine river walk behind the casinos between the Riverside and the Golden Nugget. You can take the public bus, the Silver Rider, which runs along the Strip ($1.75). You can also catch a water taxi to any of the hotels ($4 one-way, $20 day pass). Or grab a cab to where you want to go. But the easiest way, as always, is to drive. You can park in the Riverside lot to visit that casino, and then park in the Flamingo structure to see the Hilton, Ramada Express, Edgewater, Colorado Belle, Pioneer, and Golden Nugget; then drive to River Palms Resort, and on to Harrah's.

Riverside

Start your tour, naturally enough, at Don Laughlin's front-runner Riverside Hotel (1650 S. Casino Dr., 702/298-2535 or 800/227-3849, $42–79) at the northern end of the "mini Strip." The Riverside, being Laughlin's first, has a movie theater, an arcade, a 34-lane bowling alley, a showroom, a headliner room, and a classic car museum (10 A.M.–10 P.M.

This stretch of the Colorado River in Laughlin experienced a development boom in the 1980s and 1990s.

daily, free). It's an older establishment, comparatively speaking, and always crowded with regulars.

The Riverside has a 24-hour café and deli, a Mexican restaurant, a Chinese restaurant, a buffet, a snack bar, a food court, the Prime Rib Room, and the Gourmet Room. The showroom features headliners, traveling productions, and tribute bands. Something a little wild is almost always going in Loser's Lounge. There's also a Western dance hall, where a DJ spins the country tunes, and guests take the stage for karaoke night.

Aquarius

Formerly the Flamingo Laughlin, the 1,907-room Aquarius (1900 S. Casino Dr., 702/298-5111 or 800/662-LUCK—800/662-5825, $40–85) has traded pink feathers for a blue wave facade. A new 57,000-square-foot casino and room redesigns are part of the recently completed $46 million upgrade. **Splash Cabaret** is part sports bar, part dance club, part concert venue, depending on the day and

time. Big-time acts such as the Beach Boys, Kid Rock, Kenny Rogers, and ZZ Top play the **Outdoor Amphitheater.**

Windows on the River (7 A.M.–10 P.M. daily, $10–20) may be the best restaurant in Laughlin, especially the crab and prime rib on Saturday nights or the champagne brunch daily. And we'd trample people in the aisle to get to the chocolate fountain at dinner.

Edgewater

A Mandalay Resort Group hotel, the Edgewater (2020 S. Casino Dr., 702/298-2453 or 866/352-3553, $18–55) grew to nearly 1,500 rooms when the 1,000-room tower, right on the river, opened in 1992. The casino seems much larger inside than it looks from the outside: sprawling, airy, and roomy. Downstairs are the buffet, a 24-hour Coco's Restaurant, and a steak house called **Hickory Pit** (702/298-2453, ext. 3716, 4–10 P.M. daily, $15–25). There's also a snack bar and a food court. The Showroom hosts stand-up comedians most weekends.

Colorado Belle

The Edgewater's sister, steamboat-themed Colorado Belle (2100 S. Casino Dr., 702/298-4000 or 866/352-3553, $18–55) sits right on the river. The smokestacks soar 21 stories tall, strobe lights make the paddlewheel appear to turn, and a bridge over a little moat gives access to the main entrance. Red flocked wallpaper, riveted stacks for beams, fancy cut-glass chandeliers, major period murals and paintings, and a sweeping staircase with wood and brass banisters make visitors feel like first-class passengers. You can almost smell the magnolia blossoms. A Dixieland band performs 8–11 P.M. Thursday–Saturday.

The hotel offers 12 restaurants, including the **Boiler Room Microbrewery** (11 A.M.–10 P.M. Fri.–Sun., 4–10 P.M. Mon.–Thurs. $10–15); it's a great place for burgers and home brew.

Pioneer

The waving, winking, cigarette-smoking River Rick marquee and adobe hint that the Pioneer (220 S. Casino Dr., 702/298-2442 or 800/634-3469, $25–75) is a throwback to the sawdust-joint days of early gambling in Nevada. Carpet, not sawdust, covers the casino floor, of course, but dark filigreed wood and glittery chandeliers carry through the Old West theme. Wallpaper and chintz in the rooms complete the picture. The **Boarding House** (7–10 A.M. and 4–10 P.M. Mon.–Fri., 7–10 A.M. and 1–9 P.M. Sat., 9 A.M.–2 P.M. Sun., $10–15.) buffet is excellent, and it's a traditional restaurant as well, so you can order off a menu or join the pig-out line.

Tropicana Express

Across the street sits the Tropicana Express (2121 S. Casino Dr., 702/298-4200 or 800/242-6846, $25–80), originally a Ramada, the only hotel so far on the east side of the Strip. Catch Old No. 7, "The Gambler," at the new depot in front of the hotel for a 10-minute, 0.75-mile ride around the parking lot. The trip takes you fairly high above the action and supplies convenient transportation from the covered parking lot down to the casino and the street. It runs every 15 minutes on the quarter hour 10 A.M.–10 P.M. Monday–Friday, 10 A.M.–11 P.M. Saturday–Sunday. A fog machine simulates smoke from the stack and engine, and sound effects, such as the roar of fire in the engine's boiler and the whoosh of air brakes, add to the effect.

The Pavilion Theater is the big room that presents comedians, singers, and Broadway-style productions. The Caboose Lounge hosts smaller acts.

Seven restaurants insure a treat for all tastes. In addition to Italian, Mexican, and sushi establishments, there's a café, a buffet, and **The Steakhouse** (5–10 P.M. Sun. and Wed.–Thurs., 5–11 P.M. Fri.–Sat., $30–50) the reigning king for 12 years, according to local surveys.

Golden Nugget

At the Golden Nugget (2300 S. Casino Dr., 702/298-7111 or 800/950-7700, $39–79), you walk in through the familiar tropical

© RYAN JERZ

River Rick, a cousin to Vegas Vic and Wendover Will, has invited people to Laughlin for 20 years.

atrium that was inspired by the Las Vegas Mirage: verdant foliage, curvy palms, rocky waterfalls, and a winding alleyway to the right of the Gilded Cage, in which five animated birds perform show tunes every 15 minutes 10 A.M.–10 P.M. It's about as tasteful as such a thing can be, and at least it's more sophisticated than Disney's Enchanted Tiki Room. Have a coconut cocktail at **Tarzan's Nightclub,** which generally showcases the best lounge acts in Laughlin; at 9 P.M. Monday–Friday, 10 P.M. Saturday–Sunday it transforms into the city's top nightclub, with DJs spinning Top 40. Saltgrass is the steak house, and there's a Joe's Crab Shack, a deli, and a Starbucks. Our pick is **Harlow's** (6 A.M.–midnight Mon.–Thurs., 6 A.M.–3 A.M. Fri.–Sat., 9 A.M.–midnight Sun., $15–25).

River Palms Resort

The rooms at River Palms (2700 S. Casino Dr., 800/835-7904, $18–49) are cheaper but less desirable than many of its neighbors. The casino has beefed up its amenities, with the opening of the 2700 Club—stand-up comedy in the evening and no-cover dance bands later—and the boutique-like Elite Island slot lounge. The lounge is set off from the main casino—the low-budget River Palms version of a high-roller area, but with slots denominations as low as $0.25.

Harrah's Laughlin

The Mexican Riviera theme at Harrah's (2900 S. Casino Dr., 702/298-4600 or 800/221-1306, $29–99) is understated, as are the themes at its sister properties in Nevada—a touch of tile here, an adobe bell tower there. The 1,505 guest rooms are a bit more obviously Mexican, with festive comforters and wall accents. The service is stellar, just the way Bill Harrah would have insisted. Laughlin's southernmost hotel-casino opened in 1988.

The intimate, 280-seat **Fiesta Showroom** brings in tribute acts and stars your kids have never heard of, but they are still just as entertaining as you remember—Collin Raye, Don McLean, and Rich Little have graced the

stage. Bigger names pack 'em into the Rio Vista Amphitheater right on the river. The sandy swimming beach, a rarity at Laughlin casinos, is open to the public. Typical of Harrah's, the nightlife is pretty sedate, but dining is another story. With a Mexican theme, no matter how vague, it stands to reason that **Baja Blue** (702/298-4600, 5–10 P.M. daily, $10–20) would be *muy bueno.* The Fresh Market Square Buffet is above average, and the café, food court, and The Range Steakhouse mean there's something for everyone.

Avi Resort and Casino

Way down in the point of Nevada that separates California from Arizona, 10 miles south of town, is the newly decorated 455-room Avi Resort (10000 Aha Macav Pkwy., 800/284-2946, $30–80), owned and operated by the Fort Mojave Indians. Avi is a sprawling and scenic resort situated along an attractive stretch of the Colorado River, where you can play on the sandy beach or rent a Jet Ski. But the main draw here is the Mojave Resort Golf Club, a challenging but fair championship golf course surrounded by purple mountains and sand dunes. The lagoon pool hosts outdoor concerts amid palm trees and waterfalls. There are plenty of the usual restaurants—a café, steak and seafood, Italian, a buffet, and a fast food court. Start the day right and save your gambling bankroll with a $0.99 ham-and-egg breakfast at **Feathers Café** (24 hours daily, special served 6 A.M.–2 P.M.)

SPORTS AND RECREATION

Big Bend of the Colorado State Park (702/298-1859, $9 day-use, $15 boating, $20 camping, $30 hookups), five miles south of Laughlin on the Needles Highway, is a pleasant spot for camping, boating, picnicking, and hiking along the river. Be sure to bring sunscreen and swim gear—temperatures can get steamy in the summer.

Christmas Tree Pass and Grapevine Canyon (Christmas Tree Pass Rd., off Hwy. 163, 7 miles west of Laughlin) is a scenic area for picnicking, hiking, camping, and sightseeing; be on the lookout for petroglyphs on the canyon walls. The area is administered by the Bureau of Land Management's Las Vegas office (4701 N. Torrey Pines Dr., Las Vegas, 702/515-5000).

Golfers aren't neglected here either. There are two golf courses: the **Emerald River Country Club** (1155 W. Casino Dr., 702/298-0061, $50–100) in town and the **Mojave Resort Golf Club** (9905 Aha Macav Pkwy., 702/535-4650, $40–109) near the Avi Casino.

Fishing

Rainbow trout hang out in the river and Lake Mojave, which is also home to channel catfish, crappie, and carp, but striped bass are the big thing around here—30 pounds isn't uncommon. The world's record inland striper, 59.5 pounds, was landed at Bullhead City. May is the best time to fish for them, when the shad are plentiful and the water is warm enough to stimulate their appetites but not so oppressive as to make them sluggish. They run north from Lake Havasu starting in March.

Anglers age 13 and over must have a license, and you need a trout stamp if you're going after rainbows, cutthroats, or other species. The Nevada Department of Wildlife (www.ndow. org/fish) has the information. Laughlin Bay Marina, a couple of miles south of Harrah's, as well as the Avi and several sites in Bullhead City have boat launch ramps that can be used for a fee. You can launch for free at Fisherman's Access, just north of the Riverside. To boat on Lake Mojave, go across the river to Katherine Landing in Arizona.

Tours

Three tour boats cruise the Colorado River, as long as there's enough water downriver— the Bureau of Reclamation controls the levels, often not to the liking of the tour-boat operators. **Laughlin River Tours** (800/228-9825) runs the *Fiesta Queen* and the *Celebration,* both of which offer 3–5 sightseeing cruises per day and nightly dinner cruises ($40, over age 7 only). **USS *Riverside*** is a luxury casino cruiser designed to pass under the Laughlin Bridge for

a look at Davis Dam. Both are available for wedding charters.

Camping and RV Parks

On the Nevada side, there is only one true RV park. **Avi Casino KOA** (10000 Aha Macav Pkwy., 800/430-0721, $22), across the street from the casino, offers free shuttle service to the gaming floor and free access to the hotel's pool and other amenities; tents are not allowed. **The Riverside** (1650 S. Casino Dr., 702/298-1859, $29) has large sites of gravel and cement and little shade, but they include full hookups. The $99 weekly special is a bargain. **Harrah's** (2900 S. Casino Dr., 702/298-4600, free) and **River Palms** (2900 S. Casino Dr., 702/298-2242, free) make room in their parking lots for RVs.

FOOD

Overall, food outside the casinos in Laughlin is good but not great, plentiful, and cheap, much like Las Vegas of the 1980s and 1990s. And like its big brother to the north, Laughlin's buffets are ubiquitous and usually inexpensive, while quality ethnic and specialty restaurants—especially in the casinos—are on the increase.

Outside the casinos, try the **Firehouse Coffee Company** (10200 Aha Macav Pkwy., 702/535-4400, $8–10) for breakfast (Mexican quiche) or lunch (grilled panini). It has a firefighter theme and "coffee" in the name, so you know the joe is always fresh. For steak with all the sizzle and none of the pretense, hit **Daniel's** (Regency Casino, 1950 S. Casino Dr., 702/299-1220, 8 A.M.–10 P.M. daily, $14–20)—with grilled rib eye, a salad, a baked potato, a vegetable, and rolls for $16.95. The spaghetti and meatballs are a fine selection at **Alberto's Italian Restaurant & Lounge** (3100 Needles Hwy., Suite 1200, 702/298-2318, 11 A.M.–8 P.M. Mon.–Sat., $15–30), but the Mexican specialties are just as good, and you won't find better broasted chicken anywhere in Nevada. Not only the best Japanese restaurant and best sushi bar in town, **Minato** (2311 S. Casino Dr., Suite G-1, 702/298-7997, noon–10 P.M. Sun. and Tues.–Thurs., noon–11 P.M.

Fri.–Sat., 4–10 P.M. Mon., $20–35) gets our vote for the best overall place in Laughlin. The sushi is always chilled to just the right temperature to assure freshness. Grilled and tempura selections are light and never overcooked.

SHOPPING

Preferred Outlets (1955 S. Casino Dr., 702/298-3650, 9 A.M.–8 P.M. Mon.–Sat., 10 A.M.–6 P.M. Sun.) is the big game in town, with 55 stores that include Gap Outlet, Levi's, and Van Heusen stocked with factory-discounted merchandise. Most stores are aimed at the hoi polloi rather than the haute. There is also a food court and market as well as a nine-screen movie theater.

INFORMATION

The local branch of the **Las Vegas Clark County Library** (2840 Needles Hwy., 702/507-4060) is about four miles west of the casinos.

The **visitors center** (1585 S. Casino Dr., 702/298-2214 or 800/227-5245) run by the Laughlin Chamber of Commerce and the Convention and Visitors Authority is right in the heart of the mini Strip.

GETTING THERE

The **Laughlin/Bullhead International Airport** (2550 Laughlin View Dr., Bullhead City, AZ, 928/754-2134) is on the east side of the Colorado River. It is a full-service regional airport with daily flights from numerous cities. Plenty of tour operators offer day trips from Las Vegas to Laughlin. If you want to drive yourself, take U.S. 95 south out of Las Vegas. It's easy to speed on this road, and the Highway Patrol is vigilant. It's also easy to become bored with the drive and let your attention wander, so be careful. After 75 miles, take Highway 163 east through winding, hilly country before descending into the river valley and Laughlin. From Southern California or north-central Arizona, take I-40 to U.S. 95 north to Highway 163.

RENO

Reno is the *original* Las Vegas, and was at one time the hub of everything that makes Nevada famous (or infamous). But Reno is not a "poor man's Las Vegas," a watered-down or wannabe version of Sin City. On the contrary: Reno has made a deliberate, conscious decision not to emulate, compete with or—heaven forbid—*become* Las Vegas. While Vegas careens wildly down the course of excess, Reno taps the brakes.

A rambunctious child, born with a silver boom in its mouth, Reno today maintains the characteristics of rebellious adolescence and youthful conquer-the-world exuberance. But it also has mellowed a bit, matured. It still can rock out with the in crowd, but one of its car radio buttons is set to easy listening. Reno continues to run, bike, and ski, but now that after-workout massage is more of a necessity than a luxury. The town still finds inspiration in the raging rapids of the Truckee River, but it also slows down to breathe in the peach and apple aromas at the Sparks Hometowne Farmer's Market, and let the juice run down its chin.

Like all responsible adults, Reno has succeeded in achieving balance. It remains a mesmerizing resort destination with the best entertainment, gourmet restaurants, world-class spas, and some of the best outdoor recreation in the United States. But it's much more: a quaint college town, an art enclave, a riverside community, an industrial hub. A hometown.

HISTORY

The Washoe and Paiute Indians eked out a living in Truckee Meadows between the Carson and Virginia Mountain Ranges for centuries

HIGHLIGHTS

LOOK FOR 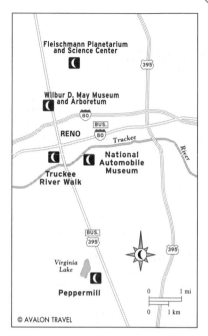 TO FIND RECOMMENDED SIGHTS, ACTIVITIES, DINING, AND LODGING.

Peppermill: A boisterous flashing rush when you want a night on the town and a quaint boutique resort when you want to get away from it all, the Peppermill has it all under one roof. Spa Toscana is the queen of the northern Nevada pamper palaces (page 147).

Truckee River Walk: An urban renewal project that worked, the walk wanders through idyllic scenes of fly-fishers making perfect casts, sophisticated connoisseurs sipping wine and contemplating the new gallery acquisition, and exhilarating kayakers challenging swirling white water (page 156).

National Automobile Museum: Elvis's Caddy and James Dean's Mercury are here, so you know this museum oozes cool. The collection is what's left of William Harrah's extensive purchases. A highlight traces the nation's turn-of-the-20th-century transition from horse to horsepower (page 162).

Fleischmann Planetarium and Science Center: The building is as other-worldly as the one-ton meteorite inside. The theater hosts surreal star shows and larger-than-life nature and space documentaries (page 163).

Wilbur D. May Museum and Arboretum: Eclectic treasures from the re-naissance man's 40 trips abroad make for an unusual collection. Several gardens give visitors a chance to calm their nerves after viewing a shrunken head, tribal masks, and other frisson-producing oddities (page 163).

© AVALON TRAVEL

before the first Europeans arrived. The land was too arid for agriculture, but they collected pine nuts, hunted rabbit and ducks, and fished in Pyramid Lake and Lake Tahoe.

Jedediah Smith was the first nonnative to visit the area, in search of beaver and a vain quest for the mythical San Buenaventura River that was hoped would provide easy transportation from the Rockies to the Pacific. And although others ventured into the Truckee River Valley over the next decade, history remembers John C. Frémont and Kit Carson's pathfinding mission in 1844 as the beginning of the region's settlement.

Reno has always been in the middle of things: the settlement of the West and the California gold rush; the unification of the country via the transcontinental railroad; and the nation's critical transportation, distribution, and supply industries. Reno is only a few hours' drive from Sacramento and San Francisco, and within a day's drive of Los Angeles, Portland, Seattle, Boise, and Salt Lake City.

The Truckee River's plentiful water and animal forage made it an attractive stop along the California Trail, and soon entrepreneurs set up stores and small farms to "mine the miners" before they reached the gold fields. Once the subsistence gold miners in the area that was to become Virginia City and Goldfield realized the bluish slag they were discarding in their quest for the yellow flakes was actually rich silver ore, the dash for the Comstock Lode erupted. The settlers around the river quickly built ore processors, livery stables, sawmills, and other businesses to cater to and take advantage of the silver rush.

Among the most intrepid entrepreneurs was Myron Lake. He appreciated the little settlement's logistical advantages and purchased the ramshackle bridge across Truckee River in 1861, charging a toll for each crossing of people, animals, and goods. He converted his profits into land holdings, which he sold when the Central Pacific Railroad came through, promising to make "Lake's Crossing" an important site in the settlement of the West. The little town was dubbed Reno in a post–Civil War patriotic tribute to Brigadier General Jesse Reno, killed at the battle of South Mountain. The town flourished, especially after the Virginia and Truckee Railroad linked the Comstock Lode to the Central Pacific Railroad. For more than 30 years, the mainline ensured a steady flow of people, products, and progress, even after the silver deposits were finally exhausted. Reno remained a whistle stop, fighting river flooding, economic stagnation, and the boom-and-bust cycles of the mining industry. After the Comstock was exhausted, Nevada's population dwindled by one-third during the 1880s.

Just after the turn of the 20th century, Reno was "discovered" as a divorce destination. The little outpost suddenly found itself at the center of a national tug-of-war between social conscience and individual freedom. Unhappily married millionaires, movie stars, socialites, and artists flocked to Reno, gracing the town with their presence for six months to meet the residency requirement to obtain a divorce decree. Newspaper society pages nationwide covered them daily, making Reno a household word. The daily train became known as the Divorcée Special, and the county courthouse was called the Separator. The mayor of Reno set the record for the number of clients granted divorce decrees in one day.

In addition, political and financial power brokers moved to Reno from the waning mining excitement of Tonopah and Goldfield in central Nevada. A national exposition celebrating the completion of the transcontinental Victory and Lincoln Highways was held in Reno, prompting the residents to install an arch at the entrance to downtown with the proud slogan, "Biggest Little City in the World."

Reno's divorce boom waned as other states liberalized their requirements. In 1931, on the same day Nevada lowered its residency requirement to obtain a divorce to a scandalous six weeks, the state also legalized wide-open gambling—again. The Territorial Legislature had banned gaming in 1861, legalized it in 1879 as a bulwark against declining state revenues as mining fortunes fizzled, and re-criminalized it as the Progressive movement pushed the country toward more Victorian morals. Finally, with the Great Depression gripping the nation, gambling once again emerged from smoky backrooms to deliver Reno from tough times. The Smith family's national advertising campaign for its casino, "Harold's Club or Bust," William Harrah's classy "carpet joint," and a spate of postwar divorces kept Reno bustling throughout the 1930s and 1940s.

By the mid-1950s, as hotels rose regularly along the new Las Vegas Strip, Reno's city planners, elected officials, and downtown business interests became concerned their town would suffer similar unbridled growth, sprawl, and a growing criminal element. They reined in the gambling industry, restricting its expansion. By the mid-1970s, however, officials removed the zoning restrictions. A major casino boom ensued: the MGM Grand opened in 1978 just east of downtown Reno. It was the world's largest casino, with an unprecedented 1,000 hotel rooms. The Comstock opened three weeks later, and the Sahara Reno, Money Tree, and Circus Circus all opened for business on the same day in 1979.

The increased job opportunities spurred another population boom, but Reno still seemed content to maintain a slower pace of development than Las Vegas, concentrating on protecting its own niche as an idyllic counterpoint.

RENO

PLANNING YOUR TIME

Whether you're a hard-core gambler, a nature lover, a gourmand, a hipster, or a culture freak, you'll want to spend at least a long weekend in Reno. And if you're intrigued by history as well as hold 'em, truffles as well as trance, even a week won't be enough to partake in all of Reno's charms.

The resort hotels on the casino corridor take customer service seriously, and the concierge desk is a font of information and insider tips. Taxicabs are always handy, and it's always easy to get around, even in winter. With more than two feet of snow per year, that can't always be said for the smaller and more rural communities around the valley. Restaurants to suit any taste are just an elevator ride away.

Unless you're a first-time visitor or have a specific restaurant, show, or attraction in mind, a casino crawl is probably a waste of time. If you've seen one slot machine, you've seen them all, so pick the casino that has most of what you're looking for, and do most of your gambling, dining, and carousing there. That doesn't mean you won't want to go out for art, history, and culture between the mai tais and the inside-straight draws. The Riverwalk district south of downtown is the anticasino—natural light, fresh air, and open spaces. The gurgling Truckee River in the background makes for a refreshing respite from the clang of the slots, and you can study the eclectic styles and media of local and widely renowned artists.

If that's not enough to keep you busy, remember that the casino lounges are hopping until the wee small hours, most resorts have at least one 24-hour restaurant, and the gaming floor never closes.

ORIENTATION

Reno sits at the crossroads of I-80, which runs east–west from New York to San Francisco, and U.S. 395, which crosses into Nevada on its way from east-central Oregon to Southern California. The Truckee River parallels I-80, running west–east through the heart of downtown Reno. The downtown area is roughly bounded by 1st Street just north of the river, I-80 eight blocks to the north, Wells Avenue to the east, and Keystone Avenue to the west. The intersection of 1st Street and Virginia Street is roughly the location of Myron Lake's bridge and inn and is the hub of the Riverwalk retail district. From this point, addresses are labeled east, west, north, and south. The higher the building number, the farther away you are from downtown. The casino district is centered around 4th and Virginia Streets.

I-80 separates the high-rise downtown hotels from the mostly low-rise buildings of the University of Nevada, Reno (UNR) campus on Virginia Street, which sits on a bluff overlooking downtown.

At the northern edge of the campus, Virginia Street, also called Business Highway 395, intersects with North McCarran Boulevard, which circumscribes the valley, encompassing Sparks and Reno-Tahoe International Airport. A trip on the 23-mile loop around Reno-Sparks is a scenic way to get oriented to the different faces of Truckee Meadows: mountains, desert, river, industry, commerce, and suburbs. There are some superb views of downtown.

From downtown, head north on North Virginia Street past the college and take a left (west) on McCarran Boulevard. You will drive right by the big whitewashed N, for Nevada, maintained by UNR students on Peavine Mountain (elevation 8,266 feet), the northernmost peak of the Carson Range; the Monument to the Basque Sheepherder at Rancho San Rafael Park provides a stark green contrast. From there, you're into the desert—sand, sage, and hills with a few residential areas sprinkled in. If you continue north to Parr Boulevard and turn right, you'll wind up at Truckee Meadows Community Collect, but it's much easier to take U.S. 395 north to the Parr exit.

The airport is south of the river in the southeast quadrant of the city. Just south of it, at U.S. 395 and Virginia Street, is Meadowood Mall and Smithridge Plaza. Across the Truckee River in the northeast quadrant is Sparks, home to the Legends at Sparks Marina, a massive outlet center.

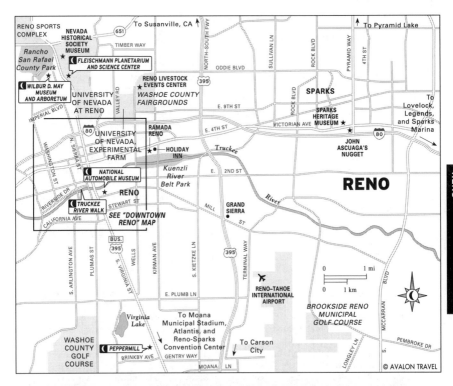

Casinos

The nature of Reno's everything-under-one-roof resort casinos means you could spend all week in just one, within a few hundred feet of your hotel room, and still experience a wonderful vacation. You could treat yourself to a café breakfast and then bask in the sun and splash around the resort's fabulous swimming pool all morning. After a salad or grilled chicken sandwich from the poolside grill, you could retire for a short power nap, gearing up for an afternoon of hand-to-hand combat with the dealer or slot machine. Treat yourself to a steak dinner in the hotel's gourmet room, have a couple of drinks in the lounge, then enjoy a variety show or musical concert in the showroom.

The next day, trade pool time for shopping in the casino's boutiques, if your gambling session was a success, or just browsing if it wasn't. Skip lunch and dinner; gorge yourself at the sumptuous buffets in the middle of the afternoon instead. Recoup your losses and celebrate by dancing the night away in the trendy club. Repeat as often as your vacation lasts and your bankroll holds out. If you exhaust all the entertainment, dining, and drinking options available at your "home" hotel, there are a dozen more within walking distance.

Reno casinos generally do not allow pets in their tower rooms. Older casinos that still rent their older motel-style rooms in the back or those with RV parks usually welcome pets.

RENO

THE FAMOUS ARCH

Reno's venerable "Biggest Little City in the World" arch received its most environmentally friendly facelift in 2009, when the city replaced its 2,076 incandescent 11-watt light bulbs with 2.5-watt LED bulbs. Spectators took home a piece of Reno history as the old bulbs were given away as souvenirs.

It was only the latest in a string of alterations in the life of one of the world's most recognizable landmarks. The main arch, across North Virginia Street at West 3rd Street, is on the site where the first arch was erected in 1926 to celebrate the completion of the transcontinental Victory and Lincoln Highways. It cost $5,500 and read "Reno Transcontinental Highway Exposition." The arch grew on local residents, who decided to keep it. As the novelty of the highways wore off, Mayor E. E. Roberts announced a contest to create a permanent slogan. The winning slogan was adapted from the ad campaign for the 1910 Jim Jeffries-Jack Johnson prizefight in Reno, which proclaimed Reno the "Biggest Little City on the Map." The sign was composed of nearly 1,000 bulbs and cost $30 a month to operate, which proved too rich for the city's Depression-era budget, so it was shut off in 1932. A great hue and cry erupted over the cost-saving measure, and downtown business owners paid the electric bill to keep the arch lit.

A new improved arch was erected in 1934.

Built of reinforced steel and lit with neon, the sign read simply "Reno." This change was again universally condemned, and in 1936 the old slogan was returned to the arch. The next time someone tried to monkey with the archway was in 1956, when Mayor Ken Harris proposed changing the slogan; it nearly cost him his job.

This arch was eventually replaced, in 1963, when it was moved to Idlewild Park, the highway exposition site, then to Paradise Park, then into storage for 40 years. It saw daylight again in 1994 when it was erected over 4th Street to add ambiance to the baseball biopic *Cobb*. In 1995 it traveled to its current spot outside the National Automobile Museum at Lake and Mill Streets.

Its 1963 replacement was installed in preparation for Nevada's centennial and reflected the slightly psychedelic sentiments that abounded in northern Nevada and California in the 1960s. This "Hippie Arch" was donated to the town of Willits, California, where it welcomes visitors to California's redwood forests.

The fourth and current arch was unveiled in front of a jam-packed Virginia Street crowd in August 1987. The contemporary design is the creation of Charles Barnard of Ad Art Company in Stockton, California, and the Young Electric Sign Company (YESCO) built the arch for $99,000, charging the city for the materials only. It uses 800 feet of tubing.

COURTESY OF RENO-SPARKS CONVENTION AND VISITORS AUTHORITY

This version of Reno's most recognizable landmark was erected in 1980, but arches bearing various slogans, of varying designs, and in changing locations have graced the city for 85 years.

Circus Circus

- **Restaurants:** Americana Café, Courtyard Buffet, Kokopelli's Sushi Bar, Main Street Deli & Ice Cream Shoppe, Smokin' Gecko's BBQ, The Steakhouse
- **Entertainment:** Circus acts; Cabaret Stage
- **Attractions:** Midway of Fun

Like its Las Vegas cousin, Circus Circus Reno (500 N. Sierra St., 775/329-0711 or 800/647-5010, $45–89 d) is a hangout for families with kids, although it occupies a comfortable position in the city's casino mainstream, perhaps because its neighboring hotels aren't as upscale as those in Las Vegas, or maybe because the Reno edition has rounded off the cotton-candy pink facade in favor of more muted tones. Whatever the reason, the property has found a way to keep pleasing budget-minded families while also giving more sophisticated travelers reasons to visit.

The world-class circus acts on the **Midway Stage** (6–11 P.M. daily, free) are always a hit with the kids, and the **Midway of Fun** gives everyone a chance to go home a winner no matter how their luck is running at the tables.

More adult fun abounds on the **Cabaret Stage** (6 P.M.–2 A.M. Fri.–Sat., free), with live music blasted through a state-of-the-art sound system. Classic rock, blues, or karaoke are on tap. Shops are scattered throughout the property, in case you've forgotten to pack sundries or sweatshirts, or if you're itching to spend your winnings on some bling.

Try the *tres leches* cake or American and Mexican comfort fare in the **Americana Café** (6 A.M.–2 P.M. daily, under $15). **Kokopelli's Sushi** (11:30 A.M.–2 P.M. and 5–9 P.M. Mon.–Thurs., 11:30 A.M.–2 P.M. and 5–10 P.M. Fri., 11:30 A.M.–10 P.M. Sat., 11:30 A.M.–9 P.M. Sun., $15–25) ignited Reno's sushi-in-a-casino trend.

Now boasting 1,572 guest rooms and suites in cinnamon or purple, the hotel connects to the neighboring Silver Legacy and Eldorado. Guest rooms are about 355 square feet in size, and on higher floors in the Sky and North Towers they command terrific mountain and cityscape views.

Some rooms adjoin to form "pseudo suites" to accommodate large families.

Silver Legacy

- **Restaurants:** Café Sedona, Fairchild's Oyster Bar, Flavors the Buffet, Sterling's Seafood Steakhouse, Sips Coffee and Tea
- **Entertainment:** *Catch a Rising Star*
- **Attractions:** Grande Exposition Hall, Mining Machine
- **Nightlife:** Aura Ultra Lounge, Rum Bullions Island Bar, Drinx, Silver Baron Lounge

Imagine yourself a 19th-century silver baron at the Silver Legacy (407 N. Virginia St., 775/325-7401 or 800/687-8733, $55–275 d) and indulge in all the luxury that bullion can buy (or rent by the night if you're on vacation). Start by fantasizing that the magnificent 1,300-piece **Mackay silver collection** on display at the hotel desk has just been delivered to your

COURTESY OF SILVER LEGACY CASINO

The Silver Legacy pays homage to Nevada's past and present as the center of America's metals mining industry.

RENO

mansion by the **Wells Fargo stagecoach.** The collection was commissioned by John Mackay and produced from 1,000 pounds of Comstock Lode silver. With a casino housing some 1,600 slot machines, 85 table games, and Reno's largest hotel with 1,700 guest rooms, the Silver Legacy has the space and resources to provide everything a vacationer requires.

Take in a show by a big-time entertainer in the 1,600-seat **Grande Exposition Hall.** Recent performers include the Beach Boys, Engelbert Humperdinck, and Cheech and Chong. Then get revved up for a night of partying at one of the Legacy's several bars and lounges. Get adventurous and sample a flambéed kava kava cocktail at **Rum Bullions Island Bar** (4 P.M.–2 A.M. daily). Laugh and sing along with the dueling pianos. Finish off the night (or morning, rather) with a nightcap at the elliptical bar at sensual and sophisticated **Aura** (11 A.M.–4 A.M. daily). After a good night's sleep, pamper yourself with a treat from **The Boutique** (800/687-7733, call for hours), featuring Michael Stars, Tribal, and Raviani, or any of the several other shops carrying everything from wine and jewelry to Harley-Davidson memorabilia.

Pan-roasted oysters, shrimp, clams, and crab get the star treatment at **Fairchild's Oyster Bar** (11 A.M.–10 P.M. Sun.–Thurs., 11 A.M.–11 P.M. Fri.–Sat., 4 P.M.–10 P.M. Sun., $20–30). The kitchen artistry is as polished as the cherrywood at **Sterlings** (5 –10 P.M. Mon.–Thurs., 5 –11 P.M. Fri. –Sat, 9 A.M.–2 P.M. and 5 –10 P.M. Sun., $35–50) The desserts—both the common sweets, such as cherry and apple pie, and the unusual, such as a caramel flan—are the draw at **Flavors!** (8 A.M.–1:30 P.M. and 4:30–10 P.M. daily, $10–20) buffet.

Skywalks connect the Legacy with the Eldorado on one side and Circus Circus on the other, allowing you to walk more than four city blocks in downtown Reno without stepping outside. Park in the Circus Circus garage (West St. and W. 6th St.) and head over to the Eldorado (N. Virginia St. and E. Plaza St.).

Remodeled in 2010, the Silver Legacy's 340-square-foot rooms are richly appointed in gold and brown. Upper rooms in the 37-story tower lord over city lights, mountain peaks, or the meandering Truckee River. Spa suites offer all that along with 50 percent more space and whirlpool tubs.

Eldorado

- **Restaurants:** Eldorado Coffee Co., Golden Fortune, La Strada, Roxy's, The Buffet, Eldorado Sushi Bar, Prime Rib Grill, Tivoli Gardens

- **Entertainment:** Eldorado Showroom, Casino Cabaret

- **Nightlife:** Roxy's Bar & Lounge, Brew Brothers, Cin Cin, Vito's Bar

The Carano family, which opened the Eldorado (345 N. Virginia St., 775/786-5700, $49–139 d) in 1973 with 282 guest rooms and a 10,000-square-foot casino, is a testament to hard work and perseverance. Ben Carano, whose Italian immigrant grandfather was a cook during the Comstock silver boom, initiated the family's road to fortune in 1929 with a modest investment in 50 feet of what was to become prime real estate near Virginia and 4th Streets. The clan extended its land holdings, and Ben's son Don opened the Eldorado in 1973, expanding its size several times and extended the casino to 40,000 square feet in 1985.

Located in the heart of the casino district and connected via sky bridge to Silver Legacy and Circus Circus, the Eldorado does a good job of segregating its sometimes-raucous gaming areas from its other resort amenities. With dark wood and marble in the lobby and common areas, the Eldorado has a quiet elegance. **Brew Brothers** (1:30 P.M.–late) often continues that sedate theme through dinner, but late at night and on weekends it becomes a boisterous college party with karaoke, battles of the bands, and all-you-can-drink beer specials. The **Eldorado Showroom** is one of the few Reno casino on-site venues delivering Vegas-style production shows and musical theater. Packages are available to combine the show with dinner at several of the casino's better restaurants, including Roxy's, **The Prime Rib Grill** (5–10 P.M. Wed.–Sun.,

There's always a party in the Eldorado's casino, but sumptuous accents and décor in the rooms, restaurants, and lobby leave no doubt this is a luxury resort.

$20–30), and for northern Italian cuisine **La Strada** (5–9 P.M. Sun.–Tues., 5–10 P.M. Fri.–Sat., $15–30). Not many restaurants can manage both huevos rancheros and wonton soup, but **Tivoli Gardens** (11 a.m.–10 p.m. Wed.–Sun., $10–15) pulls it off with flying colors. The big room at **The Buffet** (8 a.m.–10 p.m. daily, $9–19) is made less cavernous through clever use of dark wood columns and panels. The spicy curry is so good, though, we'd eat it if it were served in a gymnasium.

Standard rooms in the Virginia and Sierra Towers are an intimate 250 to 275 square feet. Now sporting a clean, light wood and an off-white color scheme, they offer the obligatory mountain and city views. A variety of suites also are available, with escalating levels of luxury and price.

Sands Regency

- **Restaurants:** Fuzio Universal Bistro & Steaks, Mel's Diner, Sands Buffet, Cabana Café, Arby's

- **Entertainment:** Empress Casino Lounge
- **Nightlife:** Pipeline Lounge, Third Street Bar

While there's much to be said in favor of Nevada's megaresorts, they're definitely not for everyone. If you're someone who finds that these behemoths leave something to be desired, Terrible's Sands Regency (345 N. Arlington Ave., 775/347-2200 or 866/386-7829, www.sandsregency.com, $39–129 d) may be just what you're looking for. If you find high gaming limits and odds heavily in favor of the house to be a raw deal, consider the Sands Regency's $2 blackjack tables and 10X odds on craps. If dealing with snooty maître d's is not your idea of a relaxing meal, the burgers and shakes at **Mel's Diner** (24 hours daily, $10–15) are as unpretentious as they were when the joint opened in 1947. If you find production shows too heavy on the wallet and too skimpy on the costumes, visit the Sands Regency's **Empress Casino** (9 P.M.–1 A.M. Fri.–Sat.) for free music and summer pool parties.

THE MACHINE THAT STARTED IT ALL

For the second quarter of the 20th century, Reno – not Las Vegas – was the center of the country's gambling culture. And it was all thanks to an ingenious yet unassuming little contraption that has come to symbolize the entire gambling industry.

Charles Fey, a young German immigrant, was tinkering in his San Francisco apartment in 1895 when he created the world's first true slot machine. Today each of the most popular of Nevada's 200,000 slots generate as much as $5,000 per month in revenue. They work 24 hours a day, seven days a week and require little maintenance; they rarely make a mistake, making them the perfect casino "employee."

Although today's machines often include electronics, complicated pay scales, multiple lines, and dozens of symbols, they're easy to play, a feature that has made them popular since Fey placed his first "Liberty Bell" machines in Reno and San Francisco saloons before the turn of the 20th century. During the first half of the 1900s, proprietors of several of Reno's legal and illegal gambling dens installed the simple devices as diversions for wives and mistresses while "serious" gamblers played poker and craps.

Fey drew inspiration from a five-reel poker machine built by a New York company, but the machinist developed several improvements still in use today, including automatic payouts for winning combinations and a "trade check separator" that could distinguish between real nickels and the plug and wooden variety.

The Liberty Bell used three reels, all painted with symbols – hearts, diamonds, spades, and Liberty Bells. For a $0.05 investment, gamblers could reap a fortune of 10 times their bet by lining up three bells. Fey and the saloons split the profits.

As the popularity of slot machines continued to grow in the early 1900s, competitors copied Fey's design, which he was unable to patent. One of these knock-offs, the Operator Bell, used oranges, lemons, and cherries instead of playing-card suits, thus creating the first "fruit machine."

When Nevada officially outlawed gambling from 1911 to 1930, the halls simply moved their slots to a back room. Other establishments used machines that dispensed cheap gum or candy with each pull, disguising the gambling devices as innocuous vending machines. When the ban was lifted, it didn't take long for slot machines to advance technologically. Electric machines debuted in 1934.

Modern machines are not mechanical. Their wheel sequences are controlled by random number generators. Many offer progressive jackpots, including Megabucks, with machines throughout the state. In 2003 it made one player $39.7 million richer – a far cry from the half-buck that three Liberty Bells were worth to patrons of Fey's original slot machine.

If you find "deluxe rooms" often means a couple of beds crammed into 250 square feet, check out the Regency's 800 guest rooms, which claim to be the largest in Reno. High rollers should consider the Presidential Suite, weighing in at 1,100 square feet and full of big-screen televisions, twin sofas, a jetted tub, a wet bar, and a dining area overlooking the mountains.

Just a few blocks off the strip on 4th Street, the Sands has the classic Las Vegas–type look of a casino that has grown up piecemeal, with the original 1964 low-rise motel units surrounding its first pool, towers rising above, and three or four different wings on the casino.

Harrah's

- **Restaurants:** Café Napa, Carvings Buffet, Harrah's Steak House, Ichiban, Joy Luck Noodle Bar, Quiznos, Starbucks

- **Entertainment:** Sammy's Showroom, The Plaza

- **Nightlife:** Sapphire Lounge

Gaming icon William Harrah's empire began here with a failed bingo parlor in 1937. Harrah reopened the joint the following year, and he acquired five bar-casinos and opened Harrah's (219 N. Center St., 775/786-3232 or 800/427-

7247, $65–225 d) in 1946. Acquisition and expansion continued with the purchase of the Golden Hotel in 1966 and the addition of a 24-story hotel in 1969. Harrah's legacy of growth continued after his death in 1978: A second tower in 1981; a renovation in 1994 as the property fought off challenges from new hotels and their ever-increasing quest for the ultimate in opulence; the incorporation of the 400-room Hampton Inn in 1999; and the purchase and implosion of two neighbors that same year to build **The Plaza,** an outdoor concert venue that is home to tribute bands on summer weekends and an occasional A-list performer. **Sammy's Showroom,** named for the Rat Packer and frequent Harrah's performer, hosts production shows that have included *X Burlesque.* Show packages often include food credit at several Harrah's restaurants, including **Café Napa** (24 hours daily, $10–20), which has a wine bar and offers fresh California wine-country edibles. Darn the calories and order the Gooey Bread—it's covered with cheeses and broiled, and arrives at the table swimming in garlic and butter. Discrete and romantic, **The Steak House** (11 A.M.–2:30 P.M. AND 5–10 P.M. Mon.–Fri., 5–10 P.M. Sat.–Sun., $25–40) should be reserved for special occasions and companions. **Ichiban's** (775/323-5550, 4:30–10 P.M. Sun.–Thurs. and 4:30–11 P.M. Fri.–Sat., $20–30) theatrical food preparation doesn't overshadow the culinary mastery of the show chefs.

Nightlife at Harrah's is more about relaxation than rowdiness. A well-made martini, some elbow room, and good company are the draws to the **Sapphire Lounge** (5 P.M.–late Wed.–Sun.).

Harrah's 828 guest rooms are arranged in its two hotel towers. The West Tower guest rooms are a bit nicer and about $10 more than their counterparts in the East Tower. The East Tower guest rooms boast 32-inch televisions, however, while West Tower guests only get 19-inchers. Pets are not allowed in guest rooms, but the hotel offers a few on-site kennels. Guests must ensure their own furry family members are fed, watered, cleaned, and exercised.

Club Cal-Neva

- **Restaurants:** Casino Grill, Copper Ledge Steak House, Pasta Shoppe, Skyway Deli, Sports Deli, Top Deck
- **Nightlife:** Cabaret Bar karaoke

Low limits, an affinity for nostalgia, and location, location, location draw locals and visitors to Club Cal-Neva (38 E. 2nd St., 877/777-7303, $34–124 d), now nearly 50 years old, making it the second-oldest casino still in operation in Reno. One of its original owners, Warren Nelson, brought keno to Nevada, giving a Chinese lottery game a horseracing theme (keno games still are called "races").

For entertainment, it's probably better to walk a few blocks to the Eldorado, Silver Legacy, Sands Regency, or Circus Circus, but the Cabaret Bar hosts karaoke (8 P.M.–1 A.M. Tues.–Sun.).

Despite some upgrades to keep pace with its neighboring gambling establishments, dim lights and a sprinkling of retro (1990s) slots among the more modern machines and table games are the hallmarks of the multilevel casino. With the exception of the **Copper Ledge Steak House** (4–10 P.M. Fri.–Sat., $12–22), the food is of the cheap and hearty variety. The **Top Deck** (24 hours daily, $5–10) is noted for its $4.99 steak and eggs.

Rooms here are cheap as well but tastefully decorated in teal (Nevadan Tower) or buff (Virginian Tower).

Siena

- **Restaurants:** Lexie's, Contrada Cafe.
- **Nightlife:** The Loft, Enoteca Wine Bar & Lounge

Only 10 years old, Siena (1 S. Lake St., 775/32-SIENA—775/327-4362 or 877/SIENA-33—877/743-6233, $69–169 d) is the Italiante remodel of the venerable Holiday Hotel, which closed its doors in 1998 after more than 40 years. Nestled between the tranquil Truckee River and the hubbub of downtown, Siena projects European sophistication. With its Tuscan architecture, notable lack of neon, emphasis on relaxation and service, an extravagant day spa, and restaurant views of the Truckee River, Siena targets guests seeking a slower pace than that offered by its glitzy compatriots in the resort corridor. Note that as of 2010, Siena does not offer table games—it's slots only here. The casino also echoes Italian elegance, with massive archways and pillars accenting the 23,000-square-foot room.

The pasta appetizers at **Lexie's** (5–9 P.M. Mon.–Thurs., 5–9 P.M. Fri.–Sat., 10 A.M.–2 P.M. and 5–9 P.M. Sun., $15–25) set the stage for a Mediterranean treatment of its steak and chop

main courses. Talented and diverse creations by local artists provide conversation starters at **The Loft** (10 P.M.–late Fri.–Sat.). The music is just as eclectic, and the drink prices can't be beat. **Enoteca** (7 P.M.–late Fri.–Sat.)—the name means "wine cellar" in Italian—serves sophisticated acoustic music along with tapas and wine by the glass.

A boutique hotel under the guise of a Riviera villa, Siena's 214 guest rooms and suites range from warm-colored standard rooms to the more muted color schemes of the larger deluxe rooms to 600-square-foot suites with a sitting area and second half-bath. Twenty-nine suites are tucked into Floor dei Nobili, where the 1,200-square-foot rooms are decked out in

THE "BLACK BOOK": A VERY EXCLUSIVE CLUB

For much the same reason that Willie Sutton robbed banks ("because that's where the money is"), plots are continually being hatched to rip off Nevada's casinos. Modern plots are rarely as sophisticated as an *Ocean's 11* caper, and the culprits are rarely as engaging as Frank Sinatra or George Clooney. But while slot-machine technology and casino security have foiled token counterfeiters, card markers, and loaded-dice artists, the villains have used technology as well.

Those who get caught often wind up in a most exclusive club – the Nevada Gaming Commission's List of Excluded Persons. The "Black Book" is full of geniuses and the not-so-bright who designed and used mechanical devices, sabotage, bribery, or their inside position to steal from the casinos. The book – which is silver, not black – also contains names of known organized-crime figures and other unsavory characters whose affiliation or association with gambling parlors would give the appearance of impropriety. Eleven mob associates made up the book's first class in 1960. Dozens have been added since, although more than a few have wiggled off the hook for various reasons. Today 39 people grace the book's pages.

The newest additions are two slot cheaters added in 2004.

Anyone with a felony conviction, a rap sheet that includes a crime of moral turpitude or violation of any state's gaming laws, an interest in a gaming establishment that they did not disclose to authorities, or a history of willfully evading taxes is eligible for Black Book membership. Excluded persons face gross misdemeanor charges if they're caught entering a gaming establishment (stores, airports, bars, and other places with no gambling tables and only a few slot machines are not included in the ban).

Perhaps the most intriguing Black Book member is Ronald Dale Harris. For 12 years he was an employee of the Nevada Gaming Control Board, where he evaluated the security of gaming machines. He used his familiarity to rig several Nevada machines, winning several small payouts over three years before he and an accomplice got greedy. Harris gaffed a video keno game's random-number generator and sent the accomplice to Atlantic City to win a $100,000 jackpot. Casino authorities became suspicious because – well, because nobody ever wins at video keno – and the investigation led back to Harris.

warm hues reminiscent of a Tuscan sunset and come with guaranteed mountain or Truckee River views.

Peppermill

- **Restaurants:** Romanza, Bimini Steakhouse, Chi, Biscotti's, Coffee Shop, Island Buffet, Oceano, Saucy's Smokehouse, Sports Deli, Café Espresso
- **Entertainment:** Tuscany Event Center, Cabaret Lounge, Terrace Lounge
- **Attractions:** Arcade Xreme
- **Nightlife:** Edge, Fireside Lounge, Lobby Lounge, Video Cube Bar, Sports Bar, Fish Bar, Flamingo Bar, Banyan Bar

No matter how well hotels appoint their gambling areas with replicas of art masterpieces or carry their casino theme through to their restaurants, nightclubs, and hotel rooms, reconciling the thrills of casino gaming with a desire to project luxurious resort amenities is never seamless. The Peppermill (2707 S. Virginia St., 866/821-9996, $69–349 d) avoids these problems by segregating—both physically and stylistically—its glitter-and-neon gambling den from its more traditional resort amenities. The 100,000-square-foot casino is as flashy, loud, and bright as any in Nevada, but the rest of the property, decked out in marble, leather, and rich wood, might easily be mistaken for a rich-and-famous retreat in the Caribbean or Mediterranean. The Peppermill delivers this best-of-both-worlds scenario using attractions common to most Nevada resorts, but it does them bigger and better than most. A swimming pool is almost a given at resort hotels, but at the Peppermill, a "mountain stream" cascades down rocky outcroppings at the main outdoor swimming pool. Spas are a dime a dozen in Nevada, but the Peppermill's **Spa Toscana** (7 A.M.–9 P.M. daily), a highlight of the $400 million expansion in 2008, envelops guests like a terrycloth robe in 30,000 square feet of luxurious treatments and relaxation in its indoor pool and sun deck.

Top gamers can win video game systems, iPods, and more with just the flick of a wrist at **Arcade Xtreme** (9 A.M.–11 P.M. Sun.–Thurs., 9 A.M.–1 A.M. Fri.–Sat.).

All that fun is sure to work up an appetite; for breakfast and lunch, you can't go wrong with the Peppermill's original **Coffee Shop** (24 hours daily, $12–25), a local favorite for burgers, salads, and hearty omelets. Northern Italy is features at **Romanza** (5:30–11 P.M. daily, $25–40), where the food is prepared in a massive wood-fired oven. Hit **Oceano** (11 A.M.–9:30 P.M. Sun.–Thurs., 11 A.M.–10 P.M. Fri.–Sat., $25–35) for the breathtaking underwater theme and shrimp quesadillas.

The Peppermill hosts top musical talent and conventions in the **Tuscany Event Center** along with live music throughout many of its 17 lounges and other watering holes. The best is at **Cabaret Lounge** (7 P.M.–1 A.M. Mon.–Thurs., 7 P.M.–4 A.M. Fri.–Sat., 7–11:30 P.M. Sun., free) and the **Terrace Lounge** (9 P.M.–1 A.M. Fri.–Sat.) for rock and blues amid pool-and-gardenscapes.

Standard guest rooms in the Peppermill Tower feature lacquer and mirrored accents for a touch of classic elegance. For even more elegance, choose a suite in the Peppermill or the new 600-room Tuscany Tower with its 550-square-foot accommodations, sweeping views, and Old World charm. The Montego Bay Wing conjures the Caribbean with mahogany accents and vibrant colors. Hand-painted artwork, panoramic mountain views, a large dining room, and a pool fill the 2,200-square-foot house-sized Palace Suite.

Atlantis

- **Restaurants:** Atlantis Steak House, Bistro Napa, Café Alfresco, Chicago Dogs, Gourmet Grind, Manhattan Deli, Oyster Bar, Purple Parrot, Sushi Bar, Toucan Charlie's Buffet
- **Entertainment:** Atlantis Cabaret
- **Attractions:** Fun Center

Atlantis's tower rooms have crisp, clean stylings with attractive buff, cream, and chocolate décor.

- **Nightlife:** Atrium Lounge, Sports Bar

With always up-to-date amenities and design along with resort-quality entertainment and food, Atlantis (3800 S. Virginia St., 775/825-4700 or 800/723-6500, $100–200 d) is a favorite among frequent Reno visitors. With a skywalk connecting the hotel to the adjacent Reno-Sparks Convention Center, Atlantis also provides convenient accommodations for business travelers. Its restaurants offer menus and prices to suit every occasion and budget. Unlike many casinos, you can actually tell whether it's day or night, sunny or snowing: Atlantis gives gamblers inspiring views of the surrounding mountains through tall windows.

The **Atlantis Cabaret** (4 P.M.–3:30 A.M. daily, free) hosts two musical lounge acts per night.

From classic video games to the latest multimedia and virtual reality, the **Fun Center** (9 A.M.–10 P.M. Sun.–Thurs., 9 A.M.–1 A.M. Fri.–Sat.) offers a 24-hour pass ($50) for hardcore gamers.

Can mashed potatoes be a gourmet dish? They can when the staff knows its way around a spud like the chefs at the **Atlantis Steakhouse.** With a 4,000-bottle cellar and an experienced sommelier, **Bistro Napa** (775/825-4700, 5–10 P.M. daily, $20–40) will deliver the perfect pairing for your choice of California cuisine. The raw bar deservedly has its fans, but for coast-influenced comfort food, try the braised hunter stew with venison and lamb. Bring a friend or a huge appetite if you order the pastrami at **Manhattan Deli** (6 A.M.–10 P.M. daily, $8–20). The chicken soup is worth catching a cold for. Seafood at a diner often is a 50–50 proposition, but **The Purple Parrot** (24 hours daily, $8–20) comes up aces with its prawn scampi. We usually consider it blasphemy to eat greenery at a buffet, but the spinach salad with hot bacon dressing at **Toucan Charlie's Buffet and Grille** (7:30 A.M.–10:30 P.M. Mon.–Sat., 11 A.M.–10 P.M. Sun., $20–30) almost makes us forget about the Mongolian barbecue.

Like its restaurants, Atlantis's guest rooms run from plush to plain. Standard tower guest rooms are only average size at 375 square feet, but marble accents, city and mountain views, and high ceilings with decorative moldings make them seem bigger. If you want to save a few bucks or bring Fido on vacation with you, opt for the pet-friendly motor lodge and its tiny 240-square-foot rooms. On the other hand, if you want to treat yourself, choose the Concierge Tower. The 450-square-foot digs on the upper floors are tastefully decorated in buffs and creams and include 42-inch TVs with DVD players. Better yet, guests here are invited to the **Concierge Lounge** for cocktails, free hors d'oeuvres, continental breakfast, Internet access, and newspapers.

Grand Sierra

- **Restaurants:** Charlie Palmer Steak, Briscola, Fin Fish, Rim, The Lodge, Café Sierra, 2nd Street Express, Starbucks, Johnny Rockets, Port of Subs, Round Table Pizza

- **Entertainment:** Grand Theatre

- **Attractions:** Fun Quest, Ultimate Rush thrill park, indoor golf, driving range

- **Nightlife:** 2500 East, The Beach, The Reserve, Crystal Bar, Mustangs, Escalator Bar, Xtreme Sports Bar, Bottom of Form

Located just outside Reno's casino core, the Grand Sierra (2500 E. 2nd St., 775/789-2000 or 800/501-2651, $119–219 d), formerly the Reno Hilton, has everything the vacationer or conventioneer could want—all under one roof. The aptly named resort is built on a grand scale, from its 2,000-room hotel with 440-square-foot guest rooms to its 100,000-square-foot casino—larger even than most Las Vegas gambling dens. You could spend a week here and never eat dinner twice in the same restaurant, and shop till you drop and never visit all the boutiques.

With the largest indoor stage in Nevada, the **Grand Theatre** hosts comedy, ballet, mixed martial arts matches, and music headliners ranging from Harry Connick Jr. to Korn.

The Beach (9 P.M.–late Fri.–Sat. May–Sept., weather permitting, $20) is Grand Sierra's sexy poolside nightclub, with designer cocktails, food from the hotel's gourmet restaurants, and celebrity DJs.

Excitement of a different stripe is to be had at **Fun Quest** (noon–10 P.M. Mon.–Thurs., noon–11 P.M. Fri., 10 A.M.–11 P.M. Sat., 10 A.M.–10 P.M. Sun.), a state-of-the-art video and virtual reality parlor. You can join the virtual PGA tour with the resort's championship **golf course simulator** (9 P.M.–midnight daily). Challenge Pebble Beach, Pinehurst, and others using regulation clubs. Advanced electronics measure your swing and determine the ball's flight on a video screen. You can even warm up before your round at Grand Sierra's **aquatic driving range** (7 A.M.–midnight Sun.–Thurs., 7 A.M.–2 A.M. Fri.–Sat). If you're still hungry for adventure, the Grand Sierra Adventures Desk in the hotel lobby serves as a sort of nature concierge and can arrange off-site golf, skiing, boating, and sightseeing tours.

Celebrity chef Charlie Palmer operates three restaurants at Grand Sierra. **Fin Fish** (5:30–9:30 P.M. Sun.–Thurs., 5:30–10:30 P.M. Fri.–Sat., $24–40) is the best of the lot, especially the gourmet seafood variations of fast food staples. The buff-and-aqua color scheme evokes the seaside. **Charlie Palmer Steak** (4:30–10:30 P.M. daily, $35–60) cooks up new twists on generational favorites. Palmer's Italian entry, **Briscola** (5:30–9:30 P.M. Sun.–Thurs., 5:30–10:30 P.M. Fri.–Sat., $10–20) is casual and family-friendly, with gooey, cheesy dishes designed with kids in mind and more subtle selections for adults. Sorry, Charlie, but the Italian is almost as good as the Lodge Buffet's lunch. Some of Reno's best sushi tops the menu of pan-Asian favorites at **Rim** (11 A.M.–10 P.M. daily, $20–30).

With 500-square-foot standard rooms, some of which adjoin to form two-bedroom suites, the Grand Sierra's accommodations meet even the largest family's needs. Sage, brown, and buff accents add to the home-away-from-home aura. Suites have sumptuous leather furnishings,

RENO

microwaves, mini fridges, and flat-screen TVs. Brown velour and black leather add to the contemporary sophistication in the Imperial Suite at the Summit at Grand Sierra.

Boomtown

- **Restaurants:** Cassidy's Steakhouse, Whole Maine Lobster Buffet, Reno Peet's Coffee and Tea, Denny's

- **Attractions:** Family Fun Center

In the Old West, wherever travelers converged, a boomtown sprang up to sell supplies, food, and animal forage. The covered wagon gave way to the automobile and the semitrailer, and Bill and Effie's, on this site at the head of a mountain pass traversed by I-80, continued to serve as a wayside for truckers in need of coffee, fuel, and respite from the asphalt trail. Today the site is another Boomtown (2100 Garson Rd., 775/345-8550, $80–120 d). The massive truck parking lot is gone, sold to make way for a huge Cabela's sporting goods showroom, and the clientele is more likely to arrive in a minivan than a wagon or big rig.

The 30,000-square-foot **Family Fun Center** (10 A.M.–10 P.M. Sun.–Thurs., 10 A.M.–midnight Fri.–Sat.) houses a 3-D digital motion theater, a climbing wall, a flight simulator, an antique carousel, a Ferris wheel, and 200 video games.

North Tower rooms, at 350 square feet, have 42-inch TVs, iPod docking stations, and Wi-Fi. South Tower rooms and their TVs are smaller, but so is the price. You can also upgrade to one of the several dozen suites with jetted tubs and balconies.

John Ascuaga's Nugget

- **Restaurants:** Steakhouse Grill, Restaurante Orozko, John's Oyster Bar, Rotisserie Buffet, Rosie's Café, Trader Dick's, Noodle Hut, Gabe's Pub & Deli, Starbucks

Boomtown hosts a cool 3-D motion theater, along with its full-scale gambling, dining, and nightlife.

COURTESY OF PINNACLE ENTERTAINMENT, INC.

HAROLD'S CLUB OR BUST

At 250 North Virginia Street, Harold's Club was once the center of the casino gambling universe. Raymond "Pappy" Smith, a carnival operator, sent his son Harold to Reno to open a little roulette concession (one wheel, two nickel slots) in 1935, a time when gambling, although legal, was still very much a Douglas Alley backroom scam-riddled enterprise. That first little excursion into legal gambling proved profitable, so the Smiths expanded, and in the process changed the face of casino gambling forever. They not only ushered gambling into the daylight of Virginia Street, but they also launched a campaign to improve the image of legalized casino gambling in the national consciousness, which also reflected on the image of Harold's Club and Reno.

In so doing, the Smiths set the ground rules for Nevada's incipient gambling industry by showing the first generation of casino operators how to make gambling palatable to the middle-class masses. Without them, Meyer Lansky and Bugsy Siegel could never have envisioned their own resort hotel in Las Vegas. And it would've been a very different world today.

In the late 1930s the slogan "Harold's Club or Bust" suddenly loomed from billboards, played on the radio, and appeared in newspapers all over the country, introducing locals and non-Nevadans to the novel concept that gambling was good clean fun. The Smiths implemented sophisticated safeguards against cheating on both sides of the table, inventing them as they went along – the original eye-in-the-sky, one-way glass, and the catwalk system, for example. Harold's Club was the first to offer free drinks, comps, and junkets and to charter trains and planes for its customers. Harold's was the first to hire female dealers, during the labor shortage of World War II, further enhancing casino respectability. The whole strategy worked so well that it immediately became standard casino operating procedure and has remained so ever since.

Pappy Smith, who has been called the Henry Ford of Nevada gambling, died in 1967. The Club was sold to Howard Hughes's Summa Corporation in 1970 and expanded in 1979. When Fitzgeralds bought it in 1988, it was the last casino property that Summa had to sell, thereby ending the 20-year presence of Howard Hughes's corporation in Nevada. (Fitzgeralds also bought the Sundance in Las Vegas in 1987, thereby ending Moe Dalitz's nearly 40-year reign as that city's King of Juice.) Fitzgeralds tried to sell the unprofitable casino for years and finally had to shut it down in 1995. Harrah's purchased it in 1999, and the casino's Plaza now occupies the site.

- **Entertainment:** Celebrity Showroom, Rose Ballroom, Casino Cabaret

- **Nightlife:** Orozko Lounge, Trader Dick's Lounge

The former general manager of Dick Graves's Nugget bought and renamed this place John Ascuaga's Nugget (1100 Nugget Ave., Sparks, 800/647-1177, $55–140 d) after himself in 1960. Two 29-floor hotel towers were added in 1984 and 1996, and the coffee shop and slot machine parlor were transformed into a full-fledged resort. Still family-owned, the Nugget is a testament to the entrepreneurial spirit. Ascuaga even fought not only city hall but the federal government—and won. In the late 1950s, the Nugget commissioned a solid gold rooster to serve as the mascot for a new restaurant, but the U.S. Treasury Department claimed the bird ran afowl (sorry) of the law prohibiting private ownership of more than 50 ounces of gold unless it was in the form of an objet d'art. The Nugget won its case that the poultry was indeed art and reclaimed possession. The restaurant is no more, but the rooster perches proudly in the hotel lobby, crowing his victory over Uncle Sam.

Country superstars such as the Oak Ridge Boys along with top comedians and the occasional rock or blues band entertain in the intimate, 700-seat, pitch-perfect Celebrity

Showroom and 2,000-seat Rose Ballroom. Lounge acts rule the Casino Cabaret (8 P.M.–midnight Thurs., 9 P.M.–2 A.M. Fri.–Sat., free).

Hearty Basque fare goes upscale at **Restaurante Orozko** (5–9 P.M. Wed.–Thurs., 5–9:30 P.M. Fri.–Sat., $25–35), and the clams and pan roasts at **John's Oyster Bar** rival Fairchild's at Silver Legacy. Despite the decidedly Western name, **Trader Dick's** (775/356-3300, 5–10 P.M. Fri.–Sat., 5–9 P.M. Sun.–Mon., $15–35) masters Asian cuisine. The bartenders mix a mean Singapore sling as well. **Rosie's Café** (24 hours daily, $7–15) is reminiscent of a neighborhood diner where families and working stiffs savor coffee and hearty sandwiches while discussing the high school football team or the latest controversy at city hall. Asian night is the best of the "featured cuisine" dinners at the **Rotisserie Buffet,** although the salads are fresh anytime.

With jazz nights, beer, wine, martini tastings, and live entertainment, Orozko Lounge is a popular after-work and weekend gathering spot.

Newly remodeled East Tower rooms include 42-inch TVs, rich wood accents, and gold and mauve textiles. West Tower rooms offer outstanding views with a retro facade. Courtyard rooms and suites also are available.

Arts and Entertainment

Reno has plenty of nongambling entertainment to offer, and a few publications can help you plan your visit and keep track of the ever-changing talent.

The daily **Reno Gazette-Journal** (www.rgj.com) publishes a special entertainment section called "Best Bets" that covers the headliners, big-name bands, comedians, and lounge groups at the hotels along with an up-to-date chart with listings of all entertainment, club acts, and events in the area. It also has blurbs on parks, museums, outdoor activities, and local recreation. Much of the information is also available on the website.

The alternative weekly **Reno News and Review** (www.newsreview.com) is published on Thursday and distributed free on news racks around town. It reviews local arts, movies, restaurants, and clubs and prints a weekly calendar of events.

SHOWROOMS AND CONCERTS

Almost all the major hotel-casinos have at least one lounge, cabaret, show bar, or bandstand with groups entertaining the masses. With the largest indoor stage in Nevada, the **Grand Theatre at Grand Sierra** (2500 E. 2nd St., 800/647-3568) ranks at the top of the casino venues. It hosts comedy, ballet, and musical acts.

Harrah's renamed its concert venue **Sammy's Showroom** (219 N. Center St.) after Sammy Davis Jr., one of the most venerable and best-loved performers in Reno, died in 1991. There is also the newer **The Plaza** for free concerts and other entertainment. Call 775/787-3773 for showtimes, prices, and reservations.

The Eldorado has three entertainment venues: **Brew Brothers, Roxy's,** and the **Eldorado Showroom** (345 N. Virginia St.). John Ascuaga's Nugget has the 750-seat **Celebrity Showroom** plus the **Rose Ballroom, Casino Cabaret,** and **Trader Dick's** (1100 Nugget Ave.); call 775/356-3300 for reservations. The Peppermill has two entertainment venues: the **Tuscany Event Center** and the **Cabaret** (2707 S. Virginia St., 775/826-2121).

Circus Circus of course, has continuous entertainment under the big top. Free circus acts are presented noon–midnight every day on the **Midway Stage.** (500 N. Sierra St., 775/329-0711).

On any given night—more likely on Friday–Saturday—the **Knitting Factory** (211 N. Virginia St., across from Harrah's, 877/435-9849, http://re.knittingfactory.com) is likely to have something cool on stage. The Knit has hosted everyone from Willie Nelson to Toad the Wet Sprocket.

NIGHTLIFE

Hip one moment, defunct the next; such is the life of the nightspot. Check the chart in the *Gazette-Journal*'s entertainment section for all the latest. Reno's best bars are too cool to waste time coming up with creative names. If you prefer to plan your weekend festivities, **210 North** (210 N. Sierra St., 775/786-6210, www.210north.com) will provide a guaranteed, though predictable, good time. Antiseptic but appealing chrome, detailed lighting schemes, a $15 cover charge many nights, and patrons decked out in their best slinky dresses testify to the 210's "intense approach to Saturday nights," as one reviewer wrote.

If serendipity is more your thing, hit **3rd Street** (125 W. 3rd St., 775/323-5005). Comfortable-clothed regulars along with blues and rock cover bands on weekends make for evening that's not as pretty but just as fun.

The Zephyr Lounge (1074 S. Virginia St., 775/324-9853) attracts an eclectic live-and-let-live crowd of music and art lovers, blue-collar types, and young professionals. Poets and singers offer open-mike performances of varying genres, sensibilities, and talent levels.

Much of the Reno nightclub scene is found in casino bars. The Peppermill sets the pace with its new **EDGE** (2707 S. Virginia St., 10 P.M.–late Thurs.–Sun.). The ultralounge–dance club invites you and the rest of the swankily attired cool crew to indulge in Epic Saturdays and Get Back Sundays with the club's go-go girls.

Brew Brothers (345 N. Virginia St., 775/786-5700) at the Eldorado offers live music as well as hand-crafted beers and a late-night menu. **Roxy's** is a bit more intimate, with its menu of 102 martinis and live piano music nightly.

For a more intimate setting, Harrah's Reno has the **Sapphire Lounge** (219 N. Center St., 775/786-3232, 5 P.M.–late Tues.–Sun.).

The Silver Legacy offers **Rum Bullions Island Bar** (407 N. Virginia St., 800/687-8733), which packs them in with exotic (and often flaming) rum drinks as well as live entertainment, including dueling pianos.

For stand-up comedy, **Catch a Rising Star** (407 N. Virginia St., 775/325-7452) is at the Silver Legacy, which also presents headliners in the **Grande Exhibition Hall.**

THE ARTS

Reno and Las Vegas both have been called cultural vacuums, but in recent years both have taken pains to cultivate an arts district. Reno in particular boasts a long history of embracing art.

Much less pretentious than you might expect, the **Nevada Opera** (775/786-4046, www.nevadaopera.org) offers preperformance explanatory discussions with artistic director Michael Borowitz, so even if you're a newbie, you'll get the gist of the story. If you lose the plot, the theater projects English versions of the lyrics as the performers sing. The opera performs on the lower level of the **Pioneer Center for the Performing Arts** (100 S. Virginia St., 775/686-6600, www.pioneercenter.com). The center, a 1,500-seat venue run by a nonprofit organization, also stages popular mainstream musicals.

The **Reno Philharmonic Association** (775/323-6393, www.renophilharmonic.com) performs year-round throughout the region, with indoor concerts fall–spring in the Pioneer Center and outdoor summer shows of family, festival, and pops music.

The **Reno Chamber Orchestra** (1664 N. Virginia St., 775/347-9413, www.renochamberorchestra.org) has been a city mainstay since 1974 when founder Vahe Khochayan plucked some of his musical colleagues from casino showrooms to play classical music in whatever venue they could find. Today the orchestra hosts the annual Nevada Chamber Music Festival and the College Concerto Competition in addition to its regular-season performances.

Advocacy, education, and funding are the goals of the **Sierra Arts Foundation** (17 S. Virginia St., Suite 120, 775/329-2787, www.sierra-arts.org), which supports local community-spirited artists to work, exhibit, and perform in

RENO

ARTOWN

Lots of towns have invested in arts districts to revitalize their downtowns, and many host First Friday or Third Thursday events to show off the resulting urban renewal. But Reno's transformation has been so remarkable that one day a month simply isn't enough time to show it off. The city presents Artown (775/322-1538, www.renoisartown.com), a monthlong celebration of the visual and performing arts highlighted by visiting world-renowned artists, children's theater performances, gallery events, and cultural experiences. Artown has grown to include some 400 events and attract 350,000 people to Reno's downtown arts district each July.

Recipient of the National Endowment for the Arts's Access to Artistic Excellence grant, Artown boasts that 63 percent of its events are free, with many others costing less than $10. Free offerings in recent years have included family movies, dances, and the wildly popular Discover the Arts children's workshops, where kids 6-12 learn about theater, dance, music, poetry, painting, and sculpture.

"There's an upbeat energy that permeates Reno each July, and we're thrilled that Artown can have that sort of impact," Artown executive director Beth Macmillan said. "To say that we've been able to grow the festival to include so many events and genres and accommodate the number of attendees seen in recent years is phenomenal and speaks to the strength of Artown."

In its 15 years, Artown's annual festival has infused $100 million into the local economy, federal grant funding, and tourism. Just as important, it has fostered the community's appreciation of art and generated valuable partnerships and collaborations among artists, arts organizations, patrons, and local governments.

COURTESY OF RENO ARTOWN

Concerts, dances, and other performance art are as important as visual art at Reno's annual Artown celebration.

the community, especially in locations in need of beautification and revitalization.

The **Bruka Theater of the Sierra** (99 N. Virginia St., 775/323-3221, www.bruka.org) brings to its venerable and stark stage everything from Shakespearean drama to contemporary comedy, children's theater, and the avant-garde.

At press time, the **Reno Little Theater** (775/329-0661, www.renolittletheater.org) was about to move into its new digs on Pueblo Street between Wells Avenue and Virginia Street, where it will continue to educate and expose adults and children to the world of live theater with performances September–June. A part of the Reno arts scene since 1935, the troupe performs at Hug High School (2880 Sutro St.) until its new theater is complete.

Directors of the **Lear Theater** (528 W. 1st St., 775/786-2278, www.leartheater.org) are working with architects and designers to preserve the theater's historical features while finding funding sources to ameliorate building code deficiencies that forced its closure in 1999.

FESTIVALS AND EVENTS

Maybe it's because Reno enjoys such a mild spring, summer, and fall that it packs in as much entertainment as it can before the winter ski season arrives. Just about any weekend early May–early October will find the city hosting a cultural or athletic festival.

May

White-water paddling is the focus of the **Reno River Festival** at Wingfield Park, but there's also a muddy two-mile obstacle course for runners as well as live bands, food and beer, and an outdoor product trade show.

June

Cowboy up for the 10-day Professional Rodeo Cowboys Association–sanctioned **Reno Rodeo,** which that draws 140,000 spectators for seven go-rounds at the Reno Livestock Events Center. From German brats and polkas to Swedish meatballs, Celtic fiddles, and Polish polkas, **EuroFest,** at the Sands Regency, celebrates the Old World. The **Nevada Humanities**

Chautauqua Festival (Hawkins Amphitheater, Bartley Ranch Regional Park) brings history to life through "firsthand" storytelling by colorful personalities from the past. Visitors can stock up on farm-fresh produce, international food tasting, and arts and crafts Thursdays throughout the summer at the **Sparks Hometowne Farmer's Market** at Victorian Square in downtown Sparks. Experience the biker lifestyle for a weekend at **Street Vibrations Spring Rally,** with musical entertainment, terrific food, poker runs and walks, and rides through the region's cultural and historic districts. Nonmotorized bikers get their chance to strut their stuff at **Tour de Nez,** a series of races and rallies. The tour includes rides throughout the region, with the Reno events centered around Wingfield Park. A trade show and musical entertainment complete the package.

July

Reno celebrates its commitment to the visual and performing arts with **Artown,** a month-long celebration in the Riverwalk district. The Eldorado Casino hosts the **BBQ, Brews & Blues Festival,** a journey through some of Reno's best food and microbrews. Chicago and Delta blues performers pack two stages throughout the weekend. Country musicians and storytellers converge on the Hawkins Amphitheater in Bartley Ranch Regional Park for the **Cowboy Poetry & Music Gathering.** Aspiring young local thespians are paired with professional actors to present condensed versions of the Bard's best throughout the area in the **Shakespeare Festival.** Pro wakeboarders show off their best "aqua-batics" at Sparks Marina in the **Mastercraft Pro Wakeboard Tour.** PGA Tour professionals vie for their share of the **Reno-Tahoe Open**'s $3.5 million purse. Heart-pounding fireworks culminate an Independence Day full of music, cool refreshments, games, and street performers in **Star Spangled Sparks.**

August

Part car show, part street party, **Hot August Nights** presents wholesome 1950s and '60s–style entertainment in Reno, Sparks, and Lake Tahoe.

RENO

Polish up the tailfins and cruise on over. Food, rides, games, a demolition derby, a competition for queen, and livestock—everything that makes Nevada great is at the **Nevada State Fair.**

September

John Ascuaga's Nugget in Sparks invites you to gorge yourself on barbequed ribs and other treats at the **Best in the West Nugget Rib Cook-Off.** Free entertainment is presented on five stages, and a kid's play area is open daily. Don't miss the professional rib-eating contest—do not try this at home. **The Great Reno Balloon Race** has more than 100 colorful hot-air balloons of all shapes dotting the skies north of Reno. A craft and souvenir show, food, balloon rides, and a student tissue-paper balloon launch add to the excitement. Pilots in several classes of planes battle for air supremacy in the **National Championship Air Races,** racing at up to 500 mph just feet off the ground. One of the 10 best and 10 largest bike rallies in the country, **Street Vibrations** is a weeklong succession of rides, vendors, and parades, all with a Harley attitude.

October

Bring the oregano and enter your spaghetti sauce in the **Great Italian Festival** cook-off, or try your hand (foot, rather) in the hilarious grape-stomping contest. There's boccie and gelato-eating contests as well as traditional Italian entertainment. Scottish and Irish games, music, dances, and food feature in the **Reno Celtic Celebration** at Bartley Ranch Regional Park.

Sights

◖ TRUCKEE RIVER WALK

"Pedestrian-friendly" has become a catchphrase for urban renewal, and Reno embraces the concept wholeheartedly with the Raymond I. Smith Truckee River Walk, a downtown promenade that can also be called artist-friendly, oenophile-friendly, and even kayaker-friendly. Named for the founder of Harold's Club and completed in 1991, the River Walk is home to art walks, beer crawls, wine tastings, and many of the city's other social events. The walkway is the centerpiece of Reno's reembracing of its history and culture—its "Reno-ssaince." Trendy eateries, quaint boutiques, art galleries, and artists lofts along the promenade have transformed the area, long forgotten as Reno nurtured its gambling, entertainment, and resort reputation.

Waterfalls and idyllic scenes of fly-fishing, rafters and waders, lush riparian landscaping, and plentiful waterfowl compete for your attention with strolling performers, Victorian homes, and the snowcapped Sierra Nevada mountains.

TRUCKEE RIVER WHITEWATER PARK

Start your walk on the river at Wingfield Park, a 0.25-mile-long island that splits the Truckee into two channels. A couple of blocks south of the casino corridor and smack-dab in the middle of Reno's fledgling arts scene at First Street and Arlington Avenue, the park is home to one of Reno's most unusual and iconic attractions: Truckee River Whitewater Park's Class II and III rapids challenge advanced paddlers while providing a safe environment for beginners as well as canoeists and rafters. Fed by clear mountain runoff, the rafting course includes 11 drop-in pools and a racing course, so the route never gets old. **Tahoe Whitewater Tours** (775/787-5000 or 800/442-7238, www.gowhitewater.com) or **Wild Sierra Adventures** (775/323-8928 or 866/323-8928, www.wildsierra.com) can set you up. If you're visiting on a summer weekend, there's a good chance you can catch a classical music, theater, jazz, or children's program at the park's **amphitheater** (775/334-2417).

TRUCKEE RIVER BRIDGES

As with most downtown renovation plans, Reno's desire to cultivate its heritage is knocking heads with its need to keep the area safe, clean, and vibrant. The Virginia Street Bridge is a case in point. More than 100 years old, the bridge's double arches, weathered facade, and historical significance have carved the span a special spot in the hearts of many Renoites; it stands very near the spot where Charles Fuller built his original log structure in 1859. Reno founder Myron Lake bought the bridge in 1861, completely rebuilt it, and collected tolls for 10 years. In 1877 the county replaced the wood with iron, matching the railroad bridge just downriver. The current 146-foot, twin-arched concrete bridge was built in 1905. Legend has it that during Reno's quickie-divorce era, the newly unwed would celebrate their freedom by hurling their wedding rings from the bridge into the river. The bridge's design and construction have enabled it to survive numerous floods, but constant battering has eroded the bridge supports. A century of service and the susceptibility of its arches to become clogged with debris has led flood control officials to call for a modern replacement.

The Sierra Street and Lake Street bridges are also being targeted for replacement as Reno works to avoid a repeat of the "100-year flood" that inundated 20 downtown blocks in 1997. Near the Sierra Street bridge, you can stroll beneath the romantic glow of an antique streetlamp. Just west of this bridge is a salmon-colored pedestrian span connecting the river's north bank with the island of Wingfield Park. A rose-colored pedestrian bridge crosses the main channel of the Truckee River west of Sierra Street between the north bank and Wingfield Park, and other interesting bridges cross the Truckee at Arlington and Center streets. The Center Street bridge was poorly constructed when it went up in 1926, and in 1994 it was in such bad shape that the sidewalks were closed; it was finally rebuilt in 1998.

LAKE MANSION

Myron Lake charged each horse and rider 10 cents to cross his toll bridge on Virginia Street in the 1860s. All those dimes added up, and in 1879 Lake purchased a stately home at Virginia Street and California Avenue. Although it's a fitting abode for the founder of the biggest little city in the world, the Lake Mansion (250 Court St., 775/826-6100, www.lakemansion. com, 9 A.M.–4 P.M. Mon.–Fri., donation) never housed Myron Lake. Jane Lake got the home as part of the settlement in her split from Myron, the first of many prominent divorces in Reno.

The home is a detailed example of the Italianate style. The veranda around the house, carved woodwork, and modern (for the 19th century) sliding parlor doors testify to the quality workmanship Reno's upper crust could afford. In the mansion's kitchen hangs a portrait by Cyrinus B. McClellan, perhaps the most prolific, if not the most talented, of the Comstock painters. In the picture, Lake stands in front of his toll bridge next to Chief Winnemucca. The library now displays art works completed by VSA students. VSA, a nonprofit organization where people with disabilities learn through, participate in, and enjoy the arts, has its offices in the mansion. The group renovated the mansion and moved it to its current location in the city's arts district.

NATIONAL BOWLING STADIUM

A bowling alley as a resort destination? A monument to one of the country's most popular recreational sports, the National Bowling Stadium (300 N. Center St., 775/335-8870 or 800/304-2695) is far removed from after-work leagues and beer frames, with a 440-foot video projection screen that would be right at home in any NFL stadium, a computer-driven system to detect even the tiniest flaw in a bowler's delivery, a pro shop with the sophisticated equipment to maximize every frame, and 80 lanes of kegling contentment. Hosting some of the sport's biggest tournaments, the bowling stadium treats pro bowlers like the elite athletes they are, whisking them in twin glass elevators to the fourth floor Tournament Level.

But bowling isn't the only attraction of the

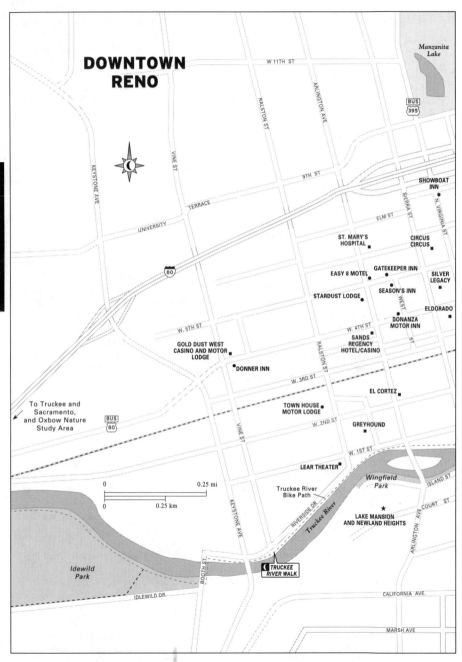

DOWNTOWN RENO

RENO

W 11TH ST

Manzanita Lake

BUS 395

RALSTON ST

ARLINGTON AVE

VINE ST

KEYSTONE AVE

9TH ST

SHOWBOAT INN

SIERRA ST

N. VIRGINIA ST

TERRACE

ELM ST

UNIVERSITY

ST. MARY'S HOSPITAL

CIRCUS CIRCUS

80

GATEKEEPER INN

EASY 8 MOTEL

SILVER LEGACY

STARDUST LODGE

SEASON'S INN

WEST

ELDORADO

W. 5TH ST

DONANZA MOTOR INN

W. 4TH ST

GOLD DUST WEST CASINO AND MOTOR LODGE

SANDS REGENCY HOTEL/CASINO

RALSTON ST

DONNER INN

W. 3RD ST

To Truckee and Sacramento, and Oxbow Nature Study Area

BUS 80

EL CORTEZ

TOWN HOUSE MOTOR LODGE

W. 2ND ST

GREYHOUND

VINE ST

W. 1ST ST

0   0.25 mi

LEAR THEATER

Wingfield Park

ISLAND ST

0   0.25 km

Truckee River Bike Path

Truckee River

LAKE MANSION AND NEWLAND HEIGHTS

ARLINGTON AVE

COURT ST

RIVERSIDE DR

Idewild Park

BOOTH ST

TRUCKEE RIVER WALK

CALIFORNIA AVE.

IDLEWILD DR.

MARSH AVE

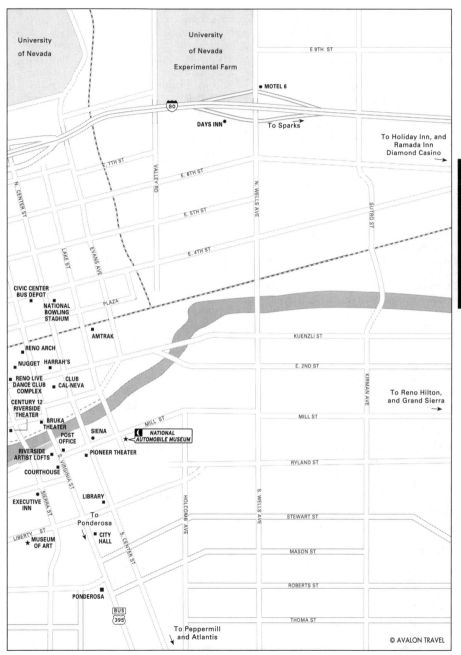

stadium. Striking design features include a 56-foot marble and glass atrium dominated by a life-size bronze of a 1940s family rushing to a bowling alley. The building's design allows it to be used for conferences, parties, and other functions, and the bowling ball–shaped top-floor I-Werks theater treats up to 172 people to epic 50-foot images and digital sound. The $35 million stadium also hosts a restaurant, gift shop, and a Reno information center.

RENO-TAHOE GAMING ACADEMY

For a couple of hours and a few bucks, you can acclimate yourself to all those confusing casino games without the embarrassment and mistakes common to novices. The Reno-Tahoe Gaming Academy (3702 S. Virginia St., Suite H-2, 775/329-5665) is the oldest dealer school in the country, training northern Nevada's next generation of casino professionals. The academy offers classes for careers in the pit: 21, craps, mini baccarat, roulette, poker, and *pai gow* poker, plus pit supervisor and bartender courses, with classes all year round. It can take students as long as six months before they achieve a level of game mastery high enough venture onto the casino floor to deal to real players for real money. The student dealers receive intensive training and practice against each other until they are proficient enough to deal to visitors who pay for the lessons and a behind-the-scenes gaming tour. You probably won't learn optimum strategy, and the academy won't teach you to count cards, but you will learn the etiquette, rules, and customs of the games. The tour of the academy includes a fine display of antique gaming equipment and memorabilia, some of it available for sale. The classes and the gaming tour are by appointment only.

NEWLAND HEIGHTS

The lucky, the ruthless, and the professionals and merchants who "mined the miners" to prosper from the Comstock Lode silver boom in Tonopah and Goldfield treated themselves to the spoils of their victories with mansions in Reno and San Francisco. The Reno nouveaux riches congregated just after the turn of the century on a bluff overlooking the Truckee River just outside downtown. Frederic DeLongchamps, Nevada's most famous architect, designed many of the homes in this historic district, which you can reach by crossing the river at the Sierra Street Bridge and turning right on Court Street.

The house at 247 Court Street, at the corner of Arlington Avenue, is one of the oldest in the district, built in 1907 for the Frisch family. Roy Frisch was a cashier in a bank who agreed to testify against two men accused of federal mail fraud in the 1930s. Frisch disappeared before the trial and was never seen again. The houses at 401, 421, 435, 457, 491, and 514 Court Street are all at least 100 years old.

The Queen Anne house at 617 Court Street, completed in 1890, was once the office of Francis Newlands, the powerful U.S. senator from Nevada at the turn of the 20th century; 7 Elm Court was the Newlands's house. The house at 4 Elm Court was built by DeLongchamps for use as a honeymoon cottage.

Follow Lee Avenue and Ridge Street around to California Avenue and turn right to find the house at 631 California Avenue, built in 1906 for U.S. senator George S. Nixon after his move to Reno from Winnemucca. The house at 825 California Avenue was designed by DeLongchamps for Mrs. William Johnson, Newlands's daughter and the granddaughter of William Sharon, a Comstock Lode mogul and another U.S. senator.

Other houses in the neighborhood are good examples of colonial revival, French château, and Spanish colonial revival styles built in the second quarter of the 20th century.

DOWNTOWN PARKS

Surrounding Wingfield Park, the island in the middle of the Truckee River on both riverbanks is **Riverside Park,** three acres of grass with a playground and tennis and basketball courts. It's a good place to stroll from downtown day or night to clear your head of all gaming.

Continue west along the north side of the river (or drive out along Riverside Drive and follow the signs) to **Idlewild Park.** Just under a mile from downtown, this park, originally developed for the Transcontinental Highway

RENO IN SONG

Reno's unique history as a frontier town, a Wild West outpost, the original Sin City, and a haven for renegades has been chronicled in songs made famous by everyone from Woody Guthrie to R.E.M. Country and folk seem to be the genres of choice for singers and songwriters setting their musical tales in the Biggest Little City.

Reno's booming divorce trade got the Guthrie treatment. He penned "Reno Blues" in 1937. Rose Maddox recorded it under the title "Philadelphia Lawyer." It tells of the title character's efforts to steal another man's wife:

Way out in Reno, Nevada
Where romance blooms and fades
A great Philadelphia lawyer
Was in love with a Hollywood maid.
"Come, love, and we will wander
Down where the lights are bright.
I'll win you a divorce from your husband,
And we can get married tonight."

The husband, Wild Bill, isn't keen on the idea, and when he gets wind of the scheme, it turns out badly for the attorney:

Now back in old Pennsylvania
Among those beautiful pines
There's one less Philadelphia lawyer
In old Philadelphia tonight.

Johnny Cash uses Reno in one of his most popular songs, tabbing the Nevada city as the site of his downfall in "Folsom Prison Blues." The Man in Black was sent up the river after ignoring his mother's plea:

When I was just a baby, my mother told me, "Son,
Always be a good boy; don't ever play with guns."
But I shot a man in Reno, just to watch him die.

Reno is the first city mentioned in the "sing-ing" part of the American version of "I've Been Everywhere," originally recorded by Hank Snow and covered by a who's who of country artists: Lynn Anderson, Asleep at the Wheel, Johnny Cash, Willie Nelson, and a dozen more. Incidentally, the song's introduction mentions another Nevada town: "I was totin' my pack along the dusty Winnemucca Road . . . "

Other bands that have found Reno the perfect setting for their tunes include R.E.M. ("All the Way to Reno"), Tom Waits ("Virginia Avenue" mentions the closing of the famous Harold's Club), Rocky Votolato ("Wrong Side of Reno"), and even the Grateful Dead ("Friend of the Devil" includes the line "I set out from Reno / I was trailed by 20 hounds"). Bruce Springsteen's "Reno" is an R-rated story of an encounter with a prostitute, and Doug Supernaw's "Reno" laments his bad luck at the gambling tables:

Couldn't roll me a seven
If you gave me loaded dice
I couldn't draw a hand
If I sat here all night
Scared money bad whiskey
There ain't no way to win
This ain't the first time
It's the way it's always been
You know the Lady's a lot like Reno
She ain't got a heart

Eddie Arnold's 1971 recording of "Roses to Reno" bemoans a different kind of loss:

Send some roses to Reno
Maybe it's not too late
If the roses reach Reno
Maybe baby will wait
Baby's gone, she's out of sight
It all happened over night
But I long, I should have stayed
And that was yesterday
Before I'd found
Baby's Reno bound

RENO

Exposition in 1927, is one of the oldest and prettiest city parks in the state. It boasts a large duck pond and outdoor swimming pool, picnic pavilions, baseball fields, volleyball courts, a playground, stately old trees, a rose garden, and Peter Toth's Nevada sculpture, *53rd Whispering Giant,* looking down from 30 feet to share a special secret with each visitor. The kiddies' amusement park opens daily at 11 A.M. May–Labor Day, weekends and holidays (weather permitting) the rest of the year. The rides are perfect for preschoolers: a merry-go-round, kiddie train, and more.

◖ NATIONAL AUTOMOBILE MUSEUM

Even the building that houses the National Automobile Museum (10 S. Lake St., 775/333-9300, 9:30 A.M.–5:30 P.M. Mon.–Sat., 10 A.M.–4 P.M. Sun., $10 adults, $8 seniors, $4 ages 6–18, free under age 5) is clad in tinted glass, sleek metallic styling, and glittering chrome. The wide hallways are decked out as streetscape vignettes depicting 100 years of car culture. The first gallery shows the transition from horse to horseless carriage. Another "street" shows the advent of the muscle car. Also among the museum's displays are a Cadillac owned by Elvis Presley and the Mercury driven by James Dean in the film *Rebel Without a Cause.* A 22-minute multimedia presentation shows cars rolling on and off the screen while video screens project special effects.

The collection is just a small percentage of the 1,000 or so cars amassed by casino mogul William Fisk Harrah. After Harrah died and his company was sold, the new owners auctioned off nearly 75 percent of the cars, many of which were bought by Ralph Engelstad, owner of the Imperial Palace in Las Vegas, and displayed in the auto collection there. The remainder was donated to the museum foundation.

A research library houses one of the most extensive collections of literature covering the development of the automobile in the world, including paint chips, photographs, owners manuals, and even wiring diagrams.

A café with hot dogs, burgers, soup, salad, and drinks and a gift shop stocked with models, wooden toys, car-related books, T-shirts, knickknacks, cups, chocolates, road signs, and more make the visit complete.

NEVADA MUSEUM OF ART

The Nevada Museum of Art (160 W. Liberty St., 775/329-3333, www.nevadamuseumofart.org, 10 A.M.–5 P.M. Wed. and Fri.–Sun., 10 A.M.–8 P.M. Thurs., $10 adults, $8 seniors and students, $1 ages 6–12) exhibits its 2,000-piece permanent collection in five focus areas, all dealing with the natural, constructed, and surreal environment. Each focus area contains works from the 18th century through the present without regard to artist, style, or period. Feature exhibits focus on the works of American and international artists, and new artists are featured every few months.

The gallery's home, designed by Will Bruder, whose Frank Lloyd Wright inspiration is evident from the first glimpse of the building, features stark white walls and a black torqued-wall exterior reminiscent of Nevada's Black Rock Desert. With a mission to "cultivate meaningful art and social experiences, and foster new knowledge in the visual arts by encouraging interdisciplinary investigation," the gallery is one of the best small art museums in the country.

The museum store sells books, posters, prints, art magnets, jewelry, cards, pottery, T-shirts, and some sculpture. And Café Musée is open for light and, of course, artistic lunches.

NEVADA STATE HISTORICAL SOCIETY MUSEUM

Nevada's oldest and perhaps best museum, the State Historical Society Museum (1650 N. Virginia St., 775/687-1190, 10 A.M.–5 P.M. Wed.–Sat., $4 age 18 and over, free under age 18) resides at the north end of the University of Nevada, Reno, campus. The museum is dedicated to collecting and preserving Nevada's past, from prehistory through the frontier and Comstock Lode era to its modern position as a resort destination. The permanent collection includes such diverse and provocative items as mining artifacts, Native

American baskets, slot machine cheating devices, and showgirl costumes.

Temporary exhibitions complement the collection and often celebrate eras or events from Nevada's past. A recent temporary exhibit revisited the centennial of the Jack Johnson–James Jeffries fight in Reno and its impact on race relations. Other exhibits have traced the influence of national policies, trends, institutions, and issues—the New Deal and the Red Cross, for example—on the state's development.

If you want to learn more about specific events in Nevada's past, there's sure to be a book about it in the museum's well-stocked gift shop, and the adjoining research department (noon–4 P.M. Wed.–Sat.) houses a huge collection of historical black-and-white photographs, books, manuscripts, diaries, brochures, pamphlets, newspapers, maps, directories, death and census records, and more. It is open to the public, in case you want to track down that long-lost Nevada ancestor to complete your family tree.

◖ FLEISCHMANN PLANETARIUM AND SCIENCE CENTER

Next door to the Historical Society Museum, the Fleischmann Planetarium (1650 N. Virginia St., 775/784-4811, www.planetarium.unr.nevada.edu) presents not only out-of-this-world star shows and public stargazing in the observatory but also large-format documentaries and other educational films in its domed theater. Built in 1964, the planetarium is shaped like a hyperbolic parabola (think the upper half of a floppy flying saucer) and is listed on the National Register of Historic Places. Get lost in space among the thought-provoking exhibits: a black hole simulator, globes of the earth and moon, a clouds display, and a collection of meteorites found in Nevada and elsewhere, one weighing more than a ton. Stick a nickel in the gravity well and play (gently) with the instruments in the gift shop. Admission to the main building (hours vary) is free. The star shows and large-format features (noon–4 P.M. Fri. and Mon.–Tues., noon–7 P.M. Sat.–Sun., $6 adults, $4 seniors and children) alternate on the hour.

W. M. KECK MUSEUM

North of the quad on the University of Nevada, Reno, campus is the Mackay Mining School, home to the W. M. Keck Museum (1664 N. Virginia St., 775/784-4528, www.mines.unr.edu/museum, 9 A.M.–4 P.M. Mon.–Fri., free). Out front is a statue of the famous and generous miner John Mackay, who became Bonanza King of the Comstock Lode and later endowed the university. The statue was sculptured by Gutzon Borglum of Mount Rushmore fame. In Borglum's depiction, Mackay holds a pile of mineral-rich Nevada earth and a miner's pick, symbolizing industry and ambition. The building, originally constructed in 1908, now rests an eighth of an inch off the ground on 66 high-tech rubber bearings and 43 Teflon slider plates to make it virtually earthquake-proof.

The museum entrance is on the first floor of the building, where you can see all the gold, silver, copper, lead, uranium, turquoise, gypsum, borax, and other minerals Nevada is famous for. Historic black-and-white photos of many mining boomtowns grace the walls, and Mackay's own vault houses two dozen rocks from the Comstock Lode itself. Upstairs on the mezzanine is a geological breakdown of minerals and some fossils from around the world, plus mining tools, machines, scales, and diagrams.

◖ WILBUR D. MAY MUSEUM AND ARBORETUM

The Wilbur D. May Museum and Arboretum (1595 N. Sierra St., at the south end of Rancho San Rafael Park, 775/785-5961, www.maycenter.com, hours vary by exhibit, $8 adults, $5 children and seniors) carries on the department store magnate, aesthete, and philanthropist' commitment to charity and education. May overcame physical challenges to become a pilot, adventurer, and financial genius (he sold his investments just before the 1929 stock market crash, and then bought them back at fire-sale prices after Black Monday). A true Renaissance man, his song, "Pass a Piece of Pizza, Please" sold 100,000 copies.

And as this gem of a museum amply illustrates, May not only had money, he had excellent taste; he collected treasures during more than 40 trips around the world. Tour the replicated tack room, living room, trophy room, and bedroom of the ranch house May lived in on a 2,600-acre spread outside of Reno. Watch the 20-minute video about his life, which has great travel and wildlife footage. Notice his passports, a spine-chilling shrunken head, and weavings, glass, silver, tribal masks, and ivory from all corners of the globe.

Visitors can relax at the indoor arboretum, with its koi ponds and waterfall. Ask at the desk for the attractive brochure with the layout of the arboretum out back and wander through the large variety of gardens dedicated to energy conservation, xeriscaping, songbirds, fragrances, rocks, the desert, roses, and many others.

Sadly, the adjacent Great Basin Adventure historical theme park has closed, a victim of Nevada's crushing budget deficit.

OXBOW NATURE STUDY AREA

Head west on 2nd Street and bear left on Dickerson Road just before the railroad underpass about two miles west of town. Just when you think the landscape can't get any more urban, the warehouses and body shops part to reveal this most unusual city park (3100 Dickerson Rd., 775/334-3808, sunrise–sunset daily). Take the nature trail that parallels the Truckee River, and make sure you take the time to peruse the interpretive signs and park brochure. Both are chock-full of interesting tidbits about the ecology of the area. But walk softly so you don't disturb the deer, coyotes, frogs, snakes, beavers, muskrat, waterfowl, and other animals. The trail is wheelchair accessible and an easy hike.

An oxbow is a river channel that has been diverted from the main flow by sediment deposits. This 30-acre park along the Truckee River encompasses a large oxbow area. A flood on New Year's Day 1997 completely changed the face of the park, and it took three years to rebuild. The park naturalist says the redesigned park is even better than it was before, with a half-mile boardwalk interpretive trail winding

through 18 acres of interesting features that include ponds and marshes and a large deck right out over the river, which is great for bird-watching. Grasses, sedges, tules, cattails, wild roses, alders, and cottonwoods dominate the riparian ecosystem.

Feathers really fly in the park early May–late July, when 150 species of migratory birds arrive here to nest and rear their young; this park is a wetlands habitat for nesting on the Pacific flyway. Hummingbirds are usually the last to leave, in August.

You can spend several enjoyable and relaxing hours walking the interpretive trail, eating lunch at the park benches and picnic tables strategically placed throughout the park.

SIERRA SAFARI ZOO

North of Reno on U.S. 395 is the Sierra Safari Zoo (10200 N. Virginia St., 775/677-1101, www.sierrasafarizoo.org., 10 A.M.–5 P.M. daily, weather permitting, Apr.–Oct., $7 adults, $6 children and seniors, free under age 3), Nevada's largest self-supporting wild-animal attraction. It as much a sad statement on the Las Vegas zoo as it is an inspiring tale of survival for Sierra Safari. More than 200 animals of more than 40 species call the zoo home, including sloths, lemurs, wallabies, zebras, monkeys, lions, and tigers. Visitors can mingle with the tamer species, and most of the animals, including the big cats, have been hand-raised from birth.

To get to the zoo, drive eight miles north of Reno on U.S. 395 to exit 76 (Stead Blvd.). Turn left onto Stead Boulevard, then right onto North Virginia Street for 1.5 miles.

ANIMAL ARK

Not far away, Aaron and Diana Hiibel care for nonreleasable wildlife on 38 acres at Animal Ark (1265 Deerlodge Rd., 775/970-3111, 10 A.M.–4:30 P.M. Tues.–Sun. Apr.–Oct., $8 adults, $6 seniors and children). The Hiibels provide the infirm or orphaned creatures permanent care in captivity in as natural a setting as possible. Their presence also gives visitors a rare glimpse into the lives of exotic

At Animal Ark, orphaned and injured creatures receive permanent care in natural settings, offering glimpses into the lives of exotic cats, raptors, monkeys, wolves, and more.

cats, raptors, monkeys, and wolves, creating a bridge between humans and animals by increasing appreciation of the natural world. Different animals are featured during special events and educational lectures at Animal Ark. "Howl Nights" celebrate the wolves' mournful baying and reward the best human imitations.

Cheetah Runs let the cats show off their 45 mph speed.

To get there, take U.S. 395 north to exit 78 (Red Rock Rd.), turn right on Red Rock Road, drive 11.2 miles to Deerlodge Road, take a right, and go 1 mile; Animal Ark is on the right.

Sports and Recreation

Reno is a fantastic recreation destination for winter as well as warm-weather sports and activities. It's a great biking town and has close access to some of the best skiing in the country. It also has some surprises—ballooning, for instance, is a popular noncasino attraction. There's plenty to keep kids entertained, as well, with amusement parks and carnival midways close at hand.

WINTER SPORTS

While several world-class alpine resorts are only a few hours away at Lake Tahoe, a few are just an hour or less from Reno. **Mount Rose–Ski Tahoe** (22222 Mt. Rose Hwy., 775/849-0704 or 800/SKI-ROSE—800/754-7673, www.mtrose.com) is the closest, 22 miles from Reno on Highway 431, with 1,000 skiable acres. It boasts the region's highest base elevation (8,260 feet) and summit elevation (9,700 feet) with five lifts to serve 43 runs and trails. Its runs are rated for every skill level, and there are beginner, intermediate, and advanced trails. Snowboarders are welcome, and you can rent equipment and take classes at the

WORLD'S FASTEST SPORT

Is the Indianapolis 500 too pedestrian for your tastes? Do you think Kyle Busch should stop being so timid? The **Reno National Championship Air Races** (775/972-6663, www.airrace.org) is NASCAR with wings – if stock cars could reach 500 mph. Piloting their craft wingtip-to-wingtip as low as 50 feet off the ground, the racers at the Reno Air Races make *Top Gun* aviators look like first-time soloists.

For nearly 50 years, pilots and their biplanes, kit-built aircraft, and jets have gathered each September to embrace the challenge of the oval courses at Reno Stead Airport, just north of the city. Six classes of racing aircraft reach speeds of "only" 250 mph in the biplane and Formula One classes,

and up to 500 mph in the unlimited class populated by modified Mustangs, Bearcats, and other World War II fighter planes. The slower classes race on three-mile courses, while the courses for the faster aircraft are as long as eight miles per lap. Races are generally 5-10 laps long.

The promoters present a first-class air show, military aircraft displays, and food and souvenir vendors in conjunction with the races. Aerobatics, skydiving demonstrations, and the Snowbirds – the Royal Canadian Air Force's answer to the U.S. Air Force's Thunderbirds – are among the recent air show performers. Demonstrations, qualifications, and competitions run about 8 A.M.-dusk. RV parking is available.

ski school. Shuttles are available daily from several of Reno's larger hotels and casinos. In addition to lodging and shopping, you can buy ski packages, season passes, and family plans. Call for pickup times, ski conditions, road conditions, and more.

If Nordic is more your style, cross-country trails abound, although most resorts are around Lake Tahoe.

The city develops a section of the Truckee River each winter for an ice skating **Rink on the River.** The location varies a little each year, depending on water and ice conditions, but it's almost always within a stone's throw of Idlewild Park. The rink is generally open weekday evenings and all day on weekends; the cost is $7 adults and $5 ages 3–12 and over age 55. Skate rental and season passes are available.

BIKING AND HIKING

Truckee River Bike Path is a paved cycling, jogging, and walking trail nearly as long as Truckee Meadows and running right along the river most of the way. It's roughly 12 miles long, running from the eastern edge of Sparks (near the Vista Blvd. exit on I-80) through

Rock Park (near the west edge of Sparks), Galetti Park (in east Reno), Idlewild Park (in central Reno), and finally to the Mayberry area (at Caughlin Ranch in west Reno). It's an idyllic chain of parks linked by the murmuring river that snakes through the middle of the city. The widening of U.S. 395, which detoured cyclists and pedestrians out of Fisherman's Park II along city streets to Fisherman's Park I, was scheduled to be completed by spring 2011.

The most popular biking hill climb is to the top of **Geiger Grade** on Highway 341 to Virginia City; it's a killer. Cyclists also work out on McCarran Boulevard between West 4th Street and Skyline Boulevard, although it's somewhat narrow. The streets of Reno-Sparks are in pretty good shape, but mountain bikes are preferred around town for their fat and cushiony tires.

Sierra Adventures (775/323-5698 or 866/323-8928, www.wildsierra.com) is one of a few outfitters in Reno that organize mountain biking tours in addition to renting bicycles. One of the best rides is down Peavine Mountain through wild horse and deer habitat and Nevada desert scrub. Other places in Reno that rent bicycles include **Sundance Bike Rental** (345 N. Arlington Ave. at 3rd St., 775/786-0222), downtown at the Sands Regency Hotel; and **Snowind Sports** (2500 E. 2nd St., 775/323-9463) at the Reno Hilton.

Huffaker Hills Trailhead, southeast of the airport just off McCarran Boulevard, is perfect for the novice hiker. Easy and moderate trails lead to elevations that command panoramic views of the valley: the Reno skyline, Sparks, Peavine Mountain, and more.

BALLOONING

One of the most popular Reno events of the year is the **Great Reno Balloon Race,** which takes place in September. More than 100 balloons take to the atmosphere from Rancho San Rafael Park starting very early in the morning. To go up in a balloon at other times of the year, call **Sierra Adventures** (775/323-8928 or 866/323-8928) or **Soaring Adventures of America** (800/762-7464). It is an experience unlike anything you've done before, but it's only for early risers. The balloons take off around 8 A.M. in the winter and as early as 6:30 A.M. in the summer to avoid being caught in warm thermals as the air heats up. The balloons float 500–1,000 feet up, somewhere between the trees and the clouds, for about three hours.

SWIMMING

Reno has two indoor and two outdoor public pools. The **Northwest Pool** (2925 Apollo Way, 775/334-2203) has eight 25-yard indoor lanes. The other indoor facility is in the **Evelyn Mount Community Center** (1301 Valley Rd., 775/334-2262), with four lanes in 3–5-foot water. Both outdoor pools, open seasonally, have eight lanes of water up to 10 feet deep: **Idlewild Pool** (1805 Idlewild Dr., 775/334-2267) also has diving boards, a water polo area, and 50-meter lanes. **Traner Pool** (1600 Carville Dr., behind Washoe County Fairgrounds, 775/334-2269) has a double-flume water slide. Public lap

RENO

COURTESY OF NEVADA COMMISSION ON TOURISM

The Great Reno Balloon Race each September is one of the city's favorite events.

swimming sessions are about $5 adults, $3 ages 6–17, and $2 for seniors and children under 6.

Sparks's **Alf Sorenson Community Center** (1400 Baring Blvd., 775/353-2385, $6 adults, $4 seniors, $3.50 children under 18) has an indoor pool as well.

FISHING

Northern and central Nevada streams are some of the best trout waters in the country. The Truckee River gives up good-size browns, especially in mid- and late spring, along with cutthroats and stocked rainbows throughout the cooler months. The quantity and diversity of the fish, the variety of habitat, and the ease of access to the river all make the Truckee a great all-around fishing destination. Not far away, the forks of the Carson and Walker Rivers are also good bets.

Idlewild Park has bluegill; Virginia Lake has brown trout, and its fishing dock is one of the more easily accessed by people with disabilities. The fishing pier at Sparks Marina Park is also accessible, and the 77-acre lake is stocked with rainbow trout.

Nevada fishing licenses are available at most sporting goods stores or at the Nevada Department of Wildlife website (www.ndow.org). Check the website for statewide and local regulations regarding catch-and-release, legal bait and tackle, and more. The site also has a reliable fishing report updated weekly. The **Reno Fly Shop** (294 E. Moana Lane, Suite 14, 775/825-FISH—775/825-3474, http://renoflyshop.com) has a top-notch guide service, rental equipment, and the latest advice on what's catching.

HORSEBACK RIDING

Rancho Red Rock (15670 Red Rock Rd., 30 miles north of Reno, 775/969-3315, www.ranchredrock.com) is open all year, weather permitting. It arranges trail rides and offers riding lessons and pony rides. **Sierra Adventures** (407 N. Virginia St., 866/323-8928, www.wildsierra.com) at the Silver Legacy leads one-day and two-day excursions into the Nevada backcountry.

GOLF

The Reno area is golf heaven, with 50 courses within a 90-minute drive of downtown. The Reno-Sparks area has more than a dozen courses, with another dozen courses just to the south in the Carson Valley. Several challenging courses designed by the some of the game's legends can be played for less than $50, even at near-peak times, and offer great 19th hole restaurants and other resort amenities. **Wolf Run Golf Club** (1400 Wolf Run Rd., 775/851-3301, www.wolfrungolfclub.com) is the University of Nevada, Reno, home course. **ArrowCreek Country Club** (2905 ArrowCreek Pkwy., 775/850-4653) has courses designed by Arnold Palmer and Fuzzy Zoeller. The course along with the entire **Resort at Red Hawk** (6590 N. Wingfield Pkwy., Sparks, 775/626-1000, www.resortatredhawk.com) are the brainchild of Robert Trent Jones, so you know it has been designed for the serious player. It's worth the trip just to stock up in the huge—and very cool—pro shop.

© RYAN JERZ

Mountain, city, and desert views make ArrowCreek Country Club one of the most beautiful courses in the Reno area.

Budget players can rejoice as well. Many of the area's courses are quite playable with greens fees of less than $25. The walkable course at **Sierra Sage Golf Course** (6355 Silverlake Blvd., 775/972-1564, http://sierras-agegolf.org) is less than $1 per hole most days. **Washoe County Golf Course** (2601 Foley Way, 775/827-6640, www.washoegolf.org, about $22) opened as a private country club in 1917 and is now a public course.

Information on golf courses and golf packages is available from area visitors centers and chambers of commerce, including the Reno-Sparks Convention and Visitors Authority (800/FOR-RENO—800/367-7366, www.visitreno-laketahoe.com).

RIDES AND GAMES

Ultimate Rush (2500 E. 2nd St., 775/786-7005, noon–10 P.M. daily year-round, $25 per jump) operates bungee jumping from its 180-foot tower in front of the Grand Sierra Resort. The tamer **Attractions** at the resort cost much less.

The **Wild Island Family Adventure Park** (250 Wild Island Court, 775/359-2927, www.wildisland.com, 11 A.M.–7 P.M. daily summer, $25.50 for 48 inches tall and over, $20.50 under 48 inches) has slides, pools, waves, and all-around splashing fun during the summer season. There's also a bowling alley, go-karts, a kids play area, an arcade, and a fun center. Inner tubes, golf, go-karts, the pool, and bowling cost extra.

SPECTATOR SPORTS

No longer a bush-league city, Reno fielded its first Triple-A baseball team in 2009 when the **Reno Aces** (http://web.minorleaguebaseball.com), the top farm club of the Arizona Diamondbacks, moved into the 9,100-seat Aces Ballpark (250 Evans Ave.) in the

RENO

SEVERAL BLOWS FOR EQUALITY

A couple of weeks before the new heavyweight champion of the world was scheduled to meet the undefeated former champion in San Francisco, Governor James Gillett of California bowed to political pressure to stop the bout. Claiming the fight would "demoralize the youth of the state, corrupt public morals, and offend senses of the great majority," Gillett pulled the plug on the July 4, 1910, bout.

San Francisco's loss was Reno's gain. Champion Jack Johnson battered Jim Jeffries through 15 rounds and struck a blow against racism while retaining the championship belt. Jeffries had come out of retirement specifically aiming not only to defeat Johnson in "The Battle of the Century" but also to teach the "uppity" African American man a lesson. The racist sporting public didn't accept Johnson as the heavyweight titlist because the son of a slave won it by beating a lackluster champion rather than the true champ, Jeffries. "I am going into this fight for the sole purpose of proving that a white man is better than a Negro," Jeffries declared, earning the sobriquet "The Great White Hope." The bigoted public and the ex-champ apparently had forgotten that Jeffries refused several chances to take on Johnson in prior years, choosing to retire undefeated when he couldn't duck the contender any longer.

Johnson incurred the wrath of racist sports fans by dating white women (he eventually married two of them), moving into an upscale white Chicago neighborhood, and challenging notions of racially based intellectual inferiority by demonstrating striking abilities as a writer, artist, performer, and inventor.

More than 20,000 spectators crowded the custom-built ring in downtown Reno, fortifying themselves with copious amounts of beer and spirits, hurling epitaphs at Johnson, and cheering Jeffries. The raucous anticipation dissipated quickly as Johnson wasted no time in establishing his dominance. Jeffries hit the canvas for the first two times in his career, and he almost certainly would have felt the humiliation of a knockout blow had his corner not thrown in the towel after 15 rounds.

riverfront Freight District for the Pacific Coast League season, which runs early April–early September; tickets run $6–23.

The **Reno Bighorns** (www.nba.com/dleague/reno) are the NBA D-League affiliates of the Orlando Magic and Sacramento Kings. The season runs November–April, and the 25-game home schedule is played at the 7,100-seat Reno Events Center (400 N. Center St.); tickets start at $10.

The nonprofit Reno Rodeo Foundation hosts the Professional Rodeo Cowboys Association–sanctioned **Reno Rodeo** (1350 N. Wells Ave., 775/329-3877) each June, with proceeds benefitting local educational outreach, children's charities, and high school rodeo programs. The 10-day rodeo features a carnival, a cattle drive reenactment, and a Western apparel trade show.

The **University of Nevada, Reno,** fields teams in 17 sports, and joined the Mountain West Conference in 2011. The Wolfpack football team has earned a bowl berth for six straight seasons. The team plays its home games at Mackay Stadium (17th St. and E. Stadium Way, tickets 775/347-7225) on campus. The men's basketball team plays at the Lawler Events Center (1500 N. Virginia St., tickets 775/784-4444) on campus and has qualified for postseason tournaments every year since the 2005–2006 season.

Reno's impressive **National Bowling Stadium** (300 N. Center St., 775/335-8870 or 800/304-2695, www.visitrenotahoe.com/meetings-conventions/facilities/national-bowling-stadium/tournament-calendar) hosts junior, teen, college, international, and professional tournaments throughout the year, including U.S. Bowling Congress–sanctioned events. Stead Airport, north of the city, hosts the **Reno Air Races** (775/972-6663, www.airrace.org) each September.

Shopping

Reno has been selling stuff to visitors since before the Civil War. Once Charles Fuller's bridge brought travelers through the area on their way to and from Virginia City, it didn't take long for merchants to set up, providing food, forage, and supplies for migrants and their livestock. The vendors tradition continues today with eclectic boutiques, massive malls, art and antique treasures, and, of course, trendy shops in every casino.

RIVERWALK DISTRICT

The pride of the city fathers, Riverwalk is a window shopper's paradise. Forty shops—mostly catering to the smart, chic, urban professional—line the shady riverbank. Start at Arlington Avenue and 1st Street, north of the river, roughly the walk's western terminus. Check out **LaBussola and Center Gallery** (254 W. 1st St., 775/348-8858) and **Sasha's Boutique** (250 W. 1st St.), and don't miss **La Terre Verte** (100 N. Arlington Ave., 775/284-5006), which sells jewelry created from reclaimed glass, purses with pull-tab accents, and other environmentally friendly fashion accessories. Take time to experience the theaters, saloons, galleries, and interesting architecture along 1st Street and its cross streets as you make your way east. Pause to peruse at **Dharma Books** (11 N. Sierra St., 775/786-8667, 10 A.M.–4 P.M. Tues.–Wed. and Fri.–Sat., 10 A.M.–5:30 P.M. Thurs., noon–5 P.M. Sat.–Sun.), the best used bookseller in town. It's cramped and a bit musty, like a bohemian bookshop should be. Head north on Sierra Street to **Antiques & Treasures** (151 N. Sierra St., 775/327-4131, 10 A.M.–6 P.M. daily). This is where your old baseball card collected ended up. Dozens of other dealers have shops here to buy, sell, and haggle over collectible coins, vintage toys, casino detritus, and other relics.

SHOPPING CENTERS

Reno is home to several shopping malls containing the usual complement of shoe, clothing, and jewelry stores. Locals prefer **Meadowood Mall**

(500 Meadowood Mall Circle, off U.S. 395 at McCarran Blvd., 775/827-8450, 10 A.M.–9 P.M. Mon.–Sat., 11 A.M.–6 P.M. Sun.) for its large retailers, ample parking, and cleanliness. Across the road is **Smithridge Plaza** and **Smithridge Center** (5081 S. McCarran Blvd., 775/827-1000), with a mix of national chains, local florists, and dry cleaners. It's also the location of Reno's Trader Joe's, in case you need to stock up on organic veggies or other foods. Other popular strip malls in town include **Southwest Pavilion** (8175 S. Virginia St., 775/851-3666) and **Shopper's Square** (370 Casazza Dr., 775/323-0430).

The Summit (13925 S. Virginia St., 775/853-7800, 10 A.M.–9 P.M. Mon.–Sat., 11 A.M.–6 P.M. Sun.), at Reno's southern tip, is an upscale outdoor plaza with lots of open spaces with fountains, fire pits, and summer musical performances.

Sparks's **Legends at Sparks Marina** (1310 Scheels Dr., 775/357-3800, 10 A.M.–9 P.M. Mon.–Sat., 11 A.M.–6 P.M. Sun.), built in 2009, is a bargain hunters' must-see, with outlets of some of the nation's top sellers, including Ann Taylor, Banana Republic, and Bose. It's also a mini-museum: Plaques and statues scattered throughout the outdoor mall pay homage to the region's legendary heroes (Mark Twain, Basque shepherds, Sarah Winnemucca, and others) and historical eras (the Pony Express, the silver boom, and railroading). Several restaurants cater to the shopping-weary, the best of which is **Jazz, a Louisiana Kitchen** (775/657-8659, 10 A.M.–9 P.M. Mon.–Sat., 11 A.M.–6 P.M. Sun., $15–30), specializing in, you guessed it, N'awlins-style Cajun and creole cuisine.

BOOKSTORES

Recently celebrating its 25th year in business, **Sundance** (1155 W. 4th St. at Keystone Ave., 775/786-1188, 9 A.M.–9 P.M. Mon.–Fri., 10 A.M.–6 P.M. Sat.–Sun.) is neck-and-neck with **Dharma Books** (11 N. Sierra St., 775/786-8667, 10 A.M.–4 P.M. Tues.–Wed. and Fri.–Sat., 10 A.M.–5:30 P.M. Thurs., noon–5 P.M. Sat.–Sun.) as the community's best locally owned shop, followed closely by **Zephyr Books** (1501 S. Virginia St., 775/322-6657, 10 A.M.–8:30 P.M. Mon.–Sat., 1:30–6 P.M. Sun.).

The chains are represented in Reno too. The **Barnes & Noble** superstore (5555 S. Virginia St., 775/826-8882, 9 A.M.–11 P.M. Mon.–Sat., 9 A.M.–10 P.M. Sun.) has more than 150,000 titles, a newsstand, and a coffee bar; and **Borders** (4995 S. Virginia St., 775/447-9999, 9 A.M.–9 P.M. Sun.–Thurs., 9 A.M.–10 P.M. Fri.–Sat.) is nearby.

RENO

Accommodations

The Reno-Sparks area's 30,000 hotel rooms give visitors a full range of rates, amenities, and locations to choose from. The options become much more limited during the summer high season, on holidays, and during the seemingly continuous special events the city and its resorts sponsor throughout the year. Rooms that can be had for $45 in the middle of the week in January, for example, command triple that rate during Hot August Nights.

Reserving a reasonable room in Reno is somewhat akin to buying an airline ticket. If you book it far enough in advance, you'll get bargain-basement rates; as it gets closer to your travel date, you'll pay a premium. If you decide on the spur of the moment to come for a weekend gambling spree, you'll have to be happy with what you can get. That doesn't mean you'll have to settle for a cramped, dimly lit space in a no-star motel; often it's just the opposite, with the reasonably priced spots snapped up in advance and only top-shelf and top-dollar digs on offer at the last minute. The law of supply and demand rules, with reserved rooms even on a nonevent Friday–Saturday 25 percent higher than the same reservation midweek.

For the sake of safety and convenience, and to ensure there are no nasty surprises on the bill come checkout time, always ask to see the room first, and check it out carefully. Make sure the windows open and lock securely and that the air-conditioning works. Don't forget to ask about telephone use, whether local calls are free and if long-distance access charges are imposed. Be sure to ask if any coupons or coupon books are available, which often include substantial food and show discounts and gambling incentives. Even if you're a once-a-year visitor, it can pay to sign up for casino affinity club or slot club. The points you earn translate to discounts, and club membership puts you on the resort's mailing list for special offers in the future.

Note that the big resort hotels are profiled in the *Casinos* section.

DOWNTOWN

If the plush accommodations at the major resort hotels are something you can live without, downtown motels can give you access to some of the best dining and entertainment the city has to offer, at significant discounts.

There are plenty of motels in the heart of downtown near the casino action. Good choices include the **Easy 8 Motel** (255 W. 5th St., 775/322-4588, $30–50). It is clean and friendly, which isn't always the case with Reno's low-price options.

The quieter area near the Greyhound station is a good intermediate location—near the downtown casinos, but the motels exude a more apartment-like feel. For example, guest rooms at the **Town House Motor Lodge** (303 W. 2nd St., 775/323-1821 or 800/437-5660, $39–105) come with microwaves and fridges. The **El Cortez** (239 W. 2nd St., 775/322-9161, $25–60), like most of the older hotels here, is adequate if not classy. El Cortez and the **Hotel Windsor** (214 West St., 775/323-6171, $40–85) each have parking available in parking lots across the street.

In the same area are the **Showboat Inn** (660 N. Virginia St., 775/786-4032 or 800/647-3960, $35–75) and the newer and sparklingly clean Seasons Inn (495 West St., 775/322-6000 or 800/322-8588, www.seasonsinn.com, $40–120). Other choices include the **Gatekeeper**

Inn (221 W. 5th St., 775/332-1730, $40–125), the **Bonanza Motor Inn** (215 W. 4th St., 775/322-8632 $37–125), and the **Stardust Lodge** (455 N. Arlington Ave., 775/322-5641 or 866/473-5946, $30–85).

OUTSIDE DOWNTOWN

The **Super 8 Reno** (1651 N. Virginia St., 775/329-3464, www.super8.com, $45–65) is next to the University of Nevada's basketball arena. **University Inn** (1001 N. Virginia St., 775/323-0321, opposite the university, $70–180) and the **Capri Motel** (895 N. Virginia St., 775/323-7979, $60–120) are among the best motels on the motel ministrip closer to downtown on Virginia Street, just north of I-80.

Just south of the Truckee River is the clean, utilitarian **Center Lodge** (200 S. Sierra St., 775/329-2101, $45–90). Ask about weekly rates. Much farther south, more removed from the downtown area, is **Quality Inn** (1885 S. Virginia St., 775/329-1001, www.qualityinn. com, $79 and up). **Comfort Inn** (1250 Plumb Lane, 775/682-4444, www.renoairporthotel. com) has rooms starting at $140.

Another ministrip occupies West 4th Street between the river and I-80. Motels here include the **Gold Dust West Casino & Motor Lodge** (444 Vine St., 775/323-2211 or 800/437-9378, www.gdwcasino.com, $39–69), with terrific early-morning breakfast specials. Other top picks include the **Donner Inn** (720 W. 4th St., 775/323-1851, $30–60) and the **Carriage Inn** (690 W. 4th St., 775/329-8848, $59–99).

East of downtown, **Baymont Inn & Suites** (2050 Market St., 775/786-2506 or 877/229-6668, www.baymontinns.com, $50–140) offers homey rooms. **La Quinta Inn** (4001 Market St., 775/347-6100 or 800/531-5900, www.lq.com, $65–160), at U.S. 395 exit 65 (Plumb Lane), has a fine reputation and a family restaurant. Other chain motels near the airport include **Best Western Airport Plaza** (1981 Terminal Way, 775/347-6370 or 800/648-3525, www. airportplazareno.com, $50–140).

The **Wildflower Village** (4300 W. 4th St., 775/827-5250, www.wildflowervillage. com, motel $50–75, B&B suites $100), in the

SCHOOL SPIRIT WRIT LARGE

Those tall whitewashed letters on the hillsides above most of the towns in Nevada – who put them there, and why?

Similar letters are scattered all around the West, but the 38 in Nevada represent the most per capita of any state. Contrary to urban legend, these mountain monograms were not built to help airmail-dropping pilots identify the communities they flew over.

University of California students put the first letter, a C, on a hill overlooking the Berkeley campus in 1905 as an imaginative way to put school spirit ahead of class rivalries. The sentiment found its way to the University of Nevada, Reno, in 1913 when students constructed a huge N on Peavine Mountain above the campus. It consisted of thousands of rocks and hundreds of gallons of whitewash (water and lime) and covered 13,000 square feet. The rage quickly spread to high school students around the state. Elko teens assembled their E in 1916, the Tonopah T went up in 1917, and Carson City (C), Battle Mountain (BM), Virginia City (V), and Panaca (L, for Lincoln County) all had their own letters by 1927. Austin high schoolers finally put up their A in the early 1950s, and Beatty's B dates back to 1971. Other southern Nevada schools are represented as well: Basic, Indian Springs, Boulder City, Eldorado, and Moapa Valley are among those with hillside letters.

Lately, however, liability worries have prevented students from maintaining some of the letters. In places, the task has been taken over by service clubs and alumni groups. In fact, the SV above Smith Valley has gone high-tech and is now kept bright with an air sprayer powered by a portable generator. It'll take more than insurance premiums to jeopardize Nevada's 85-year tradition of sweater letters on hillsides.

middle of an artists' enclave, offers a refreshing respite from clanging slot machines or a welcome bit of pampering following sweaty hikes in the Truckee Valley. Rock yourself to drowsiness on the porch with a river view, then wake to the aroma of a gourmet champagne breakfast delivered to your door (included with suite rental). Nearby galleries offer showings along with watercolor and pottery lessons.

CAMPING AND RV PARKS

If your idea of camping means tents and sleeping bags, you'll need to travel 20 miles or so beyond the city's concrete. Once you're beyond the glow of neon, plenty of options are available. By far the best spot to pitch your tent is at **Davis Creek Park** (Washoe Valley, 19 miles south of Reno on U.S. 395, 775/849-0684, $20), a Washoe County facility with 62 rustic sites dotting the perimeter of a small pond. On the road to the state capital is **Washoe Lake State Park** (4855 E. Lake Blvd., Carson City, 775/687-4319, $17). A boat launch and fishing docks provide access to fun on the water. **Lookout Campground** (Road 570, $6) is 18 miles northwest of Reno beyond Verdi in Dog Valley, California, near rockhounding areas.

If your idea of roughing it does not include communing too closely with nature or being too far from free Wi-Fi, **Chism's Trailer Park** (1300 W. 2nd St., 775/322-2281 or 800/637-2281, www.chismtrailerpark.com, $26) is a good bet. Near Idlewild Park and bordered by the Truckee River, the park has 124 permanent spaces and 28 RV spaces. The oldest private campground in Nevada, Chism's opened in 1926, and it's the closest place to downtown to set up camp. Towering elm trees and lush landscaping provide relief from the midday heat. There are full hookups, and six sites are pull-throughs. Tents are allowed. Accessible restrooms have flush toilets and hot showers; public phones, sewage disposal, and laundry are available.

Like everything else at the resort, the RV park at the **Grand Sierra** (2500 E. 2nd St., $35–39) is one of the largest in the area. It's mostly concrete, but a handful of the 178 pads, plenty of which are pull-throughs, overlook the river or the driving-range lake. Accessible clean restrooms have flush toilets and hot showers; sewage disposal, laundry, groceries, video rentals, and a heated swimming pool are available. Guests have the full run of the resort's amenities.

Reno RV Park (735 Mill St., 775/323-3381 or 800/445-3381, www.renorvpark.com, $30) has 46 spaces in two narrow alleys; all are back-in sites. It's close to downtown Reno in an older part of town, with hospitals, medical offices, and the police station nearby. Security is strong, with security cameras, a high wall, and gates to get in and out. Tent camping is not allowed. Accessible restrooms have flush toilets and hot showers; public phones, sewage disposal, and laundry are available. Good Sam and AAA discounts are offered, as are more economical weekly and monthly rates.

Keystone RV Park (1455 W. 4th St., 775/324-5000 or 800/686-8559, www.keystonervpark.com, $25 for 2 people) is a 104-space parking-lot facility with a few trees and a little grass on the western edge of the downtown business district. The casinos are about eight blocks away, so the Keystone fills up fast for the nonstop events Memorial Day–Labor Day. Tents are not allowed. Accessible restrooms have flush toilets and hot showers; sewage disposal and laundry are available. Good Sam discounts offered.

Shamrock RV Park (260 Parr Blvd., 775/329-5222 or 800/322-8248, www.shamrockrv.com, $32) dates to 1985, but its pristine pool, immaculate laundry room, and tidy picnic area make it look brand-new. It has 121 pads, 75 of which are pull-throughs, all with full hookups, that sit in a little bowl with earthen walls in an industrial part of town. From I-80, take the Virginia Street exit and go north about two miles, turn right on Parr Boulevard, and drive down the hill; the park is on the right. Tents are not allowed. It's big, all paved, and has trees and shrubs between wide sites. The recreation hall has exercise equipment and a full kitchen. It is two blocks from the small but popular Bonanza Casino. A mile south is Rancho San Rafael Park, the largest park in the urban area, and two miles south of

that is downtown. Accessible restrooms have flush toilets and hot showers; sewage disposal, laundry, groceries, a small playground, and a heated swimming pool are available. Good Sam discounts are offered.

Bonanza Terrace RV Park (4800 Stoltz Rd., 775/329-9624, www.bonanzaterracervpark.com, $34) has 80 spaces. **River's Edge RV Park** (1405 South Rock Blvd., Sparks, 775/357-8533 or 800/621-4792, $36) is an idyllic setting for an RV park, right on the Truckee River, with immediate access to many miles of paved riverside biking and hiking trails. It's lush and well shaded, and it also happens to be right on the eastern landing route for Reno-Tahoe airport, so big commercial airliners fly 300 feet overhead. But if you can stand occasional jet-engine noise, River's Edge is one of the nicest RV parks around. There are 164 spaces for motor homes, all with full hookups; 98 are pull-throughs. Tents are not allowed. Restrooms have flush toilets and hot showers; sewage disposal and laundry are available.

Victorian RV Park (205 Nichols Blvd., off Victorian Ave., Sparks, 775/356-6400 or 800/955-6405, $21) has 92 spaces for motor homes, all with full hookups; 46 are pull-throughs. Tents are not allowed. Accessible restrooms have flush toilets and hot showers; sewage disposal, laundry, groceries, a heated pool, and a spa are available. Good Sam, AAA, and AARP discounts are offered.

Boomtown RV Park (off I-80, Verdi, 775/345-8650 or 877/626-6686, $40 for 2 people) is a large, self-contained KOA-affiliated facility below the casino, with wide spaces, some greenery, and its own pool. You'll never need to ask the time as the Boomtown clock tower is right above it. Inside the casino is the Family Fun Center, featuring a 17-hole indoor miniature golf course, an antique carousel, a motion-simulation theater, and video games galore. There is also a steak house, a buffet, and a 24-hour coffee shop. The RV park has 203 spaces for motor homes, all with full hookups; 132 are pull-throughs. Tents are not allowed. Accessible restrooms have flush toilets and hot showers; sewage disposal, laundry, groceries, video rentals, a heated swimming pool, and two spas are available. Good Sam and AARP discounts are offered.

Bordertown RV Resort (19575 U.S. 395 N., 775/677-0169 or 800/217-9339, $25), near the California state line, has 50 sites. Across the street from the Peppermill Casino is **Silver Sage RV Park** (2760 S. Virginia St., 775/829-1919 or 888/823-2002, www.silversagervpark.

com, about $40). Its 43 spaces include cable, phone, fax, and Internet. **Keystone** (1455 W. 4th St., 775/324-5000 or 888/686-8559, www. keystonervpark.com, $30) is close to the downtown casinos and the Truckee River Walk. **Terrible's Gold Ranch RV Resort** (350 Gold Ranch Rd., Verdi, 775/345-6789 or 877/927-6789, www.goldranchrvcasino.com, $45) is part of the small casino off I-80's exit 2.

Food

RENO

BUFFETS

Nevada's buffets are many things: panaceas for families with finicky eaters, fodder for lounge comedians, and among the tsk-tsk types, examples of the nation's gluttony. The best buffets in Reno are based in the casino resorts, and the noncasino King Buffet is a strong bet for Chinese food.

The Atlantis's **Toucan Charlie's Buffet and Grille** (3800 S. Virginia St., 775/824-4433, 7 A.M.–3 P.M. and 4:30–9 P.M. Sun.–Thurs., 7 A.M.–3 P.M. and 4:30–10 P.M. Fri.–Sat., $11–28) has one lunch and dinner feature that gives it a leg up on its competition: Mongolian barbecue, where your vegetables and meats are stir-fried on a round grill. It also has a specialty salad buffet with Caesar and hot spinach salads made to order, and at breakfast, omelets prepared to your specifications. There's also a varied and very good seafood selection, along with Italian, Asian, Mexican, and Cajun favorites and decadent desserts.

After a $5 million renovation and expansion a few years ago, **The Buffet** (Eldorado, 345 N. Virginia St., 775/786-5700, 7:45 A.M.–2 P.M. and 4–9 P.M. Mon.–Fri., 7:45 A.M.–2 P.M. and 4–10 P.M. Sat., 7:45 A.M.–2 P.M. and 4–9 P.M. Sun., $9–19) has emerged to challenge Atlantis's perennial status as Reno's best. The atmosphere certainly compares favorably, with dark wood columns and high ceilings that make dining with 250 of your fellow travelers seem almost intimate. Another transglobal

journey, The Buffet's ravioli and Asian curry are epic.

At the Grand Sierra, **The Lodge Buffet** (2500 E. 2nd St., 775/789-2000, 7 –10:30 A.M. and 4–9 P.M. Mon.–Fri., 7 A.M.–2 P.M. and 4–10 P.M. Sat. –Sun., $12–25) is spacious and offers foods from around the world. Pizza, salads, and pastas are among the best lunchtime choices. The peel-and-eat shrimp, snow-crab legs, and ever-present prime rib make for belt-loosening dinners. Save room for dessert and create your own ice cream version of the Sierra Nevada mountains. Don't forget the hot fudge and caramel mountain streams and crushed peanut boulders.

A more limited menu and a little less imagination shown in preparation and presentation drop **Flavors!** (Silver Legacy, 407 N. Virginia St., 775/325-7401 or 800/687-8733, 8 A.M.–1:30 P.M. and 4:30 –10 P.M. daily, $10–20) just a notch below Reno's big two. Its oysters on the half shell and fruit pies are better than you'd expect at a buffet.

Limited selection is not a problem at **King Buffet** (3650 Kietzke Lane, 775/827-7997, 1 A.M.–9 P.M. daily, $10–15); there is even a sushi chef on-site. The garlicky green beans and sesame balls are addicting and could make a satisfying meal by themselves.

John Ascuaga's Nugget's **Rotisserie Buffet** (1100 Nugget Ave., Sparks, 800/647-1177, 11 A.M.–2 P.M. and 5–9 P.M. Mon.–Fri., 8:30 A.M.–2 P.M. and 5–9 P.M. Sat.–Sun., $15–30) serves different cuisine-themed lunches and dinners, including Mexican on Thursday, Seafood on Friday, and Western barbecue on Saturday. The food is consistently good, especially the salads and desserts.

CASINO QUICK BITES

At halftime or between innings, grab a dog and a beer at the **Cal-Neva**'s Sports Deli (775/323-1046) in the corner of the sports book. A big fat frankfurter and a bottle of Heineken will only set you back $4.75 and won't keep you waiting in line while your team rallies. Other great deals are the tacos and French fries.

Baldini's Brickyard (865 S. Rock Blvd., Sparks, 775/357-0116, 9 a.m.–10 p.m. daily) is nearly unbeatable for lunch and dinner specials. A burger, fries, and soda is $2. **The Grille** at Gold Dust West (444 Vine St., 775/323-2211, 6 a.m.–10 p.m. daily) is similar, with cheap specials that include prime rib with a potato, a vegetable, a roll and butter, and a dinner salad for $7.77.

The Peppermill (2707 S. Virginia St., 775/826-2121, 24 hours daily, $12–25) started life as a humble coffee shop, and the original eatery still serves up sandwiches and salads as well as a darn good chow mein.

Tivoli Gardens (Eldorado, 345 N. Virginia St., 775/786-5700, 24 hours daily) is head and shoulders above your usual coffee shop, with food from every continent, including Vietnamese, Thai, and sushi specialties, plus 24-hour breakfasts.

The Purple Parrot (Atlantis, 3800 S. Virginia St., 775/825-4700, 24 hours daily, $8–20) lets you pile on all the toppings you want on your three-quarter-pound Angus patty at its Big Burger Bar. It also has all the other traditional coffee shop fare along with a few surprises like prawn scampi and shrimp Louis.

Carnivores' eyes glaze over and stomachs begin to rumble at the mention of the Awful Awful Burger, a half-pounder served with enough salty seasoned fries to choke a horse (or at least clog an artery) served at **The Nugget** (233 N. Virginia St., 775/323-0716, 24 hours daily, $10–15). It's awfully big and awfully

good—it's said that when one entrepreneur opened a restaurant in town, he advertised that his joint served "the second-best burger in town" in tribute to the Awful Awful.

Not surprisingly, the **Iron Skillet** (Alamo Casino Travel Center, off I-80 at the Sparks Blvd. exit, 775/355-8888, 24 hours daily) caters to the working person's appetite with hearty meat-and-potatoes breakfasts and dinners at affordable prices. The menu is tractor-trailer size, the fried chicken and chicken-fried steak will fill the void of the open road, and the coffee is hot and robust enough to wash away the loneliness. The real treats here are the potatoes: Bakers are available 24 hours a day, home fries are thick and chunky, and hash browns are crispy on top and suitable for egg-yolk dipping.

DINERS AND DELIS

Archie's (2195 N. Virginia St., 775/322-9595, 24 hours daily, $8–12) has a 1950s-style diner menu in a contemporary campus setting. The burgers are filling and a bit pricy, but they come with fries. It's worth the $2 to substitute the fries with beer-battered onion rings. Splurge on a chocolate malt or vanilla shake. More old-fashioned shakes and burgers await at **Mel's: The Original Diner** (Sands Regency, 345 N. Arlington Ave., 775/337-6357, 24 hours, $10–15), and the atmosphere is right out of *American Graffiti*. The **Gold 'N Silver Inn** (790 W. 4th St., 775/323-2696, 24 hours daily, $8–12) has been in business for more than 50 years. It's more popular than ever after being featured on *Diners, Drive-Ins and Dives,* Guy Fieri's Food Network show, and the burgers are huge. Get to the **Empire Diner** (Baldini's Sports Casino, 865 S. Rock Blvd., 775/358-0116, 24 hours daily, $10–15) before 10 a.m. to take advantage of their two-for-one breakfast specials.

Some have found that the service at **Josef's Vienna Bakery Café & Restaurant** (933 W. Moana Lane, 775/825-0451, 8 a.m.–5:30 p.m. Mon.–Fri., 8 a.m.–4 p.m. Sat., 8 a.m.–3 p.m. Sun., $8–12) leaves much to be desired, the portions leave too big a hole in the belly, and the prices leave too little in the wallet, but the food receives unanimous praise. We dare you to resist the dessert. Portions are more generous—overwhelming, even—at **Black Bear Diner** (2323 Virginia St., 775/829-5570, 6:30 A.M.–9 P.M. daily, $12–20). It's not gourmet quality, but it is honest fare at fair prices.

If you're in the neighborhood, try the beef brisket sandwich at the Atlantis Casino's **Manhattan Deli** (3800 S. Virginia St., 775/825-4700 or 800/723-6500, 6 A.M.–10 P.M. daily, $8–20). Just like the Jewish delicatessen in the old neighborhood, it sells knishes, latke, lox, chicken salad, and other favorites.

BREAKFAST

You just can't beat the $4.99 steak and eggs at the **Top Deck** (38 E. 2nd St., 775/954-4540, $5–10) on the third floor of the Cal-Neva. The French toast is a winner too, filled with fruit and sprinkled with cinnamon.

If breakfast can ever be considered haute cuisine, **Peg's Glorified Ham & Eggs** (420 S. Sierra St., 775/329-2600, 6:30 A.M.–9 P.M. daily, $10–20) is about as close as you'll find in Reno. It's no secret—there's often a line out the door, even on frigid mornings—but the locals agree that the huevos rancheros and eggs Benedict with crab are worth a little frostbite. A family home renovated into a neighborhood restaurant, **Daughters Cafe** (97 Bell St., 775/324-3447, 9 A.M.–2 P.M. Tues.–Sun., $15–25) is run by the family matriarch as cook and her daughters serving as business manager and waitress. Breakfast often evokes French provincial, with crusty baguettes, beignets, and goat-cheese omelets.

STEAK

Rich ambiance and flamboyant tableside preparation make nationally recognized **Sterling's Seafood Steakhouse** (Silver Legacy, 407 N. Virginia St., 775/325-7401, 5–10 P.M. Sun.–Thurs., 5–11 P.M. Fri.–Sat., $30–45) a multisensory gastronomic destination. Starched white linen tablecloths contrast pleasingly with the deep red decor as candlelight reflects off polished cherrywood wine racks and wall

accents. Servers delivering the aged steaks and other beef, chicken, and fish dishes are as professional and proficient as you'd expect from a five-star establishment.

Harrah's resorts are all about quiet luxury, so it's no surprise that **The Steak House** (219 N. Center St., 775/786-3232, 11 A.M.–2:30 P.M. and 5–10 P.M. Mon.–Fri., 5–10 P.M. Sat.–Sun., $30–50) caters to every culinary desire, from the buttery premium steaks aged for 28 days to red leather booths and woodwork as dark as any romance-minded couple could ask for. The food and service are impeccable, leading to The Steak House's inclusion in the *Nation's Restaurant News* Fine Dining Hall of Fame.

Charlie Palmer Steak (Grand Sierra, 2500 E. 2nd St., 775/789-2000, 5:30–10:30 P.M. daily, $30–42) presents an inventive "neo-traditional" menu that includes a fontina-crusted pork chop in mustard-rosemary sauce. Ceiling-high terra-cotta banquets, ash-blond walls, and dark furniture give the room an uninhibited opulence. But it's all about the steak, and the 17-ounce rib eye is the star. At $42, however, you're definitely paying for the atmosphere and celebrity chef's name as much as for the quality of the food.

An Italian approach to steak, an impressive cellar, and casual dining overlooking the Truckee River make **Lexie's** (Siena, 1 S. Lake St., 775/327-4362, 5–10 P.M. Tues.–Sat., 10 A.M.–2 P.M. Sun., $25–40) special.

Renovations in 2010 give the **Atlantis Steakhouse** (3800 S. Virginia St., 775/825-4700, 5–10 P.M. Wed.–Sun., $30–60) an old-time photo appearance in black, white, and sepia. But the accents and lighting along with the 1,100-gallon saltwater aquarium are ultramodern. The three-course prix fixe menu ($45), also available with wine pairings ($60), is an attractive option.

For an unassuming little casino, Club Cal-Neva sure delivers some cool stuff. **Copper Ledge** (38 E. 2nd St., 775/954-4540, 4–10 P.M. Fri.–Sat., $15–22) is one such treasure that has managed to create an elegant setting high above the fray on the casino floor without the high prices or pretense sometimes found in the best steak houses. A half-dozen of Copper Ledge's best meals—prime rib, coconut shrimp, and steak and lobster Alfredo included—are just $13 and include soup or salad, a vegetable, and a choice of a potato or rice.

SEAFOOD

Rapscallion (1555 S. Wells Ave., 775/323-1211 or 877/932-3700, 11:30 A.M.–10 P.M. Mon.–Fri., dinner 5–10 P.M. Sat.–Sun., brunch 10 A.M.–2 P.M. Sun., $25–35) has an interesting interior: lots of wood, some of it walling in very private, dimly lit dining alcoves; a lively, attractive bar; and stained glass. Lunch is served daily until 4:30 P.M. with salads and sandwiches for about $12. For dinner, start with escargot, calamari, or Cajun coconut prawns and continue with salads, fish, and beef. Good food, good prices, and attentive yet unobtrusive service make this place very popular.

Lulou's (1470 S. Virginia St., 775/329-9979, 5–10 P.M. Tues.–Sat., $35–55) infuses its seafood and other outstanding fare with tinges of California, Asia, and the continent. It's a truly world-class restaurant that just happens to be located in Reno. The prices, especially if you spring for wine, are eye-popping as well.

Fin Fish (2500 E. 2nd St., 775/789-2000, 5:30–9:30 P.M. Sun.–Thurs., 5:30–10:30 P.M. Fri.–Sat., $24–40), Charlie Palmer's deluxe crab shack inside the Grand Sierra, sets the beachfront mood with sand-colored tiles, aqua furnishings, and driftwood-hung walls. An open kitchen area adds to the community-clambake ambiance, but the menu is a far cry from *Gidget* and *Beach Blanket Bingo*. Start with lobster corn dogs or codfish sliders, then move on to your choice of the sea's bounty; the shellfish and wine sauces make the meal.

A ship's wheel and a swordfish that would make Santiago blanch greet visitors to **Fairchild's Oyster Bar** (Silver Legacy, 407 N. Virginia St., 775/329-4777, ext. 4335, 11 A.M.–10 P.M. Mon.–Thurs., 11 A.M.–11 P.M. Fri.–Sat., 4–10 P.M. Sun., $20–30). The facade announces a more casual dining experience reminiscent of the dockside. Pan-roasted

seafood in cream and wine sauces is the top choice.

BASQUE

Come hungry if you visit **Louis' Basque Corner** (301 E. 4th St., 775/323-7203, 11:30 A.M.–2:30 P.M. and 5–9 P.M. daily, $24–35). Traditionally prepared soup, salad, and beans complement the lamb, steak, and chicken served family style. If you're prepared to sit at tables with strangers and have a good time, you'll leave satisfied and socialized—especially after a few glasses of Picon Punch, a sour brandy concoction popular among Basque shepherds.

Basque gets a gourmet spin at **Restaurante Orozko** (John Ascuaga's Nugget, 1100 Nugget Ave., Sparks, 775/356-3300, ext. 4232, 5–9 P.M. Wed.–Thurs., 5–9:30 P.M. Fri.–Sat., $25–35). The entrées have a Mediterranean influence, and the room features walls painted to resemble the Basque countryside.

ITALIAN

With Renaissance art and Tuscan marble ubiquitous in Reno's casinos, it's no surprise that just about every hotel resort boasts a stellar *ristorante italiano*.

La Strada (Eldorado, 345 N. Virginia St., 775/786-5700, 5–9 P.M. Sun.–Tues., 5–10 P.M. Fri.–Sat., $20–40) is not only one of the top Italian restaurants in Nevada, it is among the best in the country: It has been named among the nation's top 10 Italian eateries and has claimed *Wine Spectator*'s Award of Excellence six years running. All the pasta is handmade on-site, and the prosciutto-wrapped prawn and scallop appetizer almost makes you forget about the entrées. Everything is baked in wood-fired brick ovens. The rigatoncini and Italian sausage served on egg noodles is excellent. Chicken and veal is prepared picatta, marsala, or parmesana. You can also get T-bones, grilled quail, and fish.

Towering statues, Corinthian columns, a ceiling fresco, and glowing torches at **Romanza** (Peppermill, 2707 S. Virginia St., 775/689-7178 or 800/647-6992,

5:30–9:30 P.M. Wed.–Sun., $22–32) are sure to make an impression on that special someone. The large room, on the Peppermill casino floor, is cloistered from the noise and made more intimate by a curved seating arrangement. The menu covers the Italian gamut, heavy on the north, and also features dishes cooked in a wood-fired oven.

Johnny's Ristorante Italiano (4245 W. 4th St., 775/747-4511, 5–9:30 P.M. Tues.–Sat., $30–50) has water and city views from atop a hill north of Reno. A nice little bar is on the right, and the big red-leather booths are quite conducive to settling back and enjoying your ravioli, lasagna, or chicken cacciatore (it's served with a truly inspired polenta) with your choice of wine from a limited by comprehensive cellar.

Other strong choices include **La Famiglia** (170 S. Virginia St., 775/324-1414, 5–10 P.M. daily, $20–30) for gnocchi and **Mario's Portofino** (1505 S. Virginia St., 775/825-7779, 11 A.M.–2 P.M. and 5–10 P.M. Tues.–Fri., 5–10 P.M. Sat.–Sun., $15–30) for just about everything Italian.

MEXICAN

Miguel's (1415 S. Virginia St., 775/322-2722, 11 A.M.–9 P.M. Tues.–Thurs., 11 A.M.–10 P.M. Fri.–Sat., noon–8 P.M. Sun., $10–20) is one of the original Mexican restaurants in Reno, pleasing patrons for more than 50 years. It's very bright and friendly, has excellent service, and is inexpensive—one of the highlights of Reno.

A couple of blocks south of Miguel's is **El Borracho** (1601 S. Virginia St., 775/322-0313, 4:30–9 P.M. Mon. and Wed.–Thurs., 4:30–10 P.M. Fri.–Sun., $12–25), the other original Reno Mexican eatery. Try one of the 13 interesting shrimp dishes (salads, cocktails, stew, brochette, seviche) or the usual tostadas, enchiladas, burritos, and other specials while relaxing amid the Mexican fiesta interior.

Bertha Miranda's (336 Mill St., 775/786-9697, 10 A.M.–10 P.M. daily, $15–25) has a deservedly good reputation among locals; the carnitas is especially tasty.

ASIAN

Chef Quoc Nguyen calls upon his vast experience in San Francisco and Reno to find the perfect blend of Asian flavors for American palates at **Jazmine** (9333 Double R Blvd., 775/851-2888, 11 A.M.–2:30 P.M. and 5–9 P.M. Mon.–Sat., $15–25). A sushi bar and takeout service is available.

Despite its reasonable prices, **Palais de Jade** (960 W. Moana Lane, 775/827-5233, 11 A.M.–9:30 P.M. daily, $12–20) is the ritziest Chinese restaurant in town. In an extremely tasteful room done in mostly black and white, it is quite understated and elegant. Sticklers for authentic cuisine may find a few things to question, but there are traditional moo shu, cashew, and kung pao dishes. The food is delicious, and the service is on top of things. Just as good is **Francis' Asian Bistro** (4796 Caughlin Pkwy., Suite 102, 775/827-3111, 11:30 A.M.–10 P.M. Mon.–Fri., 5–10 P.M. Sat., $20–30). Unexpectedly terrific views, all-you-can-eat sushi, and an unusual curried sea bass attract a lot of folks, but we're partial to the crab and seaweed salad.

Among the casinos, try the upscale **Golden Fortune** (345 N. Virginia St., 775/786-5700, 11 A.M.–10 P.M. daily, $10–15) for Hong Kong cuisine inside Tivoli Gardens at the Eldorado, or **Trader Dick's** (John Ascuaga's Nugget, 1100 Nugget Ave., Sparks, 775/356-3300, 5–9 P.M. Sun.–Mon., 5–10 P.M. Fri.–Sat., $15–35), a palm-fronded Polynesian tiki bar. The garlic pork with bamboo shoots, mushrooms, and water chestnuts is a favorite, as are the planters punch and the Rangoon Ruby at the bar near the largest aquarium in town.

Don't let the strip mall location fool you: **Green Papaya** (4786 Caughlin Pkwy., Suite 303, 775/826-8116, 11 A.M.–9 P.M. Sun.–Thurs., 11 A.M.–9:30 P.M. Fri.–Sat., $10–15) delivers authentic pad thai and curries just as hot as you dare order them. The portions are big. For Vietnamese, head for the **Golden Flower** (205 W. 5th St., 775/323-1628, 10 A.M.–3 A.M. daily, $7–10). Choose from 25 different kinds of *pho* (traditional noodle soup) along with the must-eat imperial egg rolls and shrimp stickers.

EUROPEAN

As you might expect, **Bavarian World** (595 Valley Rd. at 6th St., 775/323-7646, 8 A.M.–8:30 P.M. Tues.–Sat., $15–25) is right out of a Black Forest village, with a bakery, deli, and convenience store stocked with German imports: clocks, chocolates, and strudel on one side and the Oktoberfest-like restaurant on the other. German immigrants Klaus and Lura Ginschel started the bakery so that they'd have a steady supply of the heavy rye bread they missed when they moved from their native country. Although they lacked restaurant experience, they learned

by trial and error. Decades later, their business is still thriving. There are American dishes on the menu, but you'd be remiss if you didn't try the Wurst Wurst Wurst Platter, perhaps the Germanic cousin of the Awful Awful Burger offered at The Nugget. It's heaped with sausages, sauerkraut, and fried potatoes.

The Siena eliminated its table games in 2010 as the boutique hotel-casino battles financial setbacks. Part of the resort's current strategy is to expand its entertainment offerings. That's good news for fans of the Euro-style lounge **Enoteca** (1 S. Lake St., 775/321-5886, 7 P.M.–late Fri.–Sat., $15–25). The lounge and wine bar under the casino serves tapas, desserts, and dinner.

Information and Services

The **Reno-Sparks Convention and Visitors Authority** (4001 S. Virginia St., 775/827-7600 or 800/FOR-RENO—800/367-7366, www.re-nolaketahoe.com, 8 A.M.–5 P.M. Mon.–Fri.), at the back of the Reno Town Mall, carries loads of useful literature, brochures, and other information for visitors here and at its other visitors center (634 Pyramid Way, Sparks, 8 A.M.–5 P.M. Mon.–Fri., 8:30 A.M.–5 P.M. Sat.–Sun.). Be sure to ask for the excellent *Travel Planner*, published annually. The website also offers a hotel booking service, vacation packages, and a listing of current entertainment, casino activities, conventions, and special events.

MARRIAGE AND DIVORCE

The County Clerk's office is in the courthouse (75 Court St. at S. Virginia St., 775/327-3274, 8 A.M.–5 P.M. Mon.–Fri., www.co.washoe.nv.us). Bring your ID, your betrothed, and $60 in cash, money order, traveler's check, credit card, or debit card for a marriage license; no blood test is required, and there is no waiting period. You can then get married at any of Reno's dozen wedding chapels. Prices start at $150, and most are in the same part of the strip along North Virginia Street.

To get married for cheap, with no muss and no fuss, go to the **Commissioner of Civil Marriages** (350 S. Center St., Suite 100, 775/337-4575). In Reno-Sparks, the County Clerk doubles as the Commissioner of Civil Marriages, who appoints deputy commissioners whose sole function is to marry people. Just show up at their office 1–4 P.M. Monday–Friday with your license and $50 cash, Visa, or MasterCard.

If it doesn't work out, at least one of the divorcing parties must be able to prove Nevada residency for six weeks. Several companies advertise fast cheap divorces. They start at about $150 for the paperwork, although many circumstances will drive the cost higher. The filing fee is $170.

LIBRARIES

The extensive main branch of the **Washoe County Library** (301 S. Center St., 775/327-8300, www.co.washoe.nv.us/library, 9 A.M.–5 P.M. Mon.–Thurs., 10 A.M.–5 P.M. Sun.) is a nifty architectural specimen with curved, flowing lines. It's filled with trees and even a pond—added by the architect when his desire to build the library in a park went unfulfilled.

LOVESICKNESS AND "THE CURE"

Couples intent on tying the knot quickly and with minimal ceremony have been coming to Reno since the 1930s. The region's natural beauty, plenty of honeymoon-worthy hotel resorts, Washoe County's liberal laws, and its proximity to military and naval bases on the West Coast drew the lovestruck throughout World War II and the postwar era. One judge single-handedly married 5,888 couples in 1946, winning an unofficial "wedding derby" by 174 ceremonies over his closest competitor. Five years later, Reno was the site of 2,489 nuptials in just one month, July 1950, when couples raced to the altar before new grooms were sent to fight in the Korean War. Reno's marriage tourism industry spurred the erection of quickie wedding chapels beginning in the late 1950s.

Nevada still does not require a blood test or waiting period for lovers intent on plunging immediately into wedded bliss. Other states began relaxing their requirements in the 1970s, however, eliminating some of Reno's advantages when it came to fast weddings. The romance and history associated with a Reno wedding keeps couples coming to town, whether to get hitched or to renew their vows. The city's wide range of entertainment options makes it an attractive all-inclusive location – a bachelor or bachelorette party, wedding, and honeymoon destination in one.

As far back as Reno's wedding tradition goes, it's divorce that made a name for the city. After the Civil War, as much of the country sought a return to idyllic sensibilities, many states required a one-year wait time before granting a divorce petition. Nevada kept its law at six months, and as the principle city in Nevada, Reno was a beacon for betrayed wives, cuckolded husbands, and irreconcilable couples from as far away as New York. Bill Murray, in his 1910 ditty "I'm on My Way to Reno," captured the city's lure:

The love she once declared was mine
Has simply turned to hate.
So I've made up my mind
To visit old Nevada State
I'm on my way to Reno. I'm leaving
town today
It's liberty or death with me, my hair is
turning gray.
Reno life is simply great, they grant divorces while you wait . . .

The Progressive movement won a short-lived victory when Nevada joined the majority in increasing the waiting period to one year in 1913. But money talks, and the decrease in tourism was too much for the state to bear. The wait time was cut back to six months in 1915, cut again to three months in 1927, and then to six weeks in 1931, unleashing a flood of disillusioned spouses on Reno. In the first month that the liberal laws were on the books, 517 divorce suits were filed and 331 decrees issued in Nevada. By 1940 one out of every 20 U.S. divorces were settled in Nevada.

The marriages of Mary Pickford, Jack Dempsey, and Cornelius Vanderbilt II ended in Reno, lending an air of sophistication to divorce Nevada-style. And the highly publicized divorces of Lord Earl Russell and the betrayed wife of U.S. Steel Corporation president William Ellis Corey brought the practice a touch of scandal.

Like the lucrative marriage market, the Reno divorce cash cow died when other states liberalized their laws in the 1970s.

RENO

Much smaller branch libraries are scattered throughout the area; check the website for the location nearest you.

The University of Nevada, Reno's library, the **Mathewson-IGT Knowledge Center** (1664 N. Virginia St., 775/784-4636, http://knowledge-center.unr.edu, usually 7:30 A.M.–8 P.M. daily) has extended and weekend hours during the school year. The state-of-the-art facility contains 1 million books and an extensive section on Basque culture and history. The **Truckee Meadows Community College Library** (7000 Dandini Blvd., off U.S. 395 about 10 miles north of downtown Reno, 775/674-7600) has varying hours, but it's usually open 8 A.M.–5 P.M. Monday–Friday.

Getting There and Around

BY CAR

Reno is 15 miles east of the California state line. The Reno-Sparks area is served by two major highways: I-80, which crosses the country from San Francisco to New York, bisects the region from east to west, and U.S. 395, which runs from southeast Oregon briefly through Nevada, from Reno to Topaz Lake, then heads south through California toward Los Angeles. Be aware that severe winter storms can make road travel treacherous, especially through mountain passes, and road closures due to inclement weather are not uncommon in winter.

The standard rental-car companies operate out of the airport, which makes it convenient if you're flying in and out. If you aren't flying and don't want to deal with the airport, most of the rental companies also have offices in town. RentACarNow.com (www.rentacarnow.com/city/reno.html) offers a convenient service that allows you to compare models, rates, and locations.

BY BUS

Buses depart the **Greyhound** bus terminal (155 Stevenson St. between W. 1st St. and W. 2nd St., 775/322-2970) roughly 24 times throughout the day and night, with services west to Sacramento, Oakland, and San Francisco and east to Salt Lake City. These destinations connect to cities to the north and farther east. Oddly, considering the frequency of flights between the two cities, there is no direct bus service from Reno to Las Vegas; travelers are forced to connect in Salt Lake City, making for one long day.

RTC Ride (www.rtcwashoe.com, $2 adults, $1 youth, seniors, and disabled) is the Reno-Sparks public bus system and has 70 buses on 26 routes that operate about 6 A.M.–11 P.M. The most popular routes operate 24 hours; others, such as routes to ski areas or business centers, run less frequently depending on the season or the day of the week. The main terminals are at 4th Street in Reno and Centennial Plaza in Sparks. Routes and schedules are available on the website.

BY TRAIN

Amtrak (280 N. Center St., 775/329-8638 or 800/USA-RAIL—800/872-7245) runs cross-country rail service on the transcontinental line that was laid through Nevada in 1869. The *California Zephyr* passes through downtown Reno (blocking traffic twice a day for 5–10 minutes) and stops in Reno once daily in each direction, heading west to Sacramento and Emeryville in the San Francisco Bay Area and east to Salt Lake City, Denver, Omaha, and Chicago. In Nevada, the *Zephyr* stops in in Reno, Winnemucca, and Elko. Amtrak also operates several buses daily between Reno and Sacramento to connect with other trains there. There is no direct rail service from Reno to Las Vegas; take the *Zephyr* to Salt Lake City, then the bus to Las Vegas.

BY AIR

About 5.5 million people pass through the 23 passenger gates at **Reno-Tahoe International Airport** every year. American, Delta, Horizon,

Southwest, United, and U.S. Air transport passengers between Reno and West Coast and Midwestern destinations, including Chicago, Dallas, Denver, Las Vegas, Los Angeles, Phoenix, Salt Lake City, San Diego, San Francisco, and Seattle.

Conveniently located, the airport is only a 10-minute drive from downtown; take U.S. 395 south to the airport exit. Complimentary hotel shuttles run about 5 A.M.–midnight, stopping at the airport along the curb outside the D Doors, which are located north of the baggage claim area. The shuttles stop at the Atlantis, Circus Circus, Grand Sierra, John Ascuaga's Nugget, Eldorado, and Silver Legacy.

RTC Ride bus route 19 operates weekdays between the airport and the downtown Reno bus terminal. Travelers to other destinations can connect at the terminal.

TOURS

Reno Tours (888/317-1593) organizes custom sightseeing tours in a limousine as well as chauffeured transportation to concerts and sporting events.

LAKE TAHOE AND VICINITY

Lake Tahoe snuggles into the basin formed a few million years ago when faulting pushed up the Carson Range to the east and the Sierra Nevada mountains to the west. As Mark Twain once said, the lake presents the "fairest picture the whole earth affords": Majestic 10,000-foot peaks stand sentinel over the pristine alpine treasure 6,000 feet above sea level. Sun, clouds, and perspective change the lake's surface from slate gray to ice blue to navy, but it is always 99 percent pure—clear enough to see a dinner plate 75 feet down on the bottom. The lake is 12 miles wide, 22 miles long, and has 72 miles of shoreline. Averaging 1,000 feet deep, Lake Tahoe is the 10th-deepest lake in the world and is the largest alpine lake in North America. Its 40 trillion gallons of water could supply every person on the planet with a shower a day

January–August. With a surface temperature of 68°F in summer, a refreshing dip is much more likely.

About one-third of Lake Tahoe lies in Nevada. While many of the recreational opportunities—skiing, golf courses, beaches, water sports—are in California, Nevada boasts its fair share as well. Annual snowfall averages 40 feet, with a snowpack of around 20 feet— perfect skiing and snowboarding conditions. Mackinaw trout, a few tipping the scales at 30 pounds or more, and Kokanee trout, a variety of landlocked sockeye salmon, call the lake home. And the casinos, of course, are only in Nevada.

Tahoe's watershed encompasses 520 square miles, including more than 60 inlets from tributaries, and a single outlet—the Truckee River,

COURTESY OF THE NEVADA COMMISSION ON TOURISM

HIGHLIGHTS

LOOK FOR **(** TO FIND RECOMMENDED SIGHTS, ACTIVITIES, DINING, AND LODGING.

(Tahoe Rim Trail: Nearly 20 years in the making, this ski, horse, hiking, and bicycle trail circles Lake Tahoe, climbing and dipping among peaks and ridges, weaving among thick pine groves, and skirting the shoreline. Go hard-core and cover the entire 150-mile loop, or take it easy and tackle shorter stretches suitable for all fitness levels (page 189).

(Thunderbird Lodge: Heir to a fortune, George Whittell had this summer "cottage" built in 1936 so he'd have a place to indulge his whims. Slip through the hidden tunnel to the Card House, where George and his friends gambled huge sums. Check out the scion's 40-foot yacht. And see the Elephant House, where Whittell's enormous wrinkly gray pet resided (page 198).

(Lake Tahoe-Nevada State Park: Bike along the path of the flume that supplied water to Virginia City's silver mining operations. The pine, aspen, fir, and cedar forest still hasn't fully recovered from the Comstock mines' voracious appetite for timber that stripped the hillsides 130 years ago (page 199).

(Piper's Opera House: Lillie Langtry, Harry Houdini, John Philip Sousa, and other superstars of the era played this well-preserved testament to Nevada's silver boom. The theater's 1880-vintage state-of-the-art features include canvas walls for enhanced acoustics, railroad springs under the stage for more acrobatic dance steps, and interchangeable sets for quick scene changes (page 211).

(Virginia & Truckee Train Rides: The iron horse transports riders through tunnels, over bridges, and back 130 years to one of the most dynamic times in Nevada history. Lively and humorous narration brings the Comstock Lode era to life (page 214).

© AVALON TRAVEL

(Nevada State Museum: Housed in the Carson City Mint building, the museum's collection of gold and silver pieces bearing the collectable "CC" mint mark will make numismatists drool. The museum also contains excellent representations of Nevada's frontier days, its native fauna, and its geologic history (page 221).

(Genoa Bar: Of all the gin joints in all the towns in all Nevada, this is the oldest. The red stains on the ceiling and the trap door in the floor make for some pretty harrowing tales, although the best ones aren't true (page 234).

which drains the lake at Tahoe City, flows north through Truckee, California, then cuts east through Reno, finally emptying into Pyramid Lake at Nixon, nearly 100 miles northeast.

Shoreline roads circumscribe Lake Tahoe. The full 72-mile circle can be driven in about 2.5 hours, but with all there is to see and do, you could easily spend a full enjoyable day circumnavigating the lake.

Beyond Tahoe, a drive up Geiger Grade or Devil's Gate gives you the opportunity to capture a touristy, yet authentic, piece of Nevada's—and the nation's—glorious past. Virginia City preserves the boomtown spirit of the gold rush with boardwalks, saloons, mansions, mines, an opera house, and cemeteries. The Nevada state capital, Carson City, exists to keep the wheels of state government greased and the cogs of the federal bureaucracy turning. It is home not only to the governor's mansion and the state legislature but also to 56,000 souls who appreciate the city's central location, small-town friendliness, and big-city facilities. The valley south of Carson City has the oldest permanent settlement in Nevada, nestled amid fertile fields, pastoral cattle ranches, and homey small towns punctuated by the early-20th-century architecture of Nevada icon Frederic DeLongchamps.

HISTORY

Few who have seen it have escaped Lake Tahoe's haunting, spiritual attraction. The Washoe people made pilgrimages to Da-ow ("Big Water") for millennia, harvesting the teeming trout and thanking the spirits for their benevolence and abundance.

John C. Frémont and Kit Carson came upon the cobalt waters in 1844. The settlers who followed them appreciated the area less for its majesty than for its practical and commercial potential. The lake's pine-covered shores literally fueled miners' and developers' exploitation of the Comstock Lode. Logging operations to power steam locomotives, build boomtowns and silver-mining camps, and provide mine timbers gouged ugly scars into the verdant landscape. Most of this lumber was

manhandled into the lake, pulled by steamer to Glenbrook or Incline, railroaded to Spooner Summit, then shot down flumes to mills at Washoe Valley and Carson City and delivered to Virginia City first by freighters and then by railroad. By 1870 only 500 Washoe people remained, and by the 1890s the lake was nearly fished out and 50,000 acres of forest had been cut. Those ravages have largely healed, and Tahoe's natural beauty has been restored to its fullest, despite subsequent periods of overfishing, commercial development, and even schemes to drain the lake.

Even before the mines played out, entrepreneurs with a more aesthetic bent began to take notice of the region. It may surprise many who crowd the Tahoe region's powder-covered slopes in winter today that its life as a premier resort began as a beat-the-heat retreat. As early as 1863, Comstock Lode millionaires treated their families to the soothing coolness of an alpine summer. The lake's first resort and the insatiable logging and fishing industries were established at Glenbrook in the mid-1860s. A narrow-gauge short line railroad reached Tahoe City from the transcontinental stop at Truckee in 1900, and the first automobile arrived in 1905. Paved roads reached the lake in the 1930s, transforming this playground of the rich into one for everybody.

Still, the Tahoe Basin managed to maintain a kind of pristine second-growth remoteness well into the 1950s, with a total year-round population of under 3,000. But then Tahoe's development began in earnest with several water, power, and subdivision schemes. Small, reasonably priced hotels attracted more and more visitors, and private ownership of more and more shoreline encouraged an influx of residents. Harvey Gross and Bill Harrah built casinos at South Shore, land values skyrocketed, and the 1960 Winter Olympics at Squaw Valley completed Lake Tahoe's rise to a world-class year-round vacation and recreation destination. After the Olympics, development began to spiral out of control.

Lake Tahoe is the main reservoir for the entire Truckee River water system. The dam at Tahoe City (6,229 feet) regulates the six feet

THE CREATION OF LAKE TAHOE

It wasn't that long ago, geologically speaking, that the basin housing Lake Tahoe began to form. Probably less than 10 million years ago, a fault pushed massive blocks of rock through the earth's surface, creating new mountain ranges. The area between the mountains dropped between these uplifted blocks, the Sierra crest on the west and the Carson Range on the east.

A great river soon flowed through the Lake Tahoe valley floor from the south and an outlet at the north. Magma generated by the tectonic pressures and rapidly rising temperatures that also caused the faulting and uplifting gurgled beneath the now-extinct Mount Pluto volcano until andesite flows from these vents bisected and dammed the valley. Over time, the valley filled and the Truckee River found a new outlet, at the northwest corner of Lake Tahoe

in present-day Tahoe City. Glaciers from the Pleistocene epoch did not bring sheets of ice to northwest Nevada, but they did push boulders into the canyons between mountains, forming dams and preventing the Truckee River from finding an outlet, allowing Lake Tahoe gradually to fill up.

These relatively recent events are the culmination of millennia of geologic and geographic changes in the area around Lake Tahoe. Once part of the supercontinent Pangaea, the Tahoe Basin was under a shallow sea some 675 million years ago when sediment on the sea floor hardened into rock. When the North American Plate broke from Pangaea, it collided with the Pacific Plate, igniting the powers of heat, cooling, friction, volcanism, and pressure that created the incubator for Lake Tahoe.

of reservoir water above the lake's natural rim (6,223 feet). A decade-long drought plagued the area beginning in 1964, greatly diminishing the winter snowpack in the Tahoe Basin, which supplies more than 60 percent of Lake Tahoe's water. The lake level dropped below its natural rim in July 1991, and except for a brief trickle in 1993 and 1995, not a drop of water flowed into the Truckee River. Downstream storage (Donner Lake as well as Stampede, Boca, Prosser, and Independence Reservoirs) fell to precipitously low levels in summer. Finally, the lake dropped to its lowest level in recorded history, 6,220 feet.

A couple of wet winters in 1996 and 1997 replenished the reservoir and filled it a little too full; in January 1997, lake water started pouring over the dam, out of control. The Truckee River flooded its banks for most of its 100-mile length, submerging downtown Reno under five feet of water in some places and causing hundreds of millions of dollars' damage.

PLANNING YOUR TIME

Plan to spend at least a long weekend in Nevada's elbow with Tahoe as your focus. A

week or so gives you enough time to hit all the high spots along the lake and in the mountains, along with day trips to Carson City and Virginia City.

Winter visitors spend as much time as possible on the slopes, fueling up for the day's runs, and winding down afterward. All the major resorts are designed with the needs of ski bums in mind. Most offer combination room–lift ticket specials throughout the season, and many include free shuttle pickup and drop-off sites throughout the North and South Shores. Nonskiers should consider visiting in summer, when hotel rooms are cheaper, the area is less crowded, and you won't have to pack your parka.

Whether you're here for the snowpack or the sunshine, consider making one of the casino resorts at Incline Village, Stateline, or Zephyr Cove your home base. In addition to gaming, they offer fine restaurants and sometimes even spa service. If you hit the slopes and the slopes hit back, you can soak, soothe, steam, and massage out all the kinks.

Virginia City and Carson City, at the top of the day-trip list, are northwest and west of the lake, respectively, so you could save a few

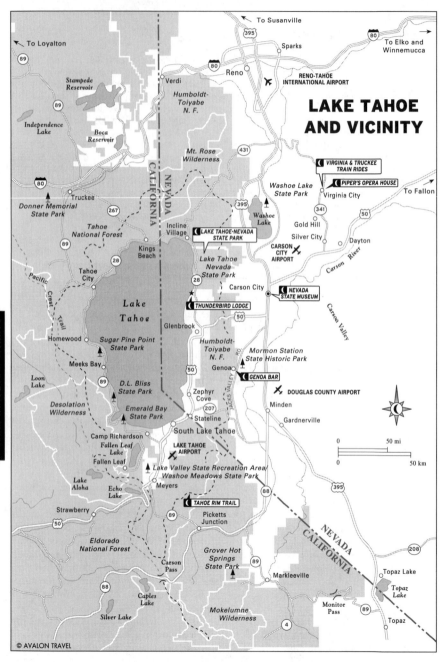

minutes' commute by opting to stay at Incline Village. Washoe Lake, Lake Tahoe–Nevada State Park, and also Reno are closer. If the history, pastoral peace and quiet, and unlimited recreational activities of Genoa, Minden, Gardnerville, Walker, and Topaz Lake are more your speed, you might decide to stay on the South Shore.

Road conditions can change without much notice, particularly during winter. If you're motoring in from California, consult the Caltrans website (www.dot.ca.gov); if you're approaching through Nevada, contact the Nevada Department of Transportation (877/NV-ROADS—877/687-6237, www.nevada-dot.com). Officials often declare snow tires a requirement for travel on I-80 and other roads around Lake Tahoe. If you're not sure, check your tires' sidewalls for an M/S (mud/snow) designation. Extreme conditions may call for front-tire snow chains. It's a good idea to have a pair in the trunk. Better yet, use the ski-resort shuttles and public transportation during difficult driving weather.

ORIENTATION

Incline Village and Crystal Bay hug Lake Tahoe's north shoreline in Nevada. These communities are surrounded by Lake Tahoe State Park and the Tahoe National Forest, which extends a couple of miles southward along the ovoid lake. Glenbrook is about midway along the eastern shore on U.S. 50. Further south is Zephyr Cove and Stateline. Stateline, of course, is on the border between Nevada and California, just at the point where the lakeshore turns westward; the small communities of Minden and Gardnerville sit due east of Stateline. Genoa is due east of Zephyr Cove. Carson City is 10 miles east of Lake Tahoe, and Virginia City is 20 miles north-northwest of Carson, east of Washoe Lake.

The South Shore and Stateline

The town of Stateline on Lake Tahoe's South Shore is the quintessential California–Nevada border town, a representation not only of the economic and cultural glue that binds the two together but also of the discrete elements that make them unique. The California side of town is an elephantine freeway exit ramp fronted by hundreds of low-rise motels, fast food spots, service stations, shopping centers, apartments, and condominiums. On the Nevada side of the border are a half-dozen casinos as well as the compact and vertical peaks of the Carson Range.

SIGHTS AND RECREATION
(Tahoe Rim Trail
The Tahoe Rim Trail encircles Lake Tahoe for 150 miles along ridges and mountaintops. The trail winds through national forests, state parks, and wilderness lands, passing through a variety of vegetation zones and providing spectacular views of dense conifer forests,

wildflower-dotted meadows, and pristine alpine lakes. The trail offers something for everyone, with stretches ranging from easy to difficult, a number of loop trails, and an average grade of 10 percent. Hiking, horseback riding, and skiing are allowed on all parts of the trail; mountain biking is allowed on specified portions.

In the 1980s a National Forest Service recreation officer here came up with the idea of a trail circling Lake Tahoe, and the nonprofit Tahoe Rim Trail Association was organized in 1981. The officer's brainstorm was to link the trail with 50 miles of the Pacific Crest Trail that runs along the west side of the Tahoe wilderness. Volunteers began making the trail a reality in 1983, and a year later the TRTA had attracted 50 members. By 1988 the 1,500 members had helped clear 30 miles of the trail, working only May 1–October 15. They completed the work in 2001, and the entire trail officially became a loop.

a clear morning in Zephyr Cove, with views of the California side of Lake Tahoe

You can easily walk part of the trail by beginning at any of nine trailheads, or if you are ambitious, you can complete the whole circle and become a member of the "150 Mile Club." Camping is permitted along most of the trail, allowing extended trips into the solitude of the backcountry and wilderness regions; the numerous trailheads give day users abundant opportunities to tackle smaller portions of the trail and explore the beauty of the mountains. On the Nevada side, trailheads include the Spooner Summit trailhead (U.S. 50), the Kingsbury trailhead (2 miles north of Hwy. 207), and the Tahoe Meadows to Spooner Summit trailhead (Hwy. 431). California-side trailheads include the Brockway trailhead (Hwy. 267), the Tahoe City trailhead (230 yards north of Hwy. 89), the Barker Pass trailhead (Blackwood Canyon Rd., 4 miles south of Tahoe City), and, on the south side of the lake, the Big Meadow trailhead (Hwy. 89) and the Echo Lakes and Echo Summit trailheads (U.S. 50).

Trail maps are posted at the trailheads, but users are urged to carry maps with them on the trail. A detailed map ($10) is available at the **Tahoe Rim Trail Association**'s office (948 Incline Way, Incline Village, 775/298-0012, www.tahoerimtrail.org); it can also be ordered on their website.

There are lots of opportunities for involvement with the Tahoe Rim Trail Association. You can join a trail construction or maintenance party, buy a T-shirt, or volunteer in a variety of capacities.

Round Hill Pines Beach and Marina

Much of the summertime activity around Stateline is centered at Round Hill Pines Beach and Marina (775/588-3055), on a 0.5-mile-long sandy beach two miles north of the casinos and 0.5 miles north of the Round Hill Shopping Center. Facilities include a large deck area, a heated swimming pool, a tennis court, volleyball courts, horseshoe pits, barbecues, a deli, and a bar. Activities include waterskiing, fishing, parasailing, and private lake tours. **H2O Sports** (775/588-4155 or 775/588-3055) rents

Sea-Doos, kayaks, Seacycles, and paddleboats. Guided two-hour Sea-Doo excursions to Emerald Bay depart in the morning. You can also take advantage of the **Don Borges Water Ski School** (530/541-1351). Fishing guides include **Mile High Fishing Charters** (530/541-FISH—530/541-3474), **Tahoe Sportfishing** (800/696-7797), and **O'Malley's Fishing Charters** (775/588-4102).

The *Tahoe Star* (775/586-6534, $40 adults, $28 children), a 54-foot luxury yacht operated by Harrah's, offers cruises to Emerald Bay and other specialty cruises and charters.

Shore Line Ski and Sports (4100 Lake Tahoe Blvd., South Lake Tahoe, 530/544-1105) rents mountain bikes, mountain boards, inline skates, and off-road and inline skateboards in summer as well as skis and snowboards in winter. Sleigh rides, hayrides, and carriage rides offered by the **Borges Family** (775/588-2953 or 800/726-RIDE—800/726-7433) depart from near the casinos.

Nevada Beach

This large U.S. Forest Service beach, day-use area, and campground, only two miles north of Stateline on U.S. 50 (take a left at Elk Point), is one of the most popular beaches along the lake. It is nearly 0.75 miles long, and it is deep—more than 600 feet in some spots. Its parking lots are spread well apart, which spreads the people out as well. There's a $7 per vehicle entrance fee for day use.

Nevada Beach Campground (877/444-6777, $28–34) is one of the most popular beaches and campgrounds on Lake Tahoe, with 54 sites that fill up fast. Make reservations as far in advance as possible, up to 240 days ahead, especially if you want a primo spot near the water; if you don't have a reservation, you can show up at 9 A.M. to see if someone has left early. Checkout time is officially 2 P.M., but many campers spend a few extra hours on the beach and before heading off. A good method is to pay the $7 for the day, hang out on the beach, then take a walk through the campground every so often to see what's vacant (see the campground host to pay for first-come, first-served sites). The camp is equally popular among tenters and RVers; sites

have shade or sand but usually not both. The beach is a two-minute walk. Piped drinking water, flush toilets, picnic tables, grills, and fire pits are provided. There is a campground host. The maximum stay is 10 days. A pretty walk or aerobic run from here is north up Elks Avenue to Elk Point, a fairly exclusive residential neighborhood overlooking Zephyr Cove.

Zephyr Cove

Zephyr Cove is an action-packed small marina a few miles north of Nevada Beach on U.S. 50; its long pier is home base for the *Dixie II* and *Tahoe Queen* paddle-wheelers. You can also arrange sailing and fishing charters, sailboarding, Jet-Skiing, boating, parasailing, horseback riding, and weddings. There's a bar and grill, a resort, an RV park, and a campground.

The original *Dixie* started her illustrious career on the Mississippi River in 1927 and was brought to Tahoe in 1947 to become a floating casino. Legal squabbles over ownership prevented the *Dixie* from fulfilling that mission, and she sank under mysterious circumstances in shallow water off Cave Rock in 1949. The boat was raised in 1952 but didn't start tour cruises until 1972. The *Dixie I* made an estimated 17,000 trips on the lake in 22 years, but the repairs necessary to pass the 20-year Coast Guard inspection in 1993 would have cost nearly $2.5 million. Instead, the owners decided to dry dock *Dixie I* and build *Dixie II* from scratch.

The *Dixie II* has a capacity of 400 people. It cost $4 million to build at a shipyard in LaCrosse, Wisconsin, and was shipped to Tahoe in four pieces in spring 1994. The main deck has a dining area for 200 as well as the galley; the upper deck is enclosed for dancing and cocktails and houses the captain's cabin. The "hurricane deck" is open-air and hosts the snack bar and pilothouse.

The authentic *Tahoe Queen* recently received a facelift and now accurately reflects the grandeur of her former life on the Mississippi River. A variety of cruises (tickets and information 775/589-4906, www.zephyrcove.com) depart from the cove on both boats year-round, including the two-hour Emerald Bay trip ($39

CALIFORNIA SKI RESORTS

In Tahoe, alpine skiing and snowboarding are king. While several prime downhill ski areas have been carved out of the Sierra Nevada on the Nevada side, the California side claims some of the most famous ski areas in the world.

The **Heavenly Resort** (3860 Saddle Rd., South Lake Tahoe, CA, 775/586-7000 or 800/HEAVENLY – 800/432-8365, $77-88) lies right on the Nevada–California state line. Heavenly has a summit elevation of 10,067 feet, a base elevation of 7,200 feet, a vertical drop of 3,500 feet, 4,800 acres for skiing, 30 lifts, 94 trails, and a ski school. More than 20 percent of the runs are suitable for beginners; nearly half are classified as intermediate.

Climb the Sierra on I-80 and take Highway 267 to reach **Northstar at Tahoe** (100 Northstar Dr., Truckee, CA, 800/GO-NORTH – 800/466-6784, $88-92). The 3,000-acre resort, with a summit elevation of 8,610 feet, base elevation of 6,400 feet, and a vertical drop of 2,200 feet, has 19 lifts and is open to snowboarders. Its 93 trails are 60 percent intermediate, 25 percent advanced, and only 13 percent beginner. It also has a ski school with more than 100 instructors. There are 25 miles of groomed cross-country trails. Child care is available on-site.

Back on I-80, take the Donner State Park exit to reach **Tahoe Donner** (11509 Northwoods Blvd., Truckee, CA, 530/587-9400, $39). Best known for its cross-country skiing, this area has 60 miles of trails, all double-tracked with wide skating lanes and lighted nighttime skiing on Wednesday and Saturday. A favorite for beginning downhillers and children, 14 of the wide-bowled alpine runs are for beginners; an-

other five are rated intermediate, and four more are for experts. Four lifts ferry skiers to the 120 acres of runs.

The next resort west on I-80, also serving less-advanced skiers, is **Boreal** (19659 Boreal Ridge Rd. Truckee, CA, 530/426-3666), just off I-80 on the Castle exit. Beginner packages (from $25) include lift tickets and lessons. Snow fans ski day and night down 500 vertical feet from a summit elevation of 7,800 feet. One-third of the runs are suitable for beginners. Kids who prefer to ride the snow on their backs or bellies can opt for the several tubing lanes. Associated with Boreal is **Soda Springs** (10244 Soda Springs Rd., Soda Springs, CA, 530/426-3901 or 530/426-1010, $35), a resort set up for families. It has summit elevation of 7,400 feet and a vertical drop of 652 feet. Two lifts and three carpets lead fun-seekers to the runs, a terrain park, and 15 lanes of tubing down a 400-foot incline. Little tikes who feel the need for speed can climb aboard a mini snowmobile for a 10-lap ride.

Three miles off I-80's Norden/Soda Springs exit, the 500-acre **Donner Ski Ranch** (19320 Donner Pass Rd., Norden, CA, 530/426-3635, $25-42) is more ski and less resort. With tubing as well as boarding and skiing, Donner was built in 1937 and strives to maintain that old-fashioned ski value with a laid-back pace and uncrowded slopes. It has six lifts, a summit elevation of 7,031 feet, and a vertical drop of 750 feet.

Catering more to more highly skilled skiers, close by is the recently expanded **Sugar Bowl** resort (629 Sugar Bowl Rd., Norden, CA,

---

adults, $15 children) and the 3.5-hour dinner-dance excursion ($65 adults, $35 children).

Zephyr Cove Resort Marina (775/589-4906) runs a parasailing concession and rents open-bow runabouts, ski boats, cruisers, deck boats, pedal boats, canoes, kayaks, electric Sun Kats, water skis, wetsuits, and more. Reservations are advised.

Hop on a horse at **Zephyr Cove Stables** (775/588-5664), where friendly cowpokes

guide riders along the lake and over tree-lined trails on excursions of 1–2 hours. Chuck wagon meals are provided on some rides.

A snack shop offers burgers, and a bar and grill restaurant overlooks the pier. A free shuttle runs back and forth to the casino area. Finally, after an exciting day on the water with your honey, why not get married by **The Dream Maker** (775/831-6419, www.wedtahoe.com), along the shoreline or on a cruise?

530/426-9000, $71-77). With half its runs catering to advanced skiers and nearly one-third to intermediates, it has a summit elevation of 8,383 feet, 13 lifts, 95 runs, and a vertical drop of 1,500 feet.

The famous **Squaw Valley** resort (1960 Squaw Valley Rd., Olympic Valley, CA, 530/583-6985, $86-92), site of the 1960 Winter Olympics, lies northwest of Tahoe City. Seventy percent of its runs are geared for beginners and intermediates. It has 33 lifts, a summit elevation of 9,050 feet, a vertical drop of 2,850 feet, and more than 4,000 acres of terrain served by lifts in its 8,300-acre spread. It also offers a ski school, child care, and cross-country trails. Closer to the lake on Highway 89 is **Alpine Meadows** (2600 Alpine

Meadows Rd., Tahoe City, CA, 530/583-4232 or 800/441-4423, $71-77). Serving skiers of all abilities, it has 13 lifts, a summit elevation of 8,637 feet, and a vertical drop of 1,800 feet. Its runs are 25 percent beginner, 40 percent intermediate, and 35 percent advanced. Its ski schools include lessons for disabled people. The "Shreadows" is Alpine Meadows' four-run terrain park.

Just south of Tahoe City off Highway 89 is Tahoe's oldest resort, **Granlibakken** (725 Granlibakken Rd., Tahoe City, CA, 800/543-3221, $23), with one lift, a summit elevation of 6,500 feet, and a vertical drop of 300 feet. It is set up for beginners and families, with low rates and lessons. Forty percent of its runs are beginner, the rest intermediate.

© JOHN DICKINSON/WWW.123RF.COM

Donner Lake California, from old Soda Springs Road

Then spend the night in one of Zephyr Cove Resort's guest rooms (778/589-4907, $150–350). The resort was built in the early 1900s, and much of the original architecture and charm remain. A variety of accommodations includes six guest rooms in the lodge that sleep 2–6 people; there are also bungalows, cabins, cottages, studios, and chalets that can accommodate up to 10.

In winter, the **Zephyr Cove Snowmobile Center** (775/589-4908) outfits riders with one of its 100 late-model Yamaha and Ski-Doo snowmobiles, as well as certified helmets, bibs, gloves, and boots.

The **Pine Cone Resort** (601 U.S. 50, 800/624-3887, $70–110) right on the highway about five miles on the Nevada side of the state line, just north of Nevada Beach, has condo-like rooms with kitchenettes and fireplaces. It books quickly in the summer.

You can also camp or park an RV across the highway from the lodge at **Zephyr Cove RV Park** (800/23-TAHOE—800/238-2463, $29) a recently renovated campground under the pine trees. There are 93 spaces for motor homes, all with full hookups; seven are pull-throughs. There are also 47 walk-in tent sites. Restrooms have flush toilets and hot showers; public phones, sewage disposal, and laundry are available.

Cave Rock

Continue north on U.S. 50 four miles to this legendary Tahoe landmark. One tunnel through the rock dates from the early 1900s; another dates back into prehistory, fashioned by the Great Spirit with a spear. Just before you reach the tunnel, there's a turnoff for a parking lot, a lakefront picnic area, and a boat launch, with Cave Rock towering overhead. Day-use fees ($7 per vehicle, $17 to camp) are charged at Cave Rock beach. This is a popular boat-launch spot, and the fishing is good too. Keep an eye out for the Loch Ness Monster's cousin, Tahoe Tessie, who may just live under an out-cropping here.

Glenbrook

Another four miles north on U.S. 50 is the Glenbrook historical marker. Glenbrook was the site of the first non-Washoe settlements at Lake Tahoe, dating to 1860. Friday's Station opened that year a few miles above Glenbrook along the Placerville Road to Genoa over Kingsbury Grade. A year later, A. W. Pray established a sawmill at Glenbrook, and in 1862 the Lake Bigler Toll Road connected Friday's Station to Carson City by way of King's Canyon, the route U.S. 50 follows today. Finally, in 1863 Tahoe's first hotel was constructed at Glenbrook.

CASINOS
Harveys

- **Restaurants:** 19 Kitchen, Cabo Wabo, Hard Rock Café, Sage Room Steakhouse, Sierra Choices deli, Starbucks, Cinnabon

Beautiful and imposing, Cave Rock is sacred to the Native Americans of the area.

- **Entertainment:** Cabaret Theater, Harveys Outdoor Arena
- **Nightlife:** Cabo Wabo Cantina

◖ **Harveys** (18 Hwy. 50, Stateline, 775/588-2411 or 800/HARVEYS—800/427-8397, $89–199) is a Harrah's-owned 740-room hotel, the largest on the lake; the Lake Tower was completed in 1987. The casino is also monumental at 52,500 square feet; a wooden "path" helps you to navigate the gaming area. On the back wall of the poker room is the world's largest hand-tooled leather mural, commissioned by Harvey Gross in 1946. It recreates a scene from Virginia City at the height of the Comstock Lode era, taking some liberties with the characters and the setting.

Interestingly, the front desk is on a level lower than the casino, under a two-story chandelier, so you don't have to lug your suitcases past the blackjack pit. The guest rooms are the best in South Lake Tahoe, with the best mountain and lake views. Accommodations are large and tastefully decorated in soft mauve or rustic vermillion.

Harveys boasts several restaurants. The top of the lot is the casually elegant **19 Kitchen** (775/588-2411, 6–9 P.M. Tues.–Thurs., 5:30–10 P.M. Fri.–Sat., $25–40), which has the best panoramic lake views of any restaurant in Stateline, set off by two-window alcoves and three levels of tables.

Downstairs on the tunnel level is **Cabo Wabo** (8 A.M.–10 P.M. daily, $10–20) for Mexican and Caribbean dishes and specialty drinks made from Sammy Hagar's infamous Cabo Wabo tequila. The lounge portion of the restaurant features live entertainment until early in the morning. Upstairs in the casino, the **Sage Room** (5–10 P.M. daily, $25–40) is a steak house that looks just as it has for more than 60 years. Harveys also has a **Hard Rock Café** (11 A.M.–11:30 P.M. Sun.–Thurs., 11 A.M.–midnight Fri.–Sat., $15–30).

Harveys **Outdoor Arena** is busy throughout the summer, with superstars such as Elton John, Stevie Nicks, and Bob Dylan among the recent performers. Inside, the **Cabaret Theater** hosts top names and budding comics

at The Improv. Typical of a Harrah's property, the bars and nightlife are relatively sedate, although **Cabo Wabo** presents live rockers on weekends.

Harveys has an interesting history: Gross's Wagon Wheel was the first bona fide casino at South Lake Tahoe. Harvey Gross was a meat wholesaler in Sacramento who supplied the beef to the restaurants and resorts at the lake in the 1940s. Gambling on growth, he and his wife, Llewellyn, bought some property near the California state line across from two existing slot joints. They started in a one-room log-cabin saloon with six slot machines, three blackjack tables, and a six-stool snack bar and quickly added a dozen more slots and a gas pump out front—the only one at the time on the old Lincoln Highway (U.S. 50) between Placerville and Carson City. Harveys grew steadily and quietly over the years and was owned solely by the Gross family until 1994, when Harveys went public.

In 1980 it played a central role in one of the most bizarre episodes in recent Nevada history. Casino executives arrived on August 26 to find a new piece of equipment in their offices. A note on the new copy machine indicated that it contained a bomb and demanded $3 million. The executives and FBI agents quickly evacuated the hotel; the machine, packed with 800 pounds of dynamite, exploded, blowing a massive three-story hole in the casino's west wall but injuring no one. John Birges Sr., a Fresno, California, landscaper who had lost nearly $1 million in Lake Tahoe casinos, was arrested, convicted, and sentenced to life in prison for the crime; he died in custody in 1996.

Harrah's

- **Restaurants:** Friday's Station Steak and Seafood Grill, Gi Fu Loh, Forest Buffet, American River Café, Cliché, Manchu Wok, LA Italian Kitchen, Fatburger
- **Entertainment:** South Shore Room, Casino Center Stage

- **Attractions:** Reflections Spa, Family Fun Center

- **Nightlife:** Vex

Harveys' sister property, Harrah's (15 U.S. 50, Stateline, 775/588-6611 or 800/HARRAHS—800/427-7247, $99–189) is one of the country's top 10 resorts. This is luxury, pure and simple: Each of its 525 sage- and maple-accented guest rooms has two full bathrooms with a phone and TV in each, along with a minibar, great mountain or lake views from the picture windows, and 500 square feet in which to spread out. The 65,000-square-foot L-shaped casino is isolated from most of the resort's restaurants. The **Reflections Spa** (8 A.M.–8 P.M. daily) lets you take a trip around the world of indulgence with Turkish steam rooms, Roman baths, and Swedish massage. The kids arcade was tripled in size and is now the **Family Fun Center,** and families also enjoy the hotel's unique dome-covered swimming pool. Lounge acts perform in the **South Shore Room.**

Lovers of grand views can still get their fill at the resort's **Friday's Station Steak and Seafood Grill** (775/588-6611, 5:30–9:30 P.M. Sun.–Fri., 5–10 P.M. Sat., $40–60). On the other side of the top floor is the **Forest Buffet** (5–10 P.M. daily, brunch Sat.–Sun., $10–15) boasting art deco lighting fixtures and a gorgeous sight line to the lake.

The **Vex** nightclub presents a mini "Cirquesque" show of aerialists as well as the "Vex Girls," a bevy of dancing beauties starting at midnight Friday–Saturday.

Horizon Casino

- **Restaurants:** Four Seasons, Town Square Buffet, Starbucks

- **Entertainment:** Golden Cabaret, Horizon Stadium Cinemas, Arcade Worl

- **Nightlife:** Aspen Lounge

Horizon Casino (50 U.S. 50, Stateline, 800/648-3322, $50–120) was opened in 1965 by Del Webb, owner of the Sahara and Mint

hotels in Las Vegas. Webb first arrived in Las Vegas in 1946 to build Bugsy Siegel's fabulous Flamingo, and in 1951 he was hired to build the Sahara in return for shares in the hotel. By the time he opened the Sahara Tahoe he was one of the largest hotel-casino operators in the state. His company sold the casino in 1990, and it is now the brightest and airiest casino on the lake. It also has the GameWorld arcade, an eight-screen movie theater, and the largest outdoor pool in Lake Tahoe. The **Golden Cabaret** brings in impressionist and musical acts.

Montbleu

- **Restaurants:** Ciera, Café del Sol, the Buffet, The Zone, Montbleu Café

- **Entertainment:** Blu, Opal, Montbleu Theater

- **Attractions:** Onsen spa

- **Nightlife:** HQ, The Zone

Caesars Entertainment shed this property, formerly Caesars Tahoe, in 2005 in preparation for its merger with Harrah's, and while Montbleu (55 U.S. 50, Stateline, 775/588-3515 or 888/829-7630, $69–239) has lost its Roman theme, it continues to impress with its amenities and overall atmosphere. Opened in 1980, the 440-room hotel features a picturesque indoor pool with boulder borders and a big rock waterfall in a secluded lagoon setting. After a day on the hiking trails or slopes and a rug-cutting evening with **Blu** nightclub's top DJs or live music most weekends, the Roman tubs and luxurious bedding in the rooms, along with Montbleu's Onsen spa services, will have you rejuvenated and ready to do it all again.

Four Diamond award–winner **◖ Ciera** (800/648-3353, 5:30–10 P.M. Wed.–Sun., $35–60) delivers melt-in-your-mouth New York strip steak; complement it with the blistered asparagus. And with a menu longer than a *New Yorker* article, **Café del Sol** (24 hours daily, $10–20) will wake up your taste buds at any time of day.

Lakeside Inn

- **Restaurants:** Latin Soul, Timber House
- **Nightlife:** Tavern Bar, Casino Bar, Timber House Bar

Small, rustically designed, and locals-oriented Lakeside Inn (168 U.S. 50, Stateline, 775/588-7777, $79–169) has pet-friendly rooms decorated with lodge paneling and comfortable bedding. The casino offers liberal odds and even conducts courses on the most popular games. Nightlife is sparse, but its location puts guests in the middle of the action.

Go on island time at ◖ **Latin Soul** (775/588-7777, 8 A.M.–10 P.M. daily, $10–20). Its pan-Caribbean fare—get the jerk chicken with coconut rice, fried bananas, and okra—will have you feelin' irie, mon.

ACCOMMODATIONS

Aside from the casinos, lodging options are slim on the Nevada side. The best is the remote **Ridge Tahoe** (400 Ridge Club Dr., Stateline, 775/588-3553, $72–148), accessed via a steep and snaking four-mile climb. The views make it a popular site for outdoor weddings. Many of the guest rooms and suites are fairly old but terrifically maintained. Even the standard rooms contain refrigerators and microwaves. On-site recreation includes a theater; a miniature golf course; racquetball, basketball, and tennis courts; an indoor-outdoor pool; and a spa and exercise room. The casually gourmet **Hungry Bear** (775/588-3553, hours vary, $25–40), a deli, and a bar complete the full-service amenities.

The guest rooms at the all-suite **Lodge at Kingsbury Crossing** (133 Deer Run Court, Stateline, 775/588-6247, $85–157) sleep 4–6 in queen beds and queen sofa-sleepers. Each suite has a bathroom, a balcony or patio, and a kitchenette with a microwave and a refrigerator.

Family ski weekenders will appreciate **Tahoe Summit Village Stateline** (750 Wells Fargo Lane, Zephyr Cove, 775/588-8571 or 866/265-2041, $89–215), located between Heavenly Ski Resort North's Boulder and Stagecoach chairlifts. Two-bedroom and loft suites are smoke-free and overlook Carson Valley. They all have full kitchens, spa tubs, and wood-burning fireplaces. Guests can enjoy the spa, common room, and access to the swimming pool next door.

Doc's Cottages (151 Stateline Ave., Stateline, 775/588-2264, $60–90) are very rustic but clean and cheap, with plenty of character (including uneven floorboards). There are few amenities, but the location is unbeatable—it's next door to Harveys and a stone's throw from the Heavenly Ski Resort. Each cabin has a full kitchen, but you'll have to supply your own cookware and silverware.

There are hundreds of quaint and cheap motel rooms just across the California state line. California also offers lakeside tent and trailer parking. For more information, contact the **Lake Tahoe Visitors Authority** (169 U.S. 50, Zephyr Cove, 530/544-5050, reservations 800/210-3429, www.virtualtahoe.com). The *Lake Tahoe Travel Planner* (www.laketahoe.com/tahoeguide) has a good amount of useful information, including a lodging guide. Also check out **www.tahoeinfo.com** for heaps of useful brochures, magazines, and other information about the California-side attractions.

FOOD

Stateline is also blessed with many stand-alone eateries for folks who want to escape the resorts. Gaze across emerald fairways at pink sunsets and creamy peaks at **Edgewood Tahoe** (100 Lake Pkwy., Stateline, 775/588-2787, 6–11 P.M. daily, $25–35). The fresh fish and steaks are deceptively simply prepared and complemented by sauces and flavors from around the world. The restaurant's chalet decor completes the idyllic alpine setting and seals our vote as the best noncasino restaurant on the south shore.

Veteran chef Camille Schwartz's **Mirabelle** (290 Kingsbury Grade Rd., Stateline, 775/586-1007, 5:30–11 P.M. Tues.–Sun., $22–38) serves classic, traditional, and rich French cuisine. The sauces drive home the flavor, especially the red wine reduction served with the lamb.

LAKE TAHOE AND VICINITY

Camille's tender ostrich fillet comes at a perfect medium-rare.

The **Chart House** (392 Kingsbury Grade Rd., Stateline, 775/586-6276, 5–9:30 P.M. Sun.–Thurs., 5–10 P.M. Fri. –Sat., $25–40) could charge diners a seating fee just to watch the sun set over Lake Tahoe from its cliff-side perch; thankfully it doesn't, nor does it try to cover the view and ambiance in the check. Prices are hefty, to be sure, but not out of line for top seafood and steak in a resort destination. Bypass the prime rib and stick with the Maine lobster or shrimp. Order the lava cake even if you have to spend two hours on the treadmill before dinner.

For a completely different atmosphere, head to **Fox and Hound** (237 Tramway Rd., Stateline, 775/588-8887, 7:30 A.M.–2:30 A.M. Sun.–Thurs., 7:30 A.M.–4 A.M. Fri.–Sat., $8–15) just off Highway 207 (Kingsbury Grade Rd.).

Grab a beer, pizza, or chicken wings and settle in for some live music on weekends or video poker anytime. Other casual meals worth leaving the slot machines for include the raw fish at **Sushi Pier** (177 Lake Tahoe Blvd., Stateline, 775/588-8588, 11:30 A.M.–9:30 P.M. Mon.–Sat., 11:30 A.M.–9 P.M. Sun., $15–30), the pancakes at **Red Hut Café** (229 Kingsbury Grade Rd., Stateline, 775/588-7488, 6 A.M.–2 P.M. daily, $10–20), and the shrimp tempura at **Thai Delight** (177 U.S. 50, Stateline, 775/588-5888, 11 A.M.–3 P.M. and 5–9 P.M. Mon.–Sat., $20–30).

INFORMATION

The **Tahoe-Douglas Chamber of Commerce** (169 U.S. 50, Stateline, 775/588-1728, www.tahoechamber.org) visitors guide can supply tons of information on everything from casinos to nature trails, ski packages, weddings, coupon booklets; it also has a reservation service.

The North Shore

Head over to Lakeshore Drive in **Incline Village** to check out one of the most valuable and scenic two-mile stretches of real estate in Nevada. Tool around the town's own golf courses, tennis clubs, beaches, and ski resorts and you may get the idea that Incline Village is, well, prosperous. Consider this: Incline Villagers make up 3 percent of the population of Washoe County and pay 10 percent of the total property taxes that the county collects. All that disposable income supports myriad cultural opportunities. Sierra Nevada College offers degrees in fine arts, humanities, and social sciences, and the community has thriving arts and historic preservation groups.

Incline also has the best weather on the lake, with 300 days of sunshine per year, and the lowest accumulation of snow, so it's not surprising that the village has more outdoor-related stores—outfitters, ski and ski repair, sportswear, camping, running shoes, cycling, fishing, and the like—than anywhere else in Nevada. The population increases by more than double in the balmy summer months.

Nearby **Crystal Bay** is similarly exclusive. Dating to 1960, the original layout of the development is still very much intact, with mansions on the lake, chalets on the mountainsides, and condos on the flats all surrounded by dense forest, thanks to second-generation growth and strict tree-cutting regulations. The commercial zones stretch in a thin line along Highway 28 and down Southwood Boulevard, designed to prevent congestion and preclude the establishment of a town center.

The luster and lure of Crystal Bay casinos has worn thin since the days when Judy Garland and Marilyn Monroe came here to rub shoulders with Jack Kennedy, but efforts are under way to revitalize the area's appeal as a resort destination.

SIGHTS AND RECREATION
◖ Thunderbird Lodge

This spectacular example of historic preservation, just south of Incline Village on Highway 28, is well worth taking the time to explore.

The lodge was built in 1936 as a summer cottage for the fabulously wealthy George Whittell and designed by noted Nevada architect Frederic DeLongchamps. It has two master bedrooms, a great room with a movie screen, and extensive servants' quarters. Whittell, a colorful playboy and bon vivant in his day, entertained guests in the Card House, a beautiful stone room that was connected to the house via a tunnel that visitors can still go through. Whittell also had a penchant for wild animals, and visitors can inspect the Elephant House, which was once home to the millionaire's pet pachyderm, Mingo.

Whittell's taste for personal indulgence is manifest in his yacht, the *Thunderbird,* a mahogany and stainless steel speedboat he commissioned in 1939 for $87,000, or $3.3 million in today's dollars. Embellished by Whittell with crystal accents, the floating palace was further renovated by subsequent owner Bill Harrah into the casino pioneer's "70-mph speedboat."

Now under the loving care of a nonprofit association, the lodge is open for 75-minute **guided tours** (800/GO-TAHOE—800/468-2463, Tues.–Sat. June–Oct., $39 adults, $19 ages 6–12) that include a shuttle from the Incline Village–Crystal Bay Visitors Center (969 Tahoe Blvd., Incline Village, 775/832-1606). Tours take visitors through the servants' quarters, the original kitchen, and the Lighthouse Room. Walk through the 200-yard tunnel to visit the Card House and boathouse where the yacht resides.

The 40-foot *Tahoe* (888/867-6394) departs from the Tahoe Keys Marina (2435 Venice Dr. E., South Lake Tahoe, CA) for the lodge at 10 A.M. Tuesday–Saturday on a narrated five-hour voyage ($110 adults, $55 under age 12) with continental breakfast and full bar. Cave Rock, the shoreline mansions, and birds of prey are included on the tour.

Skiing

Most resorts make snow when nature falls short; call their snow-phone lines for current conditions. In addition to lodging and shopping, most resorts offer equipment rentals and ski schools. You can also buy ski packages, family packages, and lift tickets for the North Shore downhill ski resorts. Cross-country packages are available too. For detailed information, contact the **North Lake Tahoe Resort Association** (530/583-3494 or 888/434-1262, www.nltra.org), the **Reno-Sparks Convention and Visitors Authority** (800/FOR-RENO—800/367-7366, www.visitrenotahoe.com), or the individual resorts.

Billing itself as a family ski resort with great views of the lake, **Diamond Peak at Ski Incline** (1210 Ski Way, 5 miles north of Incline Village off Hwy. 431, 775/832-1177, $49) offers a summit elevation of 8,540 feet, seven lifts, and a vertical drop of 1,840 feet, the fourth longest at Lake Tahoe. The resort has expanded into the peak's upper reaches, upgraded its snowmaking system, and installed new quad chairlifts, with a new Child Ski Center in 2010. It also offers a ski school and day care. Diamond Peak is also known for its cross-country skiing, with 16 trails on 22 miles of groomed track, one-third advanced, half intermediate, and the rest beginner.

With 1,000 skiable acres, **Mount Rose-Ski Tahoe** (22222 Mt. Rose Hwy., 775/849-0704 or 800/SKI-ROSE—800/754-7673, www.skirose.com, $69–74) has Tahoe's highest base elevation (8,260 feet) and summit elevation (9,700 feet), five lifts, 43 runs and trails, and a 1,440-foot vertical drop evenly divided among beginner, intermediate, and advanced trails. You can also rent equipment and take classes at the ski school. It's on Highway 431 just 22 miles from Reno; several of Reno's larger hotels and casinos offer twice-daily shuttles.

◖ Lake Tahoe-Nevada State Park

On the east shore of the lake south of Incline Village is Lake Tahoe–Nevada State Park. It preserves three miles of shoreline along with a 10-mile-long stretch of the wooded Carson Range adjoining Toiyabe National Forest. There's a lot of wilderness to explore on several high-country trails at elevations of

LOGGING SCARS SLOW TO HEAL

Only 100-125 years ago, 50,000 acres of virgin forest around Lake Tahoe, mostly sugar and Jeffrey pine, cedar, and some fir, were clear-cut. As much as 80 percent of the lake basin's trees were then milled, shipped, and buried forever in the shafts, drifts, and tunnels of undermined Mount Davidson. The big Jeffreys were what the loggers were after, and they took them all, leaving only a few firs that provided the seeds of today's forest. The second-growth firs have regenerated the lake's forests, but they are completely lacking in species, age, and size diversity, and therefore in health.

Furthermore, thanks in part to aggressive fire-suppression policies, these young trees have overpopulated their habitat, and fir, unlike pine, is extremely drought-intolerant, which has left most of the forest susceptible to attack by fir beetles. Since most of the lakeside is also thickly populated by humans, fires that naturally thin out the forests have been suppressed, and conservation policies strictly inhibit logging activities. These factors together are why so many of Tahoe's trees are dead or dying.

Although some tree die-off is beneficial to the health of the forest, the recent ravages are unprecedented. Tahoe National Forest officials estimate that 25-33 percent of the trees in the 200,000-acre Tahoe Basin are dead or dying, and half the forest, roughly 4 million trees, is in grave danger from drought and insects. Of course, the danger is only relative to people, houses, and to some extent wildlife. The natural cycle of a forest is growth, decay, fire, and regeneration. Native Americans found it possible to live with fire, simply moving their settlements to escape the danger. Nonnative settlers, however, built houses that couldn't easily be moved out of the way of the flames and therefore saw forest fires as destructive. For the last 100 years, the lack of fire has been the primary element that has prevented the forest from recovering its health.

On the other hand, it's possible that the beetles are doing fire's work for it by thinning the forest. The insects also supply food for birds and other predators. Soon, predator populations will increase and eliminate the beetles. Then it'll rain, and a new forest will emerge. Nature could be providing an alternative cycle to cope with the human suppression of fire.

More recently, the U.S. Forest Service has begun to work diligently to lessen the possibility of catastrophic fire and to improve forest health by thinning the forest.

6,200–8,900 feet. Most of the trees are second growth, at most 120 years old: pine, fir, cedar, and aspen up to 7,000 feet, red fir and lodgepole pine above that. Countless birds and rodents live here, and the black bear population is increasing in the area, so be careful.

HIKING

An easy 2.3-mile nature trail circles Spooner Lake, which takes about an hour; keep an eye out for ospreys prowling the shoreline for a fish dinner. A post marks the five-mile trail through aspen-dotted North Canyon to Marlette Lake, which still supplies water to Virginia City, as it has for 120 years; the moderate 10-mile round-trip trail takes 4–6 hours to traverse. The trail continues 11 miles to the far trailhead at Hidden Beach and has become part of the Tahoe Rim Trail.

From the Memorial Point overlook and parking lot, it's just under a mile to the state park's **north trailhead,** which is unmarked but obvious at a fire track between two posts. You can also park 0.25 miles farther along on the north side of the trailhead just beyond the park boundaries, but here you're competing with visitors to Hidden Beach and from the south residential section of Incline Village. The trail starts climbing quickly up the granite slopes of the Carson Range. It's one hour (1.5 miles) to Tunnel Creek Station, another hour (1 mile) to Twin Lakes, and one more hour to Hobart Creek Reservoir, where you loop back past Red House camping area to Tunnel Creek. Or walk across the park down to Spooner Lake, which is 16 miles and takes at least 10 hours.

BIKING

In summer, activities at Spooner Lake include mountain biking on the **Flume Trail.** This ride, an exciting single track 1,600 feet above Lake Tahoe, is one of the most scenic rides anywhere, providing spectacular views of the lake; the trail follows the path of a historic flume line that once provided water to the silver mines of Virginia City. Most mountain bike groups start at Spooner Lake: Take North Canyon Road to Marlette Lake dam (6 miles, 800-foot elevation gain) and follow the historic flume line 4.4 miles to Tunnel Creek Road. From there you can return to Spooner Lake, a 21-mile round-trip that takes 3–5 hours; descend 1,600 feet (2.5 miles) to Highway 28, a 13-mile one-way trip, which takes 3–4 hours; take a backcountry loop back to Spooner Lake (24 miles round-trip, 4–6 hours); or a different backcountry loop back to Spooner Lake via the Tahoe Rim Trail (22 miles, 2,000-foot elevation gain).

Nevada's Division of State Parks published a pamphlet with a basic map and information about these trails called *Lake Tahoe Nevada State Park Backcountry*; look for it at the state park office (Sand Harbor, Hwy. 28, 775/831-0494) or at the Incline Village–Crystal Bay Visitors and Convention Bureau (969 Tahoe Blvd., Incline Village, 775/832-1606).

You can bring your own bike and use the **Flume Trail Shuttle Service** ($10 pp) to bring you back up to Spooner Lake, or rent a bike ($45–65) from **Spooner Lake Outdoor Company** (Hwy. 28, Glenbrook, 775/749-5349).

WINTER SPORTS

In winter, Spooner Lake has 53 miles of

TAHOE GOING FOR GOLD IN 2022

Dedicated sports fans and several northern Nevada and California tourist boards are working to make their Olympic dreams come true by bringing the 2022 games back to the Sierras. The organizing committee is evaluating venues, athlete housing options, visitor accommodations, marketing plans, financing, and more in order to present a statement of interest to the U.S. Olympic Committee in spring 2012. Selected cities will then bid for the chance to be the U.S. choice to host the games. The International Olympic Committee will make its choice in the second half of 2015, giving the winner enough time to build the infrastructure and organize the Olympics.

The Reno-Tahoe area has several advantages. Its ski resorts can easily accommodate the alpine ski events, and it would not take much work to groom local areas into world-class cross-country courses. The University of Nevada, Reno, campus and Tahoe resort hotels along with plenty of hotel and motel rooms across the California border could be used to house athletes, spectators, and media. If that's not enough, Las Vegas is only an hour's plane ride away. Mackay Arena, on campus, could host opening and closing ceremonies as well as medal presentations.

Northern Nevada also appears to have an advantage over Denver, its U.S. challenger, identified as a promising American site by the same key U.S. Olympic Committee that tabbed Lake Tahoe. Denver had a chance to host the Winter Olympic Games in 1976, but a referendum by Colorado voters led to the city backing out. Innsbruck, Austria, was named the host city for that year.

If Lake Tahoe were to win the sweepstakes to host in 2022, it would mark the return of the Olympics to the region after 62 years. Squaw Valley, California, near Lake Tahoe, hosted the 1960 Winter Olympics. Lake Tahoe's competition promises to be formidable; cities in China, Romania, Switzerland, Spain, Ukraine, Canada, New Zealand, and Chile have expressed interest in hosting the 2022 games.

LAKE TAHOE WATER TRAIL

What the Tahoe Rim Trail is to hikers, the Lake Tahoe Water Trail is to kayakers. Billed as a "water route through paradise," the water trail is designed as a six-day paddle tour around the lake's 72-mile shoreline. While it's an intensive workout for beginning kayakers and canoeists, the trail also provides plenty of opportunity to rest, explore, and learn.

The trail starts at Sand Harbor in the northwest corner of Lake Tahoe, just south of Incline Village. The first day takes you west past Incline Village and tiny, boulder-strewn Bucks Beach. Upscale steak houses and hearty Tex-Mex restaurants as well as a variety of hotel options will be welcome sights as you tie up in the Agate Bay enclave of Tahoe Vista. On Day 2 you'll round the bend and head south along the Tahoe National Forest. Lunch at Carnelian Bay, then get back in the boat and finish your day's journey at Tahoe City, with its upscale shops and restaurants. Or if you want to save a few dollars, paddle two miles farther and pitch your tent at William Kent Campground. You'll see some of the lake's palaces on Day 3 along the western shore. There are plenty of sandy beaches here too to take advantage of.

There's even a water slide at Meeks Bay. On Day 4, you'll float past the Rubicon Trail and Emerald Bay, home of the Vikingsholm mansion. Turn eastward to begin Day 5 and make your way along the south shore and back into Nevada. Stateline offers Nevada-style entertainments and restaurants. Live it up, you're almost done. Continue north a bit and camp at Zephyr Cove. On the final day, point your kayak northward along the lake's eastern shore in Nevada. You'll go past the beautiful sacred Cave Rock – keep an eye out for Tahoe Tessie, the lake's sea serpent. You'll also see magnificent secluded beaches before arriving back at Sand Harbor.

The Lake Tahoe Water Trail Committee (www.laketahoewatertrail.org) publishes the waterproof *Lake Tahoe Water Trail Map & Guide* to help independent paddlers find their way around. It includes GPS waypoints, points of interest, restaurants, camping areas, and more. Several outfitters and tour companies in both Nevada and California can guide individuals and groups along the full circumnavigation of Lake Tahoe or on shorter daylong or weekend paddle trips.

groomed cross-country skiing trails spread over 9,000 acres with skiing for beginners up to experts. The **Spooner Lake Lodge** (information 775/749-5349, conditions 775/887-8844, 8:30 A.M.–5 P.M. daily) is right off Highway 28. Trail fees are $21 adults, free under age 7 or over age 70; ski rentals ($5–20) and lessons are also available.

BEACHES

Sand Harbor (Hwy. 28, parking $8) is the main beach in the park. A spit of land, crowded with pines and boulders, juts into the lake, on the south side of which lies a gorgeous long, sandy, and sunny crescent beach. Because of the spit and the prevailing winds and currents, the swells are occasionally high enough to surf on; foam boards are best as freshwater is not as buoyant as the ocean. The term often used to describe the

water temperature is "bracing," and the water reaches its highest temperature, 68°F on the surface, during the last two weeks of July.

The north side of the spit is a different scene entirely: calm and clear water, rugged rocky land, and little beach. Known as Divers Cove, it's a great spot for snorkeling and sunbathing.

Sandy Point, at the end of the spit (left of the first parking lot), has an excellent 0.75-mile nature trail with interpretive displays in summer. It takes an easy half-hour and is well worth the time for a close look at the lake's ecology. Pick up free handouts at park headquarters near the entrance.

Sand Harbor has a wheelchair-accessible boardwalk, three large parking lots, restrooms, group picnic facilities, lots of water fountains, and no concession stands. This is effective for limiting litter, but bring everything you need with you, except glass bottles, which are prohibited. Get there early on weekends.

Hidden Beach is a 0.5-mile-long stretch of prime Tahoe shoreline where nude bathing and skinny-dipping are de rigueur. The U.S. Forest Service and the Trust for Public Land protect nearly 11,000 acres of Tahoe real estate in this area. How to get to Secret Harbor is kind of a secret, but here's a hint: Grab a parking space near other cars on the stretch of Highway 28 between the north edge of the state park and the south edge of Incline Village, then bushwhack through the undergrowth and overgrowth down to the lake.

ARTS AND EVENTS

During the summer, Sand Harbor is the site of a fine music and drama festival in an excellent venue with a new outdoor stage. Every summer since 1978 the North Tahoe Fine Arts Council has sponsored four days of music in mid-July and a Shakespeare Festival during the entire month of August. Call 800/74-SHOWS—800/747-4697 to order tickets and for current details; you can also buy tickets at the Incline Village Visitors Center (969 Tahoe Blvd., Incline Village, 775/832-1606).

CASINOS

Of the five casinos on the north shore, one is in Incline Village and the other four are in Crystal Bay.

Hyatt Regency

· **Restaurants:** Lone Eagle Grill, Sierra Café,

STEAMSHIPS ON THE LAKE

The tree-covered slopes surrounding Lake Tahoe presented an irresistible temptation for the entrepreneurs serving the mines of the Comstock Lode. The mines gobbled up tons of timber shoring; railroads shuttling ore out and supplies in needed wood to fire their steam locomotives; miners' campfires and cook stoves, assays, mills, and other businesses needed wood in order to operate.

But for would-be lumber barons to exploit Tahoe's vast lumber resources, they first had to access the trees and get the logs to their sawmills. They used trains, flumes, horses, and various other transportation methods to process lumber for use on the Comstock. The need for efficiency led lumber moguls such as Duane Bliss to commission construction and delivery of steamships. Among Bliss's commissions was the *Meteor,* built in a shipyard in Wilmington, Delaware. Bliss had the ship disassembled and the sections transported to the shores of the lake by railroad and oxcart. Skeptics doubted the iron-hulled ship would even float, let along provide valuable service. But float it did, and it moved at an impressive 20 knots, towing vast rafts of logs from all over the lakeshore to Bliss's mills at Glenbrook. The *Meteor* was well worth Bliss's investment, serving faithfully for two decades until a road was completed around the lake. With automobile transportation made more reliable and economically viable, the need for lumber freighted by steam waned; the *Meteor* carried mail and tourists for another 30 years before being scuttled in 1939.

The end of the Comstock era did not mean the end of steamships on Lake Tahoe. Bliss, his fortune secure, had the majestic 169-foot *Tahoe* built in San Francisco and transported in sections across the Sierra. The biggest and most luxurious ship ever to ply the lake, the *Tahoe* gleamed in brass, mahogany, teak, and glass. Guests reveled in the leather upholstery, marble bathrooms, and the latest amenities, like running water in the staterooms, electric lights, and steam heat. The ship made a circuit of the lake daily during summer, delivering not only passengers but freight and mail. Alas, the road around the lake made the steamer redundant, and after languishing unused for several years, she was sent to the bottom in 1940.

For more on the fascinating history of steamboats on Lake Tahoe, read *Steamboats of Lake Tahoe* by Lyndall Baker Landauer.

Lakeside Beach Bar & Grill, Stillwater Pool Bar & Grille

- **Nightlife:** Cutthroat's Saloon, Pier 111, Sports Bar, Lobby Bar

Incline's Hyatt Regency (111 Country Club Dr. at Lakeshore Blvd., Incline Village, 775/832-1234, $180–280) is the closest hotel-casino to forest and lakeside in Nevada. Its quaint alpine lodge exterior masks the resort's size. It boasts 422 guest rooms, a massive stone fireplace, and a full-service casino that includes a high-limit area and old-money atmosphere. Guest rooms are 400 square feet in crisp white, rustic hunter green, and rust red decor with big-game accents and outdoor prints. A saltwater spa, a private beach, tennis courts, bike and nature trails, golf, lake jaunts on the Hyatt's private boats, and gourmet dining complete the getaway-from-it-all experience.

Cal-Neva Resort Spa and Casino

- **Restaurants:** Lakeview Dining Room

The class act of the north shore for five decades has been ◖ **Cal-Neva Resort Spa and Casino** (2 Stateline Rd., Incline Village, 775/832-4000 or 800/225-6382, $105–162), a nine-story, 220-room boutique resort on a narrow spit of land at the edge of Crystal Bay. Hard times closed the casino in 2010, but it's now under new management, with plans to reopen the gaming floor. Meanwhile, the hotel, restaurants, and bars remain open. The hotel was part-owned by Frank Sinatra in the early 1960s before the Chairman's gaming license was revoked for showing hospitality to Chicago organized-crime figure Sam Giancana. Cal-Neva embraces the area's ubiquitous alpine architecture, with a dramatic sloped-roof facade, extensive stonework, and a log-wall exterior. The lodge part of the resort is actually in California; the state line runs smack down the center of the huge stone hearth and through the middle of the swimming pool outside. Cabins—Marilyn Monroe stayed in one—are a more rustic option for accommodations.

Known as the Indian Room for the poignant Washoe artwork and artifacts, the lobby has a fireplace burning real wood, massive granite boulders topped with a big stuffed bobcat, a wooden cathedral ceiling, and big-game trophies; take some time to absorb the graphically presented story of the Washoe. Peek out the back door to see the Washoe bedrock mortar in a stone boulder on the deck.

The menu changes with the seasons at the **Lakeview Dining Room** (800/225-6382, 7 A.M.–10 P.M. daily, $14–30), which has big picture windows overlooking Lake Tahoe. Many of the ingredients are harvested locally, and the brunch buffets on Mother's Day and other special occasions are sublime. Be sure to check out the Circle Bar, with its massive stained-glass ceiling.

The Cal-Neva opened on Memorial Day weekend in 1926. Supposedly it operated as an illegal casino until 1931, when gambling was legalized in Nevada; Prohibition barely made a dent in its patrons' alcohol consumption. The original lodge was restored in the 1980s, and today weddings and honeymoons account for 30 percent of the Cal-Neva's business.

Tahoe Biltmore

- **Restaurants:** Conrad's, Cafe Biltmore

The Tahoe Biltmore (5 Hwy. 28, Incline Village, 775/833-6724 or 800/BILTMOR—800/245-8667, $70–120), right on Highway 28 a block before the California state line, is homey compared to the places at the other end of the lake. Gaming includes blackjack, craps, and roulette. The 113 guest rooms and suites in the main hotel, as well as the lake-view cottages, qualify as bargain accommodations in Lake Tahoe. All come with cable television and access to the outdoor spa and pool, gift shop, and arcade.

Conrad's Restaurant (5–10 P.M. Wed.–Sun., $25–35) does grilled steaks, seafood, pasta, and a top-notch grilled chicken breast stuffed with goat cheese and chives. **Café Biltmore** (7 A.M.–10 P.M. Sun.–Thurs., 7 A.M.–midnight Fri.–Sat., $9–15) is a typical diner with atypically huge burgers and hand-cut fries. It also serves a decent—and inexpensive—pot roast at dinnertime.

Crystal Bay Club

· **Restaurants:** Steak and Lobster House, Bistro Elise

Next door to the Biltmore, the Crystal Bay Club (14 Hwy. 28, Incline Village, 775/833-6333, $229–299) is just as homey. The club opened in 1937 as the Ta-Neva-Ho and underwent a total transformation in 2003.

Continental cuisine served in a manner designed to preserve the continents and the oceans is the theme at **Bistro Elise** (8 A.M.–midnight daily, $9–15), named for Elise Norman, who owns the resort with her husband, Roger. All meals are served on recycled dishes and consumed using potato-based utensils, doggie-boxes are made from sugar cane, and the vegetable oil used in cooking goes straight to the recycler, all helping to keep the planet healthy. Bistro Elise

also works to keep its customers happy. Burgers come on a wheat bun with a side salad. You can also get French fries, capellini, and fettuccini Alfredo—all prepared with no trans fats. It's best to come for breakfast—the cafés and lattes are strong enough to jump-start guests even on the coldest of mornings—or lunch for the glorious paninis.

The wine list at the **Steak and Lobster House** (5:30–10 P.M. daily, $25–35) keeps winning awards, and the beef and lobster provide the perfect foundation for the vintages to perform their magic. The resort's wine consultant gives diners a wide selection with recommendations that make perfect pairings.

Nugget

· **Restaurants:** Izzy's Burgers

· **Nightlife:** Nugget Bar

As classy in its way as the Hyatt, Jim Kelley's Nugget (20 Hwy. 28, Incline Village, 775/831-7156) is a slot shop and video poker room with

© RYAN JERZ

LAKE TAHOE AND VICINITY

The state line runs right through the Cal-Neva. You can straddle it in the hotel or swim across it in the resort's pool.

no table games (unless you count a blackjack machine with a virtual dealer). This could be the state's only redbrick casino, which fits in nicely at the lake. Cozying up to a burger and fries from **Izzy's** on the patio is a pleasant way to spend a summertime lunch.

ACCOMMODATIONS

Gabrielli House (593 N. Dyer Circle, Incline Village, 800/731-6222, $99–179) is the only true bed-and-breakfast in Incline Village. Each of the five bedrooms has a private bath and a TV. The common-area living room is perfect for reading or dozing by the fire.

Parkside Inn at Incline (1003 Tahoe Blvd., Incline Village, 775/831-1052 or 800/824-6391, $69–149) is just south of Country Club Drive. There's no casino, but the Hyatt is three blocks away, and the Inn has a surprise in the basement: a rudimentary indoor swimming pool, hot tub, and sauna. Complimentary Internet and continental breakfast are offered for those staying in the 38 guest rooms, which are clad in knotty pine and decorated with outdoor equipment on the walls.

Cabins and Camping

Spooner Lake Cabins (775/749-5349, www.spoonerlake.com, $95–275 summer–fall, $149–350 winter), in Lake Tahoe–Nevada State Park, offer self-contained cabins with fully equipped kitchens.

Two hike-in **campgrounds** (775/831-0494), Marlette Peak and North Canyon, are available in the Lake Tahoe–Nevada State Park backcountry; each has around 10 campsites, all first-come, first-served.

FOOD
Incline Village

Along Tahoe Boulevard, Incline Village has more eclectic eateries. The **Grog n' Grist** (800 Tahoe Blvd. at Southwood Blvd., 775/831-1123, lunch daily, $10–15) is a local lunch legend, sometimes cranking out 500 sandwiches a day from its big bustling deli counter in the back.

In the Christmas Tree Center is **Mofo's**

Pizza and Pasta (884 Tahoe Blvd., 775/831-4999, 11 A.M.–10 P.M. daily, $10–20). It does subs, individual pizzas, chicken wings, and quite a decent salad bar in addition to lasagna and pasta primavera.

A great place for breakfast and lunch is the ◖ **Wildflower Cafe** (869 Tahoe Blvd., 775/831-8072, 7 A.M.–2:30 P.M. daily, $8–15). This place is no secret, and there's usually a line for breakfast, but tough it out; you'll be glad you did when your fluffy biscuits slathered in savory gravy arrive.

T's Rotisserie (901 Tahoe Blvd., 775/831-2832, 11 A.M.–8 P.M. daily, $10–15) is another local favorite. It's well hidden, tucked away in the little shopping center beside the 7-Eleven and the Incline Cinema, but the villagers have ferreted it out for its big Mexican and Tex-Mex gut-busters.

For more sophisticated fare, venture closer to the river or farther inland from Tahoe Boulevard. ◖ **Big Water Grille** (341 Ski Way, 775/833-0606, 4:30–10 P.M. daily, $20–40) has terrific, if a bit unoriginal, seafood dishes, but the wild mushroom risotto and onion-potato hash side dish make us consider becoming vegetarians.

Two of the better spots are neighbors just off Lakeshore Boulevard. **Le Bistro** (120 Country Club Dr., 775/831-0800, 6–9:30 P.M. Tues.–Sat., $30–50) serves top-notch French and Italian dishes à la carte as well as a well-regarded prix fixe menu. Across the street, **Lone Eagle Grill** (Hyatt, 111 Country Club Dr. at Lakeshore Blvd., 775/886-6899, 11:30 A.M.–10 P.M. Mon.–Thurs., 11:30 A.M.–10:30 P.M. Fri.–Sat., 10:30 A.M.–10 P.M. Sun., $30–50) has lake views and serves hearty dinners for refueling after a day on the slopes or light lunches before you hit the beach.

Crystal Bay

The top restaurant outside the casinos, and perhaps the best in town, ◖ **Soule Domain** (Stateline Rd. and Cove St., 530/546-7529, 6–10 P.M. daily, $17–30) is right on the state line, west and across the street from the Biltmore's parking lot. The two-room log cabin with a hand-laid stone fireplace, a timbered ceiling, and rail-fence posts contrasts with the sophisticated Mediterranean and American delicacies from the kitchen, including lamb with cheese, olive, and tomato filling and fowl, beef, and seafood entrées such as curried cashew chicken with snow peas and shiitake mushrooms.

INFORMATION

The **Incline Village-Crystal Bay Visitors and Convention Bureau** (969 Tahoe Blvd., near the south end of town, 775/832-1606 or 800/GO-TAHOE—800/468-2463, www.gotahoe.com) has all the brochures and information you'll need, including everything from hiking trails and outdoor activities to restaurants and resorts. You can download their helpful vacation planner (www.gotahoenorth.com/about-tahoe/vacation-guide).

The **library** (845 Alder Ave., Incline Village, 775/832-4130, 9 A.M.–6 P.M. Tues.–Thurs., 10 A.M.–4 P.M. Fri.–Sat.) is just north of the Christmas Tree Center, set back from the road; a road sign points the way. This is a branch of the excellent Washoe County library system and has a thorough collection of Nevada history resources. There's a coffee bar and a big comfy fireplace.

Virginia City

Starting as early as 1851, a backwash of disillusioned California gold seekers filtered east to search Nevada's high desert for the precious metal. One pair of miners on Sun Mountain optimistically called their gopher hole the Ophir Mine, after the biblical land where the wealth of King Solomon was located. Yet they remained unaware of the real riches right beneath their feet. The more they dug, the more they got bogged down by blue-gray mud. It polluted the quartz veins, settled quickly to the bottom of the sluice boxes, diluted the quicksilver—in general, it seriously impeded the recovery of the gold. The miners flung it aside until a visitor carried a chunk down to Placerville in July 1859 and had it assayed. The mud was found to contain $875 per ton in gold and an incredible $3,000 per ton in pristine sulfuret of silver. The news spread immediately west and east, and an estimated 10,000 fortune seekers flooded the ragged settlement on Sun Mountain. The Comstock Lode, Virginia City, and Nevada were about to explode.

By 1863, the first golden age of Virginia City—a boomtown the likes of which had never been seen before—had begun. The mines got deeper (to the 300-foot level), the ore got richer, and stock speculation and property litigation ran rampant. Thousands of claims—badly recorded—overlapped to the extent that the Comstock Lode was "owned" in its entirety 3–4 times over. The wildly fluctuating value of the famed "feet" of pay dirt turned paupers into princes and back into paupers in a single day.

Today, more than 3 million visitors a year drive up beautiful Geiger Grade or Devil's Gate to recapture a piece of Virginia City's boomtown glory. While small-scale prospecting operations continue near here even today, Virginia City has staked its claim in the travel industry, mining deep-pocketed tourists.

Despite its occasionally kitschy souvenirs, the town's attractions are authentic and as close as you're likely to come to imagining yourself a miner on payday, eager to soak up all the entertainment, culture, whiskey, and social accompaniment your money can buy. You'll get a feel for all aspects of those heady Comstock days, from the sweltering, claustrophobic working conditions endured by the common miner to the opulent mansions of the silver kings; from the heavenly architectural treasures of Virginia City's churches to the tools of the sex trade at the Red Light Museum.

Yes, Virginia City may be a tourist trap, but it's one you won't mind being caught in.

LAKE TAHOE AND VICINITY

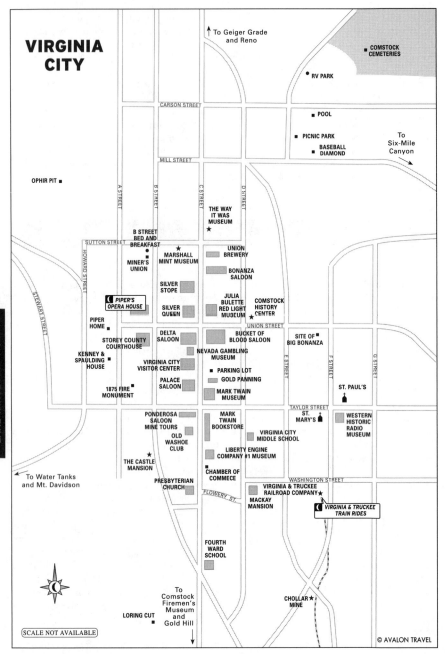

VIRGINIA CITY

To Geiger Grade and Reno

COMSTOCK CEMETERIES

RV PARK

CARSON STREET

POOL

PICNIC PARK

BASEBALL DIAMOND

To Six-Mile Canyon

MILL STREET

OPHIR PIT

A STREET

B STREET

C STREET

D STREET

THE WAY IT WAS MUSEUM

B STREET BED AND BREAKFAST

SUTTON STREET

HOWARD STREET

STEWART STREET

MINER'S UNION

MARSHALL MINT MUSEUM

UNION BREWERY

BONANZA SALOON

SILVER STOPE

SILVER QUEEN

JULIA BULETTE RED LIGHT MUSEUM

COMSTOCK HISTORY CENTER

PIPER'S OPERA HOUSE

PIPER HOME

STOREY COUNTY COURTHOUSE

DELTA SALOON

BUCKET OF BLOOD SALOON

UNION STREET

SITE OF BIG BONANZA

KENNEY & SPAULDING HOUSE

VIRGINIA CITY VISITOR CENTER

NEVADA GAMBLING MUSEUM

PARKING LOT

GOLD PANNING

E STREET

F STREET

G STREET

1875 FIRE MONUMENT

PALACE SALOON

MARK TWAIN MUSEUM

ST. PAUL'S

TAYLOR STREET

PONDEROSA SALOON MINE TOURS

MARK TWAIN BOOKSTORE

ST. MARY'S

WESTERN HISTORIC RADIO MUSEUM

OLD WASHOE CLUB

VIRGINIA CITY MIDDLE SCHOOL

THE CASTLE MANSION

LIBERTY ENGINE COMPANY #1 MUSEUM

To Water Tanks and Mt. Davidson

CHAMBER OF COMMECE

PRESBYTERIAN CHURCH

FLOWERY ST.

WASHINGTON STREET

VIRGINIA & TRUCKEE RAILROAD COMPANY

MACKAY MANSION

VIRGINIA & TRUCKEE TRAIN RIDES

FOURTH WARD SCHOOL

To Comstock Firemen's Museum and Gold Hill

CHOLLAR MINE

LORING CUT

SCALE NOT AVAILABLE

© AVALON TRAVEL

SIGHTS

With dozens of storefronts strung along five blocks of C Street, you could spend a long day just walking in and out of museums, saloons, eateries, and shops from the near end of the street to the far end, then back up the other side. That doesn't include the mine tours, mansions, opera house, churches, train, trolley, and stagecoach rides, or hiking around. In short, Virginia City is so full of history, adventure, excitement, and curiosities that it's too hectic to do it all in one visit. Either plan on going full-bore from sunup to sundown or hit a half-dozen highlights in a casual day trip.

For a look at the conditions in which the lowliest miners worked, the richest executives lived, and the whole spectrum of Comstockers was entertained, the top three attractions are an underground mine tour, the Mackay Mansion, and Piper's Opera House.

Underground Mine Tours

The heart and soul of Virginia City was the Comstock Lode. Two mine tours allow you to get under the ground to see what the miners saw. Most authentic is the tour of the **Chollar Mine** (615 S. F St., 775/847-0155, 1–5 P.M. daily Mar.–Oct., $7 adults, $2 ages 4–14), the last of the Comstock's old original mines. The Chollar Mine was the fifth highest in production, producing more than $18 million in gold and silver, and this tour shows you the real thing, with the square-set timbering, ore, and old tools and equipment as well as knowledgeable, experienced guides. The Chollar claim was filed in 1859, production started in 1861, and the mine was worked for almost 80 years until it closed in 1942. It was reopened in 1961 for tours, 100 years after its first began producing.

The 30-minute guided walking tours go over 400 feet into the mountain. The Chollar Mine is not far from the center of town; you can get there by going downhill from C to F Street, turning right (south) on F, and continuing for about 0.5 miles; or head south from town on C Street, turn left (east) onto the truck route just past the Fourth Ward School, and follow the road around.

Virginia City's other underground tour, of the **Ponderosa Mine** (106 S. C St., 775/847-0757, 10 A.M.–6 P.M. daily, $4.50 adults, $1.50 under age 12), departs from the rear of the Ponderosa Saloon. The mine tunnel snakes 315 feet from the rear end of the saloon into the Best and Belcher diggings, whose pay dirt yielded 55 percent silver and 45 percent gold. Displays include gold-rich ore, the powder room where "monkeys" (young boys) worked, square-set timbering, minerals under black light, and all the heavy buckets, drills, winches, and rods the miners used to muck the rock, tunneling 6–8 feet per day. The guide enumerates myriad dangers: the perpetual threats of cave-ins, fire, scalding steam and water, the terrible heat, and bad air, not to mention the back-breaking, head-knocking, bone-crushing work itself. At $4 per day, the equivalent of $232 today, the miners were well paid, considering that most hard-rock miners around the world earned less than $1 per day; still, this tour is graphic evidence that the Comstock miners earned every penny. At the far end, the guide might light two candles and kill the overheads. If he blows out the candles, an early-warning signal of gases or a lack of oxygen, you'll feel like you're back in 1873. The only inconsistency is the 52°F temperature; you could take a jacket, but it isn't really necessary.

Mackay Mansion

The Mackay Mansion (129 S. D St., 775/847-0373, 10 A.M.–5 P.M. daily summer, winter hours vary, free) reigns as the best way to see how the other half lived during the Comstock's heyday. John Mackay, heir to William Sharon as king of the Comstock Lode, lived and worked in this three-story Italianate-style edifice with a wraparound veranda and a large deck, using it as the offices of the Gould & Curry Mine Office. Up until 1950, visitors could purchase gold bars straight from the vault. Mackay occupied the home after George Hearst—William Randolph Hearst's father—made his Comstock fortune and headed back East. The house's grand parlor and staircase offer the best examples of original and period

CAMELS IN CARSON VALLEY

As might be expected in a state whose major historical landmarks include the Sands, the Dunes, the Desert Inn, and the Sahara, camels played a role in Nevada's development. Ships of the desert first came to Nevada in 1856, when the U.S. Army took up Lieutenant Edward F. Beale's offer to train dromedaries (one-humpers) to haul military supplies throughout the arid West. Camels, after all, are bigger and stronger than horses and mules, required little water, and were accustomed to the dry heat. Beale and roughly 30 camels crossed the Colorado River into present-day southern Nevada in 1857, but his experiment eventually failed, and the Army sold the stock that survived.

The Army's mistake, San Francisco mining interests posited, was that it put its trust in the wrong camel: Business owners in 1861 imported several dozen Bactrian camels (two-humpers) from China and sent the beasts across the Sierra to haul salt from southern Nevada to the mines and mills in Virginia City and Austin. According to reports, the camels handled the job fairly well; they toted large loads, but they also had trouble negotiating rock-strewn paths, scared the horses, and they reeked. By 1875 camel-induced stampedes had become such a problem that the Nevada legislature banished them from public highways. Drovers sold their animals to traveling circuses or abandoned them to their fate in the desert. As late as the 1960s, desert rats in Nevada, California, and Arizona reported spotting feral camels roaming the playa.

While camels were a small part of the working life of the Comstock Lode, they were never raced for sport. In fact, the first reported camel race in Virginia City came 100 years after the Comstock's heyday. And true to the spirit of Western journalism, that report, as Mark Twain might have said, was greatly exaggerated: In 1959, Bob Richards, a reporter for the revived *Territorial Enterprise* in Virginia City, "reported" on the town's camel races and invited other newspapers to take up the challenge. Whether duped by Richards's story or simply calling his bluff, representatives from the *San Francisco Chronicle* and the *Phoenix Sun* showed up in Virginia City, camels in tow. John Huston, in town to direct Clark Gable and Marilyn Monroe in *The Misfits*, took the reins for the *Chronicle* and galloped (er, plodded) to victory.

After a few years' hiatus, the races returned and have been a much-anticipated annual event in Virginia City.

What started as a hoax has been a Virginia City tradition for more than half a century.

furnishings. The parlor's centerpiece, a burgundy upholstered set, fronts a mirror framed in 24-carat gold leaf and backed by crushed diamonds. The tour includes the upstairs bedrooms used by Mackay and his children as well as the children's play area, complete with dolls from the 19th century and a rocking horse from the Comstock era.

Other silver barons' homes are nearby on **Millionaires Row.** While you're here, take a look at the Chollar, Bowers, and governor's mansions. You can also view the exterior of the Castle, the 16-room gem that still contains all-original furnishings. Built in 1868 by Robert Graves, superintendent of the Empire Mine, its olivewood shutters are visible, but the exquisite antiques inside are not open to the public.

◖ Piper's Opera House

The well-preserved and restored Opera House (B St. and Union St., 775/847-0433 or 888/422-1956, 11 A.M.–4 P.M. daily summer, winter hours vary, guided tours

11 A.M.–1 P.M. and 3 P.M., $5 adults, $2 ages 6–12) was built by John Piper in 1885, after the first two opera houses burned down. Canvas walls to aid the acoustics as well as balconies and chandeliers designed to throw patterns on the ceiling, the original round-backed chairs, the railroad spring-loaded floor (a dancer enhancer), and a stage raked higher in the back—from which the terms *upstage* and *downstage* originate—are among the unusual features. Advertisements appear on top of the curtain. Three slotted stage sets (a parlor, a forest, and a street scene) could be rolled into and out of view by stagehands. Proscenium box seats are on one side of the stage. Signs inside tell of the performers who appeared here, including Mark Twain, Harry Houdini, John Philip Sousa, Lillie Langtry, Al Jolson, and John Barrymore, among many others. Circles and keys painted on the floor date from when Piper's was used as a basketball court and roller rink in later years. Today the opera house hosts weddings, school plays, and dances.

Houdini, Jolson, Twain, and more enthralled audiences at Piper's Opera House in Virginia City.

COURTESY OF THE NEVADA COMMISSION ON TOURISM

LAKE TAHOE AND VICINITY

Fourth Ward School

Once educating as many as 1,000 students per year (the classrooms were huge), the Fourth Ward School (537 S. C. St., 775/847-0975, 10 A.M.–5 P.M. daily May–Oct., $5 adults, $3 ages 6–12), at the south end of town, was one of four public schools during Virginia City's heyday. Built in 1876, it boasted many revolutionary modern conveniences: a cut-stone foundation reinforced and anchored to the granite of Mount Davidson with steel rods, newfangled heating and ventilating technology, and water piped to all four floors, including indoor drinking fountains. The last class graduated in 1936, and today the Nevada State Museum has set up an excellent exhibit on the ground floor about the Comstock community's culture, letter-press printing technology, mining, and education. Exhibits include a 3-D viewing machine and a model of a stamp mill. Some of the 16 original classrooms have been restored with original desks, maps, and books. The preservation society has done a terrific job restoring the building and making it a learning tool.

The Way It Was Museum

With the largest and most impressive collection of Comstock mining artifacts, maps, minerals, and photos, The Way It Was (113 N. C St., 775/847-0766, 10 A.M.–6 P.M. daily year-round, $3 adults, free under age 12), on C Street at Sutton Street, is a valuable link to Nevada's past. You can see how the silver ore was processed with the museum's working scale models of stamp mills, mine reproductions, and Cornish pumps, all built by J. E. Parson of Oroville, California. Three *American Frontier* videos with Charlie Jones and Merlin Olsen discuss the Comstock, Piper's Opera House, and Mark Twain; they alone are worth the price of admission. Also check out the scale model of the underground mine workings and Jim Fair's personal stamp mill.

Marshall Mint Museum

More mint than museum, the Marshall Mint Museum (96 N. C St., 775/847-0777 or 800/321-6374, 10 A.M.–5 P.M. daily), located in the 1861 assay office building, sells Christian-themed medallions, handcrafted gold jewelry, collectible coins, and silver-cast currency reproductions.

Mark Twain Museum

The Mark Twain Museum (53 S. C St., 775/847-0155, 9 A.M.–6 P.M. daily Apr.–Oct., 10 A.M.–5 P.M. daily Nov.–Mar., $3 adults, $2 children) was once the pressroom for Nevada's oldest publication, *Territorial Enterprise,* which started up in Genoa in December 1858, moved briefly to Carson City, then in October 1860 settled down into a long and profitable run in Virginia City, with writers like Mark Twain and Dan DeQuille keeping things lively. The museum displays 19th-century printing technology, such as an 1894 linotype, an old binding machine, and a hot-type cabinet. There's an interesting recording about Twain and his time in Virginia City, including his two years at the newspaper. Twain's original desk is on display along with some of his books and journals. The press area, where Twain's desk was spared from the great 1875 fire, was insulated from the conflagration by the debris from the charred offices above. The current office was build around the press area the next year, and the *Enterprise* continued to publish until 1893. Also called the Territorial Enterprise Museum, it's located in the center of town, in the basement of the *Territorial Enterprise* Gift Shop.

Comstock Firemen's Museum

Located in Virginia City's original firehouse, built in 1864, the Comstock Firemen's Museum (1117 S. C. St., 775/847-0717, 10 A.M.–5 P.M. daily, free, donations accepted) is one of only a few buildings that survived the big fire of October 1875. The brick building's collection includes silver trumpets, belts, and helmets that the Virginia City volunteers used as well as photographs and memorabilia from other fire departments around the state. As Virginia City grew, its fire department also grew to include a hook-and-ladder company, six engine companies, and seven hose companies. An 1874 Clapp & Jones steam fire engine

CRADLE OF JOURNALISTS

For most, life on the Comstock Lode was a dusty, lonely existence. Prospectors who ventured west with visions of stuffing their pockets with silver to bankroll a life on easy street for their families often found frontier life a bitter reality. A few of these disenchanted would-be silver barons, such as Mark Twain, quickly learned

> the real secret of success in silver mining – which was, not to mine the silver ourselves by the sweat of our brows and the labor of our hands, but to sell the ledges to the dull slaves of toil and let them to the mining!

Twain found wielding a pen more enjoyable and lucrative than wielding a shovel, wasting no time in liquidating his mine holdings shortly after arriving in Unionville. Twain, of course, is the most famous journalist to make his name on the Comstock. His dry observations – many self-deprecating – earned him a spot on the *Territorial Enterprise* in Virginia City, where he never let the facts get in the way of a good story. Twain became a master at hoax journalism, fabricating tales of petrified men and bloody shootouts.

Unionville also was where veteran California gold rush journalist William J. Forbes got his start in Nevada. The hard-bitten and hard-drinking Forbes did not suffer fools lightly, especially when those fools were running the territory. When Governor James W. Nye's pet project, a dam and a mill, ran way over budget and ran out of money with the job half completed, Forbes noted that "Governor Nye has a dam by a mill site, but he has no mill by a dam site." Forbes eked out a living in several Nevada boomtowns before opening a saloon, writing that "of 20 men, 19 patronize the saloon and one the newspaper. I'm going with the crowd." While the gin joint may have been the only profitable business Forbes ever owned, ink ran in his veins. He soon sold out and returned to his rattletrap press.

Twain's friend and mentor in Virginia City, William Wright, under the pen name Dan De Quille, was king of the hoaxes, though his serious accounts of life in the mining camps, especially *The Big Bonanza*, are still considered classics of mainstream reporting and are often credited with establishing the criteria for modern journalism.

Affectionately known as "Lying Jim," James Townsend's tales were tall. When he came to work at one newspaper, he introduced himself to readers by telling his "life story." According to Jim's biography, his shipwrecked mother had been captured by cannibals. After his birth, Jim was fattened for a dozen years in anticipation of being the main course at a tribal feast. He escaped, became a successful businessman, and ran up a considerable fortune. Then disaster struck. He became a journalist, squandered his fortune, and was reduced to continue writing for his supper.

Other notable writers who cut their teeth or honed their trade on the Comstock include Myron Angel, Fred Hart, and Jock Taylor of the *Reese River Reveille*. Angel wrote the definitive Comstock-era chronicle, the *1881 History of Nevada*. Wells Drury edited the *Gold Hill News* for a dozen years. When he applied for a job with Alf Doten, he was informed that citizens of the rough-and-tumble frontier didn't settle their differences with lawyers and libel suits. "You write what you please. Nobody censors it," Doten told Drury. "But you must defend yourself if anybody has a kick."

has been restored to operating condition and is one of the coolest artifacts in the collection. It participates in the fire company musters that the museum regularly hosts. Nevada's oldest piece of fire equipment is an 1839 four-wheel hose carriage originally used in Philadelphia and bought for use in Virginia City in 1870. It was used in Gold Hill until it was retired in 1938.

Other well-restored pieces include an 1856 hand-drawn, hand-pumped engine bought for the Virginia City firefighters in 1870 and restored to its 1870s appearance.

Western Historic Radio Museum

More interesting than you might expect, the Western Historic Radio Museum (109 S. F St., 775/847-9047, 1–5 P.M. daily May–Oct., off-season and off-hours tours by appointment, $5 adults, $2 under age 15) looks like an ordinary house; it used to serve as the rectory for the Catholic church next door. The museum entrance is in the rear. Whether you're a radio buff or not, this is a fascinating museum, with more than 200 antique and classic radios on display along with antique wireless apparatus, a ham radio room with vintage ham radios and a collection of QSL cards from around the world, and a collection of photos of famous old-time radio personalities. The displays are arranged in chronological order and include comprehensive descriptions of the unit's use and contribution to radio's evolution, making for a step-by-step walk through telecommunications history from 1910 through the mid-20th century.

In addition to radio receivers, the museum houses horn speakers, cone speakers, early vacuum tubes, microphones, telegraph keys, and more. Pride of place goes to an original, complete 1912 Spark Station, discovered in Reno in November 1999. Owner and curator Henry Rogers will give you a guided tour of the museum, if you like. Radio buffs from far and wide contact Rogers with radio issues and for antique radio repair.

Comstock History Center

Mining and railroad history are on display at the Comstock History Center (20 N. E. St., 11 A.M.–4 P.M. Thurs.–Sun., free) including Engine No. 18, *The Dayton* of the historic Virginia & Truckee Railroad. The center also contains railroad and other historic photos and reference material.

Comstock Gold Mill

Virginia City offers several chances to see how miners got the ore out of the mines, but the Comstock Gold Mill (F St. at the railroad crossing, 775/742-9694, 10 A.M.–5:30 P.M. daily mid-May–Labor Day, $10 adults, $5 ages 5–12) is their chance to see how they got the gold out of the ore. Stamp mills crushed the ore, and the slag was placed on a steel table, where mercury was added, attracting the gold pieces. Burning drove off the mercury and left the gold. Mercury is toxic, however, and millers died from working with it, so the process changed in the 1880s. The new process screened the ore and then washed away the small rocks and dirt, leaving the heavier gold. Narrated tours explain it all.

The mill equipment was originally built in the 1860s at the Murrietta Mine in Goldfield. It was brought here and rebuilt next to the Arizona-Comstock Mill.

🄲 Virginia & Truckee Train Rides

Free your imagination as you spy exposed silver ore veins along this historic railroad's Virginia City–Goldfield route that shuttled rich Comstock ore to quartz reduction mills. The return trip supplied the richest city on earth with lumber, mining timbers, and cord wood for fuel. The 35-minute narrated ride (370 F St., 775/847-0380, 10:30 A.M.–4 P.M. daily late May–late Oct., $9–10 adults, $5 ages 5–10) takes passengers from the F Street depot past several famous mines and through Tunnel No. 4, one of five burrowed through rock walls for the line's 1,600-foot change in elevation. As they chug past the Chollar, Potosi, Yellow Jacket, Crown Point, and other historic mines, passengers can spot the telltale blue-gray veins still exposed. The conductor relates the history and regales riders with

COURTESY OF THE NEVADA COMMISSION ON TOURISM

Rail fans can ride the Virginia & Truckee Railroad's mine-to-mill route from Virginia City.

exciting and romantic tales of the Comstock Lode era.

The V&T also offers one-way and round-trip rides from Virginia City to Carson City. The one-way voyage is through a 566-foot tunnel, over the highway via a dramatic bridge crossing, past a scale and water stop that serviced 40 trains a day during Virginia City's heyday, and through American Flat, a contender for the state capital until the ore ran out and the town disappeared.

Several special trains run throughout the year, such as the haunted Pumpkin Train in October, the Santa Train in December, and other themed rides for Memorial Day and Independence Day.

Trolley, Carriage, and Stagecoach Rides

Virginia City's **Silver Line Express** (775/847-4FUN—775/847-4386 or 800/718-SLVR—800/718-7587) offers several package deals with discount rates for most of the town's top attractions; most include a V&T Railroad jaunt and a short 20-minute trolley ride around town. It's a

quick history and geography lesson, a good way to begin your day and do a quick reconnaissance. To see the town in style, book a splendid carriage ride with **Happy Hoofers** (775/849-0959, $20 pp for 30 minutes). The driver will regale you with tales of Julia Bulette, Piper's Opera House, and more. The tour company can set you up with period clothing and hats so you'll really look the part. A much less sumptuous journey is in store when you climb aboard for an authentic **stagecoach ride** (at the Comstock Gold Mill, F St. at the railroad crossing, 775/742-9694, 11 A.M.–5:30 P.M. daily, weather permitting, $10, family packages available). The ride only lasts about 10 minutes, but the bumps and jostles are authentic, and most folks are ready for the ride to end. Speeds approach a plenty-fast 25 mph.

St. Mary in the Woods Church

Still offering Saturday mass, St. Mary's in the Mountains (Taylor St. and E St., 775/847-9099, 10 A.M.–5:30 P.M. daily, donation) is Nevada's oldest Catholic church. Volunteers offer free tours of the museum and wine cellar; St. Mary's also has an extensive gift shop that supports the small parish and restoration project. The sanctuary's Victorian and Gothic architecture features a 17th-century Florentine canvas, *The Visitation,* over the altar and a 4- by 6-foot depiction of the Virgin Mary done in needlepoint by nuns who spent five years creating it.

Burly Paddy Manogue built the church after the 1875 fire and ministered to the Irish-Catholic miners of Virginia City for almost 20 years.

Storey County Courthouse

Built after its predecessor succumbed to the great fire, the Italianate courthouse (26 S. B St., 10 A.M.–5 P.M. Mon.–Fri., donation) was completed in 1877 for the then unheard-of sum of $117,000. Justice is not blind in Storey County; the statue outside depicts the scale-wielding goddess sans blindfold. But contrary to the local legend that justice needed all its faculties to tame the Wild West town, several courthouses throughout the country at the time presented their justice with eyes wide open.

Within the courthouse's jail, the **Silver State**

THE CROOKEDEST RAILROAD IN THE WORLD

Bank of California owner William Ralston and his agent William Sharon had very nearly cornered the silver production and processing market in Virginia City by 1861. And like true entrepreneurs, they were looking to expand their holdings and vertically integrate their supply chain. Recognizing an opportunity in the nearby approach of the Central Pacific Railroad, the barons schemed to build a rail connection from Virginia City to the transcontinental line. Freight costs to and from the mines and settlements could be reduced, mining interests would beat a path to their door, and profits would soar.

Sharon started making money even before he laid a foot of track. Business owners paid him $500,000 to divert from his original plan to run the spur directly to Reno and instead choose a path through Carson City and up the Washoe Valley. The first Virginia & Truckee Railroad train arrived in Gold Hill from Carson City in December 1869. Passenger service to and from Virginia City started the next month. Winding its way from Virginia City through six

tunnels, the V&T twisted its way 0.5 miles south to Gold Hill across the vertigo-inducing Crown Point trestle and slithered through narrow canyons and steep grades to American Flat. From there, it dropped into Moundhouse and through Brunswick Canyon to Carson City. "The Crookedest Railroad in the World" was not a mere slogan. There were so many turns that the 16-mile trip required 21 miles of track.

The railroad purchased rolling stock and five engines and completed the line from Virginia City to Lakes Crossing in 1873, just as it appeared the Comstock Lode was exhausted. But the "Big Bonanza" was a windfall not only for the mine owners but for the V&T as well. Renewed activity on the Comstock Lode meant plenty of business for the railroad. Soon it had more than tripled the number of locomotives and rail cars and was making an incredible 40 runs a day, shipping ore out and supplies and timber in. At its peak in 1874, the railroad's income was $400,000 per month ($10 million in today's dollars).

Peace Officers Museum (775/847-7800, 11 A.M.–5 P.M. daily, $5 adults, $3 ages 6–12) sparks the imagination and tugs at the heartstrings. Step through the iron bars of the 1876 jail; a cell wall is still decorated with vintage inmate artwork. Uniforms, badges, police cars, weapons, and newspaper accounts trace the history and development of law enforcement from the founding of the United States.

The darker side of police work is depicted as well in the Nevada Officers Memorial Room, with a searchable computer kiosk with a page dedicated to each Nevada officer killed in the line of duty while serving the community.

Comstock Cemeteries

A far cry from the verdant contemplative gardens they were considered when Virginia City was a thriving community, cemeteries nevertheless are another valuable resource for studying and preserving the history of the Comstock era.

Daily **tours** (772/847-0281, $5 adults, $2 students) of the major burial grounds leave from the main gates of the Virginia City cemetery at the north end of town. Admission without a tour is free. Cemeteries are segregated by ethnicity and economic class, which explains the different sizes and frills of the monuments.

Julia Bulette Red Light Museum

Bulette, Virginia City's prostitute with a heart of gold, became prosperous plying the world's oldest profession and popular by supporting the fire department and many other civic and charitable causes. This museum (5 N. C St., 775/847-9288, hours vary, $1 adults), in the basement of the Mandarin Garden Chinese Restaurant, has only a nebulous connection to the world's oldest profession as practiced in the mining towns or to Bulette, who was murdered in 1867. The exhibits are more sophomoric than serious—old condom wrappers and sexual aids, snake oils, a walking stick made from an elephant's penis, and nudie shot glasses.

Saloons

When you visit Virginia City, a visit to the **Bucket of Blood Saloon** (1 S. C St., 775/847-0322) is a must, if only to get the conversation-starting T-shirt. Built just after the big fire atop the destroyed Boston Saloon, the origin of the Bucket's name is the subject of some debate. There are several plausible stories, but our favorite is that miners sweated a bucket of blood daily, justifying their indulgence in a few cold ones.

The Bucket is well-populated with cowboy hat–wearing tourists. It's light and airy thanks to the big picture window in back overlooking Six-Mile Canyon. Belly up to the old-fashioned bar with its ornate woodwork and brass accents and groove to the country, rock, and bluegrass acts on stage most weekends.

The **Delta Saloon** (18 S. C St., 775/847-0789), a half-dozen doors north, is as close to a casino as it gets in Virginia City, with 125 slots and video poker machines (there are no table games in town). The Sawdust Corner coffee shop, named after another of the Comstock era saloons, is on one side and the Delta Gift Shop on the other. Be sure to traipse upstairs, if it's open, to check out the period carpeting, wallpaper, and chandeliers that greeted customers visiting the "soiled doves." There are bright skylights, four big banquet rooms, and restrooms up here as well. The Delta is also the home of the infamous Suicide Table, where legend has it no less than three of its owners offed themselves after losing their fortunes at faro or blackjack. At the opposite end of the casino is an 1880s globe, built at a cost of $450 of rosewood, complete with mariner's compass, for James Fair, king of the Comstock Lode bonanza. It's estimated that this unique globe is now worth $100,000.

A few shops north on the boardwalk is the **Silver Queen** (28 N. C St., 775/847-0440), home of a 16-foot-tall lady on the wall. This silver queen is made of 3,261 silver dollars, her belt of 28 gold pieces, and her jewelry of dimes and half-dollars. At the back of the huge and ornate back bar is a small wedding chapel. The Captain and Tennille tied the knot here in 1975. The shop has reproductions of vintage clothing, so you can get your Butch and Sundance on. The biker favorite **Union Brewery** (63 C St., 775/847-9016), across the street at the north end of town, was built in 1862; the exterior is original.

Across the street and up the block is the **Ponderosa Saloon** (106 S. C St., 775/847-0757) in the old Bank of California building. The highlight is the original bank vault, with a half-inch steel-plate cage surrounded by two-foot-thick walls where Billy Sharon kept his spare change. Study the historic photos and the portraits of the early celebrities: Julia Bulette, James Finney, Henry Comstock, and Mark Twain.

The **Old Washoe Club** (112 S. C St., 775/847-7210) is a bit to the south, built in 1875 after the great fire. This was the hangout of the local millionaires, frequented by Ulysses S. Grant, Thomas Edison, and Wyatt Earp, among others. The posh upstairs digs were accessed by the spiral staircase, still viewable in the back, which is listed by Ripley's as the longest spiral staircase without a supporting pole. Buy a drink and get the scoop on the bar, the rich guys, and the ghosts, then check out the displays in the back.

The **Crystal Bar** (86 S. C St. at Taylor St., 775/847-7500) is the home of the Crystal Visitors Center, where the Virginia City Chamber of Commerce and tourism offices are located. The crystal and gold-plated chandeliers are original, and many mementos line the walls.

SHOPPING

While much of Virginia City is authentic, it's also a tourist town, full of kitschy souvenir stores, ice cream parlors, and old-time photo studios. Despite the retail shtick, you may want to take home some souvenirs of your visit. You won't believe what they can do with semiprecious stones at **Comstock Rock Shop** (20 C St., 775/847-0383). Pick up a carved memento, a stunning piece of jewelry, or a knickknack carved from one of nature's gifts. You'll find yourself pining for Elvis and tail fins even if you didn't grow up in the 1950s when you visit **Virginia City Mercantile** (85 C St., 775/847-

LAKE TAHOE AND VICINITY

0184). Wax nostalgic over the vintage advertising signs and soda in real glass bottles. While you're here, stock up on 32 flavors of taffy by the half-pound. Make sure to include big scoops of apricot and cinnamon.

Mark Twain Books (111 S. C St., 775/847-0454, www.marktwainbooks.com) has an excellent selection of new, used, out-of-print, and rare books. The shop specializes in books about Nevada, Western Americana, the Comstock Lode, Virginia City, and Mark Twain along with Nevada travel guides, kids books, postcards, and plenty more. The store is a mini museum with Twain memorabilia on the walls in one of very few buildings to survive the great fire of October 1875; built in 1862, it survived because it is made of stone and brick, whereas other Virginia City buildings in 1875 were primarily wood.

The best thing about the toys and games at **Little City Items** (145 S. C St., 775/847-4200, 10 A.M.–5 P.M. daily) is that you don't have to hook them up to the television to play them—they are vintage, classic, and just plain good old-fashioned fun toys.

Virginia City offers a handful of old-time photo shops: **Silver Sadie's Old-Time Photos** (116 S. C St., 775/847-9133), **Priscilla Pennyworth's Photographic Emporium** (203 S. C St., 775/847-0333), **Rotten Rowdy's Old Time Photos** (63 S. C St., 775/847-7978), and **Garters & Bloomers** (63 S. C St., 775/847-7979). The props and costumes turn you into practically any kind of character from the roaring 1870s that you'd like to be: a barmaid, a piano player, a cocktail waitress, a cowboy or cowgirl, or a gunslinger. Get an 8-by-10 for about $20.

ACCOMMODATIONS

Virginia City's accommodations run from rustic to regal. **The Assay House** (398 N. B St., 775/847-0702 or 775/830-7343, $135–155), built in 1862, is a survivor of the great fire. You can rent the one-bedroom brick structure that originally performed the ore assessments that could make or break miners and investors. Since then, it has served as a grocery store, antique shop, and postmaster's home. Other original

features include the unique front windows and wood flooring in the front main section of the house. Period furniture and modern upgrades (a gas fireplace and a ceiling fan) strike a balance between authenticity and comfort. The back of the house, a 20th-century addition, contains a full modern kitchen, bath, and bedroom done in Italian quarry tile. Outdoors you'll find a garden, a patio, and park benches with views of the mountains and St. Mary's Church.

Built in 1863 and used as a cider factory, ◖ **Edith Palmer's Country Inn** (416 S. B St., 775/847-7070, $95–140) opened for overnight trade in 1948, and reopened in 2003 after extensive expansion and renovation. Eight rooms and two suites are contained in three Victorian houses; the Cider Factory restaurant completes the package. Open spring–fall, the elegant **Cobb Mansion Bed & Breakfast** (18 S. A St., 775/847-9006 or 877/847-9006, $99–199) offers six rooms appointed in period antiques in a mansion setting. Once owned by a prosperous Comstock-era merchant, the three-story

Sugarloaf Mountain Motel

mansion overlooks the Carson River. Start each morning with a full breakfast in the regal dining room. Constructed just after the Great Fire, the **B Street Bed & Breakfast** (58 N. B St., 775/847-7231, $99–139) delivers variety and freshness at breakfast with homemade pastries and hot daily entrées. Tea with cocoa, coffee, and cookies is served in the parlor of the former home of Henry Piper, of opera house fame. Antiques and reproductions recreate the prim and proper Victorian ideals under which Virginia City's Comstock wealthy lived. The B&B's three rooms were renovated in 2008 and include private baths, cable TV, queen beds, and free Internet. A decent library downstairs contains Nevada and Western history books, and the parlor or garden areas are restful places to read and doze.

Oozing with authenticity, the **(Silver Queen Inn** (28 N. C St., 775/847-0440, $55–170), in the center of town, offers rooms with brass beds and desolate canyon views. There's a small slot casino and a real-deal 1870s bar. Similarly, the **Gold Hill Hotel** (Hwy. 342, 1 mile south of Virginia City, $55–200) dates to 1859. All 19 rooms are individually decorated. It has a bar, a restaurant, and a Nevadiana bookstore. Fair warning: Both the Gold Hill and the Silver Queen are said to be haunted—rumors that the owners encourage.

The **Comstock Lodge** (875 S. C St., 775/847-0233, $50–70) has 14 rooms, all done in period antiques. The **Sugarloaf Mountain Motel** (430 S. C St., 775/847-0551 or 866/217-9248, $60–100) was an 1878 boardinghouse, but the bright and airy rooms of today contain no bunkhouse connotations. Rooms include cable TV, microwaves, and refrigerators. Coffee and teakettles are on by 7 A.M. along with breakfast snacks in the trading post.

The **Virginia City RV Park** (Carson St. and F St., 775/847-0999 or 800/889-1240, www.vcrvpark.com, $23 RVs, $14 tents) is down the hill on a bluff; to get there, turn downhill at Carson Street and drive three blocks to F Street. Some sites overlook the cemetery. It's a bit cramped, but there's a delicatessen, a market, propane sales, restrooms, shower houses, a laundry, and a dumping station to make things convenient. The park has 47 full-hookup RV sites, a small tent-camping area, and three rental cabins. It's next to the town park, which has tennis, basketball, and a community pool, and it's within walking distance of downtown Virginia City and other historic attractions, including the historic cemeteries and trail rides.

FOOD

The homemade salsa gives **(Café Del Rio** (394 S. C St., 775/847-5151, 11 A.M.–8 P.M. Mon.–Sat., 10 A.M.–8 P.M. Sun., $10–25) the title of best Mexican and Southwestern joint in northern Nevada. Anything in the tacos, enchiladas, and carnitas line will serve you right, especially the steak fajitas and steak tacos. The interior and decor are modern and inviting, although the exterior maintains the Old West feel.

On the former site of the *Territorial Enterprise,* the **Palace Restaurant and Saloon** (54 S. C St., 775/847-4441, 9 A.M.–2 P.M. daily, under $10) has been slinging hash and frying burgers for 125 years. Its coffee and hot chocolate are almost necessities on winter mornings, and pancakes are the draw.

The **Bonanza Cafe** (27 C St., 775/847-7122, 11 A.M.–8 P.M. Tues.–Sat., 11 A.M.–3 P.M. Sun., under $10) does salads and sandwiches and has a nice view from up top, if the weather cooperates.

Fine dining is tough to find here, but if you're willing to drive a mile south to the **Crown Point** (1540 Main St., 775/847-0111, 11 A.M.–3 P.M. and 5–9 P.M. Wed.–Sat., 5–9 P.M. Sun.–Mon., 5–7 P.M. Tues. summer, 5–9 P.M. Wed.–Mon., 5–7 P.M. Tues. winter, $25–40), in the Gold Hill Hotel, you'll find steak, chops, salmon, and shrimp along with a nifty cellar with the perfect pairings.

The **Firehouse Restaurant & Saloon** (171 S. C St., 775/847-4774, 7 A.M.–4 P.M. daily, under $10), at the south end of town, is a coffee shop and bar that serves a variety of inexpensive breakfasts and lunches. Have the barbecue if you're here at lunchtime.

The café attached to the **Delta Saloon** (18 S. C St., 775/843-8503, 10 A.M.–3 P.M. daily,

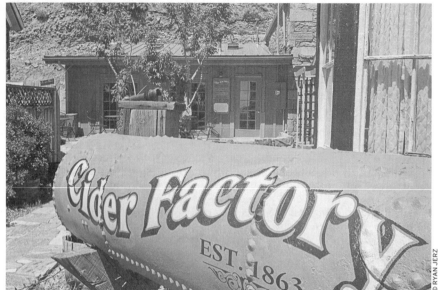

© RYAN JERZ

The Cider Factory restaurant at Edith Palmer's Country Inn really was originally used for making cider.

$10–20), known as Sawdust Corner, is a justifiably popular place for breakfast or lunch.

You'll certainly see, probably smell, and maybe even taste the fudge being slopped around on tables in the picture windows in front of **Grandma's Fudge Factory** (20 N. C St., 775/847-0770).

INFORMATION

The Virginia City **Convention and Tourism Authority** (86 S. C. St., 775/847-7500 or 800/718-7587) is on the northwest corner of C and Taylor Streets. The **Chamber of Commerce** can be contacted at http://virginiacity-nv.net.

Carson City and Vicinity

Carson City could be thought of as the center of Nevada. The geographic center of the state is roughly 200 miles away, 30 miles southeast of Austin, and Las Vegas and Reno are the financial and entertainment centers. The claim of historic center rightly belongs to Virginia City, but Carson City is the power center, where the state looks for vision, leadership, and order, bureaucratic though it may be.

While Nevada's state capital shared the boom-and-bust cycles of the Comstock Lode era throughout the last half of the 19th century,

it missed the worst of the crashes thanks to the business supplied by the burgeoning bureaucracy. The state prison, gaming commission, department of transportation, commission on tourism, and myriad other state and federal agencies keep the cogs turning.

Carson City is not just the state capital and center of political power. Some say this calm, comfortable, pretty, and friendly town sits atop a rare locus of planetary power. These emanations from the earth may have infused its founders and partisans with a special zeal and authority, and they may continue to infuse residents and visitors who appreciate the city's excellent size, central location, friendliness, excellent facilities—and the subtle sensation of powerful forces still at play just below the surface.

HISTORY

With a population of more than 500 in 1860, Carson City was just the kind of burgeoning city Congress was looking for when it came time to bestow the title of territorial capital, and it beat out Genoa and Virginia City for the honor. City father Abraham Curry befriended fellow New Yorker James Nye, territorial governor, and helped induce him to convene both the territorial and the new Ormsby County governments at Carson. Finally, on Halloween 1864, Nevada became a state with Carson City its capital.

By then, Uncle Abe, as he was henceforth universally known and revered for his civic spirit and generous soul, was Carson City's major landowner, contractor, hotelier, saloon keeper, and road builder. He wasn't content, of course, as merely a prophet and property mogul, and quickly made another transition to politician: he acted frequently as sheriff, delegate to an early constitutional convention, and aide to Governor Nye. Probably with ulterior motives, Curry also his hastily constructed the Warm Springs Hotel for use by the first territorial legislature. The hotel was two miles from town, and the ever-solicitous Curry transported the legislators in his horse-drawn streetcar—Nevada's first. Next, Curry sold his second hotel, the Great Basin, to the government to serve as a courthouse and legislature. The Warm Springs building later became the territorial prison, with Curry as the first warden. Prison labor quarried the limestone for many of Carson City's distinctive buildings, some of which are still standing. He later sold the prison and quarry to the territory. In 1865, Carson City received federal approval to build a branch of the U.S. Mint, and Curry—by now the go-to guy of patronage-wielding politicians—not only oversaw construction of the

building but also was appointed its first superintendent when it opened in January 1870.

Uncle Abe resigned his commission at the mint in September 1870 to run on the Republican ticket for lieutenant governor, a campaign that he lost. He then turned his attention to building the mammoth stone roundhouse and shops for the Virginia & Truckee Railroad. The Grand Ball, held to celebrate the opening of the railroad facilities on July 4, 1873, proved to be Curry's swan song. He died in October 1873 from a stroke at age 58. All in all, Abe Curry had lived one of the richest lives of any early Nevadan and had earned and maintained a reputation for being one of the most warm-hearted, civic-spirited, generous, and honest men during those turbulent times.

SIGHTS
◖ Nevada State Museum

Nevada's premier museum, the Nevada State Museum (600 N. Carson St., 775/687-4810, 8:30 A.M.–4:30 P.M. Wed.–Sat., $8 adults, free under age 17) is inside the famous Carson City Mint, which operated 1870–1893 coining 57 different silver issues, all with the very collectible "CC" mint mark. After the mint closed, the stone building, erected by town father Uncle Abe Curry, served as a federal office building until 1933, when it was abandoned because of neglect. Five years later, Judge Clark J. Guild noticed a "For Sale" sign on the building and promptly mobilized a coalition of his friends, local residents, Senator Patrick McCarran, Nevada philanthropist Max Fleischmann, and the state legislature to repair the building and outfit it as a museum. It opened to the public in 1941, and the rear wing was added in 1959.

After paying admission, head into the mint exhibit, which illustrates the entire coining process from depositors' bullion through ingot melting to gold and silver "cakes," which are rolled, annealed, and cut into blanks, then washed, weighed, and coined by the likes of the huge Coin Press No. 1 (on display) into $1, $5, $10, and $20 silver and gold pieces.

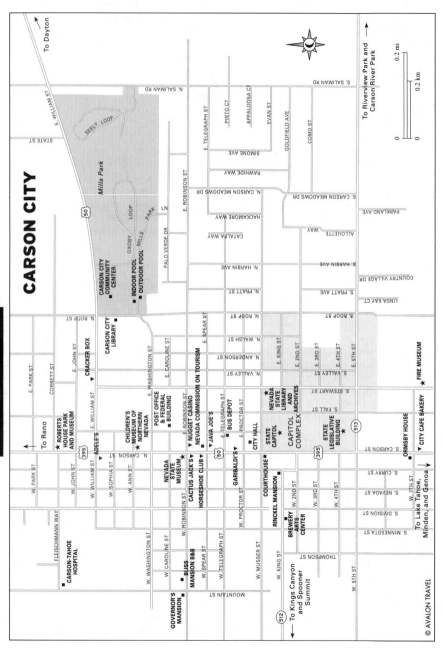

CARSON CITY

To Dayton

STATE ST.

E. WILLIAM ST

SEELY LOOP

Mills Park

N. SALIMAN RD.

S. SALIMAN RD.

PINTO CT.

E. TELEGRAPH ST

APPALOOSA CT.

EVAN ST

GOLDFIELD AVE.

COMO ST.

SIMONE AVE.

RAWHIDE WAY

N. CARSON MEADOWS DR.

S. CARSON MEADOWS DR.

PARKLAND AVE.

HACKAMORE WAY

E. ROBINSON ST.

PALO VERDE DR.

CATALPA WAY

ALLOUETTE WAY

COUNTRY VILLAGE DR

N. HARBIN AVE.

S. HARBIN AVE.

N. PRATT ST.

S. PRATT AVE.

LINDA KAY CT.

OXOBY LOOP

PARK LN.

MILLS PARK DR

CARSON CITY COMMUNITY CENTER ■
■ INDOOR POOL
● OUTDOOR POOL

CARSON CITY LIBRARY ■

N. ROOP ST.

N. ROOP ST.

S. ROOP ST.

E. SPEAR ST.

N. WALSH ST.

N. ANDERSON ST.

E. KING ST.

E. 2ND ST.

E. 3RD ST.

E. 4TH ST.

E. 5TH ST.

E. WASHINGTON ST.

E. CAROLINE ST.

E. JOHN ST.

E. PARK ST.

N. ROOP ST.

CORBETT ST.

■ CRACKER BOX

E. VALLEY ST.

S. VALLEY ST.

E. STEWART ST.

S. FALL ST.

★ FIRE MUSEUM

E. TELEGRAPH ST.

■ BUS DEPOT

E. PROCTOR ST.

★ NEVADA STATE LIBRARY AND ARCHIVES

CAPITOL COMPLEX

STATE LEGISLATIVE BUILDING

STATE CAPITOL ★

CITY HALL ■

▼ CITY CAFE BAKERY

ORMSBY HOUSE ●

To Reno

To Riverview Park and
Carson River Park →

0.2 mi
0.2 km

E. PARK ST.

W. PARK ST.

W. JOHN ST.

W. WILLIAM ST.

N. CARSON ST.

W. JOHN ST.

N. SOPHIA ST.

N. ANN ST.

N. CARSON ST.

N. ROBINSON ST.

★ ROBERTS HOUSE PARK AND MUSEUM

■ ADELE'S

CHILDREN'S MUSEUM OF NORTHERN NEVADA ■

POST OFFICE & FEDERAL BUILDING ■

● JAVA JOE'S

● NUGGET CASINO

NEVADA COMMISSION ON TOURISM ■

NEVADA STATE MUSEUM ★

CACTUS JACK'S ●

HORSESHOE CLUB ●

GARIBALDI'S ▼

COURTHOUSE ■

RINCKEL MANSION ■

CARSON-TAHOE HOSPITAL ■

FLEISCHMANN WAY

W. WASHINGTON ST.

W. CAROLINE ST.

W. ROBINSON ST.

W. SPEAR ST.

W. TELEGRAPH ST.

■ BLISS MANSION B&B

CARSON-TAHOE HOSPITAL ■

GOVERNOR'S MANSION ■

MOUNTAIN ST.

W. MUSSER ST.

W. KING ST.

W. PROCTOR ST.

W. 2ND ST.

W. 3RD ST.

W. 4TH ST.

W. 5TH ST.

THOMPSON ST.

BREWERY ARTS CENTER ■

To Kings Canyon and Spooner Summit →

S. CARSON ST.

S. CURRY ST.

S. NEVADA ST.

S. DIVISION ST.

S. MINNESOTA ST.

W. 7TH ST.

To Lake Tahoe, Minden, and Genoa →

© AVALON TRAVEL

The mint produced $49.2 million from 56.6 million coins in its 23 years of operation, and you can see a sample of every coin minted here—including a complete set of CC Morgan Dollars. The mint wing also houses the silver collection from the USS *Nevada,* made from 5,000 ounces of silver from the Tonopah mines and inlaid with gold from Goldfield.

Nevada's Changing Earth Exhibit walks visitors through a Nevada timeline from 1,750 million years ago to 40 million years ago as the climate and the geology morphed. Rock specimens, photo illustrations, and an interactive walk through the Devonian Sea fully explain this part of history. This region of Nevada was once part of the Columbian mammoth's home turf, and the biggest one on display in the country is here at the museum; visitors can see its recreated unsuccessful battle with death in a Black Rock Desert water hole. The skeleton of another old-time Nevadan—an ichthyosaur—is on the stairs.

The Environmental Gallery celebrates Nevada's native and endemic plants and animals, including a big black bear, bobcats, porcupines, a big Lahontan cutthroat trout, a cui-ui, and the Pyramid Lake pelicans and cormorants. Other exhibits center on Native Americans and their culture, food, tools, and weapons.

The underground mine recreation is quite realistic, using reclaimed timbers, vents, and ores from once-active mines around the state. It meanders through a large maze under the whole building and imparts a lifelike sense of working in tunnels underground.

There's a big selection of Nevada books and gifts in the shop on the second floor.

Nevada State Railroad Museum

Under the control of the Union Mill & Mining Company and the Bank of California, the Virginia & Truckee Railroad was an immediate financial success and is at least partly responsible for extending the life of the Comstock Lode. The standard-gauge short line connecting Reno, Carson City, Virginia City, Minden, and eventually the rest of the country made it more efficient and less costly to move silver ore to nearby reduction mills. That meant even low-grade ore could be profitable, keeping miners at work and investors opening their pocketbooks. Once the line connected with intercontinental service, an opulent passenger trade began as well.

The focus of the Nevada State Railroad Museum (2180 S. Carson St., 775/687-6953, 8:30 A.M.–4:30 P.M. Fri.–Mon., $5 adults, free under age 19) is its collection of Nevada's railroad heritage depicted through the locomotives and rolling stock of the V&T and other railroads. Many came to the museum from the Hollywood studios that made them famous on the big and small screen. Of 65 painstakingly restored locomotives and cars in the collection, 40 were built before 1900, and 31 are pieces that operated on the V&T Railroad.

In addition, some 15 astonishingly realistic model railroad layouts show the workings and hardships of the V&T, Southern Pacific, and Nevada Copper Belt from both the steam and diesel eras. Modeled in strikingly detailed HO scale, some of the stock and engines on the layouts are replicas of actual pieces in the museum collection, allowing visitors to compare details and put the machinery into historical context.

Museum visitors also can ride the trains and handcars, attend lectures, and conduct research on railroading in Nevada.

The Capitol and Legislature

The state capitol building (101 N. Carson St., 775/687-5030, 8 A.M.–5 P.M. daily, free) just south of the state library between West Musser Street and West 2nd Street, was built in 1870, when it was one of only a few structures in the city. Improvements, including the iron fence, were made five years later; the library annex, now the controller's offices, was added onto the back of the building in 1905; the two legislative wings were constructed in 1913; and the entire structure was gutted and restored in 1977.

A fine museum on the south side of the second floor, in the old senate chambers, displays a collection of Nevada historical artifacts: William Stewart's Wooten Patent Cabinet desk, an 1862 map of the Nevada Territory, the 36-star flag, the silver trowel from the capitol's cornerstone ceremony, and the goblets used by Abe Curry and James Nye to toast statehood. Spend some time following the history of the building, especially the photographs of the gutted interior during the 1977 restoration and the installation of the new fiberglass dome. Don't miss the Capitol room, and in the old assembly chambers down the hall is a display on the USS *Nevada*.

Today the capitol and legislative building anchor a complex of government structures. Nearby are the Nevada Supreme Court and State Library and Archives, all surrounded by a lush landscape of native plants.

The Legislative Building across the plaza hosts lawmakers who sit beginning in February during odd-numbered years. As you're wandering around the building, peek into the Assembly (south) and Senate (north) galleries. During the other 660 or so days when they're not in session, you will be alone in the public galleries in air-conditioned meditative luxury.

Brewery Arts Center

Brewery Arts Center (449 W. King St., 775/883-1976, 10 A.M.–4 P.M. Mon.–Sat., free) sponsors more than 100 classes and workshops in visual and performing arts, art exhibits, crafts fairs, concerts, plays, storytellers, and other cultural programs throughout the year. Stop in and check the schedule; you're sure to find something that appeals to your tastes.

The center is housed in a building constructed in 1865 for the Carson Brewery. For 80 years the formidable two-story brick structure produced several brands of beers, lagers, and ales, most notably Tahoe Beer, touted as "Famous as the Lake."

Children's Museum of Northern Nevada

It took six years of fund-raising to collect $400,000 and another year of renovating to unveil the Children's Museum of Northern Nevada (813 N. Carson St., 775/884-2226, 10 A.M.–4:30 P.M. Tues.–Sun., $5 adults, $4 over age 54, $3 ages 2–14). The museum is one block north of the Nevada State Museum on the opposite side of the street. There are 25 exhibits in fine arts, humanities, and science aimed at the 6–13 age group, but it is fun for the whole family.

Fire Museum

Chronicling the service of Warren Engine Company No. 1, the Fire Museum (777 S. Stewart St., 775/887-2210, 9 A.M.–5 P.M. Mon.–Fri., donation) is housed in the city's main fire station. Warren Engine Company No. 1 began as a volunteer firefighting fraternity in 1863 and has served Carson City uninterrupted ever since, making it the oldest volunteer company in the West; mostly professional firefighters now make up its ranks. That first year, 20 charter members of the company raised $2,000 at a fireman's ball to buy the first firefighting equipment in town: a Hunneman Engine built in the early 1800s and used by the Warren Engine Company of Boston. Later it was shipped around the Horn and worked in San Francisco and Marysville, California, before arriving in Carson City, where the company named itself for the Warren Company of Boston. In 1913, on its 50th anniversary, the company bought a Seagrave fire engine, Nevada's first motorized fire truck. Check out the Seagrave, the wild old goggles, masks, helmets, and caps, the 1870s two-wheeled hose cart, and the familiar Currier & Ives original prints of New York conflagrations. One of the firefighters will show you around; ask your guide to explain the trumpet trophies.

Historical Houses

The **Roberts House Park and Museum** (1207 N. Carson St., 775/887-2714, 1–3 P.M. Fri.–Sun. Apr.–Oct., donation) is Carson City's oldest house, but the Gothic Revival with its gingerbread bargeboard, lancet windows, and steeply pitched roof was not originally built here. It is believed that it was a kit house shipped from New England to San Francisco and then transported by rail and wagon to Washoe City, where it was assembled around 1859. In 1875 the house, home of James Doane Roberts and family, was moved to Carson City. Today it has been restored and contains period furniture.

The **Kit Carson Trail** leads modern-day explorers on a walking path through Carson City's historic homes district. A painted blue line and bronze medallions along the sidewalk mark the trail of Victorian-style homes, museums, and churches. Pick up the trail map at the visitors center (1900 S. Carson St., 775/687-7410 or 800/NEVADA-1—800/638-2321) next to the Nevada State Railroad Museum. The flyer is beautifully illustrated, and the accompanying podcast is quite informative. The tour itself is long, with 60 stops, so you might want to rely more on the map for navigation, skipping some sites to focus on those that interest you.

Some residential highlights include the **Bliss Mansion** (710 W. Robinson St.), a two-story house built in 1879 by Duane L. Bliss, who made his fortune with the Lake Tahoe Narrow Gauge Railroad transporting timber from Lake Tahoe to Virginia City's mines. The 1860 **Stewart-Nye home** (108 N. Minnesota St.) was built for Senator William Steward and later sold to territorial governor James Nye. It's the oldest extant building originally constructed in Carson City. The **Governor's Mansion** (N. Mountain St.) has classic Southern colonial columns and a curvilinear porch; it was completed in 1907 and completely rebuilt in 2000 with private donations.

History buffs can design their own mini tour, perhaps soaking up the creative atmosphere at the **Orion Clemens House** (502 N. Division St.). Mark Twain almost certainly slept here in the two-story stucco house (originally it wood siding) that his brother built in 1863 while serving as secretary to territorial governor Nye. See the sandstone **home of city father Abe Curry** (406 N. Nevada St.), built in 1871 using materials from the state prison's quarry, formerly owned by Curry.

Other Comstock-era homes include the **Niles-Sadler House** (310 N. Mountain St.), constructed in 1878 by the Virginia & Truckee Railroad paymaster and ticket agent. It later housed Governor Reinhold Sadler, as Nevada didn't complete its governor's mansion until 1907; early chief executives either had houses built in town or bought or rented existing properties. The plantation-style **Bender-Pozzi House** (707 W. Robinson St.) has a deep porch overlooking mature trees and an expansive lawn. It was owned by Comstock lawyer George Nourse and later by David Bender, another V&T official. The **Sears-Ferris House** (311 W. 3rd St.) is where George Washington Gale Ferris Sr. planned and imported many of the now-mature trees from back East. More recognizable, perhaps, the house was the boyhood home of George W. G. Ferris Jr., inventor of the famous Ferris wheel that debuted at the Chicago World Columbian Exposition of 1893.

Homes of later Victorian vintage are represented in Carson City as well. The **Brougher-Bath House** (204 W. Spear St.) was completed at the turn of the 20th century after its owner—a state senator—struck it rich in the Tonopah boom after the Comstock bust. Notice the two-story circular porch, stained glass windows, and circular turret. Fans of *The Shootist,* John Wayne's last movie, might recognize the **Krebs-Peterson House** (500 N. Mountain St.), built in 1914 by a surgeon and shown in the film.

Stewart Indian Boarding School

A visit to the campus of the Stewart Indian Boarding School (5366 Snyder Ave., 775/687-8333) is one of the highlights of Carson City. Thirty years after the complete dislocation of Nevada's Native American population, U.S. Senator William Stewart in 1890 secured federal funds to open the school on a 240-acre campus with three teachers and 37 students from local Washoe, Shoshone, and Paiute groups. The first students consisted of orphans, sons and daughters of tribe leaders, and children who were forcibly removed from their parents. At that time, federal policy was to assimilate Native Americans, carried out as little more than forced conversion to nonnative ways. In the early years of the school, this was enforced with military rigidity, and though students were taught reading, writing, and arithmetic, emphasis was placed on vocational skills, and observing traditional customs was actively discouraged.

A more enlightened policy evolved, and the school relied less on indoctrination and more on achievement and an appreciation of Native American culture. By the time the federal government closed the school in 1980, nearly 3,000 students had gone through the program.

The museum, in the former superintendent's home, is closed, but visitors can still see the distinctive stone buildings currently used as state offices and follow the Stewart Indian School Trail, a self-guided walking tour of the campus with 20 points of interest and audio stories. Using your cell phone, you can hear recorded messages from school alumni and employees about their experiences and remembrances of specific places on campus. If you're here in June, immerse yourself in Native American culture at the annual Stewart Father's Day Powwow, which presents traditional competition dancing, Stewart School alumni recognition, and arts and crafts.

Carson Hot Springs

"Gentleman Jim" Corbett trained at Shaw's Warm Springs, predecessor to Carson Hot Springs (1500 Old Hot Springs Rd., 775/885-8844 or 888/917-3711, www.carsonhotspringsresort.com, 7 A.M.–11 P.M., $10–15), while preparing for his prizefight with Robert Fitzsimmons in 1897. Abe Curry built his Warm Springs Hotel next to these waters and ferried the territorial legislators out here when they met at the hotel in the town's early days. Today, there's a pool with 100°F soft spring water containing no sulfur odor or chlorine; no city water is added, only the geothermic heated water from far below ground. The water emerges at about 127°F but is cooled by the air

before guests take the plunge. The resort drains the pool every night and fills it up again every morning. Private in-room hot pools are also available (bathing suits are optional in private rooms), and the resort offers massages ($45 per half hour), a restaurant, and a nightclub.

Jack C. Davis Observatory

Zoom in on other worlds with the array of telescopes at the Davis Observatory (2699 Van Patten Dr., 775/445-3240, www.wnc.edu/observatory, free). The research-quality equipment, including 16-inch, 14-inch, and 10-inch scopes, can collect data from the stars, observe solar prominences, and project images onto television screens for group viewing. The public is invited to Saturday "star parties" (sunset–11 P.M.) for stargazing, observatory tours, and lectures. Additional parties are held to observe eclipses and meteor showers.

RECREATION

Mills Park (1111 East William St.), four blocks east of U.S. 395 on U.S. 50, is an excellent city facility with lots of recreation choices: expanses and shade trees for stretching out and napping, picnic tables, barbecue grills, and a tot lot. But there's also tennis courts, horseshoe pits, a big skate park, indoor and outdoor pools, and a fitness facility next door at the **community center** (775/887-2242, $4 adults, $3 ages 4–17 and over age 54). Perhaps the biggest draw is the **Carson and Mills Park Railroad** (775/887-2523, 2–7 P.M. Wed., 11 A.M.–7 P.M. Sat., 1–5 P.M. Sun., $2, free under age 3), a one-mile, 15-minute ride in two-foot-gauge toy gondolas or covered passenger cars behind a diesel switcher.

Carson River Park (775/887-2115, 8 A.M.–dusk daily) is on both sides of the Carson River about four miles out of town. Heading south on U.S. 395 from U.S. 50, turn left (east) on East 5th Street and drive through the middle of the grounds of the state maximum-security prison. Just the sight of the pen, roasting in the desert within high barbed-wire cyclone fencing and with gun towers at the corners, will make you appreciate the wide-open spaces and refreshing breezes that await you at the riverside park. Cross Edmonds Drive, take a right on Carson River Road, and head across the green valley down to the lazy river. Cross the little bridge and explore the network of dirt roads. Turn right (south) onto Mexican Dam Road, and in about 1.5 miles you'll come to Mexican Dam. You can't go onto the dam itself—it's private property—but there's a fine one-mile trail called the **Mexican Dam Ditch Trail.** Kayakers, canoeists, and rafters can put in here for a tranquil 3.3-mile Class I and II float down the river to the new **Morgan Mill Road River Access Area,** where a concrete boat ramp provides a safe takeout point. The same ramp marks a put-in point for Class II and Class III white-water rapids through the Carson River Canyon, 9.3 miles to the Santa Maria Ranch in Lyon County. This section of river is not for beginners. Stocked 10-inch trout patrol the ramp in summer, challenging anglers.

On the way to the river, you'll pass **Silver Saddle Ranch Park,** operated by the Bureau of Land Management (775/885-6000). The park is on the south side of Carson River Road, 0.25 miles north of Mexican Dam between the river and Prison Hill; another section of the ranch is on the east side of the river. The intention for this park is that it remains natural and undeveloped. You can walk down to the river on the old farm roads and enjoy the quiet open space.

Alternately, if you don't turn onto Carson River Road, you can continue straight ahead on East 5th Street until you come to **Riverview Park** (775/887-2115), a lovely riverside park with a wetland area, exercise stops along a trail, and people walking their dogs. A Korean War veterans memorial is next door.

Centennial Park (775/887-2115) is one of the largest municipal recreation facilities in Nevada. It's off U.S. 50 east of town to the south along Centennial Drive. It boasts several softball and soccer fields, many pleasant and shady picnic sites, tennis courts, and even an archery range. This is the place for a long walk after a soak at Carson Hot Springs and a meal at Garibaldi's and before hunkering down for some craps at Carson Station.

The **Sunridge Golf Club** (1000 Long Dr., 775/267-4448, $30–50), five miles south of Carson City at the north end of the Carson Valley, intersperses beautiful meadow holes, beautiful water holes, and uncannily breaking hillside greens that will cause seasoned golfers to question their abilities and duffers to consider trading their clubs for a tennis racket.

CASINOS
Carson Nugget

- **Restaurants:** The Steakhouse, Le Nougat, Garden Café, Snack Bar

- **Entertainment:** Live Music Show Bar

CARSON CITY'S FADED GRAND DAME

The **Ormsby House** (600 S. Carson St., Carson City) still stands, rickety, unadorned, and seemingly neglected, but its owners vow it will return to glory, a comeback more than a decade in the making. The various incarnations of Ormsby House date back to 1859, when it was opened by Major William Ormsby, who was killed in the Pyramid Lake skirmish with Numaga's Paiute in 1860. It was sold and expanded and by the 1870s was regarded as one of the fanciest hotels between Denver and San Francisco. In 1880 the name was changed to the Park Hotel, and it operated into the 1920s. It was reopened in 1931 after the legalization of casino gambling by the Laxalts, possibly the most famous Nevadan family. Paul Laxalt was Nevada governor, a U.S. senator, and a close friend of Ronald Reagan, and he built the existing hotel in 1972. It was subsequently sold, expanded, went bankrupt, and was resurrected again in the 1990s, but it closed, perhaps for the final time, in 2000. Perhaps a motivated owner with deep pockets can achieve another resurrection.

LAKE TAHOE AND VICINITY

• **Nightlife:** Cork & Bottle

With no end in sight to the decade-long "renovation" of the Ormsby House, the Carson Nugget (507 N. Carson St., 775/882-1626) is the main action downtown for gaming and nightlife, with seven tables along with 650 slots and video poker machines as well as bingo, keno, and poker. This is one of four Nuggets opened in northern Nevada in the mid-1950s. There's also a steak house, a café, a coffee bar, and a snack bar. Lounge entertainment includes local rock and country cover bands and the *Nugget Follies*. On weekends it's always crowded with locals and some visitors, which gives it the typical air of casino excitement.

The **Nugget Hotel** (651 N. Stewart St., 775/882-7711, $45–65), across from the casino, also has weekly rates. The pedestrian decor is pleasant enough, with knotty pine headboards and raspberry bedspreads.

The **Steakhouse** (507 N. Carson St., 775/882-1626, 5–9 P.M. Wed.–Thurs. and Sun., 5–10 P.M. Fri.–Sat.) is perhaps the closest thing to fine dining in a Carson City casino. The beef dishes are perfectly fine, and the requisite poultry and seafood are available too. But unlike some other casual fine-dining establishments, the vegetables aren't considered second-class citizens—and they come with the entrée, not as an extra. The sautéed spinach and grilled asparagus are particularly sublime.

Carson Station/Best Western

• **Restaurants:** The Station Restaurant, The Snack Bar

• **Entertainment:** Cabaret Lounge

Just a bit smaller than the Carson Nugget, the Carson Station/Best Western (900 S. Carson St., 775/883-0900 or 800/501-2929, $52–83) has five tables and 323 slots and video poker machines. Formerly the Mother Lode Casino, Carson Station is comparable to the Nugget in terms of gaming variety, and it claims the title for best entertainment venue. Its cabaret doubles as a sports bar, and the bands it attracts generally bring better production values and stage polish to their shows. That makes the Carson Station the best choice among the limited nightlife in town. With the Best Western brand gracing its side, there are no surprises when staying at the hotel. The rooms are airy and well lit, and an on-site gift shop will bail you out if you've forgotten your toothbrush. The snack bar will fill you up without taking you away from the action in the sports book.

You won't find many delicacies at **The Station Restaurant** (775/883-0900 or 800/501-2929, 7 A.M.–10 P.M. daily, $8–12), where the four main food groups are beef, gravy, potatoes, and salad. Locals flock to the Station for hearty fare and a $1.99 soup and salad bar with entrée purchase. The chicken fried steak is exceptional.

Casino Fandango

• **Restaurants:** Ti Amo, Duke's Steak House, Rum Jungle Buffet, Palm Court Grill

• **Entertainment:** Cabaret Lounge, Galaxy Theatres

The tropical-themed Casino Fandango (3800 S. Carson St., 775/885-7000) has more than 700 slots and the requisite table games claiming favorable odds, such as 5x odds on craps, 99 percent payback video poker, and 100 percent payback penny progressives. We can't vouch for the odds, but the free cabaret entertainment—heavy on Motown and other classics—is free and pretty good. A 10-screen Galaxy Theatre, a sports book and bar, and plenty of dining options complete the package.

Top of the restaurant picks is **Ti Amo** (775/886-1690, 5–9 P.M. Thurs.–Tues., $15–28). You can't go wrong with the lobster ravioli ($19) with an unusual hint of lime in the cream sauce. We like our meat, but we'd gladly trade most hamburgers for the vegetarian capellini pomodoro ($14) or eggplant parmesan ($14).

Gold Dust West

• **Restaurants:** Ole Ole, The Grille, The Snack Bar

• **Entertainment:** Bowling Center

The Gold Dust West (2171 U.S. 50 E., 775/885-

9000 or 877/519-5567, $65–140) has a 32-lane bowling alley in addition to 400 slot machines and a Cal-Neva sports book outlet. Booking one of its 146 good-sized guest rooms includes all the amenities, such as a swimming pool, a fitness center, and a spa. If you're here on business, the office center is open all night.

The menu at Gold Dust West's top restaurant, **The Grille** (775/885-9000, 24 hours daily, under $10), features some intriguing gourmet-like touches at budget prices, such as the chicken cordon bleu sandwich ($7, including a side dish) and the Cajun-spiced blackened salmon Caesar salad ($8).

Carson Horseshoe Club

• **Restaurants:** Juan's Grille

The Carson Horseshoe Club (402 N. Carson St., 775/883-2211) is slot heaven, but it's worth seeking out for **Juan's Grille** (402 N. Carson St., 775/883-2211, 7 A.M.–10 P.M. Sun.–Thurs., 7 A.M.–midnight Fri.–Sat., $8–15), with a $5 huevos rancheros breakfast special and burritos as big as a baby's head. The American standbys are just as filling. Head over for the Wednesday-night steak special ($7.77) and get $5 in free casino play.

ACCOMMODATIONS

In Carson City, just like anywhere else in Nevada, hotel-casinos are good places to start your search for accommodations; see the *Casinos* section.

The **City Center Motel** (800 N. Carson St., 775/882-5535, $28–54) is affiliated with the Carson Nugget, and a shuttle runs continuously between the two properties. The motel and the Nugget also offer room, gaming, and golf packages.

Although it has a small gaming area, **Hardman House Motor Inn** (917 N. Carson St., 775/882-7744, $50–99) isn't a hotel-casino. It's geared toward early-rising business types, with continental breakfast beginning at 6 A.M., free high-speed wireless Internet, and dry-cleaning service; there's even an evening manager's reception with cookies and

beverages to help you wind down after a long day of meetings.

Business travelers and family vacationers will especially appreciate the **Plaza Hotel** (801 S. Carson St., 775/883-9500 or 888/227-1499, $59–89). Make the Plaza your branch office with free wireless Internet, copy, fax, and mail service, a conference room, an airport shuttle, and baggage check. Amenities include an outdoor pool, the location in the center of the city's attractions, free continental breakfast, in-room fridges and microwaves, and cable TV.

Bed-and-Breakfasts

For a truly relaxing stay, book one of the nature-themed rooms at **Bliss Bungalow Bed & Breakfast** (408 W. Robinson St., 775/883-6129, $88–145). Built in 1914 and fully restored in 2005, this arts and crafts home has the original fir floors, bay windows, pine molding, and leaded glass windows accented with intricately designed Oriental rugs in the five individually-themed guest rooms. The tranquility of the rooms is matched only by the views from the front porch during balmy summer afternoons and comfortable spring and fall evenings.

Motels

Carson City has a full complement of comfortable motel rooms, with nightly rates starting in the $35 range. They fill up quickly on weekends but are useful if you're looking to save some cash and just need four walls and a clean bed.

Unless you're a light sleeper, a good place to start your search is the centrally located **Pioneer Motel** (907 S. Carson St., 775/882-3046, $35–50). The central location means it's in the middle of busy streets, but the rooms are large enough and stores and restaurants (and casinos, of course) are within walking distance. There's even a small swimming pool. Another workable option is the **Frontier Motel** (1718 N. Carson St., 775/882-1377, $33–55). Its 58 rooms have recently undergone renovation, and many contain kitchenettes, making it a prime choice if you'll be staying in town for a while.

For slightly more uptown digs, the simplicity is

the draw at **America's Best Value Inn** (2731 S. Carson St., 775/882-2007, $35–65). Each guest room contains a microwave and a refrigerator.

All the usual moderately priced chains are represented in Carson City, all offering similar accommodations and similar rates, including **Super 8 Motel** (2829 S. Carson St., 775/883-7800, $29–80), **Motel 6** (2749 S. Carson St., 775/885-7710, $30–50), and **Rodeway Inn** (400 N. Carson St., 775/882-3446, $39–75).

Camping and RV Parking

The tree-lined **Comstock Country RV Resort** (5400 S. Carson St., 775/882-2445 or 800/638-2321, $40) has a great location just south on U.S. 395 past the junction with U.S. 50. There are 160 spaces for motor homes, all with full hookups; 133 are pull-throughs. Tents are allowed. It is a bit pricy, but the restrooms have flush toilets and hot showers; public phones, sewage disposal, laundry, groceries, a game room, and a heated swimming pool and spa are available, and the casinos are close.

Although it's right off the freeway, the **Gold Dust West RV Park** (2171 U.S. 50 E., 775/885-9000 or 877/519-5567, $27–33) is peacefully shady. Sites might be a bit tight for larger rigs.

With 49 tent sites and no hookups, **Washoe Lake State Park** (4855 Eastlake Blvd., 775/687-4319, $14), five miles north of town, is not for the pampered camper, especially in winter, when nighttime temperatures routinely dip below 20°F. But what it lacks in creature comforts, the park makes up for in natural amenities: Hike the Mount Rose Trail, explore Deadman's Canyon Dam, or shoot the Truckee River rapids; they're all nearby.

A little farther north and on the other side of Washoe Lake, **Davis Creek Campground** (25 Davis Creek Rd., 775/849-0684) has 43 tent spaces and 19 dedicated RV spots, most with breathtaking views of the lake. There are also fine hiking trails, including Ophir Creek Trail, which leads past a waterfall and steep canyons on a 12-mile roundtrip. Davis Creek Park Pond teems with stocked 10-inch rainbows. But the

campground is not tranquil; traffic noise tells visitors that U.S. 395 is just beyond the tree line.

FOOD
Diners

Venturing beyond the casinos, the best place in Carson City—some say in all Nevada—to start your day or refuel is the **(Cracker Box** (402 E. William St., 775/882-4556, 6 A.M.–2 P.M. Thurs.–Tues., $9–15). This is the real diner deal, with an eight-seat counter and tables for 50 crammed into a squat green-and-white box of a building. The basic $9 breakfast has slabs—not slices—of bacon, a big mess of home fries with bits of pepper and onion, and two large eggs cooked exactly the way you order them; the orange juice is freshly squeezed. The egg dishes are the mainstay, but locals fill the place for lunch as well. Try the soup of the day. The bustling joint closes at 2 P.M., so don't be late.

The few who insist the Cracker Box isn't the best breakfast restaurant in town most likely cast their lot with **Heidi's** (1020 N. Carson St., 775/882-0486, 6 A.M.–9 P.M. daily, $10–15). With locations in South Lake Tahoe and Reno as well, Heidi's plate-sized omelets are as much as one person can handle, and families can dine here without taking out a second mortgage. Its long north and south walls are now graced by detailed trompe l'oeil murals: The south wall is a V&T steam engine with a cow catcher pulling out of the Engine House (a historic stone building constructed by Abe Curry and torn down amid controversy in 1992), and the north wall is a view of the desert from inside the Engine House.

For dinner, the combination of a fun atmosphere, pretty good beef dishes, conversation-piece decor, and plenty of beer variety on tap make **Red's Old 395 Grill** (1055 S. Carson St., 775/887-0395, 11 A.M.–late daily, $15–25) a go-to place for locals. Women on designated nights out, softball teams, and other groups dig the patio with its gas-log fire. The eclectic decorations include a 1907 fire department pumper and a 1923 steamroller.

Italian

Right in downtown Carson City is the Italian restaurant (€ **Garibaldi's** (307 N. Carson St., 775/884-4574, 11 A.M.–2 P.M. and 5–10 P.M. Mon.–Fri., 5–10 P.M. Sat.–Sun., $20–30). The exposed red brick and wood decor oozes Old World style, and we'd swim the Po for the Italian seafood dishes—especially the swordfish and wonton shrimp. The lemon-rosemary sauce makes everything that much better— even the spumoni.

Another good Italian option downtown is **B'Sghetti's** (318 N. Carson St., 775/887-8879, 11 A.M.–9 P.M. Mon.–Sat., 4–9 P.M. Sun., $12–20).

Mexican

For some of the best Mexican food anywhere, pull up an appetite at **El Charro Avitia** (4389 S. Carson St., 866/603-9778, 11 A.M.–9 P.M. Sun.–Thurs., 11 A.M.–10 P.M. Fri.–Sat., $10–20). El Charro opened in Carson City in 1978, the second outlet of a restaurant founded by a family of hardworking Mexican immigrants. The seafood enchiladas, burritos, and gorditas are worth the drive from Tahoe or Reno. Try the Tacos Nacionales with chicken, cream cheese, and almonds. The tamales are stuffed with barbecued pork, and the mini fajitas are a steal, as are the three-item combos; the guacamole shrimp cocktail is exquisite.

Asian

Top-notch sushi in Carson City? Believe it, and get some for yourself at (€ **Ming's Chinese Restaurant** (2330 S. Carson St., 775/887-8878, 11:30 A.M.–9:30 P.M. daily, $8–15). The sushi bar is on one side of the restaurant, and a sit-down family-style place is on the other. If you're not in the mood for sushi, crab Rangoon and vegetable shrimp make a tasty meal. Also very good is **Panda Kitchen** (1986 U.S. 50 E., 775/882-8128, 11 A.M.–11 P.M. daily, $10–15).

Authentic, fresh, and healthy Thai cuisine—the owners are first-generation Thais— greets diners at **The Basil** (311 N. Carson St., 775/841-6100, 11:30 A.M.–2:30 P.M. and 5–9 P.M. Mon.–Thurs., 11:30 A.M.–2:30 P.M. and 5–9:30 P.M. Fri., 11:30 A.M.–1:30 P.M. and 5–9 P.M. Sat., $12–20). Choose the spiciness of your dish while dining in an atmosphere reminiscent of tropical Southeast Asia with silk and rattan.

Fine Dining

The class act of Carson City, (€ **Adele's** (1112 N. Carson St., 775/882-3353, 11:30 A.M.–2 P.M. and 5–9 P.M. Mon.–Fri., 5–9 P.M. Sat., $20–45) is located in the 19th-century house of Nevada attorney general and Supreme Court justice M. A. Murphy. It is extremely elegant in all its Second Empire appointments, and you can read about it on the huge and varied dinner menu—practically anything you want that's in season is available at Carson City's finest restaurant. Inside, the bar is in the living room and several tables are in the dining room, with Victorian-style carpet, stained-glass windows, and fine lamps.

INFORMATION AND SERVICES

For information on Carson City, the **Chamber of Commerce** (1900 S. Carson St., 775/882-1565, www.carsoncitychamber. com, 8:30 A.M.–5 P.M. Mon.–Fri.) is downstairs in the building next door to the Railroad Museum; you can pick up local maps and brochures.

Upstairs in the same building, the **Carson City Convention and Visitors Bureau** (1900 S. Carson St., 775/687-7410 or 800/ NEVADA-1—800/638-2321, www.visitcarsoncity.com, 8:30 A.M.–5 P.M. Mon.–Fri., 10 A.M.–3 P.M. Sat.–Sun.) is another good place for visitors to ask questions. Call ahead or email and they'll send you a visitors packet.

The **Nevada Commission on Tourism** (401 N. Carson St., 775/687-4322 or 800/237-0774, www.travelnevada.com), in the historic brick Paul Laxalt State Building, has information on the entire state of Nevada, with the primary goal of promoting tourism in Nevada's rural areas. It publishes the colorful and informative *Nevada* magazine, and you can pick up brochures on events around the state, the Nevada Scenic Byways brochure, regional brochures, Great Basin National Park brochures, and a good state map.

Books and Maps

The office of the U.S. Forest Service's **Carson Ranger District** (1536 S. Carson St., 775/882-2766, 8 A.M.–4:30 P.M. Mon.–Fri.) is a block north of the Railroad Museum. The staff can supply good literature, maps, and information on Mount Rose, Lake Tahoe, and the Humboldt-Toiyabe National Forest, which comprises all the national forest lands in Nevada in many different places. The office also sells maps and a number of useful books and other items, which is unusual for a Forest Service office. Ten percent of the sales goes back to the Carson District for recreation and wilderness programs.

The **Carson City Library** (900 N. Roop St., next to Mills Park, 775/887-2247, 10 A.M.–8 P.M. Mon.–Thurs., 10 A.M.–6 P.M. Fri.–Sat.) is preparing to expand.

If you're serious about your maps, head to Room 206 of the **Nevada Department of Transportation** building (1263 S. Stewart St., 775/888-7-MAP—775/888-7627, 8 A.M.–4:30 P.M. Mon.–Fri.) for the graphics and cartography department. Beautiful huge prints grace the foyer; beautiful huge maps are for sale upstairs. Pick up the catalog plus free mileage and public transportation maps. Huge state maps, poster-size city maps, enlarged area maps, and quad maps as well as the excellent *Nevada Map Atlas* are available.

Transportation

The public bus service **Jump Around Carson** (775/841-RIDE—775/841-7433, 6:30 A.M.–6:30 P.M. Mon.–Fri., 8:30 A.M.–4:30 P.M. Sat., $1) operates 10 routes throughout town. Greyhound and the major airlines are based in Reno; no regularly scheduled flights serve this capital city.

Carson City has four rental car companies: **Enterprise** (1063 S. Carson St., 775/883-7788), **Hertz** (135 Clearview Dr., 775/841-8002), **Avis** (3911 S. Carson St.,

775/841-6758), and **Budget** (860 U.S. 50, 775/882-1944).

DAYTON

Stopping along the trail to the California gold fields, Abner Blackburn scraped around some outcroppings in Gold Creek near Dayton in 1849 and found a bit of color. It was the first gold discovered in the silver state. Dayton bills itself as Nevada's town of firsts, claiming to be the state's oldest permanent settlement as well as the site of Nevada's first marriage—and first divorce.

Sights

The **Dayton Museum** (Shady Lane at Logan Alley, 775/246-6316, 10 A.M.–4 P.M. Sat., 1–4 P.M. Sun., or by appointment, call for winter hours, free), located in an 1865 schoolhouse, chronicles all this early history and collects artifacts from the town's peak years. Dayton's role in the history of gold prospecting, railroading, milling, mining, farming, and ranching come to life through photographs, documents, machinery, and housewares.

The museum also has maps for a half-hour walking tour of the town. Sights along the path include Nevada's oldest cemetery, the first-ever depot for the Carson & Colorado Railroad (currently under restoration), camel stables, the famed Odeon Hall & Saloon (where, contrary to a plaque's assertion, Ulysses S. Grant did not make a speech in 1879), the Rock Point Mill, the jail, the firehouse, and much more.

North of town, the Carson River, raging with spring runoff or a muddy trickle in the arid summer, and U.S. 50 cut through **Dayton State Park,** which provides picturesque and easily accessible spots for picnicking, fishing, bird watching, and camping (10 sites, no reservations, free). Rangers often lead interpretive hikes to the remains of the Nothing but the Rock Point Mill, the largest stamp mill in these parts, built to process the silver ore from Virginia City, Gold Hill, and Silver City. The mill was powered by water transported via flume from the Carson River.

Carson Valley

Home to ranches that have been in families for generations, Carson Valley presents small-town treasures at every turn, from antiques shops to 150-year-old saloons. And this is cattle country, don't forget, so the steaks are among the best in Nevada.

GENOA

Genoa (juh-NO-uh) is the oldest town in Nevada, settled by Mormons in 1851 to serve California- and Oregon-bound emigrants. Mormons and non-Mormons alike were drawn to the valley's scenic, agricultural, and commercial assets, and the settlement, Mormon Station, was the site of the first house, first public meeting, first written records, first land claim, and first squatter government in what would soon be Nevada.

In the late 1940s the state rebuilt the original Mormon station and fort. That attraction and others, along with the beautiful setting, historical significance, and mushrooming tourism, have turned Genoa into a popular destination, especially as a day trip from Carson City, 12 miles north. Today Genoa is actually a growing suburb of the capital, with large new houses surrounding the historical center of town.

The sweet smell of alfalfa is a fitting background for a visit to Mormon Station State Park, commemorating the original trading post that sold fodder and other supplies along the Emigrant Trail. Genoa was also an important stop for the Pony Express, and that heritage comes alive at the city's Courthouse Museum.

Genoa Courthouse Museum

In public service for nearly 150 years, the Genoa Courthouse Museum (2304 Main St., 775/782-2555, 10 a.m.–4:30 p.m. May–Oct., $3 adults, $2 ages 7–17, free under age 7), across from the park, deserves reverence. The building was a courthouse 1865–1916, then a school for 40 years, and since 1969 it

has been a museum that captures everyday working, home, and government life in the 1800s. There is a poignant nursery scene with a collection of old dolls lining an exquisitely carved toddler's bed. Another display shows what the courthouse looked like when it handled divorces, civil suits, and the occasional murder trial. Decorated with original oak furniture from the Genoa and Minden courthouse, the display is as authentic as it gets. Realistic recreations of a blacksmith shop and pioneer kitchen as well as opulent velour burgundy furniture in the Victorian parlor offer additional insights.

Don't miss baskets created by the Washoe artisan Dat-So-La-Lee from roots, saplings, and willows. Her handiwork is perhaps the finest example of Native American basket weaving. You can also marvel at the accomplishments

Despite his nickname, John "Snowshoe" Thompson used a version of cross country skis to deliver mail over the snowy Sierras.

of Snowshoe Thompson, who braved the elements to carry mail over the Sierra Nevada to Placerville, California, and back.

The offerings in the gift shop include books on Nevada, mining, Basque culture, and native plants and animals along with Nevada souvenir T-shirts and more that make terrific keepsakes.

Mormon Station State Historic Park

Just across the street, Mormon Station State Historic Park, the site of Nevada's first permanent nonnative settlement, is home to a museum (Main St., 775/782-2590, 10 A.M.–4 P.M. Thurs.–Sun. May–Oct., $1). The log stockade replicates one built by the earliest settlers to keep livestock—it's doubtful they were much afraid of the mild and peaceful Washoe. The relics of pioneer days are housed in a replica of the original 1851 trading post; take some time to read the signboards.

The park offers plenty of shade for picnicking. Barbecue grills and picnic tables dot the site. Throughout the summer, the park hosts family-oriented entertainment such as performances by the Reno Philharmonic, a Chautauqua for youngsters, and re-creations of Pony Express rides.

◖ Genoa Bar

A block or so down the road is Nevada's oldest watering hole, the Genoa Bar (2282 Main St., 775/782-3870), built in 1853, when it operated as Livingston's Exchange. Belly up to the bar (half the bar top is original, as are the diamond-dust mirror on the back bar, the medallions on the ceiling, and a red oil lamp). The electric lamps are also original oil burners converted to electricity at the turn of the century. It doesn't make for as good a story, but the red stains on the ceiling are not blood but tomato juice. Similarly, the trap door by the pool table is not—as local parents sometimes claim—where naughty children will be sent to

While it sometimes gets a bit rowdy, the Genoa Bar has always been a "gentleman's saloon... kept in first-class style in every particular way," according to an old advertisement.

deal with alligators and bogeymen if they don't behave. It's actually an old ice box. Ice harvested from small lakes in the area was packed in burlap and straw to keep the bar's food fresh and drinks cool.

Historic Buildings

Genoa was not immune to fire, the bane of frontier boomtowns. Most of the town's original buildings perished in one conflagration or another, but a few have survived. South of the courthouse is the old **Masonic Hall** (2286 Main St.), built in 1862 and expanded in 1874. The **Genoa Country Store** (2299 Main St.) was built in 1879 and is one of the great country stores in Nevada, with an interesting assortment of cards, bottles, and jams. Stock up on soda, beer, ice cream, and some of the best sandwiches around. Genoa **Town Hall** (289-A Main St.) began life in 1886 as the Raycraft Dance Hall and remained in the family for 55 years before the town bought it. The structure hosted the Genoa Candy Dance from its inception in 1919 until the event outgrew the venue. Today, it hosts community events, meetings, and weddings. It has been renovated and expanded over the years and now contains a bar salvaged from the Globe Saloon in Carson City. Built with donated materials and community volunteer labor after a huge 1910 fire devastated the business district, the nondenominational **Genoa Community Church** (182 Nixon St.) is a quaint house of worship and pleasant wedding venue.

Candy Dance

Genoa is also the scene of one of the oldest annual events in Nevada. The Genoa Candy Dance originated in 1919 when the town was trying to raise funds to install lights on the streets of the town. The fund-raiser started out as a dance and midnight dinner and eventually turned into a bake sale after the Genoa matriarchs mixed up batches of fudge to sell by the pound to the partygoers. The candy proved to be the star of the show, and the Candy Dance tradition began. In modern times, the proceeds from the Candy Dance have paid for most of Genoa's town services. Genoa celebrated the 90th edition of the Candy Dance in 2010 with craft fairs, musical entertainment, dinner, and, of course, candy and dancing.

The Candy Dance takes place the third weekend of September with events all over town. The crafts fair is usually held at Mormon Station, the town park, and the Volunteer Fire Department. On Saturday night, a buffet dinner and dance is held at Genoa Town Park.

More than 4,000 pounds of candy—plain, nut, and mocha fudge as well as Almond Roca, nut brittles, dipped chocolates, divinity candy, mints, almond clusters—35 different kinds altogether—are sold during the two-day fair.

Accommodations

Genoa boasts two attractive bed-and-breakfast inns. **Genoa House Inn** (180 Nixon St., 775/782-7075, $150–165) was built in 1872 by A. C. Pratt, publisher of the *Carson Valley News,* the valley's first newspaper. The fine example of Greek Revival architecture is on the National Register of Historic Places. It features three guest rooms upstairs, each with distinctive features. The Rose Room is illuminated by church-quality stained-glass windows; the Blue Room comes with a jetted tub; and the Garden Room boasts a faux fireplace and garden views.

Just up the street from the Genoa House is the **Wild Rose Inn** (2332 Main St., 775/782-5697, $150–240), a three-story Queen Anne Victorian-style mansion built in 1989 specifically for use as a B&B. All five guest rooms and suites have private baths. Innkeeper Sue Knight is a font of local knowledge and a wizard in the kitchen. You won't leave for your daily excursions hungry, and she'll be ready with a glass of wine before bedtime. Guests can get discounts to Walley's Hot Springs.

Nestled in the Sierra foothills you'll find **Genoa Country Inn** (2292 Main St., 775/782-4500, $89–119), decorated in clean white and neutral tones.

Walley's Hot Springs (2001 Foothill Rd., 775/782-8155 or 800/622-1580, $78–145) is just over a mile south of Genoa on Highway

206. The springs, whose water reaches 160°F, have had a hotel since 1862. The original hotel burned in the 1920s and was rebuilt in the late 1980s with no expense spared and attention paid to every detail. Today it's a beautifully landscaped, luxurious, and reasonably priced hotel-spa. Room rates include the use of seven mineral pools, a large heated swimming pool, a steam room and sauna, and other hotel amenities. You can also get a massage, play tennis, take exercise classes, or just use the facilities for the day ($20).

Food

Formerly the Pink House, **La Ferme** (2291 Main St., 775/783-1004, 5:30–10 P.M. daily, $30–50) delivers French provincial cuisine in a pastoral setting. Sip white wine in the garden while preparing for a delectable meal of venison, duck, or fillet. The restaurant and bar sit in a quaint two-room guest cottage and bunkhouse on the grounds of the Pink House, built in 1855 by Captain John Reese, the earliest non-Mormon settler at Mormon Station and therefore the first in Nevada. The guest house was added in 1904. There's also a gallery of jewelry, pottery, and art.

Authentic Italian with attractive vistas both inside and out grace **Antoci's** (1 Genoa Lakes Dr., 775/783-6645, 4–9 P.M. Thurs.–Sat., $20–30) at Genoa Golf Club. The European bistro–style clubhouse perfectly complements the Sierra views from big picture windows. Pasta is a specialty, along with chicken, seafood, and beef dishes with an Italian flair.

MINDEN AND GARDNERVILLE

In 1879 Lawrence Gilman, previously from Genoa, bought nearly eight acres of land on the East Fork of the Carson River. He moved a building there from Genoa and opened the Gardnerville Hotel. He also opened a blacksmith shop and saloon that served the local ranchers as well as the miners and freighters heading from Washoe to the mining activity in Esmeralda. In the 1880s, a number of Danish immigrants settled in Gardnerville; their Valhalla Hall became the social center

of the valley. Then, at the turn of the 20th century, Basque sheep ranchers swelled the ranks, both human and ungulate, of Carson Valley. Basque boardinghouses flourished in Gardnerville, and their legacy is alive today.

In 1905, the Virginia & Truckee Railroad extended its line from Carson City down into the southern Carson Valley to serve the farmers and take their produce to market. The railroad right-of-way was provided by Henry Fredrick Dangberg, a rancher in residence from the early days of Mormon Station who owned 36,000 acres. Dangberg was the first to grow alfalfa in Nevada; he married Margaret Ferris, sister of Carson City's George Ferris, who invented the Ferris wheel. Dangberg died in 1904, and Dangberg Land and Livestock Company, run by his three sons, established a town to capitalize on the railroad depot. They named it Minden for their father's birthplace in Westphalia, Prussia, now northwestern Germany.

A tidy little town with square blocks and a central plaza was laid out around the V&T depot. Within 10 years, Minden scooped the county seat from Genoa and got a courthouse in 1915. Gardnerville got the high school the same year. Minden developed its residential aspect while Gardnerville developed its businesses. In the 1930s, both towns claimed a combined population of only 500, but in the 1960s the area got an economic boost when Bently Nevada, maker of electronic instruments, moved into the old Minden flour mill and creamery buildings.

Only two miles apart, Minden and Gardnerville have grown contiguous over the years, with most of the action strung along both sides of U.S. 395 for several miles.

It's worthwhile to wander the thin strip of back streets on each side of the highway; you'll get an instant sense of Minden's tranquil European charm and Gardnerville's farm-to-market tradition.

Sights

Starting at the northwest end of Minden and heading south U.S. 395, you pass the Carson

Valley Inn; at the stoplight, notice the big **flour mill** (1609 U.S. 395 N.) and **butter company** (1617 U.S. 395 N.) buildings. Bently Nevada Corporation, which produces vibration-monitoring and measuring machinery, now owns the buildings. The flour mill is straight out of a 1910 model railroad layout. It's a must-see for anyone who appreciates sturdy, utilitarian construction of yesteryear with its distinguished, faded brick facade, stately 45-foot steel silos, and old-time lettered signage. A couple of historical markers provide additional information. Next door, the brick Minden Butter Manufacturing Company building replaced the original wood structure in 1916 to increase production and pasteurize the butter, as mandated by a new California law.

For an overview of nearly 50 historic sites in Minden, download the well-designed walking tour map or pick up a paper version at the CVIC building (1602 Esmaralda Ave., Minden, 775/782-5078, www.townofminden.com).

Down the street is the **C.O.D. Garage** (1593 Esmaralda Ave.) and other brick buildings on Esmeralda Avenue in old downtown Minden. The garage was founded in 1910 as a Model-T dealer by Clarence O. Dangberg (C.O.D.). The garage's Union 76 sign on Esmeralda Avenue makes for one of the great retro photo ops in Nevada. Across the street, the county office building is the former **Minden Inn** (1594 Esmeralda Ave.), one of several structures downtown and across Nevada designed by Frederic DeLongchamps. The classy inn, completed in 1916, was the home-away-from-home of Clark Gable, Jean Harlow, and other Hollywood biggies.

Follow Esmeralda Avenue northwest a few more blocks past the homes and businesses of some of Minden's prominent early residents, built in the 1910s and 1920s, to **Minden Park,** laid out by H. F. Dangberg across from his house for his workers. The **courthouse** (1616 8th St.) was another of DeLongchamps's creations.

Heading southeast into Gardnerville, you pass the old high school building, built in 1915, again by DeLongchamps. The Carson Valley Historical Society spent several years restoring the building, now the **Carson Valley Museum and Cultural Center** (1477 U.S. 395, Gardnerville, 775/782-2555, 10 A.M.–4 P.M. Mon.–Sat., $3 adults, $2 ages 7–17). Inside you'll find exhibits on the solo life of a Basque sheepherder in the desolate Pinenut Mountains, Washoe art, and circa-1880 state-of-the-art medical equipment. There's also a small art gallery and the requisite gift shop. Just up the road, the **French Hotel and Bar** (1437 U.S. 395, Gardnerville) is another example of a Basque hotel. In the 1930s it hosted traditional pelota tournaments at a fronton out back. The game was so popular and the competition so keen that the championships offered $1,000 purses.

Continuing along U.S. 395, stop at the **East Fork Hotel Building** (1441 U.S. 395, Gardnerville), one of the first businesses in town. It later served as a Basque boarding-house. Sadly, the building has been damaged by fire and is not open to the public. Virtually next door, the **Adaven Building** (1435 U.S. 395, Gardnerville) still sports original granite blocks made by the Carson City Penitentiary on one exterior wall. Now home to a bar, the Adaven ("Nevada" spelled backward) has served as the Odd Fellows hall, a retail store, a soda fountain, a hotel, and a restaurant.

Recreation

Three golf courses grace the area. **Carson Valley Golf Course** (1027 Riverview Dr., south of Gardnerville, 775/265-3181, $28–46) is the local favorite. With lots of water, the par-71 course is only 6,020 yards, but there's plenty of challenge even for long hitters. **Genoa Lakes Golf Club** (1 Genoa Lakes Dr., Minden, 775/782-4653, $45–130) has two championship courses. The watery Lakes Course places a premium on distance and accuracy off the tee; the Resort Course is more of a short-game challenge. **Sierra Nevada Golf Ranch** (2901 Jacks Valley Rd., Genoa, 775/782-7700, $40–90) sits in the Sierra Nevada foothills on a former cattle ranch.

A well-established glider-ride company, **Soar**

Minden (1138 Airport Rd., Minden, 775/782-7627 or 800/345-7627, $155–295) has been taking people soaring since 1978. The scenery over Lake Tahoe is breathtaking, and there's no distracting engine noise (although strong winds do whip up). The most popular flight is the Mile High Flight; other popular flights include the Emerald Bay Excursion and a looping, rolling aerobatic experience. Introductory flying lessons are $180. Soar Minden operates out of Douglas County Airport, three miles north of Minden.

Take your first plunge or fall for the lake vistas with **Skydive Tahoe** (102 Wass Way, Minden, 775/783-8708, 8 A.M.–sunset Sat.–Sun., tandem dives $229). The drop zone offers solo jumps for first-timers as well as experienced skydivers. Video and photo packages are available. Heading east of U.S. 395 on Airport Road, turn left onto Heyborne Road, then right on Firebrand Road, and head for the large hangers on the right. Skydive Tahoe is in the leftmost hangar.

Carson Valley Swim Center (1600 Hwy. 88, Minden, 775/782-8840, 11 A.M.–8 P.M. Mon.–Fri., 11 A.M.–6 P.M. Sat.–Sun., $3.50 adults, $1.75 over age 55 and under age 18) has two cool water slides, diving boards, a competition pool, a family pool, and water toys.

Casinos

The gaming action in the twin towns is at **Carson Valley Inn** (1627 U.S. 395, Minden, 775/782-9711), which dates to 1984. The inn completed a top-to-bottom refurbishment in 2010, the latest in a string up expansions and upgrades that have transformed it from small slot joint on the highway to a modern, classy resort-style casino, a reflection of the area's growth and prosperity over the last 25 years. The casino now houses more than 500 new and classic-favorite slots, a new sports book, bars, and a cabaret showroom. There's a small poker room and a handful of table games.

Sharkey's (1440 U.S. 395, Gardnerville, 775/782-3133) makes no pretense of competing with the Carson Valley Inn in terms of opulence, but what it lacks in sophistication, it makes up for in value. The late Milos "Sharkey" Begovich learned the gambling business at his parents' boardinghouse in the California gold country. He worked as a pit boss at Harrah's Tahoe in the 1950s and 1960s, and one night ran a lucky streak up into six digits on a blackjack binge at Harvey's, across the street. The money eventually bought Sharkey's. It's mostly slots, with three blackjack tables and keno.

Accommodations

At about 340 square feet, the 152 standard guest rooms at the **Carson Valley Inn** (1627 U.S. 395, Minden, 775/782-9711 or 800/321-6983, $65–160) are not the most substantial, but they're attractively appointed in rusts and pastels. They have bright and decent-sized bathrooms as well as 25-inch televisions. Next door is the **Carson Valley Motor Lodge** (1627 U.S. 395, Minden, 775/782-9711 or 800/321-6983, $49–75), with 76 guest rooms. Behind the Inn is **Carson Valley RV Resort** (1627 U.S. 395, Minden, 775/782-9711 or 800/321-6983, $31). It's parking-lot camping but is surprisingly quiet for being so close to the highway. There are 59 spaces for motor homes, all with full hookups; 26 are pull-throughs. Tents are not allowed. Accessible restrooms have flush toilets and hot showers; public phones, sewage disposal, laundry, groceries, and gas are available.

Your other hotel choices in Minden are chains: **Holiday Inn Express** (1659 Hwy. 88, 775/782-2288, $105–148) and **Minden Best Western** (1795 Ironwood Dr., 775/782-7766 or 800/441-1234, $75–100).

Gardnerville motels are of the mom-and-pop variety. The best is probably **Historian Inn** (1427 U.S. 395 N., 775/783-1175 or 877/783-9910, $59–99). Other perfectly fine options include the close-to-shopping **Westerner** (1353 U.S. 395, 775/782-3602 or 800/782-3602, $35–65), whose rooms have small fridges and big TVs; the **Sierra** (1501 U.S. 395, 775/782-5145 or 800/682-5857, $35–70); and the small-roomed **Village** (1383 U.S. 395, 775/782-2624, $32–68).

The **Cottonwood Creek B&B** (1702 Sanchez

Rd., Gardnerville, 775/782-3057, $125–145) is an idyllic horse-boarding farm. The equines as well as the old dogs and barn cats are friendly. All guest rooms have private baths. You'll experience life on a working horse ranch, minus the chores, and a three-course breakfast awaits to fuel you up for the nearby rafting, golf, or gambling.

Food

Minden–Gardnerville, like much of north-central Nevada, is Basque-food country, where you can experience the Basque version of all-you-can-eat hospitality. A good place to start is the **The Overland Hotel** (1451 U.S. 395 N., Gardnerville, 775/782-2138, noon–2 P.M. and 5–10 P.M. Mon.–Sat., $15–22), in a 1909 building that once housed a butcher and later bunked Basque shepherds. Get cozy with your tablemates as servers deliver a big tureen of soup along with salad, beans, and more. You don't need a menu; just pick fish, chicken, steak, or lamb. You won't leave hungry.

In an even older building that also housed Basque shepherds, built in Virginia City at the height of the silver boom and moved to Gardnerville after the bust, is another vintage Basque establishment, **J&T Bar and Restaurant** (1426 U.S. 395 N., Gardnerville, 775/782-2074, 11:30 A.M.–2 P.M. and 5–9 P.M. Mon.–Sat., $22). The restaurant celebrated its 50th anniversary in 2010. The menu is similar to the Overland's, but includes rabbit, which is recommended, as well as occasional special dishes such as oxtail stew and beef tongue.

Monochromatic photos at each booth complete the arts and crafts interior architecture at **CV Steak** (Carson Valley Inn, 1627 U.S. 395, Minden, 775/783-6650, 4:30–10 P.M. Wed.–Sun., $20–30), formerly Fiona's. The remodeled restaurant is just as classy as the old space. A fine wine selection complements the pasta, seafood, and top-notch beef dishes, especially the porterhouse. The menu prices include a house salad and potato selection. Even if you're not a fan of au gratin, order the au gratin. If you're not in the mood to get gussied up, the inn's **Katie's Country Kitchen**

(24 hours daily, $7–12) deals out big four-egg omelets for breakfast and hearty nightly dinner specials such as pork loin, prime rib, and Swiss steak.

The owner has died and his eponymous casino has changed hands, but **Sharkey's** (1440 U.S. 395, Gardnerville, 775/782-3133, $7–15) is still open 24 hours daily. The new owners have made good on their promise to carry on the tradition of the prime rib special. You can also get the diner food you've come to expect from 24-hour casino eateries: bacon and eggs, omelets, burgers, club sandwiches, and so on.

It's worth finding **Café Girasole** (1483 U.S. 395, Gardnerville, 775/782-3314, 10:30 A.M.–5 P.M. Mon.–Tues., 10:30 A.M.–7 P.M. Wed.–Fri., 10:30 A.M.–3 P.M. Sat., $5–10), especially if you're fan of California-fresh sandwiches and grilled veggies, caramelized onions, artichokes, and sun-dried tomatoes.

Information

The **Carson Valley Chamber of Commerce and Visitors Authority** (1477 U.S. 395, Suite A, Gardnerville, 775/782-8144 or 800/727-7677, 8 A.M.–5 P.M. Mon.–Fri., www.carson-valleynv.org) has information on the entire Carson Valley. The website is more insightful and helpful than most.

TOPAZ LAKE

This underappreciated little gem, like its famous big sister to the north, sits half in Nevada and half in California. It's also fringed by the mighty Sierra mountains and has a state-line lodge with gambling just across the Nevada border on the highway. Unlike Tahoe, however, Topaz is an artificial water-storage basin that impounds water from the West Walker River for recreation and irrigation in Lyon County's Smith and Mason Valleys. It's also a treeless desert compared to forested Tahoe.

The Walker River Irrigation District, created in 1919 to manage the river, built a feeder canal from the West Walker River into a dry lake bed, renamed Topaz Lake, in 1921. An outlet tunnel was dug in the rim of the lake, allowing the river to continue on its way through the Smith and Mason Valleys and into Walker Lake. The Army Corps of Engineers built a rock-face wall in 1937 that added storage capacity. At its deepest, Topaz Lake is 100 feet deep.

Topaz Lake Park

Topaz Lake Park (775/782-9828, camping $18, $25 with hookups) on the northeast side of the lake near the boat launch, is a perfect base for the outdoor enthusiasts the lake attracts. It's a big spot with a mile of beachfront. The 29 RV hookup sites come with electricity, water, and dump stations. Tenters can make use of 40 developed campsites or can camp just about anywhere in the park. There's a grassy playground for the kids. The maximum stay is 14 days, and reservations are required. The lake is stocked twice a year with trout, and the fishing season runs January 1–September 30. The browns and rainbows can reach seven pounds, and 3–4 pounders are not uncommon. Waterskiing and picnicking are other popular diversions. To get to Topaz Lake Park campground, head south on U.S. 395 past Highway 208. At the sign, turn left and drive one mile to the campground.

Topaz Lake Lodge and RV Park

The Topaz Lake Lodge (1979 U.S. 395 S., 775/266-3338, $60–80) has a small poker room, a few table games, and a boatload of slots and keno games. If you're not particularly fond of roughing it, the lodge makes a great base for waterborne or lakeside outings. A steak house (5:30–9:30 P.M. Wed.–Sun., $20–40) and coffee shop (24 hours daily, $7–15) with views of the Sweetwater Mountains as well as a general store will keep you well fed and well supplied.

The RV park ($25) next door has full hookups plus showers and cable TV. It has 36 spaces for motor homes, all with full hookups; six are pull-throughs. Tents are not allowed. Accessible restrooms have flush toilets and hot showers, and public phones, sewage disposal, groceries, and a heated swimming pool are available. Reservations are recommended for summer.

To get here, drive 18 miles south of Gardnerville on U.S. 395; it's three miles beyond the intersection of U.S. 395 and Highway 208 east, and 38 miles to Yerington.

HUMBOLDT VALLEY

His mules hungry and his water barrel empty, in 1849 Elisha Perkins found little relief on the banks of the Humboldt River. Disgusted, he noted in his journal that "The 'Humbug'… does not deserve the name of river, being only a good sized creek…a stream of so little pretension." Although he meant it derisively, Perkins' assessment of the Humboldt's unpretentiousness describes perfectly not only the river but the entire valley and the people who would come to occupy it over the years. The Humboldt Valley provides a fitting setting for the rugged self-sufficient trappers, shepherds, miners, merchants, and ranchers intrepid enough to carve out a livelihood in it. But for all its splendor, the region—like the people of Winnemucca, Elko, Battle Mountain, Lovelock, Carlin, and other small northern Nevada outposts—maintains a Spartan dignity tinged with neighborliness and humor.

The Humboldt River, fed by Ruby Mountain spring snowmelt and small tributaries trickling down the Jarbidge, Independence, and Humboldt Ranges, runs west for 300 miles, but it never reaches the ocean, instead disappearing into the dusty desert floor. The Humboldt Valley's most striking features run the gamut—the unassuming river, towering crags, a huge lake with a pyramid in the middle, no less, and the otherworldly Black Rock Desert.

You'll find surprises like these throughout your travels in the northern region of Nevada, from quaint small towns straight out of *Brigadoon* to astonishing natural beauty.

© KARIN LAU/123RF.COM

HIGHLIGHTS

LOOK FOR 【 TO FIND RECOMMENDED
SIGHTS, ACTIVITIES, DINING, AND LODGING.

【 **Anaho Island:** Awkward on the ground but as majestic as swans in the air, thousands of pelicans call this refuge in Pyramid Lake home, returning year after from their winter retreats in Baja California. The island is off-limits to humans, but with a boat and binoculars, you can see them nesting and raising chicks on the tufa formations (page 248).

【 **Lovers Lock Plaza:** Truly devoted couples can symbolize their commitment by fastening their love lock to a chain and throwing away the key. It's an Americanized version of an ancient Chinese custom. The courthouse is next door, in case lovers decide to make their commitment more formal (page 258).

【 **Grimes Point and Hidden Cave:** Home to some of Nevada's original residents, Hidden Cave contained 2,500 basket fragments, leather pieces, stone tools, food, arrowheads, and other artifacts after its rediscovery in the 1920s. The trails along Grimes Point and the area's caves reveal petroglyphs and pictographs in two distinct styles, tracing the development of the Native American culture here (page 263).

【 **Buckaroo Hall of Fame:** Nevada's ranch hands have turned riding, ropin', and wranglin' into an art form, and their individualism and style in the face of hardship are celebrated at this Winnemucca museum. And if you see a real live one while you're here, remember he's a buckaroo, not a cowboy. Forget that and you may find yourself hogtied and branded (page 272).

【 **Northeastern Nevada Museum:** Long gone are the days when a desert rat with a pick or a pan could make his fortune with a rucksack full of almond-size gold nuggets. Today's prospectors use heat, acid, cyanide, and a dozen more methods to claim gold crumbs from tons of hard rock. A multimedia presentation at this Elko museum shows the painstaking process from blast to brick. Two-million-year-old mastodon bones, recovered near here, are another highlight (page 280).

【 **Western Folklife Center:** Sophisticated oils, poignant photographs, the Great Western Songbook, and the renowned National Cowboy Poetry Gathering celebrate the ranch and trail lifestyle at this top-notch museum, gallery, and performance venue (page 282).

【 **Newmont Gold Company:** With nary a pick in sight, Newmont is one of the world's largest producers of gold, with strip mines all along the lucrative Carlin Trend. The company locates and extracts lode deposits, assays and refines the precious metal, and turns it into bars of 92 percent pure gold. Tours reveal the entire process; no free samples (page 283).

【 **Ruby Mountain Heli-Skiing:** Drop nearly 40,000 feet in six runs over unblemished powder on perhaps the most beautiful mountains in Nevada. If the three-day package price doesn't take your breath away, the altitude and scenery will (page 288).

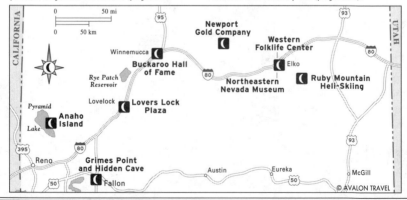

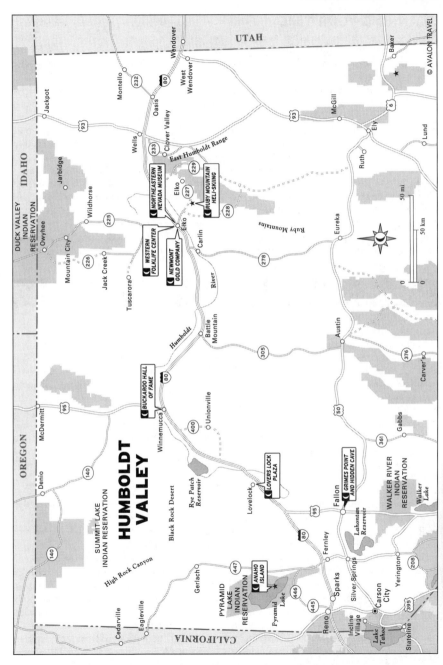

UTAH

IDAHO

OREGON

CALIFORNIA

HUMBOLDT VALLEY

Baker

Wendover

West Wendover

Montello

Oasis

Clover Valley

McGill

Ely

Lund

Jackpot

Ruth

Wells

East Humboldt Range

Jarbidge

NORTHEASTERN NEVADA MUSEUM

RUBY MOUNTAIN HELI-SKIING

Elko

Eureka

Wildhorse

Mountain City

Owyhee

DUCK VALLEY INDIAN RESERVATION

WESTERN FOLKLIFE CENTER

NEWMONT GOLD COMPANY

Jack Creek

Tuscarora

Carlin

Ruby Mountains

Humboldt River

Battle Mountain

Austin

Carver's

Humboldt

BUCKAROO HALL OF FAME

Winnemucca

Unionville

McDermitt

Denio

Gabbs

SUMMIT LAKE INDIAN RESERVATION

Black Rock Desert

Rye Patch Reservoir

LOVERS LOCK PLAZA

GRIMES POINT AND HIDDEN CAVE

Lovelock

Fallon

WALKER RIVER INDIAN RESERVATION

Walker Lake

High Rock Canyon

Gerlach

Fernley

Lahontan Reservoir

Silver Springs

Yerington

Cedarville

Eagleville

AMAHO ISLAND

PYRAMID LAKE INDIAN RESERVATION

Pyramid Lake

Sparks

Reno

Incline Village

Carson City

Lake Tahoe

Stateline

50 mi

50 km

PLANNING YOUR TIME

Perhaps more than any other region of Nevada, the Humboldt Valley captures the spirit of Nevada past and present. Elko makes the most sense as a home base; its airport accommodates several daily connecting flights from Salt Lake City, and there are plenty of intriguing ways to spend an afternoon or a weekend. The legacy of Nevada's mining history comes fascinatingly to mind with a tour of the **Newmont Gold Company,** where the latest technology extracts tiny flecks of gold from determined hard rock. The **Northeastern Nevada Museum** and **Western Folklife Center** honor those hardy pioneers who laid the groundwork and scoped out the geography in search of their own golden dreams. The museum also helps visitors hark back to the days when mastodons trod the earth. And **Sherman Station** gives new life to the just-as-intrepid Pony Express adventurers who brought mail—and a semblance of civilization—to the frontier.

As you make your way east and south, delve into the attractions every bit as romantic and fanciful as their names connote. You can vicariously live the life of a buckaroo and take your lumps along the **Bloody Shins Trail** in Winnemucca, gaze at **Purgatory Peak,** and dig for fiery treasure at the **Rainbow Mine.**

In late summer the **Burning Man** festival in the **Black Rock Desert** transforms this patch of playa into a small city of individuality, art, and self-expression that exists for one week then vanishes like a puff of dust—till next year.

Pyramid Lake

Rounding a bend in the road, it seems like a hallucination. The stark desert setting makes its pewter-blue existence even more improbable. Its shorelines are smooth and treeless, its inlets gentle and graceful, and its beauty strange and unsettling. A huge unmarred stone pyramid rises above it, as incongruous as those rising from the sands of Giza. As you descend to its edge, the cool clear water finally convinces you that Pyramid Lake, a rare remnant of ancient Lake Lahontan, is no mirage but a very welcome reality.

It has been called the most beautiful desert lake in the world, and it's one of the largest freshwater lakes in the West: 27 miles long, 9 miles wide, 370 feet at its deepest point, and 3,789 feet above sea level, with a water temperature a swimmable 75°F in summer and a forbidding 42°F in winter. Its source, the Truckee River, flows from Lake Tahoe, travels 105 miles down the east face of mighty mountains, through thirsty cities and across reclaimed desert, then trickles into the southern end of the lake, which has no outlet. Anaho Island juts up off the eastern shore slightly south of the pyramid, providing breeding grounds for the American white pelican and other shorebirds. Jagged pinnacles stand sentinel over the northern end, where hot springs drain into the lake and a steam geyser vents from a rusty wellhead. Great Lahontan cutthroat trout grow to 15 pounds, and the endemic cui-ui sucker fish haunt the ancient depths. Nearly 500,000 acres of lake and surrounding desert are enclosed by the Pyramid Lake Reservation, a sacred area managed and preserved by its traditional Paiute caretakers.

HISTORY

Pyramid Lake is the larger vestige (Walker Lake, 90 miles south, is the smaller one) of great Lake Lahontan, which covered much of the western Great Basin only 50,000 years ago. Glacial incursions during the ice ages of the previous 2 million years touched Nevada only in the high ranges, but the accompanying cold, wet climate created and nurtured this giant prehistoric body of water. A complicated inland sea with branches spreading over basins and between mountain ranges, Lahontan stretched from McDermitt in the north, Honey Valley in the west, Hawthorne

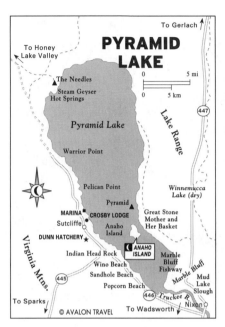

New Arrivals

In late 1843, mountain man, mapmaker, and explorer John C. Frémont found the Black Rock Desert's appearance "so forbidding that I was afraid to enter it." He and his party marched south in early 1844 along the edge of the Fox Range, beyond which they climbed a hill where "a sheet of green water...broke upon our eyes like the ocean.... For a long time we sat enjoying the view [of the lake] set like a gem in the mountains." Frémont named the lake for the smaller of its two islands, which "presented a pretty exact outline of the great Pyramid of Cheops." Continuing south, Frémont and his men encountered Paiute in a village near present-day Nixon. They were served up a feast of "trout as large as the salmon of the Columbia River...the best-tasting fish I had ever eaten." The explorers went on to name and map the Carson and Walker Rivers, then crossed the Sierra into California.

Less than two decades later, tension between the nomadic Native Americans and ore-seeking nonnative immigrants already ran high. Nonnatives ignored the 1855 Treaty of Friendship negotiated by federal agents and the great Chief Winnemucca, trespassing on prized—even sacred—ground, killing the game, clear-cutting the trees, wasting precious food and resources, and bullying the natives along the Humboldt River Trail. Still, the Northern Paiute, a strong, industrious, and peaceable people, knew the futility of waging war on the newcomers. In the spring of 1860 the vast horde of fortune-seekers bound for Washoe overran prime pine nut land in the Virginia Range and fouled cui-ui spawning grounds along the Truckee River in their mad dash for the Comstock Lode. Only when traders at Williams Station on the Carson River kidnapped and abused several Native American women did the Indians seek revenge. They killed the traders and burned the station. The incident spread hysteria, fear, and bloodlust through Washoe, and a ragged troop of volunteers set out on an ill-conceived, ill-prepared, and ill-fated retaliatory expedition. The avengers shot at a Paiute bearing a flag of

in the south, and the Stillwater Range in the east. Its covered 8,600 square miles at an average depth of several thousand feet.

The warming and drying trend that has prevailed since the last ice age, which ended roughly 15,000 years ago, has shrunk the vast lake, concentrating it into this "minor" remnant. And unless a new ice age arrives, it will continue to shrink until sometime in the not-too-distant future when the Truckee River, like the Humboldt and Carson Rivers, will disappear into a desert playa that was once an improbable turquoise lake.

Paleo-Indians of the Lovelock period, 11,000–4,000 years ago, dwelled in lakeside caves, wore pelican-skin robes, chipped arrowheads from obsidian, carved fishhooks from deer antlers, and fashioned fishnets, baskets, and even duck decoys from willow and tule reeds. It's undetermined whether the Lovelock people abandoned the area, were driven away by the encroaching Paiute, or were incorporated into the Paiute, a nomadic people who gravitated here for fish feasts during the spawning of the cui-ui's and the Lahontan cutthroat.

COURTESY OF NEVADA COMMISSION ON TOURISM

Pyramid Lake's namesake outcropping rises serenely from the water.

truce and blindly chased the Paiute into a ravine, where the Indians turned and slaughtered them. A month later, a force of regular troops from California took two Paiute lives for every white life that had been lost, effectively ending the Nevada Indian Wars.

Water Troubles

After the diversion of the Truckee River in 1905 at Derby Dam to irrigate farmland around Fernley and Fallon, the water supply to the lake diminished, depleting its fisheries and causing frequent irrigation problems for the Paiute farmers and ranchers. The lowered inflow created a silty, swampy delta where the river entered the lake, preventing the big Lahontan cutthroat from spawning. Along with massive overfishing, it rendered the trout almost extinct by the 1930s, further exacerbating the financial instability of the reservation. In 1975 the Paiute began to stock the lake with purebred cutthroat, and today 15-pound trophies are not uncommon.

The depth of the lake dropped continually throughout the 20th century, and the surface level has fallen nearly 100 feet. Diverting the river for irrigation and urban growth upstream has also increased the amount of pollution finding its way to the lake. During periods of prolonged drought, the surface level of Lake Tahoe, source of the Truckee River, falls below its natural rim, and with all flow of Lake Tahoe water into the river cut off, there's no inflow to replenish Pyramid Lake or the system's reservoirs in California.

FISHING AND BOATING

Fishing season for cutthroat trout is October 1–June 30. Record cutthroat are generally 15–20 pounds. Fishing permits cost $9 per day, or $74 for the season; boating fees are the same. If you're going to fish from a boat, it's therefore $18 per day or $148 for the season. If you buy a fishing permit, you don't pay the reservation's $7-per-vehicle day-use fee, levied on nonfishers visiting the lake. There's also a $9 camping fee. If you catch a cui-ui, you have to release it unharmed immediately; the penalty for being caught with an endangered species is a $10,000 fine (and very bad publicity). Fishing

CUI-UI FISH

The endangered cui-ui (kwee-wee) is a sucker fish that lives only in Pyramid Lake. A prehistoric species, cui-ui inhabited Lake Lahontan for tens of thousands of years; as the inland sea slowly evaporated, these fish of the deep were able to survive at the bottom of the little Pyramid Lake remnant.

Cui-ui grow as large as seven pounds and can live 40 years. They spawn between the ages of 12 and 20, as early as April and as late as July, when they swim upstream as far as 12 miles west to lay their eggs. In the old days, before the Derby Dam water diversion lowered the lake's level, the Paiute spearfished and snagged them at the mouth of the Truckee River during the spawn.

The Works Progress Administration's 1940 *Nevada – A Guide to the Silver State* reported:

> Now that the flow into the lake has been curtailed by upstream storage, the fish runs have practically ceased. Cui-ui schools circle through the shallows near the river mouth, searching in vain for spawning grounds, and pelicans step in and gorge themselves.

The cui-ui were nearly extinct by the 1940s. They managed to recover slightly in 1952 with one of the largest spawning runs (120,000 fish) in recent history, but compared to the millions of cui-ui that spawned in past, the population was decimated, prompting the federal government to list the fish as an endangered species in 1967. Another large run was recorded in 1969 (110,000 fish), but only a handful of cui-ui spawned between 1976 and 1982, and a census in 1984 counted only 150,000 of them. No cui-ui spawned between 1987 and 1992. The Paiute members voluntarily stopped eating them in 1979.

In the early 1970s, federal courts directed that water in Stampede Reservoir be used exclusively to benefit the cui-ui. A small pulse of fresh reservoir water is released as early as January to tickle the spawning instinct; the pulse reaches its peak by April, which helps the fish reach the spawning grounds. The fresh water also incubates the eggs and helps the microscopic larvae to swim back to the lake.

The Marble Bluff dam and fishway were built in 1976 to stop the erosion of the riverbank, which threatened the stability of Nixon, just upstream. The dam also protects critical cui-ui spawning habitat. Some cui-ui will use the three-mile clay-lined fishway, which resembles an irrigation canal with a number of terraces known as ladders, but many won't. During large spawning runs, the fish jam the entrance to the fishway, and some are smothered before they can be gathered onto a large elevator platform, which raises them up to the river and washes them into it. In 1993, after one of the wettest winters and springs in the 20th century, so many fish struggled onto the elevator that it couldn't lift them, and 3,000 died. Officials had to load nearly 5,000 cui-ui into trucks, drive them past the fishway, and drop them back into the river.

After the failure of the fish elevator, the federal government in 1996 allocated $2.5 million to redesign the Marble Bluff dam, fishway, and elevator. Aided by high water and other factors, more than 250,000 cui-ui spawned in the spring 1997 run, a 50-year high. The Cui-ui Recovery Team now estimates the total adult cui-ui population at 1 million. John Jackson, director of water resources for the Paiute reservation, says down-listing the cui-ui on the Endangered Species List from endangered to threatened status is under consideration.

Today, anglers sometimes land cui-ui when fishing for Lahontan cutthroat trout at Pyramid. The fish remain on the endangered species list, and there is a zero-kill policy. This policy, the Paiute hatcheries, and timed water releases from Boca and Stampede Reservoirs work to ensure the cui-ui's survival.

HUMBOLDT VALLEY

and boating permits and information are available at the Pyramid Lake Marina (off Hwy. 445, Sutcliffe, 775/476-1156), Crosby's Lodge (30605 Sutcliffe Dr., Sutcliffe, 775/476-0400), and several other places around the lake.

You can bring your own boat, or rent one at the **Pyramid Lake Marina** (off Hwy. 445, Sutcliffe, 775/476-1156). Two small, locally owned companies operate fishing charters on the lake. Jim Hartfiel's **Just Rite Fishing** (775/575-7850) and George Molino's **Cutthroat Charters** (775/476-0555, $125–175) guide excursions on Pyramid Lake throughout the season. Both provide all equipment and refreshments. Secure your own licenses and permits.

While you're here, visit **Dunn Hatchery** (63 Sutcliffe Dr., Sutcliffe, 775/476-0500, 9–11 A.M. and 1–3 P.M. daily), up the hill from town, to learn about the Paiute people's Pyramid Lake fisheries. There are displays on prehistory, history, tufa, fishing, and past problems and future solutions in front of the main hatchery. Next, a Paiute employee will show you around the work area. These hatcheries are considered among the most advanced and successful in the world. A million cutthroat (and a handful of cui-ui) are planted yearly in Pyramid and Walker Lakes. Pregnant fish are captured and artificially spawned at the Marble Bluff fish passage facility. The fertilized eggs are brought to the hatchery and incubated; they hatch in 1–4 weeks. The fry are then "ponded" in freshwater tanks. After a year, they're planted in the lakes. You'll see the numerous ponds, the incubation chambers, and the rock-filtration room.

Head around to the back building to check on the much more specialized and intimate cui-ui hatchery. This operation provides a graphic representation of how difficult it is to artificially breed these ancient suckers. Good spawning runs make the breeding program a little less critical.

The **Numana Hatchery** (Hwy. 446, 8 miles north of Wadsworth, 775/574-0290, 7:30 A.M.–3:30 P.M. Mon.–Fri.) also grows cutthroat trout from eggs to fingerlings and gives tours. The visitors center displays the fish and the tagging operations, and a trail leads to a bird habitat.

CAMPING

Down the hill and around the corner from Crosby's Lodge is the **Pyramid Lake Marina** (off Hwy. 445, Sutcliffe, 775/476-1156), where there's a ranger station, a minimart, a small museum, and an RV park. The Pyramid Lake Marina Campground (2500 Lakeview Dr., Sutcliffe, $35) is a small RV park right on the water's edge. The campground has 44 spaces, each with full hookups. There are no picnic tables or fire rings, but guests are welcome to bring their own. Campground amenities include a laundry, hot showers, and a small camp store. A boat launch facility is two miles away on Pelican Point.

Stop off at the ranger station or minimart and pay $7 per vehicle for a day-use permit, which is required for everyone visiting the lake, even if you're just passing through. If you want to tent-camp on the beach, it's only $9 and includes the $7 vehicle permit.

Two miles north of Sutcliffe is **Pelican Point,** with a boat ramp, a good beach, and at most times of the year several tents already pitched right at water's edge. Farther north on paved Highway 445, you pass many turnoffs and dirt roads down to the shore—the sites aren't exactly secluded, but there's plenty of opportunity to be by yourself on the beach, although there is little shade and no facilities. The pavement runs out in eight miles at **Warrior Point Campground** ($9 per vehicle) which has a phone that may or may not work, picnic shelters, drinking water, and little else. There are no campsites per se, but any open spot is claimable.

【 ANAHO ISLAND

Anaho Island floats in Pyramid Lake like a giant stingray, its wide, flat wings spreading out gradually to meet the water. For centuries this rocky, 600-foot-tall island provided a breeding ground for the largest colony of American white pelicans in the United States. Because these birds—clumsy and comical on the ground, majestic and dignified in the air—have such sensitive nesting instincts, they have long been considered a symbol of the wild country and a measure of its wildness. Predictably, the number of nesting pelicans on

ALEXANDER VON HUMBOLDT

As you've probably gathered by now, the area around Winnemucca is Humboldt Land. There is Humboldt County, the Humboldt Mountains plus the East and West Humboldt Mountains, Humboldt National Forest, Humboldt Sink, Humboldt Mining District, Humboldt Trail, and of course Humboldt River. So who was Humboldt, anyway, and how did his name become attached to so many important features in northern Nevada?

Surprisingly, for all his accomplishments in Europe, Russia, and Latin America, Alexander von Humboldt not only never discovered anything in Nevada, he never set foot in the state! Still, his resume apparently made enough of an impression on John C. Frémont that when he happened upon an unpretentious northern Nevada stream in 1844, he designated it the Humboldt River. And the Humboldt River it has remained.

The first nonnative known to have stumbled on the river was Peter Skene Ogden in 1829, and his humble name for it, Ogden River, stuck at least until 1833, when Joseph Walker followed its entire length west through Nevada and continued from there into California. But it appeared on Bonneville's 1837 map as Mary River. John C. Frémont designated it the Humboldt River in 1844 in honor of Alexander von Humboldt, and the Humboldt River it has remained.

Alexander von Humboldt was born in Berlin in 1769. He received a college education in mining technology and advanced quickly in his field. At the age of 27 he inherited a substantial sum of money, with which he embarked on a scientific expedition that ranged from Venezuela, Cuba, and Colombia to Mexico and the United States. He collected botanical, zoological, geological, and astronomical data, studied Pacific Ocean currents, the Cuban plantation economy, and pre-Columbian cultures. He climbed to 18,000 feet in the Andes, surveyed the headwaters of the Amazon, followed ancient Inca trails in Peru, and sipped mint juleps with James Madison in Washington, D.C.

Humboldt settled in Paris in 1808 and began publishing the reports and results of his travels and inquiries. The subsequent 30-volume, 12,000-page encyclopedia earned him an international reputation as a "one-man institution" at the same time that it ruined him financially. Humboldt then embarked on several years of diplomatic missions for Frederick William III of Prussia, traveled through Siberia at the invitation of Czar Nicholas I, and finally settled down to a position as lecturer and author in Frederick's court in Berlin.

For the last 30 years of his life, Humboldt concentrated on his five-volume *Kosmos,* an epic survey of the earth and the rest of the universe. In it, he attempted to determine, through scientific knowledge, the place of humanity in the cosmic order. Alexander von Humboldt died in Berlin in 1859 at the age of 90.

Anaho Island has dropped dramatically in recent years.

Pelicans could be the easiest birds in the world to recognize. Their creamy white feathers, black-tipped wings with 10-foot spans, and huge orange bills cause them to stand out among the cormorants, herons, terns, ducks, geese, gulls, hawks, owls, and smaller species that call Anaho home for several months of the year. For thousands of years, tens of thousands of these creatures have migrated to Anaho from Southern California and western Mexico in the spring to set up nests in this makeshift pelican city. A pair of pelicans settle into a nest, barely a hole in the ground, softened perhaps with some dry grass and sage twigs.

Into it the female lays two eggs, incubating them for a month with the webs of her feet. The male flies off every day to bring back a fish dinner. After hatching, the chicks mature quickly, reaching flight size in two months and full size (15–20 pounds) by migration time in the fall.

Contrary to common misconception, pelicans do not store fish in their large beaks; the pouch stretches or contracts to control body temperature. They swallow the fish, traditionally tui chub and carp from Winnemucca Lake—now dry—just east over the Lake Range, then regurgitate and redigest them. Pelicans, in fact, are the bulimics of the animal kingdom, vomiting their food when faced with intrusion or danger.

They're so skittish that fast-growing chicks exposed to chronic emotional distress can't hold their food down and will starve to death. Adult pelicans, startled by noise, will abandon their nests, leaving their eggs to fry in the hot desert sun, if the gulls don't eat them first. Unprotected days-old chicks will quickly succumb to starvation, exposure, or predation.

In 1913, President Woodrow Wilson signed a bill preserving Anaho Island as a bird sanctuary, and today it's a 750-acre national wildlife refuge. In 1948, there were 10,000 pairs of pelicans nesting here; by 1968 only 5,000 were showing up. In 1988 an all-time-low 350 pelican pairs arrived to breed, from which a mere 50 chicks matured.

Since then, the numbers have improved dramatically. The solution was simple: a big inflow of water into the lake and the Stillwater marsh country 60 miles southeast, traditionally the feeding grounds for the pelicans. Nature ended the drought in 1995 and supplied the area with plentiful freshwater—until the next drought. The island is closed to visitors; you can view the pelicans and other wildlife from boats. Bring a scope or binoculars.

INFORMATION AND SERVICES

Pay your usage, camping, fishing, and boating fees at the **Pyramid Lake Store** (29555 Pyramid Hwy., 775/476-0555, 6 A.M.–6 P.M. daily), just inside the boundary of the reservation if you're coming from Reno, or the store or ranger station at **Pyramid Lake Marina** (off Hwy. 445, Sutcliffe, 775/476-1156).

Crosby's Lodge (30605 Sutcliffe Dr., Sutcliffe, 775/476-0400) has trophy cutthroats mounted over the bar, video poker, a big TV, and a pool table. A DJ spins country and rock on Saturday nights, and you can stock up on groceries, fishing supplies, and gas. Cabins ($55–70) and trailers ($70–120) are available if you're planning to stay awhile.

Black Rock Desert

The Black Rock Desert's lunar landscape is so forbidding that as eminent an explorer as John C. Frémont, on his way to discover Pyramid Lake, was afraid to approach it. Today the Black Rock, the largest playa in North America, is a magnet for rock hounds and history buffs, hikers and pilgrims, hot-rodders, UFO fans, and free spirits.

In *Hiking the Great Basin,* John Hart observes that overall, the Great Basin Desert is not generally referred to as the desert. "That word," he writes, "is reserved for sections that stand out as barren among the barren, wastes among wastes," among which the "Black Rock Desert, at least one million acres in extent, is second only to the Great Salt Lake Desert." Doug Keister, photographer and author of a book called *Black Rock: Portraits on the Playa,* says, "I see the playa as the world's largest stage. It's so pure and clean that anything you put on it becomes significant."

The Black Rock encompasses 1 million acres, split into two fingers by the encroaching thrust of the Black Rock Range, the volcanic outcrop that gave bearings to an estimated 30,000 migrants who crossed the desert between 1849 and 1870. Because of its remoteness and hard surface, the Black Rock section of the Emigrant Trail is the best preserved in the West, and conservation groups want to set aside large tracts as a National Conservation Area with a visitors center.

PLANNING YOUR TRIP

The best descriptions of this country and its unlimited hiking potential are found in John Hart's *Hiking the Great Basin.* The **Sierra Club** (775/851-5185) and the **Friends of Black Rock High Rock** (775/557-2900, http://blackrockdesert.org) lead occasional outings into the desert to camp, view meteor showers, photograph geographical formations and wildflowers, or visit the area's hot springs. Group outings like

DeWayne "Doobie" Williams created the folksy monuments and cheery aphorisms along "Guru Road" in the Black Rock Desert near Gerlach.

these are the best and safest way to experience the spirituality of Black Rock.

If you're soloing, be careful: This place is treacherous, and people die out here every year. It's very easy to get lost, and if your car breaks down, you might be in serious trouble. If you're planning to explore the Black Rock in any depth for an extended period, it's recommended that you carry detailed topo maps and a compass, five gallons of water per person per day, emergency food for a week, sunblock, a first-aid kit, warm clothes, portable shade, two spare tires, tools, a hand winch, rope and chain, a shovel, an ax, extra gas, belts, hoses, and fluids, and a CB radio. Many people actually tow an extra car in. Late spring–fall is the safe season for cruising the cracked desert; winter is too muddy. And for a week in late August–early September each year, tens of thousands of people flock to this desert for Burning Man, an ambitious art festival that attracts more seekers each year.

Finally, don't forget to pack and consult Sessions Wheeler's classic travelogue *Black Rock Desert*.

ORIENTATION

Heading north on Highway 447 on the east side of Pyramid Lake, you'll see the **Lake Range** between the highway and the lake and the dry bed of Winnemucca Lake east of the highway. Known as Little Lake of the Cui-ui by the Paiute, this transient body of water came and went often through the ages, since its depth was dependent on the overflow of the Truckee. In 1876, for example, a gravel bar partially blocked Pyramid Lake from the mouth of the river, which emptied much of its mountain and desert water into Winnemucca Lake to a depth of 85 feet. In wet years, it provided an important rest stop for migrating waterfowl. After the Derby Dam diversion in the early 20th century, Winnemucca Lake received a continually diminishing supply of water and was completely dry by the late 1930s. The **Nightingale Mountains** rise up from its extinct eastern shoreline.

This road is pencil-straight, and 20 minutes north, the tufa begins appearing on the west side of the road. Keep an eye out for **Tufa**

Snoopy. Thirty miles north of Marble Bluff you can clearly make out the old shoreline at the north edge of Winnemucca Lake. The **Selenite Range** picks up where the Nightingales leave off; Mount Limbo's **Purgatory Peak** rises to 7,382 feet. North of it, **Kumiva Peak** scrapes the sky 900 feet higher. About 40 miles north of Nixon, a turnoff leads to a geothermal power plant. In days gone by, excess heat from the generators was used to dry onions and garlic.

The valley narrows as it ushers you into the U.S. Gypsum company town of **Empire,** a thin strip of green along the highway backed by the southern edge of the great **Black Rock Desert.** Giant mine trucks haul dusty, chalky-white salt into the plant, passing flatbed 16-wheelers hauling out heavy loads of sheetrock. The mine is a little east, up in the Selenite Range. The mine and mill employ around 140 people. Empire is a shady, breezy, comfortable company town four blocks wide and four long. Cruise up and down the streets to get a glimpse of company housing, the community pool and park, a nine-hole golf course (free and open to the public), tennis and basketball courts, and the small airport.

Drive down onto the playa (a broad mud plain, another dry lake bed of ancient Lake Lahontan) and accelerate for miles without the need to steer. The edge of a shimmering lake that you seem to be hurtling toward is always just ahead. It's the same body of water that enticed gold-rush pioneers to struggle onward to slake their crushing thirst. Like them, you'll never reach it. Now the surface starts to feel like thin ice, which you're always just about to crack through. Other cars' tracks race up to you, crossing under you in a flash, then disappear behind you—while you're standing still. Even the illusions are on a grand scale.

To get onto the Black Rock, take the right-hand fork just north of Gerlach and continue on the paved road that travels along the upper edge of the playa; in several miles an obvious entrance ramp presents itself.

GERLACH

Just beyond Empire is the green oasis of Gerlach, huddled directly below distinct **Granite Peak,**

more than 9,000 feet tall, the southernmost peak of the Granite Range. At first glance, Gerlach is a tiny town that serves as a division point for the Southern Pacific Railroad as it chugs through northwestern Nevada. With fewer than 500 souls, the town is nevertheless the largest settlement in an area of about 10,000 square miles—from Reno to the south; Lakeview, Oregon, to the north; Susanville, California, to the west; and Winnemucca to the east. Gerlach, in fact, is one of the few places in the whole northwest corner of Nevada with a gas station, slot machines, a restaurant, and a motel. It's also the gateway to the Black Rock Desert and a friendly, comfortable town in its own right, boasting the best ravioli in the state, a surprising variety of residential architecture, a cool pottery ranch, and a dramatic view of the railroad snaking across the desert.

This area was settled by Native Americans, who appreciated its good spring water, wild game, and sheltering mountains. More recently, pioneers en route to Northern California and Oregon paused at the springs here, marking the end of the Black Rock Desert and the beginning of the arduous journey through High Rock Canyon.

Louis Gerlach began ranching in this area around the turn of the 20th century. A few years later, the Western Pacific Railroad laid tracks along the northern route out of Winnemucca, crossing Desert Valley and the Jackson Mountains, skirting the edge of the Black Rock and Smoke Creek Deserts, then crossing Beckwourth Pass north of Reno and down into Oakland. Gerlach was founded as a rail division point in 1906 and named for the ranch.

Rocket Cars and Land-Speed Records

The most exciting times in Gerlach are the land-speed record-setting events on the Black Rock playa, which happen every so often. It all started in October 1983 when Project Thrust was rained out of the Bonneville Salt Flats on the other side of the state near Wendover. Driver Richard Noble and his team of Brits relocated their rocket-car operation to the Black Rock Desert northeast of Gerlach. They set up a 10-mile straightaway on the flat cracked-mud playa (another dry lakebed of vast Lake Lahontan) with a 10-mile overrun—in case the braking parachutes failed to deploy. Noble cranked up the Rolls Royce Avon engine (with afterburners) of *Thrust II*, the rocket car, and attained a speed of 633.606 mph, finally breaking Gary Gabelich's record of 622.407 mph set at Bonneville in 1971. Local residents and the racers adopted each other.

Gerlach's rush over speed was rekindled in 1997 as Noble and former record holder Craig Breedlove (407 mph in 1966) of the United States made plans to face off on the Black Rock playa in the first-ever head-to-head challenge for the land-speed record. The Bureau of Land Management imposed a series of conditions on the racers intended to address concerns from the Paiute people about possible damage to cultural sites, from environmentalists about possible impacts on wildlife, and from history buffs about the proximity to nearby emigrant trails.

Breedlove had partly blamed the failure of his 1996 attempt to top Noble's record on a last-minute appeal that postponed his run into the windy season. His hopes, though luckily not his brains, were dashed when a gust lifted the nose of his *Spirit of America* rocket car, clocked at going 677 mph, sending him careening through the world's fastest—and longest—U-turn. Even though he exceeded Noble's record by over 40 mph, Breedlove's time didn't count.

The Breedlove and Noble camps eyed the record—and the 741.4 mph sound barrier—as both descended on the Black Rock in October 1997, near the 50th anniversary of Chuck Yeager's first supersonic flight.

Breedlove's single jet engine with afterburners from an F-4 fighter delivered 48,000 hp. Royal Air Force pilot Andy Green piloted Noble's sinister-looking twin-jet design. Engine, design, weather, and money woes left both teams well short of the record until, on September 25, it finally became official:

Green put together runs of 700 and 728 mph within the specified one-hour time limit to set the new land-speed world record at an average of 714 mph, 80 mph faster than the previous record. Noble's team didn't rest on its laurels. On October 14 *Thrust II* achieved supersonic speeds of 760 and 764 mph, breaking the sound barrier on land for the first time in history. When the speed of the rocket car exceeded Mach 1, it set off a light sonic boom; much of the noise was absorbed by the acoustically soft desert. It didn't set a new record, however—the runs were 61 minutes apart.

Practicalities

The reason that ⟨ **Bruno's Country Club** (445 Main St., 775/557-2220, 7 P.M.–10 P.M. daily, $6–13) has been called the social center of northern Washoe County can be summed up in a single surprising word: ravioli. These big fat fatties, swimming in Bruno Selmi's old-country meat sauce and covered with home-cured imported cheese, go for a bargain $12.65. The adjoining bar has video poker and reel slots, a pool table, and photographs of the racers and local artwork. The bar also serves as the front desk for the 40-unit **Bruno's Motel** ($45–75). Deluxe rooms have a stove and a refrigerator.

For such a small community, Gerlach has more than its share of drinking establishments. Just up the street from Bruno's is **Joe's Gerlach Club** (385 Main St., 775/557-2260), its clientele mostly U.S. Gypsum workers killing time between shifts. The retired set seems to prefer the **Miners Club** (480 Main St., 775/557-2389) next to Bruno's café.

Bruno's Shell Station is at the south end of town, the last gas before Eagleville (80 miles) or Denio (110 miles). You can pick up local brochures here.

Sixty miles north of Gerlach, the **Soldier Meadows Guest Ranch & Lodge** (Soldier Meadows Rd., 775/849-1666, www.soldiermeadows.com, $80–175) is a working cattle ranch with a 600,000-acre range. Accommodations run from bunkhouse-and-bedroll to lodge suites. RV parking ($15) and tent sites ($12) are available as well. Guests can ride horses, mountain bikes, hike, tag along on history and nature tours, hunt, or join the ranch hands in their ranch activities. The ranch serves hearty breakfasts ($13) and dinners ($28) using mostly local produce and quality meats. They can pack you a lunch ($13) as well if you're headed for the trails. Meals are a few dollars more for nonguests, a bit less for children under 12.

HIGH ROCK CANYON

A long series of canyons make up High Rock, with 800-foot-high sheer walls of polychrome volcanic rock jutting from mineral-infused and lichen-encrusted rock debris. Stands of willow and chokecherry populate the valley floor. The dark basaltic rock near the top of the walls is from the last volcanic activity, somewhere around 15 million years ago, when massive lava flows obliterated the landscape and laid down a uniform layer of tuff. The bright red band below the dark rock is the fine layer of soil that was turned red when the hot lava flowed over it. The beige bands below it are ash deposits from earlier volcanic eruptions. The sage, yellow, rust-red, and sea-green lichens add to the area's Technicolor. The craggy peaks above are perfect homes for nesting golden eagles, prairie falcons, hawks, and owls. In the valley below, chukar, quail, mule deer, pronghorn antelope, and bighorn sheep attract hunters from around the world; wild horses find refuge as well.

John C. Frémont made the first recorded nonnative passage through High Rock Canyon in 1843 and described it in his diary. In 1846 the Applegate brothers, following Frémont's directions, blazed a trail through the canyon, which Peter Lassen used in 1848 to lead a wagon train from near Winnemucca on the main Emigrant Trail to Goose Lake in the northeast corner of California.

The area around the canyon is ranching country, with alfalfa fields, ranch houses under big cottonwoods surrounded by cypress windbreaks, and frequent cattle guards. It's also where four Basque shepherds became the victims of the last Indian massacre in American history. The unfortunate Basques ran across a group of camping Bannock Indians in 1911, and according to the Bureau of Land Management's *Emigrant Trails in the Black Rock Desert,*

> Their mutilated bodies were found frozen in the streambed one month later and a posse was formed for a manhunt. After a chase, which covered hundreds of miles, the band and their leader, Shoshone Mike, were gunned down in Rabbit Creek Wash northeast of Golconda near Kelly Creek Ranch.

Orientation

As you get deeper into the Granite Range, some 35 miles from Gerlach, Highway 34 veers off to the west toward Vya while a very ugly road runs northeast to High Rock Canyon. It's rough going on a one-lane primitive dirt road full of chuckholes, washboards, and sage scratching both sides of the car as you negotiate boulders in the middle of the lane and bounce down deep gullies and washes like a dinghy on the high seas. You should not even consider this canyon excursion unless you have a high-clearance 4WD vehicle, but if you do, you are rewarded with some of the best rugged beauty Nevada has to offer.

After a while, you come to an intersection; bear left to enter **Little High Rock Canyon.** There's a very narrow jeep track into this canyon, and it is easier to hike in than to drive, but two hours and 15 miles from the turnoff, three hours and 50 miles from Gerlach, you reach the brown Bureau of Land Management sign for High Rock Canyon. It's still another couple of hard miles, though. A pullout in the middle of the first (and most spectacular) canyon has firewood, campfire rocks, and a cozy carbon-covered cave. The dusty road slows to about 1 mph because of the rocks, dips, ruts, and creek crossings. Again, the road is only passable in a high-clearance 4WD vehicle with heavy-duty-suspension.

If you're really interested in this country, you can continue the hard driving. Topo maps from the U.S. Geological Survey or DeLorme's *Nevada Atlas & Gazetteer* show side trips to historical sights such as cabins, pioneer graffiti, and old Emigrant Trail camping grounds. Along the main track is a lone cabin with a pullout if it gets dark and you need to stop for the night or if you want a break from the physical pounding of the drive. The surface improves around 25 miles from the entrance to the canyon; it's back up to 20 mph, and there are some cattle around.

At the next fork in the road, go straight; you have to open and close a wire gate behind you. From there you climb up to Stevens Camp, the only place along the road with potable water. At Stevens Camp you can cut around to the northwest and drive for a short time at around 25 mph until you come out on Highway 8A. This road is wide and smooth and supports speeds up to 45 mph, although it is a bit slippery and has washboards in the gravel—but it's still velvet compared to the previous 35 miles.

SHELDON NATIONAL WILDLIFE REFUGE

Like the American bison, pronghorn once roamed the West in the millions, but within 100 years of the first mountain men entering Nevada, their numbers were decimated to the brink of extinction by overgrazing, hunting, disease, and deliberate poisoning. One pocket of pronghorn holdouts remained in the remote corner of northwestern Nevada. In the early 1920s, Edward Sans, state director of predator control and a representative of the U.S. Biological Survey, began a campaign to carve a pronghorn refuge out of the large ranches here. He lobbied government bodies and the New York conservation societies and big-game clubs. The Boone and Crockett Club donated $10,000 for the effort in return for naming the refuge after its leading member, Charles Sheldon, a hunter, explorer, and writer who had studied and reported on the pronghorn over the years.

By 1928 ranch land had been purchased, and the federal government set it aside as a refuge. Experts and money from the Audubon Society managed the 34,000 acres until 1933, when the refuge was officially taken over by the federal Department of Biology, forerunner of the U.S. Fish and Wildlife Service. Edward Sans was appointed director, and by 1937 the refuge had expanded to 575,000 acres. Since then, programs have been implemented to manage the pronghorn, mule deer, and burros. The highway across the refuge was completed in 1962; bighorn sheep were introduced in 1968.

Today the pronghorn at the refuge have built up to a winter population of 3,500. They are more dispersed in summer as they range widely for food and water. In the spring and summer many antelope leave Sheldon for the Hart Mountain Refuge across the border in Oregon. The best times to spot them is morning and evening, although because they feed during the day—a boon to hunters—you might see them anytime. Early in the morning, especially, you can see hundreds of these graceful and skittish creatures all over the park. They're very fast, and they'll keep distance from your car, but when they feel safe they'll resume their camel walk, bouncing over the sage as if on springs, bobbing their heads back and forth, and flashing their white rumps.

Orientation

The **ranger's residence,** a beautiful stone house built in 1934, is a little past Bald Mountain summit on Highway 34, on the west side of the refuge; it has a shop next door. If you enter the refuge from U.S. 140 on the east side, pick up a map and a brochure at the information signpost.

Continuing east from the ranger's residence, the narrow but smooth dirt road supports speeds up to 35 mph, but you'll probably want to poke along at 25 mph. From the top of a gentle grade, you get a nice overlook of **Swan Lake Reservoir.** If the pronghorn are out, there could be scores of them on the flats south of the lake. The road then turns north, into unusual country for Nevada: vast and rolling high volcanic plains, which are good for spotting wildlife. Little humps on the plateau carry names such as Sage Hen Hills,

Round Mountain, and Blowout Mountain; flattop crests are called Bitner Butte, Big Spring Butte, and Gooch Table. The road runs along, then around, Rubble Ridge and comes to **Catnip Reservoir** and a primitive campground with a fire pit, picnic table, and outhouse; fishing is not allowed. Shortly past the county line, when you cross from Washoe County into Humboldt County, is the junction where Highway 34A ends at Highway 8A, which returns south to Vya. Coming from the south before the junction, Highway 8A climbs a low rise between Fish Creek Table and Fish Creek Mountain. There's no sign, but a change in county road maintenance is evident as you're forced to slow to 20–25 mph as you cross into Humboldt County. Razor-sharp shards of obsidian glisten on the roadbed. Locals say the road eats tires, so be careful. Five miles farther north is U.S. 140, the Winnemucca-to-the-Sea Highway, which means pavement, glorious pavement.

Turning left (northwest) on U.S. 140 leads eventually to Lakeview and Medford, Oregon, and finally to Crescent City, California. But take a right on U.S. 140 toward Denio. A half mile east is a turnoff to Big Springs Reservoir Campground, just two miles north of the highway. When there's water (or ice) in the reservoir, there are trout. Beyond the campground, the road descends to Virgin Valley, where a long, straight, flat plateau points at the road—the *Nevada Road Atlas* calls it **Black Ridge,** and the USGS two-degree map calls it **Railroad Point.**

Camping and Hot Springs

Heading east on U.S. 140, about 10 miles west of Denio, you'll come to a sign pointing out the turnoff to the **Virgin Valley Campground and Hot Springs.** Another sign here advertises the Royal Peacock Opal Mine, which features recreational opal mining for a fee. A good gravel road takes you one mile south to the campground—and back into the refuge—past the Dufurrena Ponds. The free campground has about eight loosely defined spaces with fire pits and tables, pit toilets, and a tap with drinking water. The ponds offer fishing for bass and perch; state regulations apply. A group called Friends of the Refuge has done an excellent job fixing up the place. The stone-rimmed hot pool has a fresh gravel bottom, and the adjacent showers, in an old stone building, are clean and in good repair. At about 85°F, it's more of a warm springs, but pleasurable nonetheless. A colony of guppies lives in the lightly mineralized water. Some are fantails with orange, yellow, and blue spots, just like the ones you might have had in your aquarium as a kid.

It's a nice place, marred only by the halogen lights outside a nearby ranch house and the minimal privacy afforded by the open campsites. In summer you'll fall asleep to a serenade by bullfrogs, which populate the two dozen or so ponds in the area. While you're here, check out **Thousand Creek Gorge,** visible east of the road, on the left as you drive in to the campground. It's a four-mile open wound in the earth delimited by towering golden-red walls and dotted with former ponds and willows. There's no real trail to follow, so tread carefully, not only because you're in sensitive mountain habitat but because the wild burros leave their calling cards all around.

Driving eight miles farther into the refuge on the same road brings you to the **Royal Peacock Opal Mine** (10 Virgin Valley Rd., Denio, 775/941-0374, 8 A.M.–4 P.M. daily May 15–Oct. 15, $75–180), 10 miles in from U.S. 140, where you can search for elusive fire opals. Volcanic ash, silica chips, buried organic material, superhot water, and a few million years combined to create these light-refracting gems. Kids can dig free with paying adults in the mine tailings. Sifting through the bank diggings is more expensive but potentially more rewarding.

The RV park at Royal Peacock (775/941-0374, $35) has full hookups, showers, restrooms, and a laundry room, and it offers tent camping ($7 pp) and a couple of fully furnished trailers ($65).

Other than in the Virgin Valley, there are about a dozen primitive campsites in the refuge; most have vault toilets but no water or other amenities.

Lovelock

Focused on its plentiful forage and water—an all too rare commodity in many parts of Nevada—Oregon-bound farmers and California-bound gold seekers in the mid-19th century circled this area on their hand-drawn maps. That same abundant water and grass-sustaining land also lured George Lovelock, a Welsh quartz miner who came to California by way of Australia and Hawaii in 1850. He homesteaded a ranch in Humboldt County in 1861; in 1866 he bought 320 acres at Big Meadows and took title to the oldest water rights along the Humboldt River—just in time to donate 85 acres for the Central Pacific Railroad right-of-way in return for naming the new railroad town after him. Railroad construction brought a large and thriving Chinese community, and one of Nevada's first Chinatowns sprang up in Lovelock.

The rich land and good grass attracted cattlemen and ranchers. By the early 1900s, reservoirs on the Humboldt River irrigated 8,000 acres, but the supply of river water, never dependable, seemed to diminish year by year as settlers, spread over several hundred square miles to the east, diverted more and more of the water. Eventually the federal Bureau of Reclamation helped build the Rye Patch Dam, completed in 1936. Its reservoir, when full, provides irrigation water to 40,000 acres of the Lovelock Valley as well as great fishing and other recreational activities.

In 1919 Nevada split Humboldt County in half, and Lovelock became the seat of the new Pershing County, named after the World War I general. Pershing County encompasses 6,000 square miles, roughly twice the size of Connecticut. In addition to agriculture and ranching, mining has become economically important in the Lovelock area. Nearby operations include Coeur Rochester, the seventh-largest producer of silver in the world, as well as other gold and silver prospecting sites and a large EP Minerals diatomaceous-earth mine.

Interestingly, former Nevada governor Charlie Russell, former U.S. senator Alan Bible, and former congressman and Nevada Supreme Court

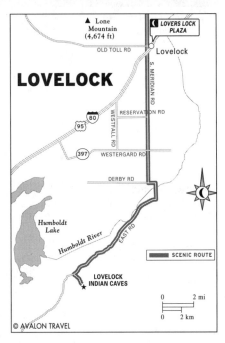

chief justice Cliff Young were all born within a block of each other in downtown Lovelock. The town's other claim to fame is Edna Purviance, Charlie Chaplin's on-screen foil and off-screen lover for decades, who grew up in Lovelock and was discovered by Chaplin in San Francisco. They appeared in 40 movies together, and she was the leading lady in Chaplin's famous *The Tramp.*

The town's current most famous resident is O. J. Simpson, who arrived at Lovelock Correctional Center in 2008 to serve a minimum of nine years after being found guilty of kidnapping and armed robbery in Las Vegas.

SIGHTS
Marzen House Museum
Originally the big house on Colonel Joseph Marzen's 3,400-acre Big Meadow Ranch outside of town, this two-story structure served as

HUMBOLDT VALLEY

Marzen's home and showplace. Built in 1874, the fully restored structure was transported to its current location and now serves as the Marzen House Museum (25 Marzen Lane, 775/273-4949, call for hours, donation), home to relics and artifacts of Pershing County's history. Many of the items displayed are related to agriculture and mining, including large pieces of equipment, a relocated assay office, and vintage stock certificates. Other displays are vignettes of everyday life in the late 19th and early 20th centuries—a carpet sweeper, a pump organ, and household furniture and fixtures. Other items are associated with early Native Americans, the Emigrant Trail, Lovelock Cave, and movie star Edna Purviance.

◖ Lovers Lock Plaza

If you stop at the **Pershing County Chamber of Commerce** (350 Main St., 775/273-7213) for brochures and information, you are already at a downtown attraction. Lovers Lock Plaza (400 Main St.), adjacent to the circular courthouse, carries on the Chinese tradition of symbolizing undying love by affixing a lock to a chain, then throwing away the key. More than 1,000 locks adorn the Lovelock chain, an American version of the links that wind their way around the Great Wall of China and the Yellow Mountains. Most shops in town can supply the lock; put it on any available link on the chains snaking around and among the pillars in the plaza. If you're ready to formalize your love, Lovelock has a few quaint churches and a justice of the peace who can do the deed. You can get a marriage license here at the county clerk's office (8 A.M.–5 P.M. Mon.–Fri.). The Courthouse, designed by prolific Nevada architect Fredrick J. DeLongchamps, recalls the Pantheon in Rome. Completed in 1921, it's the only round courthouse still in use in the country. If you get married here, you can start going around and around with your spouse right away; why wait till the honeymoon is over?

Town Tour

From the courthouse and plaza, head south along Cornell Avenue (old Hwy. 40) to 8th Street; take a right and go one block down to Broadway, the old business district along the tracks. The **Union**

Lovers can symbolically lock their commitment in Lovers Lock Plaza, then make it official in the Pershing County Courthouse.

Pacific Depot (1005 W. Broadway) was in use until the early 1990s. Built in 1880s Eastlake or "stick" style, it gave more than 100 years of service. Politician and noted orator William Jennings Bryan spoke here in 1915. Across the street, stop in for a cold one at the **Longhorn Saloon** (925 W. Broadway Ave., 775/273-7015) and gaze at the intricate beauty of the murals on the interior walls. The Longhorn is one of the few original buildings still standing along this stretch of what used to be Railroad Street.

Lovelock Cave

At the Marzen House Museum (25 Marzen Lane) or the Chamber of Commerce (350 Main St.), pick up a map and informational booklet about the 20-mile trek known as the **Lovelock Cave Back Country Byway.** It begins at the Marzen House and heads through the town, irrigated fields, and along the Humboldt River. The road traces the base of the West Humboldt Mountains and follows a section of the California National Historic Trail to Lovelock Cave (Hwy. 397/S. Meridian Rd., 22 miles south of Lovelock). The cave and nearby **Leonard Rock Shelter** can be considered the beginning of Nevada civilization. The shelter, protected by petroglyph-decorated tall tufa, yielded relics and other evidence of continual though sporadic occupation by Native Americans about 4000 B.C.–1400 A.D.

The horseshoe-shaped cave achieved archeological significance some years after a company began excavating its bat guano in 1911 for use in fertilizer. Near the bottom of the five-foot-deep guano piles they found basketry, intricate tule duck decoys, and other evidence of human occupation. Unfortunately, treasure hunters and vandals looted or destroyed many relics before archaeologists were brought onto the site. Some people believe they also found eight-foot-tall human skeletons, broken arrows that had been shot from the cave mouth above, and other evidence supporting the Paiute legend of the "red-haired giants."

Rye Patch State Recreation Area

One of the many efforts to control the Humboldt River, the designated purpose of **Rye Patch Reservoir** (2505 Rye Patch Reservoir Rd., 775/538-7321, $7) was to serve the irrigation needs of farmers and ranchers in Lovelock Valley. Secondarily, when it's full, the 72 miles of shoreline and 11,000 acres of surface water have created a multiple-species fishing bonanza and a sublime camping and outdoor recreation complex. Located 22 miles north of Lovelock on I-80, the reservoir anchors the Rye Patch State Recreation Area. It's ideal for picnicking, with two designated day-use locations complete with restrooms.

Springs feeding the Humboldt River attracted

THE ROAD TO LOVELOCK CAVE

Lovelock Cave was discovered by teenagers in 1887, although it was not explored until 1911 when guano miners excavated 250 tons of bat scat, uncovering numerous Native American artifacts in the process. The 160-foot-wide, 40-foot-deep cave, created by Lake Lahontan, served as a shelter to Native American inhabitants around 2000 B.C. and was the first Great Basin site to be excavated by archaeologists. The artifacts, which include baskets, textiles, and the famous Lovelock Cave duck decoys, are exhibited at museums around the country.

The route from downtown Lovelock to Lovelock Cave has been declared a Cultural Back Country Byway by the state. Begin at the Marzen House Museum on the southwest side of town. Drive northeast through town and then turn right on Main Street. Go two blocks and turn right on Amherst Avenue. Past the park, the road becomes South Meridian Road (Hwy. 397). The first half of the 20-mile route takes you through irrigated fields; after crossing the Humboldt River the road changes to dirt. This byway is at its best in summer and early fall.

prehistoric horses, camels, bison, and elephants nearly 25,000 years ago; humans arrived to hunt them some 8,000 years ago; nonnative trappers arrive 150 years ago and named the area for the wild rye they found.

While water levels play a huge role in the quality of angling, the reservoir's water teems with crappie, white bass, wipers (a white bass–striped bass hybrid), catfish, and walleye. Live bait is allowed but is not available in the recreation area; bring your own, and don't forget your fishing license. Two **campgrounds** ($14), one below the dam and the other on the reservoir's west side, have flush toilets and showers. Primitive camping, with some sites accessible via rough roads, others by boat only, is allowed along the water.

Unionville

An hour's drive from Lovelock, Unionville sits in the aptly named Buena Vista Canyon. During the Civil War, Confederate sympathizers founded the site and named the town Dixie. When Northerners arriving to work the mines outnumbered the Southerners, they quickly voted to rename the town to show support for Lincoln's government. A few remnants of those roaring 1860s times are still present, but there is no preservation effort. A few dozen people still live among the rustic ruins that include a schoolhouse and the shack where Mark Twain lived for a few weeks while he entertained dreams of making a fortune in mining.

Today you can still explore the region's mining history not only in Unionville but also the nearby mining ghost towns of Rochester, Star City, and Seven Troughs. If you're looking to relax in Unionville's tranquil, scenic canyon locale, take advantage of the hiking, hunting, and fishing spots nearby, or walk in Twain's footsteps, establish a base at the **Old Pioneer Garden Bed & Breakfast** (2805 Unionville Rd., 775/538-7585, $85–100), the only commercial operation in town. The owners, looking to get away from it all themselves, moved to town in the 1970s and quickly set about restoring the Hadley House, one of Unionville's first structures. The two-

Nevada's state-record walleye came out of Rye Patch Reservoir. White bass, crappie, largemouth bass, bluegill, brown bullhead, and channel catfish also challenge anglers here.

story renovation incorporated the home's original stone walls; the restored home now includes six guest rooms. A second restored home has additional rooms for rent.

ACCOMMODATIONS

The part of I-80 that runs through northern Nevada wasn't completed until 1983, and Lovelock was one of the last towns to be bypassed; for a long time the traffic light at Main Street and Cornell Avenue was the only one on the route between New York and San Francisco. This also accounts for the dozen or so motels along Cornell Avenue—all the I-80 traffic had to drive right by them. Those listed here are all clean, comfortable, and invitingly friendly, with basic rooms, Wi-Fi, microwaves, and refrigerators. Entering town from the north, the first you'll encounter is the **Super 10** (1390 Cornell Ave., 775/273-0703, $28–45). Freight trains might rouse light sleepers at the **(C Cadillac Inn** (1395 Cornell Ave., 775/273-2798, $30–40), but that's just part of the charm of this quaint establishment. The building is old, but management is keeping up with repairs and maintenance. A recent visit showed new windows, landscaping, and shower tiles. A block off Cornell Avenue on Dartmouth Avenue at 9th Street, the **Covered Wagon** (945 Dartmouth Ave., 775/273-2339 $35–55) is capably managed by Lisa Wu, who ensures guests' every need is attended to.

The **Lazy K Campground and RV** (1550 Cornell Ave., 775/273-0577, $20) is just off of I-80; from exit 105, go north to Cornell Street, then take a right (east) for a mile to the campground. The Lazy K was a KOA for years but reopened in 1995 as an independent. It's right off I-80, but the large trees and landscaping hold down the noise. This is the only camping in Lovelock, with 49 spaces for motor homes, 30 with full hookups; nine are pull-throughs. There are 10 tent sites ($12) in the trees. Restrooms have flush toilets and hot showers; laundry and groceries along with a deli, a bar, a game room, and a playground are available.

FOOD

Ranch-land diner-style grub is the rule in Lovelock. Slow down a pace and duck into the **Cowpoke Café** (995 Cornell Ave., 775/273-2444, 6 A.M.–8 P.M. Tues.–Sat., 6 A.M.–3 P.M. Sun., $7–15), which has the best pie in town. Try the brisket sandwich; folks also rave about the chicken noodle soup and the veggie burger.

Sturgeon's (1420 Cornell Ave., 775/273-2971, 24 hours daily, $10–20) has terrific New York strip and prime rib specials that include a grapefruit-size baked potato, vegetables, and the salad bar. It's part of a casino, restaurant, and motel complex, so you can try your luck at the machines after dinner.

From Mexican dinners (especially the chiles rellenos) to purely American burgers and rib-sticking breakfasts, **(C La Casita** (410 Cornell Ave., 775/273-7773, 6 A.M.–8:30 P.M. daily, $10–20) has it all.

Fallon

Spend a few days here and see for yourself why Fallon has been called the "Oasis of Nevada." Push the smog from your lungs with fresh alfalfa-scented air wafting from the productive farmland and rolling hills. Thrill to the sight of birds—both the F-5E/Fs and other war birds at Naval Air Station Fallon or the ibises, sandpipers, stilts, and avocets prowling the shores of Carson Lake. Enter the surreal worlds created by glaciers eons ago and populated by ancient civilizations.

HISTORY

Native Americans from the prehistoric to the Paiute made gentle use of the Stillwater marsh for thousands of years before the first non-natives trampled the surrounding grasslands in their quest for beaver. A few decades later, the mass westward migration of pioneers and

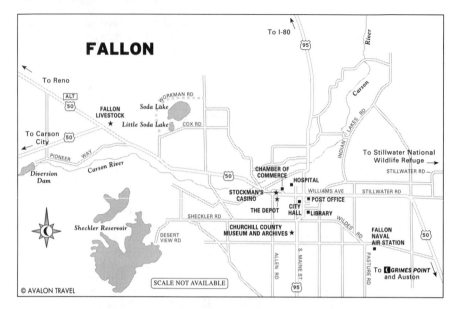

gold seekers couldn't get through west-central Nevada fast enough on their way to the rich Willamette Valley and the gold fields of northern California. During and centuries before the great migration, the lives of the Toidikadi (Cattail Eaters) band of Northern Paiute centered on the bountiful marsh; it provided not only their physical needs—food, clothing, and building materials—but also spiritual observances, which focused on the migratory cycles of the waterfowl.

Asa and Catherine Kenyon established a way station at Leeteville, west of Fallon, in 1855 to sell much-needed supplies to the pioneers who survived the treacherous stretch of the Emigrant Trail known as the Forty-Mile Desert. The Pony Express and Overland Stage also rode through Leeteville, or Ragtown, as it was sometimes known because of the discarded mattresses and household goods strewn around the area or for the ragged clothes washed in the Carson River and laid out on the banks or hung on tree branches to dry.

Reclamation

Mining for soda and salt, freighting supplies along a route between Virginia City–Carson City and Austin, and some ranching ushered the county into the 20th century. The area's early ranchers dug their own irrigation ditches by hand, sometimes for miles, from the Carson River to their homesteads. One of the first water reclamation projects after the federal Reclamation Service was established in 1902 was an irrigation project in western Nevada using water from the Carson and Truckee Rivers. Workers began building the Derby Dam and digging the Truckee Canal in June 1903 to divert Truckee River water 32 miles southeast into the Carson River, and from there to the farms of the irrigation district. The engineers grossly underestimated the amount of water needed to irrigate the planned 400,000 acres, and the agricultural project nearly failed during the first 10 years. Lahontan Dam was built on the Carson River 1911–1915, and it impounded enough water to irrigate about 75,000 acres.

Cantaloupes and Fighter Pilots

Even with a reliable supply of water, the

alkaline soil of Carson Sink had to be fertilized for years before profitable crops could be reliably produced. Beets failed, but Heart o' Gold cantaloupes proved more successful, even enjoying a national reputation for a time. Fallon turkeys were similarly briefly popular, but alfalfa endured as the major crop, and in a normal water year 30,000 acres produce nearly 150,000 tons of stock feed. Garlic, some vegetables and grains, and some Heart o' Gold cantaloupes are also grown. (Even as the number of melons grown in the vicinity drops, the number of people who attend the annual Hearts o' Gold Cantaloupe Festival grows. The Labor Day weekend event at the Churchill County Fairgrounds draws 15,000–20,000.)

The arrival of a small airfield in 1942 boosted the local economy. It closed after the war, reopened during the U.S. intervention in Korea, and now aircraft carrier–based pilots are trained here. The Navy Fighter Weapons School, more popularly known as "Top Gun," moved to the airbase in 1996 from Miramar, California.

SIGHTS

Fallon's seeming incongruities extend to its attractions. Visitors can commune with the simple yet poignant petroglyphs created by ancient civilizations at Grimes Point or feel the adrenaline rush as fighter pilots put their powerful aircraft through their paces across the road.

Churchill County Museum and Archives

The Churchill County Museum and Archives (1050 S. Maine St., 775/423-3677, www.cc-museum.org, 10 A.M.–5 P.M. Mon.–Sat., noon–5 P.M. Sun. Mar.–Nov., 10 A.M.–4 P.M. Mon.–Sat., noon–4 P.M. Sun. Dec.–Feb., donation) is one of the state's top museums. In 1968, Alex and Margaret Oser, Southern Californian philanthropists who owned land in Churchill County, bought an old supermarket building to donate to the county for the museum. Today the huge building and a

couple of annexes are packed with fascinating exhibits to keep you occupied for most of the day.

The collection includes the mineral specimens and mining equipment that all Nevada museums are required by state law to display (kidding), but the real stars are the Native American and pioneer life exhibits. The Native American collection includes hand-woven baskets, a tule hut, a Paiute village, arrowheads, duck decoys, clothing, and other necessities. The pioneer section shows a turn-of-the-20th-century kitchen, complete with cast-iron stove, utensils, and cookware; a bedroom; a parlor; an old-time "family room" with pianos, cameras, dolls, and other luxury items; a quilt display; and period hats and other feminine accoutrements like those sold in Fallon's Bluebird Hat Shop in the 1920s.

The museum also chronicles the excavation of Hidden Cave, 12 miles east of town, and sponsors tours of the cave (9:30 A.M. 2nd and 4th Sat. of every month, free) starting from the museum.

The museum gift shop sells a large stock of books, postcards, and gift items.

◖ Grimes Point and Hidden Cave

Petroglyphs had a religious and cultural significance far beyond simple rock doodles or literal depictions of the world around the artwork's creators. The carvings traditionally were performed by a shaman before a hunt or ceremony. The petroglyphs at Grimes Point are believed to have been carved sometime between 5000 B.C. and A.D. 1500.

At Grimes Point (U.S. 50, 7 miles east of Fallon) you'll see one of Fallon's remarkable contrasts. You walk along a mile-long trail (pick up an information booklet at the trailhead; it identifies the eight signed stations on the route), viewing these carvings on the rocks made by ancient people. The deadly technology on display across the way at the airbase makes a surreal contrast. This prehistoric rock art site, one of the largest and most accessible petroglyph collections in northern Nevada, contains about 150 basalt boulders covered with carvings.

COURTESY OF NEVADA COMMISSION ON TOURISM

Once the shoreline of ancient Lake Lahontan, Grimes Point contains exquisite examples of "pit and groove" petroglyphs, the oldest type of rock art in existence.

Two types of petroglyphs are visible along the trail: primitive "pit and groove" formations, created by striking the boulders heavily with a sharp stone; and "Great Basin pecked" creations, in which flat stones were used to sand the shapes into the rock. There are also two distinct styles, curvilinear and rectilinear, basically meaning lazy eights and stick figures. Some of the artwork's symbolism is obvious—the sun, snakes, and people—but you'll also see pictographs that resemble mushrooms, tic-tac-toe games, the Great Lahontan butterfly, menorahs, tadpoles, treble clefs, and even fire trucks. By the end of the trail, you'll have had enough petroglyph exposure to invent your own theories about their shapes, meanings, ages, and scientific descriptions.

Hidden Cave is only a mile northeast of Grimes Point, and two signs near the trailhead point you in the right direction. But you'll still have to look carefully to find the small camouflaged entrance (it ain't called Hidden Cave for nothing). Dusty roads fork off every which way, and if you take the wrong one, you're lost in the desert. The Bureau of Land Management has installed an information kiosk at the trailhead parking lot for Grimes Point and Hidden Cave. Signs along the trails are intended to make it harder to get lost.

Once you find the site, the loop of three caves includes petroglyphs, tufa, and obsidian. Signs inside the first Hidden Cave chamber are helpful in identifying the main cave's features and some of the tools used for excavation. There is the distinct aroma of bat guano. Passing another large chasm, a rocky half-mile trail winds up a slope to a tiny opening that you crouch low to get through. Inside, lamps light the yawning cavern and reveal evidence of excavations conducted through the 1970s. Sedimentary deposits here have helped geologists date natural events throughout the West; one whitish layer marks the ash of Mount Mazama, a volcano that erupted 6,600 years ago and formed Oregon's Crater Lake.

Stumbled on by four schoolboys in the 1920s, Hidden Cave eventually yielded 2,500 artifacts in excavations from the 1930s through the 1970s, including leather pieces, basketry, carved wooden and stone tools, arrow shafts and points, and stored food.

Fallon Naval Air Station

Take either Maine Street or South Taylor Street for about five miles down U.S. 95 until you see the sign for the Naval Air Station to the left on Union Lane. Go another few miles on Union Lane until you get to the south gate. Then take a right on Pasture Road and a left on Berney Road to view the runways on the other side of the high cyclone fence. Watching the planes taking off is the excitement outside the fence.

The Top Gun air combat school arrived in May 1996, and 25 pilot trainers are stationed at the base year-round. An aircraft carrier's entire fighter wing can train together here at the same time using realistic fight scenarios and comprehensive air combat tactics. Ten trainees at a time are assigned to the school for 10-week flight and air-combat classes offered four times a year. F-18 Hornets and F-14 Tomcats can sometimes be seen engaging each other in mock dogfights over the Navy training area east of the Stillwater Range. The area's 300 days of crystal-clear skies, an extensive training facility that includes 13,000 miles of airspace and four live-ordnance target ranges, and a 14,000-foot-long runway make it an ideal location for practicing combat scenarios.

Soda Lakes and Carson Dam

Heading west on U.S. 50, take a right on Lucas Road and follow it north, then around to the east where it meets Cox Road. Follow the signs over the hill to Soda Lake and Little Soda Lake. Unexpected islands of blue in a sea of beige, these lakes occupy the craters of basalt volcanic cones about 3,000 years old. They're fed by underground tributaries of the Carson River. Entrepreneurs scooped up the pure soda (sodium carbonate) on the lake beds for use in the Virginia City mines during the 1850s. After the federal government constructed several dams and ditches, water levels in the lakes' rose hundreds of feet, not only diluting the soda but also drowning the mine and mill. Today divers and boaters use the lakes as recreational sites. Magma Energy operates a geothermal power plant here, exploiting the many subterranean hot springs in the area.

Continuing west on U.S. 50, a left onto Pioneer Way and following a back road along the Carson River leads between big trees and fields of green to **Carson Diversion Dam.** The 23-foot-tall, 241-foot-long concrete dam diverts river water into two main canals used to irrigate surrounding farmland.

Livestock Auctions

Every week the **Fallon Livestock Exchange** (2055 Trento Lane, 775/867-2020, 11 A.M. Wed.) auctions sheep, goats, pigs, cattle, calves, and horses. A real throwback to the Old West, modern actions use technology (live Internet streaming video) to link stock buyers from around the world to the local sale, which is conducted in a 200-seat ring corral. The Livestock Café (6:30 A.M.–1:30 P.M. Mon.–Tues. and Thurs.–Fri., 6:30 A.M.–auction's end Wed., $10–20) uses farm-fresh ingredients in its breakfast and lunch specialties.

Top Gun Raceway

Speed freaks can have their time in the spotlight and the cockpit, competing in the super pro, pro, sportsman, high school, and junior classes at the Top Gun Raceway Motor Sports Complex (15550 Schurz Hwy., 775/423-0223 or 800/325-7558, $10 adults, $5 ages 6–12, free under age 6). Overflow crowds of spectators flock to the stands on selected weekends March–November. The 2,500-seat complex, owned and operated by Motor Sports Safety Inc., is located 15 miles east of Fallon on U.S. 95. The track has state-of-the-art staging and timing equipment, lights for night racing, and a concession stand.

The **Rattlesnake Raceway** (Rattlesnake

Hill and Rio Vista Dr., 775/423-7483) is also going strong. The stock car dirt track is operated by the Lahontan Auto Racing Association. Saturday evening races start at 7 P.M.

Fallon National Wildlife Refuge

After a long reclamation and conservation effort, the Stillwater National Wildlife Refuge, which includes Fallon and Anaho Island on Pyramid Lake, is one of the most productive refuges in the country. In a good wet year it accommodates 80,000 migrating shorebirds—pelicans; 12,000 swans; several thousand pintails, canvasbacks, teals, and other ducks; a large colony of nesting white-faced ibises; and 150 other species. The Fallon section (Indian Lakes Rd., 15 miles north of town, 775/423-5128, daily year-round, free), however, established in 1931 as a refuge and breeding ground for birds and wild animals and covering more than 15,000 acres of playa and wetland habitat, seldom sees sufficient water flow to attract shorebirds in large numbers. Still, the desert landscape and a few individual winged creatures can provide visual diversion.

Lahontan State Recreation Area

Drive nine miles west of Fallon to the cutoff of the Carson Highway (main U.S. 50) and turn toward Carson City; in another eight miles is the entrance to the Lahontan State Recreation Area (1971 Fir Ave., Silver Springs, 775/577-2226, $7). From the entrance, follow the road around to the junction and take a right to get to the day-use picnic area and beach right at the south side of the Lahontan Dam. There's another picnic area at Silver Springs Beach near the Fir Avenue entrance to U.S. 95A.

Lahontan boasts 25 picnic, camping, and swimming beaches at three different locations. From Lahontan Dam, follow the gravel shore road southwest past 10 separate beaches; the 7th has wheelchair access. There are 40 campsites (Apr.–Oct., $14) for tents or self-contained RVs up to 30 feet long along with piped water, flush toilets, showers, picnic

tables, grills, and fire pits. Primitive on-the-beach camping is permitted anywhere along the shoreline except the day-use areas and boat ramps. The 17-mile-long reservoir invites shore and boat anglers to try their luck for walleye, catfish, trout, and wipers.

ENTERTAINMENT

Stockman's Casino (1560 W. Williams Ave., 775/423-2117) is the full-service gambling and entertainment palace in Fallon. In addition to 260 slots and video poker machines, the blackjack tables open in the early evening, and there's an outpost of Leroy's Sports Book and a keno lounge. Typical of small-town casinos, it has a café, a steak house, and a catch-all lounge for DJs, live music, and big-screen TV sporting events. Up the block, the **Depot** (875 W. Williams Ave., 775/423-2411), located in the town's original 1907 railroad depot (although the building itself has been relocated a few times), has almost as many gaming machines as Stockman's but no table games. Bingo is upstairs. The bar-lounge, dubbed the Midnight Flyer, is the Fallon party spot on Wednesday nights. The live band takes the stage at 10 P.M.

Under the same management, the **Fallon Nugget** (70 S. Maine St., 775/423-3111), **Bonanza Casino** (855 W. Williams Ave., 775/423-6031), and **Silver Springs Nugget** (1280 U.S. 95A, Silver Springs, 775/577-4263) are locals-oriented, with cafés, entertainmentless bars, and rows of slots.

ACCOMMODATIONS

Many of Fallon's motels are along U.S. 50 (Williams Ave.) west of town, more than a few of them associated with casinos. **Holiday Inn Express** (1560 W. Williams Ave., 775/428-2588, $100–133) is the Stockman Casino's hotel option. Clean and fresh in a chain-hotel way, it attracts families with its indoor-outdoor swimming pool and free continental breakfast. The top budget stay can be found at **Value Inn** (180 W. Williams Ave., 775/423-5151, $45–65). It has lightning-fast Internet, microwaves, fridges, and peace and quiet. The room rates make it worth putting up with a few inconveniences, such as slightly frayed towels and nicked furniture.

Modern amenities are even fewer and farther between at the 100-year-old **Overland Hotel** (125 E. Center St., 775/423-2719, $40–60). Soundproofing apparently hadn't been invented when the hotel was built in 1908. The draw is the history and local rusticity, especially the old jukebox and just-as-old 45s playing on it in the kitschy, memorabilia-strewn barroom. If you plan to do your gambling or socializing at Bonanza Casino, or if you're bringing Fido and Fluffy, you may prefer to stay close by at the **Super 8 Motel** (855 W. Williams Ave., 775/423-6031, $45–65).

Fallon also has the historic **1906 House B&B** (10 S. Carson St., 775/428-1906, $65). It's a lovely Queen Anne Victorian house with turret and wraparound porch, furnished with all Victorian period furnishings. When the owners bought the house, they were told it had been built in 1906, hence the name; it was only later that they found out the house was actually built in 1904. It has two guest rooms sharing one bath.

RV Parks

Of the two standard RV parks west of Fallon on U.S. 50, **Fallon RV Park** (5787 U.S. 50, 775/867-2332, $30) is the nicer. The trees are larger, the grass is greener, and the spaces are wider. There's a small market nearby and the cable and Wi-Fi are free. There are 44 spaces for motor homes, all with full hookups; 20 are pull-throughs. Tents are allowed. It's not perfect—not every site has one of those big mature shade trees, the cement roadways are starting to crumble, and it can get noisy if you're parked close to the highway. You could opt to save a few bucks and pull into **Sage Valley RV** (4800 U.S. 50, 775/867-3636), but even though it's a mile closer to town, you'll probably wish you hadn't. The Sage is showing its age, and the sites can be cramped if your rig is of any size. In fact, there's a lot

HUMBOLDT VALLEY

The Overland Hotel in Fallon hosted Teddy Roosevelt during water reclamation projects.

about the place that seems small: the pads and the restrooms, for example. The one advantage the Sage has over Fallon RV is that the noise from the highway doesn't seem to carry to the sites.

The **Bonanza Inn RV Park** (855 W. Williams Ave., 775/423-6031, $17) has 20 sites and access to the casino's amenities. **Churchill County Fairgrounds** (99 Sheckler Rd., 775/423-7733, $15) has 48 full-hookup sites, a dump station, and showers. People attending the livestock shows fill the place quickly, but if there are no events, you can have your pick of prime sites.

FOOD

The **Steakhouse** (1560 W. Williams Ave., 775/423-2117, 5–9 P.M. Tues.–Thurs., 5–10 P.M. Fri.–Sat., $15–30) is the fine-dining option at Stockman's Casino. You could make a meal out of the fabulous appetizers, but save room for the Cajun rib eye. Stockman's also has **Stockman's Cafe** (1560 W. Williams Ave., 775/423-2117, 6 A.M.–midnight Sun.–Fri., 24 hours Sat., $8–15) with cheap full breakfasts and nightly dinner-platter specials.

The **Depot Diner** (875 W. Williams Ave., 775/423-3233, 8 A.M.–9 P.M. daily, $7–15) serves good home-style cooking, including specials for seniors and children. **Aniceta's** (475 W. Williams Ave., 775/423-3111, 6 A.M.–9 P.M. Wed.–Sat., 6 A.M.–2 P.M. Sun. and Tues., $8–20), at the Fallon Nugget, is similar in price and fare. **J. D. Slingers** (855 W. Williams Ave., 775/423-3050, 11 A.M.–9 P.M. daily, $7–15) prides itself on its big half-pound burgers but also serves chicken, ribs, and mountain oysters. The ◖ **Basque Dining Room** (125 E. Center St., 775/423-2719, 5–9 P.M. Wed.–Sun., $10–20) at the Overland Hotel dishes up traditional family-style Basque dinners. Come hungry and in the mood for conversation with your tablemates.

Away from the casinos, your best bets are to try some of the very good though perhaps not terribly inventive ethnic joints. **The Wok** (250 S. Maine St., 775/423-5588, 11 A.M.–9 P.M. Mon.–Thurs., 11 A.M.–10 P.M. Fri.–Sat., $15–20) is half sushi bar, half traditional Chinese sit-down. The lunch

combo ($12) of soup, an appetizer, an entrée, and fried rice can't be beat. The more adventurous can try the raw fish, while kids can order the cooked crab, beef, and chicken dinners from the menu. The coup de grâce: They deliver.

Top honors in the Mexican category go to **La Fiesta** (60 W. Center St., 775/423-1605, 11 A.M.–10 P.M. Sun.–Thurs., 11 A.M.–11 P.M. Fri.–Sat., $10–20) for carnitas and cheesy enchiladas. In a world where if you've tasted one, you've tasted them all, the white salsa and tortilla chips at La Fiesta really stand out. You can find cheaper Mexican fare in plenty of other places, but life is too short.

Some prefer the enchiladas at **Julio's Mexican & Italian** (1941 W. Williams Ave., 775/423-7721, 24 hours daily, $10–15) over those at La Fiesta. Blasphemy! The lasagna, on the other hand, as well as pretty much all the Italian side of the menu is something we can recommend with confidence. In fact, unless pizza counts as an Italian menu, it's the best in town. If pepperoni pie does count, we opt for ◖ **Pizza Barn** (1981 W. Williams Ave., 775/423-7155, 11 A.M.–9:30 P.M. Sun.–Thurs., 11 A.M.–10:30 P.M. Fri.–Sat., $10–20). Try the "hot sack" ($5), pizza dough made into a sort of pita pocket, stuffed with meat, cheese, and vegetables, and baked. It comes with chips and a pickle wedge.

For traditional American, the catfish, collard greens, and ribs at **Big Ed's Brickhouse** (610 W. Williams Ave., 775/867-2823, 11 A.M.–10 P.M. daily, $15–25) come in huge tasty portions. The cornbread is melt-in-your-mouth fluffy.

INFORMATION AND SERVICES

Fallon Chamber of Commerce (85 N. Taylor St., 775/423-2544, www.fallonchamber. com) has all the statistics and information on the area, as well as hotel and restaurant deals. The **Churchill County Library** (553 S. Maine St., 775/423-7581, 9 A.M.–6 P.M. Mon. and Thurs.–Fri., 9 A.M.–8 P.M. Tues.–Wed., 9 A.M.–5 P.M. Sat.) has a Nevada room overflowing with interesting books and reports.

Winnemucca

Winnemucca has always been an overnight stop on a variety of long-distance journeys. A traditional crossroads for Native Americans, trappers, mountain men, pioneers, miners, and maybe—just maybe—one of the most infamous outlaw bands in history, this part of Nevada attracted non-natives even before silver was found nearby, even before the place had a name.

Beaver trappers established an outpost on the Humboldt River as early as the 1830s. The site of Winnemucca was originally named Frenchman's Ford, after Joe Ginacca, who operated a ferry service across the river for California- and Oregon-bound pioneers who opted for the Applegate-Lassen Cutoff and the Humboldt Trail route. By 1865, Winnemucca was growing to accommodate mining operations in the region, and it was a logical stop for the Central Pacific Railroad, which arrived in 1868. Railroad company officials renamed the town Winnemucca in honor of the famous Paiute chief.

After years of steady growth, burgeoning Winnemucca battled declining Unionville for the Humboldt County courthouse. A writer for the Unionville *Silver State* wrote, "The principal production of Winnemucca consists of sand hills, vapid editorials, and a morbid hankering for the county seat." Nevertheless, Winnemucca got the courthouse in 1873.

A large Chinatown sprouted after the

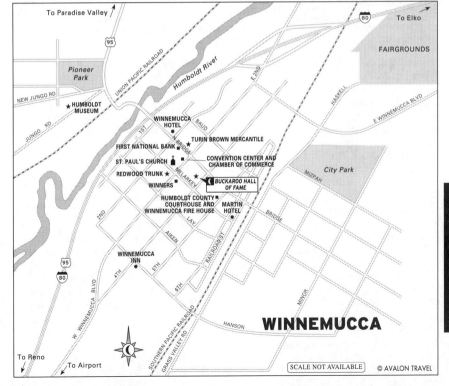

HUMBOLDT VALLEY

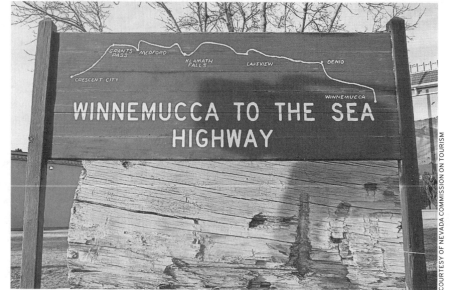

COURTESY OF NEVADA COMMISSION ON TOURISM

This 8-foot-wide section of California redwood washed up at Crescent City, CA, the other terminus of the Winnemucca-to-the-Sea Highway.

railroad was completed, and Basque shepherds settled around Winnemucca to labor on ranches and herd sheep. The Chinese were eventually hounded away, and little remains of their time here, but the Basque influence is still evident in the town's restaurants and cultural events. George Nixon, a telegraph operator on the Central Pacific Railroad, opened a bank here and founded a regional financial empire and a political career that extended to Washington, D.C. In September 1900, Butch Cassidy may or may not have ridden into town with the Wild Bunch and stolen $2,000 in gold from Nixon's bank.

Winnemucca maintained a passable level of prosperity in the early 20th century, thanks to the railroad and highway construction. The population never exceeded 3,000 until the mid-1980s, when a boom began in new mining of gold, silver, dolomite, and specialty limestone. Since then the population has nearly tripled, and Winnemucca has visibly burst its small-town boundaries, spreading north into Paradise Valley and south into Grass Valley.

Even so, Winnemucca has retained its old-time homey feeling and friendliness for visitors. It is still a service center for a large chunk of northern Nevada and has been making a name for itself as the Buckaroo Capital of the country, with the Buckaroo Hall of Fame located right downtown.

SIGHTS

The site of Winnemucca's main claim to fame is George Nixon's First National Bank (352 Bridge St.). While Butch Cassidy's role in the town's most famous bank robbery is uncertain, it is known that members of Butch's gang were responsible, one of the robbers even holding a knife to Nixon's throat. Understanding the value of a good story, Winnemuccans insist Butch masterminded and directed the robbery. From here you can embark on a walking tour of Winnemucca.

Town Tour

At the main intersection downtown, the corner of Winnemucca Boulevard (locally known as

THUNDER MOUNTAIN

Frank Van Zant, a member of the Creek nation who renamed himself Chief Rolling Mountain Thunder, is responsible for the **Thunder Mountain Monument** (www.thundermountainmonument.com), an eclectic folk art collection near Imlay, 33 miles southwest of Winnemucca on I-80. Using abandoned car parts, scrap metal, concrete, and treasures salvaged from junkyards, over 30 years the chief built what is described as "a monument to the American Indian, a retreat for pilgrims aspiring to the pure and radiant heart," according to a website maintained by his son, who is working to restore the roadside museum and art gallery.

Van Zant created the five-acre site along I-80 after serving in World War II and careers in law enforcement and the ministry. He retired, remarried for the third time, and set out for rural Nevada – where he reinvented himself as Chief Rolling Thunder Mountain. The chief at times said his inspiration came in a dream that a giant eagle swooped down from the sky and told him "this is where I should build his nest." Other times, he claimed a less spiritual beginning: his truck broke down, so he set up camp and started foraging.

Whatever the origin, the monument soon took on a life of its own, growing into a monument to the American Indians' struggle, a plea to take care of the environment, and other ideals. In the 1970s, the monument's messages attracted rebellious young people who helped in the art's creation and added a hostel house, underground hut, and even a playground. The hippies looked to Rolling Thunder as a spiritual guru. Though he never claimed mystical powers, some believers claimed Rolling Thunder could teleport objects, create rain, and heal wounds and diseases. The interfaith community thrived in the 1970s, serving the spiritual needs of such notables as Buckminster Fuller and the Grateful Dead, and remained in operation until 1985. A lifelong addiction to cigarettes caught up with Van Zant in the 1980s; his wife left and took their children with her; and fewer counterculture allies visited to help with the site. He committed suicide in 1989, and his life's work fell victim to fire, vandalism, and neglect.

Thankfully, Frank's son Dan Van Zant and his wife have taken on the responsibility to restore Thunder Mountain Monument. There is plenty to spark interest and imagination in what's left of the hostel and playground, and to contemplate in the art created from civilization's castoffs.

Rolling Thunder's grandson Sidian Morning Star Jones is a founder of Open Source Religion, which explores and melds beliefs and rituals of various religious traditions, including those preached by Rolling Thunder.

Main St.) and Melarkey Street, is an eight-foot-diameter cross-section of a **redwood tree trunk** that washed ashore in Crescent City, California, in 1964. It was presented to Winnemucca to mark the beginning of the Winnemucca-to-the-Sea Highway, which ends in Crescent City. Where the Winnemucca Convention Center (30 W. Winnemucca Blvd.) now stands was the location of the Nixon Opera House, built in 1907 by George Nixon, who wanted to leave Winnemucca a memorial when business compelled him to move to Reno. It operated for 80 years and was slated for restoration until it was destroyed by arson in 1992. The Convention Center houses the **Chamber of Commerce** (30 W. Winnemucca Blvd., 775/623-2225,

www.humboldtcountychamber.com), which can provide you with a free copy of the *Take a Walk Through History* map of the town. Go up a block to Bridge Street, and then turn east. The restored commercial building at 355 South Bridge Street used to house the **Turin Brown Mercantile,** built in 1898. Continue on to 5th Street to the **Humboldt County Courthouse,** constructed in 1921 from the designs of quintessential Nevada architect Frederick DeLongchamps. The classical Greek pillared dispensary of justice was built after its predecessor was destroyed by fire in 1919. On the same corner is the **Winnemucca Fire House,** completed in 1935; the art deco structure, like the courthouse, remains in operation.

HUMBOLDT VALLEY

Winnemucca Hotel

Retrace your steps and cross Main Street. In another block, you'll reach the town's oldest surviving building. The Winnemucca Hotel (95 Bridge St.) was believed to have been erected in 1863 by Frank Baud and others. Baud was one of the town's founders and the first postmaster; he constructed the first toll bridge across the Humboldt River. His legacies include Winnemucca's first schoolhouse, constructed with funds from his estate. The restaurant still serves some of the best and most reasonably priced Basque dinners in Nevada; plan on coming back when you're really hungry.

Grammar School and Martin Hotel

Cut over the southeast quadrant of town, and if school's not in session, peek in at the Winnemucca Grammar School (522 Lay St.). Built in 1927, the redbrick white-trimmed schoolhouse is just as lovely and Rockwellian as ever. While you're in the neighborhood, visit the Martin Hotel (94 W. Railroad St.). Built just before World War I, its Basque cuisine rivals that of the Winnemucca Hotel. It's busy all the time, but not as busy as in the era when it fed trainloads of hungry travelers.

St. Paul's Church

The location for the final scene in the 1926 film *The Winning of Barbara Worth*, **St. Paul's Catholic Church** (350 Melarkey St.) brings you full circle from your wanderings around town. Constructed in 1924, the church is on the original site of the town's first Catholic mission. It's striking Spanish colonial architecture makes it one of the most photographed structures in town.

◖ Buckaroo Hall of Fame

At the Convention Center, pay tribute to the working ranch hands whose strong backs and calloused hands built this part of Nevada at the Buckaroo Hall of Fame and Western Heritage Museum (50 W. Winnemucca Blvd., 775/623-2225 or 800/962-2638, 8 A.M.–5 P.M.

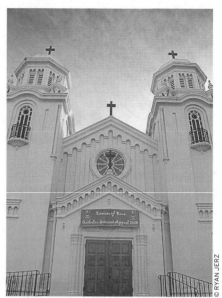

St. Paul's Catholic Church in Winnemucca had a co-starring role in *The Winning of Barbara Worth*.

© RYAN JERZ

Mon.–Fri., free). Remember, they're buckaroos (a bastardized pronunciation of the Spanish *vaquero,* or "skilled horseman"). They get touchy if you call them cowboys, with the term's dusty, style-less connotations. Buckaroos have flair as well as function. Charles Russell, chronicler of all things Western, in 1927 contrasted the buckaroo with the cowboy, noting that buckaroos were:

> generally strong on pretty, using plenty of hoss jewelry, silver-mounted spurs, bits, an' conchas.... Their saddles were full stamped, with from 24 to 28 inch eagle-bill tapaderos. Their chaparejos were made of fur or hair, either bear, angora goat, or hair sealskin. These fellows were sure fancy....

Displays not only honor the 70 or so vaqueros inducted so far but also present the rugged lifestyle they led through artwork, equipment, song, and other media. Buckaroo Hall of Famers must have been born in the 19th century and worked as cattlemen within a 200-mile radius of Winnemucca. Next door, **Riverview Park** is well shaded and a fine place to have a picnic or just a drink and watch the river flow.

Humboldt Museum

Across the river at Pioneer Park, the Humboldt Museum (175 Museum Ave., 775/623-2912, 9 A.M.–4 P.M. Mon.–Fri., donation) showcases the courage of westward emigrants and Native Americans, the wonder of Hollywood and the automobile, and the region's history from the last ice age until today. Housed in the former St. Mary's Episcopal Church, built in 1907 on 5th Street and later moved here, you'll see Winnemucca's first piano, retrieved from the Winnemucca Hotel; a square grand piano brought to Winnemucca in 1868; Native American relics from Lovelock Cave; paintings of the Jungo Hotel and Golconda School; posters of Charlie Chaplin and Edna Purviance; and a scrapbook from *The Winning of Barbara Worth,* starring Gary Cooper, Ronald Coleman, and Vilma Banky and filmed 30 miles west of Winnemucca at the edge of the Black Rock Desert in 1926.

The newer rear building boasts a beautiful floor, a wall-length mural of what downtown Winnemucca looked like around the turn of the 20th century when Butch's gang robbed the bank, a pump organ from Paradise Valley, couches from Unionville, and an original hand-inked mint-condition survey map of Winnemucca from 1867. The antique auto collection includes a 1901 Merry Oldsmobile, the county's first car. An old grain store on the grounds serves as a thrift shop to raise funds for the Historical Society.

Bloody Shins Trail

This provocatively named collection of mountain bike trails east of town has trails for every level of mountain biker as well as facilities for horseback riding and hiking. Conveniently located but usually not crowded, the trails are one- and two-track dirt paths that form

the Sundance Casino in Winnemucca

7–24-mile loops. There are no gates to open and close, and the 4,500–5,200-foot elevation, inspiring views, and adrenaline-pumping turns, drops, and rises provide plenty to take your breath away. For directions or more information on Bloody Shins or the more off-the-beaten-path Blue Lakes Trail, contact the Bureau of Land Management's Winnemucca Field Office (5100 Winnemucca Blvd., 775/623-1500).

CASINOS

The "resortiest" entertainment venue in town, **Winners** (185 W. Winnemucca Blvd., 775/623-2511 or 800/648-4770) is also the only place in town to find live hold 'em. Other table games include blackjack, three-card poker, and craps, also a rarity in Winnemucca. There are a few hundred slots, of course, as well as a bingo parlor. The lounge hosts stand-up comedians (7:30 P.M. Thurs.), and Top 40 and vintage rockers perform on selected weekends throughout the year.

Winnemucca Inn (741 W. Winnemucca Blvd., 775/623-2565) is a compact slot palace

HUMBOLDT VALLEY EVENTS

The towns of the Humboldt Valley celebrate every aspect of their culture and history, and there's plenty to celebrate. The region has been at the forefront of mining milestones, farming and ranching breakthroughs, military successes, and Western heritage.

JANUARY

The **National Cowboy Poetry Gathering** in Elko is a weeklong celebration of the rural West through modern and traditional arts born of the land. Elko overflows with thousands of cowboys and cowgirls, poets and musicians, artisans and scholars, ranch hands and city dudes who value and practice the artistic traditions of the region and are concerned about the present and future of the West.

MARCH

Winnemucca's **Ranch Hand Rodeo** has 30 teams from Nevada's vast ranches competing for bragging rights and prizes in saddle bronco riding, calf roping, wild mugging, team roping, ranch doctoring, and team branding.

MAY

Cowboys and cowgirls compete for top honors in barrel racing, roping, bull riding, and bronco busting at the **Senior Pro Rodeo** in Wells. Amateur and professional chefs compete in Dayton's **Oodles of Noodles** to see whose linguini, macaroni, and fettuccini recipes can "pasta" test as best noodle dish in town. A craft fair gives attendees a chance to work off all the carbs. **Run-A-Mucca** in Winnemucca is a big motorcycle rally that tempts riders with big prices. In addition to free live music, barbecue feasts, and vendors, bikers can win $1,000 in the burnout contest or poker run. And some lucky raffle-ticket holder goes home with a new ride.

JULY

Hot rods and cool cats roll into Wells for the **Fun Run Classic Car Show,** a chrome-filled party with street dances, "show & shine," a poker run, and more. **Frontier Days** in Lovelock is old-fashioned fun that includes feats of strength (arm wrestling), speed (bicycle races), and daring (a scavenger hunt) along with clowns, cribbage, tractor pulls, parades, poetry, and music. Since 1964 the Elko Euzkaldunak Club has or-

---

with additional amenities not always found in small casinos. A few table games, a rowdy sports bar complete with big-screen TVs and a Leroy's Sports Book outlet, and a much more sedate coffee shop make the inn feel bigger than it is. Its location in the middle of casino row as well as plenty of red and blue border neon outside and opulent decor, all stuffed into a space the size of the Harrah's Tahoe women's restroom, add to the illusion. The **Model T** (1130 W. Winnemucca Blvd., 775/623-2588) is a casino, hotel, and RV park with gaming options similar to the Winnemucca, including more than 200 slot machines.

R & L's Express (1985 W. Winnemucca Blvd., 775/625-1777) is a lounge and casino with 104 slots and a Dos Amigos Restaurant inside. The **Sundance Casino** (33 W. Winnemucca Blvd., 775/623-3336) is downtown across from the Chamber of Commerce at Bridge Street and Main Street, with slots and video poker.

ACCOMMODATIONS

Finding a room in Winnemucca generally doesn't present a challenge, but reserving in advance often will get you a break on room rates. Pay close attention to all the factors that can change the rates: summer or winter, weekend or weekday, two people in one bed or two beds, and so on.

The **Winnemucca Inn** (741 W. Winnemucca Blvd., 775/623-2565 or 800/633-6435, $99) has a few suites to accommodate families and strong sound- and light-proofing to accommodate anyone who needs a good night's sleep. The bathrooms aren't terribly large, but they ganized the **National Basque Festival,** an annual celebration of Basque musical, historical, and artistic culture. The celebration typically includes fold dancing, Basque songs, art, and traditional games such as weightlifting, tug-of-war, and wood-chopping.

SEPTEMBER

The highlight of **Fallon Air Show** is the Blue Angels, the U.S. Navy's fighter demonstration team. At Naval Air Station Fallon, the event attracts some 50,000 spectators each year. Other acts include skydivers, aerobatics, and Air Force and Navy fighters from World War II vintage to the most advanced F-22s. **Burning Man,** in the Black Rock Desert, sees tens of thousands of workaday slobs shed their inhibitions (and often most of their clothes) to live on the fringe for a week of self-expression, art appreciation, environmental stewardship, and rebellion against The Man, commercialism, consumerism, government oppression, and anything else that sticks in their craws. Small-town celebrating at its best, **Dayton Valley Days** in Dayton brings together community members for a pet parade, crafts fair, musical entertainment, an art show, silent auction, games, and good ol' American fun. From barely-over-highway-speed jalopies to 400 mph performance machines, drivers test their cars' metal and their own mettle as they go mano a mano with the stopwatch at **World of Speed** in Wendover. Cars don't compete in classes or against one another, so you never know what you may see challenge the course next. A similar exhibition, the **Bonneville Salt Flats World Finals,** is held in October.

OCTOBER

History buffs, strong Unionists, and unreconstructed Confederates converge on Fort Churchill in Dayton for **Civil War Encampment** to reenact battles in the war between the States and celebrate American military history. Another encampment is held in May. The **World Cowboy Fast Draw Championship** in Fallon has modern-day Doc Hollidays face off against the stopwatch to earn the title of fastest gun in the world. Between the high noon showdowns, celebrities try their hand at wielding the six-shooter.

---

have vanity sinks with good storage space. The TVs are 37-inch flat screens, and there's plenty of sitting room even in the standard rooms.

The accommodations part of the Model T Casino, the **Quality Inn** (1130 W. Winnemucca Blvd., 775/623-2588 or 800/645-5658, $55–70) is due for renovation. The location, pool, and free Internet are pluses. Families will probably want to explore other options, but gamblers and those passing through who just need a place to rejuvenate will have their needs met. The 120 rooms at **Winners Hotel and Casino** (185 W. Winnemucca Blvd., 775/623-2511 or 800/648-4770, $55–70) also are showing their age. Everything's clean, but the hotel has that frayed-around-the-edges feel.

The best choice for the budget traveler is the park-outside-your-room **Town House Motel** (375 Monroe St., 775/623-3620, $70–80) on the west side. The rooms, especially those at the back, are far enough away from traffic to be relatively quiet. Rooms are about average size, the pool is refreshing, and the Wi-Fi is free. It is also an older motel, but it has been lovingly cared for. The rooms have tables and chairs outside so you can enjoy the summer breeze or the crisp fall air. Just as recommendable, **Scott Shady Court** (400 1st St., 775/623-3646 or 866/875-3646, $50–80) has a cozy setting off the main drag and a luxurious year-round indoor pool. A perfect family option, there's a safe and grassy playground area.

As a crossroads, Winnemucca also has its full complement of chain outlets. You'll find Motel 6, Best Western, and a very good **Holiday Inn Express** (1987 W. Winnemucca Blvd., 775/625-3100 or 800/HOLIDAY—800/465-4329, $115–165). The

HUMBOLDT VALLEY

price may put you off unless you're here on an expense account, but the business amenities and free breakfast can't be beat.

RV Parking

Winnemucca RV Park (5255 E. Winnemucca Blvd., 775/623-4458 or 877/787-2755, $32) has been in the same location, about a mile east of downtown Winnemucca, for more than 20 years. The trees are mature, there's plenty of green space that includes a very nice grassy tenting area, and the sites are spacious. There are 132 spaces for motor homes, 83 with full hookups, and 70 are pull-throughs. The seasonal pool is heated, and the on-site owners provide a shuttle service to the town's casinos and restaurants.

With plenty of recreational activities, **Hi-Desert RV Park** (5575 E. Winnemucca Blvd., 775/623-4513, $30–36) is one of the larger and nicer RV stopovers for I-80 travelers. Each of the 132 sites (80 pull-throughs) has a patch of grass, and most are tree-shaded. The park is a mini town, with downsized versions of a library, a kitchen, a dance floor, a playground, a putting green, and a store. The game room is full-size, with a pool table, video games, and a TV; there are also a weight room, a swimming pool, and a shower room. A handful of tent sites are available (about $25).

Model T RV Park (1130 W. Winnemucca Blvd., 775/623-2588, $30) is in the parking lot of the Model T Casino, a somewhat urban setting. There are 58 spaces for motor homes, all with full hookups, all pull-throughs. The whole "park" is paved, and tents are not allowed. Restrooms have flush toilets and hot showers; laundry, a convenience store, and a seasonal pool are available.

FOOD

Any discussion of food in this part of Nevada starts with Basque cuisine, and if you're talking Basque, you're talking the ◖ **Martin Hotel** (94 W. Railroad St., 775/623-3197, 11:30 A.M.–9 P.M. Mon.–Fri., 4–9 P.M. Sat.–Sun., $25–35). Built in 1898 to serve the passenger and commercial traffic generated by the Southern Pacific Railroad next door, it also served cattle ranchers and sheep herders when business forced them off the range

and into town. A quasi–community center, the Martin brings in locals for the camaraderie and conversation as much as for the food, which is bountiful. Two entrées and all the sides will feed a family of four. There's a charge for the endless sides and additional charges for the entrées, which management doesn't seem to mind if you share.

Ormachea's Dinner House (180 Melarkey St., 775/623-3455, 4:30–10 P.M. Tues.–Sun., $20–35) also observes the tradition of oversize entrées that anchor sides of bread, rice, beans, fries, salad, and soup. A quite serviceable all-you-can-drink wine is a few dollars more. Sharing the "Taste of Basque" platter is not only an inexpensive introduction to the food; it's quite filling and not a little romantic. You'll sample the Basque takes on chicken (tomato glazed), pork (wine-garlic sauce), and beef.

There's more family-style Basque dining at the **Winnemucca Hotel** (95 Bridge St., 775/623-2908, 6:30 A.M.–8 P.M. daily, $20–40). The old hotel's barroom is so lovely that you won't mind if you have to wait for a table.

Ambrosia takes the form of shredded beef at **Chihuahua's Restaurant** (245 Bridge St., 775/625-4613, 11 A.M.–9 P.M. daily, $7–15). Tender and perfectly seasoned, the beef is a carnivore's dream and a vegetarian's potential downfall (although they also have vegetarian entrées). Dine in front of a trompe l'oeil arch opening onto a Mexican village courtyard. Start with a cerveza in the bar; finish with fried ice cream.

A Winnemucca institution for half a century, **The Griddle** (460 W. Winnemucca Blvd., 775/623-2977, 5:30 A.M.–2 P.M. daily, $10–15) is the best and most popular breakfast restaurant in town—the food, from basic bacon and eggs to the haute-ier tomato and basil omelets, is delivered fast and friendly. The pancakes, French toast, and crepes, all served with fresh fruit, are more like decadent desserts than breakfasts. Lunch consists of good but ordinary sandwiches, so come for breakfast.

At the ◖ **Flying Pig** (1100 W. Winnemucca Blvd., 775/623-4104, 11 A.M.–9 P.M. daily, $10–20) the sauce is so tangy that you'll want to buy a bottle to take home. Dinner ribs are fall-off-the-bone perfect, but it's the lunchtime pulled pork sandwich and that spicy sauce with a touch of honey sweetness that keeps us coming back. Crispy onions make just the right textural complement, and homemade curly fries make a sandwich a meal. The Flying Pig can be forgiven for its halfhearted attempt at a side salad. It's a meat place, after all, and they have ice-cold microbrews on tap. Apology accepted, swine.

The Winnemucca Inn and Model T casinos both have 24-hour coffee shops. The Winners casino's coffee shop is open 6 A.M.–10 P.M. daily.

INFORMATION AND SERVICES

Park Cinemas (740 W. Winnemucca Blvd., 775/623-4454) is the only theater between Sparks and Elko. The duplex shows first-run features weeknights and matinees on weekends.

Winnemucca has a fine **library** (85 5th St., 775/623-6388, 9 A.M.–5 P.M. Mon. and Thurs.–Sat., 9 A.M.–9 P.M. Tues.–Wed.). The Nevada room has lots of primary sources; local newspaper indexing cuts hours off research time.

The **Greyhound** office is at Winnemucca Gas (240 W. Winnemucca Blvd., 775/623-4464). **Amtrak**'s (209 Railroad St., 800/USA-RAIL—800/872-7245, www.amtrak.com) *California Zephyr* stops in town once daily eastbound toward Salt Lake City, Denver, and Chicago and once daily westbound toward Reno and Northern California.

Battle Mountain

As you head southeast along I-80 out of Valmy, the skyscraping stacks of Sierra Pacific Power Company's huge Valmy power plant are visible a few miles north. This 522-megawatt generator, completed in 1985, burns nearly 2 million tons of coal annually. Off to the right in the distance is Battle Mountain (8,550 feet).

According to miner George Tannihill, a band of Shoshone attacked him and a few dozen comrades near this spot in about 1857; the pioneers regrouped and counterattacked the Indians in the hills southwest of town. The mountain was named for the battle, and the town was named for the mountain. Despite extensive records of area happenings in 1857, there's no mention of a major Indian battle, so Tannihill may have made it up.

The Central Pacific Railroad arrived in the town from Winnemucca in 1869, coinciding with a mining rush to Copper Canyon over by the mountain. Mining and the main line attracted three more railroads: The Nevada Central ran a spur line straight down the Reese River Valley 90 miles to the old mines at Austin. The Battle Mountain and Lewis short line ran 12 miles to Lewis and operated for a total of 18 months. Western Pacific arrived around the turn of the 20th century.

A new boom erupted in the late 1960s when the Duval Company reopened the Copper Canyon operation, initiating a resurgence of mining in the area for gold, copper, silver, turquoise, iron, mercury, and barite (Battle Mountain is the barite capital of the world). After coveting the county seat for 110 years, Battle Mountain, at one end of long thin Lander County, finally usurped the courthouse from Austin, at the other end, in 1980. By 2010, after major mine layoffs, the town's population was down to 3,000 people, but despite the boom-and-bust cycles, it remains a pleasant small town with a slow pace of life.

SIGHTS

Unlike other towns along the Humboldt River, Central Pacific, U.S. 40, and I-80 corridor, downtown Battle Mountain hasn't budged for over 120 years. Front Street still fronts the railroad yards, with most of the businesses (and no vacant storefronts) lining

THE HERO AND THE COWARD

At the end of the Civil War, General James H. Ledlie resumed his successful career as a civil engineer. He helped direct construction of the transcontinental railroad and the Nevada Central line from Battle Mountain to Austin. He had proven an able leader and organizer, his virtues commemorated with a locomotive and a siding named in his honor. Ledlie was in Battle Mountain in October 1879 when his old commanding officer, Ulysses S. Grant, came to town as part of his triumphant world tour after his time as U.S. president.

But this would be no time for back-slapping camaraderie and sharing war stories. While there is no record of Grant's activities in Battle Mountain that day, it is certain he did not meet Ledlie, whom Grant once called "the greatest coward of the Civil War." The slur, by most accounts, was one Ledlie deserved. Ledlie was to lead the charge after the detonation of explosives in a tunnel under Confederate troops outside Richmond, Virginia. When the time came,

however, Ledlie cowered in a bunker, throwing back shots of liquor. His troops, badly prepared and poorly led, plunged into the bomb crater, became trapped, and were shot like fish in a barrel. More than 5,300 Union troops fell at the Battle of the Crater. Roundly criticized by both Grant and a court of inquiry, Ledlie faced dismissal from the Army. Instead he resigned his commission on January 23, 1865.

Grant, by contrast, was a hero of the Civil War and served two terms as president. More popular even than Abraham Lincoln, Grant was the first president to visit northern Nevada. He spent two years traveling the world after his second term ended in 1877. The last part of the tour took him through Nevada's Comstock Lode. He visited Glenbrook and Spooner Summit at Lake Tahoe, spoke at Carson City, Virginia City, and Battle Mountain, and took an underground mine tour, jokingly suggesting the journalists accompanying his tour be left behind in the shaft.

the opposite side of the thoroughfare. Natural attractions and outdoor adventure, not museums or amusement parks, are what draw visitors. You don't have to go far to find yourself on public land bursting with opportunities for wildlife viewing, hiking, fishing, hunting, biking, and off-roading.

Lander County Courthouse

A symbol of county seat–dom, the Lander County Courthouse (315 S. Humboldt St., 775/635-2885) began life in 1916 as a schoolhouse. The simple, neoclassical hand-me-down with its broad front elevation and full-height entrance is a far cry from the elaborate Greek Revival style of Austin's courthouse, built with pedimented gables, a narrow entrance, and porch colonnades.

Galena

At one time larger than the town of Battle Mountain, Galena boomed and busted its way from the 1870s through the 1920s.

Right in the middle of the mining action at Copper Canyon south of the mountain, Galena came to life with a run of silver and lead mining in 1869. Two hotels and four stores had opened by the next year. The first boom ended in the late 1870s, and most residents left after the 1889 fire that claimed much of the downtown area, including the mill and assay office.

Military needs jump-started Galena again during World War I, with three mining companies at work. Peacetime saw the machinery silenced again, but World War II and other 20th-century conflicts revived the mines for a while. Today only a few wooden buildings remain in town, but there's plenty of mining equipment and tailings ruins that are of interest. Of particular note is the town's large cemetery, complete with a serene park.

CASINO
Owl Club

The only action downtown, the Owl Club (72

E. Front St., 775/635-5155) is a casino and restaurant with a variety of slots and, on busy nights, a blackjack table or two. The restaurant (6 A.M.–11 P.M. Fri.–Sat., 6 A.M.–10 P.M. Sun.–Thurs., $7–15) gets high marks for its fried chicken and sandwiches. The bar gets even higher marks for its cheap and potent cocktails.

ACCOMMODATIONS

Nearly all of Battle Mountain's motels are along Front Street. Coming in from the west on I-80 and taking exit 229, you first come to **Broadway Flying J Plaza,** a full-service minimart, truck stop, 24-hour diner, and motel, the **Battle Mountain Inn** (650 W. Front St., 775/635-5200 or 877/342-6099, $50–65). Rooms come with pillow-top beds, a refrigerator, a microwave, a coffeemaker, and free HBO and Wi-Fi. Suites with jetted tubs are usually the same price as standard guest rooms and are located at the back of the property where there's less ambient noise. Next along the motel strip is the **Big Chief Best Western** (434 W. Front St., 775/635-2416 or 800/528-1234, $45–65). It has pretty much the same amenities as its neighbor plus a free continental breakfast. It doesn't advertise jetted tubs, but there's a spa and a pool. It's more of the same at **America's Best Value Inn** (521 Front St., 775/635-5880, $50–55).

The **Super 8** (825 Super 8 Dr., 775/635-8808, $70–95) is right on I-80, but thanks to sturdy walls, good insulation, and double-paned windows, you'd never know it. Rates are a bit more than the motel-strip accommodations, but the rooms are quite large; most include a sofa bed, so Super 8 is a good choice for families.

Broadway Flying J RV Park (650 W. Front St., 775/635-5424) has 96 full-hookup spaces for motor homes; 79 are pull-throughs. Tents are not allowed. Wheelchair-accessible restrooms, in the truck stop, have flush toilets and hot showers; public phones, laundry, and groceries are available. For more greenery and scenery but no amenities, head to the

Mill Creek camping area (50 Bastian Rd., 775/635-4000, free), 19 miles south of Battle Mountain off Highway 305 toward Austin. It's a former Civilian Conservation Corps camp with a small, shady, secluded little camping area beside Mill Creek; there is a footbridge across the creek.

FOOD

You can't fairly compare rural Nevada's restaurants with those in the resort cities, but **El Aguila Real** (254 E. Front St., 775/635-8390, 11 A.M.–9 P.M. daily, $10–20) has all the flavor—even the usually pedestrian rice and beans are quite tasty—without a pretentious atmosphere and pricing. Make like a local and head on over. Don't forget the fried ice cream. **Mama's Pizza** (515 E. Front St., 775/635-9211, 11 A.M.–9 P.M. Mon.–Sat., 11 A.M.–8 P.M. Sun., $10–15) has good but pricy pizza and killer cheesy breadsticks. **The Hide-A-Way** (872 Broad St., 775/635-5150, 5–9 P.M. daily, $15–25) is the town steak house.

INFORMATION AND SERVICES

Check with the **Chamber of Commerce** (625 S. Broad St., 775/635-8245, www.battlemountainchamber.com), inside the Civic Center, for information on local cultural and recreational activities, including gold mine tours. The **library** (625 S. Broad St., 775/635-2534, 11 A.M.–5 P.M. Mon., noon–6 P.M. Tues., 2–6 P.M. Wed., 4–8 P.M. Thurs., noon–4 P.M. Fri., 1–3 P.M. Sat.) is next door. For sundries, magazines, prescriptions, and whatnot, stop in at **Mills Pharmacy** (990 Broyles Ranch Rd., 775/635-2323). The **Battle Mountain Swimming Pool** (560 Altenburg Ave., 775/635-5850) is open June–August. A true desert course, **Mountain View Golf Club** (205 Fairway Dr., 775/635-2380, $20 for 18 holes) recently got a lot tougher with more bunkers, larger water hazards, and greater length added. These improvements, along with the tight fairways and small greens, make shot-making paramount.

Elko

Modern extraction and ore processing techniques have made the pick and the pan obsolete, and pickup trucks make for quicker work than the one-horsepower steeds of the past, but Elko remains dedicated to its mining and ranching heritage. Indeed, Elko has been gentrified and citified, but it's still the same place local vaqueros visit on Saturday nights and where Basque sheepherders flock (sorry) to bask (sorry again) in their unique culture.

Elko was founded at the same time the Central Pacific Railroad arrived in the area in 1868, when the company laid out a town site for a division point and sold land. The origin of the name Elko is obscure but is believed to be a lyrical form of the word *elk*.

Elko immediately turned into a major supply and freighting center for the eastern Nevada mining boom. It also became the seat of huge new Elko County and site of the first University of Nevada. Elko suffered boom-bust cycles through the rest of the 19th century and lost the university to Reno. Cattlemen grazed large herds on public lands around the county, but the mercilessly severe winter of 1889–1890 wiped out most of the stock. Soon afterward, the Basque sheepherders arrived.

Elko prides itself as a can-do sort of town. When gambling was legalized in 1931, Elko started up its casino industry in the venerable Commercial Hotel and began booking big-name acts for the floor show. Later, the people of Elko managed to relocate the railroad tracks from downtown streets to out by the river—something that no other town along the northern Nevada main line has managed to accomplish. When Elko wanted a community college, it got one. Parks? No problem—the town raised the money and built them with volunteer labor. Downhill skiing? Someone bought a hill, dug a well for snowmaking machinery, and put in a rope tow. Museum? Convention center? Cowboy poetry gatherings? Yup—they're all here. Elko also some of the most irresistible outdoor recreation

anywhere and the most legal brothels in the country (eight).

This booming town has a brash and modern frontier energy all its own. There's a strong hustle and bustle but also a warm homespun vitality. Coming into Elko after a long drive is like stepping up to a blazing campfire on a cold desert night.

SIGHTS
(Northeastern Nevada Museum
The remarkable Northeastern Nevada Museum (1515 Idaho St., 775/738-3418, 9 A.M.–5 P.M. Tues.–Sat., 1–5 P.M. Sun., $5 adults, $3 ages 13–18 and over age 64, $1 ages 3–12, free under age 3), toward the east end of town, is one of the largest, most varied, and most interesting collections in the state. Even those not interested in museums will want to spend an hour or so examining the animal displays. Half a day would ensure you can take in all the highly informative and artistic exhibits and displays and take in some of the anecdotal tidbits offered by volunteers and staff.

The 300-specimen animal collection is a veritable safari to a mountain peak covered with Great Basin critters in their recreated natural habitat. Other vignettes show animals from Africa, the arctic, Australia, Asia, and all over North America in natural settings. Two million-year-old Murray the Mastodon's bones get their own separate place of reverence. A construction company dug up Murray in 1994 at nearby Spring Creek.

The region's cultural history is covered as well; the Native American and Chinese sections poignantly describe these peoples' contributions through history. The beautiful burnished Halleck Bar was salvaged from an early gin joint in the town of Halleck that dated to 1916. The history gallery also has the original printing press from the *Elko Daily Free Press* and memorabilia from Bing Crosby's time as an Elko resident. The art gallery hosts traveling exhibits that have included familiar

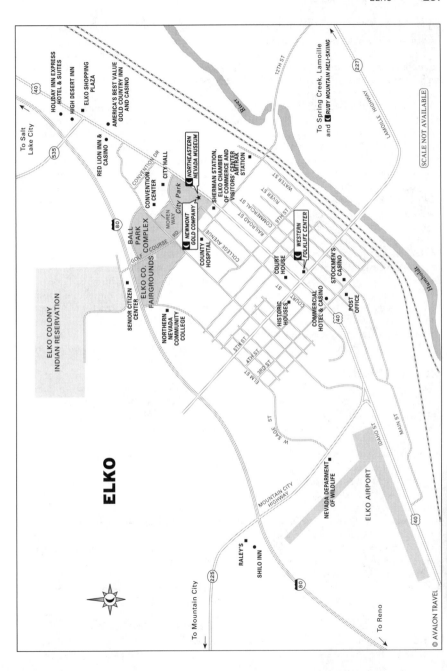

ELKO

To Salt Lake City

To Spring Creek, Lamoille and ◩ RUBY MOUNTAIN HELI-SKIING

(SCALE NOT AVAILABLE)

HOLIDAY INN EXPRESS HOTEL & SUITES
HIGH DESERT INN
ELKO SHOPPING PLAZA
AMERICA'S BEST VALUE GOLD COUNTRY INN AND CASINO
RED LION INN & CASINO
CONVENTION DR
CITY HALL
CONVENTION CENTER
City Park
BALL PARK
MOREN WAY
GOLF COURSE
ELKO CO. FAIRGROUNDS
SENIOR CITIZEN CENTER
NORTHERN NEVADA COMMUNITY COLLEGE

NORTHEASTERN NEVADA MUSEUM
SHERMAN STATION, ELKO CHAMBER OF COMMERCE AND VISITORS CENTER
AMTRAK STATION
NEWMONT GOLD COMPANY
COUNTY HOSPITAL
COLLEGE AVENUE
RAILROAD ST
COMMERCIAL ST
RIVER ST
LS HILLS
WATER ST
12TH ST
River
Humboldt

WESTERN FOLKLIFE CENTER
COURT HOUSE
STOCKMEN'S CASINO
COMMERCIAL HOTEL & CASINO
POST OFFICE
HISTORIC HOUSES
COURT ST
5TH ST
4TH ST
3RD ST
ELM ST

NEVADA DEPARMENT OF WILDLIFE
W SAGE ST
MOUNTAIN CITY HIGHWAY
IDAHO ST
MAIN ST
ELKO AIRPORT

RALEY'S
SHILO INN
To Mountain City
To Reno

ELKO COLONY INDIAN RESERVATION

LAMOILLE HIGHWAY

HUMBOLDT VALLEY

© AVALON TRAVEL

watercolor desert landscapes and rustic sketches to abstract oils and urban photography.

Perhaps the most relevant display is the one on mining, which features multimedia displays explaining how companies retrieve the microscopic gold flecks found along the Carlin Trend, which is so rich and extensive that some say it won't be mined out for another generation. Watch how the ore is blasted, scooped, hauled, dumped, vibrated, separated, crushed, limed, conveyed, ground, pulped, thickened, settled, leached, cyanided, charcoaled, stripped, steel-wooled, retorted, acid-treated, inductothermed, poured, and bricked—all to recover microscopic specks of gold. It requires up to 100 tons of ore to produce a single ounce of gold. Marvel over the 100-ton dump trucks with their 10-foot-diameter tires that dwarf their drivers as well as all the equipment that is used to make Nevada the number-one gold-producing state.

The gift shop sells a variety of books of historical and local interest. Peruse local cookbooks along with some art and jewelry. Admission is free for everyone on the last Sunday of each month.

Sherman Station

Next door to the museum, Sherman Station (1405 Idaho St., 775/738-7135, 9 A.M.–5 P.M. daily, free) was part of the historic home of Valentine and Sophie Walther, who homesteaded 600 acres on Sherman Creek in Huntington Valley, about 60 miles south of Elko, in 1875. This group of five buildings, all built of logs between 1880 and 1903, includes the main house, which is a two-story, 4,800-square-foot structure filled with interesting historical exhibits, Walther family portraits and personal items, a gift shop, brochures, and the Elko Chamber of Commerce and Visitors Center. The smaller buildings are a historic blacksmith shop, a schoolhouse, a creamery, and the stable that housed the horses used to pull stage coaches to and from Sherman Station on the Hill Beachy toll road to Hamilton.

City Tour

Mature trees invite picnickers and frolickers to 21-acre **Elko City Park** (1435 Idaho St.)

between Sherman Station and the Northeastern Nevada Museum. Visitors can enjoy a large playground as well as tennis, basketball, and handball courts; basketball and softball fields; horseshoe pits; and a large lawn area for Frisbee and croquet. Before it was a park, in the 1870s this area was known as China Ranch for the big vegetable patches the Chinese railroad workers planted after they were discharged when the transcontinental line was completed. The gardens fed residents and miners for miles around. Nine blocks south, you'll come to the **Elko County Courthouse** (571 Idaho St.). Built in 1910, the two-story neoclassical structure incorporates a dome and a two-story portico with pediments and cornices. The current building was constructed on the site of the first permanent courthouse, finished in 1869, where Nevada executed its only woman. Elizabeth Potts and her husband, Josiah, were hanged in 1890 for the murder and dismemberment of neighboring rancher Miles Faucett. Interestingly, the judge who presided over the Potts's trial was unconvinced of Josiah's culpability and pleaded with the Board of Pardons to commute their sentences.

Take Court Street, one block north of Idaho Street, back downtown to view a number of **historic houses.** Mostly brick, with big lilac trees and rose bushes blooming in mid-May, the oldest is on Court Street near 4th Street, refurbished and now inhabited by an engineering firm. The shop next door on the corner was the first schoolhouse in Elko, built in 1869; you can buy topo maps here.

Make sure to stop off at **J. M. Capriola's** (500 Commercial St., 775/738-5816 or 888/738-5816, 8 A.M.–5 P.M. Mon.–Sat.), one of the largest cowboy outfitters in the state. Downstairs, ranch and Western wear, boots, and hats are sold; check out the artwork on the stairway and the tools of the buckaroo trade upstairs, where craftspeople hand-make saddles, bits, and spurs.

◖ Western Folklife Center

The Western Folklife Center (501 Railroad St., 775/738-7508 or 888/880-5885, 9 A.M.–5 P.M.

Mon.–Fri., closed some Mon., donation) found a new home in the Pioneer Saloon in 1991. The saloon's 40-foot mahogany, cherry, and pearl bar remains a centerpiece.

The National Cowboy Poetry Gathering is in Elko each January with the center's sponsorship. It began in 1985 when a small group of folklorists and poets organized the event, which has become an annual tradition for thousands of people who value and practice the artistic outlets of the American West and work hard to preserve its future.

The ground floor houses a gift shop full of CDs and books of cowboy poetry and music; posters and photos from Cowboy Poetry Gatherings; and songbooks full of the music of Gene Autry, Roy Rogers, and Dale Evans from the heyday of cowboy culture. The center focuses on the Western spirit and cowboy code of self-reliance, honesty, fair play, and hard work. Traveling exhibitions celebrate the cowboy lifestyle from the Western United States, South America, Australia, and Europe through artwork, leatherwork, and performances through the year.

◖ Newmont Gold Company

Witness firsthand what is igniting Elko's boom with a visit to a working gold mine. There's a new sense of urgency and prosperity at Newmont Gold Company (775/778-4068, tours 9 A.M.–noon second Tues. of the month Apr.–Oct., free) since the precious metal has skyrocketed past $1,400 per ounce. It's a good idea to reserve a tour at least a week ahead. Children age 12 and older are welcome if accompanied by an adult. Tours leave from the Northeastern Nevada Museum (1515 Idaho St.), where an introductory film is shown. Transportation is provided to the mine, where visitors can see the pit, dump leach, and milling facilities. Newmont revolutionized gold mining by using processes to recover specks of gold almost invisible to the naked eye. It has developed strip mines all along the Carlin Trend, one of the most lucrative gold deposits in the world. The company's sophisticated operation is a far cry from the hit-and-miss attempts by Nevada's earliest prospectors to strike it rich.

RECREATION

Elko SnoBowl (6 miles north of town via 5th St., 775/777-7707 or 775/738-4431, dawn–dusk Fri.–Sun. and holidays Jan.–Mar., $10–15) is Elko's ski and winter recreation area. With a north-facing slope, a base elevation of 6,200 feet, and a maximum elevation of 6,900 feet, it offers good skiing even when there's no snow in the valley. The ski hill is served by two rope tows and a chairlift. Saturday ski lessons are offered for children and beginners; more advanced skiers can try the expert run. Sledding and snow tubing are also popular. A shuttle bus leaves hourly on the hour from the end of 5th Street.

The Downtown Business Association sponsors a **Wine Walk and Farmers Market** (second Sat. July–Oct.). The market (10 A.M.–3 P.M., free) present locally grown fruits and vegetables and ends just in time to prepare for the wine walk (4–7 P.M., $20), a meander through the business district where wine samples are distributed along the way.

Raconteurs keep Elko's railroad history alive with storytelling, music festivals, and other events at **Railroad Park** (7th St. and Commercial St., 775/738-4091, days and times vary).

Stock cars of various classes compete at the **Summit Raceway** (Errecart Blvd., 775/778-6622, www.summitraceway.com, 6:30 P.M. Fri.–Sat. Apr.–Sept., $8 adults, $4 seniors and students, free under age 12).

Rodeos, equestrian events, and other Western activities have a home at the **Horse Palace** (670 Bronco Dr., 775/753-6510 or 775/753-6295, www.springcreeknv.net/HorsePalaceEvents.html, 10 A.M.–6:30 P.M. daily) in Spring Creek at the foot of the Ruby Mountains. It has a 1,500-seat indoor arena surrounding a 150- by 300-foot show floor. There are warm-up rings, dressage rings, hunt rings, miles of trails for riding, and boarding facilities as well as a bar.

CASINOS

For such a bustling little town, Elko's entertainment options are a bit thin. Even the major casinos offer little outside the occasional lounge act, and these aren't promoted heavily.

HUMBOLDT VALLEY

The White King on display at the **Commercial** (345 4th St., 775/738-3181 or 800/648-2345) is the largest polar bear exhibited in Nevada and probably the country. This guy stands over 10 feet tall and weighs more than a ton. Formerly the Commercial Hotel (it hasn't offered rooms for several years), this place has been around for nearly 140 years; the small dance floor and band alcove in the bar created one of the first lounges in Nevada in 1937.

Across the plaza and under the same management as the Commercial, **Stockmen's** (340 Commercial St., 775/738-5141) has more slot machines than hotel rooms. Craps, blackjack, and three-card poker tempt table game players.

Farther east, the **Red Lion Casino** (2065 Idaho St., 775/738-2111 or 800/545-0044) is the closest thing to a Reno-style resort in Elko. The Red Lion's roomy 17,000-square-foot casino has a Vegas-style pit of eight table games (blackjack, three-card poker, craps, and roulette). The only poker room in town, a sports book, keno, and row after row of slots are packed in as well. At the **Sports Bar,** next to the sports book, you can toast the winning touchdown or curse that ill-timed interception. Catch every replay on big TVs while enjoying a range of cocktails and beverages. The **Casino Bar** is a bit more eclectic, with poker machines and TVs.

Just across the street, **Gold Country Inn & Casino** (2050 Idaho St., 775/738-8421 or 800/621-1332) is a slots and video poker emporium. On the west side, near the airport, the **Gold Dust West** (1660 Mountain City Hwy., 775/777-7500) has even more slots and a few table games, but no hotel.

ACCOMMODATIONS

Being the biggest town for several hundred miles in every direction and a boomtown to boot, Elko can be a tough place to get a room, especially in the summer and on weekends year-round. Still, Elko has more than 1,800 hotel rooms, so if you call even a day or two in advance, you'll probably be able to come up with an adequate place to stay in your price range.

Stockmen's (340 Commercial St., 775/738-5141, $45–85) has 141 basic but clean guest rooms (the TVs are old, but in working order), and there's an outdoor pool and 24-hour room service for relaxing between gambling sessions. If you seek peace and quiet, ask for an upper-floor room on the east side. It's away from the pool with rooms off an interior hall.

The biggest hotel in town is the **Red Lion Inn & Casino** (2065 Idaho St., 775/738-2111 or 800/545-0044, $89–109). It's a step up from Stockmen's in amenities and price. All guest rooms boast bathrooms accented with imported granite vanities, ceramic tile floors, and premium shampoos and lotions. Microwaves and refrigerators come with upgraded rooms. The pool is open spring–fall, and the kids can while away the hours in the extensive game room. A fitness center and gift shop round out the all-inclusiveness of this resort destination.

The 150 rooms at **Gold Country Inn & Casino** (2050 Idaho St., 775/738-8421 or 800/621-1332, $70–80), across from the Red Lion, have been upgraded with new Western motifs. A recent visit showed it to be just as impeccably clean as its sister properties in the Humboldt Valley.

Idaho Street is motel, inn, and motor lodge strip in Elko. Entering town from the north, you'll be greeted by the **Hilton Garden Inn** (3650 E. Idaho St., 775/777-7307, $119–189), with 84 guest rooms, and **Holiday Inn Express** (3019 Idaho St., 775/777-0990, $97–159). They're both a bit pricy for Elko but have the chains' seal of approval, so there are no worries about service or amenities. Next is the large **High Desert Inn** (3015 Idaho St., 775/738-8425 or 888/394-8303, $69–99), with 171 guest rooms and an indoor swimming pool. A half-dozen economy chain motels then appear in quick succession along with the Red Lion and Gold Country Inn, and farther south are the independents. The **Thunderbird** (345 Idaho St., 775/738-7115, $37–69) has big rooms, careworn furniture, a cute little pool, and breakfast vouchers, making it a top pick in this class.

The friendly **Once Upon A Time B&B** (537

14th St., 775/738-1200, $65–100), operated by Michael and Madeline Johnson, is walking distance to downtown. They have three guest rooms and offer a full breakfast.

For more convenient airport access, try the smoke-free **Shilo Inn Suites** (2401 Mountain City Hwy., 775/738-5522 or 800/222-2244, $80–120). A fitness facility, pool, and the usual in-room necessities as well as easy check-in and getaway to catch your flight make it perfect for business travelers. **Oak Tree Inn** (95 Spruce Rd., 775/777-2222, $65–105), on the other side of Mountain City Highway, is a little cheaper and almost as convenient. It boasts quiet, dark rooms and extralarge beds to ensure a refreshed start to the day.

RV Parking

Double Dice RV Park (3730 E. Idaho St., 775/738-5642 or 888/738-3423, $35) is a full-scale urban RV park atop a hill in East Elko. The park has its own sports bar and lounge complete with pool tables, TVs, and sandwiches and burgers for sale (for more dining options, catch the shuttle down the hill to town). The Double Dice makes its showers available to noncampers ($3 for 15 minutes). There are 140 gravel spaces for motor homes, all with full hookups; 55 are pull-throughs. Tents are allowed, and reservations are recommended in summer. Free continental breakfast is included in the rates.

Gold Country RV Park (2050 Idaho St., 775/738-8421 or 800/621-1332, $26) is right in the thick of the urban action at the east end of Elko; it is behind the Gold Country Inn. There are 26 spaces for motor homes, all with full hookups.

The management at **Iron Horse RV Resort** (3400 E. Idaho St., 775/777-1919 or 800/RV-2-ELKO—800/782-3556, $35–45) is as professional as it comes, and the grassy sites are a welcome change from the dirt, gravel, and cement often found at in-town parks. Although the swimming pool is tiny, campers here have access to the pool and other amenities, as well as discount meal coupons, at the Hilton Garden, a short distance up the road.

FOOD

Not surprisingly, the main theme in this cow town is beef—at coffee shops, diners, burger joints, steak houses, and Basque restaurants.

Of the four Basque dinner houses in Elko, three are along Silver Street, one block south of Idaho Street behind Stockmen's Casino. The **Star Hotel Basque Restaurant** (246 Silver St., 775/753-8696, 11:30 A.M.–2 P.M. and 5–9:30 P.M. Mon.–Sat., 5–9:30 P.M. Sun., $20–45) is the oldest. It opened in 1910 as a Basque boardinghouse with 11 rooms. The seating is family-style, and they keep the tureens of soup, salad, beans, veggies, fries, and bread coming to accompany trout, pork, lamb, and steak entrées.

With a name that means "Come to This Place," **Toki-Ona** (1550 Idaho St., 775/738-3214, 6 A.M.–9:30 P.M. daily, $15–25) serves Basque breakfast, lunch, and dinner and gold old American favorites like chicken and rice soup and prime rib. Go for lunch and order the garlicky sirloin steak sandwich.

The slant at **Nevada Dinner House** (351 Silver St., 775/738-8485, 5–10 P.M. Tues.–Sun., $20–30) is Basque dining with regular restaurant seating and a very discernable Italian bent. Lasagna seems to be the new chef's specialty.

Slightly less expensive than the other Basque eateries is **Biltoki** (405 Silver St., 775/738-9691, 4:30–10 P.M. Thurs.–Tues., $15–25).

Elko is blessed with a handful of authentic and inexpensive Mexican restaurants. Our favorite is **Dos Amigos** (1770 Mountain City Hwy., 775/753-4935, 11 A.M.–10 P.M. daily, $7–15). The locals agree, especially when it comes to Amigos's extravagant brunch buffet ($10). And if refried beans can be gourmet cuisine, then Dos Amigos is the Cordon Bleu. Served with perfectly salted chips and a cheese enchilada, they're sublime.

There are plenty of other taquerias in town that are serious contenders for Dos Amigos's sombrero-shaped crown. Although it's essentially fast food, the quality ingredients and careful preparation at **9 Beans and a Burrito** (2525 Argent Ave., 775/738-7898,

7:30 A.M.–9:30 P.M. Mon.–Sat., under $10), in the Raley's plaza, make it popular with locals and a worthy stop for travelers. Big burritos are the specialty, but we're partial to the hard-shell tacos as well. Even though it's right there in the name, we hesitate to put **Sergio's Mexican Restaurant** (743 Idaho St., 775/777-7736, 9 A.M.–9 P.M. daily, under $10) in the Mexican category—the burgers are outstanding. A true hole-in-the-wall, Sergio's doesn't sweat the small stuff like decor or ambience, but the food is a thing of beauty. The homemade chips and salsa bar and enchiladas earn this joint its Mexican stripes, but we agree with Sergio's modest description of "the best hamburger in northern Nevada."

The Chinese choices are much more limited, but there are a couple of standouts. **◖ Chef Cheng's Chinese Restaurant** (1309 Idaho St., 775/753-5788, 11 A.M.–9 P.M. daily, $15–25) is one. It's consistently ranked among the best in the country, in fact. Cheng has quite a knack for seafood: His walnut prawns are the equal of anything in San Francisco, and the sautéed fish is fluffy and juicy. If you're more into turf than surf, opt for the salt-and-pepper pork.

Flying Fish (382 5th St., 775/777-3594, 11 A.M.–2 P.M. Mon., 11 A.M.–2 P.M. and 5–10 P.M. Tues.–Fri., 5–9 P.M. Sat., $15–25) is the place for Asian-inspired fish and sushi. Start with the *pho* and move on to the spicy crab and other rolls. There's teriyaki chicken, a few Italian entrées, and some other "non-Asian" dishes to keep the whole crew satisfied.

Traditional pasta and chops get the gourmet once-over at **J'Ossie's** (1430 Idaho St., 775/738-2254, 4–9 P.M. daily, $20–30). The sauces (fig, chipotle) complement but don't overwhelm the casually elegant steak-house offerings.

There is a bar at **JR's Bar & Grill** (Gold Country Inn, 2050 Idaho St., 775/738-8421, 24 hours daily, $10–15), and some of the food is grilled, but it's really more of a family restaurant and separate neighborhood bar. The food and decor are typical, but it's open all the time, so you can always find dependable bellyfillers. At **The Brand** (Commercial, 345 4th St., 775/738-3181 or 800/648-2345, 5–9 P.M.

Tues.–Sat., 9 A.M.–2 P.M. Sun., $10–20), ranchers burned their brands into the walls in the 1950s, giving it a unique decor and its distinctive name. Look for Bing Crosby's "+B" mark. Other casino options include the 24-hour coffee shops at the Commercial and Stockmen's, and the Red Lion Inn & Casino has the **Coffee Garden Restaurant & Buffet** (2065 Idaho St., 800/545-0044, 24 hours daily, $10–20), the only buffet in town, with buffets for breakfast, lunch, and dinner as well as an à la carte menu. **Aspens** (Red Lion, 2065 Idaho St., 800/545-0044, 5–11 P.M. daily, 775/753-0562, $20–30) is the first-class dining room hereabouts. Just opened in the summer of 2010, it serves steak, prime rib, and upscale pub grub in a Western-style woodland lodge setting.

INFORMATION AND SERVICES

Started in 1907, the **Chamber of Commerce** (1405 Idaho St., 775/738-7135, www.elkonevada.com) is Nevada's oldest. Located in the historic Sherman Station, the office has a good amount of information, brochures, and free newspapers. The town boosters working here are a friendly, efficient, and busy bunch. Much of their work involves sending out relocation and employment information to people eager for a stake in Elko's continuing economic boom.

The **library** (720 Court St., 775/738-3066, 9 A.M.–8 P.M. Mon.–Tues., 9 A.M.–6 P.M.Wed.–Thurs., 9 A.M.–5 P.M. Fri.–Sat.) has a big wall of bookcases full of Nevadiana; ask the librarian to open them up for you.

The **Bookstore** (1372 Idaho St., 775/738-5342 or 800/580-5342, 8:30 A.M.–5:30 P.M. Mon.–Fri., 8:30 A.M.–5 P.M. Sat.) is the area's only bookseller, with a large selection of new and used books, magazines, paperbacks, books of local interest, and Louis L'Amour books.

Whatever your outdoorsy hankering, Bill Gibson of **Elko Guide Service** (775/744-2277) and his expert guides are sure to put you onto your prey of choice—big game, ducks, turkeys, bass, trout, and more. They also organize summer horseback pack trips and cabin camping adventures.

Other local licensed outfitters serving the Ruby Mountains and beyond include **Nevada High Country Outfitters & Jaz Ranch** (Lamoille, 775/777-3277), **Ruby Valley's Secret Pass Outfitters** (775/779-2232), **Prunty Ranch Outfitters** (775/738-7811), **Humboldt Outfitters** (Wells, 775/752-3714), and **Hidden Lake Outfitters** (Ruby Valley, 775/779-2268).

To get outfitted for your outdoor adventure, visit **Anacabe's General Merchandise** (416 Idaho St., 775/738-3295), owned by the same family for 75 years. Pick up your Elko and Basque trinkets here too.

GETTING AROUND

The **Greyhound** depot is at the Tesoro Gas & Food Store (1950 E. Idaho St., 775/738-3210).

On the *California Zephyr* route, one **Amtrak** (800/USA-RAIL—800/872-7245, www. amtrak.com) train stops in Elko daily in each direction: westbound toward Reno and Northern California, and eastbound toward Salt Lake City, Denver, and Chicago. They stop at two shacks on either side of the tracks at 13th Street. To get there, take the 12th Street overpass and follow the signs.

SkyWest Airlines, the Delta (775/738-5138 or 800/453-9417) connector, operates flights to and from Salt Lake City out of **Elko Regional Airport** on Mountain City Highway at the west end of town. Historical artifacts and black-and-white photos and captions line the wall behind the baggage carousel. Services at the airport include a travel agency, vending machines, a café, and rental cars.

The Ruby Mountains

Southeast of present-day Elko, the rugged Ruby Mountains were traditionally Shoshone territory. They hunted its peaks and collected nuts from its vast pine forests. The Native Americans revered the land, but treaties with the U.S. government deprived them of their traditional homeland. For westbound pioneers, these "Alps of Nevada" represented the beginning of the final arduous challenge in a succession of trials to reach the fertile Oregon and gold-crusted California valleys. On the other hand, this most daunting of obstacles—including a harrowing waterless crossing of the Forty-Mile Desert—came just as supplies had dwindled, pack animals were weak, and determination waned.

LAMOILLE

Lamoille Valley was originally an alternate route to the denuded Fort Hall main stretch of the California Emigrant Trail. Pioneers cut south from Starr Valley near Wells, traveled along the western foot of the East Humboldts on a well-worn Shoshone trail,

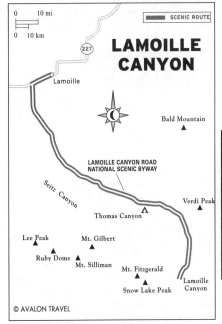

0   10 mi
0   10 km

SCENIC ROUTE

LAMOILLE CANYON

227

Lamoille

Bald Mountain ▲

LAMOILLE CANYON ROAD
NATIONAL SCENIC BYWAY

Seitz Canyon

Verdi Peak ▲

Thomas Canyon ∧

Lee Peak ▲   Mt. Gilbert ▲

Ruby Dome ▲
          Mt. Silliman ▲

Mt. Fitzgerald ▲

Snow Lake Peak ▲   Lamoille Canyon

© AVALON TRAVEL

G. THOMAS/WIKIMEDIA COMMONS

Snow Lake Peak, looking northwest from the Ruby Crest Trail in Lamoille Canyon

availed themselves of Lamoille Valley's water and forage, then rejoined the main trail near Elko. The first homesteaders settled here in 1865, and within a few years a small village grew up around the farms and ranches. The post office arrived in 1883, but it took another 50 years for an actual road to reach the valley.

A favorite place in Lamoille is the **Pine Lodge** (Hwy. 227/Main St./Lamoille Hwy., 775/753-6363, $70–100). The lodge was built in 1947 and recently expanded. Next door is the restaurant and bar (5–9:30 P.M. Wed.–Sun., $25–50) in a beautiful cabin; check out the trophies and fantastic wildlife photography.

Also in town is **The Bitter End Tavern** (Main St., 775/753-6451, 8 A.M.–4 P.M. daily, $15–30), with solid Asian and Italian food, and **Swisher's General Store** (Main St., 775/753-6489, 8 A.M.–7 P.M. daily).

The Presbyterian **Little Church of the Crossroads** (Hwy. 227 and Crossroads Lane), on the corner where the pavement runs out, has a fine steeple and stained glass; it might have the most heavenly location of any church

in the state. It celebrated its 100-year anniversary in 2005.

Red's Ranch (Country Lane, 775/753-6281, $150–270) offers accommodations on a beautiful Lamoille ranch. Activities include horseback riding, swimming, hiking, and skeet shooting, and there's a spa; in winter, Ruby Mountains Heli-Skiing trips operate from the ranch. It has 10 rooms, each with a private bath; reservations are required.

RECREATION
【 Ruby Mountain Heli-Skiing

The Rubies are a mighty 100-mile-long range with nearly a dozen peaks higher than 9,000 feet. They can get 400 inches of snow at higher elevations, and have patches of snow year-round. Since 1976, when the U.S. Forest Service allowed a heli-skiing business to operate in the Rubies, **Ruby Mountain Heli-Ski** (775/753-6867, www.helicopterskiing.com) has introduced adventurous skiers and snowboarders to some of the most pristine snow and awe-inspiring mountains in the world. The helicopter allows the company to put skiers right where they want to be: gentle or extreme terrain, narrow tree-lined runs, or open bowls.

The company offers three-night ski packages ($4,250 pp) that include lodging at Red's Ranch, all meals, ski rentals, helicopter rides, guide service, and a guarantee of 39,000 vertical feet of skiing. One-day packages ($1,375 pp) are available for part of the season. The season runs late January–early April; make reservations as far in advance as possible. They do an average of six runs per day in perfect powder in the 1,500 square miles of terrain.

Hiking

Highway 227 (Lamoille Hwy.) runs southeast from Elko and in 19 miles, just west of Lamoille, meets National Forest Road 660, a scenic drive that winds through Lamoille Canyon. Twenty-nine miles from Elko, Forest Road 660 ends at a parking area and trailheads for the Island Lake and Ruby Crest National Recreational Trails. The **Island Lake Trail** heads north for two miles to 9,672 feet; the trailhead is just to the right at the fork near the entrance to the parking lot. The 40-mile **Ruby Crest Trail** heads south from the far edge of the parking lot; looking up at the top of the mountain, you'll see a prominent V-shaped saddle just down to the left of what can only be called "Bald Eagle Crest." That's Liberty Pass.

The Ruby Crest Trail starts out in primeval forest and quickly leads up into the cirque. It crosses three creeks on nice Forest Service bridges, then passes **Dollar Lakes** (9,600 feet). Before you know it you're at **Lamoille Lake** (9,740 feet), where signs point the way. A hiker in fair shape can make it here in 40 minutes. From here the trail continues upward, twisting and turning toward the pass. **Bald Eagle Crest** has a visible head, shoulders, wings, and in late August even some snow patches that you could imagine to be wingtips. Finally, another 40 minutes above Lamoille Lake, is **Liberty Pass** (10,450 feet), where you can see that the other side is even more beautiful than the side

LAMOILLE CANYON: THE YOSEMITE OF NEVADA

If you go back a mile toward Elko from Lamoille and turn left up Lamoille Canyon, you'll be on the **Lamoille Canyon National Scenic Byway,** a 13.5-mile road that takes you straight into the heart of the Ruby Range. These metamorphic mountains occupy a sacred place in the hearts of most Nevada hikers, climbers, skiers, photographers, picnickers, and writers. Wettest of the high ranges, they combine the best aspects of the nearly 250 other discrete ranges in the Great Basin – long (100 miles) and thin (10 miles), tilted, and geologically labyrinthine with dramatic features all their own. Glacial ice has played a large part in their erosion, with U-shaped valleys, cirques, kettles, valley-bottom moraines, and glacier-swept cliffs. This rainmaker range also supports lush vegetation, including large alpine tundra. In addition, the 8,800-foot level is accessible by car, and you can follow a good trail for days through some of the most beautiful mountain country in the West.

After long debate and some controversy, in 1989 the Ruby Mountains were designated one of 14 official wilderness areas in Nevada. The Ruby wilderness area is mostly in the higher elevations of the mountains, which along with the East Humboldt wilderness area comprises 25 percent of the local U.S. Forest Service ranger district.

Lamoille Canyon Road runs around **Ruby Dome** (11,249 feet), the highest peak in the range. Massive skyscraping outcrops loom high overhead on both sides of the canyon in two continuous lines up the road. Explanatory signs along the way describe the glacial features. In the winter, the road often closes to cars but is alive with snowmobilers and cross-country skiers.

HUMBOLDT VALLEY

you just climbed. **Liberty Lake** and **Favre Lake** await those with more time and energy, as does **Harrison Pass,** 30 miles and several days' hike from the parking lot.

The hiking season starts around June 15 and lasts roughly 12 weeks. You'll meet a few other people on weekdays, but weekends get crowded, especially on the first few miles. Backpackers, however, can leave the crowds behind on any number of explorations to high-country lakes (many filled with trout) and isolated canyons.

For detailed and up-to-date information on campgrounds, hiking trails, and road conditions in the Rubies, call or write the U.S. Forest Service, Ruby Mountain Ranger District, 140 Pacific Ave., Wells, 775/752-3357. Office staff will send you a copy of *A Guide to the Ruby Mountain Ranger District* (very informative) and all kinds of other brochures and pamphlets about the area.

Picnicking

Driving up Forest Road 660, the **Powerhouse** (6,200 feet, $5 per vehicle day-use) picnic area at the mouth of Lamoille Canyon has one group site and four single-family picnic tables, barbecue grills, and pit toilets. There's no water, however.

Terraces, at 8,400 feet, is for picnickers only; it has picnic tables, barbecue and fire pits, vault toilets, potable water, and trailheads nearby.

At the end of Forest Road 660 is **Roads End** picnic area (8,800 feet), the trailhead for the Island Lake and Ruby Crest Trails. The area has parking and one picnic site, water, and toilets, and there is no fee.

Camping

At 7,600 feet, Forest Road 660 passes **Thomas Canyon Campground** (877/444-6777, late May–Oct., $15 single, $30 double), which has 40 paved sites; 30 have tent pads, five are double-family sites, and four are pull-throughs. Facilities include picnic tables, barbecue and fire pits, vault toilets, and water from a pump. The campground is officially open late May–October, but they try to keep a loop open all year, depending on weather conditions. The campground is

situated in a spot in the canyon where downhill is due west, and the sun setting beyond the valley turns the rugged ridges a distinct ruby hue. The mountain range, however, was named for its garnets. Sunrise is right over the cirque, imbuing the canyon with golden light.

South Fork Reservoir

The **South Fork State Recreation Area** is at the South Fork Dam, 16 miles south of Elko on Highway 228. The dam, constructed 1986–1988, is made up of 1 million cubic yards of earth that dam South Fork Creek roughly 10 miles from the Humboldt River. The reservoir, when full, stretches 3.5 miles and covers 1,650 surface acres. The reservoir is surrounded by 2,200 acres of wildlife-filled meadowlands and rolling hills. Swimming, boating, fishing, hunting, wildlife viewing, camping, and picnicking are popular activities. The Nevada Department of Wildlife stocks trout and bass, and the park is known for its trophy-class trout and bass fishery. Facilities include a campground, a trailer dump station, a boat launch, and a picnic area. The 24-site **campground** (off Hwy. 228, 10 miles south of Hwy. 227, 775/744-4346, 14-day maximum stay, year-round, $10) has showers and running water but no hookups. It is on the reservoir shore about two miles from the dam. You can also camp anywhere else you like around the park outside the developed campground; this costs $5 per night, and you can come to the campground to shower. The park is open year-round, but winter access may be difficult due to extreme cold and snow.

Twelve miles south of Elko and 0.5 miles from the South Fork reservoir, the **Ruby Crest Guest Ranch** (Spring Creek, 775/744-2277, $150–300) is also the home of the Elko Guide Service, which offers a wide variety of activities such as horseback trail riding, summer horseback mountain pack trips, fishing and hunting trips, sightseeing and photography trips, and nature tours. Winter activities include cross-country skiing, snowmobile trips, ice fishing, and chukar hunting. Ranch vacations are a specialty, with accommodations ranging from a room at the ranch to rustic log cabins at the base of the Ruby Mountains and tent camps.

Ruby Marshes

South of the reservoir, visit **Ruby Lake National Wildlife Refuge,** open every day from an hour before sunrise until two hours after sunset. This is an unusual sight for the Great Basin Desert—a freshwater bulrush marsh that is host to a large variety of birds, fish, and mammals. Within the 38,000-acre refuge, created in 1938, is a network of ditches and dikes built to manage the riparian habitat. More than 220 species of birds, including trumpeter swans, canvasback and redhead ducks, cranes, herons, egrets, eagles, falcons, and small birds are found in the refuge in a normal year, along with five types of introduced trout and bass. In summer, rattlesnakes and garter snakes stretch out along the roadsides, and sometimes right in the traffic lanes, to get sun. You might see one feeding on a leopard frog, the refuge's only amphibian.

The water is collected up on the porous slopes and peaks of the southern Rubies, then flushed out at the bottom from more than 200 springs into **Ruby Lake,** which, along with **Franklin Lake** farther north, once covered 300,000 acres 200 feet deep in this valley. The current drought has the lakes at their lowest level in 30 years. In 1986, before the drought, the largest bass harvest on record saw 300,000 fish caught; by 1992 the catch was down to a few thousand. Refuge officials say both lakes are at normal levels now; in this desert environment "normal" includes quite a bit of fluctuation.

Take a left at Bressman's Cabin onto the causeway to see the birds, birders, fish, and anglers. Make the big loop around the marsh and rejoin the road at the south end of the East Sump.

Camping is not allowed inside the refuge, but if you head south on County Road 767, you'll reach the **South Ruby Campground** (877/444-6777, $12) at 6,200 feet. It has 35 gravel sites, water, toilets, and an RV waste dump. Most sites have tent pads. Near the Gallagher Fish Hatchery, sites are on a rise overlooking the marsh. Primitive camping is allowed on U.S. Forest Service land 300 feet west of County Road 767 and on Bureau of Land Management land east of the refuge.

Two miles south is **Shantytown,** a small settlement that dates to the 1940s when the Bureau of Land Management leased half-acre parcels for $5 per year. In 1967 the bureau sold off the parcels for $499; they now go for around $30,000. Shantytown has no services.

Wells

Eastbound from Elko on I-80, at the end of the East Humboldt Range, a spot a little northwest of the present-day town of Wells was once a famous camping site on the Emigrant Trail. Called Humboldt Wells for the dozen springs providing freshwater and grass, it was the easternmost source of the Humboldt River. The Central Pacific Railroad established a division point nearby, around which the town, its name shortened to Wells, slowly grew up. You can easily trace the evolution of the business district, from 7th Street at the railroad tracks to 6th Street along old U.S. 40 to the developing exit ramps on I-80. Wells has embraced each transition to keep up with the times.

Mining and ranching have long contributed to the local economy. The Works Progress Administration's 1940 *Nevada—A Guide to the Silver State* has a story about the brutal winter of 1889–1890, when most of the cattle froze or starved to death: "Wealthy stockmen went bankrupt almost overnight, and some were forced to begin all over again as cowboys." More adversity came in the early 1980s, when a con man named Michael Wilwerding set up shop in Wells, claiming he could convert used tires into oil. He got all kinds of tax breaks and state aid money, and he even produced a small amount of oil. But the site turned out to be a secret dump for highly toxic liquid waste, and Wells received the first Superfund money in Nevada to clean up the mess.

Wells is not only a crossroads town where I-80 meets U.S. 93, with excellent facilities for travelers and truckers; it is also a border town of sorts due to its proximity to Idaho and Utah.

SIGHTS

Wells's tourism suffered a potentially fatal blow in February 2008 when a 6.0 earthquake struck, severely damaging the town's historic district on Front Street along the railroad tracks. What was once an 1880s town center of two dozen buildings in various states of preservation is now is a fenced-off safety hazard with little prospect of being repaired.

Front Street

Despite the devastation, the district is worth a look through the fence. Wells's historic section contains the most intact railroad row on the entire original Central Pacific line. This might be your last chance to see the structures. Among the "if these walls could talk" buildings is the **Bulls Head Saloon and Hotel** on the corner. It opened as a log hut on Christmas Eve 1869. You can also see the shell of the Bank of Wells, the town's only depository until 1960. Built in 1911, it was once robbed by a lone gunman. Livery stable owner Harry Tuttle tackled the villain as he made his escape. It was later learned that the robber's revolver featured a carved wooden (and inoperable) cylinder, probably to Tuttle's great relief. You'll also be able to see the **Nevada Hotel,** which was turned into a movie theater until it closed, and the **Coryell Residence,** the oldest house in town.

Casinos

At the junction of I-80 and U.S. 93, the **4 Way Bar, Café, and Casino** (1440 6th St., 775/752-3344) has 150 slots in every denomination, including some with progressive jackpots, and a couple of blackjack tables. **Lucky J's Casino** (193 S. U.S. 93, 775/752-2252) has 50 slot machines in denominations from $0.01 to $1. **Luther's** bar downtown has slots too.

California Trail Back Country Byway

Nearly 100 miles of gravel roads beginning 25 miles north of Wells off U.S. 93 take adventurers on a rugged and informative drive into the heart of the gold rush. Half the route parallels the California National Historic Trail, where you can still see the ruts made by the wagons toting migrants to the California gold fields. Walk the well-marked path taken by 240,000 hopeful pioneers more than 160 years ago. An information kiosk four miles into the byway near the Winecup Ranch tells of the trail's history. The **Bureau of Land Management Field Office** (725 Aspen Way, Elko, 775/753-0200) has information on the route.

East Humboldt Range

The 13-mile road from Wells to Angel Lake makes a lovely drive, especially in spring when the fields along the way are full of wildflowers. It's so pretty that it has been designated an official scenic route, the **Angel Lake Scenic Byway.** However, roads can be treacherous or closed in winter. Piñon pines, mountain mahoganies, and aspens dot the lower elevations, while the surrounding mountains scarps and pinnacles pierce the sky before parting to reveal the lake. On the way to the lake, set up camp at one of the 19 sites at **Angel Creek** (775/752-3357, year-round, weather permitting, $12) or continue to the top of the road to **Angel Lake Recreation Area** (775/752-3357, July–Sept., $27), a 26-site campground and picnic site. Both campgrounds have potable water and restrooms. Keep an eye out for Chimney Rock on the eastern horizon. The trailheads for trails to **Winchell Lake** (10 miles), **Greys Lake** (6 miles), and **Smith Lake** (1 mile) are nearby. These alpine waters are just as beautiful as Angel Lake but much less crowded on summer holiday weekends.

U.S. 93 runs south from Wells along the magnificent eastern scarp of the East Humboldts. About six miles from the highway is a distinct right turn onto a narrow 4WD track up into

THE DONNER PARTY

For most on the grueling overland wagon route to California, the sight of Truckee Lake would inspire determination to complete the journey and begin a new life in the promised land. But for one group of migrants from the Midwest, the snow falling on the Sierra Nevada to the west that greeted their arrival on the lakeshore in October 1846 provided a grim reminder that they were way behind schedule.

Eager to reach California, the party, led by George Donner, put its trust in a "shortcut" discovered by Lansford Hastings. The Hastings Cutoff across the Wasatch Mountains and the Great Salt Lake Desert promised to trim hundreds of miles from the journey. Instead, the new route took the Donner Party 68 days to travel from Little Sandy River, Wyoming, to Truckee (now Donner) Lake. The main California Trail was 28 days shorter, and would have left them plenty of time to cross the mountains before the first snowfall.

Desperate to beat the winter storms that would close the pass until spring, the pioneers were forced to stop for several days to rest their animals and forage for food and water. The extra 100 miles spent traversing the for-bidding terrain of the cutoff and along the Humboldt River, it would turn out, effectively closed their window of escape. Hopelessly snowbound, members of the party built what structures they could – cabins for some, tents made from wagon canvases for others, crude brush *wikiups* for others.

As those who made it across the mountains to Sutter's Fort organized rescue parties, those left behind ate the last of their provisions and turned to boiled ox hides, bones, and tree bark for sustenance. Some of the desperate tried to hike out on makeshift snowshoes. The 10 men and five women quickly ran out of provisions, and eight died. The others made the ghastly decision to eat their fallen comrades. The seven survivors reached safety in late January. Relief parties finally arrived on February 19, 1847, finding 12 dead and 48 clinging to life. The party retrieved 23 survivors, but two children died on the way out. Additional relief parties made their way to the various camps, often finding more evidence of cannibalism.

The tragic events claimed 41 of the 87 members of the Donner Party.

Lizzie's Basin, below the East Humboldts' highest mountain, Hole in the Mountain Peak (11,276 feet). The feature that gave the peak its name is one of the strangest and most compelling in the west. Roughly 300 feet below the summit is a large (30- by 25-foot) natural window in the weak and thin marble of the mountaintop. This hole, oriented east–west, was known as Taindandoi ("Hole in the Top") to the Shoshone and Lizzie's Window to the early settlers, named for the first local to mention the hole.

Pilot Peak

On your way to Wendover through passes in the Pequops and Toanos, to the north you'll see the Pilot Range and its most prominent mountain, Pilot Peak. Named by John C. Frémont in 1845, this is one of the most beautiful and historic mountains in Nevada. Pioneers along the Emigrant Trail focused on it during their brutal four-day ordeal crossing the blazing Great Salt Lake Desert. Finally arriving at Pilot Peak's base, just over the Nevada state line, they found water and grass, the knowledge of which sustained them during the desert trudge to the mountain, and the presence of which replenished them for the next leg to Humboldt Wells. Pilot Peak is classically conical—it looks like a kindergartner's drawing of a mountain, wooded at the waist with a long and tapered *bajada* beckoning to the salt flats in the southeast. It also slopes off to the northwest, pointing to California and the promised land.

ACCOMMODATIONS

Combining the history—and a bit of the bawdiness—of the frontier days with all the modern conveniences of a modern resort, the **Wild**

West Inn (455 6th St., 775/752-3888, $45–65) downtown has brass and wood accents and soothing pastel colors in its 30 rooms. There's also a laid-back bar where you can relax by the fire, shoot pool, or catch a game on the big-screen TVs while sipping a martini or pounding the brews. Have a few and you might even spot the Lady in Red, the resident ghost.

The **Rest Inn Suites** (1509 E. 6th St., 775/752-2277 or 800/935-5768, $44–60), across from the 4 Way, recently renovated its 57 guest rooms and mini suites. All come with free continental breakfast, microwaves, fridges, hair dryers, remote-control TVs, and queen beds.

The other choices are strictly in the budget or chain categories. Good bets include **Griff's Wagon Wheel** (340 6th St., 775/752-2151, $32–45), **Shell Crest Motel** (573 6th St., 775/752-3755, $30–42), and **Lone Star** (676 6th St., 775/752-3632, $30–40). The national chains represented include the **Best Western Sage Inn** (576 6th St., 775/752-3353 or 888/829-0092, $57–95), which was remodeled a few years ago.

RV Parks

The spic-and-span bathhouse and laundry, trees, and greenery between sites make **Mountain Shadows RV Park** (807 S. Humboldt Ave., 775/752-3525, Mar. 1–Oct. 31, $25) one of the coziest, cleanest, and friendliest RV parks on I-80 through northern Nevada. They don't have a swimming pool, but there is a playground nearby. Mountain Shadows contains 38 spaces for motor homes, 33 with full hookups and 13 pull-throughs. Tents are allowed. Reservations are recommended Memorial Day–Labor Day, especially for the pull-throughs.

Depending on how your trip is going, the nearby train whistles are either soothing or annoying at **Crossroads RV Park** (734 6th St., 775/752-3012, Apr.–Oct., $10). The 25 RV spaces with full hookups are smallish but not cramped. The price is right, but a TV room at the office is the only amenity. **Welcome Station** (I-80 exit 343, 775/752-3808, $25) is open June–November and offers 35 spaces; tents are allowed.

FOOD

The **4 Way** (1440 6th St., 775/752-3344, 24 hours daily, $8–15), on the east side of town at I-80 exit 352, has a coffee shop with a resort-worthy 40-item salad bar and big from-scratch breakfasts.

Visitors rave about the espresso and corned beef hash at **Bella's Espresso House** (143 U.S. 93, 775/752-2226, 6 A.M.–2 P.M. daily, $10–20). Basic breakfasts and smoothies also get top marks. Folks seem amazed to find touches of civilization on the road in northeastern Nevada, so they appreciate the gourmet coffee and quaint aprons in the windows. They often have quite different reactions when they discover the owner is the Bella from Bella's Hacienda Ranch, a legal brothel. Families rest assured: The businesses are nowhere near each other.

For Italian, head to **Mamma Miners** (Wild West Inn, 455 6th St., 775/752-3888, 6–10 P.M. daily, $15–25).

INFORMATION AND SERVICES

Wells is a good place to wait for the sun to go down if you're heading west. I-80 aims directly into the fiery orb, which makes shadows of everything other than the blinding sun.

The **Chamber of Commerce** (395 6th St. at Lake St., 775/752-3540, www.wellsnevada.com), in the Kelly Kreations building, has extensive although sometimes outdated information.

You can also stop in at **City Hall** (1279 Clover Ave., 775/752-3355) and read the bulletin boards and rifle the info rack. Next door is the **library** (208 Baker St., 775/752-3856, 11 A.M.–5 P.M. Mon.–Wed. and Fri., 1–5 P.M. and 7–9 P.M. Thurs.).

The U.S. Forest Service office for the **Ruby Mountain Ranger District** (140 Pacific Ave., 775/752-3357, 7:30 A.M.–4:30 P.M. Mon.–Fri.) supplies maps, trail guides, and general information on the Ruby and East Humboldt Ranges. Read the proclamation by Teddy Roosevelt naming Ruby National Forest in 1906, and check out the picture of Hole in the Mountain Peak.

Wendover

Wendover (more properly, West Wendover—the town of Wendover is across the state line in Utah) sits on the western side of what was once Lake Bonneville, which covered a large area of northwestern Utah to a depth of 1,000 feet. The lake had no outlet, and roughly 16,000 years ago, as it shrank and then disappeared (except for what is now the Great Salt Lake), it deposited a smooth layer of salt and other minerals in the lowest point of the Bonneville basin, where the salt flats are now.

The Central Pacific Railroad bypassed this area by 30 miles to the north in the late 1860s, but the Western Pacific Railroad pushed tracks across the salt flats in the early 1900s. Wendover was founded to supply water to the railroad, piped in from Pilot Peak springs, 25 miles west, the only stop with water on the main line for 100 miles.

In 1914 the anonymity of this sleepy railroad village, with its roundhouse, saloon, and railroad-tie cabins, was lost forever. Speedsters discovered the advantageous features of the flats; one Teddy Tezlaff set the first land-speed record driving a Blitzen Benz just under 142 mph and put Wendover in the media and on the map. U.S. 40 arrived in the mid-1920s, the start of Wendover's destiny as a travelers oasis, and Wendover Air Force Base was created in 1940. At 3.5 million acres, it was one of the largest in the world. Pilots, navigators, and bombardiers learned their skills over this range, and the crew of the *Enola Gay,* which dropped the first atomic bomb on Hiroshima, Japan, in 1945, trained here.

Potash (potassium chloride) has been mined from the flats over the years for use as fertilizer; magnesium chloride, a by-product of potash processing, is used in refining sugar beets. And speed freaks have kept coming back with hotter and faster wheels. Jet cars such as the *Meteor,* the *Green Monster,* and Craig Breedlove's famous *Spirit of America* set and reset records;

Breedlove was the first to break the 600-mph mark. Gary Gabolich's *Blue Flame* set a record in 1970 of 622 mph, which held for 14 years until Richard Noble broke it in the Black Rock Desert.

Today Wendover is a booming border town with a backyard that is a shimmering expanse of earth so white that even in the summer's scorching heat, the surface remains cool. Another weird feature is that the heat waves and blinding silver reflection do strange things to radio and TV signals. Also, the bases of telephone poles on the flats become permeated with salt water; when the water evaporates, the salt crystals expand, swelling and splitting the poles. Fierce thunderstorms are caused by the rising heat, but then everything dries and brightens in a matter of minutes. Against such a backdrop, the big hotels and bright lights are as inviting to modern-day travelers as Pilot Peak on the western horizon was to the pioneers of the past.

The white state line is painted across Wendover Boulevard; the Wendover Will statue points at it with two moving arms. As in South Lake Tahoe and Laughlin, the big hotels are on the Nevada side, and low-rise services line the main street next door in Utah.

Note that Wendover is in the mountain time zone, while most of Nevada is on Pacific time; move your watch ahead one hour.

BONNEVILLE SPEEDWAY

To drive on the **salt flats,** take I-80 into Utah, get off at exit 4, and head five miles northeast. Obey the signs carefully if you don't want to have to dig your wheels out of the mud or walk out for a tow truck, and watch for jet cars whizzing around at 500 mph.

Three weeks of official races are held on the flats. **Speed Week** has occupied the third week in August since 1948, with 350 cars and motorcycles participating. **World of Speed** is in September, with 100 cars and bikes.

The **Bonneville Salt Flats World Finals,** held in October, is when the really fast cars come out. The race course has to be prepared from scratch every year, as "temporary Lake Bonneville" inundates the flats with six inches of water November–May and wipes out the markings. But the water's movement also levels the desert, making it perfect for ultrahigh speeds. After a landplane scrapes the surface, clearing an area 80 feet wide and 10 miles long between black spray-painted lines, it's ready to go.

The whole speedway encompasses 28 square miles—3,700 feet wide and 13 miles long, of which about half is normally used in speed trials. The speedway is run by the Bureau of Land Management, which works closely with the event organizers, the Utah Salt Flats Racing Association (801/785-5364, www.saltflats. com) and the Southern California Timing Association (559/528-6279).

CASINOS

Start where it all started in Wendover: right at the state line. The **Wendover Nugget** (101 Wendover Blvd., 800/848-7300) is attractive, big, and classy. The table-game pits deal blackjack, royal match, roulette, craps, three-card poker, and *pai gow* poker under 42-inch TVs tuned to news and sports. The sports book has 18 more 42-inchers and three mammoth projection screens. The nearby bar and food court mean you'll hardly have to move while watching football all weekend. The poker room deals nine tables' worth of various games and limits. The serve-yourself beverage station means never having to wait for a cocktail waitress. And more than 800 of the latest real and video slot machines grace the 47,000-square-foot casino, all with automated player tracking systems, so the comps pile up quickly. The steak house, coffee shop, and buffet provide plentiful dining options.

Right across the street, the **Montego Bay Casino and Resort** (100 Wendover Blvd., 800/217-0049) is part of the Peppermill family that includes the Wendover Peppermill and

the Rainbow. Another resort-class operation, Montego Bay's expansive 40,000-square-foot casino houses nearly 1,000 slots and poker machines and 50 table games, along with a race book, sports book, and poker room. Other top amenities include a shop, a spa, a swimming pool, and four restaurants. The **Peppermill** (680 Wendover Blvd., 775/664-2255 or 800/648-9660) is almost as large: 1,000 slots and 27 tables.

The Peppermill bought Mac's Casino in the mid-1990s and transformed it into the **Rainbow** (1045 W. Wendover Blvd., 775/664-4000 or 800/648-9660), a Wendover-scale version of the Peppermill Reno with a rain forest motif and multicolored neon befitting the casino's name. Since then, the Rainbow has evolved into one of the top stand-alone resorts in town, with 1,000 slots, expanded blackjack, craps, and other games on 46 tables as well as five restaurants, more than 400 hotel rooms, and large convention and entertainment facilities.

The more intimate option in town is the **Red Garter** (1225 Wendover Blvd., 775/664-2111 or 800/982-2111). More than two-thirds of the 363 machines are of the penny, nickel, and quarter variety, and you can usually find low-limit craps, blackjack, and roulette. The sports book and bar is the place to be during football season.

ACCOMMODATIONS

Wendover has more than 1,400 hotel and motel rooms, and there are another 540 on the Utah side to accommodate the overflow, including the chains Motel 6, Best Western, Bonneville, Knights Inn, Days Inn, and others. As you might expect, the casinos are the big hotel players in town. The Peppermill family's three entries are the best of the bunch, with **Montego Bay** (100 Wendover Blvd., 800/217-0049, $59–129) nosing out its sister properties for top honors. Its dark room decor, with café au lait walls and dark chocolate furniture and carpeting, is more noir than stylish, but floor-to-ceiling windows help mitigate the gloominess. By contrast, the bathrooms, highlighted by marble double basins, are bright and cheerful. The 🌙 **Peppermill** (680 Wendover Blvd., 775/664-2255 or 800/648-9660, $45–139) has been renovating its guest rooms in phases. The spiffed-up accommodations are much brighter than those at Montego Bay, with buff and neutral draperies, plush seating, and padded headboards. Bathroom vanities are all granite, and the double queen rooms come with mini fridges. If you're traveling with easily bored teenagers, be aware that there is no Wi-Fi in the guest rooms and no swimming pool at the property. Striking a happy medium decor-wise, the 429 guest rooms at **The Rainbow** (1045 W. Wendover Blvd., 775/664-4000 or 800/217-0048, $55–119) are more colorful in royal blue (east wing) and hunter green (west wing).

The **Wendover Nugget** (101 Wendover Blvd., 800/848-7300, $60–120) offers very basic to luxury guest rooms and suites with jetted tubs. Standard rooms have granite vanities and Southwest decor in dusky rose, sage green, and gold. Deluxe rooms have cherrywood furniture. The Wendover Nugget's guest rooms are not in the same class as its casino, pool, and other common areas; the old gal is due for some renovations.

The **Red Garter** (1225 W. Wendover Blvd., 775/664-2111 or 800/982-2111, $45–69) is the budget option among the casinos. Its 106 guest rooms are plain but clean.

Wendover KOA Campground (651 N. Camper Dr., 775/664-3221 or 800/562-8552, $35–47) is just south of the Red Garter. With 120 sites, it is a big and bustling RV park on the southern edge of town, between the back doors of the Red Garter casino and the wilderness. Tent sites (about $22) are available along with cabins ($44–55). The swimming pool is open spring–fall, and there's a playground, tetherball, volleyball, basketball, horseshoes, a miniature golf course, a rec room, a minimart, and a gift shop to ensure everything you need is at your fingertips.

FOOD

The Wendover Nugget, Peppermill, Rainbow, Montego Bay, and Red Garter all have 24-hour coffee shops, and the food and prices are similar, although the spicy chicken salad at Montego Bay's **Paradise Grill** (100 Wendover Blvd., 800/217-0049, 24 hours daily) makes a satisfying, not-too-filling lunch. The one-size-fits-all mentality extends to the big five casinos' snack bars as well. For casual specialty dining, **Trino's Tacos** (Wendover Nugget, 101 Wendover Blvd., 775/664-2221, 10 A.M.–10 P.M. Wed.–Mon., $8–15) is an authentic treat. If the spice is too much, **Dreyer's Creamery** (101 Wendover Blvd., 775/664-2221, 10 A.M.–10 P.M. Wed.–Mon.) is next door.

Wendover is a snack-bar kind of town. All five major casinos have at least one snack bar, and they're all good and cheap. The one in the sports book downstairs at the Wendover Nugget (101 Wendover Blvd.) is the most comfortable.

It wouldn't be a Nevada resort town without expansive buffets, and Wendover is home to a bunch. The Friday-night Seafood Extravaganza at the **Rainforest** (Rainbow, 1045 W. Wendover Blvd., 775/664-4000 or 800/217-0048), **Grand** (Peppermill, 680 Wendover Blvd., 775/664-2255 or 800/648-9660), and **Oceano** (Montego Bay, 100 Wendover Blvd., 800/217-0049) are cruise-ship expansive and decadent; shrimp fans will think they've died and gone to heaven. The sister properties' buffets all keep the same hours and prices (11 A.M.–9 P.M. Mon.–Thurs., 11 A.M.–11 P.M. Fri., 9 A.M.–11 P.M. Sat., 9 A.M.–3 P.M. Sun., $16–25). The **Nugget Buffet** (Wendover Nugget, 101 Wendover Blvd., 800/848-7300, 11 A.M.–10 P.M. Mon.–Fri., 9 A.M.–11 P.M. Sat., 9 A.M.–10 P.M. Sun., $12–20) is for those who prefer the turf more than the surf. Broiling stations keep the chops and chicken breasts rolling out nightly, complementing the prime rib, crisp salads, and build-your-own root beer floats.

Fine dining starts and stops at 🌙 **The Steakhouse** (Rainbow, 1045 W. Wendover Blvd., 800/537-0207, 5–9 P.M. Sun. and Wed.–Thurs., 5–10 P.M. Fri.–Sat., $25–40).

HUMBOLDT VALLEY

All the steaks and seafood are primo, and the wine selection is the best for hundreds of miles. The peppercorn and cognac–glazed fillet with steamed asparagus, paired with a full-bodied vintage, is manna and nectar. **Bimini** (Montego Bay, 100 Wendover Blvd., 800/537-0207, 5–9 P.M. Sun.–Tues., 5–10 P.M. Fri.–Sat., $25–40) is similar but with more seafood selections. Our favorite is the Bimini trio, with a petite fillet, mini halibut, and shrimp scampi.

The best lobster bisque in town is found at the **Nugget Steakhouse** (Wendover Nugget, 101 Wendover Blvd., 775/664-2221, 5–10 P.M. Wed.–Sun., $25–40).

INFORMATION AND SERVICES

The West Wendover Tourism and Convention Bureau operates the **Nevada Welcome Center** (735 Wendover Blvd., 775/664-3138 or 866/299-2489, 9 A.M.–5 P.M. Mon.–Fri.). Staff not only hand out brochures but also share insiders' tips for making the most of your visit. The Tourism and Convention Bureau promotes Wendover's citywide annual festivals, such as Cinco de Mayo and Independence Day.

The Wendover branch of the **Elko County Library** (590 Camper Dr., 772/664-2510) is open weekday afternoons.

THE GREAT BASIN

The Great Basin, the largest watershed in the country that does not drain into an ocean, covers nearly all of Nevada as well as parts of Idaho, Utah, California, Oregon, Wyoming, and Mexico. At turns remote and self-contained, central Nevada celebrates the history and natural beauty of this unique geological feature.

While much of Nevada panders to the visitor's desire to live fully in the moment, the Great Basin region welcomes those who want to step back into the past. It is home to quintessential icons of the American West: Native American petroglyphs near Pioche and Cathedral Gorge speak of ancient civilizations. The relics of ghost towns like Rhyolite, Goldfield, and Manhattan provide insight into the lure of precious metals and the rush to riches. Sulfurous hot springs, great marine lizard fossils, and the calcite formations of Lehman Caves take travelers even further back to an era before human habitation. Spying on coyotes, eagles, elk, rattlesnakes, and mountain lions reminds us that although it's harsh, the Great Basin has always been a thriving ecosystem. And on a star tour of Tonopah, visitors can gaze up at the diamonds-on-black-velvet sky while contemplating the wonders of the galaxy.

HISTORY

In the early 1920s, the U.S. 50–Lincoln Highway Association was actively competing against the U.S. 40–Victory Highway Association for automobile traffic across Nevada. The northern Victory Highway had the edge: It was the first and always the more

© BETHANY DRYSDALE

HIGHLIGHTS

LOOK FOR (TO FIND RECOMMENDED SIGHTS, ACTIVITIES, DINING, AND LODGING.

(**Nevada Northern Railway:** Not some mildew repository, this "museum" is actually comprised of most everything needed to operate a short line railroad, and just about everything is in working order. Learn about the depot, freight warehouse, 32-mile track, machine shops, roundhouse, and rail cars, then climb aboard Old No. 40 or one of the other powerful steam and diesel engines for a nostalgic ride through ghost towns, tunnels, copper mine remains, and mountainous ridges (page 304).

(**Cave Lake State Park:** Tucked into the Schell Creek Range at 7,300 feet, Cave Lake's wintergreen water is the perfect subject for nature photography and an idyllic backdrop for picnicking, hiking, ice skating, and cross-country skiing (page 307).

(**Ward Charcoal Ovens:** These big furnaces turned native pine and juniper into hot-burning charcoal to feed the area's smelters. Well-built by true craftspeople, the kilns have survived fire, wind, rain, and vandalism. Willow Creek runs through here; it's full of rainbow and brook trout (page 308).

(**Lehman Caves:** Stalagmites, stalactites, and all the other cool formations we think of when someone says "cave," this centerpiece of Great Basin National Park has attracted visitors for more than 125 years. Rangers lead informative hour-long and 90-minute tours (page 314).

(**Echo Canyon State Recreation Area:** Spire-like hoodoos seem to spring from amid the alfalfa fields as you plunge through Horsethief Canyon into Dry Valley. Picnic sites nestle in the shade of sheer canyon walls, and the stream-fed reservoir is stocked with crappie and trout (page 323).

(**Berlin-Ichthyosaur State Park:** A few dozen ichthyosaurs beached themselves and were covered with silt until their fossils were unearthed in the early 20th century. See their calcified skeletons and a life-size 50-foot sculpture, and learn about their ecosystem. The ghost town of Berlin gives a glimpse into a much more recent but just as intriguing part of Nevada's past. The mine is closed for safety reasons, but there's plenty of mine-related ephemera about, highlighted by the well-preserved mill (page 335).

popular byway for travelers after Peter Skene Ogden and Joseph Walker pioneered the route in the 1820s and 1830s. It came to be known as the Emigrant or Humboldt Trail and was used by the vast majority of pioneers who crossed Nevada in the 1840s and 1850s.

The central route, however, had its advocates. Jedediah Smith had blundered across it in 1827, almost dying of thirst, on one of the bravest and most desperate explorations of the American West. After Smith's torturous march, however, it was nearly 30 years before a trail was surveyed through central Nevada by Howard Egan, then mapped by Captain James Simpson four years later in 1859. The Overland Stage, Pony Express, and transcontinental telegraph all used the shorter central route, but the Central Pacific Railroad opted for the Humboldt Trail.

Rough wagon ruts were developed between the major towns along both trails, but when the automobile necessitated actual roads and the new breed of automobile adventure traveler began to go distances on them, constructing statewide highways was an idea whose time had come. Immediately, every town wanted a highway. Savvy promoters began publicizing routes through their towns before government surveyors stepped in and brought some order and logic to the routes. Like the railroads before them, the highways made or broke many small towns in Nevada.

The rivalry between backers of the Victory Highway through Elko, Winnemucca, and Reno and the Lincoln Highway through Ely, Eureka, Austin, Fallon, and Lake Tahoe was sometimes good-natured and

◖ Spencer Hot Springs: The rough road to get here will be worth it when you submerge your aching back and jarred bones into the slate-tiled pool commanding a view of the Toiyabe Mountains in the distance. Another hot spring flows into a big steel tub someone thoughtfully brought (page 337).

◖ Tonopah Historic Mining Park: Look down from a suspended cage into Jim Butler's original diggings, the birthplace of Tonopah's long mining history. On the tour you'll see a two-foot-wide exposed silver ore vein and experience the frisson Butler must have felt when he hit pay dirt not far away (page 343).

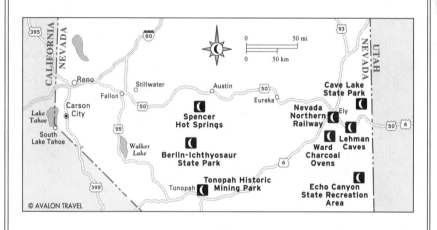

sometimes heavy-handed. The Victory Highway Association installed signs designating its road the "Main Line" across Nevada, and the Lincoln Highway Association set up shop at a Wendover gas station to try to divert westbound traffic to the central route. The northern Victory route won out, and in 1940 was designated a national defense highway, which gave it priority over other roads in the state in terms of expenditures for improvements. U.S. 40 fans combined forces with backers of connecting routes in Utah, Wyoming, Nebraska, Iowa, and California to promote the lengthening of the "49er Trail." The interstate highway era had come.

The Highway Act of 1956 included the creation of I-80, spurring competition among the half-dozen or so towns along the new highway in northern Nevada and cutting into

U.S. 50 traffic even more. Before long, the old Lincoln Highway's fortunes had plummeted to the point where Eastern writers and editors were calling it the country's loneliest road. The story goes that *Life* magazine ran an article telling travelers of the lack of services on U.S. 50 through Nevada, suggesting they avoid the road entirely. The article inspired a lighthearted and extremely successful advertising campaign by the Nevada Commission on Tourism. Far from being apologetic about it, state publicists actually celebrated U.S. 50's remoteness, challenging adventuresome drivers to get off the established interstate and rejoice in the loneliness. The magazine editors hadn't planned it, but they had given the 65-year-old traffic competition between the central and the northern routes across Nevada an unwitting shot in the arm.

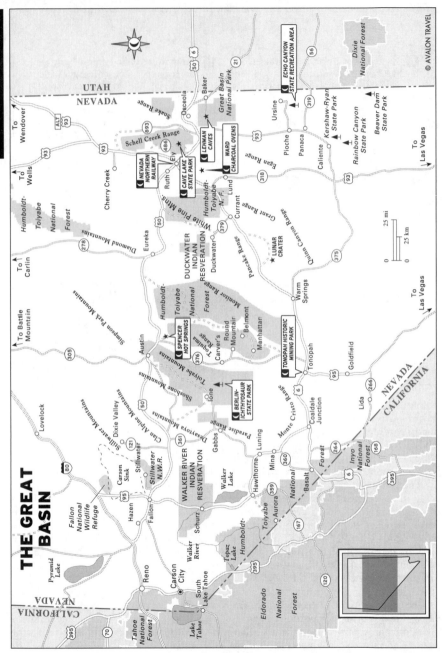

© AVALON TRAVEL

Ely

Ely has certainly benefited from the U.S. 50 "Loneliest Road" campaign. But this town is much more than a mere whistle-stop on an old highway. Indeed, there's much to do in and around Ely. The town's connection to mining is evident everywhere: the open copper pits, charcoal ovens to produce fuel for smelters, and the painstakingly restored Northern Nevada Railroad short line.

Nature and outdoor recreation aficionados will find much to appreciate here too, from picturesque Murry Canyon to the elk herd that returns like the Capistrano swallows year after year to share habitat with visiting bald eagles, ravens, and other fauna.

HISTORY

Explorers Jedediah Smith and Howard Egan, mapmaker James Simpson, the Pony Express, and the transcontinental telegraph all passed through this neighborhood between 1827 and 1861. In 1863 small-scale gold and silver mining began in the Egan Range while it was still part of Utah Territory. In 1866 Nevada's eastern boundary was moved one degree east, which incorporated the Egan District. A year later, Treasure Hill on Mount Hamilton created a stir, attracting the "requisite 10,000" (more likely half that number) boomers. When White Pine County was carved out of vast Lander County in 1869, Hamilton became the county seat. The final bust at Treasure Hill was in 1878. Hamilton's courthouse burned down in 1885, and the county seat transferred to Ely in 1887.

It had long been known that major copper deposits were here for the taking, but the task, especially during Nevada's 20-year depression (1880–1900), remained too unwieldy. Gold and silver could be mined and refined with hand tools and small machines and hauled away in the form of valuable bullion on mule trains. But copper meant tonnage: Every 60 pounds of raw copper required dumping 25,000 pounds of tailings and smelting 6,000

pounds of ore and was worth roughly $10. Only big bucks could buy and bring in the giant equipment required for mining, crushing, smelting, and shipping the astronomical quantities of pay dirt, ore, and refined copper. As is typical, however, it was a couple of little guys who got the ball rolling. David Bartley and Edwin Gray, copper miners from California, appeared in September 1900, secured a grubstake, and started digging into a hill in the Egan Range just up from Copper Flat. They went 300 feet in and 200 feet down and discovered the richness and vastness of the deposit.

Within two years the original mine had been opened into a pit and the immense smelter had been located at McGill, 12 miles north of Ely. The Nevada Northern Railroad operation, however, remained based in East Ely, and track connected it with the pit at Ruth, the smelter at McGill, and the main line at Cobre.

Thus began Nevada's longest-lived and most prolific mineral venture, lasting a full 70 years. The granddad Liberty Pit expanded to more than a mile long, half a mile wide, and 700 feet deep. The dizzying descent to the bottom eventually required 14 miles of track. In the mid-1960s the mine hit the $1 billion milestone, but the ore started to thin, profits began to sag, and new pollution regulations finally shut down the mine in 1979. The smelter closed a couple of years later, and the railroad ceased operating in 1982.

In 1986 local politicians, the Chamber of Commerce, and the White Pine Historical Railroad Foundation convinced the mine's owners to donate the railroad property and equipment to the town; the trains have been running and the yard has been a museum since 1987. In addition, Great Basin National Park was created 70 miles east, and a new state prison was built just outside of town. A few gold and silver mines still operate in the area.

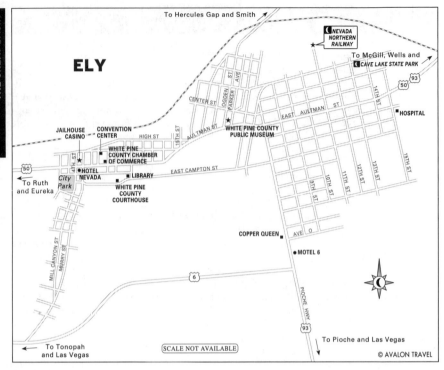

© AVALON TRAVEL

SIGHTS
🎧 Nevada Northern Railway

While most museums offer a glimpse into the past, the Northern Nevada Railway transports visitors back 110 years to relive it. The railway museum (1100 Ave. A, East Ely, 775/289-2085 or 866/40-STEAM—866/407-8326, www.nevadanorthernrailway.net, 8 A.M.–5 P.M. Mon. and Wed.–Sat., 8 A.M.–4 P.M. Sun., $4 adults, $2 ages 4–12, free under age 4) actually encompasses the entire Nevada Northern rail yard, its facilities, and the rolling stock. The tour, one of the most thrilling in the state, takes you through the most complete and authentic working remains of any short-line railroad in the country—and then you get to ride on it.

Altogether there are more than 30 buildings here from the 1906–1907 era, including an old water tower and sand and coal bins. Start your exploration of this workhorse operation at the old depot, built in 1907 with local sandstone and restored to its original grandeur. Check out the ticket office and big black-and-white historical photos.

From the depot, walk by the freight barn, the oldest building in the complex, dating to 1905, past the bus barn and master mechanics offices, and then into the engine house, where most of the equipment is stored: locomotives, cabooses, a passenger coach, a rotary steam-driven snowplow, a steam crane, and track-repair cars. Next stop is the rip-track building, or car-repair shop. Old No. 40 lives here. This steam engine was restored in 1939 and almost immediately retired after Nevada Northern passenger service was discontinued, having transported nearly 5 million people over a 35-year period. You'll learn how the engineer and the fireman used the valves, gauges, faucets, pipes, boiler, and controls to get the behemoth stoked and rolling. Behind the Ghost Train are a converted flatcar, a Pullman sleeper, and a passenger car.

By now you're itching to fire up a train and light out for the territory. Weekends April–November and daily Memorial Day–end of September, the No. 40 and the No. 93 steam engines or No. 109 and No. 105 diesels pull passengers on the 105-minute Keystone and Adverse routes ($24 adults, $15 ages 4–12, free under age 4, $10 surcharge to ride in the caboose). The Hiline diesel is brought out for the trip to Adverse, 11 miles north. Schedules may change from year to year, so call ahead. The Hiline trip is a relaxing ride as the train rocks gently to and fro on its trip north toward McGill along a low eastern rise of the Duck Creek Range above Steptoe Valley.

The Keystone ride (diesel or steam power) parallels Aultman Street up the hill for a great view of downtown and Ely's red-light district. Then it parallels U.S. 50 through Robinson Canyon and passes through Tunnel No. 1, blasted out in 1907. The canyon broadens into Lane Valley, where the train goes by the Lane City ghost town, site of the original strike in 1869. The steamer then runs up to the copper-tailing mountains just this side of Ruth, then turns around.

A snack bar in the last car sells drinks and snacks. The museum also offers a variety of special-event train rides, including the popular Polar Express at Christmas, a Fourth of July Fireworks and Barbecue Train, Sunset at Steptoe (with wine tasting), and the Haunted Ghost Train. Call for schedules and prices; advance reservations are required.

You can also charter the equipment for special runs. You can even rent the engines by the hour and receive instruction on driving the confounded things. Advance reservations are required, and you must do it on days the museum is operating. Call or write for schedules and reservations.

Bristlecone Convention Center

The remains of the world's longest-lived organism are on display at the convention center (150 6th St., 775/289-3720 or 800/496-9350)—depending on your viewpoint, a testament to advances in climatology or to the willful destruction of the earth's precious and unique resources. A cross-section of the 5,000-year-old bristlecone pine, dubbed Prometheus, occupies a framed place of honor. It was cut down by a graduate student studying climate history with the approval of the National Forest Service. It had lived at the tree line on Wheeler Peak, Nevada's highest, now a focal point of Great Basin National Park. In fairness, the student, Donald Curry from the University of North Carolina, had no reason to believe the tree was the oldest in existence. Still, the felling remains controversial among scientists and environmentalists alike. The whole Prometheus story is recounted in Jim Sloan's excellent *Nevada—True Tales from the Neon Wilderness.*

White Pine County Public Museum

Opened in 1959, the eclectic and unstuffy White Pine County Public Museum (2000 Aultman St., 775/289-4710, 9 a.m.–3 p.m. Mon.–Fri., 10 a.m.–2 p.m. Sat.–Sun., donation) is near East Ely. Outside is Nevada Northern rolling stock, a drilling rig, and the original Cherry Creek depot, which was transported to the museum in 1991. Cherry Creek, like much of the area around Ely, was an important mining district in the 1870s and 1880s. The museum pays tribute to this legacy with a comprehensive 300-specimen mineral collection. Among the pieces on display are samples of gold, silver, and copper ore, polished semi-precious gemstones, petrified wood, and ancient marine fossils.

The museum displays diverse holdings, including a large collection of Hesselgesser dolls, a model of a prehistoric bear whose bones were discovered in a nearby cave, Indian baskets, Baker's one-room schoolhouse, a jail cell, a 1917 xylophone, and turn-of-the-20th-century furniture.

A great introduction to Ely, the museum also

BRISTLECONE PINE FAQ

Are bristlecone pines really the oldest living things on Earth?

In 1964, only six years after Edmund Schulman of the Arizona Tree-Ring Research Group published an article in *National Geographic* announcing the discovery of bristlecone pines, a scientist doing research on Wheeler Peak found the tree called Prometheus, later determined (when it was felled by a graduate student and the Forest Service) to be 4,900 years old. This ancient organism was older, by more than 1,000 years, than the largest California sequoia. It predated the pyramids in Egypt by 1,200 years.

How do they live so long?

In his excellent and lyrical *Trees of the Great Basin,* Ronald Lanner comments that in the case of the bristlecones, "Adversity breeds longevity." Because these trees inhabit such a harsh environment − at the highest elevations, on exposed and rocky slopes, bearing the full brunt of the elements − they enjoy a suitable lack of competition; only limber pine and Engelmann spruce keep these timberline ancients company. Also, since bristlecone stands are somewhat sparse, fire presents less danger. Finally, these slow-growing trees produce an extremely dense wood, which is highly resistant to infection, parasites, and decay.

How do they die?

A very little at a time. Even 3,000-year-old trees continue to be reproductively active and bear cones. Incredibly, the inexorable forces of erosion finally overtake their mountain habitat and expose the root system, which dries out and rots or becomes susceptible to fungus or parasites. The upper limbs connected to the lower roots then die off one by one. Next, the wind and rain scour off the bark, leaving a bleached and polished trunk. Still, 90 percent of a bristlecone pine can be dead while, in Lanner's words, "a single sinuous strip of living bark connects the occasional live limb to the occasional live root."

Also, an old bristlecone can stand for 1,000 or so years after dying off completely.

What does science learn from the mighty memories of these trees?

Thankfully, scientists have developed core-sampling techniques that enable them to "read" the rings without having to cut down the whole tree to do it (although Prometheus wasn't so lucky). Bristlecones are sensitive to drought conditions, which restrict their ring formation. In this way, these trees provide dendrochronologists a natural calendar of climatic events dating back nearly 9,000 years using long-dead trees. When you consider that scientific weather records have only been kept for the last 100 years, it becomes clear that the bristlecones add immeasurably to our knowledge. In addition, the trees can help us measure the action of erosion itself.

© BETHANY DRYSDALE

Bristlecone pines have been dated to 5,000 years and older, making them the oldest living organisms on earth.

offers maps, brochures, postcards, souvenirs, and books.

Murals and Sculpture
The White Pine County Museum proudly displays the first of two dozen **murals** (www.elyrenaissance.com/muralmap.html) commissioned by professional artists or undertaken by local residents. The museum's mural, on an outside wall, depicts an early Fourth of July celebration. Other realistic murals, mostly along Aultman and Clark Streets between Mill and 10th Streets, also pay homage to Ely's past. There are tributes to Basque sheepherders, the Pony Express, mining, Italian immigrant labor, railroading, and others celebrate small-town life: the joys of children, high school spirit, and more. Sculptures are interspersed with the murals, giving another artistic perspective on Nevada history. Check out the sculpture of the Shoshone woman gathering pine cones (Clark St. and 8th St.).

Conclude your tour with a look at the restored homes in **Renaissance Village** (6th St. and Ely St., June–Sept.) that explore the cultures of the various people that built the town. Most Saturdays in fall, the village hosts a farmers market; cultural demonstrations, art festivals, concerts and more find a home here throughout the summer in 10-seat courtyard.

Success Summit Loop
North on U.S. 93, six miles past McGill, follow the long white pipeline running for nine miles from Duck Creek Reservoir parallel to the highway along the lower slope of the Duck Creeks. The pipeline delivered nearly 300 million gallons of water to the smelter and still supplies all of the town's water. The former copper mine's owner, Kennecott Copper Corp., still owns the pipe and the water, and in 1994 threatened to shut off the flow to the town in order to redirect it to a 3,500-acre project to restore Steptoe Valley, covering mill waste with dirt and vegetation. After an uproar in the town, the company decided to use nonpotable water for the restoration.

Take a right on Highway 486 and head through **Gallagher Gap,** on the other side of which the road cuts south. Picturesque **Duck Creek Ranch** is three miles off to the right, and **Bird Creek** Forest Service campground is off to the left, up into the Schell Creeks. This is a classically beautiful eastern Nevada ranching valley, with **Timber Creek** Forest Service campground four miles east, and **Berry Creek** campground five miles east from the junction at the end of the pavement. Any of these campgrounds (June–Sept., $8) provide access to productive elderberry and chokecherry bushes and trout streams in the area. The fruit is free for the picking, but if you try your fishing luck, make sure you have a Nevada license and trout stamp. Haul in your own firewood and boil creek water before you drink it.

The road now turns rocky and rough and can support speeds of only 20 mph, in some places 10 mph. In a few miles, there is an unmarked fork in the road—go right. You descend into Boneyard Canyon, then up to aptly named Success Summit (if you haven't slid off the road, ruined your suspension, or had a flat tire), which has great views. The growing season is short, but if you've timed it right, you'll be rewarded with the sight of vibrant wildflowers. This is also where Nevada's largest elk and deer herds are found, so keep an eye out for them; they are most often seen in the early morning and evening or at night. From here the road switches back about a dozen times and descends along Steptoe Creek to **Cave Lake State Park,** where the pavement resumes after 25 miles of rough road.

Cave Lake State Park
This is one of the most beautifully situated parks in Nevada. Perched high in the Schell Creek Range at 7,300 feet, the mint-green lake is backed by a sheer slope and stocked with rainbow and German brown trout. An earthen dam maintains an average lake depth of 20 feet, at the deepest 60 feet. Two campgrounds have a total of 36 sites: Both the first campground as you approach from Success Summit, **Elk Flat** (775/867-3001, May–mid-Oct., $14), and **Lake View** (775/867-3001, year-round, $14), farther on, have heated showers and flush

toilets. With more than 100,000 visitors to this park yearly, these sites fill up fast.

Steptoe Creek Trail parallels the road for three miles from the park entrance to the lake. Cave Springs Trail, a moderate five-mile hike, meanders throughout the surrounding hills.

◖ Ward Charcoal Ovens

Coming down from Cave Lake, turn left (south) onto U.S. 93/50/6 and go a few miles to the historic sign for the Ward Charcoal Ovens. Turn right (west) onto a well-graded gravel road, which can support speeds of 40 mph, and go six miles to Cave Valley Road. Turn left and enjoy the view of the beehive-shaped ovens lined up in the desert, hemmed in by a broken ridgeline.

The Ward Mining District was founded in 1872, and a San Francisco company began digging in 1875. These six charcoal ovens, the largest in Nevada, were built in 1876 to supply smelters with superhot-burning fuel in order to refine the complex lead-silver-copper ore. The mills shut down in 1879, a big fire razed the town in 1883, and the post office closed in 1887. Only $250,000 in silver was reportedly recovered. The kilns, however, built by a master mason, survived it all and lasted through another 100 years of the elements and vandalism.

Each oven is 30 feet high and 27 feet wide at the base, with a door, window, and chimney hole. Each oven held 35 cords of piñon and juniper wood stacked inside; the openings were shut with iron doors, and a fire was started. By controlling the fire and using small vents around the base of the ovens to limit and regulate the amount of oxygen feeding it for 13 days, tenders charred the wood to perfection and then smothered the fire by closing all the vents. Each oven yielded 300 bushels of charcoal per batch.

Ward Charcoal Ovens State Historic Park (775/867-3001 or 775/289-1693, $7) has camping, ATV and interpretive hiking trails, and access to Willow Creek, a tiny stream with cagy rainbow as well as brown and brook trout.

Six beehive furnaces at the Ward Charcoal Ovens, outside Ely

© BETHANY DRYSDALE

Willow Creek Campground ($14) has two pull-throughs and 12 smaller sites for rigs or tents. Water is available May–September.

Ely Elk Viewing Area
Heading south from Ely for 11 miles on U.S. 6/50/93 brings you to this mile-long corridor where you can pull off the highway to view a diverse variety of wildlife, including the largest herd of elk in Nevada. They return here year after year during both the March–April and October–November seasons to feed and rut. The area is also home to golden eagles, ravens, black-tailed jackrabbits, and chipmunks. Bald eagles arrive in late fall and spend the winter here as well.

CASINOS
The action in Ely centers on the corner of Aultman and 5th Streets. The **Hotel Nevada** (501 Aultman St., 775/289-6665 or 888/406-3055) is your only option in White Pine County if you're interested in hold 'em, three-card poker, or blackjack. More than 200 slot machines will happily gobble your pocket change. There's a 24-hour restaurant, and the bar is especially lively at times.

Across the street, the **Jailhouse** (211 5th St., 775/289-3033 or 800/841-5430) is all machines: 146 of them in denominations a penny to a dollar along with games from traditional reel slots and video poker to keno, spin poker, and multigame machines. There's a sports bar in the casino, so you can toast your good fortune or drown your sorrows, as the case may be.

Out on the Pioche Highway, the **Copper Queen** (805 Great Basin Blvd., 775/289-4884) has slots, both vertical and horizontal, but no table games. It's the only casino in the state that shares a room with the motel pool. The pool and 80 slots are housed in a 9,000-square-foot atrium area.

The **Holiday Inn Prospector** (1501 E. Aultman St., 775/289-4607 or 800/750-0557) opened in 1995 and has expanded to 100 slots in the lobby and a café.

There are no craps in Ely—in fact, there isn't a craps game on U.S. 93 for nearly 500 miles in eastern Nevada between Jackpot and Las Vegas.

ACCOMMODATIONS
Nearly two dozen lodging options offer more than 650 rooms at quite reasonable rates. Most of the older and less expensive places are bunched along Aultman Street between 3rd and 15th Streets; some newer ones are on U.S. 93 South (Pioche Hwy.).

The six-story ◖ **Hotel Nevada** (501 Aultman St., 775/289-6665 or 888/406-3055, $35–100) is among the oldest hotels in the state and has an appropriate exterior with neon slot machines and a big die-cut Unknown Prospector, a combination of the two most enduring and recognizable images of the state's identity. This 67-room piece of Nevadiana was the tallest in the state (six stories) when it was built in the 1920s. It's still the tallest structure in town. Guest rooms are small but charming. Some of the better guest rooms are named for and decorated with Hollywood memorabilia of entertainers such as Gary Cooper, Jimmy Stewart, and Mickey Rooney. Other decorations pay tribute to cowboys, hunters, and motorcyclists.

Across the street is the **Jailhouse** (211 5th St., 775/289-3033 or 800/841-5430, $58–70), which offers a total of 60 "cells." There's a small weight room and spa.

The **Ramada Inn/Copper Queen Casino** (805 Great Basin Blvd., 775/289-4884 or 800/851-9526, $60–120) has an interesting lobby. Walk around the front desk; the slots stand between it and the pool and whirlpool tub. Have a drink downstairs in the barroom, or walk upstairs and lounge on the deck. This is the only casino in Nevada that has a pool in the middle of it. Guest rooms are warmly decorated in burgundy and navy; bathrooms are utilitarian, but other amenities lend a touch of home: a free newspaper, free Wi-Fi, and free microwave popcorn in the room.

Unexpectedly, a turn-of-the-20th-century hearse greets guests in the lobby of the **Prospector Hotel & Casino** (1501 E. Aultman St., 775/289-8900 or 800/750-0557, $69–120). Hallways and public areas are decorated with lithographs and mementoes of Nevada's past. Some rooms are themed: Asian, hunter, miner, and risqué.

Towering six stories, the Hotel Nevada was the state's tallest building when it opened in 1929.

Motels near the casinos include **Motel 6** (770 Ave. O, 775/289-6671 or 800/4-MOTEL-6—800/466-8356, $40–55), across from the Copper Queen, the largest in town with 99 rooms; and the **Four Sevens** (500 High St., 775/289-4747, $40–60), behind the Jailhouse and across from the Bristlecone Convention Center.

For motels, our picks in Ely include the weathered-brick and wood-shingled **Rustic Inn** (1555 Aultman St., 775/289-2800, $40–75), which despite the rustic look is quite modern and spacious; and the **Bristlecone Motel** (700 Ave. I, 775/289-8838 or 800/497-7404, $60–100), which is spotless with country quilt–like bedspreads and a Western motif.

If you're not averse to chain motels, Ely is home to some fine examples. Only a few years old, **La Quinta** (1591 Great Basin Blvd., 775/289-8833, $80–120) will send you on your way with a killer free hot breakfast. Rooms are decked out in gold and maroon and come with free wired and wireless Internet, mini fridges, and microwaves. The

pool area and fitness center are immaculate. **Best Western–Park Vue** (930 Aultman St., 775/289-4497 or 888/297-2758, $45–90) has clean, comfortable, budget-motel furnishings and decor as well as a complimentary breakfast. As in nearly all motels in this part of Nevada, small pets are welcome.

For infinitely more atmosphere, book in at the **Steptoe Valley Inn Bed and Breakfast** (220 E. 11th St., 775/289-6991 or 877/289-6991, $81–99), just up 11th Street from the Nevada Northern depot. Built in 1907 to house the Ely City Grocery, the inn still reflects that dusty Old West era. Inside, Victorian paint, wood trim, tile, marble, fixtures, and glass details stand out from the 1990 full restoration. The inn features a library upstairs among the five guest rooms named for early Ely settlers. Downstairs is a comfortable living room and the bright breakfast room. All guest rooms have private baths and balconies. Among the rooms are the feminine McGill, with a white wrought-iron bed with dusty pink and white palette and lace curtains; and the yellow-and-peach Gunn

& Thompson, overlooking the rose garden. Breakfast—your choice of the specialty entrée of the day or traditional eggs with sausage or ham—is served along with fresh-baked breads and pastries beginning at 7 A.M.

RV Parking

Valley View RV Park (65 McGill Hwy., 775/289-3303, $26) opened in 1976, and its mature landscaping—tall trees and thick, lush, grassy central park—is a definite advantage. On the other hand, the sites, though level and large enough, could use a facelift. It is friendly, convenient, and usually quiet. There are 46 spaces for motor homes, all with full hookups, and 12 pull-throughs. Tents are allowed. Accessible restrooms have flush toilets and hot showers; public phones are available. Reservations are recommended spring–fall, especially for the pull-throughs.

Holiday Inn/Prospector Casino RV Park (1501 E. Aultman St., 775/289-8900, $15), on the east side of town, has 22 spaces with full hookups, six of them pull-throughs, for a very attractive rate. Guests are welcome to use the swimming pool at the Holiday Inn next door. All the spaces are first come, first served; the park often fills up by early afternoon. Nearby road traffic noise can be a nuisance.

KOA of Ely (Pioche Hwy., 3 miles south of Ely, 775/289-3413 or 800/562-3413, $32–40) is the largest RV park in all of eastern Nevada. Mature cottonwoods rim the perimeter, and Chinese elms line the sites. Ward Mountain in the Egan Range broods directly behind the park, which sits up above the valley a little, so at night you can look down at the lights of town. There are 80 spaces for motor homes, most with full hookups; 38 are pull-throughs. The overnight RV sites are set on dirt or gravel pads. Tents are allowed in a separate grassy area. Groceries, a playground, and volleyball are available, but there is no pool.

FOOD

You're in for a new experience (we hope!) when you dine in your own prison cell in the **Cell Block Steak House** (Jailhouse, 211 5th St., 775/289-3033, 5–9 P.M. daily, $15–25). Hardly bread and water, this is top-of-the-line beef, lamb, and seafood at reasonable prices in a fun and unstuffy atmosphere. Plan to do a little hard time when you're in town.

This is cowboy country, so you won't find much radicchio salad or soy mousse on the menus, especially at **Evah's Restaurant** (Copper Queen, 805 Great Basin Blvd., 775/289-4884, 6 A.M.–9 P.M. daily, $10–20). Red meat and buttery pasta are served up in generous portions; damn the cholesterol. The Hotel Nevada **coffee shop** (500 Aultman St., 775/289-6665 or 888/406-3055, 24 hours daily, $5–10) delivers a huge selection of simple American diner fare at the counter or in booth seating.

Locals love ◖ **La Fiesta** (700 Ave. H, 775/289-4114, 11 A.M.–9 P.M. daily, $10–20) for Mexican food with some authentic kick. They serve their homemade tortilla chips with a spicy cabbage salsa—hot and cool. Other safe bets in town include the **Silver State** (1204 Aultman St., 775/289-8866, 24 hours daily, $10–20) for primo diner food such as fried chicken, country fried steak, and apple pie; and **Twin Wok** (700 Park Ave., 775/289-3699, 11 A.M.–10 P.M. daily, $10–15) for Chinese food in huge portions. The hot and sour soup and fried wontons make a fine lunch.

Finally, for a real old-fashioned treat, stop in at ◖ **Economy Drug** (696 Aultman St., 775/289-4925, 9 A.M.–6 P.M. Mon.–Fri., 9 A.M.–5 P.M. Sat.) and pull up a stool at the soda fountain. The milk shakes, floats, sodas, and malts are heavenly, and the lunchtime sandwich specials are pretty good too.

INFORMATION AND SERVICES

The White Pine County **Chamber of Commerce** (636 Aultman St., 775/289-8877, www.whitepinechamber.com) can point you in the right direction and answer questions. The **library** (950 Campton St., 775/289-3737) is next to the courthouse.

Great Basin National Park

Officially designated in October 1986, Great Basin is the only national park in Nevada. It was carved out of Humboldt National Forest and surrounds Lehman Caves National Monument. National Park status was first proposed in 1922 when Lehman Caves was designated a National Monument, but the idea was defeated by a powerful lobby of mining and ranching interests in the remote area. A second movement gained momentum in the late 1950s, but local opposition this time included miners, cattlemen, loggers, hunters, and even the U.S. Forest Service. A 28,000-acre Scenic Area was the result of a compromise on the proposal for a 150,000-acre park; the paved road up to 10,000 feet on 13,000-foot Wheeler Peak was laid in 1961.

Finally, in the mid-1980s, after the copper mine closed and unemployment in White Pine County reached 25 percent, the White Pine Chamber of Commerce resurrected the issue. This time the political climate was more favorable, and another broad compromise was worked out: Boundaries were drawn to exclude private mining land, grazing was permitted, and the 174,000-acre park proposal was cut in half to its present 77,000 acres.

One of the nation's smallest national parks, Great Basin receives an average of 80,000 visitors per year. It gets crowded on weekends during the short peak season, and late arrivals can be turned away from the cave and campgrounds. All the park's campgrounds are first come, first served, but you can make advance reservations by phone for the cave tours—a wise idea on summer weekends. Many visitors treat the park as a day-trip detour and view the caves, drive to the peak overlook, and then continue on their way. Since it's extremely remote from urban areas and interstate highways, there is little of the carnival atmosphere that pervades many other national parks in the West. For anyone acquainted with often crowded parks like Yosemite, Grand Canyon, and Yellowstone, Great Basin seems like solitude personified.

Great Basin National Park was created to preserve and showcase a preeminent example of the vast Great Basin ecosystem, which covers 20 percent of the Lower 48 land mass and almost all of Nevada. The Snake Range packs a more diverse ecology into a discrete mountain range than any of the other 250 ranges in this vast western desert. All five Great Basin biological zones occur in the roughly 8,000 feet from the valley to Wheeler Peak, the second-highest point in Nevada. The range contains the only permanent glacier-like ice in the state. It boasts a large forest of 4,000-plus-year-old bristlecone pines, the oldest living creatures on the planet. Within the quartzite limestone are corridors of caverns that have been carved by water over millions of years. The park's major attractions are easily accessible: There is a road to 10,000 feet, the highest in Nevada; day-trip trails to the peaks, ice, and bristlecones; and rough 4WD tracks to the most solitary backcountry. The air is fresh, the views are grand, and the vibe is reverent in this hallowed temple of the wilderness.

Tiny Baker (population 382), five miles from the park entrance, is the nearest settlement. Ely, the largest nearby town, is 70 miles by road.

SIGHTS
Driving Tour

Head east on U.S. 93/50/6, past Comins Lake and the cutoffs for Cave Lake State Park and the Ward Charcoal Ovens. The road starts to climb into the piñon pines and junipers of the **Schell Creeks**. Right over **Connors Pass** (7,780 feet) the very big **Snake Range** comes into view. **Wheeler Peak** (13,063 feet) towers above tree line, with permanent snow around the peak. For a short distance, as you cross **Spring Valley** toward the Snake Range, you're heading right at Wheeler Peak.

At Majors Junction, U.S. 93 cuts south (right) at the fork; follow U.S. 6/50 left. Continuing east, the road drops into Spring Valley between the Schell Creek Range and behind and the Snake Range ahead. The road up Spring Valley is worthy of an afternoon's scenic drive on its own.

An alternate route is a right turn at the sign for **Osceola**. This very rough gravel road is passable, though just barely, with a low-clearance vehicle. The road climbs straight up into the Snakes and past a cemetery and old gold pit. Some rusty mining junk and ramshackle shells of buildings are scattered around near the top. Placer gold was discovered here in 1872, and hydraulics were used to sluice out the nuggets and dust. Primitive grinders were employed in the early days, and later a small stamp mill was built. In order to supply more water for sluicing, a ditch was dug in 1889 around the mountain from Lehman Creek on the west side of the Snakes. The rough road rejoins the highway on the east side of the mountains.

If you don't take the Osceola detour and stay on the main highway, you make a big loop north, through the low point of the Snakes, **Sacramento Pass** (7,154 feet). To the north, **Mount Moriah** rises to a peak 1,000 feet lower than Wheeler Peak. Nevada's fifth-highest peak, Mount Moriah is now a designated Wilderness Area, one of 14 created in 1989. Its 82,000 acres feature a one-square-mile rolling-tundra Table at 11,000 feet bordered by bristlecone pines. Hampton Creek Trail is a steep 15-mile round-trip hike to the summit of Mount Moriah that requires a 4WD vehicle; Hendry's Creek Trail is a 23-mile round-trip backpack hike up to the Table. For complete descriptions and instructions for these trails, see *Nevada Wilderness Areas* by Michael White.

Turn off U.S. 6/50 at the boarded-up Y Truck Stop onto Highway 487 and take a look-see around **Baker.** At a site just north of Baker, archaeologists have discovered the ruins of a settlement of the Fremont Indians, who were based in central and southwestern Utah around the time the Anasazi were predominant in southern Nevada. The Fremonts had the largest population of any native civilization in the area, about 10,000 people at its height. The Baker site is believed to be a western outpost of the agricultural Fremont. Like the Anasazi, they also disappeared from their western frontier around 1270 because of a 20-year drought. Three pit houses, pottery, arrowheads, and artifacts have been found.

Next, double back to the road up to the park. Keep an eye peeled for Doc Sherman's whimsical roadside art gallery that extends from Baker to the park entrance. On the left is *Horse with No Name,* a skeletal horse at the wheel of an old jalopy; on the right is *It's All Downhill from Here,* a bony bike rider with flame-red hair, and *Too Tall Tony,* a desert rat whose legs were too long for his coffin, along with several others.

Visitors Center

The park visitors center (775/234-7331, www. nps.gov/grba, 8 A.M.–5:30 P.M. daily summer, 8:30 A.M.–4:30 P.M. daily winter) is where you buy tickets for the **cave tour** ($8–10 adults, $4–5 ages 5–15 and over age 54), if you haven't already bought tickets in advance. Allow time to study the exhibits on park flora, fauna, and cave formations and to enjoy the 3-D Landsat thematic image. You could easily spend an hour just looking at the books, slides, and videos.

Borrow a trail guide from inside and take the Visitors Center Nature Trail at the side of the building. Stop first at **Rhodes Cabin** to see the historical exhibit on the caretaking of the national monument. Then stroll the gentle 0.3-mile trail, stopping to read about juniper and piñon pine, mountain mahogany and mistletoe, limestone and marble, and cave entrances.

In front of the visitors center and down the hill slightly are some giant apricot trees that were planted more than 100 years ago. They produce a ton of very fine sweet and juicy fruit the second week of August. Help yourself; they're better than candy.

Various activities are centered around the visitors center; check the bulletin board or with a naturalist when you arrive. Next door to the visitors center is a gift shop (Apr.–Oct.), stocked with quality artwork and books as well as T-shirts and other take-homes. Quite a bit of the inventory comes from Nevada, some from the immediate area: silver and turquoise jewelry by Jan Everitt of Austin and Erman Blossom, a member of the northern Paiute from Pyramid Lake, and T-shirts by Virginia City's Tom Gilbertson.

At the **Lehman Caves Cafe** (775/234-7221, 8 A.M.–5:30 P.M. daily summer, 8:30 A.M.–4:30 P.M. daily winter, $10–20) the food is gratifyingly good, and considering it's a monopoly, it is pretty reasonably priced. Breakfast and lunch are served, and homemade soups are distinctive and well-seasoned. Try the "incredible ice cream sandwich," a double scoop crammed between a giant pair of oatmeal cookies ($3.75), easily big enough for 2–3 people.

The Western National Parks Association operates a **bookshop** (775/234-7331, ext. 268) in the park visitors center and another at the Lehman Caves Visitors Center.

◖ Lehman Caves

Five hundred million years ago, nearly everything everywhere was under water. Nevada's sea was shallow, teeming with creatures like the ichthyosaur (now Nevada's official state fossil). The eons of pressure changes, incessant heating and cooling cycles, erosion, and calcification acted on that primordial seabed, pushing into mountain ranges, changing sandstone into marble, and cutting deep gashes in the rock. The result, countless calcite dribbles later, is the Lehman Caves (775/234-7331, ext. 242, 9 A.M.–4 P.M. Mon.–Fri.), with ornate and incredible stalagmites, stalactites, "soda straws," and other features.

The true story is lost to history, but depending on which legend you believe, either Absalom Lehman, his brother, his hired hand, or his horse discovered the cave in 1885—unless Native Americans had found it 800 years earlier, as bones found in the cave suggest. Lehman explored the cave and altered it; additional changes since the federal government took it over include entrance and exit tunnels and trail improvements.

Lehman Cave tours are of varying lengths; options include a 60-minute Lodge Room tour and a 90-minute Grand Palace tour ($8–10). Each tour usually departs every two hours 9 A.M.–4 P.M. daily in summer, and twice 9 A.M.–3 P.M. daily in winter. You can reserve space on a tour in advance, which is a good idea if you're planning a weekend visit. If you don't reserve in advance, there is a chance the cave's visitors center will have no tickets available.

The National Park Service has also surveyed

40 other caves and rock shelters scattered throughout the park between the 8,000-foot and 12,000-foot levels. A permit system allows people to visit some of these "wild caves" while others (especially those containing sensitive bat habitats) are off limits. Contact the park's Resources Management department (775/234-7331, ext. 228) for information on exploring the wild caves.

HIKING AND CAMPING

The park has four developed campgrounds (775/234-7331, $12). Three—Baker Creek, Creek, Upper Lehman Creek, and Wheeler Peak—are open generally May–October, although water may not be available early and late in the season. The Upper Lehman Creek campground has one wheelchair-accessible site, and the Baker Creek campground has two. Lower Lehman campground is open year-round, although there's no water in winter. Fees are reduced when water is unavailable. All four campgrounds are first come, first served. Claim your site early on summer weekends. The park also has primitive camping facilities (free) along Snake Creek and Strawberry Creek roads; campsites have fire grates and picnic tables, and only a few have pit toilets. They're open year-round but are often muddy in spring and snow-covered in winter. These sites are difficult to reach and are definitely not for RVs.

Baker and Johnson Lakes

Baker Road leaves the main park road just below the visitors center and runs south, then west, up to 7,000 feet. It's a good gravel road that supports speeds of 25 mph through piñons and aspens and past massive stone outcrops. A little less than three miles from the main road is **Baker Creek Campground** (775/234-7331, May–Oct., $12). Three loops contain 34 sites, two of them wheelchair accessible, with outhouses and running water. The choice spots are under big evergreens right on the creek.

A little more than three miles from the campground is the steep, 13-mile **Baker Lake and Johnson Lake Loop Trail.** Both lakes are five miles from the trailhead with one mile

between them over Johnson Pass (10,800 feet) of Pyramid Peak (11,921 feet). Much of this area in the central and southern part of the park is generally accessible to high-clearance vehicles on dirt roads from Highway 487 near Garrison, Utah. Several points on the trail provide 360-degree vistas, including inspiring looks at Baker Peak and Wheeler Peak.

Just short of Johnson Lake, you'll see the remains of a mining camp. Johnson Lake Mine has been reduced to the ruins of a few cabins, some discarded mining equipment, and a 1,000-foot aerial tramway that transferred tungsten ore from the mine to a packing station where it went by mule to the on-site mill. Tungsten was important during World War I, when it was alloyed with steel for use in radio transmitters.

A well-graded gravel road heads into the southeast corner of the park from south of Garrison. At the end, a 1.7-mile trail brings you to **Lexington Arch,** a six-story natural limestone arch. Ask at the visitors center about the **Big Wash** hike. No permits are required for backcountry hiking or camping, but the National Park Service strongly encourages you to fill out a voluntary backcountry registration form.

Lehman Creek and Wheeler Peak

Just below Baker Creek Road, down from the visitors center, take a left onto Wheeler Peak Road and go up the mountain toward the peak. **Lower Lehman Creek Campground** (775/234-7331, year-round, $12) at 7,500 feet has 11 sites, mostly used by trailers and RVs, and pit toilets. **Upper Lehman Creek Campground** (775/234-7331, May–Oct., $12) is 0.25 miles ahead at 7,800 feet, with 22 tent sites and better scenery. The trailhead for Wheeler Peak Campground is here. If there's no water at the campsites, get it from the Lehman Caves Visitors Center, 3.5 miles down the road.

Continuing up this extraordinary road (RVs or vehicles over 24 feet not recommended) at around 8,500 feet are a couple of curves, then the peak, from tree line to summit, takes your breath away. At 9,000 feet the views get even better. The road keeps climbing, with the peak ahead and the vast valley behind, until you get to the end of the road at the parking lot for the trailheads and the loop through **Wheeler Peak Campground** (775/234-7331, June–Sept., $12). The campground is 13 miles from the visitors center at a breath-sucking 10,000 feet. It has 37 sites and pit toilets.

Warm up your hiking boots on the **Theresa Lake** and **Stella Lake** trails, which you can do in an aerobic hour or a lethargic two hours. The grades are easy, the lakes are pretty, and the peaks are mighty. After acclimating on this loop, head up to the **bristlecones** and the **ice field,** 2–3 hours round-trip (4.6 miles) and not especially strenuous. Signs point the way at the forks and intersections with the other trails. An interpretive trail 1.4 miles from the trailhead circles the bristlecone sanctuary, where these ancient beings cling to life with a tenacious yet precarious grip. The spirituality here is palpable, and hikers unconsciously adopt a light step and a reverent tone as they move in awe through this divine forest. Don't be shy about caressing the trees—the barkless wood, burnished by thousands of years of wind, rain, snow, and sun, invites touch. The bottlebrush needles are soft, sensual, and surprisingly young feeling. The living parts of the trees are triumphal, but even the dead parts are beautiful. This forest is exquisite proof that wood can remain attractive long after death and does not demand to be buried.

Past the temple of the pines, the trail becomes steep and rocky, but your perseverance over the next mile will be rewarded. In no time you enter the cirque, a valley carved by the extant glacier, visible at the end of the valley. The Great Basin's only glacier, it is bookended by sheer cliffs, the summit of Wheeler Peak in full view. One of the many political skirmishes in the effort to create a national park here was over whether the ice field was a true glacier. Ranchers and miners opposed to the park derisively called it a snow field. Park supporters rallied behind the little patch of ice, insisting it was Nevada's only glacier and thus needed the protection of national park status. According to park supporters, it has now been determined that Wheeler's ice does move, so technically it is a glacier. But anyone who has spent time in Alaska or Yukon might think it looks more like an ice cube.

Wheeler Peak Trail branches off near Stella Lake and climbs 3,000 feet in four miles; it is steep, high, and exhilarating. This trail is open year-round, but in winter you'll need winter gear such as crampons to hike it.

ACCOMMODATIONS AND FOOD

The tiny town of Baker (population 55), five miles from the park entrance, has a couple of options for accommodations and a bite. The **Silver Jack Inn** (10 Main St., Baker, 775/234-7323, $49–69) is the most whimsical and offers several options for recreation, meals, and rooms. The proprietor can rent you guidebooks and cross-country skis, snowshoes, or mountain bikes for individual exploration or lead you on sightseeing ventures into the surrounding mountains. If the seven standard motel rooms don't do it for you, you can get an efficiency apartment ($69), an RV space with hookups and showers ($22), or a primitive campsite ($8).

Morning coffee along with home-baked muffins and scones await each morning at the inn's 'Lectrolux Gallery Café & Movie House. The restaurant can also supply lunches for your outings into Nevada's outback and will provide something hearty and eclectic on the menu for dinner when you return, along with a soothing scotch, brandy, or wine. They screen movies during dessert and coffee on Wednesday and Saturday evenings. Check out the gift shop and art gallery: The Great Basin T-shirts, among other things, are original, and there's a fine selection of art, both fine and folksy.

The 29 remodeled guest rooms at **Border Inn** (Hwy. 6/50, 13 miles east of the park entrance on the Utah-Nevada line, 775/239-

7300, $50–60) are paneled and plain. The bunkhouse-like hotel also has a restaurant (6 A.M.–10 P.M., $10–20), a bar, slots, a pool table, RV parking, and gas. The gas pumps are in Utah, where transportation taxes are lower, making it about 15 cents cheaper than in Nevada.

Similar remodeled guest rooms and a bar can be found at **Whispering Elms** (195 Baker Ave., Baker, 775/234-9900, $57), which has horseshoe pits and satellite TV. It also has RV parking ($25–30) and tent camping ($17).

Hidden Canyon Guest Ranch (2000 Hidden Canyon Pkwy., 15 miles south of Baker, 775/234-7175) is a complex with lovely lodge rooms ($119), "condotel" suites ($245), cabins ($58), and campsites ($30). It offers horseback riding, hiking, fishing, and other Western activities. Packages can be arranged to include meals, activities, and tour guides.

Cathedral Gorge and Vicinity

CATHEDRAL GORGE STATE PARK

Yet another unexpected delight in eastern Nevada, Cathedral Gorge State Park (U.S. 93, near Panaca, 775/728-4460, $7) is more a place to exercise your imagination than your legs and lungs. It's a wash that has weathered and eroded into a fantasyland. What separates this 1,578-acre area from countless other washes and gulches is that its walls are made of chalky-soft suede-colored bentonite clay that has created pillars, gargoyles, dragons, and of course, cathedrals. Baroque features—lacy, filigreed, fluted, and feathered—decorate its walls.

One million years ago, streams washed silt, clay, ash, and other volcanic and igneous products from rock outcrops surrounding the valley into a Pliocene freshwater lake. These sediments were eventually deposited on the lake bottom up to 1,500 feet deep, the coarser materials at the edges with finer materials in the deep middle. Faults in the mountains at the southern end of the lake allowed the water to seep away slowly, carving the canyon deeper along the fault line. After the lake dried up and exposed the bed, the elements did the rest.

More recently, petroglyphs in Meadow Valley indicate Native Americans used this lush region for hunting and traveling. In the 1920s, Shakespearean plays, local pageants, and fairs used the gorge as a dramatic backdrop, and the area was designated a state park in 1935.

Exploring the Park

Park at the pullout near the sign at the main part of the gorge. Notice the horizontal line running along the formation; the darker rock on top is compacted clay hardened by lime from decomposing limestone, while the light greenish rock below is the siltstone from the middle of the lake. The hard clay protects the

Wind, water, and time carved the spires, hoodoos, and monuments at Cathedral Gorge.

soft siltstone from accelerated erosion, which has already worn away roughly 1,000 feet of deposits from the lakebed.

From here, hikes disappear into Moon and Canyon Caves. They're not really caves but areas where the canyon walls become so narrow that they almost create natural bridges. The best time for photos is in the evening because the cliffs face west. A one-mile trail continues from the end of the paved road to the base of Miller Point Overlook; a four-mile nature trail leads through the desert and around to the campground; signs along the way identify plants and animals in the lower gorge.

The historical sign for **Bullionville** stands between the entrance and Miller Point. The discovery of silver deposits spurred the founding of Bullionville in 1869, and the town's remains are still visible east of the park entrance. The Bullionville Cemetery is north of the park entrance, off U.S. 93. Beyond Miller Point, the road begins to climb into the juniper forest on the slopes of the Highland Range. In a few miles the road passes the Castleton Cutoff, then in three miles the left fork leads into Pioche.

Information and Services

Cathedral Gorge is open year-round. There is a visitors center at the entrance that has interpretive exhibits and park information. Be sure to check out some of the ranger programs that cover topics ranging from bird-watching to stargazing. You'll also find shaded picnic areas in strategic locations, drinking water, and restrooms.

The **campground** (maximum stay 14 days, $17) is a pleasant spot with introduced Russian olive and locust trees. In spring, the Russian olives bear a little yellow flower that gives susceptible locals a bad case of hay fever; birds love to eat the pea-size olives but can't quite digest them. There are 22 developed sites for tents or self-contained motor homes up to 30 feet; the two pull-throughs can handle longer rigs. Piped drinking water, flush toilets, showers, sewage disposal, public telephones, picnic tables, grills, and fire pits are provided. Bring your own firewood, or buy it at the campground.

Another mile north from the main entrance of Cathedral Gorge is **Miller Point Overlook,** with a superlative view of the whole wash plus four sheltered picnic tables, pit toilets, and explanatory signs.

PANACA

One mile south of Cathedral Gorge and 15 miles north of Caliente (turn east from U.S. 93 onto Hwy. 319) are lush irrigated fields of grain and vegetables, apple orchards, barns, farm equipment, haystacks, and grizzled farmers. Panaca hasn't changed much in the 130 years since it was founded in 1864 by Mormon missionaries and colonists. The town's name was an anglicized version of *pan-nack-ker,* a Southern Paiute word meaning "metal" or "wealth." The Panaker Ledge was actually at Pioche, and the boomtown of Bullionville thrived slightly north of Panaca 1870–1875 until it was supplanted by Pioche.

The Mormons, miners, and Native Americans were wary neighbors. The miners were disrespectful of the Mormons' water rights, religious beliefs, and lifestyle; the Mormons disapproved of the miners' lawlessness; and both groups infringed on the Native Americans' ancestral home. A mutual dependence arose as the miners provided an excellent market for Mormon produce, and both groups defended their common interests against Indian threats. The fate of the valley farmers and the mountain miners became intertwined. Pioche and Panaca today remain excellent reminders of that frontier tension. Pioche settled into a semblance of law and order by the mid-1870s, and real quiet arrived with the inevitable decline of the mining boom.

Serious dust was stirred up, however, after an 1866 survey revealed Panaca to be within Nevada's boundaries, not Utah's or Arizona's, to which the townspeople had already paid taxes. Panacans thought it unjust for Nevada to try to collect back taxes from them, and many left in protest, but the town itself persisted.

Driving Tour

Highway 319 becomes Main Street as you enter

Panaca. At 4th Street, peek into the **Mercantile,** known to locals as the Panaca Co-op. Mormons built the institution in 1868. Across the street another adobe building, **Panaca Ward Chapel,** served as a Mormon meeting house, school, and community center. Built in 1867, it is the oldest building in town.

Go up a block and take a left on 5th Street. Notice the brick-and-stone Italian Victorian house on the east corner; this was the second house of N. J. Wadsworth, a member of one of the founding families. Take the first left onto E Street, then past the gymnasium and ball field, which dominate the town and where you'll find the whole populace during a basketball or baseball game. The street runs past schools and the church, all presided over by the incongruous but striking chalk formation known as **Court Rock.** This public square is a graphic example of how seriously this town takes its education, religion, and civic responsibilities.

Go right at the stop sign and take the first left on D Street. Go to the end and take a left onto 2nd Street at the **Henry Matthews** house. Look back for a view of this pretty house, built in stages from crude adobe to wood-frame cottage to two-story Victorian home. Heading north one block to Ernst Street and turning east is the way to **Panaca Spring,** whose warm freshwater is part of Meadow Valley Wash, which makes farming possible in this valley. It's deep and warm, with kids swimming in it at all hours and a beautiful view of the valley and mountains beyond.

Practicalities

If you're looking to stay in Panaca, there is only one option—but the **Pine Tree Inn and Bakery** (412 N. 3rd St., 775/728-4675, $70–85) is a lovely option for relaxation or adventure. Guest rooms are decorated country style with quilted spreads on the four-posters. Guest rooms have big flat-screen TVs and wireless Internet, and a library full of page-turners and plenty of bright, quiet reading nooks is available. Outdoors, choose from horseback riding or guided ATV tours offered by the inn.

The innkeepers can rustle up a steak dinner afterward or pack a lunch for the ride. A hot Western breakfast complete with scrumptious muffins gets the day started, and the on-site bakery will grubstake you for the next leg of your journey with fresh bread, big cookies, and a variety of cakes and pies at reasonable prices.

PIOCHE

They came in waves from Virginia City across the Great Basin of central Nevada— prospectors in search of rich lodes, speculators in search of boomtown profits, and camp followers in search of new lives to lead. Pioche, in the Highland Range, mushroomed in 1869 atop a promising ore body in the rush to riches eastward across the new state.

Pioche (pee-OACH) was named for a San Francisco financier who bankrolled the original strike and quickly gained notoriety as one of the most dangerous towns on the Western frontier. As in Bodie and Tombstone, the distinction between law enforcement and lawbreaking in Pioche depended on which side of the gun you were standing. And since Pioche attracted the most violent and lawless the frontier had to offer, inevitably groups of "regulators" were organized to protect the various claims, further contributing to the mayhem. Pioche's enduring (and almost certainly exaggerated) claim to fame is that 40–50 men died of violence or accidents before anyone lived long enough to die of natural causes. Records show that two men were punished during this time. During a particularly rowdy celebration in 1871, a fire got out of control and touched off an explosion of 300 powder kegs, killing a dozen, wounding many more, and destroying nearly the entire town.

By the mid-1870s, after the Lincoln County seat was transferred to Pioche and the population had increased to 12,000, some order had been established on the streets and in the mines. One explanation credits the influx of women to the town; they married the miners and put them on short leashes. In fact, it got to the point where men were afraid of "walking

THE EXTRATERRESTRIAL HIGHWAY

While the federal government advises everyone to "move along, there's nothing to see here," self-styled ufologists, conspiracy theorists, aviation buffs, and seemingly the Nevada Department of Transportation (NDOT) beg to differ. Getting into the spirit of UFO sightings and the oh-so-secret federal facility at Groom Lake, NDOT in April 1997 designated the desolate 92-mile stretch of Highway 375 the "Extraterrestrial Highway," putting up four signs to that effect. During the ceremony, Nevada governor Bob Miller quipped that some of the signs should be placed flat on the ground "so aliens can land there." Governor Miller also commented that the designation shows Nevada has a sense of humor. This is UFO country, folks, and the town of **Rachel** is its headquarters.

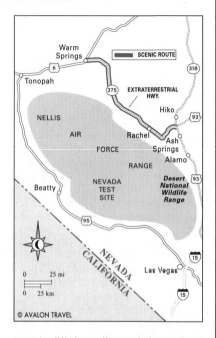

When you cruise in from a remote stretch of state highway it all seems a little unlikely that this tiny hamlet of less than 100 souls (not counting extraterrestrials), a leftover development of the aborted MX missile project of the early 1980s, garnered almost as much publicity in the late 2000s as Las Vegas. Rachel was at the center of a controversy that encompasses two Air Force facilities, government secrecy, military land grabbing, UFOs, toxic waste, and a computer programmer from Cambridge, Massachusetts.

It all started in 1989 when Bob Lazar, a self-described former engineer at the Los Alamos labs in New Mexico and a Nevada brothel owner, told a Las Vegas journalist that he'd been working on extraterrestrial aircraft at a top-secret Air Force facility near Rachel known as Papoose Lake. Although a media inquiry turned up no record of Lazar's claimed degrees from MIT and Caltech nor any mention of him in scientific circles (the government erased the records as part of its cover up and to discredit him, Lazar said), his story launched a feeding frenzy that turned up Papoose Lake and a second previously unknown Air Force installation, Groom Lake, also known as Area 51, in the far northeastern corner of the vast 3.5-million-acre Nellis Air Force Range.

Meanwhile, UFO fans from around the planet descended on Rachel, convinced that the an-

swers to all their questions rested somewhere in the alkali flats of dried-up Groom Lake.

All the hoopla attracted the attention of Glenn Campbell, a young computer programmer from the East. He made the pilgrimage to the now infamous "black mailbox" (29 miles south of Rachel) serving the Medlin ranch, a landmark where UFO enthusiasts gathered to await a close encounter. Campbell never caught a glimpse of any intergalactic spacecraft, but he did see fighter jets galore doing bombing target practice over the nearby desert and simulating dogfights in the big sky. But it wasn't until the Air Force, under media scrutiny from around the world, denied that Groom Lake even existed that Campbell found his true calling.

Rachel townsfolk lined up on both sides of the UFO uproar, some claiming to have seen and been visited by saucers, the rest convinced that any extraterrestrial worth his higher intelligence wouldn't be bothering with a dusty village in an unfriendly desert on a small planet. But Pat and Joe Travis, owners of the Rachel Bar and Grill, changed its name to the **Little A-Le-Inn** (pronounced "alien") and redecorated it in an ET motif with a giant wooden saucer outside and extraterrestrial-themed trinkets (bumper stickers, doormats, cigarette lighters, and T-shirts) for sale inside. Try an Alien Burger or a Beam Me Up, Scotty (made from Jim Beam, 7 Up, and scotch). There are also 13 motel rooms ($45–58) and free RV parking (775/729-2515, no hookups or dump station).

While the UFO research story won't die, military aircraft testing seems a more plausible raison d'être for the facilities at Papoose and Groom Lakes. According to what's been pieced together from the sketchy reports of local eyewitnesses, former Groom Lakers, and government whistle-blowers, the installation has field-tested top-secret aircraft since the 1950s, including the U-2 spy plane, the Stealth series, the Manta craft used in the first Gulf War, and the Aurora speed demon, rumored to fly at 5,000 mph. Reports say that the three-mile-long runway is the longest in the world. In the past decade, some former employees of the base have filed a class-action suit, claiming that the Air Force's mishandling of toxic materials affected their health. Finally, the Air Force has applied for an additional 4,000 acres of land surrounding the base for security; this would effectively seal off all known vantage points of the facility that officially doesn't exist.

One current theory is that, as a result of the notoriety received by Groom Lake and Area 51, the Air Force has surreptitiously moved whatever was there to an even more secret location but maintains the illusion of security at Groom Lake to keep the curiosity and interest focused there where it can do no harm, rather than somewhere else where the truth may accidentally be discovered.

Nevada took a good-natured jab at the federal government with this designation on the section of Route 375 that runs near the "top secret, but absolutely not UFO-related" Area 51.

down the street for fear of coming home married," and the Single Men's Protective Association was formed in 1876 to help "the bachelors withstand the wiles of the fair sex."

Meanwhile, especially during the freewheeling days at the peak of the boom, local politicians developed a fondness for spending money—to build the courthouse, for example—far beyond their capacity to raise revenues. They floated bonds, printed local scrip, and quickly doomed the county to 70 years of debt. Part of the problem was that the citizens weren't interested in paying taxes, especially in the decline period of the late 1870s. This prompted the sheriff to assume tax-collection responsibilities, which helped line his pockets and those of his cronies. The 1871 courthouse was finally paid off in 1938.

Pioche's boom-and-bust cycles have continued ever since. Mines and short lines came and went; a small boom developed when cheap power reached Pioche from Hoover Dam just before World War II. The war effort also kept the mines open and producing manganese and tungsten. Since then, Pioche has managed to survive in large part due to highway traffic, some mining, ranching, and farming. Historical sites, the visitors center and library, two museums, and the tramway structure will keep you happily occupied for an afternoon.

Sights
DRIVING TOUR
U.S. 93 forks south of town, giving you the choice of two routes: the higher, westerly road, Highway 321, goes left into Pioche, 6,060 feet up in the hills; the lower, easterly road bypasses the town. The lower bypass runs under the **tramway buckets** suspended on a cable between the mine and the mill. The upper road takes you right to the **headframe** of the aerial tramway built by the Pioche Mine Company in 1923. The weight of the buckets carrying ore down to the mill helped propel the empty buckets back up to the mine. A 5-hp engine, about the size of the motor in a large washing machine, got the whole thing going. Visit the 80-foot-high structure to see where the small

motor turned the little pulley that turned the big pulley that helped propel the cable and its dozens of buckets. The whole monstrous structure—headframe, gears, cable, and buckets—is in the same spot it was in when the tram was shut down for the last time some 70 years ago. Climb around on it at your own risk; if the risk doesn't bother you, it's jungle-gym heaven.

Stop in at the **Commerce Cottage** (752 Main St., 775/962-5544, 11 A.M.–3 P.M. Mon.–Fri.) for a historical map and plenty of handouts on Pioche. The building was a store before the turn of the 20th century, in 1940 became the first town library, and became home to the Pioche Chamber of Commerce in 1984. Down Main Street from the visitors center is the current **library** (93 Main St., 775/962-5244, noon–4 P.M. Mon.–Fri.).

Take Main Street through town, and at the fork of Main Street and Pioche Street are the **Commercial Club** and **Amsden Building,** both of which managed to survive fires, explosions, and gunfights and are now two of the oldest buildings in Nevada. Two doors down is the old firehouse.

Next door is the **Thompson Opera House.** The interior still has the original 1873 footlights, seats, and scalloped picture frames, plus an adit to an old mining tunnel running out the back. The theater hosted performances, movies, and community events during the town's boom years.

Down the street are the **Wells Fargo Building** and a **miner's cabin,** with historical information signs in front. Take a right on Comstock Street to get to the cemetery with its renowned Boot Row. Find the grave of John H. Lynch, killed by James Harrington, according to his tombstone, in an argument over a dog on July 6, 1873. Harrington wounded three other men at the same time. (Must've been a hell of a dog.)

MILLION DOLLAR COURTHOUSE
The courthouse (69 Main St., 775/962-5207, 10 A.M.–3 P.M. daily, donation) is one of Nevada's ultimate symbols of the boom-bust economy and mentality. Originally designed to

cost $16,000, graft and construction overruns forced the price up to $26,000 when it was finally completed in 1876. Discounted bonds to finance the construction immediately put the county deep in debt, from which it took nearly 70 years to recover. By 1890 officials had yet to make a payment on the principal, and $400,000 in interest had accrued—nearly 70 percent of the assessed value of the entire county. The state refused to allow the county to default, and the commissioners refinanced the debt, by then $650,000, in 1907. They finally finished paying off the bonds in 1938, four years after the building itself had been condemned and the same year a new courthouse was constructed.

The building is now home to the Lincoln County Museum. Walk in, sign in, and the volunteer will take you through the historical photo room, sheriff's office, DA's office, and assessor's office. Upstairs are the fire department's room, the judge's office, and the courtroom. The judge's bench and nearby chairs are originals. Out the back door is the jailhouse; the middle cell has the original bunk and leg iron. The jailhouse is possibly the most graphic evidence remaining of the tough hombres that hung around this town 120 years ago. New to the courthouse in 1994 was a series of large watercolors painted in the late 1800s–early 1900s by R. G. Schofield, a watchmaker and jeweler by trade.

◀ ECHO CANYON STATE RECREATION AREA

Echo Canyon State Recreation Area (775/962-5103, maximum stay 14 days, no reservations, $7) has a reservoir and a campground; it is four miles east of Pioche on Highway 322 (the Mount Wilson National Back Country Byway), then eight miles southeast on Highway 86. This narrow two-lane road winds around and drops fast into the beautiful and inappropriately named Dry Valley, part of the Meadow Valley Wash water system. The road passes well-irrigated and verdant alfalfa fields, then approaches the small earthen dam stretching across Echo Canyon on the far side of the valley. When you arrive at the park, take a right to get to the ranger station and group picnic area; drive straight ahead and past the earthen dam, which is about 40–50 feet high and holds back a fairly large body of water, to get to the **campground** (775/962-5103, $17), which has 33 big sites, is lush with tall sagebrush, has piped drinking water, flush toilets (turned off at the end of Oct.), sewage disposal, public telephones, picnic tables under roofed shelters, and barbecue and fire pits.

The reservoir is fed from the northeast by a stream that flows through a long, narrow farming community dedicated to growing hay. The canyon in which the park is set has high walls of volcanic tuff that has been eroded and carved by wind and rain. The reservoir is stocked with rainbows and crappies, and the campground has a fish-cleaning shed. Boating costs $10 per day.

The road continues up the wash into Echo Canyon under big white sandstone walls, 100 feet high with eroded pinnacles. It emerges in Rose Valley, another beautiful little basin full of alfalfa fields hemmed in by hills and canyon walls. At Rose Valley Ranch is a T intersection. To the left the road climbs a mile back up to Highway 322; instead, take the road right through another lesser canyon into Eagle Valley for more farm-canyon scenery.

Continue on this good dirt road all the way to **Ursine,** a stunning little farm town with huge cottonwoods and fruit trees, idyllic farmhouses, horses, and sheep along the creek that runs through. Watch for kids and dogs in the road in this pastoral village. The road rejoins the pavement of Highway 322 again at the far end of Ursine; take a right. **Eagle Valley Resort** (775/962-5293, $21) has 50 spaces for motor homes, 36 with full hookups and no pull-throughs. A few cabins ($79–105) are available as well. The grocery store and bar, which has slots and video poker, are across the highway. Beyond the resort, the road winds around **Eagle Canyon** past the precarious gravel- and slate-covered slopes of the White Rock Mountains until you reach Spring Valley Recreation Area.

SPRING VALLEY STATE PARK

Spring Valley (775/962-5102, $7) has the same facilities as Echo Canyon: a dam, a reservoir, and a campground. A canyon cliff makes up about 15 percent of the dam wall. This park is bigger and a bit more crowded. There's pretty good fishing for rainbow trout at the 65-acre Eagle Valley Reservoir, evident in the large number of anglers around the lake. There are plenty of spots to stake out around the shoreline, or you can rent a boat from **Big Fish Boat Rentals** (775/962-1405 or 775/728-4692). Ice fishing is growing in popularity here: Die-hard anglers bundle up and trek onto the reservoir, which freezes over for about two months in the winter. Docking and launching facilities are available. The reservoir water is muddy, precluding swimming.

Horsethief Gulch Campground (775/962-5102, $17), just west of the reservoir, has 36 campsites for tents or self-contained motor homes up to 28 feet. Shade ramadas, picnic tables, and fire pits come with each site. The campground also has flush toilets, showers, piped drinking water, a fish-cleaning station, and public telephones.

The road continues along the reservoir, although the pavement ends at the dam. The road, the Mount Wilson Back Country Byway, continues far into the wilderness; you'll need the *Nevada Map Atlas* to explore back here. The drive, with panoramic views of junipers, piñons, aspens, and ponderosas as well as wildflowers and wildlife, is beautiful in the spring.

PRACTICALITIES

Pioche has a dozen motel rooms and a few hotel rooms. Rooms at the **Overland Hotel** (662 Main St., Pioche, 775/962-5895, $58–95) cater to outdoorsy types, with leather furniture, hunting and fishing memorabilia, and wood-frame beds. Others have garden or Victorian themes. The saloon has plenty of slots and video poker along with one of the coolest bars anywhere. The mahogany bar top dates to 1868 and fronts a solid cherry back bar. Built in England in 1863, it is sturdy

© BETHANY DRYSDALE

With its lengthy history, it's perhaps unsurprising that Pioche's Overland Hotel's guests have reported seeing ghosts prowling the hallways.

enough to have survived a trip around the Horn, the 1906 San Francisco earthquake, shipment across the Sierra Mountains, and the 1948 Pioche fire that destroyed the original Overland Hotel.

The **Hutchings Motel** (411 Lacour St., Pioche, 775/962-5402, $50–70) has lower rates and less character. The **Silver Cafe** (673 Main St., Pioche, 888/344-6922, 7 A.M.–4 P.M. Mon.–Sat., $10–20) brings on unpretentious and tasty offerings such as steak sandwiches and fried seafood platters. They bake their desserts themselves, and the lunch specials are just $6.95.

Tillie's Mini Market (1 Main St., Pioche, 775/962-5205 or 866/810-7303) sells groceries, hunting and fishing supplies, and sundries and rents **Wright's Country Cabins** ($55–75) out back. If anything exciting is going on in town, it'll probably be at the **Alamo Club** (28 Main St., Pioche, 775/962-5116) or the **Nevada Club** (59 Main St., Pioche, 775/962-5170).

Caliente

The first Anglo settlers in the area, the Culverwell family, bought a large tract of land in 1879 for farming and ranching. This southeast corner of Nevada, too far to connect with the transcontinental main line in northern Nevada, was neglected by the railroads until late in the 19th century. In 1894 the Union Pacific Railroad surveyed a route between Salt Lake City and Los Angeles, but it found competition in the upstart San Pedro, Los Angeles, and Salt Lake Railroad, which claimed title to the narrow right-of-way south of the Culverwell ranch. Each company deployed thugs to interfere with its competitor's progress. The inevitable violence ensued in Clover Valley with shovels and ax handles—the only major confrontation between railroads in Nevada history. A federal judge sided with Edward Harriman of Union Pacific, who shortly thereafter reluctantly went into partnership with the other company's William Clark, ending the Clark-Harriman Railroad War. From 1903 they continued construction along the dangerous Meadow Valley Wash south toward the little ranch known as Las Vegas. Caliente was created as a division point on the San Pedro, Los Angeles, and Salt Lake Railroad thanks to the abundant water gushing out of springs near the wash, which quelled the perpetual thirst of the steam engines.

The moguls built row houses for their workers north of the repair shops and offices, and the new town enjoyed nearly continuous prosperity until the 1940s. The only disruptions came when disastrous floods wreaked havoc on the railroad in 1907 and 1910, necessitating massive track replacement. The branch line between Caliente and Pioche ran for a full 60 years, 1907–1967. By the time it shut down, U.S. 93 had already been built through town, three state parks had been created nearby, agriculture prospered, and the railroad never completely abandoned Caliente. Freight trains still rumble through town regularly.

Today, Caliente has a vitality all its own. The streets follow an orderly company-town grid,

with two main business streets downtown, one on each side of the wide railroad right-of-way. The hot springs for which the town was named are a surprise treat. Along with the depot mural, Rainbow Canyon, and the low-stress residents, Caliente ("cally-anti," pronounced like the Spanish but with an American West inflection) is an undiscovered gem.

SIGHTS
Walking Tour

Start your walking tour of Caliente at the **Union Pacific Railroad Station** (100 Depot Ave., 775/726-3129, 10 A.M.–2 P.M. Mon.–Fri.), built in 1923. Once the nerve center of the railroad, it is now the center of the town. City hall, the **library** (1–6 P.M. Mon. and Thurs., 10 A.M.–3 P.M. Tues.–Wed.), and an art gallery call the historic two-story mission-style depot home. As the steam era came to an end, the depot housed the railroad station, the stationmaster's quarters, the telegraph office, a restaurant, a community center on the ground floor, and a hotel above. A huge historic mural, a source of justifiable pride in Caliente, hangs in silent homage to that romantic era inside the depot. The big painting covers the history of the entire southern section of Nevada 1864–1914, from Pioche in the northeast to Las Vegas in the south and all the way up to Tonopah in the west. Locals Mary Ellen Sadovich and Rett Hastings designed and painted it. The **Boxcar Museum** (10 A.M.–2 P.M. Mon.–Fri., $1) next door adds to the depot and mural experience with vintage photographs and memorabilia as well as rolling stock.

Lots of local buildings have been standing since 1905; pick up a walking tour brochure at the depot or at http://lincolncountynevada.com and wander along Clark Street past the town's iconic stone structures. A block from the depot you'll come to the **Culverwell House.** Built in the 1870s, it is one of the oldest stone houses in town. The square abode was built into a hillside, which insulates the house, keeping it cool in summer and warm in winter. Other stone houses in the area are the **Crawford House,** south on Spring Street, and the **Underhill House** at Clark Street and Denton Avenue. This area, the Underhill District, includes a **Mercantile Store** and the **Underhill Rock Apartments,** built entirely of stone in 1907. After you pass the apartments (turn right off Clover St. at the end of town) you'll come to the **Union Pacific Railroad row houses,** standing grandly on Spring Street just north of town, that were built in 1905; notice the two choices of floor plans. Near the corner of Market and Culverwell Streets, back of town, the **Community Methodist Church** (140 Culverwell St., 775/726-3665) is an attractive historical and cultural structure.

Rainbow Canyon and Kershaw-Ryan State Park

Beginning at the intersection of U.S. 93 and Highway 317 at the south end of Caliente by the Mormon Church lies **Rainbow Canyon,** one of the most beautiful in southern Nevada. Mark your odometer mileage at this point because many of the most interesting sites farther on can only be located by knowing the miles you've driven from this intersection.

The road turns a corner and passes under the first of many trestles into this stunning and remarkable wash. The cliff rock is volcanic tuff, which settled over all of Nevada 34 million years ago; The stunning spectrum of colors is the result of hot mineral-carrying water flowing through and filling fissures and faults; the water seeped out or evaporated, leaving the minerals to stain the rock a variety of colors (rusty iron, powdery yellow calcium, acidic blue, green copper, black manganese, and white ash).

Many elements combine to make this one of the most scenic and least explored roads in the state: the dips in the road in the flood zones; the many railroad trestles and bridges; the idyllic ranches, farms, big trees, and creek; the petroglyphs and other historical sites; and, of course, the sheer and colorful canyon walls.

The area's beauty and bounty were not lost on Native Americans, and 10,000 years ago Desert Archaic, Fremont, and Southern Paiutes were

© BETHANY DRYSDALE

Both native and cultivated trees and plants help make Kershaw-Ryan State Park one of central Nevada's most verdant locations.

drawn to Rainbow Canyon by seasonal water, cool Etna Cave, relatively fertile flood plains suitable for growing crops, and the trail of bighorn sheep, deer, and rabbits. The gouged and painted petroglyphs are the most obvious evidence of these early residents, but digs have also turned up pottery shards, stone tools, leatherwork, and basket fragments. The informative and colorful *Lincoln County Rock Art Guide* (http://lincolncountynevada.com) explains the significance of the Rainbow Canyon artwork and provides directions to petroglyph sites throughout the area.

Two miles into Rainbow Canyon you come to **Kershaw-Ryan State Park** (775/726-3564, $7), destroyed by flash floods in 1984 and reopened in 1997. Camping ($17) and facilities were completed in 2009. The entrance to this gem is well marked on a graded dirt road leading east into a box canyon off Highway 317. The park is 240 acres of cliff and canyon country liberally shaded by groves of ash and cottonwoods and laced with hiking trails. The rugged cliff walls enclosing the canyon are heavily overgrown with scrub oak and wild grapevines. The sound of running water is everywhere since the end wall of the canyon has a series of seeps that send water trickling down its face into a pond and a little brook at its base. Spring returns early and winter arrives late at this protected canyon, making it a good place to visit most of the year.

The park has modern restrooms amid a profusion of ivy and grass. The picnic area has tables and barbecue grills. Just above the picnic area is a small wading pool for children. Above that is a beautiful seep dripping water from the canyon wall in an undercut that creates a beautiful hanging garden of riparian plant life, including grapevines. Two short hikes, one a mile long and the other 0.25 miles, lead to other springs and lush canyons. Kershaw Canyon is a favorite destination within the park; a spring here has been channeled into a watering trough used by wild horses, deer, mountain lions, lizards, and other animals.

Continuing down Rainbow Canyon, at mile 3.8 you come to the **Old Conway Ranch,** which was turned into a public golf course that went bankrupt. At mile 5.0, you arrive at **Etna Cave.** Park on the right shoulder, walk under the train trestle, follow the sandy wash though the tunnel for about 400 feet, and then look up to the left on the tan cliff face to see the abundant petroglyphs and pictographs carved and painted into the cliff face.

At mile 6.0 you come to the **Tennille Ranch.** Tennille sold the ranch to a Las Vegas man who conducts stress-management classes in the beautiful ranch house. The place is now called the Longhorn Cattle Company. At mile 8.7 you come upon the remains of **Stein Power Station,** a steam-generated power plant that supplied electrical power to the mines 1902–1909. Farther up this road are the remains of the old Delamar pumping station and pipeline, which pumped water over the high cliffs to Delamar on the other side of the mountains to the west.

At mile 11.0 you come to a vantage point where you can view the few remaining piñon pines and juniper trees that were much more abundant in the canyon prior to massive cutting

for fuel and building materials at the turn of the 20th century. This stand has grown back.

At mile 14.7, watch for a turnoff to the left just after crossing under another railroad trestle. Park off the road and take a short drive (0.7 miles) up a good dirt road into **Grapevine Canyon.** Bear left at the fork. Park at the barbecue-pit area and enjoy a picnic under the shade of huge ash and hackberry trees. Walk back down the road about 100 feet, and then follow the well-marked foot trail up the slope to some tuff overhang. You'll spot another abundance of petroglyphs and pictographs dating back thousands of years. More such artifacts can be found along the cliff face and on the south side of Grapevine Canyon.

At mile 17.5, just past the railroad bridge, look for a short dirt road on the right. Park and walk north along this access road about 400 feet. You'll see a small railroad tie structure and **Tunnel No. 5,** dated 1911–1925. Look west and uphill from the structure. You should see several dark-stained talus blocks strewn along the hillside with petroglyphs of bighorn sheep carved on the tops and sides.

At mile 19.9, park along the right shoulder of Highway 317 and look for a boulder covered with petroglyphs. Across the highway, lush willows dominate a wetland zone and protect the stream bank from erosion by flooding. They also provide food for deer, beavers, and livestock.

At mile 20.2 you come to **Bradshaw's "End of the Rainbow" Ranch,** established in the 1880s and the only ranch in the canyon still owned by descendants of the original settler. The pavement ends here. If you visit in fall, you might be able to pick a bucket of Jonathan or Delicious apples in the ranch's orchard. Check for a sign on the ranch gate for the dates when End of the Rainbow is open to the public. In another few miles, Rainbow Canyon starts to peter out and becomes an ordinary desert wash in the summer months. The stream that you've followed all the way down the canyon either dries up or goes underground.

Elgin Schoolhouse

Although Meadow Valley Wash had been homesteaded and several ranches existed here as early as the 1870s, there were few children in the area until the Salt Lake, San Pedro, and Los Angeles Railroad came through the valley in 1903. Several small communities popped up to serve the railroad and its passengers. Many of these workers had children, and so the need for a school arose. The Elgin Schoolhouse (775/726-3564, 10 A.M.–4 P.M. Thurs.–Sat. Apr. 1–Oct. 15, $1 adults, free under age 13), built by Reuben Bradshaw, a second-generation resident, educated first- through eighth-grade students for 45 years, 1922–1967. Bradshaw's descendants restored the school and furnished it with mostly original and some authentic period items.

Kane Springs Road

This road starts at the south end of Rainbow Canyon where the paved road turns into dirt and ends 38 miles southwest on U.S. 93. It's a shortcut or a good circle tour for anyone traveling between Caliente and Las Vegas and can support speeds of 45–50 mph. It's also a great drive across high desert with clean, clear air and lots of yucca. As you traverse the high-desert green valley running between the Meadow Valley Mountains on the south and the Delamar Mountains on the north, shut off your air-conditioning, open your windows, and taste, smell, and feel the desert—don't seal yourself off from it. Toward the end, the Sheep Range grows bigger straight ahead.

Beaver Dam State Park

One of Nevada's remotest state parks is accessed from Caliente. The park (775/728-4460, $7) is so irrepressibly cheerful a place that the long dusty drive to get there is a small price to pay for a visit. The 2,393-acre park is set high in mountain piñon and juniper forests. Hiking trails wind under the trees and cliffs and through the canyons. Anglers may try their luck along the cottonwood-lined beaver-dammed stream. Flooding destabilized the dam creating Schroeder Lake in 2005, and officials breached the dam as a safety precaution and began to restore the streambed to its predam flow. There are picnic sites and developed campsites ($14) in the park. There are no visitors centers or concessions, so bring everything you'll need.

The well-marked turnoff for the state park is 5.3 miles north of Caliente on U.S. 93. For the next 25 miles the well-graded dirt road climbs gently, but you can't travel faster than 35–40 mph because the road twists and turns a great deal, and you don't know what's coming up around the next turn or over the next hilltop. After 14 miles you come to a fork in the road. Stay on the left branch to Beaver Dam. The right branch, which rapidly becomes 4WD territory, goes to the dry remains of Matthews Canyon Reservoir and then winds its way through the mountains south into the Utah backcountry.

After another 4.5 miles, you cross the Union Pacific tracks. Four miles later you come to the beginning of a steep incline down the side of Pine Ridge into Beaver Dam State Park. While it may look like a nail-biting ride, any passenger vehicle can make it with no trouble. From this point it's three miles to the campground. Do what the stop sign says (yes, a stop sign way out here) and register. The park is open year-round, weather permitting.

There are three campgrounds available with a total of 33 campsites. The first (to the left) is the best, with tables, grills, running water, vault toilets, and camping spots for RVs as well as tents. The other campgrounds are similar but a bit more primitive.

Delamar

About 24 miles east of Alamo, you come to a dirt road on the south side of the highway proclaiming "Delamar 15 miles." This straight-arrow dirt road heading southwest is well graded and easy for passenger vehicles. The striking broad Delamar Valley is west of the Delamar Mountains. The first gold discovery was made here in 1891. The town of Reeves was laid out below one of the mines, but the name was later changed to De Lamar (Delamar) when a Dutch immigrant of that name purchased the group of mines in 1893.

Delamar was a principal gold-mining center that supported a thriving business district of stores, saloons, theaters, and professional offices. As many as 120 mule-drawn freight wagons continuously brought supplies from the

DELAMAR'S WIDOW-MAKER MINES

Desolate and dry, the Delamar's productive hard-rock mines nevertheless attracted more than 1,500 residents to the desert outpost 30 miles southwest of Caliente. The sparsely distributed springs were barely enough to supply townsfolk with water for drinking and household needs in the 1890s. That forced the mines and mill to use dry-extraction and dry-procession methods to coax the precious gold from quartzite – an unusual bed for the lode mineral.

At the height of production, the mill processed 260 tons of ore each day, crushing the surrounding quartzite and kicking up clouds of dust – sharp, glasslike particles known as "dagger dust." Unaware miners and townspeople breathed the dust, often resulting in minute tears in their lung sacs, inflicting victims with silicosis. Hundreds of miners died from the disease, earning Delamar the ominous nickname "The Widow Maker." In fact, as many as 400 of the town's 1,500 residents fit that description, their miner husbands taken by the disease.

By 1896 the Delamar mill was handling up to 260 tons of ore daily. Near the turn of the century, the town built a pipeline to transport water from Meadow Valley Wash, 12 miles away. The water's arrival transformed the mining and milling processes, but it was too late for many who had already breathed in the deadly quartz dust. A fire destroyed the town in 1900, and although it was rebuilt, a rich ore discovery in Tonopah helped ensure the town's demise. Town founder Captain John Delamar closed up shop in 1909 after producing $15 million in gold and hundreds of corpses. A short-lived mining revival began in 1929, but Delamar itself breathed its last in 1934.

---

nearest railroad stop at Milford, Utah. Today what remains at the site are old stone walls, a crumbling mill, and a large cemetery from which many of the old tombstones have been stolen by souvenir seekers. The rock ruins, crowded as they are into the shallow canyon above the mine dumps, make a fascinating picnic site.

From Delamar, you can continue southwest on the dirt road to Alamo, or return to U.S. 93 to the north and drive on to Caliente. Six miles from the Delamar turnoff you top **Oak Springs Summit** (6,237 feet). A campground a short distance off the south side of the highway has picnic tables, grills, and a green shady picnic area. It's a nice cool place at high elevation to enjoy a rest and a picnic, and to listen to Air Force jets streaking up and down the Pahranagat Valley.

From here you start dropping down to Caliente. One last scenic treat awaits before the town: **Newman Canyon** has high, sheer sandstone cliffs, some of them completely vertical and smooth. It is not as dramatic, however, as Rainbow Canyon on the other side of town.

Hiko

A few miles north of the intersection with U.S. 93 and Highway 375 on Highway 318 is Hiko (HY-ko). This is a small ranching hamlet spread along the highway for a mile or two behind range fencing. The silver strike in 1867 at Irish Mountain, 15 miles north of Hiko, was a flash in the pan compared to the silver strike in the Highland Range at Pioche in 1871. Almost overnight the population of Hiko moved to Pioche, as did the county seat, where it remains today. Hiko rests in the center of a pretty little basin with a string of ranches, a post office, the state's Key Pittman Wildlife Management Area, and Nesbitt Pond. A sign here warns that the next gas is 100 miles away in Lund.

Named to honor Key Pittman, a former U.S. senator from Nevada known for his vigorous support of legislation to assist the silver-mining industry of the West, **Key Pittman Wildlife Management Area** comprises two lakes, Nesbitt and Frenchy. The lower lake, Frenchy, is usually dry about half the year since it's used to supply irrigation water for the farms in the area. Frenchy Lake is reputedly named after an old sourdough miner who worked the old Logan Mines up in the Mount Irish mountains to the west. Just under five miles north on Highway 318 is Nesbitt Lake, a beautiful lake that does not go dry. It's surrounded by tules, tall cottonwoods, and oaks and is inhabited by an abundance of birds and other small animals.

When you come to the entrance to **Nesbitt Lake,** stop, open the cattle gate, drive in, and close the gate behind you so you don't let grazing cattle out onto the road. Then take a leisurely drive around the lake. You can park at several shady areas at the beginning of the road around the lake. Nonmotorized boats are allowed on the lake. There are no fees for picnicking or camping in this lush oasis.

Directly across from Nesbitt Lake is a barbed-wire gate to a dirt road leading 18 miles up into the Mount Irish Range and the Mount Irish Archeological Site. The range and site are rich with ancient petroglyphs and other Indian artifacts. Up here you'll also find the remains of the old mining town of Logan. This is a dirt road and pretty isolated, so be sure to take water, a digging tool, a spare tire, and other desert survival equipment in case you get a flat tire or get stuck; it's a long walk back. Passenger vehicles can easily make the 18 miles to Logan, but avoid going off this road. All other access roads are strictly for 4WD vehicles.

PRACTICALITIES

The **Rainbow Canyon** (880 Front St., Caliente, 775/726-3291, $49–60) has clean, comfortable, quiet guest rooms with big TVs and spacious bathrooms. Family-owned **Shady Motel** (450 Front St., Caliente, 775/726-3106, $53–63) is similar, although the bathrooms are a bit more cramped.

Young's RV (1350 Front St., Caliente, 775/726-3418, $20) is on U.S. 93 behind the Bureau of Land Management office. Spaces are wide with trees and grass at each; facilities are limited, but it's right in town. There are 27 spaces for motor homes, all with full hookups; 16 are pull-throughs. Tents are allowed in a separate grassy area. Restrooms have flush toilets and hot showers; sewage disposal is available. Reservations are accepted.

The best food in Caliente is of the cowboy diner variety. The **Brandin' Iron** (190 Clover St., Caliente, 775/726-3164, 6 A.M.–8 P.M. daily, $7–15) is representative. Cowboy art graces the walls, and the fare is trail-ride hearty: burgers, meat loaf, real meat, and taters.

The **Knotty Pine** coffee shop (690 Front St., Caliente, 775/726-3194, 6 A.M.–8 P.M. Sun.–Thurs., 6 A.M.–9 P.M. Fri.–Sat., $7–15) is similar, although the menu is less extensive. The coffee's good, and the local gossip is sometimes juicy.

The Toiyabe and Toquima Ranges

The Toiyabe Range is the preeminent stretch of mountains in central Nevada, anchoring a vast network of mountains and valleys, busted boomtowns, and dusty outposts. They are home to Austin, which bathed in the radiant glow or silver mining in the 1870s, and Eureka, whose brick structures were built to survive boomtown floods and fires and still stand today. The Toiyabe—a Shoshone word variously translated as "black mountains," for the thick piñon, juniper, and mahogany cover, and "big mountains" for their length, height, steepness, and ruggedness—stretch from Toiyabe Peak near Austin to Mahogany Mountain opposite Carvers. This mansard roof tops the middle of the state in a thin straight line more than 10,000 feet high for 50 miles. The southern slope extends for another 20 miles, hooking up with the Shoshone Range to the west and gradually squeezing off the Reese River Valley in between. Numerous tributary creeks converge here to create the mud-puddle Reese River and fertile ranch land.

The upper range elongates for another 50 miles, rising to a head at mystical Mount Callaghan, paralleled by the Toquima Range to the east across Big Smoky Valley. Austin, at 6,500 feet one of the highest towns in Nevada, sits on the western slopes of the Toiyabes. Monitor Valley and the Monitor Range, with their adjoining mining towns and ghosts towns, complete the pattern.

Three peaks in the Toiyabes tower over 11,000 feet, with **Arc Dome,** near the convergence of the Shoshone and Toiyabe Ranges, the highest at 11,788 feet. Another four peaks in the range rise over 10,000 feet. The top of mighty Mount Jefferson of the Toquima Range right across the valley actually looks down 200 feet at the crown of Arc Dome. This is one of the finest mountain scenes in the state.

John C. Frémont appears to have been the first European to set foot in **Big Smoky Valley** in 1845; he named it after the late summer haze that partially obscured it. He followed it for three days, camping at Birch Creek, the hot springs, and Peavine. James Simpson passed along its northern edge in 1859 as he surveyed the central alternative route through the territory. After Austin attracted its horde of fortune seekers in 1863, prospectors crawled all over the Toiyabes, finding some minerals within the granite intrusions. Toiyabe City, Kingston, Canyon City, Geneva, Amador, and Yankee Blade all sprouted and withered at the finds.

Today, Arc Dome is the largest U.S. Forest Service Wilderness Area in Nevada at 115,000 acres. *Hiking the Great Basin* by John Hart covers a baker's dozen hikes here in detail, including two for Arc Dome, several from Twin Rivers and Jett Canyon, and the 65-mile Toiyabe Crest National Recreation Trail. *Nevada Wilderness Areas* by Michael Rose covers seven hikes here, including two Twin River loops, Cow, Tom's, and Jett Canyons, and the Toiyabe Crest Trail. If internal combustion is more your style, the roads down Big Smoky from Austin to Tonopah and up Reese River Valley from Ione Canyon to Austin provide two of the most breathtaking scenic cruises in the West.

EUREKA

Miners began to notice Eureka when silver turned up in 1864, but the difficulty processing the lead-laden ore prevented much interest. The complex refining required the ore be sent overseas for processing, cutting deep gouges into potential profits. In the 1870s, smelters sprung up in Eureka, greatly simplifying the process and spurring renewed mining interest—in the lead more than the silver—in the remote town. By 1879, large-scale exploitation of the deposits was underway, and Eureka was on its way to earning the nickname "Pittsburgh of the West." The town grew to 9,000 residents, but the 1880s saw the once-lucrative mines peter out.

Eureka is a charming town with many well preserved 19th-century buildings. To mitigate the damage from frequent floods and fire, boom-era residents built many structures out of brick. Today, several of these intriguing structures, many still in use, can be seen. In addition to mining, which is still susceptible to boom-and-bust cycles, agriculture remains a vital part of Eureka's economy, as does outdoor recreation.

Sights

Nevadans have a knack for turning negativity on its head. Potential nuclear fallout in Las Vegas? Celebrate it with a Miss Atomic Bomb beauty contest. *The Washington Post* calls Battle Mountain "the armpit of America"? Get a deodorant sponsor and host the Armpit Festival. And so it was with the lonely outposts along U.S. 50. In 1986 *Life* magazine called the byway "the loneliest road" and quoted a AAA spokesperson as saying the road was

totally empty. There are no points of interest. We don't recommend it. We warn all motorists not to drive there unless they're confident of their survival skills.

Recognizing a golden opportunity, the state

and the towns along U.S. 50 quickly appropriated the title. They developed the *Official Highway 50 Survival Guide* (http://travelnevada.com) to encourage adventurous motorists to test their skills. And contrary to the AAA's assertions, Eureka and U.S. 50 are full of fun and educational roadside stops.

Start at the **Eureka Opera House** (31 S. Main St., 8 A.M.–5 P.M. Mon.–Fri., free). Originally intended as a union hall, the unfinished building was purchased for a song when the striking union needed emergency funds. A regular stop for touring operas and other professional productions, the opera house also hosted boxing matches, debates, school functions, and the Nob Hill Fire Company's annual New Year's Eve masquerade balls. Later, silent films and talkies were shown here until 1958. Sadly, a carelessly placed lantern ignited the magnificent Italian hand-painted stage curtain in 1923, but the "new" curtain, brought in from Minneapolis in 1924, is just as striking.

A couple of blocks away, the **Eureka County Courthouse** (10 S. Main St., 775/237-5270) continues to mete out frontier justice as it has since 1880. The great fire of 1879 burned the original wooden courthouse to the ground around the iron jail and fortified vault. The county constructed the current brick structure around these two fireproof elements. Architecture and design fans will enjoy the details of the vaguely Italianate building: a second-floor balcony, brick pilasters, cornices, a filigreed parapet wall outside, and an imported Spanish cedar judge's bench and balustrade, gilded accents, a 19-foot pressed metal ceiling, and a suspended spectators gallery inside the courtroom.

Unlike the courthouse, the *Eureka Sentinel* is no longer functioning, but the press equipment on the ground floor of the **Eureka Sentinel Museum** (10 N. Monroe St., 775/237-5010, 10 A.M.–6 P.M. Mon.–Fri. Nov.–Apr., 10 A.M.–6 P.M. daily May–Oct., free) looks like it could do the job if anyone has the urge to start it up again. The paper kept residents in the know 1879–1960; posters printed at the office during the run adorn the pressroom walls.

Virtually every aspect of boomtown Eureka life is depicted at the museum, including residents' work—early mining tools, stock certificates, and miners' possessions; their leisure life—a recreated parlor and kitchen using authentic items, fraternal organization displays, and a barber shop representative of the era; and their school life—books, desks, and other items. Finish your tour at the gift shop, which sells soap and pottery made in Eureka along with books, postcards, and souvenirs. Dozens of other historic houses, hotels, and stores dot the town. To see more, get the town tour brochure at www.rainesmarket.com/eureka.

Just outside of town, Barrick Gold Corp. operates the **Ruby Hill Mine** (U.S. 50 and Hwy. 278, 775/237-6060). Tours of the open-pit heap-leach operation that recovers 4,000 ounces of gold per year are offered by appointment.

Accommodations

Clean, comfortable, and cheap are about all you can ask along this stretch of desolate desert highway. Thankfully, a couple of family-owned establishments hit the mark on all counts. In addition, the **Sundown Lodge** (60 N. Main St., 775/237-5334, $48–65) has location going for it. It's across the street from the **Best Western Eureka Inn** (251 N. Main St., 775/237-5214, $99–125). Some travelers may appreciate the consistency of chain hotels, and this place is as good as any, with free breakfast and more modern decor and amenities than the town's other choices. But we're sure the Sundown gets its share of sticker shock–weary travelers who opt for rooms at half the Best Western's rates, especially if all they really want is a roof and a bed for the night. The Sundown is also within sight of a market and the Owl Club, the only place in town that passes as a night spot. With nightlife almost nonexistent, the Sundown's large flat-screen TVs are a godsend for passing the time.

If you don't need TV or a phone, microwave, or coffee pot, spend an authentic 19th-century luxury-free night at the ◖ **Jackson House Hotel** (11 S. Main St., 775/237-5247, $79). Its nine rooms give a taste of how the well-heeled traveled at the turn of the 20th century. Grand Victorian-style furnishings, claw-foot tubs, crystal, cherrywood, and gilt grace the rooms and the elegant dining room and bar.

Front-porch rocking chairs offer the perfect vantage point from which to watch deer pluck apples from the trees at **Eureka Bed and Breakfast** (400 Edwards St., 775/237-7555 or 877/403-6868, $60–110). The hillside location also provides commanding views of the town. Children and pets are not allowed.

Eureka is home to two small RV parks with fewer than 20 spaces each. **Silver Sky Lodge** (U.S. 50 S., 775/237-7146, $20) and **Scotty's RV Park** (131 Richmond St., 775/237-5170, year-round, $19) have level spaces that are mostly pull-throughs.

Food

There are a couple of fast-food joints in town, but the only recommendable traditional restaurant is the **Owl Club & Steakhouse** (61 N. Main St., 775/237-5280, 5:30 A.M.–1:30 A.M. daily, $15–25). The establishment has a few dozen slots, a bar, a gift shop, and a horseback riding and mountain bike concession.

AUSTIN

Austin's history reaches back to the days of the Pony Express. The story goes that an Express horse kicked over a stone near the Reese River, revealing high-grade silver ore and kicking off a rush in 1862, but that story's just too good to be true. However it happened, the "Rush to the Reese" got underway in early 1863, and by spring of that year 1,000 claims had been staked in newly named Pony Canyon and on nearby hills, and by summer, Austin was a bona fide boomtown with 10,000 residents.

Entrepreneurs dismantled Virginia City's International Hotel board by board, hauled it across the desert, and reerected it in downtown Austin. The territorial government carved out Lander County around Austin in 1863; eventually, Eureka, Elko, White Pine, and Nye counties were sliced from it. Austin rivaled Virginia City's output of silver production

for the next 10 years. Roughly $50 million in gold and silver were recovered from the Reese District through 1873 Like all of Nevada, Austin experienced the long melancholy decline of resources and population until quite recently with the latest resurgence of mining. Turquoise and barium are abundant in addition to the gold and silver. There are even some uranium deposits, but their quality is too low for use in energy or weapons.

Sights

Coming from the east into town, the first business you reach is **Tyrannosaurus Rix Mountain Bike and Specialties** (270 Main St., 775/964-1212), which is trying to lead Austin to its rightful place at the forefront of the mountain biking world. This corner of the Toiyabes is chock-full of lung-searing hill climbs, heart-stopping downhills, and killer views for off-road bikers of any ilk. The terrain is not well known even though Austin straddles U.S. 50, the most direct route from California to the mountain biking mecca of Moab, Utah.

Beginners and younger riders will appreciate Castle Loop, a 4.5-mile relatively flat trail that gives a gentle sample of what the sport can offer, with twisting turns, a few jumps, and one or two short climbs. More seasoned cyclists may want to test their mettle on Gold Venture Loop. There are plenty of steep climbs as the trail gains 4,500 feet over 27.5 miles. But it rewards riders with an exhilarating spin through a mine road and the rollercoaster ride down to Birch Creek. The Austin Ranger District (775/964-2671) and the Austin Chamber of Commerce (775/964-2200) can provide information and directions to the trailheads for these and dozens more mountain rides.

If you're passing through on a summer weekend, stop in at **Main Street Shops** (99 Main St., 775/964-1100, 10 A.M.–2 P.M. Sat.–Sun. summer). Housed in an 1881 mercantile, the co-op shops sell jewelry, artwork, and collectibles.

Austin's only two bona fide tourist attractions bookend the town. Entering from the east, you can't miss the **Gridley Store,** a stone building at Main and Water Streets that now houses the Austin Historical Society (247 Water St., 775/964-1202, by appointment). The store was opened in 1863 by Rueul Gridley, whose name lives on in conjunction with a 50-pound sack of flour. Gridley paid off a losing bet by carrying the flour from his store to a bar across town, then auctioning it off for a donation to the Sanitary Fund. The highest bidder auctioned it off again, then again, and again. Townsfolk raised $6,000 by the end of the afternoon. From there, Gridley took the sack to Virginia City and repeated the process, then on to California and eventually the East Coast, raising $275,000 for Civil War relief. Gridley himself died penniless six years later. Some believe his restless soul still haunts the building, toting the famous flour sack on his shoulder. The house next to Gridley's store was originally the town brothel.

On the other side of town is **Stokes' Castle.** From Main Street, turn left on Castle Road at the west end of town and follow a precipitous road about 0.5 miles around to the back of the hill. It is a curious attraction that could only be found in Austin, a rare three-story stone "castle" built by mining baron Anson P. Stokes, who admired the castle towers he saw on a visit to Italy. He had this reproduction built of hand-cut native granite, the huge blocks hoisted into place with a hand winch and held in place with rock wedging and clay mortar. Incredibly, after all that work, it was only occupied for a month or two in the summer of 1897 before Stokes sold his Austin business interests and never returned. The castle has stood here for over 100 years and is a fine place to have a picnic or stretch your legs in the piñon forest up the hill, which has a great overlook of Reese River Valley. You could also camp here in a pinch.

Accommodations

There are a total of 39 hotel rooms in Austin, none of which could be considered luxurious. Call for reservations, as Austin is a popular overnight stop for tour buses. One busload of tourists can monopolize all the rooms in town.

The most up-to-date accommodations in town await at the **Cozy Mountain Motel** (40 Main St., 775/964-7433, $40–50), a string of 17 recently remodeled "modular" units that resemble mobile homes or construction-site mobile offices. It's more inviting and attractive than it sounds, with flower boxes, clean restful beds, and flat-screen TVs, although the rooms aren't terribly large.

The rooms at the Cozy Mountain are positively palatial compared to those at the 17-unit **Lincoln Motel** (60 Main St., 775/964-2698, $40–49). The Lincoln somehow manages to fit a queen bed, a TV, a dresser, and a tiny bathroom into its eight- by 10-foot guest rooms, which were renovated in 2007; you can fluff your pillow, shave, and watch TV all at the same time. Pets are allowed.

There are 10 plank-built guest rooms in the shade of some tall trees at the **Pony Canyon Motel** (Main St., 775/964-2605, $38–60). Following town tradition, the guest rooms are small and utilitarian.

A converted and renovated 1860s boarding house, **Union Street Lodging** (69 Union St., 775/964-2364, $65–95) is Austin's first full-service bed-and-breakfast. Four guest rooms have en-suite baths; two others share facilities. The bigger guest rooms feature four-poster beds. All of the guest rooms are tidy and snug. Coffee is on in the wee hours, and the full breakfast is of the appropriately hearty variety. You can rent the two-bedroom **Pony Express House** (269 Main St., 775/964-2306) for $35 (one room) or $70 (both rooms). The house is historic, built in the late 1860s; this is a "bed and fix your own breakfast."

Austin RV (244 Water St., 775/964-1011, $20), at 6,900 feet in elevation, has good shade, although the pull-through sites can be a bit uneven. Fee collecting is somewhat based on the honor system (read the signs on the information board and drop the night's payment in the drop box on the front of the office). There are 15 RV sites and four tent sites.

Pony Express RV Park (260 Main St., 775/964-2005, $20) offers 12 RV sites and four tent sites. It's close to a town park and public swimming pool.

Food

Austin has two places to eat, each with unique charms. At **Toiyabe Café** (150 Main St., 775/964-2220, 6 A.M.–9 P.M. daily Apr.–Oct., 6 A.M.–2 P.M. daily Nov.–Mar., $10–20) try the green chili and Swiss or Spanish omelet or bacon and eggs for breakfast. Lunch and dinner fare includes good soup and burritos, burgers, steak sandwiches, and fish; beer and wine are available.

The **International** café (59 Main St., 775/964-1225, 6 A.M.–8 P.M. daily, $8–18), on the west side of town, is in the second-oldest hotel building in Nevada, although lodging is no longer available, and makes a mean bacon-topped sirloin with all the fixings for $11 along with a range of traditional breakfasts for under $7.

Information

The **U.S. Forest Service Station** (100 Midas Canyon Rd., 775/964-2671), on the west side of town overlooking the junction of Highway 305, sells detailed maps and can advise you on hikes in the area.

The **Austin Chamber of Commerce** (122 Main St., 775/964-2200, www.austinnevada.com/chamber) has a large rack of brochures in the foyer of the courthouse; the chamber office upstairs is open most weekday mornings.

❰ BERLIN-ICHTHYOSAUR STATE PARK

Austin is the starting point for exploring the Reese River and Smith Creek valleys west of the Toiyabe Range. Back on U.S. 50 headed west, the road drops down out of Austin onto Highway 722, heading through the **Reese River Valley** flats toward the **Shoshone Range,** still in national forest. Here you cross the "raging" Reese River. This perfect description appears in David Toll's well-written *Complete Nevada Traveler*:

© BETHANY DRYSDALE

Superbly preserved, the mill at Berlin processed ore throughout the region's productive first decade of the 20th century.

The Reese at floodtide has barely the breadth of a man's wrist and the depth of his fingers. Stagecoaches forded it at a full gallop with only the suggestion of a bump, and in the dry season the Reese is even less spectacular.

Still, it was a well-known river in the 1860s and appeared on all the contemporary maps to flow confidently north from south of Austin in the Toiyabes to Battle Mountain and the Humboldt River. It provided a perfect apparition for starting up a paper business, called the Reese River Navigation Company, which sold phony stock to unsuspecting investors.

Berlin is one of the best-preserved ghost towns in Nevada and has been a state park since 1955. It owes its early history to mining claims begun in 1863 by prospectors from Austin. Berlin's later history involved the Tonopah excitement at the turn of the 20th century when the Nevada Mining Company built a large mill here that operated for nearly two decades. Berlin's post office closed in 1918. Note that tours of the Diana Mine are no longer offered due to safety concerns.

The **Berlin-Ichthyosaur State Park office** (775/964-2440) is in the former mine superintendent's home, where you can pay the $7 park entry fee and pick up a brochure with a good map; the office keeps irregular hours. If it's closed, just up the road is a sign with a map of Berlin in 1905. Up the hill are the ruins of the assay office, a stagecoach stop, a machine shop, and the hoist building over the main mine shaft. Down the hill a trail passes the sites of bunkhouses, a union hall, and a saloon; still standing are homes, shops, and the infirmary. The trail continues out to the cemetery.

The biggest building in Berlin, down by the road, is one of the last original mills in Nevada. Check out the tongue-and-groove joints and wooden pegs holding the whole thing together. Four big steam engines on the floor powered 30 stamps, and you can easily imagine the deafening din of metal on rock. For all that, Berlin produced less than $1 million worth of precious metals between 1900 and 1907.

Take Primitive Road up from Berlin and turn right into the **campground** ($17), which has 14 sites, some suitable for RVs up to 25 feet, among pines and junipers; there are fire rings, good outhouses, and running water (spring–fall). A trail from site number 8 leads 0.5 miles to the **fossil shelter,** or you can drive up to it on Primitive Road. Rangers lead 40-minute **tours** (10 A.M. and 2 P.M. Mon.–Fri., 10 A.M., noon, and 2 P.M. Sat.–Sun. Memorial Day–Labor Day, $3 adults, $2 children).

As you're driving up into the Shoshones toward the park, try to imagine what it might've looked like when ichthyosaurs swam in the warm ocean that covered central Nevada 225 million years ago. Fossils of these giant marine creatures were first found in 1928, and extensive excavations in 1954 uncovered partial remains of 40 individual ichthyosaurs. Apparently they became stuck in shallow water, covered by silt and mud, and hardened into fossils. These creatures were great predators 50–60 feet long and weighing 50–60 tons, with 10-foot heads, 8-foot-wide jaws, and foot-wide eyes. It's believed that Nevada's ichthyosaurs were the world's largest, and today they're honored as the official state fossil.

Outside the shelter is a sculpted relief of the creatures dating to 1957. If the shelter isn't open, descriptive signs and big picture windows provide a self-guided "tour" of the skeletal features of the fossils. Inside, you'll see the remains of nine ichthyosaurs that seem to have died together and were left where they were found; the shelter was built around them. You have to use a little imagination to visualize their size and shape from the fossils. There's also a cabinet full of fossils, a geologic timetable, a fossil dig, and a mural on the late Triassic landscape.

Ione

Seven miles north of Berlin-Ichthyosaur State Park is the surprising town of Ione (EYE-own), founded in 1863. The mineral discoveries here catalyzed the creation of vast Nye County, and Ione had a brief moment in the sun as county seat until Belmont took over in 1867. The nearby mines produced $1 million in gold and some mercury before the town died in 1880.

A major resumption of gold mining in 1983 turned Ione into something of a showpiece. Half-subterranean log cabins with dead sod roofs predominate, and the old schoolhouse was beautifully refinished into a general store with wood shelving and cabinets and tasteful old lamps. Just north of here is a pen of bison (keep your distance). Up the street the old post office was also renovated for use as the field office of the new owner of the mining operations and most of the town. Across the street is the town park. With its stone picnic tables, old London street lamps, scalloped concrete benches, white picket fence, trees from the 1860s, and swings and slides, it is an idyllic place for a picnic.

Don't count on the **Ore House Saloon** (775/964-2003), built in 1864, being open, but if it is, the proprietor can supply, as the sign says, "vittles, gas, and spirits" and even a trailer ($45), Ione's version of hotel accommodations, or overnight RV spots ($10).

◖ SPENCER HOT SPRINGS

Twelve miles east of Austin on U.S. 50, turn south onto Highway 376. A dirt road immediately heads off east (left) toward the Toquima Range. The dirt starts out rough, with a maximum speed of 30 mph, and gets worse, at 15 mph and one lane. Roughly halfway across the valley, a left turn (unmarked, but easily recognizable) leads up to Spencer Hot Springs. Far from a resort spa, the springs nevertheless combine fine views—the Toiyabes stretch into the background, and the Monitors reach out in front—with a soothing hot soak. These springs are not only quite civilized and not too far off the beaten track; they are also expertly "developed." The big main pool at the top ledge is sandbagged, tastefully tiled with slate, and offset by a little wooden deck. Toward the road a bit is a big galvanized tub. Hot water flows in through a pipe; put the pipe in the tub to regulate the temperature. Then lie back, breathe deeply, and offer up a prayer of thanks from your nerve endings.

BIG SMOKY VALLEY

If you decide to forgo a dip at Spencer Hot Springs, stay on Highway 376 southbound. You'll spy **Toiyabe Peak** (10,793 feet) and **Bunker Hill** (11,474 feet) as you approach the first ridgeline. About 15 miles south of the U.S. 50 junction is a turnoff into **Kingston.** In the late 1960s a developer attempted to transform the ranch land around present-day Kingston into a town like Venice, California, with cobblestone streets, outdoor cafés, and upscale boutiques; it didn't happen. Today there's a little gold mining, supported by a small settlement, the third-largest population center in Lander County after Battle Mountain and Austin.

The pavement continues through Kingston but ends on the way into **Kingston Canyon** (Big Creek Rd.). The next couple of miles present opportunities for primitive camping, trout fishing, or hiking the **Toiyabe Crest Trail.** Another half mile brings you to the Forest Service station, and from there the road continues over the Toiyabes in the shadow of massive Bunker Hill to connect with the Reese River Valley road into Austin.

Continuing south, Highway 376 passes **Sheep Canyon, Crooked Canyon,** and **Toiyabe Range Peak** (10,960 feet), with a few 8,000–9,000-foot "hills" in between. Ten miles from the Kingston junction you leave Lander County and enter Nye County, with the perpendicular granite walls of the Toiyabes shielding a string of ranches. The bottomland below that is an alkali bed of an ice-age lake. Roads head up into Summit Creek, Ophir Creek, and Twin River below Toiyabe Range Peak to the old mining sites. Directly across the valley to the east in the Toquima Range loom **Mount Jefferson**'s three summits, all over 11,000 feet.

CARVERS

Just beyond the private Darrough's Hot Springs is the town of Carvers. The settlement started as a restaurant and bar in 1947 when the road was built. Twenty years later, as mining grew in fits and starts, enough people had settled nearby that the name Carvers started showing up on state maps, and in the 1980s gold mining made Carvers a full-fledged boomtown.

Jumping Jack Motel (Hwy. 376, Round Mountain, 775/377-2566, $65) has only 17 guest rooms, which might be plenty in this out-of-the-way place, but salespeople visiting the nearby gold mine sometimes book all the rooms, so it's a good idea to phone ahead for reservations. Be sure to stop in and have a look at the **Full Moon Saloon** to experience directly how similar the words *bar* and *barn* are. The Full Moon is party central for Big Smoky Valley and also serves lunch and dinner.

At Carvers, Highway 376 turns southeast, aiming right at Round Mountain, where miners dig for gold and pile up overburden at one of the largest operations near a major road in Nevada. At the turnoff, the road to the right leads to **Hadley,** one of the largest company towns in Nevada. It's occupied by roughly 500 miners and their families. There's a 24-hour day care center, an elementary and junior high school, a medical clinic, a swimming pool and rec center, and a golf course.

The **Round Mountain Golf Club** (100 Electrum Dr., Round Mountain, 775/377-2880, $18–35) operates the longest nine-hole course in Nevada at 3,679 yards. William Howard Neff, a top golf course architect from Utah, designed the par-36 course, which boasts three lakes. The course has a café and lounge, cart rentals, and one of the best pro shops north of Las Vegas.

The **Smoky Valley Museum** (Hwy. 376, near Carvers, 775/377-2243, by appointment, free) offers a glimpse at some of the area's mining and ranching history. The museum is housed in a 1935 schoolhouse, so you can check out the class ledgers and old photos.

ROUND MOUNTAIN

Round Mountain is the name of the town, the hill it sits on, the circular tailings piling up around the pit, and the company doing the digging. They provide an excellent history of the different forms of gold mining that have been practiced around the West over the last 140 years.

In 1906, Prospectors discovered the placer gold (waterborne deposits of sand or gravel containing gold eroded from original bedrock) that had washed down from ledges in the Toquimas, transforming sleepy ranches and farmland into yet another Nevada boomtown. The gold occurred in small high-grade veins that could be dug out with hand tools and hoisted up with gasoline engines. Later, dry-wash machines worked the surface gravel deposits. Individual miners and small partnerships took $1 million before the big players got involved in 1914. That year, a larger syndicate laid a pipe across Big Smoky Valley from Jett Canyon in the Toiyabes to sluice the gold out of the lower-grade ore. A half dozen mills also set up shop to serve the growing gold operations and population, which also helped the town develop through construction of hotels, restaurants, banks, and stores. Despite the amenities, Round Mountain's middle-of-nowhere status discouraged all but the hardiest settlers. In the mid-1920s, the Nevada Porphyry Gold Mine Company installed a dredge, and it became the largest gold-gravel washing operation in the state's history.

A number of companies tried mining at Round Mountain until large equipment was installed in 1950. Huge power shovels scooped the pay dirt into equally huge hoppers that funneled it onto long conveyor belts. These belts, 36 inches wide and miles long, traveled at three mph to stockpiles. From there, the ore was weighed and sent to crushers and washers, which could handle 500 tons per hour.

A lull in the mining quieted the area and nearly emptied the town in the 1960s, but by 1977 the mine was processing 7,000 tons a day. In 1985 an extensive expansion began, culminating in 1991 with a system that could handle 135,000 tons of ore every day. In 1983 the mine produced 92,000 ounces of gold leached from 3.6 million tons of ore at a cost of $265 per ounce; in 1990 the mine produced 432,000 ounces of gold from 16 million tons at a cost of $174 per ounce.

Today it takes 300 tons of ore to produce one ounce of gold. The open pit is 8,200 feet long,

5,000 feet wide, and 1,200 feet deep. Enormous shovels, excavators, and trucks working at the bottom of the pit are dwarfed by its magnitude. But when those dump trucks come barreling by with tires as tall as your house, and you realize that it takes two full loads to make just one ounce of gold, you get the true sense of what "microscopic gold" really means.

You can't tour the operation, but you can tell from the size of everything as you drive by on Highway 376 and Highway 378 that this place means business. As you drive up Highway 378 past the round mountain surrounding the pit, the colorful overburden is eye-catching. The town of Round Mountain is up the hill past the pit and has a grand total of five actual houses. The few dozen other dwellings are mobile homes.

MANHATTAN

After gold was discovered in the shadow of Bald Mountain in the Toquimas in 1906, the rush was on. The first excitement, financed by San Francisco capital, was prematurely aborted by the great earthquake that year, but Manhattan recovered in 1910. Successful placer operations necessitated the building of a large mill in 1912. Rich pay dirt was discovered in the lower levels of the hard-rock mine in 1915, and the mill had to be reconditioned. In the late 1930s, advanced gold-mining technology arrived in the form of a great gold dredge, an Alaska-size contraption that looked like a cross between an oversize houseboat and a crane. An endless conveyor on the dredge circulated dozens of steel buckets that scooped the gravel, conveyed it to the top end, and dumped it onto a revolving screen. The screen separated the larger rocks, shunting them off to the tailings piles, from the golden gravel, which was sifted by the screen onto riffles, where quicksilver (mercury) formed an amalgam with the gold. The riffles were cleaned and the amalgam was further processed into bullion, which was assayed and shipped to the mint. The dredge operated for eight years, and Manhattan produced $10 million in gold over its 40-year run, and a comparatively small operation continues at the site.

Today, Manhattan is a tiny, attractive village in a lovely canyon in the lower Toquimas. Highway 377 passes the Manhattan pit. Old headframes overlook the pit from the hill above; the company production plant is behind the pit on the other side. The town of Manhattan is up the road, with abandoned shacks, old houses, big trees, and a couple of bars. **Miner's Saloon** (422 W. Main St., 775/487-2379) has video poker, bar food, collectible rocks and bottles, jewelry, and apple trees outside. **Manhattan Bar** (246 W. Main St., 775/487-2304) is darker and more rustic, with a tumbledown exterior. About 60 people live in Manhattan year-round.

Highway 377 continues to the top of the canyon, where the pavement ends; the road continues 12 miles over to the east side of the Toquimas to Belmont. This is a fun road, full of ups and downs, twists and turns, even at 30 mph (but don't push it). At the first fork, bear left, and at the second fork, bear right to connect to the main gravel road from the original right fork off Highway 376 just north of Tonopah. In a few miles you come to pavement, pass the big stack from the Belmont-Monitor mill, and then cruise into Belmont.

BELMONT

Silver indications were uncovered high up on the east side of the Toquimas in 1865, in the lee of big Mount Jefferson. The rush was so great that 2,000 people lived in and around Belmont within a year. The mines and mills began producing millions of dollars of silver, and the state legislature decided to move the Nye County seat from Ione to Belmont in 1867, but the town's gradual decline meant the seat moved to Tonopah in 1905. Still, Belmont enjoyed a good run: It produced $15 million in silver during its 15-year stint in the spotlight. Fire, vandals, souvenir hunters, and entropy took their toll for the next 60 years until the state stepped in to stabilize the courthouse building and protect the town as a park. Belmont was also declared a National Historic District, which eliminated further scavenging.

Today Belmont is a restored beauty with fewer than 10 full-time residents. Historic and new houses are full of character and surrounded by well-tended yards. The **Belmont Courthouse** (775/867-3001, call to arrange a tour) is open to the public, and the ruins are picturesque, but be aware that tramping in, around, and through them is trespassing, and the locals are very protective of their town. In fact, the town's only paid employee is a caretaker (read: security guard); he'll no doubt check you out in his 4WD vehicle.

The **Belmont Saloon** (775/790-1100) was temporarily closed at press time, but you can get a good look through the front windows at the bar, taken from the ruins of an 1880s hotel up the street, as well as the denim-covered bar stools, sardine-can ashtrays, 1950s refrigerator,

potato-sack ceiling, and the infamous "jug mug" atop the 1905 cash register.

Continuing on the Monitor Valley road for 17 miles brings you to a sign for **Pine Creek Campground** (free); follow the sign to the left and drive another 2.5 miles to the U.S. Forest Service camp's 26 sites at the entrance to the **Alta Toquima Wilderness.** If you have the equipment, a valid license, and a trout stamp, wet a line in Pine Creek where it pools around the campsites after careening down Mount Jefferson's spine. You'll find plenty of cool, shady fishing holes thanks to the vibrant green trees nourished by the creek water.

The Pine Creek Trail travels just under 14 miles to the South Summit and the ridgeline that connects it to the Middle and North Summits. See *Nevada Wilderness Areas* by Michael Rose for all the details.

Tonopah and Vicinity

Tonopah is a great Nevada crossroads town, a natural stop that rewards pit-stopping travelers with a hands-on mining lesson and overnight visitors with one of the darkest starry skies in the country.

The federal Departments of Energy and Defense maintain the supersecret Tonopah Test Range, which is within the Nellis Air Force Range; its northern border is only a few miles southeast of Tonopah. The F-117A stealth fighter and Soviet MiG jet fighters bought from defecting pilots were test-flown here. The Air Force moved the stealth planes to New Mexico in the early 1990s. Although the military has only a marginal impact on the local economy, according to most people, Tonopah may be the only place in the world where shopkeepers smile when sonic booms shake windows around town. If the old merchants were still around, the din would probably remind them of the heady days when mines rumbled just two blocks off Main Street, giving Tonopah the nickname "Queen of the Silver Camps."

HISTORY

The boom at Austin in the mid-1860s sent prospectors into the rugged and remote desert south through Big Smoky Valley, and the decline of Nevada's mining fortunes over the final two decades of the 19th century busted and embittered more than its share of prospectors. Even prodigious pick-wielder Jim Butler hung up his shovel and took to hay ranching in Big Smoky Valley near Belmont. Butler had been born at the California gold rush and had been a prospector and miner in Nevada for decades. One morning in 1900 Butler awoke to discover that one of his burros had wandered away. He found it on what was soon to be called Mizpah Hill. Picking up a rock with which to plunk the donkey, Butler noticed the would-be projectile seemed unusually heavy. Assays confirmed the rocks were packed with silver.

The story—probably apocryphal—continues that Butler was a lackadaisical miner and rancher who hung around Belmont all

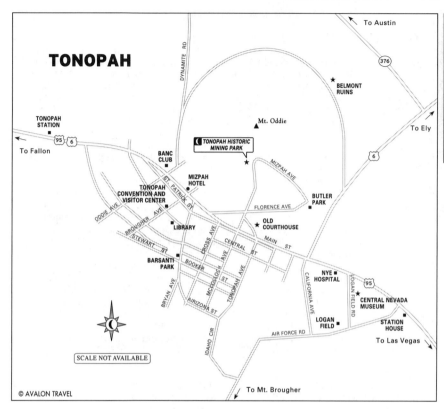

TONOPAH

To Austin

376

BELMONT
RUINS

To Ely

TONOPAH
STATION

Mt. Oddie

DYNAMITE RD

95 6

To Fallon

TONOPAH HISTORIC
MINING PARK

BANC
CLUB

ST. PATRICK ST

MIZPAH
HOTEL

MIZPAH AVE

6

TONOPAH
CONVENTION AND
VISITOR CENTER

ODDIE AVE

BROUGHER AVE

FLORENCE AVE

BUTLER
PARK

LIBRARY

CROSS AVE

OLD
COURTHOUSE

STEWART ST

CENTRAL ST

MAIN ST

BARSANTI
PARK

BOOKER

McCULLOH ST

TONOPAH AVE

CENTRAL ST

CALIFORNIA AVE

NYE
HOSPITAL

LOGAN FIELD RD

95

BRYAN AVE

ARIZONA ST

CENTRAL NEVADA
MUSEUM

IDAHO CIR

LOGAN
FIELD

STATION
HOUSE

AIR FORCE RD

To Las Vegas

SCALE NOT AVAILABLE

© AVALON TRAVEL

To Mt. Brougher

summer to watch his hay grow. Butler's wife, Belle, had to drag him back to Tonopah to stake a few claims. But a more likely version might be that word of the valuable ore started to get around and Butler deliberately delayed his return, using the hay harvest as an excuse to defuse the rush and maintain personal control of the property, which only he knew the location of. In the fall, he sneaked off with his wife and partner, Tasker Oddie, and laid out the ground.

When Butler finally showed up at Tonopah, miners crept out of the woodwork to grab their piece of the pie. Butler and Oddie worked out a lucrative inventive system of verbal leases; leaseholders paid 25 percent in royalties for the right to work the ore until the end of the year. Of the 112 handshake agreements made, not one

formal contract was signed and not one lawsuit was ever filed. Times were hard during the first winter, with everything, especially water, scarce. But by the spring of 1901 the rush was on and all the boomtown rats arrived to serve the feverish miners, who were trying to recover every last cent of silver from their leased holes before the deadline arrived at the end of the year. On New Year's Eve, the miners surfaced, brushed off, and celebrated both their own prosperity and the beginning of Nevada's most promising silver strike in 25 years. On January 1, 1902, a Philadelphia mining venture paid Butler more than $300,000 for all the leased property, incorporated the Tonopah Mining Company, and hired Oddie as general manager. Jim and Belle Butler bought a big ranch at Inyo, California, and moved there in 1903.

GREAT BASIN EVENTS

In many parts of the country parades are a lost art, but in Great Basin territory you can find one just about any summer weekend. As *Las Vegas Review-Journal* columnist John L. Smith notes, Nevada's small towns host more parades than Russia under Stalin. They are usually attached to quaint festivals celebrating the bygone days of a bypassed town and are a not-to-be-missed opportunity to loosen your tie, turn off the cell phone, and sink into quaint, idyllic, pastoral times of yore.

JANUARY

Cave Lake State Park hosts the **Fire and Ice Festival,** highlighted by ice and snow sculptures, both massive and dainty. At night, spectacular fireworks illuminate the hauntingly stark white landscape.

MAY

Tonopah's **Jim Butler Days** are a big community fair with stock car races, a parade, a craft show, food, games, raffles, gold panning, a queen contest, and the Nevada State Mining Championships. **Walker Lake Education Day** at Walker Lake provides the opportunity to view loons as they stop to feed and breed on their way back to their nesting grounds in Canada, along with grebes, pelicans, cormorants, and geese. Preservationists demonstrate efforts to save the lake. The event includes boat rides, water sports demonstrations, and fund-raising. Vintage models, muscle cars, and classic roadsters vie for attention at the **Show What Ya Brung Car Show** in Austin. Events include a community yard sale, a pancake breakfast, music, kiddie rides, and a Main Street gunfight at high noon. At the **Nevada Open Road Challenge** in Lund, drivers race along Highway 318 for 90 miles through rural Nevada, ending in Lincoln County. The two-lane course challenges drivers with speed-friendly straights, hair-raising hairpins, and ramp-like hills. Several classes of cars ensure competitive races. The Silver State Classic in September covers the same course and has the same rules. Transportation old and new, airborne and terrestrial, take center stage at the **Lyon County Fly-In** in Silver Springs, with restored early jets, state-of-the-art fighters, and radio-controlled planes lining up with hot-air balloons, hang gliders, monster trucks, and Aston Martins. Raffle drawings, plenty of food, and gunfights in the street keep the event lively.

JUNE

Nothing says good old American fun like guns and alcohol. Ely's **Cocktails and Cannons**

After surrendering $150 million in silver, the mines began to play out around 1915. Tonopah's population fell to under 2,000, and mining ceased completely at the start of World War II. The Tonopah-Goldfield short line railroad stopped running in 1947.

Bonanza Highway (U.S. 95) traffic, the Army Air Field south of town, and the Nye County seat kept the town alive into the early 1950s. Howard Hughes himself was an admirer, frequent visitor, and sometime investor in Tonopah in the 1950s. When Hughes married Jean Peters in March 1957, he did it in Tonopah. Also, when he set up shop on the ninth floor of Las Vegas's Desert Inn and proceeded to spend $300 million between 1966 and 1969 on Nevada hotels, casinos, airports, TV stations, and real estate, a large part of the $10 million he spent on mining property was centered on Tonopah and Round Mountain.

In the mid-1970s, the deregulation of gold sparked a new mining boom in the area. Anaconda Copper Company operated a large molybdenum mine and mill 25 miles north of Tonopah for a few years beginning in 1979. In 1999 an Australian company began mining copper.

SIGHTS
Central Nevada Museum

The large and varied Central Nevada Museum (1900 Logan Field Rd., 775/482-9676, celebration is actually a pretty tame family event with bathtub races, a barbecue, and yes, cannon shots. The racing tubs are studies in creativity and engineering, and the barbecue includes steak and seafood. Afterward, relax with beer, wine, and cocktails as fireworks explode over Cave Lake. **Gridley Days** in Austin have a county-fair feel, complete with a rodeo, to help the town celebrate Reuel Gridley's 1860s flour-sack tote to benefit the Sanitary Commission. Contests test participants' skills in hula-hooping, horseshoe pitching, sack racing, and sandcastle building. There's also music and food.

JULY

Tonopah's **Fourth of July Barbecue and Fireworks** are good wholesome fun that includes raffles, swimming, a softball tournament, a parade, fireworks, and food.

AUGUST

Break out your turn-of-the-century garb at **Goldfield Days** in Goldfield and witness Old West gunfights, street dances, tours of the historic town, games, parades, and barbecue and chili cook-offs.

SEPTEMBER

Drivers in the **Silver State Classic** race along Highway 318 through rural Nevada for 90 miles near Lund, ending in Lincoln County. The two-lane course challenges drivers with speed-friendly straights, hair-raising hairpins, and ramp-like hills. Several classes of cars ensure competitive races. The Nevada Open Road Challenge in May covers the same course and has the same rules. The **Spirit of Wovoka Powwow** in Yerington features Native American crafts, singing, and dancing that recall the true meaning of the Ghost Dance and the Paiute prophet Wovoka. Crafts booths, food vendors, and a raffle as well as Powwow Princess and Lil' Miss pageants are held along with the traditional entertainment. A final outdoor-activity splurge in Pioche before bundling up for the winter, **Pioche Labor Day** has a parade, softball, horseshoes, and road races along with mucking and other mining-related contests. When the sun goes down, people take to the streets for dancing to live music.

DECEMBER

Find Western treasures for everyone on your holiday list while sipping hot cocoa to ward off the crisp valley wind in Tonopah for the **Christmas Stroll and Tree Lighting.** Santa is on hand to help with the tree-lighting ceremonies.

---

9 A.M.–5 P.M. Tues.–Sat., free), just off U.S. 95 at the south end of town near Logan Field, emphasizes the region's mining legacy. The Old West town re-creation outside, with cabins, a saloon, a blacksmith shop, and a stamp mill, is especially impressive. More mining and ranching artifacts are inside, as well as intriguing and empathetic studies of the contributions of various ethnic groups to the area's history, culture, and art. An extensive photo collection shows central Nevada towns during the boom and the abandoned mines following the bust, aerial views of Tonopah and maps of the state, a purple bottle collection (manganese in the glass reacts to sunlight to create the unique color), and lots of Shoshone artifacts such as baskets. Another special exhibit looks at the contributions of the Tonopah Army Air Field during World War II.

The research room is available for modern-day prospecting. Hundreds of books, photographs, newspapers, videos, and genealogical files can help you strike research gold. The gift shop sells books, historical journals, postcards, and souvenirs. An hour or so here provides an appreciation of the history of the town and this part of Nevada, which is sure to inform the rest of your visit.

Tonopah Historic Mining Park

A video at the 70-acre Tonopah Historic Mining Park (520 McCulloch Ave., 775/482-

9274, www.tonopahhistoricminingpark.com, 9 A.M.–5 P.M. daily Apr.–Sept., 10 A.M.–4 P.M. daily Oct.–Mar., free) will introduce you to Jim and Belle Butler as well as the rest of Tonopah's colorful mining history. After the video in the park's visitors center, originally the Tonopah Mining Company's power substation and telephone exchange, poke around the Silver Top and Mizpah Mines, sorting rooms, hoists, and railroad trestles. The centerpiece of the walking tour ($5 adults, $3 ages 7–12, free under age 7) is the **Burro Tunnel Underground Adventure,** where Butler took some of his original samples. You'll have a bird's-eye view of a 500-foot stope as you enter the viewing cage suspended above.

In buildings along the tour route, spare parts and cases of core samples sit gathering dust, pretty much the way they have since the mines shut down. The tour offers a close-up look at the snaking stopes and cracks where the lease miners removed the ore in their hustle to make their fortunes before their agreements with the mine owners expired.

On the way over to the Mizpah Mine, you'll walk right across an exposed two-foot-wide vein of silver ore just like the one Jim Butler found in 1900. Curiously it was never mined. Peer into the 100-foot-deep crater of the Glory Hole site of a 1922 cave-in caused by mining too near the surface. No one was killed, but only because the collapse occurred at night. Miners returned to work the next morning to find the assay office in splinters at the bottom of the pit. The museum also has an extensive mineral display enhanced by black lighting.

The park offers an excellent view of downtown Tonopah. Look across Main Street at the Silver Queen Motel and you'll see that the upper wing of the inn is built on the huge tailings pile from the Silver Queen Mine. The motel swimming pool sits above the old shaft.

Town Tour

The Tonopah Development Corporation (TDC), in addition to its other duties, has commissioned a dozen **murals and sculptures** honoring the Butlers, the military, heroic miner Big Bill Murphy, and other pride-instilling icons. As you drive around town, keep an eye out for these mini tributes. For locations, contact the TDC (200 S. Main St., 775/482-9680).

Start at the 1907 **Knights of Columbus hall** (Brooker St. and Brougher Ave.), originally the home of George Bartlett, an attorney who lived in the mansion for less than a year before losing it in the 1907 silver panic. Sadly, much of the home's splendor—leather walls, spiral staircases, and stone hearths—has been lost to "salvagers." Several restoration efforts have failed, and the once-glorious abode is quickly losing its battle against time.

Around the corner is the mansion that mining executive, banker, and Nevada radio pioneer Arthur Raycraft built around the same time. Known as the **Castle House,** the twin turrets added Queen Anne accents to the neocolonial-style original building. It has been said that Raycraft's wife held séances complete with a crystal ball in the tower room. Perhaps that's why the shy and mischievous spirit of "George" still occasionally appears in the castle.

The once and hopefully future "Grand Lady of Tonopah," the **Mizpah Hotel** (100 Main St.) sits vacant a few blocks east at Brougher Avenue. Investors took advantage of the coming of the railroad in 1907 and constructed this opulent 76-room gem. They spared no expense, installing an elevator, imported brass chandeliers, and stained-glass windows for the five-story building, the tallest in Nevada until 1948. It's doubtful that the Mizpah witnessed much rowdy behavior; Wyatt Earp tended bar here for a time, and boxer Jack Dempsey (according to legend, and who are we to stand in the way of a good story?) worked as a bouncer. Families of Army Air Corps members lived at the Mizpah during World War II while their loved ones—including Chuck Yeager—trained on B-24s. A few restorations kept the hotel up-to-date until the 1990s, when the owners lost their gaming license. Subsequent owners fared little better, but another restoration effort is under way. Although the Mizpah has been closed for 20 years, a few guests have apparently not got the message: The ghosts of two murdered miners and a too-young-to-die "soiled dove" (prostitute) from the hotel's early years are still said to roam the hotel's corridors.

Near the corner of Brougher Avenue and Summit Street are the chamber of commerce and convention center (301 Brougher Ave., 775/482-3859) and the library.

Tonopah Star Trails

Just a few hours from Las Vegas, which probably has more lights per city block than anywhere else, Tonopah nights are the darkest in the country. That makes the town and its surroundings an optimal spot to view the treasures of the night sky. City dwellers can see only a few dozen of the brightest stars, but on a clear moonless winter night in Tonopah you can see 7,000 heavenly bodies make an appearance. Uranus and stars in the Milky Way are clearly visible to the naked eye. Even small telescopes bring Saturn's rings, frozen Neptune, the Ring Nebula, and even the Andromeda galaxy into view. The Tonopah Development Corporation (775/482-9680, www.tonopahstartrails.com) publishes *Tonopah Star Trails,* a guide to paved and unpaved roads around town that afford the best sky views. The Tonopah Astronomical Society (http://tas.astronomynv.org) hosts regular star parties; check their website for times and locations.

Old Tonopah Cemetery

Opened for business in 1901, the Old Tonopah Cemetery is the final resting place for more than 300 early residents of the town, including the victims of the "Tonopah Sickness." To this day, no one knows what caused the 1902 epidemic that took the lives of more than 30 local miners during the winter of 1901–1902. The outbreak spurred a mass exodus from Tonopah that winter. Also buried here are the 14 victims of the Tonopah Belmont Fire of 1911—including "Big Bill" Murphy, who rescued several of his fellow miners before succumbing to toxic fumes. Murphy and those he couldn't save are buried near each other. A statue commemorating Murphy's heroism can be seen in front of the post office. Nye County Sheriff Tom Logan, killed in a 1906 shoot-out at a brothel in nearby Manhattan, is also buried here. The Old Tonopah Cemetery is near the Clown Motel on Main Street; ask at the chamber of commerce for directions.

Mount Oddie

Take Florence Avenue, behind the Silver Queen Motel, to McCullough Avenue, which leads to the south side of Mount Oddie, where you'll see the **Mizpah Headframe.** Sited and named by Belle Butler, according to legend, the Mizpah Mine was the richest of the Butler properties. **Butler Park** is up here, near the corner of Valley View Avenue and Mizpah Circle; with picnic tables and restrooms, it's a pleasant place to get out of the car. Return on Florence Avenue to go by the **County Courthouse,** built in 1905 on land donated by the Tonopah Mining Company.

Turquoise Mine Tours

Tonopah sits in the center of some of the most beautiful turquoise deposits in the world. Otteson's Turquoise lets customers tour and dig in the tailings at its **Royston Mine** (101 N. Main St., 775/482-9889, Wed. and Sun. Apr.–Oct., $100 adults, $50 ages 12–18, free under age 12). The four-hour adventure allows guests to keep a bucketful of blue-green treasure. Otteson's can cut, polish, and set the stones. Visits need to be booked and a deposit paid at least two weeks in advance.

Lunar Crater

Volcanism is one of earth's most dramatic processes, and Nevada rests on one section of the most active belt of volcanoes in the world: the Pacific Ring of Fire. Lunar Crater, in the Pancake Range 80 miles east of Tonopah on U.S. 6, is an excellent example of both recent and ancient volcanism at work in Nevada. During the Oligocene epoch 40 million years ago, a colossal eruption obliterated the existing Nevada landscape. Through fractures, fissures, and vents, an unimaginably titanic disgorgement of white-hot steam, ash, and particulate spewed up from the depths, burying the surface under thousands of feet of sheets of ash flow. The topmost sheet transformed the landscape into a single uniform layer. The **Lunar Cuesta** is an illustration of the welded tuft or fused volcanic rock that resulted from this cataclysm.

The cinder cones, lava tongues, and craters at Lunar Crater are manifestations of much more recent volcanism; they are only a few thousand years old. Take a right onto the Lunar loop road and drive three miles. Turn left at the sign to **Easy Chair Crater.** It's clear how this high-backed hole got its name. A 100-yard trail from the parking area leads up to the viewpoint; a sign points out some geology and the direction of lava flows. Within view is some amazingly diverse topography: buttes, craters, cones, the cuesta floor, and the mighty Quinn Canyon Range in the background. The Apollo astronauts trained in this 140,000-acre lunar landscape.

Back on the good one-lane, 35 mph dirt road, drive another few miles and climb up to **Lunar Crater,** 420 feet deep and nearly 4,000 feet in diameter. This is a typical maar, formed when the violent release of gases reams an abrupt deep crater with a low rim. Unlike the crater behind it, which is the peak of a small cinder cone, no magma was ejected with the gases. But the old lava and ash flows were exposed by the explosion; the descriptive sign points them out.

Continuing the next eight miles toward The Wall, you drive on the east side of the loop along dry Lunar Lake. (You won't wonder where or what The Wall is; suffice it to say that Pink Floyd's eponymous double album is not only apropos, but essential.) The loop ends back at the asphalt of U.S. 6. North of the highway is **Black Rock Lava Flow,** the most recent basalt ooze in the area, covering 1,900 acres. The lava cooled so fast that it is specked with green, red, and black glass.

CASINOS

The big-town casino is at the **Tonopah Station** (1137 S. Main St., 775/482-9777 or 800/272-

6232, $55–79) on the south end of town. This hotel-casino was built in 1982 during the most recent Tonopah boom next to Scolari's Warehouse Market, the town's first supermarket. The compact 10,000-square-foot casino is cramped and crowded with slots and a small blackjack pit.

The Banc Club restaurant, bar, and casino (360 N. Main St., 775/482-5409) has slot machines and occupies a building that was once the Bank of America building. Locals say it would have been named The Bank Club, since it's in an old bank, except that Nevada law prohibits using the word *bank* in the name of a casino.

ACCOMMODATIONS

Tonopah has nearly 500 motel rooms, which are enough to accommodate all comers at any time except on the busiest Saturday nights and during Jim Butler Days, the town festival that takes place the last weekend in May. Rates are inexpensive enough that you don't have to worry about getting a good deal anywhere you go. All the motels are located along Main Street through town. The rooms at **Jim Butler Motel** (100 S. Main St., 775/482-3577, $40–75) are bright and inviting, with wood furniture and faux hearths. Some rooms have fridges and microwaves; all have free Wi-Fi. We wondered if the doors to the **Clown Motel** (521 N. Main St., 775/482-5920, $35–50) might spontaneously open and spew out juggling, tumbling, grease-painted jesters, one after another. What we found instead are clean guest rooms, free of the smell of smoke, with refrigerators and microwaves. Guest rooms are basic twin doubles for a decent price, and the only overt clown references are the marquee and understated plaques on guest-room doors.

The furnishings in the 75-room **Tonopah Station/Ramada Inn** (1137 S. Main St., 775/482-9777, $50–75) are OK but beginning to feel dated; renovations may be required soon. The hotel offers nonsmoking rooms, but they bear evidence of times when no such distinction was made. The RV park ($25) is asphalt, but its 19 spaces are relatively quiet. Some spots have decent shade, and the central location makes up for the dearth of aesthetics.

Several smaller, basic motels are recommendable: the **Tonopah Motel** (325 Main St., 775/482-3987, $30–40) has 20 guest rooms. Next is the **Golden Hills Motel** (930 N. Main St., 775/482-6238, $44–65). The **National 9** (720 N. Main St., 775/482-8202, $35–60) has 52 guest rooms. For the consistent quality that chains can offer, the best in town is the **Best Western Hi-Desert Inn** (320 Main St., 775/482-3511 or 877/286-2208, $80–120), with 62 guest rooms and homemade cookies at check-in. In a world of complimentary continental breakfasts, the waffles and eggs in the morning will give you a big ol' happy face.

FOOD

If you've been traveling around on Nevada's lonely roads for a while, you will have come to realize that the small towns that dot the asphalt ribbon don't offer much in the four-star dining range. Similarly, Tonopah is not restaurant heaven, but there are a couple of standouts, especially if you're in the mood for Mexican fare.

The **El Marques** (348 North Main St., 775/482-3885, 11 A.M.–9 P.M. Tues.–Sun., $10–20), across from the Tonopah Motel, is said to be the best in town. The chiles rellenos are tender and cheesy. Service may be a bit spotty, but who's in a hurry in Tonopah? If you are in a hurry but still jonesing for Mexican, hit the drive-through at **Cisco's Tacos** (702 N. Main St., 775/482-5022, $5–10). It has burgers, pizza, and even ribs.

The coffee shop at **Tonopah Station** (1137 S. Main St., 24 hours daily, under $10) has surprisingly good food. At the snack shop you can get tacos, burritos, burgers, chili, hot dogs, root beer floats, and milk shakes.

INFORMATION AND SERVICES

Tonopah Convention and Visitors Center (301 Brougher Ave., 775/482-3558, www. tonopahnevada.com, 8 A.M.–5 P.M. Mon.–Fri.) and the **Tonopah Chamber of Commerce**

(200 S. Main St., 775/482-9680, www. tonopahchamberofcommerce.com) has all the statistics and brochures you'll need.

Down the street is the third **library** (167 Central St., 775/482-3374, 10 A.M.–6 P.M. Wed.–Sat.) ever built in Nevada, in 1912, and the oldest one still in use.

GOLDFIELD

In 1902, when Tonopah was less than two years old and already the biggest boomtown Nevada had seen for a generation, Jim Butler grubstaked two young prospectors who'd seen rich ore on a small ledge about 25 miles due south. Just like Butler, they staked several claims, mined their first pay dirt, and managed a small return. Unlike Tonopah's silver mines, Goldfield's ore produced mostly gold. The grubstakers dug in all winter and finally attracted some expert attention in the late spring. Like Butler, they proceeded to lease their remaining claims. The gold rush became frenzied when the ore was found to be so rich that $5-per-day miners could "high-grade" $250 per day worth of nuggets—in shoes, secret pockets, hollow ax handles, and body holsters—then sell it to fences for cash. The crude tent camp on the mountainside in 1903 gave way to a real town on one of the few level plats to be found. With so much precious metal lying around and everyone's pockets bulging with nuggets, real estate prices quickly went through the roof.

In 1904 the townsfolk erected large, permanent stone buildings, and the Tonopah-Goldfield Railroad arrived. Tex Rickard, a well-known character from the Klondike-Nome gold rushes in Alaska five years earlier, promoted the Joe Gans–Oscar Nelson lightweight title fight in Goldfield in the summer of 1906, which ran nearly three hours and 42 rounds. Rickart made enough money on this event to leverage it all the way to promoting prizefights at Madison Square Garden in New York City. The publicity was priceless, and prizefights have been big business in Nevada ever since.

By 1907 Goldfield boasted more than

THE EARPS OF GOLDFIELD AND TONOPAH

More than 22 years after the events that made them famous, both Wyatt and Virgil Earp plied their various trades in and around Goldfield and Tonopah at the height of the mining boom. And while some town fathers and tourist-driven businesses might lead you to believe otherwise, neither caused a commotion anywhere near the ruckus they had been involved in at the OK Corral in Tombstone, Arizona.

Wyatt was part owner of a saloon; Virgil was a security guard. Both worked on the fringes of law enforcement, but there is no evidence either ever drew a gun while in Nevada. Fresh from making a small fortune in the Alaskan gold fields, Wyatt, along with his wife, Josie, was the first of the famous brothers to invest in Nevada. He arrived in January 1902 and a few months later opened the Northern Saloon with a partner. He also hauled ore for the Tonopah Mining Company and held the position of deputy U.S. marshal without getting into a gunfight. Never one to allow the grass grow under his feet, Wyatt sold up less than a year later and set out for California. He did make sporadic visits back to Nevada, often prospecting claims on Silver Peak, west of Goldfield. Some reliable sources believe he visited brother Virgil during the summer of 1905.

Virgil had arrived in 1904 and was quickly installed as deputy sheriff of Esmeralda County. The *Tonopah Sun* on February 5, 1905, was not impressed with his demeanor:

> Verge Earp, a brother of Wyatt and one of the famous family of gunologists...is a mild looking individual and to the outward view presents none of the characteristics that have made the family a familiar one in the west.

He moonlighted as a bouncer at the National Club, but perhaps owing to his injuries from a revenge attack following the OK Corral gunfight, he was unable to fight off a severe case of pneumonia and died in Goldfield on October 19, 1905.

Their mundane lives in western Nevada notwithstanding, several legends about the brothers' exploits live on. Storytellers delight in insisting Wyatt confronted a trio of claim jumpers and ordered them to vacate the premises. "And just who the hell do you think you are?" the trespassers sneered, their weapons trained on him. "I'm Wyatt Earp," the Western legend informed them. His name alone was enough to make the would-be usurpers up and skedaddle.

10,000 people and was on its way to becoming Nevada's largest metropolis. Barroom brawls had been replaced by corporate clashes between organized labor and company-hired goons. A confrontation between labor, represented by the emerging International Workers of the World, or Wobblies, and management over high-grading and reduced wages came to a head when Wingfield and his owner cronies persuaded Governor John Sparks to ask President Theodore Roosevelt to send in the Army to "maintain order and protect property." The military presence allowed the corporations to hire scabs and break the union. The federal troops were replaced by a new law-enforcement unit that became the state police, and the owners' control was complete.

The peak of the gold-mining boom occurred in 1910, but the bust wasn't far behind. A flood in 1913, mine closures in 1919, and the great fire of 1923 made it a near ghost town. Today the population is roughly 320, although you're likely to find only a handful in town at any given time. Most of the residents mine gold in the desert or work on the highway, at the air base, or in Tonopah. Several stone buildings, including the grand old Goldfield Hotel and the high school, are remnants of the heyday.

Sights

U.S. 95 passes through Goldfield, which rests in a bowl between Columbia Mountain of the Goldfield Hills on the east and the Montezuma Range on the west. A tour of the historic town offers a glimpse into the rich history of the West.

The historic fenced-off **Goldfield Hotel** is unmistakable. It opened in 1908 as possibly the most luxurious hotel between Chicago and San Francisco. The stone-and-brick building was equipped with telephones, electricity, and a heating system, and it was decorated with rich mahogany, black leather, gold leaf, and crystal chandeliers. It boasted 150 guest rooms and 45 suites with baths. Every room had a telephone that was part of an ingenious fire-alarm system. There was a pool and a billiard parlor, a separate gaming room for ladies, and the dining room was 40 by 80 feet. On opening night, a river of champagne cascaded down the front steps, and dinner featured oysters, caviar, filet mignon, vegetables from the hotel nursery, and ice cream.

Soon after opening, mining magnate George Wingfield bought the hotel and is still said to haunt its halls. His cigar smoke can often be smelled in his room. Other purported ghosts include Wingfield's alleged mistress and his illegitimate child, two guests who committed suicide in the hotel, two children and a little person who are said to pull pranks on visitors, and "The Stabber" who is said to "attack" people with a knife, although his ghostly attacks cause more fear than harm. Whether the ghosts are real or not, many people have attested to feeling strange presences in the hotel, and in Room 109 cameras are said to mysteriously stop working and the room becomes intensely cold. The hotel has been featured in TV shows and documentaries on haunted places, and more than one psychic has named it a gateway to another world.

The hotel closed for good in 1946 and has changed hands several times since but has never reopened. In 1986 a San Francisco investment company began to renovate the place but never finished. The interior is a half-completed construction job, and boxes of hotel supplies await the next ambitious soul to tackle a reopening.

The hotel, courthouse, high school, and several other stone buildings in town survived the fires and floods that devastated the town; some have historical markers on them, including the **Southern Nevada Consolidated Telephone Company** (Ramsey St. and Columbia Ave.), the town's communications center 1906–1963. The exterior of the huge **high school** (Ramsey St. and Euclid Ave.), which graduated its last class in 1952, maintains its grandeur as volunteers race the clock to return the interior to its former glory.

The county **courthouse** (233 Crook St.), built in 1907 of native sandstone, still serves the 1,300 residents of Esmeralda County, the least populous in Nevada. You're welcome to tour the building during business hours; if the courtroom is locked, ask at the clerk's office to go inside. It's worth the trouble to see the best preserved courthouse in the state, with original 1905 Tiffany lamps on the bench; original brass, leather, and wood furniture and fixtures; the judge's chambers behind; and the bighorn sheep's head overseeing it all. **Tex Rickard's house** and the 1908 **Goldfield Fire Station No. 1,** which is still in use, are among the other Victorian structures along Crook Street.

The **Santa Fe Saloon** (925 N. 5th Ave., 775/485-3431) has been here nearly since the beginning. Constructed in 1905, the ramshackle clapboard structure was built outside of town to be closer to its target customers, miners in search of drink and company after dusty days in the shafts. Traveling the dusty highway makes the burnished 100-year-old bar inside just as desirable today. The oldest continually operating business in town, the Santa Fe survived the big flood of 1916, the great fire of 1923, and the death of its original owner in a 1912 gunfight.

Practicalities

Stop in for a drink and a chat at the **Santa Fe Saloon** (925 N. 5th Ave., 775/485-3431, $50–90). It has a handful of serviceable if plain rooms. Check out all the history on the walls. Someone interesting is sure to be sitting at the bar.

BEATTY

Tucked into the edge of Oasis Valley between the California state line and the Nellis bombing range (and Area 51), Beatty serves as a gateway to Death Valley. It was founded at the turn of the century to supply the Bullfrog Mining District and the bustling mining town of Rhyolite.

The town is the closest town to Yucca Mountain, the on-again, off-again proposed storage site for the nation's nuclear waste. Most Nevadans oppose the project for obvious reasons; locals refer to the legislation that singled out Yucca Mountain for study as a repository as the "Screw Nevada" bill. However, as the global economic downturn gripped Nevada at the end of the 2000s, tourism dollars dried up and the state suffered the highest unemployment rate in the country, and a growing minority began reexamining the financial benefits that would accompany development of the site. The project seemed doomed when President Barack Obama discontinued funding for developing the site in his 2011 budget.

Sights

The **Beatty Museum and Historical Society** (417 W. Main St., 775/553-2303, 10 A.M.–3 P.M. daily, donation) brings everyday life in a turn-of-the-20th-century mining outpost to life through photos, books, mining stock certificates, farm implements, children's playthings, kitchen items, and Native American artifacts. The gift shop has books, apparel, and souvenirs.

Head west out of town along Highway 374 for a few miles and follow the signs to **Rhyolite,** home to the "Bottle House" and several other seriously cool buildings and ruins. One of the most photographed ghost towns in the country, Rhyolite boomed to sophistication and prosperity after the discovery of rich gold veins on Bullfrog Mountain in 1904. By 1907 the 4,000 residents of Rhyolite were enjoying concrete sidewalks, electric lights, telephones, daily newspapers, an opera house, and a public swimming pool. Three banks and a stock exchange helped residents trade and protect their fortunes. The remains of the ostentatious three-story John S. Cook and Co. Bank on Golden Street, completed in 1908, still stand. By 1909 the gold veins were beginning

to thin. The banks closed in 1910, and by 1912 the mines had mostly closed.

With more than 50 saloons in Rhyolite by the end of 1905, Tom Kelly had little trouble finding building materials for his Bottle House—one of three that once graced the town. Kelly embedded some 30,000 bottles, most recently emptied of Adolphus Busch Beer but with a few snake oil bottles thrown in, into the adobe walls of his three-room house. Kelly never lived here; after completing the interior, he raffled it off. Renovated in 2005, the Bottle House is among the best-preserved of Rhyolite's relics. You can imagine yourself among the crag-faced miners stocking up at the Porter Brothers' store, the painted ladies awaiting customers outside their cribs, and shiny-suited sharpies sizing up a mark outside the railroad depot. Ruins of all these historic buildings, along with homes, the school, and several mines, make Rhyolite a fascinating place to spend an afternoon.

Just outside Rhyolite you'll find what originator Albert Szukalski called an "art situation" in the middle of the vast desert. Szukalski crated the original dozen artworks here at what has become known as the **Goldwell Open Air Museum** (24 hours daily, free), notably *The Last Supper,* a collection of 13 ghostly plaster figures arranged to mirror Da Vinci's masterpiece. Over the decades other artists, including three of Szukalski's fellow Belgians, added to the collection, using media as diverse as native rhyolite, chrome, cinderblock, and discarded furniture. Several artists-in-residence continually add to the collection, and others take advantage of the studio and workspace the museum provides. Pick up museum-logo merchandise, original artwork, and a self-guided museum tour brochure at the gift shop (10 A.M.–4 P.M. most days).

Fifty miles southeast of Beatty, more than two dozen species that don't exist anywhere else on the planet live at **Ash Meadows National Wildlife Refuge** (Hwy. 160 and Bell Vista Rd., Pahrump, 775/372-5435, free). Although it's only about an hour from Death Valley, the paragon of aridity, the 22,000-acre refuge is a vast network of springs, bogs, seeps, and small lakes ringed by walkable beaches and alluring picnic

MANLY AND ROGERS: THE HEROIC JOURNEY

William Lewis Manly and John Rogers filled their canteens with alkali-tainted water and stuffed as much ox meat as they could fit into their makeshift packs. Striking west from near Furnace Creek Wash in early 1850, they shouldered not only their meager supplies but also the forlorn hopes of a dozen men, women, and children lost in the Nevada-California desert for three months.

In the autumn of 1849 disagreements over the best route to the California gold fields splintered the original wagon train of 500 souls who crossed into what would later become the Nevada-Utah state line area. Manly's and Rogers's group, including Asahel and Sarah Bennett with their three children and Jean Baptiste and Abigail Arcan with their baby boy, struggled across Nevada. A month's trek through the arid desert left their oxen weak from lack of forage and the children begging for water. Camped at the base of the Tempiute Range, 20 miles west of modern-day Hiko, they finally thought they had found deliverance. "Suddenly there broke into view to the south a splendid sheet of water," remembered one traveler, a boy at the time. "[But] as we hurried toward it, the vision faded, and near midnight we halted on the rim of a basin of mud, with a shallow pool of brine."

After another month of broken wagons, lame oxen, and American Indian depredations, the Bennett-Arcan Party found itself stranded, reduced to slaughtering draft animals for the meager sustenance their emaciated carcasses offered. It was here, in one of the most desolate places on earth, that two heroes emerged. The youngest and fittest of the group, Manly and Rogers were selected to go for help. Ten days and 250 miles into a grueling trek through the Amargosa Desert, Manly and Rogers staggered parched and lame from yet another mountain pass and into a most welcome sight, "a beautiful meadow...and...a herd of cattle," Manly later wrote. This, thankfully, was no mirage. The friends located a stream and butchered a calf. "How we felt the strength come back to us with that food and the long draughts of pure clear water," Manly continued.

But their ordeal was far from over, for their moral obligation would find them plunging back through the unforgiving desert not once but twice more in the coming month. At Rancho San Francisquito they bought three horses, a mule, sacks of beans and flour, and an orange for each of the four children they had left behind. Even as Manly and Rogers threaded their way over California's Panamint Mountains and through narrow passes and rocky, dusty terrain, several of those they had left at the spring lost faith in the duo.

Believing that "if those boys ever get out of this cussed hole, they are damned fools if they ever come back to help anybody," Captain Richard Culverwell packed out. He turned back but perished before he could return to the camp. As the families' camp finally appeared, Manly's and Rogers' hearts sank. Three of the seven wagons they had left were gone, and the others had been burned. There was no sign of their friends. Manly wrote,

The thought of our hard struggles between life and death to go out and return, with the fruitless results that now seemed apparent, was almost more than the human heart could bear. When should we know their fate? When should we find their remains? If ever two men were troubled, Rogers and I surely passed through the furnace.

But eventually the camp stirred, and when Bennett spied the figures in the distance, he erupted with shouts of "The boys have come! You have saved us all!"

The travelers nourished themselves for a few days, made packs for the oxen, then headed toward Los Angeles, abandoning their wagons. As they reached a high point on their exodus, they paused to remember their struggles and give thanks. A lone voice summed up their ordeals and gave the barren landscape the name it's known by to this day: "Goodbye, Death Valley."

areas. From Highway 160, head west on Devils Hole Road, or from Highway 373 go east on Spring Meadows Road. Follow the signs, and just when the sand dunes and alkali flats tell you there can't be an oasis here, there it is.

At **Crystal Spring,** near the refuge headquarters, a 0.5-mile boardwalk parallels a narrow stream. The stream is a lifeline for reeds, cattails, and other riparian plants along its banks. The rill and its flora entourage create a ribbon of life through the dusty surroundings. The creek spills into a deep emerald pool, a hangout for waterfowl. No swimming, wading, or fishing is allowed anywhere in the refuge, with the exception of Crystal Reservoir. In addition to the scenic watery wonders awaiting discovery, the northeast corner of the refuge is home to **Devils Hole.** Aside from the decaying scientific monitoring equipment lying around, there's not much to see, but this vertical cave, inside Death Valley National Park, dives 32 feet to the water table, where the endemic endangered Devils Hole pupfish eke out an existence.

You can find evidence of several extinct species at the **Beatty Mudmound** (off U.S. 95, 2 miles southeast of Beatty). Hundreds of millions of years ago these dunes were under Nevada's shallow seas, where they captured brachiopods, gastropods, sponges, and tiny crustaceans, preserving them in the muck. Over the eons the sediment dried and hardened into limestone and today offers up museum-quality specimens.

Accommodations

The only true casino in town, the **Stagecoach Hotel Casino** (900 U.S. 95 N., 775/553-2419, $65–85) has all the slots and video poker variations as well as blackjack, poker, craps, and— never a given in rural casinos—a sports book. Guest rooms are larger than average and include a refrigerator as well as sturdy if not overly stylish furnishings; it is perfectly acceptable for the price. The pool area (May–Oct.) is heavy on the deck and light on the watery diversions, but it's nice and clean. Rita's Café gets high marks from travelers for the satisfying portions and food quality.

Thirty miles down the road (I-95 to Hwy.

373 to Amargosa Valley) will get you to the **Longstreet Casino** (4400 S. Hwy. 373, Amargosa Valley, 775/372-1777, $69–99), a slot palace with run-of-the-mill guest rooms. Opt for the suites and their in-room fireplaces and balconies with inspiring views of the Funeral Mountains. **Jack's Restaurant** (7 A.M.–10 P.M. daily, $7–15) has a burger, sandwich, salad, and Mexican menu as long as your arm. The **Nebraska Steak House** ($18–27) is open for dinner but keeps inconsistent hours. The casino's RV park ($24) has 51 full-hookup spots. Entertainment runs to classic and so-awful-they're-funny films, karaoke, and occasional lounge acts.

Frequented by military and Yucca Mountain workers, the **Atomic Inn** (350 S. First St., 775/553-2250, $50–70) plays up the Cold War theme with a small museum on espionage, the Soviet Union, and nuclear energy along with outdoor film noir, comedy, and action flicks from the postwar era. Formerly the Phoenix, the Atomic Inn is a park-outside-your-room throwback to the 1950s built in 1980. Its 54 guest rooms got a sprucing up in 2008 and now beckon with inviting golds and honey-blond wood.

The decor at the 25-room **El Portal** (420 Main St., 775/553-2912, $55–70) will never be mistaken for the Ritz, but the prices are reasonable.

The 660 hotel rooms at **Death Valley Inn & RV Park** (651 U.S. 95 S., 775/553-9400, $70–100) have microwaves, cable, small fridges, free Internet, and a pool, but the RV park ($27) is the real star. It's just the right size, with 50 spacious sites, 39 of them pull-throughs; it is peacefully quiet, gives guests full access to the hotel amenities, and has hot showers. **Beatty RV Park** (U.S. 95, 3 miles north of Beatty, 775/553-2732, $22–30) has big trees, 35 big spaces, and the most immaculate restrooms and showers we've seen in an RV camp. Tenters and dry campers are allowed ($15), and weekly and monthly discounts are available. **Bailey's Hot Springs** (U.S. 95, 5 miles north of Beatty, 775/553-2395, pools and restaurant 8 A.M.–8 P.M. daily) has three pools, a small RV park ($18), and a restaurant-lounge but does not allow tent camping.

Food

Ethnic restaurants in small towns aren't always a sure thing, but the fajitas and fish tacos at **Ensenada Grill** (600 U.S. 95 S., 775/553-2600, 8 A.M.–7 P.M. daily, $10–15) come up aces. The owners pride themselves on their family recipes and regional cuisine. And there's a good view of the railroad mural on the building next door.

More along the lines of what we expect in dusty backcountry Nevada, the **Sourdough Saloon and Restaurant** (106 W. Main St., 775/553-2266, $10–20) has Harleys and half-tons in the parking lot and charred meat and malted barley on the menu. The beer is cold, and while the food isn't particularly memorable, the friendly folks and the desert dive bar experience certainly are.

Whether you like your French bread slathered in tomato sauce and mozzarella or surrounding thick slabs of turkey or barbecued beef, you'll be glad to get your hands around the offerings at █ **KC's Outpost** (100 E. Main St., 775/553-9175, 10 A.M.–10 P.M. Sun.–Thurs., 10 A.M.–11 P.M. Fri.–Sat., $10–15). There's a lively barroom separate from the dining room, outdoor picnic table dining, and a faux jail cell where your darling desperados can burn off some car-trip energy.

TONOPAH TO HAWTHORNE

U.S. 95 joins U.S. 6 in Tonopah and meanders northwest for 100 miles through picturesque valleys and the occasional mountain to Hawthorne. Along the way, it enters **Coaldale Junction,** where U.S. 6 splits off and goes to Basalt, then into California past Boundary Peak (13,143 feet), Nevada's highest point. Coaldale is the second-largest "town" in Esmeralda County after Goldfield. A pretty good stand-in for the middle of nowhere, Coaldale was once a traveler's oasis, peddling gas, food, booze, and gambling; the buildings are abandoned now.

U.S. 95 from Coaldale Junction runs north 15 miles to Redlich, where a road to the left guides you through an interesting loop of Nevada history. The first stop on the loop is **Candelaria,** which produced $20 million worth of gold, silver, and copper during the 1870s. Take the seven-mile paved road to the ghost town past vast tailing piles being revegetated by the Candelaria Mining Company. The company extracted gold and silver in the area in the 1980s and 1990s, and it takes great pains to discourage visitors. Although the mine closed in the late 1990s, this vigilance kept away would-be vandals and souvenir hunters, leaving much of the town's ruins worth seeing.

What's left of the bank and mercantile, both built of native stone, look impressive even without most of their doors and some of their walls; the bank is the one with the tall steel doors. Two shacks of rock and wood built into the hillside slouch nearby. Just up the road on the left is the mill, or rather its sprawling stone foundation. A dozen other foundations, poking through the scrub, are visible from the road.

Salt and Borax Country

The road continues around to connect with Highway 360 at Candelaria Junction, where you can take another dirt road left to **Marietta.** Frank "Borax" Smith spotted borax in 1873 at Teels Marsh near Marietta and set up his first mining operation here. Nevada's first large-scale borax mine, it soon became the most important in the world. Borax was once used in pharmaceuticals and was mined exclusively in Europe, and the development of these large deposits overwhelmed the small market. But Smith was a promoter as well as a miner, one of the first American industrialists to recognize the value of a full-scale advertising campaign. Subsequently, borax became a household word for use as an abrasive cleanser. Mining at Marietta lasted for 20 years until a more profitable type of borax was discovered in Death Valley, California; Smith relocated his mines and mills there and went on to further popularize the product with the outlandish 20-mule-team wagons. Borax is still used today, primarily in fiberglass production. Secondary uses include glass and ceramics, pharmaceuticals, and cosmetics. Soap accounts for a mere 15 percent.

Highway 360 rejoins U.S. 95 at **Tonopah Junction** at a site once known as Rhodes. This is the center of numerous surrounding salt marshes, with Rhodes Salt Marsh on the left a bit north of the intersection. Prospectors from Aurora and Bodie drifted south into this part of the desert in the early 1860s and discovered the Rhodes, Teels, and Columbus Salt Flats. Soon freighters were snaking toward Aurora, Virginia City, and Austin full of salt to be used in refining silver ore. This is the time and place in Nevada history when camels, imported from North Africa, were used to cross the 100 miles of arid land to the mills. A few years later, silver was discovered at Candelaria.

On your way north to **Mina,** at the end of the Southern Pacific Railroad's Hazen branch, you'll pass through **Sodaville,** once the most important town between Reno and Tonopah. Here all travelers and freight transferred to stages and wagons for the 70-mile trip to Tonopah, a ride so dusty that a joke survives to this day about a man who had to take a shovel at the end of the ride to distinguish fellow passengers from his wife. The ride north from Tonopah was made more bearable by the presence of warm springs at Sodaville. But the Southern Pacific Railroad, rather than deal with an unscrupulous landowner from Sodaville, built its own settlement a few miles north and named in Mina, sounding the death knell for Sodaville. Mina was once a major rail junction for the Southern Pacific Railroad, the Tonopah and Goldfield Railroad, and an SP narrow gauge railroad to California that was so slow it is said passengers could shoot game through passenger-car windows, jump off the train to retrieve their kill, and hop back on to continue the journey.

Strung out along the highway, Mina's business district consists of a minimart, an RV park, a burger joint, and believe it or not, a lobster restaurant. The walkup **Socorro's Burger Hut** (710 Front St., 775/573-2444, $10–15) gets high marks for taste and portion size. Prices are a bit steep as the nearest beef wholesaler is in Reno. For little more than a wide spot in the road, Mina has had its share of bizarre history. The owners of the town's seafood establishment, **Desert Lobster** (in the cabin cruiser at 808 Front St., 775/573-2506, 5 a.m.–9 p.m. daily, $7–15) had dreams of farming and selling desert "lobsters" (actually big Australian freshwater crayfish). Their dreams were dashed by government officials after a convoluted legal battle, culminating in raids and the destruction of his breeding stock. So the Desert Lobster restaurant sells fish, chicken, and burgers but no lobster. A sign outside the ruined lobster-farming operation testifies to the irony of the state's crustacean criminalization: "Nevada: Liquor Legal 24 HR; Gambling Legal 24 HR; Prostitution Legal 24 HR; Lobsters NOT LEGAL."

At the southern edge of town, the **Sunrise Valley RV Park** (775/573-2214, $22) offers shady gravel RV spaces with pull-throughs.

Hawthorne and Vicinity

Ten miles north of Mina at Luning, U.S. 95 cuts west to Hawthorne. In 1881, the Carson and Colorado Railway, managed by H. M. Yerington, chose a spot near Walker Lake's southern tip to serve as its freighting station for nearby mines and boomtowns. In doing so, Yerington deliberately snubbed a town 57 miles northwest that had recently renamed itself Yerington to flatter the manager into locating the station there. The new town was named after Yerington's friend W. A. Hawthorne.

Once the railroad had been installed, the town layout was modeled after Sacramento's, and lots were sold at auction.

Hawthorne's fortunes were directly related to the boom-bust cycles of the railroad and mines and the foibles of county politics. Aurora had been in decline for a decade, and Hawthorne replaced it as Esmeralda County seat in 1883, only to lose it 20 years later to booming Goldfield. But it regained county seat status when Mineral County was cleaved off Esmeralda in 1911. The Southern Pacific Railroad took over the Carson and Colorado Railway in 1904, and its new track bypassed Hawthorne by seven miles. A fire in 1926 nearly finished off the town, leaving fewer than 200 residents, but in a strange quirk of fate the Naval Ammunition Depot in Lake Denmark, New Jersey, also went up in flames that year, forcing its relocation from the major East Coast population center to some remote location in the West. Thanks in large part to the tireless efforts of Nevada senator Tasker Oddie, Hawthorne was selected as the site.

Hawthorne's fortunes were subsequently tied to the country's war involvements. During World War II the barracks town of Babbitt was built to accommodate the sixfold increase in population; after the war the population dropped, and Babbitt became a plywood ghost town, and today no structures remain. U.S. 95 ensured a steady flow of traffic, and in the 1970s and 1980s Hawthorne became home to casinos, lodging, restaurants, and Walker Lake recreational opportunities.

SIGHTS

Hawthorne is surrounded by thousands of thick concrete bunkers and pillboxes. They're filled with bullets, bombs, grenades, mortars, mines, depth charges, and missiles, making Hawthorne perhaps the only community in Nevada that hopes it never becomes a "boom" town. The town's ties to the military are only partly responsible for its patriotism, evidenced by red, white, and blue bunting and business exteriors and more Old Glories than at a political convention.

Hawthorne is just a short drive from a number of attractive places, including Walker Lake. It's also a short drive from the eastern gateway to Yosemite, the historic ghost town of Bodie, and Mono Lake across the border in California. The views from the surrounding mountains, especially the top of Lucky Boy Pass, are spectacular, spanning 50 miles from north to south and showing the unique beauty of a desert lake; the nighttime skies are alive with stars. The town's memorial rose garden features many rows of roses landscaped with paths, benches to rest on, and a babbling fountain.

Mineral County Museum

The big barn of a building that is the Mineral County Museum (400 10th St., 775/945-5142, 11 A.M.–5 P.M. Tues.–Sat. summer, noon–4 P.M. Tues.–Sat. winter, free) is home to numerous interesting historical displays. First, check out the big painting of Hawthorne's history commissioned for the country's bicentennial, featuring everything from Cecil the Serpent to chromate-green bombs. Also for the bicentennial, the townspeople created a quilt that is now on display, along with Victorian clothing, shoes, hats, and furniture. There's an apothecary exhibit from Golden Key Drugs and lots of firefighting, railroad, and mining equipment, including a three-piston stamp-mill crusher, rock displays, and lots of stories, including how the collection of Spanish mission bells was discovered.

Hawthorne Ordnance Museum

The newest attraction in town is the Hawthorne Ordnance Museum (925 E St., 775/945-5400, 10 A.M.–4 P.M. Mon.–Fri., 10 A.M.–2 P.M. Sat., free), which highlights what has been manufactured over the years at the Army Ammunition Plant. The museum showcases a few big guns but it's mostly photos, uniforms, and newspapers as well as torpedoes, mines, missiles, and other now-nonexplosive pieces of military history.

Military buffs and "pry it from my cold dead fingers" types will find nothing more enjoyable than an afternoon spent browsing the Hawthorne Ordnance Museum. The small museum is locally run and dedicated to celebrating all things military. Visitors will find displays and exhibits of a range of ammunition dating back to the early part of the 20th century as well as an in-depth look at the area's munitions history.

Walker Lake

Thirty miles long and 3–8 miles wide, this pristine high-desert lake is actually just a pond left over from ancient Lake Lahontan, which once covered 8,400 square miles of western Nevada and eastern California; Pyramid Lake, 100 miles north, is the other remnant. Walker Lake's health is in serious jeopardy these days as it experiences problems similar to, though worse than, Pyramid Lake: Tributary and river water diversions for agriculture upstream, little rainfall, high evaporation, and agriculture runoff all contribute to the lake's salinity. Still, this deep-blue diamond in the dusty rough is a treat for eyes accustomed to the beige basins and gray ranges that surround it for scores of miles.

It has been a welcome sight since the earliest explorations. While seeking the mythical San Buenaventura River, which was widely assumed to run through the vast western desert to the sea, both Jedediah Smith and Peter Skene Ogden came across the lake in the late 1820s. The lake's namesake, Joseph Walker—a surveyor with John C. Frémont's expedition—himself stumbled upon the lake when dying of thirst in 1833. Long before they arrived, the lake attracted area Paiutes looking to supplement their diet of game and pine nuts with plump cutthroat trout.

Today those trout and chubs that nourish migrating waterfowl are threatened. As the lake level drops, dissolved solids such as minerals and salts become more concentrated and kill off the microscopic zooplankton that feed the fish; algae growth increases, depriving the lake of oxygen. The Walker Lake Working Group is trying to get everyone to conserve water to ensure that Walker Lake survives. Despite increasing threats to the ecosystem, Walker Lake remains an attractive destination for recreation on and near the water. Trout fishing is still some of the best and most accessible around, and the surface is plenty big enough for boating and waterskiing. Thermals trapped by the surrounding cliffs make it a popular hang gliding and paragliding locale.

Aurora

Sitting on the Nevada-California border, Aurora in the 1860s was literally a goldmine worth fighting over. Because the border hadn't been firmly established when miners found gold in the uneven volcanic Brawley Peaks in 1861, both the Golden State and the Silver territory laid claim. Both established Aurora as a county seat. In 1864, when the new state was surveyed, Aurora was placed in Nevada, and the Mono County, California, offices had to move to Bodie, the notorious camp next door.

Samuel Clemens stopped off at Aurora to try his luck, suffered a series of setbacks, and turned to writing freelance correspondence for the *Territorial Enterprise* as a salve for his prospecting failures. At his darkest moment, a letter arrived from Virginia City, offering him a job as the newspaper's city editor for a princely $25 per week. There Sam Clemens became Mark Twain.

Aurora was just warming up as Virginia City's heat was starting to dissipate, and Aurora produced more than $20 million in gold in roughly seven years before the bust. In 1940 the Works Progress Administration guide reported that "Aurora shows signs of coming to life, maintaining a remarkable resistance to complete abandonment." Right after the war a contractor from Southern California dismantled the deserted brick buildings, and scavengers grabbed the rest.

To get there from Hawthorne, continue on Main Street (Hwy. 359) at the intersection where it diverges from U.S. 95. This is the highway around the eastern slope of the Wassuks on **Whiskey Flat** and through a small saddle in the **Anchorite Hills** to California and Mono Lake. You'll see a turnoff on a gravel road to **Lucky Boy Pass,** which the road starts climbing up to immediately. Dow Corning ran a silicate mine up here, and you might find it hard to imagine big semis full of minerals barreling down this grade. Finally you come to **Lucky Boy Pass** at 8,000 feet, where you can see for miles into the East Walker River Valley. From here, the road leads down to the Aurora Crater and around to Aurora town site, where little remains.

RECREATION

The north quarter of Walker Lake is owned by the Walker River Paiute, the middle half by the federal Bureau of Land Management, and the south quarter by the Army Ammunition plant. Speed-boat races, fishing and fishing derbies, waterskiing, swimming, and camping are the main activities on the lake.

Sportsman's Beach is 15 miles north of Hawthorne along the west shore below U.S. 95. It has about 30 developed campsites ($6) and some undeveloped sites ($4), outhouses, tables, and shelters. **Walker Lake State Recreation Area** (775/867-3001) is two miles south at **Tamarack Point.** It has 12 picnic sites, outhouses, and the lake's only boat ramp. Similar dry camping can be found at **20 Mile Beach** nearby.

The best **fishing** for the 2–3-pound cutthroat trout stocked in the lake is in March–April. Like many lakes, Walker boasts a giant serpent. Cecil is the 80-foot-long monster that hides in the ancient depths. Although he's less than benign in Paiute legends, to the children of Hawthorne, Cecil is friendly and is always well represented in local parades.

Loons visit Walker Lake twice a year, although the water quality cannot support enough food fish for the roughly 700 individuals in April and 1,000 in October that once dropped in to eat and mate on their migrations. The Walker Lake Working Group (775/945-2289 or 775/677-8951) used to hold loon-viewing festivals, but because significant numbers no longer make calls at the lake, the conservation group replaced the festival with an "Education Day" to garner support and participation in sustaining the lake's ecosystem.

With the proper permits from the Four Seasons market on the Walker River Paiute Reservation, you can fish, boat ($8), and camp at **Weber Reservoir,** located on the reservation six miles west on the road to Yerington. The store also sells a huge variety of fireworks. Over the years the reservation acreage has been chipped away for mining and recreation, and declining water levels have left the Paiute with dwindling lake frontage.

At the nine-hole **Walker Lake Golf Club** (775/945-1111, $18–25) the bar serves simple snacks like hot dogs and chili. It's at the Army base about three miles north of Hawthorne between the town and Walker Lake.

ENTERTAINMENT

It's all slots, all the time in Hawthorne. Even the biggest casino, **El Capitan Resort & Casino** (540 F St., 800/922-2311) has no blackjack tables, although the floor is stuffed with some 200 slots. It opened in 1943 during the boom years of World War II.

ACCOMMODATIONS

The 100 guest rooms at **El Capitan Resort & Casino** (540 F St., 800/922-2311, $50–60) are clean and pleasant enough, although they are close to due for a remodel and replacement of the soon-to-be-antique refrigerators in each. The restaurant (6 A.M.–10 P.M. Sun.–Thurs., 6 A.M.–midnight Fri.–Sat., $10–17) deals a mean French toast breakfast and basic burgers, chicken, steak, and fish for dinner.

America's Best Inn (1402 E. 5th St., 775/945-2660 or 800/237-8466, $90–120) has basic guest rooms, and some come with microwaves and refrigerators. The hotel has some "ecorooms," with room features that save energy and water and promote recycling. Fresh cookies at check-in and the free continental breakfast are nice touches.

Bargain hunters can try the **Sand N Sage Lodge** (1301 E. 5th St., 775/945-3352, $30–50). It's pet-friendly and has in-room Internet and a seasonal pool. The two-story building has 39 guest rooms; specify if you want smoking or nonsmoking. The **Holiday Lodge** (480 J St., 775/945-3316, $30–45) is cozy, clean, and warm on those frigid central Nevada nights.

At Walker Lake Village, **Cliff House Restaurant and Motel** (315 Cliff House Rd., 775/945-2459, $55–100) guest rooms are on the beach (although the water is pretty far away these days, especially compared to 20 years ago when the motel had to be closed due to flooding).

The best RV park in the area is **Whiskey Flats** (3045 U.S. 95, 775/945-1800, $20–25), with 60 big pull-through spaces, a tiny general store, strong Wi-Fi, clean showers, and plenty of peace and quiet. The other RV parks in town—and the town itself—won't be mistaken for Beverly Hills, but for a one-nighter they're just fine. **Scotty's RV Park** (1101 5th St., 775/945-2079, $20) has 18 spaces for motor homes, all with full hookups; 17 are pull-throughs. Tents are not allowed.

FOOD

Maggie's (758 E. Main St., 775/945-3908, 7 A.M.–9 P.M. daily, $7–15) serves dinner, but its best features are the lunch sandwiches on bread baked on the premises and an eclectic, bountiful salad bar. Come for late-afternoon soup and salad and stay a couple of hours to take advantage of the strong Wi-Fi and free drink refills. In summer and not-too-breezy spring days, ask to be seated on the patio. Maggie's has won the Nevada Governor's Tourism Award, Business of the Year, and many other awards.

Happy Buddha (570 Sierra Way, 775/945-2727, 11 A.M.–8 P.M. daily, $10–15) and **Wong's** (923 5th St., 775/945-1700, 10:30 A.M.–9 P.M. daily, $10–15) serve Chinese. **Joe's Tavern** (537 Sierra Way, 775/945-2302, 4 P.M.–late Sun.–Thurs., 10 A.M.–late Fri.–Sat.) is across the street from the El Capitan. It is a bar, dance club, slots casino, pool hall, and general hangout owned by the Viani family. Joe Viani was a beloved Hawthornite and state assembly member; Joe Junior now runs the joint. There is occasional entertainment weekend nights.

INFORMATION

The **Mineral County Economic Development Authority** (901 E St., 775/945-5896 or 877/736-LAKE—877/736-5253, 7 A.M.–5 P.M. Sun.–Thurs.) provides demographic and business information as well as some visitor resources. The **Mineral County Chamber of Commerce** (www.mineralcountychamber.

com) has no public office, but the website is chock-full of local information for visitors, as is the **county library** (1st St. and A St., 775/945-2778, 10 A.M.–7 P.M. Mon.–Thurs., 10 A.M.–6 P.M. Fri., 11 A.M.–4 P.M. Sat.).

YERINGTON

The history of this hay- and barley-growing community in the Walker River Valley is as peaceful as its setting, something that cannot always be said of Nevada's frontier settlements. Known by various names throughout its existence, Yerington finally settled on an homage to the man in charge of the Carson and Colorado Railway. Residents figured by naming their home after Henry Yerington, they were sure to be placed on the train's route. But Yerington himself was above the flattery, and the railroad bypassed the town. Earlier the settlement had been known as Pizen Switch, a commentary on one of the town's saloons, which patrons claimed was serving not alcohol but poison.

Sights

The **Lyon County Museum** (215 S. Main St., 775/463-6576, 1–4 P.M. Thurs.–Sun. and by appointment, donation) documents the 150 years of settlement in the Smith and Carson Valleys. The museum comprises seven buildings, providing an overall look at valley life. The buildings include three historic schools, a general store, a blacksmith shop, and the new E. L. Wiegand building. Some of the best displays are life-size dioramas—a parlor, a pharmacy, a court clerk's office, a dress shop, and a bunkhouse. Influential local residents such as Nevada's first woman doctor, Mary Fulstone, the Ghost Dance prophet Wovoka, and Harry Warren, who won $1,500 from local residents by carrying a 120-pound grain sack 10 miles from Wabuska to Yerington, are honored here as well.

Fort Churchill State Historical Park (1000 U.S. 95A, 775/577-2345, $7), near Silver Springs, was an active U.S. Army fort built in 1860 to protect early settlers. The fort saw service for only nine years. Its ruins

Fort Churchill offered relief and protection to westward emigrants in the 1860s.

are preserved and house informational displays about the garrison, the Pony Express, and the Overland Telegraph. A haven for outdoor lovers, the park contains a campground ($17) with 20 cottonwood-shaded spots big enough for most motor homes as well as tents and trailers. Reservations are not accepted. There is a dump station but no hookups. There are also hiking and horseback trails and access to the Carson River for canoeing and kayaking. The Buckland Station stage stop and Pony Express station was built in 1870 with materials salvaged from the fort.

BACKGROUND

The Land

Half a billion years ago, Nevada rested underwater, the eastern half a narrow shelf that slanted westward into a deep ocean trench. Where Salt Lake City now sits was the shoreline; the equator was nearby, and the region teemed with tropical Precambrian life. Soft-shelled brachiopods, primitive trilobites, tiny spiny starfish, single-celled radiolaria, and algae all populated the tidal flats, reefs, lagoons, estuaries, and wide bays of the shallow sea. For roughly 150 million years, skeletons and sediments accumulated on the ocean floor and were pressurized into limestone. At least twice during the mysterious 300-million-year Paleozoic era, violent and titanic orogenies (episodes of uplift) raised the land, draining the sea and leaving towering mesas and alluvial plains. Gravity pulled the upland rubble into the low-lying basins, which sunk under their own weight, creating new lanes for the seawater to flow back. Then, toward the end of the Paleozoic in the period known as the Permian, supercontinental collision flattened massive ridges in the ocean, forcing the ocean into retreat again and incidentally triggering the first of the two near-global extinctions in the history of the earth.

This mass extinction of plants and animals created a superabundance of free oxygen, which had been bound up by carbon in living

© BETHANY DRYSDALE

organisms. The oxygen rusted the ubiquitous ferrous iron in the earth's crust, turning it red. During the Triassic period of the new Mesozoic era, 230 million years ago, the exposed and oxidized sediments eroded. Ferric red sands blew southward and collected in dunes, which petrified into sandstone mountains, to be sculpted in later eons by wind and water.

During the Jurassic, 175 million years ago, the fused supercontinent was torn asunder, a cataclysmic megashear resulting in global-scale tectonics that again caused the flooding of North America. This triggered what is known as the Nevada phase of the Cordilleran orogeny, a violently unstable era. The earth squeezed together, folded, and thrust up from the sea. Huge blocks of sediment faulted, tipped, and rose thousands of feet. Earthquakes shuffled the ranges like a deck of cards. Great crustal fissures cracked open. Molten lava, gaseous plumes, and hot springs spewed out, bearing solutions of gold, silver, copper, and silica. Volcanoes blasted hot rock and ash. During the greatest period of granite formation in Earth's history, the ancestral Sierra Nevada rose. Flash floods gouged the mountains, leaching, oxidizing, and concentrating the ores. Two families of creatures that had survived the Permian Extinction—marine and flying reptiles and dinosaurs—evolved over the 165 million years of the Mesozoic into giants. But then, 65 million years ago, another cosmic cataclysm, the Cretaceous Extinction, again erased almost all life at the end of the Mesozoic.

The Cordilleran orogeny ended shortly thereafter, followed by 25 million years of gradual erosion. Then, during the Oligocene, 40 million years ago, another colossal episode, this time of volcanism, obliterated the Nevadan landscape. Up through fractures, fissures, and vents spewed an unimaginably titanic disgorgement of white-hot steam, ash, and particulates, burying the surface under thousands of feet of ash-flow sheets, turning the topmost sheet into a single continuous and uniform plain.

Finally, 17 million years ago during the Miocene epoch, the continental collision course stretched and lifted the crust, bowing the vast volcanic-ash plain upward like an arch. The crust pulled apart, thinned, then crumpled into blocks that tilted and slid into each other—the high edges became the ridgelines of the ranges, the low edges V-shaped canyons. As they began to fill with eroded sediment, the canyons spread into basins, tilting the blocks further upward. Large cracks ripped open between the rising mountains and sinking valleys; the blocks still quake the land at the faults today as the crust continues to adjust. Still spreading, the Basin and Range could very well be cracking open a new sea lane by way of the Gulf of California, the Salton Sea, and the Mojave Desert—parts of which are already below sea level. California may become an island, and Nevada would drown again.

Meanwhile, erosion continues to litter the valleys with mountain material. Some ranges have been whittled down over the past 15 million years to a mere 12,000 feet. Others have been completely buried in their own shavings. Still other ranges are growing as their blocks tilt more steeply. Some hills are really the peaks of mountains that extend thousands of feet below the surface, iceberg-style, resting on bedrock. Roughly 200 discrete ranges have been named in Nevada, 90 percent of them oriented northeast-southwest. The other 10 percent constitute what's known as a discontinuous fault zone—hooked, curved, folded toward all points on the compass. Collectively referred to as the Walker Belt, these individually scrambled mountains at the same time occur in a line, northwest-southeast, roughly 400 miles long along the geologically uneasy California-Nevada state line.

Appropriately enough, the locale where the structural continuity is most disturbed, where the southwest-trending cavalcade jams up at a southeast-trending dead end, is at the edge of the Las Vegas Valley. With no apparent irony, geologists call this phenomenon the Las Vegas Zone of Deformation.

The final uplift of the Sierra Nevada occurred roughly 10 million years ago; the rain shadow it cast transformed the terrain east of the great range of granite mountains into a wide desert. The Pleistocene, beginning a little less than 2 million years ago, ushered four great ice ages into history. Alternately warm and cool, the humidity remained constant. The soil was moist, rich, and full of minerals from decomposed lava. Forests of giant fir, pine, and sequoia towered over a lush undergrowth of moss, fern, and willow. Great lakes covered much of Nevada, mountain peaks poking out as islands. Lakeshore grasses and woodlands supported great Pleistocene fauna: saber-toothed cats, ground sloths, tapirs, camels, two-horned *Teleoceras,* three-toed horses, and four-horned antelope in warmer times; musk oxen, woolly mammoths, bison, mastodons, and caribou in cooler periods. The last glacial epoch, the Wisconsin, ended roughly 15,000 years ago, inaugurating a warm dry climate that persists to this day.

TWO STATES IN ONE

Unlike Nevada's next-door neighbor to the west, where the demarcation between its northern and southern zones is based as much on states of mind as on geography, northern and southern Nevada can be pinpointed fairly specifically. Simply stated, Nevada's two deserts separate the state into its two distinct parts. Northern Nevada is usually considered to include everything within the Great Basin Desert, while southern Nevada occupies the Mojave Desert. The differences in the field probably wouldn't be immediately apparent to the untrained eye, but the two primary and related factors are elevation and vegetation.

The base elevation of the Great Basin Desert ranges 4,500–6,200 feet, where the predominant vegetation is sagebrush. The Mojave's elevation in Nevada starts at 490 feet (the lowest and southernmost point in Nevada at the Colorado River near Laughlin) and ascends in elevation northward to the Great Basin; the predominant vegetation below 4,000 feet is creosote.

It isn't exact, but generally speaking a line in Nevada delineating elevation, vegetation, and drainage can be drawn from around Beatty in the west to around Caliente in the east. The Works Progress Administration's

Nevada reported that roughly 15 miles south of Tonopah,

> A distinct change in the vegetation is noted; northward is the sagebrush zone, southward the creosote bush. The line of demarcation between the zones is so sharp that in this area not a single piece of sagebrush is found within a few hundred feet south of it and not a creosote bush a hundred feet north.

Caliente is also surrounded by sage above 4,000 feet, but because its Meadow Valley Wash is drained southward into the Colorado River system, it is generally not considered part of the Great Basin, where the drainage is internal, without an outlet to the sea. Of course, all the life zones are found on the mountain ranges of the Mojave, but the Great Basin does not descend to the Mojave's zone.

Although the northern part of the state accounts for 80 percent of the land, the southern part accounts for 80 percent of the population. As for climate, the farther south you travel in Nevada, the hotter and drier it gets. Las Vegas has some of the lowest precipitation and the lowest relative humidity of any metropolitan area in the country; Laughlin, at the extreme southern tip of the state, is second only to Laredo, Texas, for having the most record-high temperatures in the country.

Nevada's 110,000 square miles, or 70,264,320 acres, make it the seventh-largest state. The federal government owns nearly 60 million of those acres, or 85 percent of the total land area. Of the federal acreage, nearly 50 million acres are managed by the Bureau of Land Management, with just over 5 million acres controlled by the U.S. Forest Service. The military has over 4 million acres, which it uses for bases, training grounds, and test sites; that number is growing.

Native American reservations, national wildlife refuges, and wilderness areas account for the remainder of the federal land total. Twenty-four state parks preserve roughly 50,000 acres, and the rest is privately owned.

THE DESERTS
Great Basin

The Great Basin Desert is one of the major geographic features in the United States. It stretches 500 miles between California's Sierra Nevada and Utah's Wasatch Mountains, up to 750 miles between Oregon's Columbia Plateau and southern Nevada's Mojave Desert, and makes up a large part of the Basin and Range Physiographic Province. John C. Frémont named the Great Basin in 1844 for a curious and unique phenomenon: internal drainage. The rivers here have no outlet to the sea. They meander for various distances through arroyos and canyons before emptying into lakes, disappearing into sinks, or just evaporating.

The Great Basin is not a bowl-shaped depression between the two major mountain ranges; it is more like a square of corrugated cardboard inside a shallow box. Some of the interior ridges—the mountain ranges—rise higher than the sides of the box. All the ranges, no matter

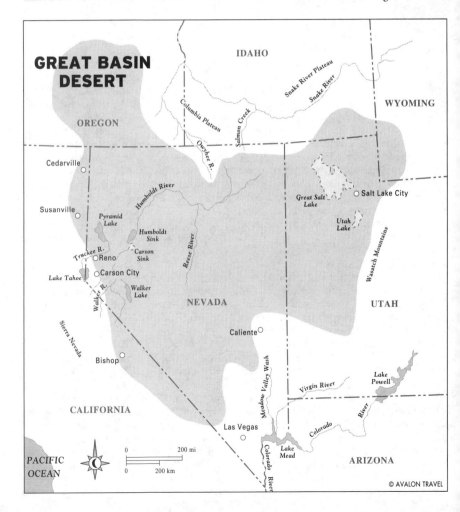

© AVALON TRAVEL

what their height, have troughs between them. The Great Basin Desert covers roughly 75 percent of Nevada, and Nevada contains roughly 75 percent of the Great Basin Desert. Only a few thousand years ago, huge lakes left over from the wet Pleistocene covered much of this desert. The earth is highly mineralized: copper, lead, iron, gypsum, salt, magnesite, brucite, diatomaceous earth, silver, and gold have all been mined in large quantities. But this desert's most unmistakable characteristic is the basin-and-range corrugation. There are upward of 300 separate mountain ranges; most are oriented northeast-southwest, are 50–100 miles long, are separated by valleys of equal length, and strongly resemble "an army of caterpillars crawling northward out of Mexico," according to early explorer C. E. Dutton. The average base elevation (where the basins meet the ranges) is 5,000 feet above sea level, slightly lower in the west, slightly higher in the east. The bottom of the basins here are higher than most mountains east of the Mississippi. The overwhelmingly predominant vegetation is sagebrush, the state flower. Piñon pine and juniper, mountain mahogany and aspen, fir, pine, and spruce inhabit the higher life zones, where many creatures, from field mice and jackrabbits to pronghorn and bobcats, reside.

Mojave Desert

At the southern tip of Nevada, the Mojave Desert borders the northern boundary of the great Sonoran Desert, which encompasses southwestern Arizona, southeastern California, Mexico's northwestern state of Sonora, and nearly the entire Baja California Peninsula. The Mojave Desert is a basin, sluicing south into the main drainage, the Colorado River. Elevations begin to plummet south of Goldfield on the west side and Caliente on the east, down to around 2,000 feet at Las Vegas, then down to around 500 feet at Laughlin. The Mojave is not only lower but also hotter and drier than its northern Nevada counterpart. Its prevalent vegetation consists of creosote, yucca, and Joshua tree. Snakes, lizards, and bighorn sheep predominate.

OUTSIDE THE DESERTS

Two tiny nondesert tableaux impinge on Nevada: the sheer eastern escarpment of the Sierra Nevada from just west of Reno to just south of Lake Tahoe, and the little bit of northeastern Nevada that separates the Great Basin from the Snake River Plateau in southwestern Idaho. Lake Tahoe sits in a mountain bowl at roughly 6,200–6,300 feet, its east shore (the Nevada side) contained by the Sierra's Carson Range. These rugged, heavily second-growth forested granite mountains drop precipitously into the desert; the Carson Range, on the California state line, is the only part of northwestern and north-central Nevada that is outside the Sierra rain shadow. The Sierras are responsible for both the paltry rainfall east of them and the Truckee, Carson, and Walker Rivers that form from the runoff from the wet peaks. The summit of Mount Rose in the Carson Range (10,778 feet) attracts more than 30 inches of precipitation in a normal year, while Washoe City, at Mount Rose's eastern foot, receives less than five inches annually.

The jumbled U-shaped ridgeline of the Jarbidge Wilderness along the Nevada-Idaho border consists of eight peaks higher than 8,000 feet and three over 10,000 feet. The Bruneau, Owyhee, and Salmon Rivers flow north from here into the Columbia River drainage system, and the vast Snake River Plateau stretches north from this part of northeastern Nevada. These three features substantiate that this corner of northeastern Nevada isn't part of the Great Basin.

THE MOUNTAINS

Depending on who's counting and how, 150–300 mountain ranges have been counted within Nevada's borders. Most were uplifted and eroded by similar forces; therefore most share similar geological characteristics. These ranges were created by the tectonic pressure exerted on the western continental crustal surface from the strain of the Pacific Plate edging north against the North American Plate at the San Andreas Fault. This colossal jostle has fractured the crust at numerous places; at the cracks, some chunks have sunk down, some have lifted up, and some have listed over. A typical Nevada range is approximately 50 miles long but can stretch 100–150 miles from one end to the other and is 10 miles wide. Each range is slanted, a long gentle slope on one side and a sheer scarp on the other. Boundary and Wheeler, the two highest peaks, reach just over 13,000 feet. Mount Moriah, Mount Jefferson, Mount Charleston, Arc Dome, Pyramid Peak, and South Schell Peak hover around 12,000 feet. A score of others rise higher than 10,000 feet.

Limestone and sandstone originated in the shallow inland sea and subsequent vast duney desert, respectively, that once covered Nevada. Limestone ranges occur primarily in eastern Nevada, from the Tuscarora Mountains to the Las Vegas Range. The Schell Creeks, Egans, and Snakes around Ely are the best known and best representatives of the limestone massifs; the Snakes contain Great Basin National Park, within which Lehman Caves provide a graphic lesson in mountain building and erosion. The sandstone ranges occur in the southern Mojave: the Spring and Muddy Mountains outside Las Vegas. After the sea retreated, massive sand dunes covered the land. Chemical and thermal reactions petrified the dunes into polychrome sandstone; wind and water erosion sculpted it into the strange and wondrous shapes on view at Red Rock Canyon and Valley of Fire.

The granite ranges mostly cluster in the west-central part of Nevada around the most magnificent granite mountains of them all: the Sierra Nevada. Granite, the major mountain-building rock, is forced up into the crust as molten magma and then cools slowly. The Granite and Selenite Ranges around the Black Rock Desert and the Pine Nut and Wassuk Ranges around Topaz and Walker Lakes are examples.

When magma cools slowly, it forms granite; when it cools quickly, it forms basalt and rhyolite. The volcanic ranges are the youngest and most active of Nevada's various types of ranges and mark the eastern edge of the famous Pacific Ring of Fire. The Virginia Range is one of the older, more eroded, and most mineralized of the volcanic ranges and has yielded hundreds of millions of dollars in gold and silver. The Monte Cristos, west of Tonopah, are an anomaly in the Great Basin—crescent-shaped, containing badlands, and brightly colored. The Pancake Range is only a few thousand years old, and the Apollo astronauts used its Lunar Cuesta to simulate the craters, lava flows, and calderas of the moon.

The rest of Nevada's many mountain ranges are composites, exhibiting a great variety of granite, sedimentary, volcanic, and metamorphic signs. The Humboldts, Santa Rosas, Stillwaters, and Toiyabes are composite ranges, and the Toiyabes have been called "the archetype of Nevada ranges."

THE RIVERS

As author John Hart wrote, "Only two large areas of North America were unexplored by 1825: the interior of Alaska and the inner areas of the Basin." The first explorers were primarily looking for rivers, seeking beaver pelts and drinking water. They also had in mind finding the mythical San Buenaventura River, believed to flow from the Rocky Mountains through the great unknown expanse of the West all the way to the Pacific Ocean.

Ten rivers of note snake around Nevada. The Truckee, Carson, and Walker Rivers flow in while the Bruneau, Owyhee, and Salmon Rivers flow out. The Humboldt and Reese Rivers are born and die in the Great Basin. The state's southeast boundary is formed by the Colorado River, which meanders for 150 miles along the edge. The Amargosa River rises in the Nuclear Test Site, slightly waters Beatty, then flows underground to Death Valley. Seven of the 10 rivers are dammed.

Only the Colorado River was large enough to be served by riverboats. The legendary Reese River, however, looked good enough on the early maps to foster one of the great scams in Nevada history: a phony navigation company. The Humboldt was both the scourge (the highly alkali water was basically undrinkable) and the salvation (both for its stock-feeding grasses and its trail along the riverbank) of thousands of pioneers. The Carson, Truckee, and Walker Rivers are life-givers and sustainers for most of western Nevada.

The Humboldt

Jedediah Smith came west from Wyoming in 1825, trapping beaver as he explored. He sniffed out a river in the great desert and named it Mary's, after his wife. Apparently, Peter Skene Ogden hadn't heard about that, because when he located it from the north in 1828 he named it Unknown River. Joe Walker, in spite of Ogden's name, found it and followed it in 1834. John C. Frémont was the last one to label it, in honor of a German scientist so eminent that not only did the name stick like glue, but the river trail, three mountain ranges, a mining district, a sink, and a county were named for him too.

Originating in northeastern Nevada, the Humboldt River flows southwest, picking up runoff from the East Humboldts, the Rubies, and a half-dozen other mountain ranges north and south of it between here and Beowawe. It cuts northwest up to Winnemucca and back southwest into the Rye Patch Reservoir. Beyond the dam, it disappears into its own sour sink. Pioneer migrants cursed its foul water and harvested all the vegetation from its banks, and reclamation projects dammed it to irrigate Pershing County. A railroad, a U.S. defense highway, and an interstate highway have been built next to it.

The Colorado

Nevada got lucky in 1866 when, only two years after its boundaries were surveyed, the state was allowed to extend its southern borders into Utah and Arizona Territories. Nevada annexed 150 miles of the west bank of the Colorado River along with Las Vegas Valley, the Muddy and Virgin Rivers, and Meadow Valley Wash. The Colorado is one big river that had made its own destiny for countless eons until the federal Bureau of Reclamation took on the Hoover Dam project in the 1930s. Davis Dam, 80 miles south of the Hoover Dam and built in 1954, further controls this now-docile dragon in Nevada.

The Sierra Three

The Truckee, Carson, and Walker Rivers all flow east out of the Sierras and fan out northeast, east, and southeast, respectively, into western Nevada. The northernmost of the three, the Truckee River, emanates from the edge of Lake Tahoe and flows northeast. It provides all the water for Reno-Sparks and some water for the reclamation projects in Fernley and Fallon. Derby Dam, which diverts Truckee River water to Lahontan Reservoir, was the Bureau of Reclamation's first dam, built in 1905. The rest of the river water reaches its original destination at Pyramid Lake.

The Carson River, which flows north to Carson City, then east between the Virginia Range and the Pine Nut Mountains, at one time spread out into the desert within the large Carson Sink. Today a dozen or so miles west of the sink, the Carson is backed up by Lahontan Dam and then sent by canals and ditches to irrigate Fallon. For years little water reached the Carson River marsh at Stillwater National Wildlife Refuge, but that is beginning to change.

The Walker River flows north from two forks into idyllic Mason Valley. It passes Yerington and then makes a big U-turn around the Wassuk Range and heads south into Walker Lake. Bridgeport Lake in California is where the East Fork is dammed early on, and Topaz Lake is where the West Fork is dammed early on; Weber Reservoir backs up the Walker River on the east side of the Wassuks, a little north of Walker Lake, its final destination.

The Idaho Three

The Bruneau, Owyhee, and Salmon Rivers flow north from the area where the Snake River Plateau protrudes into the Great Basin. They empty into the Snake River, which empties into the mighty Columbia River. The headwaters of the Humboldt cascade south from the Great Basin side of the plateau. This is a very active corner of Nevada for water, a real slice of the Pacific Northwest. The Owyhee River is dammed at Wildhorse, and the Snake River is dammed in Idaho.

THE LAKES
Artificial Lakes
Lake Mead is the largest artificial lake in the country, created by 7 million tons of cement poured 700 feet high to hold back the raging Colorado River. Lake Mojave is restrained by an earth-filled 200-foot dam. Both Rye Patch (on the Humboldt River) and Wildhorse (on the Owyhee River) Reservoirs are popular with anglers, boaters, and campers; South Fork Dam, completed in 1988, is the newest dam in Nevada, impounding 40,000 acre-feet of South Fork Creek 10 miles south of Elko; the state's newest park is also here. Lahontan Reservoir (on the Carson River) also has lots of campsites in addition to the amazing network of ditches and canals through Fallon between it and the Carson Sink.

Altered Lakes
The overflow from the Truckee River once drained out of Pyramid Lake and into Winnemucca Lake. It took only 30 years for large Winnemucca Lake to dry into a playa after the Truckee Canal diverted some river water to Lahontan Valley. Today, 100 years later, Pyramid Lake has dropped to uncomfortably low levels, the Fallon National Wildlife Refuge is gone, and the Stillwater National Wildlife Refuge is hanging on by a thread. But now it appears as if almost everyone—the feds, the state, the hatcheries, the power company, and the conservationists—although not the farmers, entirely—are starting to agree on how to satisfy the various conflicting water requirements for the lakes, refuges, irrigation systems, and urban populations.

Ruby Marsh has a number of dikes and causeways around and through it; Pahranagat is less changed. Walker Lake, like Pyramid, has had its water diverted and its fishery devastated; this lake could be one of the most endangered in the West.

For sheer beauty, Lake Tahoe—logged out, fished out, dammed, silted, but now slowly returning to a fairly pristine condition—is unsurpassed, except maybe by a few of those backcountry lakes way up in the Ruby Mountains.

Flora and Fauna

FLORA
Creosote
The Mojave Desert covers the southern quarter of Nevada, and the creosote bush covers the Mojave. Because of the extremely arid environment, these shrubs, which grow 2–10 feet tall and sprout dull-green resinous foliage, are widely scattered over the desert sand, occupying only about 10 percent of the available surface. Creosote shares the Mojave floor with a variety of cacti, yucca (especially the easily recognizable Mojave yucca, also known as Spanish bayonet), and the Joshua tree, which is endemic to the Mojave. Creosote is sometimes referred to as greasewood and is closely related to saltbush, which grows in the Great Basin at elevations lower than the sagebrush zone. Greasewood,

saltbush, rabbitbrush, shadscale, and other plants with spiny stems and tiny leaves are highly adaptable to alkali soil; their presence generally indicates conditions unsuitable for agricultural cultivation. They grow in the 450–3,000-foot elevation zone in Nevada, mostly limited to the Mojave in the south and the lowest points in the lowest valleys in the Great Basin.

Joshua Tree
This picturesque tree, also known as the tree yucca or yucca palm, is the largest species of the yucca genus. It can grow to 30 feet tall with a stout body and boldly forking branches. It blooms bright yellow March–May. The Joshua tree was named by Mormon pioneers who imagined the big yucca's branches to be

imploring, slightly grotesque "arms" pointing the way to the promised land.

Sage

Sagebrush is the state flower. It's also possibly the most memorable and enduring image of Nevada, along with neon, that travelers take home with them. The Great Basin Desert has been called a "sagebrush ocean"; the sagebrush zone, roughly 4,000–6,000 feet in elevation, could also be considered a "Lilliputian forest." Unlike shadscale and greasewood, sage grows in well-drained and minimally alkali environments. Healthy sage can grow 12 feet tall with roots up to 30 feet deep. Tall sagebrush indicated fertile soil to farmers, promising good crops if irrigated properly. Farmers considered sage a pest and cleared it with a vengeance. Migrant pioneers cursed sage as the vilest shrub on earth, more useless even than Humboldt River water.

Native Americans considered sage to be a great provider. They chewed the young leaves and drank decoctions brewed from the buds as a general tonic. They dried, ground, and made a mud of the stems and used it as a poultice. They stripped the pliable bark from the tallest sage plants, usually near streams, and made robes, sandals, and other clothing from the fiber. And they used the leaves and stems for insulation.

Covering a third of the desert surface, sage protects the earth from wanton erosion. It also gives shelter to snakes and small rodents that burrow under the bush, and it feeds sage hens, squirrels, jackrabbits, and other fauna that eat the spring buds. Sheep, cattle, and pronghorn also nibble on the young leaves.

Sage has successfully resisted nearly all attempts at commercial exploitation. Except for fuel in the absolute absence of any other wood, this bitter and oily plant hasn't been found to fulfill any modern productive purpose. Most desert rats consider that to be a good thing, since there's nothing quite so evocative of the desert as the silver-green sheen and pungent aroma of an ocean of sagebrush after a good rain.

Juniper

Utah juniper is the most common tree in the

Joshua tree, eastern Nevada

© HARRIS SHIFFMAN/123RF.COM

Great Basin. It grows on every mountain range and in some basins. Juniper is also the first tree that takes to a particular microenvironment; piñon follows later. Junipers grow to 20 feet and are sometimes as round as they are tall. They produce blue-green juniper berries (bitter but edible), pale green needles, and yellowish pollen cones. You'll normally see them at 6,000–8,000 feet.

Recent research has indicated that the Utah juniper has survived the radical climatic changes that the Great Basin has experienced over the past 30,000 years. By cross-breeding with its cousin, the western juniper, the Utah juniper altered its genetic makeup and was able to survive through the ice ages (the western juniper thrives in a cooler, wetter climate, such as in the Sierras). Forestry paleontologists compared the DNA of Utah juniper seeds and twigs discovered in ancient pack rat nests with today's juniper to decipher how plants survive climate changes—as well as which local trees will live through the current era of global warming.

Like sage, juniper provided for many Native American needs. The Puebloans favored it as a building material, especially for the roofs of their structures. They used it as savory firewood. They stripped, softened, and made the bark into baskets, rope, and clothing. In *Trees of the Great Basin* Ronald Lanner even reports that they smoked the inner bark in cigarettes. Once you learn to recognize this tree, you'll come to appreciate its shade, and also be able to use it to gauge your elevation.

Piñon Pine

If juniper is the most prevalent, then piñon is the most popular tree in the Great Basin. Juniper is the lower-growing tree of the pair in the piñon-juniper zone, and piñon grows higher. It's the only variety of 100 different types of pine worldwide that has a single needle—thus its nickname, singleleaf pine.

Piñon is a Spanish word for pine nut. The tree's nuts feed small and large rodents, birds, deer, and even bighorn sheep and bears. It was the staple food for Great Desert Native Americans, who harvested the nuts from groves that they considered sacred and ground them into flour, which they baked into biscuits, cakes, and a type of breadstick. Today the Paiute and Shoshone continue to celebrate piñon harvest festivals in the early fall; new subdivisions, especially in northern Nevada, have been encroaching perilously close to the groves. Gathering pine nuts is a popular pastime for many nonnative Nevadans in late September–early October; be sure you're not trespassing where you're picking, then let the cones dry in the sun, and roast or boil the nuts carefully.

Singleleaf pines were the preferred tree of the *carbonari,* the Italian charcoal burners. Most of the piñon woodlands of Nevada were clearcut to produce charcoal for the silver smelters, to fuel the steam engines at the mines, and to burn in woodstoves for heat and cooking. But because of the piñon's popularity with birds, seeds were widely redistributed, and the singleleaf pines have made a successful comeback.

Cottonwoods, willows, aspens, sagebrush, rabbitbrush, and Mormon tea, among other trees and plants, also grow in the piñon-juniper zone.

Other Trees

Starting at around 7,500 feet and going up to 11,000 feet or so are the trees that most people relate to the forest. In the Great Basin, the higher you go, the wetter the environment and the bigger the trees. Ponderosa, Jeffrey, and sugar pine; white fir; and incense cedar occupy the lower reaches of the forest. Lodgepole and white pine along with mountain hemlock inhabit the middle zone at about 9,000 feet. Douglas fir, white fir, blue spruce, and Engelmann spruce top off the thick growth up to 10,000 feet. Limber and bristlecone pine trees survive and thrive at or above the usual tree line in the harshest environment known to trees of the Great Basin.

Foraging

Foraging for edible foods—though not as easy as it is in California, the Pacific Northwest, or even Alaska—can nonetheless be enjoyed in the Nevada desert. Many of these edible wild plants are "escaped domestics" that grow around old ranches, settlements, and ghost towns. Raspberries and strawberries are sometimes found near remnants of civilization, although they also grow wild, mostly in damp woods or along steep well-drained slopes. They fruit in August–early September. Wild asparagus makes good forage. It's easiest to spot in summer, when the shoots are tall; return to the spot the next spring to harvest the tender 5–7-inch-high edibles. Roses grow above 5,000 feet in the sagebrush zone; look for five-petaled pink flowers on thorny stems in spring and the orange-red hips in September. In well-watered areas, the hips are juicy and delicious on their own; dry and mealy hips are generally made into jams. Remove the pips and process the flesh. Finally, pine nuts are the traditional and ultimate forage in the Great Basin. Harvesting and preparing these thin-shelled starchy seeds is almost a rite of passage for Nevadans.

FAUNA
Fish

Contrary to popular perception, Nevada is not just a great desert wasteland. In fact, nothing dispels the myth quite so forcefully as the fact that Nevada has more than 600 fishable lakes, reservoirs, rivers, streams, and creeks. *Nevada Anglers Guide* by Richard Dickerson lists 162 of the ones with the best public access and that can take the fishing pressure without too much strain.

The biggest fish are found in the biggest lakes. Mackinaw, a variety of Great Lakes trout, averages 20 pounds (the record is a monster 37-pounder); catch mackinaw deep in Lake Tahoe. Lahontan cutthroat, the "trout salmon" that so impressed John C. Frémont, grow to 15 pounds in Pyramid Lake; a 41-pounder is on display at the State Museum in Carson City, but it's a member of the original species, which is now extinct. The ancient cui-ui sucker fish is native to Pyramid Lake. Lake Mead boasts an abundance of striped bass and a regenerating population of the popular largemouth bass.

Seven pound cutthroats, five-pound browns, and three-pound rainbows are fished from Topaz Lake and a number of ponds and streams in Nevada. One-pound golden trout are catchable in the lakes (especially Hidden Lake) high up in the Ruby Mountains.

Finally, one stream in Nevada, Desert Creek near Yerington, actually has Arctic grayling, a tasteless white fish well known to anglers familiar with the lakes and streams of Alaska.

Lizards

Nevada has 26 species of lizards, about 15 of them in the Mojave Desert. Of the 3,000 lizard species worldwide, only two are poisonous, and Nevada has one of them. The **banded Gila monster** is found in Clark and Lincoln Counties between the Colorado and Virgin Rivers. Nevada's Gila monsters are nocturnal—most active right after dusk—though you might see one after a summer rain or on a cool day. They're also endangered.

The **chuckwalla** is nearly as common as the Gila is rare. This 16-inch vegetarian eats mostly blossoms and leaves and is found in Clark and Nye Counties. The **desert iguana** is another vegetarian. The **Great Basin whiptail** is found at 2,000–7,000 feet. It's easy to identify, since its tail is twice as long as its body. Another species with a distinctive tail is the **zebratail**, which is banded with black and white stripes. It wags its tail as it flees, hoping to distract its predators. If another animal gets the tail, the zebratail grows another. Zebratails are extremely fast and zigzag when they run.

The **collared lizard** has a black-and-white band around its neck. It's generally seen around rocky terrain, hunting for grasshoppers, cicadas, and leopard lizards. It bites if handled. **Leopard lizards** are extremely common in northern Nevada and prefer to hang around sage. They're easy to recognize, with thick spots all over their bodies and very long thin tails. If you creep quietly toward them, they'll tolerate you until you're very close before darting away. They also bite readily and are fierce predators.

The **horned lizard** is an unusual creature of the desert Southwest. It is black and tan and grows horns on the back of its head. Small spines cover the rest of its body. Ants are its favorite food. It relies on camouflage for protection but will puff up and hiss if threatened.

The most common lizard of Nevada is the **Western fence lizard.** It's brown with bright blue stomach patches. Like the zebratail, it can shed its tail to escape danger, then grow another.

Since lizards, like all reptiles, are cold-blooded, you'll often see them sunning on rocks in the morning and evening. They need a body temperature of 104°F to be in full fettle. Too much heat, however, is fatal; during the hottest part of the day, they hide in the shade of shrubs, rocks, or burrows. And, of course, they hibernate in the winter.

Snakes

Like lizards, most snakes in Nevada are found in the Mojave Desert. Several varieties of rattlers inhabit the Las Vegas area. The **Panamint** has a wide range (from Las Vegas to Tonopah) and a bad bite. The **Southwestern**

speckled likes the mountains and washes around Lake Mead. **Western diamondbacks** are easy to identify, as their name implies, and it's a good thing since they're especially ill-tempered as well as being the largest of the seven species of Nevada rattlers. The **Mojave rattler** is sometimes mistaken for the diamondback, although it has distinctive black and white tail rings. The Mojave rattler is less nasty but its venom is 10 times more poisonous. The **sidewinder** is a small rattlesnake, around two feet long, known for the S-curve trail its slithering motion leaves in the sand. The **Great Basin rattlesnake** has the largest range, covering more than half the state at 5,000–10,000 feet in elevation.

The **mountain king snake** is not poisonous, likes river bottoms and farmlands, and eats rattlers for breakfast; it's immune to the venom. Because it displays red and black bands, it's often confused with the highly poisonous **Arizona coral snake,** with its red and yellow bands. Though they're not supposed to exist in Nevada, coral snakes have been identified as far north as Lovelock and as far west as Carson City.

The **Great Basin gopher snake** is probably the most common and widely distributed serpent in Nevada and is active during the day. It's not poisonous; it kills small mammals by constriction.

Desert Tortoise

The desert tortoise is the state reptile. It's unmistakable with its hard shell and fat legs, the front legs larger than the rear for digging burrows. Burrows protect them on hot summer days and when they hibernate through the winter. These tortoises eat grasses and blossoms in the early morning and late afternoon. In June, females lay 4–6 eggs in shallow holes and then cover them with dirt. The eggs hatch in late September–early October. The tortoises can live to be 100 years old.

These days, however, most don't. In April 1990 the desert tortoise of the Mojave was listed as threatened due to loss of habitat to agriculture, road construction, military activity, energy and mineral development, off-road vehicles, raven predation, and private collection. The tortoises are also victims of an upper-respiratory syndrome.

Birds

Nevada is one of the best places in the West to look for raptors—eagles, hawks, falcons, and ospreys. The Goshute Mountains, specifically, between Ely and Wendover, are on the flyway of up to 20,000 migrating raptors every year. In fact, HawkWatch International (800/726-HAWK—800/726-4295, www.hawkwatch.org) has been monitoring the migrations over the Goshutes from the Pacific Northwest and Alaska since 1979: counting the individual birds among 18 different species, capturing birds to observe their health and size, banding birds to track their movements, and assessing data to estimate population fluctuations. Recently, the hawk count was the highest in a decade; the group concludes that the use of DDT and other pesticides, to which raptors are especially susceptible, is diminishing.

Both bald and golden **eagles** are found in Nevada. Golden eagles stay year-round, mostly in the northern part of the state; bald eagles migrate here for the winter and like well-watered and agricultural areas.

Ospreys have wingspans approaching those of eagles and are related to vultures. Since they feed entirely on fish (they're also known as fish hawks), osprey are mainly observed feeding in the rivers and lakes of the Reno–Tahoe area on their migration south for the winter.

Accipiters include **goshawks,** fairly large birds about the size of ravens; **sharp-shinned hawks,** about the size of robins; and **Cooper's hawks,** similar to sharp-shins. Since accipiter habitat is mostly in forests and heavily wooded areas, HawkWatch has found their populations to be on the wane because of extensive logging in the Pacific Northwest and western Canada.

Buteos are the hawks normally seen soaring above the desert. Among them are **ferruginous hawks,** which live in the juniper of eastern Nevada year-round. Common **red-**

tailed hawks prey on lizards in the Mojave. **Rough-legged hawks** winter in Nevada, while **Swainson's hawks** prefer Nevada in the summer and then fly to South America for the winter, although they're fairly uncommon these days.

Sharp-eyed birdwatchers can also spot marsh hawks, kestrels, merlins, and peregrine falcons.

Pelicans have traditionally nested in large numbers at Anaho Island in Pyramid Lake. Their numbers had fallen dramatically because of drought, reaching an all-time low of nine chicks in 1991, but the population has recovered somewhat and is now in the thousands.

Other shorebirds also nest at Anaho. The wildlife refuges at Ruby Marsh, Stillwater, Pahranagat Lakes, Railroad Valley, Kirch (south of Ely), and others are also prime bird-watching locales.

Mountain Lions and Bears

Experts consider predators and prey around the West plentiful nowadays compared to their numbers during the first half of the 20th century. Populations of pronghorn, elk, deer, sheep, wild horses, and burros have all revived in the past 30 years or so, and thus mountain lions and bears have become more common both in the remote and inhabited mountains.

Mountain lions aren't particularly shy of humans, but they're so elusive that they're not often seen. When one is, especially in a populated area, it's trapped and relocated, and it makes pretty big news. Attacks on humans are rare but not unknown. Also known as cougars, panthers (or painters), and pumas, mountain lion males weigh up to 160 pounds and females 100–130 pounds. As such, they're second in size only to bears as North America's largest predators. They hunt at night, taking coyotes, mule deer, bighorn sheep, beavers, and even porcupines.

Likewise, **black bears** are more common in Nevada than most people think. A Department of Wildlife study a few years ago concluded that up to several hundred bears live in Nevada, most in the Sierras and the rest in the Pine Nut and Sweetwater Ranges in western Nevada and around Jarbidge in northeastern Nevada. These bears can be any color from blond to cinnamon to jet-black; nearly all have a white patch on their chests. The males can be six feet long and weigh 300–400 pounds, the females five feet long and up to 200 pounds.

Coyotes

Coyotes are the West's most common predator and therefore its contemporary symbol of defiance. Coyotes are extremely smart and patient. They're fast, they reproduce readily and in large numbers, and they're utterly opportunistic, taking advantage of bumper crops of rabbits or vulnerable deer, even supplementing their diet with pine nuts. Coyotes have also pretty much lost their fear of humans and are occasionally seen in towns looking for cats and dogs. They prey voraciously on domestic stock, killing an estimated 10,000 sheep and cattle each year in Nevada. The federal Animal Damage Control (ADC) hunts them all over the West, killing nearly 100,000 coyotes in 17 Western states every year.

Bighorn Sheep

The desert (or Nelson) bighorn is the state animal. It is smaller than its cousins, the Rocky Mountain and California bighorns, but has bigger horns and is therefore highly prized as a big-game trophy. In fact, hunters have stalked this animal since records of such activities have been kept; petroglyphs and pictographs, including those in Valley of Fire State Park northeast of Las Vegas, illustrate bighorn hunting. It's even believed that sheep were a larger part of the Native American diet than deer. More than 2,000 hunters apply for the 100 or so sheep tags distributed every year to Nevadans; 1,000 nonresidents compete for the dozen out-of-state tags.

Nevada is the only state in the country that is home to all three subspecies of bighorn. Desert bighorn inhabit south and central Nevada, Rocky Mountain bighorn occupy northeastern Nevada, and California bighorn live in northwestern Nevada. An aggressive relocation program is underway; bighorn are

Desert bighorn sheep

trapped and redistributed throughout the state to ensure healthy populations.

At 1.5 million acres, the Desert National Wildlife Range is the largest wildlife refuge in the country outside Alaska. It was established to protect the desert bighorn, seen mostly in the Sheep Range, which stretches along U.S. 93 from just north of Las Vegas all the way to near Alamo. Desert bighorn have overpopulated the area around Lake Mead to the point where they can be seen grazing on the grass at Hemenway Valley Park, right in the middle of Boulder City.

Wild Horses and Burros

One of the great wildlife controversies in Nevada is over wild horses, also known as mustangs, a nonnative species introduced by Spanish colonists. Since the Wild Free-Roaming Horse and Burro Act was passed in 1971, the Bureau of Land Management (BLM) has protected these horses and burros "as a symbol of the history and pioneer spirit of the West." This legislation was enacted in part thanks to the efforts of Velma Johnson, a Reno secretary, to put an end to the brutal business of the legendary mustangers.

These cowboys chased wild horses, often with low-flying airplanes, roped them from flatbed trucks, and sold them to slaughterhouses as meat for pet food. Mustanging was graphically dramatized in the classic 1961 movie *The Misfits*, written by Arthur Miller, who took the "six-week cure" (got divorced) at Reno in 1956 and observed mustangers working around Pyramid Lake. Possibly the most famous movie filmed in Nevada, *The Misfits* shows several characters chasing and roping horses from a pickup truck and captured the last performances by Clark Gable, who died of a heart attack shortly after completing the picture, and Marilyn Monroe, who died of a drug overdose under mysterious circumstances in 1962.

Since 1971 the BLM has been in charge of rounding up wild horses. Everyone seems to agree that a definite limit to the population needs to be maintained. Ranchers insist that the horses destroy the range and pollute water sources. Herds of wild horses are occasionally found shot in remote ranching areas. Some environmentalists note, however, that when the horses are removed, ranchers run twice the number of cattle that a particular area can sustain. Others claim that horses actually benefit the range by allowing the growth of shrubs and plants that provide forage for native species such as pronghorn, bighorn, and mule deer. One expert, Joel Berger, studied horses for five years in the remote Granite Range north of Gerlach and concluded that horses account for minimal damage to the range. Still, he recommended that 90 percent of the wild horses be removed to protect native species.

In a recent roundup from a 300,000-acre horse-management area east of Eureka, upward of 1,250 of the nearly 1,500 mustangs were culled. Horses age nine and younger were transported to Palomino Valley to be offered for adoption. Horses older than nine were released back into the wild. The BLM defended the process, claiming that the older horses can reproduce until they're 16–17 years old. But critics insist that by pulling out the young horses, the government is purposely weakening the herds.

Once the horses are removed from the range, the question is what to do with them. In 1985, for example, 19,000 horses were culled from the wild herds, but only 9,000 were adopted. Since then the BLM has begun to cultivate the market, matching particular kinds of wild horses to local preferences in the Southern, Midwestern, and Eastern states. One way of dealing with a saturated wild-horse market is injecting a contraceptive vaccine into nonpregnant mares age five or older; the contraceptive is effective for two years. Even environmentalists and animal activists support this project. Other possibilities include sterilization, establishing large horse sanctuaries, destroying horses that aren't adopted within a given period, and selling unwanted horses for meat to supply the many people around the world who eat horse meat as well as to supply domestic pet-food manufacturers.

In an agreement negotiated by the Fund For Animals and Animal Protection in 1997, the BLM admitted to major abuses in its adoption system, whereby people who adopted mustangs for $125 apiece sold them to pet food manufacturers at a profit. It turns out the BLM had lost track of 32,000 adopted horses since the program began; 90 percent of the mustangs adopted each year, the Fund claimed, wound up as pet food. The BLM agreed to monitor its wild-horse adoption program more vigorously.

In the 1992 BLM census, Nevada was home to roughly 33,000 free-roaming horses, 60 percent of the nation's total. A combination of factors, including the roundups and drought, reduced the population by half by 2008. Controversy and drought notwithstanding, it's a thrill to see free-roaming herds, which is possible in nearly any rural setting in Nevada.

Environmental Issues

WILDERNESS

To many Nevadans, *wilderness* is a dirty word, a negative concept. It means controlled access and use: reduced grazing and logging as well as regulated road building, mineral exploration, and mining activity—in short, general commercial restraint of the activities that most rural Nevadans rely on for their livelihoods. All through the 19th century the term "public-domain lands" was tantamount to "lands where anything goes," with no restrictions whatsoever on grazing, mining, road cutting, and polluting.

Especially since the vast majority of Nevada land is desert, traditionally considered unattractive and useless, it belonged to whomever wanted it with no thought to preserving it in what environmentalists think of as its pristine state. At the turn of the 20th century, Theodore Roosevelt, a "preservationist" president, was elected, and Nevada became the object of some of the earliest environmental-protection and controlled-usage policies. Until quite recently, however, only small isolated chunks of Nevada's federal lands were protected.

The federal government owns more than 80 percent of Nevada, with 70 percent in the hands of the Bureau of Land Management (BLM). Traditionally, mining and ranching interests have been far too strong to be overcome by any wilderness proposals. Recently, however, the mass migrations into Nevada's two urban areas and the increasing importance of tourism to the state's economic well-being have turned the tables. The 1964 Wilderness Act empowered states to set aside peaks, canyons, forests, streams, and wildlife habitats in parks, and by 1989 the political stars were aligned properly for the federal government to designate wilderness areas in Nevada; 733,400 acres of national forest lands were protected as wilderness areas in 14 separate locations around the state.

The largest is Arc Dome in the Toiyabe Range in central Nevada, at 115,000 acres; the smallest is Boundary Peak, with 10,000 acres surrounding Nevada's highest mountain. The wilderness areas include Mount Rose (28,000 acres) and Mount Charleston (38,000 acres), within an hour's drive of Reno and Las Vegas, respectively, and the remote and trackless Quinn Canyon (27,000 acres) and Grant (50,000 acres) Ranges in eastern Nevada. Also included are the Santa Rosas (31,000 acres) in the northwest, East Humboldts (36,900 acres) and Rubies (90,000 acres) in the northeast (along with the long-established Jarbidge Wilderness Area), Mount Moriah (82,000 acres) and Currant Mountain (36,000 acres) near Ely, and Table Mountain (98,000 acres) and Alta Toquima (38,000 acres) in central Nevada.

The first guide to Nevada's wilderness areas was published in 1997. *Nevada Wilderness Areas and Great Basin National Park—a Hiking and Backpacking Guide* by Renoite Michael C. White covers a dozen wilderness areas plus the Great Basin and is indispensable for exploring these areas. Another guide covering access and backpacking routes in detail is John Hart's *Hiking the Great Basin*. The latest government publications on wilderness areas are available from the Humboldt and Toiyabe Forest Service headquarters. The Toiyabe Chapter of the Sierra Club (775/323-3162, www.nevada.sierraclub.org) publishes the *Toiyabe Trails* newsletter six times a year, covering Sierra Club activities and group outings, wilderness, water rights, and other Nevada environmental issues.

In 1976 Congress instructed the BLM to examine its land holdings (50 million acres in Nevada) to determine which areas had potential to become official wilderness. The BLM proposed 52 areas covering 1.9 million acres, which would more than double the existing wilderness in Nevada. No mechanized vehicles, including bicycles, are permitted in wilderness areas, and mining is prohibited unless the mines existed before 1976. Of course, the mining industry and environmental groups disagree over the areas and their boundaries, and the process is expected to take years, but in the meantime development is prohibited in the proposed wilderness areas.

The Wilderness Society is urging the federal government to use $15 million from the Land and Water Conservation Fund, provided by a share of the royalties from offshore oil production, to purchase Nevada land to be protected by the U.S. Forest Service. Most of the sensitive areas are near Carson City, Reno, and Las Vegas, in the Carson Range, along the Truckee River, and in the Spring Mountains.

NUCLEAR ISSUES
Nevada Test Site

This 1,350-square-mile chunk of the southern Nevada desert is a Rhode Island–sized area that's off limits to the public—but you probably wouldn't want to go there even if it weren't. Between 1951 and 1962 there were 126 atmospheric tests of nuclear weapons conducted within the Test Site's boundaries. Another 925 underground explosions rocked the desert 1962–1992, and the federal government has admitted to another 204 secret detonations.

It all started after U.S. scientists and military planners found that nuclear test explosions over the Marshall Islands in the central Pacific were politically and logistically inconvenient, and they went looking for a more suitable location on the U.S. mainland. Nevada already had the enormous Las Vegas Bombing and Gunnery Range, and there was nothing out there anyway, right? The first bomb, a one-kiloton warhead dropped from an airplane, was detonated in January 1951, initiating another bizarre episode in southern Nevada history, not to mention a deadly "nuclear war" against atomic veterans and downwinders that continues to this day.

About one bomb was tested every month for the next four years; after a two-year suspension of testing at the site, during which time larger bombs were again exploded in the central Pacific, a bomb was blown off every three weeks until the first Nuclear Test-Ban Treaty was signed in the early 1960s, eliminating atmospheric explosions.

Set off just before dawn, the tests sometimes broke windows in Henderson, 100 miles away. The fireballs could be seen in Reno, 300 miles away, and the mushroom clouds tended to drift east over southern Utah. For most of the blasts, the Atomic Energy Commission erected realistic "Doom Town" sets to measure destruction, and thousands of soldiers were posted within a tight radius to be purposefully exposed to the tests. In his classic *Been Down So Long It Looks Like Up to Me*, Richard Fariña described it thus:

> The sky changed, the entire translucent dome stunned by the swiftness of the shimmering atomic flash. The light drove their once tiny shadows to a terrifying distance in the desert, making them seem like titans. Then it shrank, the aurora crashing insanely backward, like a film in reverse, toppling, swimming into a single white-hot bulge, a humming lump, a festering core. It hovered inches above the horizon, dancing, waiting almost as if it were taking a stoked breath, then swelled in puffing spasms, poking high into the stratosphere, edging out the pale skyrocket vapor trails at either side, the ball going sickly yellow, the shock wave releasing its roar, the entire spectacle catching fire, blazing chaotically, shaming the paltry sun.

> In the echo, there was silence.

And in a less rhapsodic but no less poignant description, K. J. Evans, in his story "A Hometown Grows Up" in *Nevada Day* magazine in 1987, wrote:

> I recall an early morning in 1957, seated with my family around the breakfast table. Suddenly, an atomic blast lit up the sky. My mother stopped stirring the Wheatena, peeled back the curtain from the kitchen window and peered out. A faint rocking motion that failed to stir my kid brother, asleep in his high chair, accompanied the flash.

> Dad arose and padded to the back door.

> "A-bomb," he grunted, and went back to blotting the bacon.

Indeed, far from disturbing the local health consciousness, at the time Las Vegas turned the blasts into public-relations events, throwing rooftop parties to view them. Moe Dalitz and Wilbur Clark planned the opening of the Desert Inn to coincide with a detonation; their party garnered more coverage than the bomb test. A silent majority certainly worried which way the wind blew, and a vocal minority seemed to contract a strange "atom fever," marketing everything from atom burgers to nuclear gasoline and appointing a yearly Miss Atomic Blast. In *American Ground Zero: The Secret Nuclear War*, a coffee-table book that provides a new dimension to the word *horrifying*, author Carole Gallagher quotes a 17-year-old soldier who witnessed an aboveground explosion in 1957:

> That cloud was like a big ball of fire with black smoke and some red inside, big, monstrous, almost sickening…. It left me really

sad, real apprehensive about life.... That explosion told me I was part of the most evil thing I have ever seen in my life.

GIs were stationed as close to the blasts as was physically possible without killing them outright. Citizens in the path of the fallout wore "film badges" on their clothes to measure the amount of radiation they were subjected to. Livestock dropped dead fairly soon after exposure, and people involved with or in proximity to the tests have been dying of cancer and leukemia ever since. Today, exposed soldiers, residents of southwestern Utah, and their children are part of extremely prevalent cancer clusters. For more than 35 years the government steadfastly denied any connection between the deaths and the tests; the Justice Department spent untold millions of dollars fighting lawsuits brought by victims of the nuclear tests, primarily people who worked at the Test Site and people downwind of the tests in Nevada, Utah, Arizona, and New Mexico. Only recently have the feds begun to consider the possibility that there could be some cause-and-effect relationship between the two.

The Nuclear Waste Repository

In the 1980s the state was chosen to play host to yet another aspect of the nuclear industry—radioactive waste. Yucca Mountain, 100 miles northwest of Las Vegas, was the only site considered to become the nation's permanent high-level radioactive waste storage site. Not actually a peak, Yucca Mountain is a six-mile-long ridge rising 1,500 feet above the Amargosa Desert. The proposed repository straddled the Nevada Test Site and Nellis Air Force Range. A long line of independent scientists criticized the Department of Energy for sugarcoating, whitewashing, and even falsifying data to support the final 2002 recommendation that Yucca Mountain become the nation's nuclear waste dump. The state of Nevada filed a variety of lawsuits challenging the science, safety, and constitutionality of forcing one state to accept the nation's

nuclear waste, but the Yucca Mountain recommendation was quickly approved by the Bush administration. In 2009 the Obama administration said the Yucca Mountain site was no longer an option, and the project was effectively canceled when its funding was left out of the federal budget.

Citizen Alert (P.O. Box 5339, Reno, NV 89513, 775/827-4200, www.citizenalert.org), a statewide environmental organization working since 1975 to assure public participation and government accountability on issues affecting the land and people of Nevada, focuses on nuclear waste, nuclear testing, and Native American sovereignty. Their regular newsletters are a good resource for information and education about these issues.

LAND USE
Mining Reform

The General Mining Act of 1872, still in effect today, came under serious fire from the Clinton's administration. The law, designed to hasten the 19th-century exploration of the West, gives miners the right to prospect hundreds of millions of acres of land that is ostensibly owned by the government, lease it for $2.50–5 per acre (the 1872 prices were never raised), and dig up the minerals on the land without paying the government any royalties.

Since 1994 the BLM has not accepted new patents on mining claims, and attempts in Congress to end new patent claims and impose federal royalties on mining profits failed in 2007 and 2009.

Range Reform

Farming and ranching are no different from mining when it comes to changing perceptions of land use based on environmental values versus lifestyle and economic considerations. The argument goes that alfalfa farming, for example, produces 1 percent of Nevada's gross state product while using more than 85 percent of the available water. On the other side, ranchers argue that federal lands are owned and used by the people, more often than not third- and fourth-generation ranchers on the same land who have a strong vested interest in the health of the land for continuing their livelihoods and lifestyles. Farmers, ranchers, and miners all believe that their way of life is under attack and will soon be legislated out of existence by the powerful forces of urban environmentalism that hold an almost religious conviction to return the land to their vision of nature, an early-18th-century ideal.

These are tough issues anywhere, but out here in a state that's owned almost entirely by the federal government, they are profound and divisive concerns that will affect the future of the state.

History

INDIGENOUS PEOPLE

Excavation and carbon dating of artifacts discovered in a number of caves around the state have supplied evidence that Native Americans occupied the region now encompassed by Nevada as early as 11,000 B.C. Bones taken from a cave near Winnemucca Lake and spear tips unearthed at Leonard Rock Shelter, south of Lovelock, attest to a human presence along the shoreline of great Lake Lahontan between 10,000 and 7500 B.C. Basket remnants from the rock shelter are thought to have been woven around 5600 B.C.

At Tule Springs, an archaeological site near Las Vegas, indications are that Paleo-Indians also lived in shoreline caves at the tail end of the wet and cold Wisconsin Ice Age and hunted Pleistocene mammals such as woolly mammoths, bison, mastodons, and caribou as early as 11,000 B.C. At Gypsum Cave, also near Las Vegas, remains of humans, horses, and even a giant sloth certify a hunter culture around 8500 B.C. Beyond these finds, little is known about the earliest residents of what would become Nevada, but starting around 3,000 years ago a picture of the local prehistoric people starts to emerge.

The Lovelock Cave was a treasure trove for archaeologists, who excavated darts and fishhooks, baskets, domestic tools, tule duck decoys, shell jewelry, and human remains dating from roughly 2000 B.C. It's known that Lake Lahontan was shrinking, and these water-based people had to invent a new desert culture. The area's later Paiute demonstrated similar basket-making skills, but it is unclear whether the people who used Lovelock Cave were their ancestors. Petroglyphs from around this period have been located in the vicinity, especially at Grimes Point near Fallon, but they raise many more questions than they answer about the lives of the Paleo-Indians.

Anasazi

In the southern regions, a Native American culture began to evolve around 2500 B.C. Known as Archaic Indians, they were a foraging people who lived and traveled in small bands, built rock shelters, used the atlatl (an arrow launcher), hunted bighorn sheep and desert tortoises, and harvested screwbean mesquite and cholla fruit. By around 300 B.C. the Basket Maker culture had arisen; these people too were foragers and lived in pit houses.

At about the beginning of the common era, Native Americans in Nevada's southern desert began to develop the first signs of civilization. They lived in close proximity to each other in pit houses (holes in the ground with brush roofs), and evidence exists of cooperation during hunting and gathering chores. By around A.D. 500 these Anasazi ("Ancient Ones") had developed pottery as well as bows and arrows, begun building more sophisticated dwellings with adobe walls, learned how to mine salt and trade with neighbors, and started to bury their dead. By A.D. 800 their civilization was at its peak: They cultivated beans and corn in irrigated fields, lived in grand 100-room pueblos, fashioned artistic pots and baskets, mined turquoise, and

COURTESY OF LOST CITY MUSEUM

Lost City Museum

generally enjoyed a sophisticated lifestyle in the fertile delta between the Muddy and Virgin Rivers in what is now southeastern Nevada. Around 1150, however, the Anasazi migrated from their homeland. No one knows for sure why, but speculation includes drought, overpopulation, disease, collapse of the economic underpinnings of the culture, or warring neighbors. Whatever the reason, the Anasazi abandoned their pueblos and farms. One of the largest was uncovered in the 1920s and is now preserved at Lost City Museum in Overton.

Paiute, Washoe, and Shoshone

The Southern Paiute claimed the territory that the Anasazi had fled, but they never regained the advanced elements of their predecessors' society. In fact, for the next 700 years, the Paiute remained nomadic hunter-gatherers. The Northern Paiute migrated north to populate the high desert, where they encountered the Washoe and Shoshone. All settled into a basically peaceful coexistence, adapting to the arid land. Their fishing and hunting techniques, pine-nut harvests, tools, weapons, and baskets

are displayed in the Archaeology Gallery at the State Museum in Carson City. For hundreds of years, the Washoe of western Nevada, the Shoshone of eastern Nevada, and the Paiute of northwestern and southern Nevada developed and maintained cultures perfectly adapted to their difficult environments. Within 40 years of contact with Europeans, the Native American lifestyles had been destroyed.

EXPLORERS AND PIONEERS

The first Europeans to enter what is now Nevada were Spanish friars surveying a trail to connect missions in New Mexico and on the California coast. Two expeditions, one led by Francisco Garcés, the other by friars Silvestre Vélez de Escalante and Francisco Atanasio Domínguez, explored the region, but only Garcés touched the far southern tip of Nevada. Escalante and Domínguez, however, discovered a couple of large rivers running west from Utah and postulated a great waterway flowing from there to the Pacific. Thus the mythical San Buenaventura River, a great river that flowed from the Rocky Mountains to the Pacific Ocean, was introduced

WOVOKA: GHOST DANCE PROPHET

Orphaned at 14, Jack Wilson made his way by chopping wood and milking cows on a ranch owned by his adoptive family and listening respectfully to their Bible recitations. It is probable that the young man, named Wovoka by his Paiute parents, also spent considerable time contemplating the Native American way of life on which the newcomers had intruded. All these influences – Christianity, a strong work ethic, and his early life with his shaman father – would influence Wovoka's nascent world view.

As a young man, Wovoka awoke from a trance during a solar eclipse, telling of a coming earthly Native American paradise. In his dream, Paiute ancestors rose from the grave, the white usurpers disappeared, and the sacred earth once again teemed with buffalo and deer. Wovoka's people would live in harmony forever. Wovoka's version of paradise clearly drew on the traditions of both Christianity and Paiute mysticism; for the prophesy to be fulfilled, he told his followers, Indians must not sin nor rebel against the newcomers. To start the coming triumph, the chosen people also must perform the "Ghost Dance" ritual, he said. Wovoka described his divine inspiration:

When the Sun died, I went up to
Heaven and saw God and all the peo-
ple who had died a long time ago.
God told me to come back and tell my
people they must be good and love
one another...He gave me this dance to
give to my people.

This notion of ritualistic dancing to herald the advent of the apocalypse was common for decades among Indians frustrated by nonnative encroachment on their lands. The Paiute Tavibo, whom many believed was Wovoka's father, thrice claimed to carry word from the Great Spirit that a reverential dance would cause the land to open and swallow the white man, leaving only the Na-

tive Americans to commune with nature and their resurrected ancestors. But only Wovoka's message resonated with the desert and Plains Indians. The tribes on the Plains – Cheyenne, Arapaho, and Sioux – perhaps owing to their disillusionment with the newcomers following the Sand Creek Massacre and Great Sioux War – were especially receptive to Wovoka's teachings.

At an intertribe council in 1889, Wovoka admonished, "You must not hurt anybody or do harm to anyone. You must not fight. Do right always.... Do not refuse to work for the whites and do not make any trouble with them." Despite his movement's peaceful overtures, local bands adapted the message, taking it and teaching it as a call to arms in order to hasten the white purge. The Lakota Sioux believers made sacred shirts for the Dance that they believed to be bullet-proof.

Alarmed that the Ghost Dance at the Lakota reservation heralded another round of Indian uprisings, the U.S. government sent soldiers to protect white settlers nearby. Whether the Lakota were wont to resort to violence to end white oppression or whether their frenzied dancing was simply a manifestation of peaceful religious fervor, passions ran high on both sides. The Lakota leaders attempted to escape when the 7th Cavalry arrived. Nearly 300 Native American men, women, and children were slaughtered at the resulting "battle" of Wounded Knee.

After the massacre, Wovoka remained a powerful and respected leader among the Paiutes. Indian Agent S. W. Pugh noted years later that

He is still a power among his people
and could be used to excellent advan-
tage [on the reservation]. He is a very
intelligent Indian, and peaceably in-
clined apparently.... These people will
follow him anywhere, and he has ad-
vanced ideas.

into the frontier imagination. It took almost 70 years to bury the myth.

In 1819 a treaty between the United States and Mexico designated the 42nd parallel as the boundary between American and Spanish territories (today it is the northern border of Nevada with Oregon and Idaho). For the next 30 years all the U.S. explorers, trappers and traders, mapmakers, gold rushers, and settlers who entered Nevada were technically illegal aliens. The 1848 Treaty of Guadalupe Hidalgo, following the Mexican-American War, ceded most of the Southwest, including all of Nevada, to the United States.

In 1826, Jedediah Smith led a party of fur trappers through the same country that Garcés had crossed and spent that winter in California. In the spring he crossed the central Sierra Nevada and discovered the Great Basin Desert—the hard way. Smith's party struggled through the sand and sage with no water for days at a time, crossed a dozen mountain passes, stumbled into Utah, and reached the Salt Lake Valley an agonizing month and a half after leaving the coast.

A year later, Peter Skene Ogden entered Nevada from the north and trapped beaver along the Humboldt River. In 1829 Ogden returned to the Humboldt and then continued south, becoming the first nonnative to cross the Great Basin from north to south. Meanwhile, Kit Carson and company were following parts of the route laid out by the Franciscans, thereby helping to establish and publicize the southern Spanish Trail trade route. In 1830, Antonio Armijo, a Mexican trader, set out from Santa Fe on the Spanish Trail. An experienced scout in Armijo's party, Rafael Rivera, discovered a shortcut on the route by way of Las Vegas's Big Springs, thereby making him the first nonnative to set foot on the land that only 75 years later would become Las Vegas.

In 1833, Joseph Walker led a fur-trapping expedition west along the Humboldt and Walker Rivers through Nevada, crossed the Sierras into Yosemite Valley, spent the winter in California, then returned east along the same route in spring 1834. In both directions he encountered

and shot at the Northern Paiute—the first skirmishes in Nevada.

In 1841 the famous Bidwell-Bartleson party became the first migrants to set out from Missouri and enter California. Through a combination of dumb luck and good guides, these pioneers managed to follow Walker's route along the Humboldt River, Carson Sink, Walker River, and over the Sierras. With them were the first cattle, wagons, and white woman and child to enter Nevada. Their success encouraged a few more staggered wagon trains to attempt the long journey across the uncharted western half of the country and stimulated the first official mapmaking expedition through the Great Basin.

Frémont and the Forty-Niners

In 1843, John C. Frémont, a lieutenant in the U.S. Army's Topographical Corps, was assigned the job of exploring and mapping much of what would become Nevada; he also hoped to finally locate the elusive San Buenaventura River. Guided by Kit Carson, he marched west through the Columbia River Basin, then cut south into far northwestern Nevada. He came across and named Pyramid Lake, followed the Truckee River for a spell, turned south and "discovered" the Carson River, and continued down to the river that Joseph Walker had found. Frémont's party crossed the Sierras in January, glimpsing Lake Tahoe, then traveled south through California and reentered Nevada on the Spanish Trail, camping at Las Vegas. From there they continued through Utah, crossed the Rockies, and returned to Missouri. This initial trip resulted in the naming of the Great Basin and doubts about the San Buenaventura River. Frémont returned to Nevada a year later, this time guided by Joseph Walker himself, and further mapped the country. By then, several hundred migrants had already crossed the great desert into California.

The famous Donner incident, in which an ill-fated pioneer party became snowbound in the Sierras and resorted to cannibalism to survive, slowed migration temporarily. But one year later, in 1847, a mass migration of Mormons settled the Salt Lake Valley, advancing nonnative civilization to the eastern edge of the Great Basin. A year after that, the United States emerged victorious from the Mexican-American War and appropriated the rest of the West; fortuitously, only two weeks earlier, the country's first major gold deposits had been discovered at Sutter's Mill. Roughly 500 people had migrated to California from the east in 1847, but over the next five years nearly 250,000 frenzied stampeders flooded the West Coast. Of those who took the Emigrant Trail through the vast Utah Territory, some stopped to pan the eastside creeks of the Sierra Nevada and found gold, while others settled just short of California in the verdant valleys at the base of the great range. Mormon advance parties set up trading posts to supply the travelers; the one established in Carson Valley, called Mormon Station, attracted other settlers in 1851 who turned it into the first real town in Nevada.

Genoa and Las Vegas

Over the course of the next few years, the population of the country around Mormon Station—Washoe and Carson Valleys, Johntown, and Ragtown—started to grow. Traders, prospectors, wagon drivers, and homesteaders moved in. In 1855 this far-western corner of Utah Territory, administered from Salt Lake City, was designated Carson County and put under the direct administration of local Mormon officials and colonists. Mormon Station was renamed Genoa and became Nevada's first county seat.

Missionaries were also dispatched from Salt Lake City to southern Nevada at a rest stop along the Spanish Trail known as Las Vegas, or the Meadows. They built a stockade similar to the one in Genoa, befriended the Paiute, nourished the migrants, and even began mining and smelting lead nearby. But tensions between the Mormon colonists and miners, meager rations, and the hardships and isolation of the desert caused the mission to disband.

In addition, Mormon leader Brigham Young, concerned with the possibility of going to war with the U.S. Army over autonomy, bigamy, and manifest destiny, recalled the missionaries from Genoa. Their places were taken by the people who would soon become the first official Nevadans.

THE COMSTOCK LODE

Prospectors and gold miners had been crawling all over the Carson River and its tributary creeks for almost a decade. Chinese laborers had even been brought in to dig a canal from the river to Gold Canyon; their settlement became Dayton, the second-oldest town in Nevada. The prospectors were already following their noses up toward what could be the source of promising placer pay dirt. There were 100 or so uninformed prospectors, but only the young Grosch brothers, mineralogists and assayers from New York, knew of the gargantuan silver lode under everyone's feet. They both died suddenly one winter, and their secret was buried with them.

Meanwhile, Abraham Curry bought a ranch and opened a trading post in Eagle Valley between the county seat at Genoa and the lumber mills at Washoe City. Myron Lake bought a bridge over the Truckee River in the large basin north of Washoe. Lake had dreams of a boomtown, and Curry had dreams of a capital.

An expedition led by Lieutenant Joseph C. Ives powered the steamboat *Explorer* up the Colorado River all the way to Black Canyon, and a surveying team led by Captain James H. Simpson blazed a trail through central Nevada as an alternative to the heavily trafficked road along the Humboldt River to the north. Soon, Pony Express riders were galloping over the Simpson route, passing linemen stringing telegraph wire between poles. Several new roads were cut across the Sierras into California from the east side for the settlers at Truckee Meadows and Washoe, Eagle, Carson, Mason, and Smith Valleys.

Virginia City

In 1859 two Irish gold miners dug a hole around a small spring high up on Sun Mountain and struck gold. The respectable quantities of gold, however, were encased by a blue-gray mud, a

THE PONY EXPRESS

The Pony Express delivered mail 1,800 miles between Sacramento and St. Joseph, Missouri, for only 18 months, April 1860–October 1861. But the romantic time period, the brave riders, and the purposefulness of the operation to open the West in the face of financial and security hazards have embossed the Pony Express on the American imagination. That the Pony Express was logistically able to operate year-round proved that telegraphs and railroads could do the same and prompted the government to invest in those evolving technologies.

Horse-powered mail delivery had been in use since the time of Genghis Khan (1203–1227), who is generally credited with inventing the system: small jockeys riding flying ponies between stations every 25 miles or so. Several pony expresses were established on the East Coast to carry correspondence and news in the 1820s and 1830s, but the idea for the express route from Missouri to California originated in the imagination of California Senator H. M. Gwin on a cross-country ride to Washington, D.C., in 1854. The tensions of pre–Civil War politics in the following years prevented the government from acting on Gwin's proposals, so he turned to the freighting firm of Russell, Majors, and Waddell, which ran the Overland Stage from St. Joseph, Missouri – then the western terminus of U.S. railroads – to Salt Lake City. At Gwin's urging, the partners, against their better bottom-line judgment, accepted the challenge. Within two months they had recruited several division agents, built nearly 200 stations in the remote, barren, and dangerous 700-mile stretch between Salt Lake City and Sacramento, bought 500 horses, and hired a score of riders. The first 10-day run from St. Joseph to Sacramento was completed on April 3, 1860.

More than a quarter of the trek and one of the most grueling sections took riders over mountains, through passes, and along the sagebrush valleys of central Nevada Territory. Heading toward Sacramento, Express riders entered Nevada from Utah about midway between where I-80 and U.S. 50 cross the state

line today. The Express route then drifted south, roughly following U.S. 50's route all the way to Carson City and south of Lake Tahoe. At Schellbourne, in the foothills of the Schell Creek Range near Ely, a former Shoshone village served as an overland stage and mail station. When the Pony Express came in 1860, it made use of the same facilities, as did the telegraph when it came in 1863. A few hundred miles further along the route, just north of Austin, the Natives burned a few Express stations and killed two station tenders during the Paiute Indian War.

The efficiency, bravery, endurance, and dedication of the employees are legendary. In Nevada, each rider completed a 33-mile route with a fresh horse every 10 miles. Riders carried a pistol, a Bible, and the *mochila*, or padlocked mailbag. The stations, in eyewitness Sir Richard Burton's words, were "about as civilised as the Galway shanty – or the normal dwelling place in Central Equatorial Africa." Maintaining fresh horses, food, water, and security at the lonely stations was a continuous life-and-death struggle; several riders and many stationmasters were killed.

Ironically, completion of the transcontinental telegraph line along the Pony Express route in October 1861 spelled its immediate demise: the incredible land-speed records set by Pony Express riders across the West were still no match for the miraculous dispatch of communications through the wire.

Just beyond the Reese River are markers for the Pony Express Trail. U.S. 50 generally parallels the Pony Express Trail through central Nevada, but this stretch, between Austin and Carson City, is full of reminders of this 18-month adventure that helped open up the West. Buckland's Station, near Silver Springs, was a transfer station and home base for Robert "Pony Bob" Haslam, who once rode 120 miles in less than 8.5 hours in 1860 to help deliver the transcript of President Lincoln's inaugural address. Indian troubles in the area necessitated the construction of Fort Churchill, across the Carson River. The fort replaced Buckland's as the Express stop.

peculiar rock that polluted the quartz veins, fouled the sluice boxes, and diluted the quicksilver. But when a visitor to the diggings carried a bit of the mud down and had it assayed in Placerville, it was found to be nearly pure sulfuret of silver. A drunken prospector dropped a bottle of whiskey and baptized the ragged settlement on the eastern slope of Sun Mountain with the name Virginia, after his home state, and a shifty scheming braggart made so much noise about his claim to the riches that the whole place came to be named after him: the Comstock Lode.

The Comstock is still one of the largest silver strikes in the world, and Virginia City remains one of the most authentic and colorful boomtowns in the Wild West. The enormous impact of the riches, power, and fame of this find meant that within a year Nevada had become its own territory. The capital was placed in Abe Curry's Carson City, and of the territory's nine original counties, six surrounded the Comstock.

Meanwhile, trading posts were established all along the Humboldt Trail, at Lovelock, Winnemucca, and Carlin, among others. Boomtowns such as Aurora, Austin, and Unionville were mushrooming up in the desert. Gold was also discovered at Eldorado Canyon on the Colorado River, a short distance from Las Vegas. But Virginia City was the lodestar, the ultimate boomtown. In 1864, a mere five years after its discovery, the Comstock had earned Nevada its statehood. It also helped finance the Union Army during the Civil War, and Nevada's two new senators cast the deciding votes to abolish slavery. The unearthing of tons of silver affected monetary standards worldwide.

CARSON CITY

In 1858, Abraham V. Curry was a 43-year-old businessman who, with some partners, bought the 865-acre Eagle Ranch from John Mankin for $1,000. Curry put $300 down but Mankin, his own creditors about to catch up with him, bolted town, never bothering to collect the other $700. Perhaps aware of his destiny to become the father of Carson City, Curry bought out his partners, laid out the town, offered free

and low-cost lots to permanent settlers, and plotted his strategy to make his town the state capital. Although discovery of the Comstock was still more than a year away and the "ranch" was little more than sand and sage, Curry had found the spot where he'd base his empire.

The ambitious New Yorker knew he could never be content with a ranch. He immediately began promoting the desolate valley as the eventual site of the state capital, which he named Carson City, after the nearby Carson River, which had been named for Kit Carson, John C. Frémont's top scout. Nevada was not yet even a territory, let alone a state, and Eagle Valley could boast no more than a handful of residents and even fewer buildings. The local surveyor refused to plat a town site in return for ownership of "a full city block" of what was at the time desert scrub. The surveyor worked instead for an IOU, but soon became the first postmaster of Carson City.

Curry had him lay out wide city streets and a four-square-block area known to settlers as the Plaza, though Curry called it Capitol Square. Major William Ormsby, a businessman fed up with Genoa, was one of the first settlers. Curry used clay from the ranch to fabricate adobe bricks and constructed a few buildings in "town." He also discovered a large limestone outcrop near a warm spring on the property, which he used as a quarry; he dammed the spring and built a bathhouse, which attracted prospectors and travelers.

In the summer of 1859 miners discovered the rich silver ore of the Comstock Lode mere miles east, and the rush was on. Thousands of frenzied merchants, investors, lawyers, and scammers rumbled through Carson City's dusty streets. Curry quickly located a claim high up on the Comstock, consolidated it with a Carson City butcher named Alva Gould, and sold his share to Californians for $2,000, which financed a trip back to Cleveland to collect his wife and six daughters; his sole son was already with him in Carson. The Californians immediately became millionaires from the mine that proved to be the richest ore body in the early days of the Comstock.

The city's hosted the championship heavyweight prizefight between Bob Fitzsimmons and Gentleman Jim Corbett in 1897. The boxing match landed in Carson City after San Francisco elders caved in to public sentiment prevalent at the time against boxing and canceled it. Carson City elders felt no such squeamishness, and the 14-round bout attracted such large numbers of visitors and publicity that the legislators, most of whom had witnessed the prize-fight phenomenon firsthand, came up with the Nevada tradition that evolved into legal gambling and prostitution, quick divorce and simple marriage procedures, nonrestrictive mining laws, and nuclear testing, among other unusual revenue-attracting efforts.

The Roaring '60s

Abe Curry, founder of Carson City, not only got his capital city, he got the state prison and a federal mint as well. Myron Lake won a 10-year contract to collect tolls on his bridge over the Truckee River at a bustling little site soon to be known as Reno. The new state's eastern and southern boundaries were pushed outward, swallowing a few chunks of Arizona and Utah Territories, including 150 miles of the Colorado River. Alfalfa was on its way to becoming the star crop of Nevada agriculture. The miners of the Comstock, digging to more than 500 feet, were greedily devouring virtually every tree within 50 miles for timber supports. And Virginia Town was quickly turning into Virginia City, the largest and loudest metropolis between Salt Lake City and San Francisco.

Silver was located at Eureka, 70 miles east of Austin, and at Hamilton, 70 miles farther east. Gold and silver were mined in Robinson Canyon as well as Osceola, just west of the Utah border around today's Ely. The silver at Tuscarora opened up the northeast. A gold miner from Eldorado Canyon named O. D. Gass homesteaded Las Vegas Valley, squatting in the ruins of the Mormon fort. But the big news, in 1868, was the arrival of the Central Pacific Railroad—at Reno in May, Winnemucca in September, Elko in February 1869, and Promontory Point, Utah, in May.

It also hatched Lovelock, Battle Mountain, Carlin, and Wells as it went.

The Railroads

The transcontinental railroad across northern Nevada stimulated the building of numerous wagon roads to the north and south, interconnecting the whole top half of the six-year-old state. The Virginia & Truckee Railroad was laid from the mines at Virginia City to the mills at Carson City, then connected to the main line at Reno. Thousands of Chinese workers were abandoned by both railroads after construction was completed; they were hounded and persecuted out of every Chinatown in the state over the next 15 years. After numerous skirmishes and several major battles, the Native Americans were finally subdued, then left to fend for themselves both on and off the few reservations set up to contain them. In the late 1860s and early 1870s the Comstock Lode saw the third or fourth bust in its boom-bust cycle, but in 1872 John Mackay's Big Bonanza silver strike gave Nevada a six-year, $150-million infusion of cash. A disastrous fire in 1875 temporarily muffled Virginia City's boom, and although Big Bonanza silver restored it even beyond its previous splendor, the Comstock mines played out in the next few years.

By then Eureka was producing enough silver to rate its own railroad connection, the Eureka and Palisade Railroad, to the Central Pacific line. The Nevada Central Railroad followed suit between the mines around Austin and the main line at Battle Mountain. Other short lines were laid from mines to mills with boomtowns in between. But the demise of Comstock silver mining quickly forced Nevada to its knees. From a population of nearly 60,000 within a 20-mile radius of Virginia City in 1876, only 42,000 people remained in the whole state 20 years later.

Between 1880 and 1900 it seemed that every mining strike in the state had played out and shut down, and no new ones appeared. The boom economy deflated into a shambles. A still-unbroken record snowfall and a cold snap during the winter of 1889–1890 wiped out the entire livestock industry. Silver politics became the pastime of choice, with state residents calling for the federal government to turn more Nevada silver into circulating coins.

SINCE 1900

In 1900 Jim Butler located some very rich rock in the wilds of south-central Nevada. Butler's silver strike at Tonopah was the first news of prosperity in a generation. Two years later, Goldfield began booming even more loudly 25 miles south of Tonopah. Prospectors fanned out from there and located the Bullfrog, Round Mountain, and Manhattan districts. Railroads were quickly built between Tonopah and the Southern Pacific Railroad (which had replaced the Central Pacific Railroad). The Tonopah & Las Vegas Railroad connected the new boomtowns in central Nevada to a new transcontinental railroad—the San Pedro, Los Angeles, and Salt Lake—that crossed the southern corner of Nevada; a new town, Las Vegas, was created in 1905 as a service station for the railroad between Salt Lake City and Los Angeles. Copper in unimaginable quantities was ripped from the earth in eastern Nevada at Ruth, smelted at McGill, and shipped to the northern Southern Pacific line near Wells on the Nevada Northern Railway.

Nevada's population nearly doubled in the first decade of the 1900s. The newly established federal Bureau of Reclamation diverted Truckee River water out into the fertile desert around Fallon with the Derby Dam and Truckee Canal. Humboldt National Forest was created to manage the Ruby Mountains. The Western Pacific Railroad was laid across Nevada in 1909, from Oakland, California, across the Black Rock Desert, along the Southern Pacific route from Winnemucca to Wells, and then along a northern route to Salt Lake City. Short lines ran from Tonopah into California, from Searchlight to Las Vegas, from Pioche to Caliente, from Carson to Minden, from near Yerington to Wabuska, and elsewhere around Nevada. The railroads were in their prime, but they would last only one more generation. A company with the auspicious name of Nevada Rapid Transit had already built a road especially for automobiles between Rhyolite and Las Vegas in 1905. Floods in 1907 and again in 1910 knocked out hundreds of miles of track on both the northern and southern routes. And in 1913, the designation of Nevada Route No. 1 along the Humboldt, the first state auto road, spelled an end to the railroads' monopoly on automated transportation.

The Road

Also in 1913, Nevada passed its first motor vehicle law, the license fee based on the horsepower (any auto with more than 20 hp needed a license). In 1914 a highway between Los Angeles and Salt Lake City through Las Vegas was begun; it took 10 years to build. The Federal Aid Road Act of 1916 allocated funds to stimulate rural road building, which sent Nevada on such a road-building binge that it had to establish a Department of Highways less than a year later. In 1919, this state agency laid a road down on top of the defunct Las Vegas and Tonopah Railroad right-of-way, the first stretch of the Bonanza Highway (U.S. 95).

The Federal Highway Act of 1921 invested more money in building long-distance connectors. Over the next several years, the Highway Department improved old Nevada Route No. 1 by widening and grading it and laying down gravel. By 1927 the transcontinental Victory (U.S. 40) and Lincoln (U.S. 50) Highways were complete; a national exposition was held in Reno to celebrate, for which that city's first arch was erected over Virginia Street. The roads had an immediate negative impact on the railroads, and the downtowns along the tracks began their inexorable migrations, relocating along the highways.

The Crash

The stock market collapse of 1929 took Nevada's banks with it. The Great Depression had begun, but three events in the following two years significantly shaped Nevada's urban history: divorce residency requirements were lowered to a scandalous six weeks, wide-open casino gambling was legalized, and Hoover Dam was built. Divorces and gambling combined to focus a national spotlight on Reno, Biggest Little City in the World, and the biggest city in Nevada. Unhappily married celebrities waited out their six weeks for a divorce in the spotlight of newspaper society pages around the country—dateline Reno. Raymond and Harold Smith, veteran carnies and fledgling casino operators, embarked on a national advertising campaign to polish the image of gambling; their "Harold's Club or Bust" billboards attracted gamblers and thrill-seekers in droves. Las Vegas also hit the front pages: "Best Town by a Dam Site." Construction workers from the dam flooded the Fremont Street clubs and Block 16 cribs on payday; after the Hoover Dam was topped off, many stayed. And when the first turbine at the dam turned, Las Vegas had as much juice as it would need to do what it was destined to do.

Midcentury

A big Naval Air Station went in at Fallon, and an Army Air Base opened at Stead Field outside Reno. When the Army Airfield was installed near Las Vegas in 1941, it supplied the growing town with a steady stream of soldiers and prompted the opening of El Rancho Vegas and the Last Frontier Hotel on what would soon be known as the Strip. Basic Magnesium began mining metals at Gabbs and built factories and a town for 10,000 people at Henderson between Las Vegas and Boulder City. After the war, Mafia money and muscle, supervised by a "charming psychopath" named Benjamin Siegel, built the ultimate one-stop pleasure palace. Bugsy Siegel expanded the Las Vegas Strip, furthered the modern tourism industry, and ushered in a 20-year underworld siege of southern Nevada. Embattled state officials, caught in an unexpected squeeze play between federal heat and its growing casino revenues, slowly legislated systems to regulate the casinos.

Otherwise, the conservative moral sensibilities of the country in the 1950s did little to prevent Nevada from marching to its own unconventional drummer. In 1951, for example, Nevada welcomed the Nuclear Test Site to the state, enjoying the fireworks for 10 years until they went underground. The hotel-casinos kept opening one after another, year after year, and the brothels were left the way they've always been. Divorces were granted as routinely as ever, and the Freeport Law, instituting tax-free warehousing, was passed.

Finally, Howard Hughes rode into Las Vegas on a stretcher and bought half a dozen of the most troublesome Mafia-owned hotels. This put the seal of corporate respectability on them and paved the way for Hilton, Holiday Inn, Ramada, MGM, and other publicly traded companies to run the industry. Nevada's gambling revenues have never looked back.

Nevada Today

These days, gambling has become the country's most explosive growth industry. In 1990 only two states had legal casino gambling; by 1998 it was legal in 24 states, with more lining up. With gambling now an acceptable pastime, the big time, of course, was Las Vegas. In 2010 upward of 35 million people wagered nearly $30 billion in Clark County's legal casinos, earning $9 billion in pretax profits in Las Vegas alone. Growth continues every year. Statewide, gaming brought in revenue of $10.5 billion in 2010. For decades until the recent economic downturn, Nevada was the fastest growing state in the country. Nevada has once again become the nation's largest producer of precious metals, particularly gold.

Rapid growth and the subsequent economic downturn again introduced the stress of boom-and-bust cycles to Nevada. The state faces a bewildering combination of contemporary changes and challenges. The recent resurgence of gold and silver mining as well as the long-established policies of grazing, road building, subdividing, and other forms of developing public lands have put environmentalists on a collision course with developers. Nevada continues to try to balance boom-bust propensities with new responsibilities, to maintain the traditions that have made and kept Nevada unique and great while at the same time changing with the times to ensure a continued presence at the cutting edge of the national social and political dialogue.

Government and Economy

GOVERNMENT

Nevada's executive branch has six elected officials. The governor is elected to a maximum of two four-year terms. The current governor, Jim Gibbons, assumed office in 2007. The lieutenant governor, attorney general, secretary of state, controller, and treasurer all answer to the governor while in office and to the voters at election time. The state government's executive branch employs roughly 10,000 people.

The Nevada Legislature is one of the smallest in the country, with a 21-member Senate and a 42-member Assembly. It meets for 120 days (though often much longer) starting on the third Monday in January of odd-numbered years.

The Nevada Supreme Court's five justices are elected for six-year terms. Trials are conducted in district courts, whose judges are also elected for six years. Municipal courts handle preliminary hearings on felonies, misdemeanors, and small claims. Most municipal judges are elected for four-year terms; some are appointed. There's no appellate level in Nevada's judicial system; to be appealed, cases travel from municipal or district court directly to the Nevada Supreme Court.

Nevada has 16 counties, plus Carson City, which is a consolidated "city-county." County governments consist of 3–7 elected commissioners. Also elected are assessors, treasurers, clerks, recorders, sheriffs, and district attorneys. City councils, headed by mayors, govern Nevada's incorporated cities.

Taxes

Money magazine perennially ranks Nevada as having the third-lowest state tax burden in the country. A prosperous and hypothetical family of four that would pay $3,775 in state and local taxes in Nevada would pay $1,694 in Alaska (number 1) and $11,020 in New York (number 51). *Money* notes that

Nevada's average 7 percent sales tax is higher than that of most states nationwide. Nevada also ranks third among 90 federal judicial districts in its percentage of IRS criminal prosecutions.

Analysts agree that Nevada has the second-highest taxing capacity in the country, while the actual taxes imposed are the third lowest. However, there's a price to pay for taxes being subsidized by "export" or out-of-state taxes. Much of the state's General Fund is spent on tourist industry infrastructure, such as police and fire protection, parks and recreation, and visitor authorities and tourism agencies. At the same time, Nevada ranks low in spending on education and health care.

According to U.S. Census figures, the U.S. government spent $4,800 for every American in fiscal 1996. Thirteen cents of every dollar was spent in California, compared to half a cent of every dollar spent in Nevada. It's ironic that the federal government, which owns a larger percentage of Nevada than any other state, spends one of the lowest amounts per capita.

Incorporating

Nevada's corporation system is one of the most liberal in the country, competing with Delaware. Benefits of incorporating in Nevada include no state corporate tax on profits, no state personal income tax, very little paperwork and a low filing fee ($125), and protection from personal liability and public scrutiny. In addition, a single individual can be the sole president, secretary, and treasurer. Nevada corporations can conduct their primary business outside the state. Most attractive of all, Nevada is the only state without a reciprocal agreement with the IRS to exchange tax returns, which legally ensures maximum privacy.

Madonna is the head of a Nevada corporation, Music Tours Inc. Paul Simon, Prince,

Chevy Chase, Rodney Dangerfield, and Diane Keaton have all funneled their large incomes through Nevada corporations to legally avoid taxes and protect financial privacy; the state doesn't require income data, and it releases no information. A New York City cab company formed 50 corporations for every pair of cabs in its 100-taxi fleet; its liability is limited to 2 percent (unless a litigant wants to sue 50 companies). Ski resorts have done the same with ski lifts and oil companies with oil wells.

It's easy, it's cheap, and it's anonymous. It doesn't even require an attorney. The one necessity is a resident agent within Nevada who can receive mail and be served with any legal documents. Several incorporating companies help other businesses to incorporate in Nevada. A good one is Laughlin Associates (2533 N. Carson St., Carson City, 775/883-8484, www.laughlinusa.com). You receive a fat package explaining how to legally eliminate state income taxes, how to judgment-proof a business, how to protect your privacy and estate, and more.

Nevada's Secretary of State (202 N. Carson St., Carson City, NV 89701-4201, 775/684-5708) is another good source of information. They'll send you a free packet of information on incorporating in Nevada and on how to qualify to do business in Nevada.

ECONOMY
Tourism and Gambling

In 2009 Nevada's casinos accepted $10.5 billion in wagers. Almost exactly half the casinos' revenue comes from gambling, equaling hotel rooms, food, shows, and all other profitable operations combined. An astounding 260 casinos took in at least $1 million each.

Tourism is by far the state's largest employer, accounting for 35 percent of all jobs; in southern Nevada it's closer to 45 percent. By the end of 2009 more than 177,000 casino workers were shepherding Nevada's 45 million tourists; both numbers are down significantly due to the recent economic downturns. Given these statistics, it's amazing to think that the state Commission on Tourism wasn't created until 1983.

Mining

Mining is Nevada's second-largest revenue-generating industry. At $1,400 per ounce, gold is the most sought-after nowadays, even in the Silver State. Nevada's mines annual ferret 5.6 million ounces of the yellow metal from the earth. More gold has been mined in Nevada in the past five years than was mined at the height of the California, Comstock, and Klondike rushes combined. The Klondike, Goldfield, and Montana mines produced 5 million ounces between 1900 and 1910, and the Comstock produced 8.3 million ounces of gold between 1864 and 1889.

Silver production is significant as well, but with prices trending not much above $20 per ounce, silver production is merely a byproduct in the search for its flashier cousin, with production in the range of 22–28 million ounces annually. This is a reversal of production in the Comstock Lode era, when gold was a by-product of the silver mining. Just under 200 million ounces of silver were wrested from the Comstock. Today Nevada has just one mine, the Coeur-Rochester mine near Lovelock, that is primarily a silver mine.

Nevada is the country's largest gold and silver producer, producing a whopping 74 percent of the nation's gold and 11 percent of the world's gold each year. If Nevada were a separate country, it would be the third-largest gold-producing nation in the world after South Africa and Australia. North America's largest gold mine, the Barrick Gold Strike Mine north of Carlin, is one of several Nevada mines that each produce over 1 million ounces of gold every year.

Agriculture

Nevada farms produce alfalfa and to a lesser extent wheat and barley, alfalfa seed, garlic, onions, and potatoes. Hay crops as a whole account for well over half of all harvested acreage in Nevada. There are approximately 1,700 cattle ranches in Nevada. Cattle production dropped dramatically in the 1980s, primarily because of reduced red meat consumption, but it has seen a resurgence since 1990, with about 500,000 head of cattle in production. Nevada ranchers are largely dependent on public grazing lands, primarily federal Bureau of Land Management lands, for at least part of their forage needs.

Nevada is also home to 95,000 sheep and 7,500 hogs, figures that have decreased dramatically from previous years. In the early 1930s Nevada had 1.3 million sheep, but sheep ranching declined as it became less profitable.

People and Culture

DEMOGRAPHICS

According to official statistics, in 2000 Nevada's population topped 2 million for the first time, and the 2009 estimate was 2.6 million. A whopping 92 percent of Nevada's residents live in urban areas, the third-most urbanized state after California and New Jersey. Las Vegas's Clark County is home to 1.9 million Nevadans—remarkable considering the county was not established until 1909—while Reno's Washoe County is home to more than 400,000. Even though Nevada has an overall low population density, around 18.2 people per square mile, Truckee Meadows is filling up fast, and Las Vegas's water worries are growing.

Nevada has been the fastest growing state for decades. Clark County, for example, has grown an astounding 350 percent in the last 25 years, and Reno's population has more than doubled in the past 20 years. Only 20 percent of Nevada's residents were born here, the lowest proportion in the country. One-third of new residents come from California.

NATIVE AMERICANS

At the beginning of the 19th century, four groups of Native Americans lived in what is now Nevada. The small population of Washoe lived in the west-central region around Carson City, Lake Tahoe, and the eastern Sierras. The Northern Paiute made a large section of western Nevada their home ranging from today's eastern Nevada their home ranging from today's Humboldt County to Esmeralda County. The Southern Paiute occupied all of Clark County and the southeastern section of Lincoln County. The Shoshone were found in the east, from Elko County to southern Nye County.

The Northern Paiute (*pah* meaning "water" and *ute* designating a Utah branch) called themselves Numa, and the Shoshone called themselves Newe, both meaning simply "The People." The name for the Southern Paiute was Nuwuvi, or "Peaceful People of the Land."

These groups shared many customs and lifestyles. They spent so much of their time gathering and preparing food in the harsh environment that they had little time for warring. The only time the small bands gathered into larger groups was for cooperative hunting or harvesting efforts or to skirmish with neighbors or encroachers; otherwise each band, a single-family unit or a group of no more than 100 individuals, was mostly autonomous. The resources of the local environment tended to dictate the size of bands. The Pyramid Lake Paiute, for example, were a large group with abundant resources. Its chiefs were famous, and the band was able to hold its own against the more warlike Pitt River bands from the north. Bands had headmen as well as shamans, who were found to possess powers of prophecy, healing, or magic.

Traditionally all the bands in a given area would come together several times a year for pine-nut harvesting, antelope hunts, and rabbit or mud-hen drives. Celebrations during the get-togethers included sports such as archery, races, stick games, storytelling, music, and dance; some of the dances dictated courting rituals. The Washoe, in particular, held large gatherings twice a year, once in the fall at the Pine Nut Mountains to harvest the pine nuts for their winter flour and once in the spring at Lake Tahoe to fish.

The Family

Native Americans enjoyed extended family arrangements, usually including the maternal grandparents. Variations might consist of two wives and a husband (the second woman was adopted if she found herself alone for some reason) or two husbands and a wife. Sketchy accounts describe the society as having very little divorce, with little experience of broken homes, orphans, or child abuse. Children were loved and well cared for, assimilating into the ways of the family and the band, proving themselves worthy as they went along, and learning skills and morality mostly from the grandfathers.

Religion

Everything in nature, animate or inanimate, was embodied by a spirit. Fire, fog, even rocks were alive and required an empathy equal to that for a wolf (a good influence), a coyote (a bad influence), or a wife or husband (either). Dreams, omens, seasonal cycles and unnatural variations, prayers, and the powers of the medicine man all figured into Native American spirituality, which was as integral a part of their daily routine as eating and sleeping.

Lifestyle

The never-ending search for food in the somewhat barren desert dictated daily and seasonal activities. Native Americans had little need for shelter (except for shade) or clothing (except for a breechcloth and skirt) in the summer. In winter they stayed in a kind of tepee with a framework of poles and branches; grass or reeds made up the roof, which had a hole in it for smoke from the fire. In winter they wore animal-skin robes, hats, moccasins, skirts, or sage-bark sandals and caps, and slept under rabbit-fur blankets. Colored clay was dabbed on as makeup and to ward off evil spirits, and bones, hooves, or traded shells provided jewelry for necklaces, earrings, or bracelets.

Mostly nomadic, they had to carry everything during their frequent moves; a sophisticated basket technology evolved. Woven from split willow twigs, grasses, and cattail reeds (tule), conical baskets were used for transporting possessions or served as women's caps. Flat trays were used for winnowing seeds and sifting flour. Large pots were even used to cook in and to carry water—pitch from piñon pines, grasses, and mud kept them from burning or leaking. Decoys and snares were also fashioned from willow and tule twigs. Cradleboards attained a level of art. Properly shaped stones provided mortar-and-pestle tools for grinding, and drums, rattles, and flutes were used. The Indians were particularly ingenious in their knowledge and use of local plants. Everything had a use, and everything was sacred. They also fished and hunted rabbits, squirrels, antelope, mountain sheep, deer, ducks, and birds.

Contact

The first Anglo-Europeans who came into contact with the Shoshone, Paiute, and Washoe Indians considered them to be only slightly better off than wildlife. They had no possessions, no houses, and hardly any clothes. As James Hulse writes in *The Nevada Adventure,* "The greed, brutality, and contempt of the white man destroyed much of the beauty of Indian life and prevented the Indians from entering the white man's culture." The Native Americans were on peaceful, even friendly terms with the first trappers and traders; Chief Winnemucca prophesied, and his daughter Sarah preached, that whites and Indians could live together with a mutual respect for each other and the land, but the wagon trains quickly put an end to that utopian vision. The pioneers' migrating cattle ate all the Indians' grasses, loggers cut their sacred piñon pines, and large areas were denuded of all the living things that the native people had used to survive. Although the Nevada Paiute and Shoshone had no real organizational structure for waging war, and Nevada histories usually only describe the largest armed confrontations (Pyramid Lake, Paradise Valley, Black Rock Desert, and Battle Mountain), many skirmishes occurred with some loss of life on both sides. Treaties were repeatedly signed and violated. Within 25 years of the first wave of nonnative migrants, the Indian spirit had been broken, self-reliance was shattered, and dependence became their way of life.

Reservations

The first reservations in Nevada, Pyramid Lake and Walker Lake, were surveyed and set aside for the Paiute in 1859. Several others (Fort McDermitt, Moapa, Fallon, and Owyhee) followed over the next 15 years. But as E. A. Hoaglund writes in his *Washoe, Paiute, and Shoshone Indians of Nevada,* "The early history of Indian reservations in America is generally one of confusion and mismanagement." A near total lack of direction, financing, facilities, equipment, education, understanding of the Native American experience, and compassion for their cultural dislocation colored a full 70 years of relations. The reservations were usually too small, the land too poor, and the populations too large. Also, the reservations continued to segregate the Indians from the mainstream. "The period from 1890–1934 was one of slow moral and physical decline [for Native Americans]. Many left the reservations and found work on ranches or the fringes of towns," explains Hoaglund.

In 1887 the Dawes Act tried to disenfranchise the reservations in an attempt to ease assimilation into nonnative culture. In June 1934 the Indian Reorganization Act began a process of redressing this tragic part of American history by giving more money, land, cattle, and irrigation systems to the reservations. Self-government was made official

by way of Tribal Councils. The 1978 Indian Self-Determination Act addressed the need for economic development. Slowly, the federal government has untangled the complex questions of land issues and begun to show some responsiveness to the simple question of human rights.

For many years, smoke shops were the 24 Nevada tribes' primary revenue producers. Tribes buy cigarettes at wholesale prices, which include federal taxes. But instead of the high local taxes on smokes, the Indians charge a lower tribal tax, which is reinvested in the organization. Today, many Native American communities are finding new sources of revenue. The Las Vegas Paiute, for example, operate a large-scale casino and golf resort on reservation land 20 miles north of Las Vegas. The Washoe, whose reservation is in Gardnerville, farm and raise cattle. The Yerington Paiute have gone into the laser ground-leveling business, which local farmers rely on. The Walker River Paiute opened a truck stop and tourist center near Schurz. The Pyramid Lake Paiute fishery has helped Pyramid Lake regenerate into one of the top cutthroat lakes in the West.

A good way to observe Indian traditions and customs in action is to attend any of a number of powwows put on by the different tribes over the course of the year.

BASQUES

The Basque people are the oldest ethnic group in Europe. Evidence of their continuous existence dates to 5000 B.C., a full 3,000 years before Indo-European people arrived. There are roughly 3 million European Basques, their homeland occupying the Pyrenees mountain region of France and Spain. The true origin of these people is a mystery. Some scholars maintain that similarities exist between Basques and Iberians, their early Spanish neighbors; others believe that they share characteristics with the Irish and Welsh. Some Basques contend that they're descended from Atlantis. Their language is unrelated to any other, although researchers have tried to correlate it with languages ranging from ancient Aquitanian to modern Japanese. Although the Basques were never conquered, the Spanish and French have had a noticeable influence.

Basque argonauts migrated to Argentina and many made their way north, especially in the 1850s to the California gold rush. Following the silver exodus east to Washoe, they mined in Nevada until that work dried up. They then returned to a skill familiar from the old country: sheepherding. Basque sheepherders readily took to the pastoral life of the American West, particularly in northern Nevada. For nearly 50 years, Basque ranchers ran the largest bands of sheep in the country. They imported relatives, friends, and neighbors to herd sheep. Contract shepherds often took payment in lambs and sheep, with which they started their own ranches. Herders remained in the backcountry alone with their flocks all through the summer. It was an arduous and lonely life in a strange and barren country, but a prevalent aspect of the Basque national character is the ability to endure: Hard work, loneliness, and physical strength are part of the measure of their self-worth.

Sheepherding was seasonal. Many newcomers were laid off in the fall after the animals were shipped to market and not rehired until spring lambing season. Some sheepherders remained on the ranches, but others drifted to the hotels run by Basques in the towns. These boardinghouses quickly became the center of Basque culture in the rural towns of Nevada. Shepherds old and young spoke their own language and kept company with other Basques. Many married and remained in the towns, assimilating into the new culture. Some made their money and went home to Europe; others stayed bachelors and lived out their lives at the inns. The Basque hotel was "a crucible of birth and death, joy and sorrow; a public establishment masking many private intimacies," writes William Douglass in *Amerikanuak: Basques in the New World*.

Oso Garria!

The Basque hotel is a legacy that endures.

The Winnemucca Hotel, for example, is the second oldest in the state. Gardnerville's Overland Hotel dates from 1909, Elko's Star Hotel from 1911, and the Ely Hotel is from the 1920s. No traveler to Nevada should leave without experiencing a meal at a Basque hotel.

A Basque meal, especially dinner, is never taken lightly, nor is it a light meal. It consists of a multitude of courses served family-style: soup, salad, beans or pasta, French fries, and usually an entrée of chicken, beef, or lamb. Make sure to try a picon punch, made with Amer (a liqueur), grenadine, and topped off with a quick shot of brandy. Few northern and central Nevada towns are without Basque restaurants, where you're guaranteed a fine filling meal and a social experience. Raise your glass of picon punch and toast the house: *Oso garria!*

The Basque festival is the other enduring cultural tradition. Festivities include mass, folk dancing, strength and endurance competitions, a sheep rodeo, and the consumption of enormous quantities of red wine from the *bota*. The Basques are known for their world-class wood chopping, and contestants compete in areas of strength and will. *Soka* and *tira* are the popular tugs-of-war.

Pelota is handball, of which jai alai is an offspring. Weightlifting and carrying are the real crowd pleasers. Annual festivals take place in most of the larger towns in northern Nevada; check the events section of *Nevada* magazine in summer.

THE ARTS

People have been creating Nevada-themed art for longer than Nevada has been a state. In fact, Native Americans who haunted the sun-baked sandstone of the south and the crystal lakes of the north used sharp stones to gouge records of their never-ending search for food well before Columbus. Still, it's true that Nevada got a late start in developing European-influenced art. Few miners speeding to stake claims on the latest silver strike bothered to bring their easels and watercolors; Basque sheepherders, concerned with eking out a living, gave little thought to focal points and linear perspective.

But the state's artistic environment has been expanding exponentially. Once those pioneers found a moment of spare time, they found inspiration everywhere they looked. Nevada still boasts unspoiled views of mountains, rivers, streams, canyons, and forests, as well as art deco, beaux arts, modern, and classical architecture and signage to tempt today's painters and photographers. Many who have flocked to the state contribute to the thriving arts districts that serve as centerpieces for impressive urban renewal projects in both Las Vegas and Reno. Reno's Riverwalk District and Las Vegas's 18b district feature contemporary eateries and stylish boutiques in addition to bohemian galleries, studios, and artists lofts.

Ely is the leader, but certainly not the only Nevada city to chronicle its history through an ambitious series of historical murals throughout the town. In southern Nevada, Boulder City has commissioned not only several murals but also brass statues depicting raptors, playing children, and mythical figures. Henderson commissioned J. Seward Johnson to cast bronzes of everyday life in the bedroom community along Green Valley Parkway. His works include children frolicking with a garden hose to beat the summer heat (in front of the Green Valley Library),

friends on their way to play a set of tennis, and a mother stooping to tie her daughter's shoelace.

Other artists didn't wait around for municipal patronage. Michael Heizer has spent 30 years creating *City* near Garden Valley. This massive undertaking, like Heizer's *Double Negative* near Overton, is one of several striking pieces of sculpture (or, if you prefer Robert Smithson's term, "earthwork") in Nevada. *City* uses native boulders and caliche, among other materials, to depict a juxtaposition of ancient and modern sites. The unbounded souls who prowl the Black Rock Desert for Burning Man also have felt the urge for self-expression. Among the most notable is Jim Denevan, who "draws" geometric designs by dragging fencing behind a small plane. Many of Denevan's pictures (think crop circles in the sand) cover dozens of square miles. It was around here too that the muse told "the Guru of Gerlach," Doobie Williams, to adopt a dusty back road, name it Guru Road, and adorn it with witticisms, earthy wisdom, and Elvis tributes.

Nevada's history and eclectic citizenry have provided raw material for writers and poets as well. More than one masterpiece has been set in or focused on Nevada: Hunter S. Thompson's *Fear and Loathing in Las Vegas,* Mark Twain's *Roughing It,* Nicholas Pileggi's *Casino,* and *Moon Nevada 2011,* to name a few.

ESSENTIALS

Getting There and Getting Around

Five main roads crisscross Nevada, three east–west and two north–south. I-80 takes the long northern route west across the shoulder of Nevada from Wendover through Reno and into California. U.S. 50 cuts across the shorter waist of the state from Ely and joins up with I-80 at Fernley, then splits off to Reno or Carson City. U.S. 6 travels along with U.S. 50 from the Utah line to Ely before cutting south to Tonopah and out toward Fresno in California. U.S. 95 zigzags south, then southwest, then south, and finally southeast for nearly 700 miles from McDermitt at the north edge of the state to Laughlin at the south. U.S. 93 travels between Jackpot to Boulder City for 500 miles in a fairly straight line.

Greyhound bus routes connect terminals in Las Vegas, Winnemucca, Wendover, Reno, Lovelock, Elko, and Battle Mountain; routes heading farther afield from Las Vegas include routes to Los Angeles, Phoenix, San Francisco, and Salt Lake City, with connections to other places.

Amtrak operates the *California Zephyr* train between Emeryville (in the east San Francisco Bay area) and Chicago, stopping in Nevada in Reno, Winnemucca, and Elko. (Note that Amtrak no longer runs through Las Vegas.)

There are big airports at Las Vegas and Reno, fair-sized airports at Elko and Ely with a handful of shuttles arriving and departing each

COURTESY OF NEVADA COMMISSION ON TOURISM

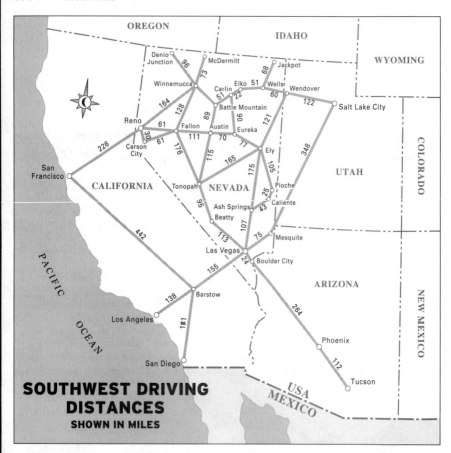

SOUTHWEST DRIVING DISTANCES
SHOWN IN MILES

day, and 10 other airports attended either 24 hours a day or during daylight hours. Carson City is one of a handful of state capitals without regularly scheduled airline service.

If you're driving in, get in your car and make a beeline; having this book along will help no matter which way you go. If you're flying in, consider touching down in Las Vegas first. McCarran International is one of the easiest airports in the country to access, and with a little research and planning, it can also be one of the cheapest. Reno is an hour by air from Las Vegas, and nowhere in Nevada is more than 10 hours or so by car.

The best way to get around the state is with your own car. Buses don't reach half the state.

Distances are long, and services are few and far between. Even the good city bus routes take a long time; taxis are expensive; and with a car you can find yourself on a lot of gravel, if you're adventurous, and if your steed is trusty you can really get out there. That's the idea, isn't it? If you do plan on some off-asphalt exploring, remember that desert driving is hot, dusty, bumpy, and can be hard on your car. Make sure your ride has the best fuel, fluids, tires, parts, and care. Carry plenty of spare water and fluids, a spare tire and a jack, a flashlight and flares, spare belts and hoses, a tool kit, and a shovel; baling wire, duct tape, and superglue often come in handy. Don't forget a rag or two.

Common-sense maintenance consciousness is required on the road. If the car gets hot or overheats, stop for a while to cool it off. Never open the radiator cap if the engine is steaming. After it has sat, squeeze the top radiator hose to see if there's any pressure in it; if there isn't, it's safe to open. Never pour water into a hot radiator—you could crack your block. If you start to smell rubber, your tires are overheating, and that's a good way to have a blowout. Stop and let them cool off. In winter in the high country, a can of silicone lubricant such as WD-40 will unfreeze door locks, dry off humid wiring, and keep your hinges in shape.

The speed limits on most of the interstate and U.S. highways outside of the cities and towns have been raised in the past couple of years. They're now 75 mph on I-80 and I-15, U.S. 95 and U.S. 93, and a few state roads. You can drive 65 mph on the interstates in Reno and Las Vegas. Most passers-through drive 80–85 mph without worrying about being noticed by the highway patrol. Since the superhighways are two lanes in each direction, road courtesy isn't much of a problem; anyone wanting to go faster than you can zip around on the left, if not the right.

Passing is generally not a problem on the two-lane highways through rural Nevada; the solid and dotted lines are well maintained, and long straight stretches through the valleys are conducive to safe zipping.

There are only a few long climbs up mountains on main roads in Nevada, and here passing can be a problem. The good news is that turnouts are common. The bad news is that some flatlanders and RV drivers don't know what turnouts are for. If you're pulling a heavy load, are nervous about mountain driving, or just have a slowpoke car, pull over and let the drivers behind you pass.

Updates on Nevada road conditions are available by calling **Road Condition Report** at 877/NV-ROADS—877/687-6237.

Recreation

Some two-thirds of Nevada is owned by the federal government, and pretty much everything that's not used for secret research or weapons testing can be used for some recreational purpose.

STATE PARKS

The Nevada Division of State Parks (775/684-2770, http://parks.nv.gov) manages and maintains 24 parks in four regions: Carson-Tahoe, Fallon, Panaca, and Las Vegas. Entrance fees are generally $7, but many are free; a few of the more popular parks, especially in the Las Vegas and Reno-Tahoe area, charge $10–12 per car. Discounted annual passes are available at the parks and by contacting the headquarters. Camping rates are a pretty consistent $17 throughout the park system.

U.S. FOREST SERVICE LANDS

The U.S. Forest Service (775/331-6444, www.fs.fed.us/r4/htnf/) oversees the **Humboldt-Toiyabe National Forest,** which encompasses all of Nevada and the far eastern edge of California. The "Humboldt" part of the name is in honor of German naturalist Baron Alexander von Humboldt. Although Humboldt never visited the area, he was something of a hero to the explorer John C. Frémont, who named the East Humboldt Mountain Range and the Humboldt River after him. *Toiyabe* is an ancient Shoshone word meaning "mountain." The Humboldt-Toiyabe is the largest forest on the U.S. mainland. The forest service's website contains information on the archeology, history, and geology; snowmobiling, hiking, biking, and horseback riding trails; camping locations; and wilderness areas in the forest.

NATIONAL PARKS

Great Basin National Park (775/234-7331, www.nps.gov/grba), administered by the

National Park Service, is the only national park located exclusively in Nevada. It charges no entry fee and has various campsites available for $12–25.

A sliver of **Death Valley National Park** (760/786-3200, www.nps.gov/deva) cuts through Nevada. The $20 entry fee is good for seven consecutive days. Camping at Furnace Creek Campground is $18 in winter, $12 in summer.

OUTDOOR PURSUITS

Whether you prefer alpine lakes, desert washes, or expansive playas, you'll find ample opportunity to hike, bike, and ride on the state's extensive network of paths and trails. Nevada is a magnet for hunters, with a variety of waterfowl; big game and predator species such as mountain lions, elk, mule deer, and whitetails; and fur-bearing animals like mink, foxes, and bobcats. Southern Nevada attracts anglers with its rainbow trout, striped bass, catfish, and black crappie, while the northern half of the state offers white crappie, perch, walleye, and several species of trout. Find information on seasons, licenses, and more from the Nevada Department of Wildlife (800/576-1020, http://ndow.org).

Las Vegas Ski & Snowboard Resort (702/385-2754, www.skilasvegas.com/winter) is the Las Vegas area's go-to ski resort, while Reno and Lake Tahoe visitors have their choice among dozens of some of the best powder in the country. For a unique experience, **Ruby Mountain Heli-Ski** (775/753-6867, www.helicopterskiing.com) promises several runs per day over pristine powder.

Gambling

Gambling and Nevada are inseparable in the national consciousness. The state's reputation since casino gambling was legalized has been predicated on Americans' image of gambling: The media, authorities, moralists, and sore losers have accused the Silver State of being a haven for organized crime, petty criminals, vice run amok, and lowlifes in general. The height of the heat centered on the 20-year period from 1946, when Benjamin Siegel, Las Vegas's most notorious gangster, built the seminal Flamingo Hotel, to 1966, when Howard Hughes introduced corporate respectability. Since then, Nevada's image has taken a turn for the better. Sixty percent of the state's massive gambling revenues come from the losses of out-of-staters. Casino jobs account for 25 percent of employment in Nevada, and taxes on casino profits make up 40 percent of state General Fund revenues. And that's just from gambling; the indirect impact of massive gambling tourism on the state's economy is incalculable. It is the major reason Nevada has no state income tax.

Although it's not often credited for it, Nevada has contributed heavily to the growing legitimacy of various forms of gambling that now exist in 48 states: lotteries, bingo, off-track betting, video gambling machines, pull tabs, card rooms, and casinos. Casino gambling was legalized in Atlantic City in 1978, the first in the country outside Nevada and the last until Iowa riverboats came online in 1991. Since then, casino gambling has become available on riverboats in Illinois, Indiana, Mississippi, Missouri, and Louisiana; in historic mining towns in Colorado and South Dakota; and on Indian reservations in a growing number of states. Gambling has become an accepted way to raise revenues without raising taxes, a sort of "painless user's tax." Certainly gambling is still generally considered frivolous by a great many Americans. It's also a highly addictive activity that has been called the deadliest psychiatric disorder. Yet its growing popularity shows no signs of abating. In fact, it was the most explosive growth industry in the country during the 1990s.

THE QUESTION OF HONESTY

In this cash-crazy business, everyone is afraid of everyone. The casinos have always been afraid of cheating customers and dishonest dealers and have evolved some of the most sophisticated security and surveillance technology, not to mention some of the heaviest private muscle, this side of the military. As the benders, crimpers, hand muckers, and past-post artists of yesteryear have turned into today's sleight-of-hand artists, card counters, and computer-equipped players, the catwalks and one-way glass above the casino ceilings have given way to video cameras and recorders in addition to all the bosses in the pit, the house guards, and outside security contractors.

The Nevada casino industry is not the most heavily regulated; Atlantic City's is. But Nevada's is the most efficient and practical. New Jersey has been overregulated to the extent that it has been difficult for Atlantic City casinos to succeed, although that's starting to change. Nevada, on the other hand, started with little to no regulation of casinos when gambling was legalized in 1931, and it took more than 50 years to reach a middle ground where the regulation was sufficient to keep things honest but also allow the industry to prosper. Mississippi, where nearly 50 casinos have opened in the past five years, copied Nevada regulations verbatim; in fact, in a few instances the Mississippi legislators neglected to change the name of the state in the documentation.

The Nevada Gaming Control Board, by way of announced and unannounced inspections, owner and employee screening, and customer-complaint services, has dealt with the state government's two main fears. The first is the house cheating the state by underreporting the action, skimming cash, and various other nefarious scams. The second is the house cheating the players. The conventional wisdom is that with the astronomical number of people playing, the small amount of money that they're risking and losing, and the profits that are accruing, the casinos don't need to cheat players; indeed they'd be crazy if they did. They'd risk losing what amounts to a license to take money thanks to the house advantage.

CASINO PSYCHOLOGY

Millions of people sample the excitement and temptations of Las Vegas every year, and the number of visitors continues to grow. Inside the casinos are a dozen different table games and scores of gambling machines, free drinks, acres of dazzling lights, expert come-ons—in short, limitless choices designed to sweep you off your feet and empty your pockets. There are nearly 70 years of marketing history and a distinct mathematical disadvantage working against you. Every inch of neon, every cocktail waitress, every complimentary highball shares the same purpose: to confuse you, bemuse you, and infuse you with a sense of saloon-town recklessness. And that's where the house advantage kicks in.

The game of roulette best illustrates the house advantage. There are 38 numbers on the wheel: 1 through 36, plus 0 and 00. If the ball drops into number 23 and you have $1 on it, the correct payoff would be $37 (37 to 1, which adds up to the 38 numbers). However, the house pays only $35. It withholds two of 38 units, which translates to a 5.26 percent advantage for the house. This advantage can be viewed in different ways. Over the long haul, for every $100 players bet on roulette, they lose $5.26. But don't make the mistake of thinking that for every $100 you carry into the casino you'll only lose five bucks. Anything can happen in the short run. You can win 13 bets in a row and make a bundle, or you can lose all your money in one bet. But the house advantage guarantees that players are the overall losers at almost all the games in a casino, and that the casino is the long-term winner.

The house advantage is the single most important concept to be aware of to understand casino gambling. As soon as you're savvy to all its implications and the varying percentages of the games, you'll begin to recognize the difference between a sucker bet, a break-even bet, and even an advantageous bet—which occurs more frequently than you might think. Then you can gamble in such a way that the percentages aren't so overwhelmingly unfavorable, and in that way you can make sure that your bankroll lasts as long as it possibly can against the omnipotent house advantage.

FIRST-TIMERS

If you've never learned to play, it's very wise to study up beforehand and practice, practice, practice. All these games move very fast, and if you try learning them as you play, you'll not only lose but everybody will get very impatient with you, which is embarrassing. Looking like a beginner is a technique that expert players use to slow down the game to minimize risk and to deflect the attention of and heat from the pit bosses so that they can make other advanced moves. But there's no upside to really not knowing what you're doing.

It's easy and fun to learn to play. Most casinos offer free lessons in all the games at specified times of day. In Las Vegas, lessons are sometimes advertised on marquees; signs are also posted in the casinos, or ask someone in the pit about them.

Loads of books have been written on how to play all the casino games. John Scarne's guides, although a little outdated, should be in most libraries. To really get into it, request catalogs from the Gambler's Book Club (5473 S. Eastern Ave., Las Vegas, 800/522-1777, www.gamblersbook.com). You can also download a catalog from Huntington Press (www.huntingtonpress.com).

ATTITUDE

Don't ever let anyone tell you differently: In a casino, it absolutely *is* whether you win or lose. You can beat the casino, but not with any of a thousand superstitions or "systems"; not with being cool, knowing all the rituals, or looking like James Bond; not even with an above-average degree of competence at the games. The gambling professionals (there are maybe a few thousand true pros, defined as people who make their entire living at gambling, mostly in Las Vegas) are part mathematician, part probability theorist, part banker, part actor, and part martial artist. They play high-level blackjack, sometimes in teams, and rarely get caught; they pounce on progressive video poker

machines when the meter goes positive; they enter all the big-money gambling tournaments, often in teams, and win regularly; they factor comps into the positive expectation; and they subscribe to the unlimited-bankroll school, which holds that "money management" is a crock. They take the big losses in stride and the big wins for granted. They eat, sleep, and dream gambling theory; they spend all their time in casinos; they carry a lot of cash and flash it when necessary; they throw big bucks at small edges; and sooner than later they go into gambling publishing, where the real money is.

The rest of us are rank amateurs. We're supposed to be in it for the fun, the recreation value, and to some extent the dream of the once-in-a-lifetime jackpot although that's only possible at bad-odds games such as keno and slots, which take your money a bit more slowly than a pickpocket. For us it's about spending the same money on gambling that we'd use to buy tickets to a ballgame, a concert, or an amusement park. It's about maximizing our vacation budgets by taking advantage of the rock-bottom room, food, beverage, and entertainment prices in Nevada, plus the slot club and comp systems for the freebies that accrue to players. It's about risking our gambling bankrolls for the excitement and adrenaline of the casino, the camaraderie with fellow players, the interaction with the dealers and cocktail waitresses and bosses, and seeing how our luck is running lately. It's mostly about risking the pain of losing for the fun of winning.

In this case, the way to play is to set a limit and not go over it. It's as simple as that. Never sit down to play with money that you can't spend; that's one of the sure signs of gambling addiction. And never try to chase your losses—another sign of the onset of problematic or compulsive gambling. Be a good loser, be a good winner, have some fun, and get some comps. Oh, and good luck.

COMPS

"Comps" is short for complimentaries, also known as freebies. These are travel amenities—free room, food, drink, shows, golf, limos, even airfare—with which the casinos reward their regular players and entice other players into their joints. Comps come in many varieties. The easiest to get are free parking (in downtown Reno and Las Vegas parking garages, you're entitled to 3–4 hours of free parking with a receipt validated at the casino cage) and fun-books that contain coupons for free drinks, snacks, and souvenirs. For these comps, you don't have to play; you only have to walk into the casino to get them.

The lowest level comp for players is the ubiquitous free drink. It doesn't matter if you're putting one nickel at a time in a slot machine or laying down $5,000 baccarat bets, the casino serves you complimentary soft drinks, cocktails, wine, and beer.

The value of comps increases with the value of your bets. The standard equation used by casinos to determine comps is: the size of the average bet times the number of hours played times the house advantage times the comp equivalency. In other words, if you play blackjack and make $10 bets for two hours, the casino multiplies 120 hands (60 an hour) by $10 and comes up with $1,200 worth of action. It then multiplies $1,200 by the 2 percent house advantage and comes up with $24—what the casino believes it will win from you on average in two hours of $10 blackjack. It then multiplies $24 by 40 percent (what it's willing to return in comps), so you're entitled to $9.60 in freebie amenities (in this case, probably a coffee-shop comp for one).

Comps returned to big bettors enter the fabled realm of high-roller suites, lavish gourmet dinners, unlimited room service, ringside seats, private parties, limos, and Lear jets. Caesars has 10,000-square-foot apartments complete with a butler and a chef, a private lap pool and a putting green, a monster hot tub, and a grand piano. The Mirage will fly you to the Super Bowl, put you in box seats at the 50-yard line, and send you to a party with the Most Valuable Player. All you have to do is bet $25,000 per hand eight hours a day over a long weekend, or have a $5 million credit line.

Comps for $25 players might include casino rate on a room (generally 50 percent of the rack rate), limited food and beverages, and line passes to the show. Hundred-dollar players qualify for full RFB (room, food, and beverage, meaning your whole stay is free) at some of the second-tier joints (Riviera, Stardust, and downtown), while the first-tier places (Caesars, Mirage, MGM) typically want to see $200–250 a hand for full RFB.

To enter the comp game, you must "get rated." This consists of identifying yourself to the casino cage (where you fill out a credit application and are entered "in the system," or given a file in the casino computer), a casino host (who will also put you in the system), or a pit supervisor (typically a floor man or pit boss, who will either look you up in the system or keep track of you on his or her own). If you're in the system, you simply identify yourself to the boss, who then fills out a rating slip that records your time in, time out, average bet size, and a few other details. The data is entered into the computer, and casino marketing determines what comps you're entitled to. If you're not in the system, you call the boss over and say something like, "How long do I have to play to get a coffee shop comp for two, or a gourmet room comp for two, or a show for two?" Then, if you fulfill his requirement, he'll write you a comp.

Herein lies the weakness in the comp tracking system. It's possible to trick the casino into thinking that you're a higher roller than you really are by practicing "comp wizardry." Casinos are especially vulnerable to attack on their comp systems because your play must be observed by pit bosses. By slowing down the game (actually playing only 40 hands an hour, instead of the 60 the casino expects to deal), betting $25 when the pit boss is watching and only $10–15 when he isn't, looking like a loser, and employing other advanced moves can greatly minimize your risk and maximize your reward in the comp game. The book *Comp City—A Guide to Free Las Vegas Vacations* by Max Rubin is the only book on the spectrum of casino comps for table-game players. It's highly recommended for anyone who plays blackjack for $5 per hand and up. It's also one of the funniest and savviest gambling books ever written.

That's the upper tier of the two-tier comp system. The lower tier encompasses the vast majority of casino players, who prefer the machines to the tables. And here we enter the world of slot clubs. Almost all casinos in Nevada have slot clubs, which are similar to the frequent-flyer clubs of the airlines. Slot clubs are free to join; all you do is sign up at the slot club or promotions booth, usually located somewhere on the edge of the casino. You're issued a slot club membership card, similar to a credit card, which you put into a slot in the gambling machine that you play. Card readers in the machine track the amount of your action, meaning the amount of money that you play. Once you play a certain number of coins, usually 20–40, you're awarded a point. And once you have a certain number of slot club points, you can exchange them for comps, just like a table-game player. Every slot club is different, so there's a science and an art to getting the most comp value out of the various slot clubs in the various jurisdictions around the state. The book to read for your slot club education is *The Las Vegas Advisor Guide to Slot Clubs* by Jeffrey Compton.

GAMBLING 101

While flashy shows and dusty museums are certainly part of the Nevada experience, the main attraction is gambling. And though casinos caution against betting more than you can afford to lose, too few people heed the warning. Unfortunately, it's very hard to stop; most of the games are fun, bordering on addictive, and the urge to keep playing until you win is hard to resist. Dream of winning big but expect to lose, and make it a goal to lose only a certain amount. Set aside a certain amount of money each day for gambling, and stop when it's gone. Remember, the only way to end a gambling session with a small fortune is to start with a large one.

Once you've played a few hands or spun a few reels on slot machines at the major casinos, you may want to try your luck at a couple of the casinos frequented by locals (in Vegas, try **The Cannery, Red Rock, Sam's Town,** and **Silverton**). Many of them advertise looser slots and offer promotions such as two-for-one dinners or inexpensive buffets to attract gamblers to their off-the-Strip locations.

Baccarat and Mini-Baccarat

Baccarat is played with eight decks of cards. It tends to be a high-stakes game, with minimums starting at $20. It's usually played in an upscale area of the casino, with dealers wearing tuxedos. Before cards are dealt by the players, players bet on the player or the banker, and each gets two cards. Aces are worth one point, face cards are worth zero, and others are face value. Depending on the totals of the first two cards, either the player, the banker, or both may draw a third. The hand closest to nine is the winner.

Mini-baccarat is played at a blackjack-style table with smaller minimum bets. It's played like baccarat except the dealer deals the cards. Wagers can be made on the player, the banker, or for a tie.

Big Six Wheel

The Big Six Wheel is the game you are least likely to win. Looking like a big carnival wheel with dollar bills inserted, it offers players a chance to bet $1 or more on $1, $2, $5, $10, and $20 symbols. You may also place a bet on the joker and house symbols. If your number comes up after the spin, you win that amount. In the unlikely event you happen to hit a joker or house logo, it pays 40 to 1. Big Six—along with keno—offer some of the worst odds in the casino.

Blackjack

Also called 21, blackjack is the most popular casino table game. The object is to have your cards total closer to 21 than the dealer, without going over. Players play against the house rather than against each other. It's one

blackjack board

of the best games to play since your odds of winning are greater than if you play a slot machine, roulette, or most other games of chance. According to "optimal" strategy, if the dealer has 7, 8, 9, 10, or ace showing on his or her hand, it's advisable to hit (take additional cards) until your hand reaches 17 or more (or you bust). If the dealer has 2, 3, 4, 5, or 6 showing, stand (don't hit) unless your hand is 11 or less, because no matter what card comes, you can't bust. If you are dealt a pair (two 7s, two 9s) you can split them and play two separate hands if you choose. Again, the conventional wisdom is to split 8s and aces. This doubles your stake so that you have two separate bets on each hand. Usually you can "double down" on certain two-card hands. Always do this with 11, and almost always (unless the dealer shows an ace) with 10. Simply turn your hand over and place another stack of chips equal to your original wager. The dealer will give you one card to complete your hand. For example, you put a $25 green chip in the betting circle. You're dealt a 6 and a 5, and the dealer's "up" card is

a 9. Flip your cards over, confidently put another greenie next to its sibling in the circle, and smile knowingly as the dealer "paints" your hand with the queen of diamonds, giving you 21.

Craps

Craps is one of the more social games in the casino, as groups of players gather around a table and whoop and scream as numbers come up on the dice. A shooter rolls two dice, and if the dice totals 7 or 11 on this "come-out" roll, everyone who has a bet on Pass wins automatically, and everyone with a bet on Don't Pass loses. (Betting on the Don't Pass Line is the opposite of betting on the Pass Line; these pay 1-to-1 odds.) If the come-out roll is 2, 3, or 12, the shooter and all Pass bettors lose. Don't Pass bettors win on 2 or 3. Any other come-out roll becomes "the point," and a marker is placed in that position on the table. The shooter must then throw the point again before throwing a 7. If the shooter succeeds, Pass wins and Don't Pass loses. If the first roll is a 12, no one wins. After the come-out roll, players can also bet on Come and Don't Come. The next throw becomes the Come number, and a Come bet wins if the thrower throws that number before throwing a 7.

To fully understand Pass Lines, points, and other rules, it's best to take one of the instruction courses offered by the casinos. There are lots of betting options, which makes craps one of the more interesting table games. Laying or taking "odds" on or against the point is the only bet in the casino where the player gets fair odds. If the point is 4, there are three ways the shooter can make his point (1–3, 2–2, and 3–1) and six ways to lose by rolling a 7. An odds bet on four, therefore, pays 2 to 1 (or 6 to 3). Lots of places let you take 5x or even 20x odds, shrinking the casino's advantage even further. This refers to the maximum you can bet at the fair odds. At a 5x table, if you bet $5 on the pass line, you can bet up to $25 on the odds. In this case (say the point is 4) if you take full odds and the shooter rolls another 4 before he "sevens out," you'll win even money on your line bet ($5) and fair odds, or 2 to 1 on your odds bet ($50).

Keno

Keno may be played in the casino or in most Las Vegas coffee shops. Every 10–15 minutes a machine selects 20 out of 80 possible winning numbers. To play you must fill out a form for each game you wish to play and pick the numbers you hope will turn up on the keno board. A keno ticket is divided into numbers 1 to 40 on top and 41 to 80 on the bottom. You can pick 1 to 15 numbers on a straight ticket. Depending on what the payout table indicates, you could win $9 on a $1 bet if five out of eight numbers match, and more matching numbers mean more winnings. (The higher value you place on your bet, the more you win if your numbers come up.) A replay ticket simply uses the same numbers you played on the previous ticket. With a split ticket, you can bet different amounts on two or more groups of numbers. The amount you bet is divided among the number of groups

you are playing. A keno runner will take your bet and return with your winning or losing ticket. Many people play $2 or $4 bets while they are having breakfast or lunch. The odds are heavily in favor of the house, but it can be a fun way to pass the time. There are myriad ways of picking numbers, splitting your bet, and so on. The rules are posted at all tables along with keno forms.

Let It Ride

Growing in popularity, Let It Ride can be played on tables with a dealer or at some video machines. Players play a basic five-card poker hand with the goal of getting the best possible hand. (In this game the dealer doesn't have a hand.) A player places three chips of equal value on the table and is dealt three cards. Two community cards are placed face down in the center. If you like your three cards you can place them under the first chip. If you are not happy with your cards, you can indicate to the dealer that you are taking back your bet by scraping the cards on the table toward you, or making a brushing motion with your hand. When all players have made a decision on their three cards, the dealer flips over the first community card, which counts as each player's fourth card. The procedure is repeated with the second community card, completing everyone's hand. A pair of 10s pays even money, two pairs 2 to 1, and so on. A royal flush pays 1,000 to 1.

Poker

Television has made poker one of the most popular casino games, and it's played much the same as you may play with your friends. But in Vegas the stakes are usually quite a bit higher. The dealer handles shuffling and dealing, and the house takes in a few dollars from each pot. Variations of poker include seven-card stud, Omaha and Texas hold 'em; the latter, especially the no-limit variety, is the most popular variation. Any casino with a poker room deals this game—both in tournaments, where all you have to lose is your entry fee, and "ring games" (cash games), where your whole bankroll could be at stake on every hand.

Race and Sports Book

Sports betting in Vegas is huge. Bets on the Super Bowl alone account for $80 million annually. Most of the major casinos have large areas where players can bet on horse races and sports events. Horse and greyhound races are broadcast live from many tracks, and fans can root for their horse or dog on large-screen televisions.

Roulette

One of the simpler games, roulette features a big wheel with numbers 00 through 36 marked in red and black. It's possible to bet on 0 or 00 but neither counts as red or black, or odd or even, so they are colored green on the wheel. Players can bet on individual numbers, groups of numbers, red or black, or odd or even, small (1–18) or big (19–36). Choosing the right number pays at 35 to 1. Choosing a pair of numbers pays 17 to 1, a block of three pays 11 to 1, and so on. Experts advise against betting on 0, 00, 1, 2, and 3, which pay 5 to 1 and offer the worst odds on the table. Many gamblers say it is better to take part in fewer spins, place what you can afford to risk on an even money bet (odd-even or red-black), and walk away whether you win or lose. While that makes statistical sense and applies to any game where the odds are against you, it's not much fun. Roulette chips are purchased in stacks of 20, and when you buy your chips you tell the dealer if you want the value to be $1, $5, $20, and so on. Most roulette tables have a minimum value of each chip, such as $1.

Slots

Every casino has rows and rows of slot machines, and they've become even more popular since slot manufacturers introduced interactive games with bonus rounds based on popular games, TV shows, and other themes. Reel-type machines, where you line up one or more symbols to win, have also

been modernized to allow more extra spins, bells, and whistles. Penny and two-cent slots are becoming hugely popular, though most people bet multiple pennies on each of several lines, making them cost more than 1 cent per spin. Nickel, quarter, and dollar machines are still widely played. Casinos also set aside high-roller slot areas for those willing to pay $5 and up per spin. The odds of winning at a slot machine are set by the casino and vary widely depending on the establishment and machine. Your chance of hitting the jackpot at a quarter slot machine is likely to be 1 in 10,000 or smaller. The house advantage on slots ranges 2–25 percent. Generally, dollar machines pay back at a higher percentage than quarter or nickel machines, but you may win smaller sums (like $50–100) more frequently on nickel and quarter slots. Nonprogressive machines have fixed payback amounts for different winning combinations, such as get three red 7s and win $100, and they pay lower bonuses more frequently. Progressive machines are linked to networks of other machines throughout Nevada and have the potential to pay off in millions of dollars but offer payouts less frequently; a fraction of every coin bet goes into the progressive jackpot pool (you can see the amount increase on a display over the slot cluster until someone hits it).

If you plan to play the slots, take the time to join each casino's slot club. Even if you aren't a heavy gambler or big winner, the time you play can earn points toward free meals, free rooms, and other promotions that you will receive in the mail. Many of the casinos under the same management have slot cards that may be used at sister casinos for cumulative points and rewards. Conventional wisdom also says casinos place their "looser" machines in high-traffic areas where frequent winners may induce others to try their luck.

Video Poker

Video poker is played like regular draw poker, except you are playing against a machine and receive set payoffs for specific hands. Several variations include Jacks or Better, Deuces Wild, and a slew of bonus machines that pay off more for four of a kind and less for the more common and mundane winners such as three of a kind and straights. Many of the machines allow players to choose the denomination played—a nickel to a dollar per hand.

Basically you are dealt a hand, choose which cards to keep or discard, and rack up winnings or losses depending on the cards you are dealt. One of the appeals to this game is that there isn't as much pressure playing a machine as sitting at a table with a bunch of other players, and it's a good way to get more familiar with the game.

Conduct and Customs

ADULT ENTERTAINMENT
Prostitution in Nevada
In Nevada, like everywhere else, sex sells, and outside the Reno and Las Vegas areas, sex is sold. Brothels opened in Virginia City long before any grocery stores and not long after the first saloons. At its peak 150–300 dens of ill repute were operating, and just as the miners fanned out from the Comstock Lode to discover mineral riches across the vast state, the women followed right behind.

Prostitution was a frontier tradition, and though prostitution was not technically legal, it wasn't technically illegal either. A modest house on the edge of town displayed a small red light near the front door. A discreet madam kept the women off the streets and somehow prevented them from scandalizing or blackmailing the married men from all walks of life who used their services.

Military bases sprang up in Nevada during World War II, bringing thousands of soldiers. The base commanders insisted that Reno and Las Vegas close up the brothels, and they never legally reopened. Today, prostitution is officially illegal in Reno's Washoe County, Las Vegas's Clark County, Lake Tahoe's Douglas County, Carson City, and Lincoln County.

Meanwhile, in the northern part of the state, a man named Joe Conforte was openly challenging the vague mishmash of law that regulated the sex industry. The state legislature had tiptoed around it, leaving it up to the counties to legislate on the issue. By the

time Conforte arrived in the 1950s, nearly 50 rules and regulations governed the brothel business. For example, no brothel can operate on a main street; no advertising is permitted; habitual clients can be charged with vagrancy; pimps are verboten; and all brothels must be at least 300 yards from a school or church. Conforte had fought for official legalized prostitution in Reno for years, doing battle with a crusading district attorney who finally succeeded in jailing Conforte for a number of years on charges relating to their disagreements. (For the whole sordid tale, see Jim Sloan's *Nevada—True Tales of the Neon Wilderness*.) But after serving his time, Conforte set up shop at Mustang Ranch, just over the Washoe County line in Storey County. Eventually, allegations that he had paid off county officials started to rankle him. The fact that Mustang Ranch was Storey County's largest taxpayer gave him a certain influence in county politics, and in 1971 Conforte convinced the commissioners to pass Ordinance 38, which legalized prostitution, the first county in the country to do so. Next door, Lyon County quickly followed suit. In 1973 the Nevada Supreme Court upheld the right of counties with fewer than 50,000 people to license brothels.

The Sex Industry Today
Today, a few dozen brothels are active at any one time, with anywhere from a few to 20 working girls on-site. They're regulated by the sheriffs, district attorneys, and

health department. The brothel sex workers are tested regularly for diseases, and brothels pay taxes. Joe Conforte fled the United States in 1991 ahead of several indictments for tax fraud; the federal government seized the Mustang Ranch and auctioned it off in 1999.

Prostitution is still illegal in Las Vegas and Reno. Of course, that doesn't mean it doesn't happen, often under the guise of to-your-room strippers, massage parlors, and nude modeling. Both the client and the prostitute can go to jail if arrested in a street prostitution sting, and although the prostitutes are arrested more often than the clients are, clients are taking a risk when they engage in illegal prostitution. Las Vegas police spend $3 million per year enforcing anti-prostitution laws.

The "gentlemen's clubs" work hard to walk the fine line between tease and please, adopting strict no-nonsense policies against prostitution. If found guilty of encouraging the world's oldest profession, they risk losing their liquor licenses or being shut down (in reality, both amount to the same thing). Still, the strippers (most prefer to be called "exotic dancers") are independent contractors, not employees. While bouncers keep a pretty close eye on the action, even in the clubs' VIP rooms, they can't monitor conversations. Assignations and negotiations could be going on anywhere.

More innocent but hardly subtle use of sex appeal can be found all over Nevada, from topless showgirls and tanned beefcake reviews to corseted cocktail waitresses and model-like blackjack dealers. One of the newer manifestations of casinos' come-hither use of cheesecake is the party pit. Go-go girls gyrate on elevated stages around the blackjack pit. The shows are free; the casino figures the less attention you pay to your cards, the better it is for the house. Party pits also traditionally offer less favorable player rules.

SMOKING AND DRINKING

So many things in Nevada are extreme that it tends to attract extremists. In terms of health, deaths from heart disease and cancer are high. The state has been the highest per-capita consumer of alcohol in the country for decades and also ranks first in deaths from smoking-related diseases: 24 percent of all deaths in Nevada are caused by smoking. (By comparison, in Utah the number is 13 percent.) The large number of seniors who move to Nevada to retire might skew the statistic somewhat, but one in three Nevadans is a smoker. Nevada also claims the largest number of chronic drinkers in the country, twice the national average, and alcohol is as good as free in casinos.

The drinking age in Nevada is 21. If you're of age, you can drink more readily and cheaply than anywhere else in the country. Every casino in the state and many bars remain open 24 hours, and every casino serves free drinks to players. The easiest way to get free booze is to plop down at a video poker bar, stick in a 20, and tip the bartender well. You don't even have to play: Simply buy in, get your comp drink, and cash out. Then go next door and do it all over again. As Max Rubin says in *Comp City,* this technique "has carried many an alkie through some desperate nights in Glitter Gulch."

If you don't even want to buy in, ask any bartender about drink specials. In Las Vegas, $1 draft beers, $2.50 margaritas, and $2 well drinks are common. Most of the casino bars outside Las Vegas offer some variation of the same, but don't drink and drive.

A few years ago Nevada passed laws prohibiting smoking in areas that serve food. While the law is not universally observed in bars, most have erected barriers between their drinking areas and their dining areas. It's not uncommon to see signs proclaiming, "Smoker-friendly bar; smoke-free dining." Smoking is part of the deal in casinos. Some have adopted smoke-free areas, usually an area with a few slot machines and a section of the race and sports book. But they're usually separated from the tobacco users by empty floor space, with nothing to prevent the smoke from wafting over.

Tips for Travelers

DISABILITIES

Nevada is always rebuilding and reinventing itself, so its major casinos and other tourist attractions are usually accessible for people in wheelchairs or with other mobility issues. Most hotels have plenty of wheelchair-accessible rooms and ramps and have at least a few low roll-up tables. Taxis and buses are equipped to ease entering and exiting. Even some nature attractions have boardwalks, transportation, or viewing platforms to make them fun for everyone. Still, casino properties are huge and often crowded, so people with limited mobility may have difficulty maneuvering around and among the casinos, especially on the Las Vegas Strip.

CHILDREN

No one under 21 can play in the casino, but they can walk through. Older kids on their own and younger kids with their parents must be moving along toward some destination—the arcade, movie theater, or restaurant. If you're with your kids and stop somewhere in the casino for some reason, security guards not far behind will ask you to continue on your way. The guards will tell you that both you and the casino can be fined for having youths in a gambling area. You and your kids can stop in a gambling area only if you're standing in a line to see a show or enter a buffet that winds through the casino.

What about 19–20-year-olds who sit down to play? That depends on the casino. The unwritten rule used to be that minors could play but they couldn't win. In other words, a 20-year-old could feed the slots until he was broke, but if he hit a jackpot that required a slot host to fill out IRS paperwork (anything more than $1,200), for which he needed to see identification, the underage player not only wouldn't get paid, he'd get the bum's rush out the door to boot. Court case after court case have upheld the casino's right to refuse to pay; in fact, if the casino did pay, it could get fined or lose its license.

These days, with more and more kids roaming around Las Vegas, some joints check ID religiously; others don't. A few years ago, for example, Bally's found itself in a hassle with the Nevada Gaming Commission for dealing blackjack over a several-hour period to three underage players, one of whom was said to have looked 14 years old. After hearing that the boys lost upward of $6,000, one parent complained to the Gaming Control Board, whose agents reviewed the videotapes of the game and recommended a heavy fine. They didn't require Bally's to return the $6,000, of course.

GAY AND LESBIAN TRAVELERS

Las Vegas prides itself on being a cosmopolitan metropolis. Nevadans are proud of their long-nurtured "if it feels good, do it" philosophy. Yet for all that and the fact that Liberace, Elton John, and Frank Marino all have enjoyed long runs here, neither the Sin City nor the Silver State is all that gay-friendly. It's not that Nevada is hostile to alternative lifestyles; no one outside the occasional redneck or Bible literalist cares who you sleep with. But there are double standards. The age of consent for same-sex relations, for example, is 18; for opposite-sex couples it's 16. Vice cops pay close attention to gay cruising areas and clubs, while well-known hetero swinger clubs often operate with impunity; and, of course, same-sex marriage remains illegal in Nevada.

For the most part, gay and lesbian travelers will find themselves at home in casinos, showrooms, and nightclubs. Las Vegas, Reno, and Lake Tahoe are home to decent gay bars, while the pickings are much slimmer in rural areas. Gay-friendly bars can be found all over Las Vegas, but the biggest concentration lies on Paradise Road just south of East Harmon Avenue. The once and possibly future queen of the "Fruit Loop," as it's affectionately called, is **Gipsy.** Other bars in the area include the

Backdoor Lounge, with drag pageants and a largely Latino clientele. Farther south, **Free Zone** has great pizza, drink specials, and a fun mix of gays and lesbians. Here too is **Buffalo,** a macho denim-and-leather bar.

While same-sex marriage remains illegal in the state, several progressive chapels in Reno will perform commitment ceremonies for same-sex couples. The gay community seems more organized in Reno-Tahoe than in Las Vegas; there's a Gay Pride parade and a Miss Gay Reno pageant held annually. The Winterfest gay and lesbian ski week is held each March.

Health and Safety

WEATHER

Two generalizations apply to Nevada's weather: It's hot in the summer and dry year-round. Always carry water; it's a desert out there. If you're hiking, have a canteen on your belt and a gallon jug on your pack.

The prevailing winds in the southern part of the state are southerlies, which have crossed the fierce Sonoran Desert and hold little moisture. Las Vegas is the driest metropolitan area in the United States, receiving an average of just 3–4 inches of precipitation a year. On top of that, the southern part of the state gets scorched 7–8 months of the year. Temperatures in Las Vegas that reach 110°F are not uncommon in May and September; highs can rise to 115°F in July–August. Laughlin can hit 120°F and usually registers over 20 days per year of the country's highest temperatures. A record-high temperature for the state was recorded in Laughlin in June 1994: a sizzling 125°F. If you're driving, a five-gallon container of water will get you or someone you happen upon through almost any emergency. Any supermarket will sell gallon jugs of spring water; don't run out. You might also buy canned or boxed juices.

Cloudbursts and thunderstorms can strike anywhere in the state but happen mostly in the south. They can dump more rain in an hour than many places receive in six months. These torrential downpours tend to be extremely localized and dangerous, giving rise to raging and roiling water that surges down gullies, washes, and drainages that might have been dry for a decade. The "wet" season is December–March; summer storms and flash floods, known in Las Vegas as "monsoon season," occur June–August.

Since most of the state is around a mile high, winters can be surprisingly severe. The harshest locations for this season are northeastern Nevada from Jarbidge to Ely, with temperatures regularly dropping below zero and the snow remaining for 4–5 months and even longer in some places. Central Nevada is similar. The western and southern sections from Reno to Laughlin have milder and shorter winters, one reason that 80 percent of Nevada's population lives in this "sun belt."

ANIMALS

Nevada is home to scorpions, black widow and brown recluse spiders, mountain lions, bears, and plenty of other animals that can deliver a nasty wound, but by far the most feared is the snake. There are seven different types of rattlers in Nevada, and a couple of them are extremely venomous, but your chances of seeing one or being bitten are slim, and your chances of having a fatal encounter are almost zero. Still, to truly enjoy all Nevada has to offer, you have to tread in areas snakes sometimes like to hang out. Only two deaths in the state have been attributed to snakebites in the last 55 years, so if you give them a wide berth, they'll most likely leave you alone as well.

Rattlesnakes are mostly nocturnal, although they do move around during the day. Most daylight sightings, however, turn out to be Great Basin gopher snakes. These are harmless, but they do make a hissing noise that might sound like a rattle.

The best way to protect against snakebite is by wearing hiking boots. Use caution when walking in rocky areas, around ledges, or near any area that might be a snake den. Try to keep night strolling to a minimum, and if you can't, be extra careful. If you bump into a snake, stay calm, stay still, and when you can, edge away. Experts recommend that you try for a soft footfall so as not to disturb the snakes, which are sensitivity to ground vibration.

In the unlikely event of a bite, stay calm; this slows the heart rate and prevents the poison from spreading as quickly. Keep the bite below heart level. If you can, try to ascertain what kind of snake bit you, but don't catch it; it could bite you again. A fang mark or two will be apparent, the area will swell and discolor, and it will hurt. Loosely bandage above and below the bite and wash it with soap and water. The old way of dealing with a snake bite, which some still subscribe to, was to take a sterilized knife, cut a quarter-inch incision between and slightly past the fang marks, then keep squeezing out the venom until you reach a doctor. But this technique removes only a small amount of poison. If you have one of the suction-cup snakebite extractors handy, you can try that. But the best thing to do is hightail it to a doctor.

Remember that snakes are as afraid of you as you are of them. Because they'll sense your presence before you will theirs, they'll generally be long gone by the time you get to where they were. Caution is always the rule, but don't let the fact that you share the backcountry with snakes deter you from using and enjoying it.

CRIME

The transience and low economic status of many people attracted to Nevada by a boomtown mentality are evident in a number of ways. Nevada has the highest rate of high school dropouts in the country and one of the lowest proportions of college-educated citizens. This makes for a large population of undereducated and economically challenged people. Add to that lots of cash floating around and hordes of unwary tourists, and it's no wonder Nevada's crime rate is among the highest in the country. One study ranks the state as the fifth-most litigious, based on the number of lawsuits filed. Crimes inside casinos are rare, but alcohol flows freely, so brawls on the street are not. Common sense is to stay in well-lighted areas and travel in groups, which will go a long way to ensuring you don't become a victim.

Maps and Tourist Information

The biggest, most beautiful, and most informative Nevada landscape map is produced by **Raven Maps** (800/237-0798, www.ravenmaps.com). It's available for $30 (paper) or $50 (laminated). The Nevada **Department of Transportation** (1263 S. Stewart St., Carson City, 775/888-7627, www.nevadadot.com/traveler/maps) also has wall-size maps of the roads, counties, and natural features. In addition, it publishes an indispensable *Nevada Map Atlas* of 127 quadrangle maps of the state, which include all the unpaved roads.

Every major library in the state has a Nevada room or a special collection of local-interest titles.

The three main libraries for researching specific aspects of the Nevada experience are the **Getchell Library** on the University of Nevada, Reno, campus (1664 N. Virginia St., 775/784-1110), the **Lied Library** on the University of Nevada, Las Vegas, campus (4505 S. Maryland Pkwy., 702/895-2286), and the **State Library** (100 N. Stewart St., Carson City, 800/922-2880).

The best general source of information about the state, *Nevada Magazine* (401 N. Carson St., Suite 100, Carson City, 775/687-5416, www.nevadamagazine.com), has been financed by the state government since the 1930s. The "Nevada Events and Shows" section provides comprehensive listings of things to do around the state; the website provides contact information for convention and visitors bureaus, chambers of commerce, events hotlines, and more.

Visitor information is also available through a number of state and federal agencies: List:**Nevada Commission on Tourism:** 401 N. Carson St., Carson City, 775/687-4322 or 800/NEVADA-8—800/638-2328, www.travelnevada.com

Nevada Division of State Parks: 901 S. Stewart St., 5th Floor, Suite 5005, Carson City, 775/684-2770, www.parks.nv.gov.

Great Basin National Park: 100 Great Basin National Park, Baker, 775/234-7331, www.nps.gov/grba

Lake Mead National Recreation Area: 601 Nevada Hwy., Boulder City, 702/293-8906, www.nps.gov/lake

Bureau of Land Management: 1340 Financial Blvd., Reno, 775/861-6400, www.nv.blm.gov/nv/st/en

Humboldt-Toiyabe National Forest: 1200 Franklin Way, Sparks, 775/331-5644, www.fs.fed.us/r4/htnf

Nevada Division of Wildlife: 1100 Valley Rd., Reno, 775/688-1500, www.ndow.org

State Library and Archives: 716 N. Carson St., Suite 6, Carson City, 775/687-8393, www.nevadaculture.org

Road Condition Report: 877/NV-ROADS—877/687-6237

RESOURCES

Gambling Glossary

call In poker, to match a previous player's bet.

double down In blackjack, the player's option to double the amount of his bet and receive one additional card to complete his hand.

expectation The statistical profit or loss that would accrue if a bet were made thousands of times. If you won $1 every time a coin came up "heads" and lost $1 every time it was "tails," your expectation would be $0. But if you won $2 for every head and lost $1 for every tail, your expectation would be $0.50 (50 heads = $100; 50 tails = -$50, for a profit of $50; $50 / 100 iterations = $0.50). Expectation can be positive or (in casino games, almost always) negative.

field in craps, an even-money bet that the shooter's next roll will total 2, 3, 4, 9, 10, 11, or 12. There are 16 dice combinations that come up winners and 20 that are losers.

flop the first three shared cards that are revealed all at once in poker games with five community cards. The next card is called "the turn" or "fourth street"; the final community card is "the river" or "fifth street."

odds the potential payout for a winning bet; 2-to-1 odds means the winner will receive $2 for every $1 he bets (he also gets his original $1 wager back). Also, a craps bet made after the come-out roll, in which the player receives true odds that the shooter will (or will not, if the bettor played the "don't pass" line) make his point before rolling a 7.

pari-mutuel The pools of money from which winning bets are paid. Under this system, used by North American racetracks, the odds are determined by the amount bet on each entrant in the race. A horse with $20,000 worth of bets on it out of the $100,000 total wagered in the race would pay 4-to-1 because four times more money was bet on the other horses ($80,000) than was bet on him.

reel machines Mechanical slot machines with three or more wheels with symbols on them. Line up the right combination of symbols to win.

ring game In poker, a game played for cash rather than for tournament prize money.

toke A tip given to a casino dealer or cocktail waitress. Short for "token of appreciation."

Suggested Reading

For an exhaustive bibliography on Nevada and gambling, see *Nevada—An Annotated Bibliography* by Stanley Paher (Las Vegas: Nevada Publications, 1980); and *Gambling Bibliography* by Jack Gardner (Farmington Hills, MI: Gale, 1980). Although both were published over 30 years ago, they are still the most comprehensive general bibliographies available.

More recently published titles on Nevada are available from **University of Nevada Press** (775/784-6573 or 877/NV-BOOKS—877/682-6657, www.nvbooks.nevada.edu); **Huntington Press** (800/244-2224, www.greatstuff4gamblers.com), Nevada's largest commercial publisher, is another fine resource.

For the best current books about gambling, request catalogs from the **Gambler's Book Club** (800/634-6243, www.gamblersbook.com). Huntington Press also publishes and distributes a number of books about gambling.

A visit to any bookstore specializing in Nevada themes will turn up many books on interesting Nevada-related topics including the California Trail, the Pony Express, Native Americans, the Basques (check out the University of Nevada Press's Basque series), ghost towns, and the natural history and geology of the Great Basin. Larger museums in the state usually offer a good selection of Nevada-related books.

TRAVEL AND DESCRIPTION

Compton, Jeffrey. *The Las Vegas Advisor Guide to Slot Clubs.* Las Vegas: Huntington Press, 1995. The ratings may be out of date, but Compton's tips on making the most of your gambling dollar and how slot clubs operate make it worth picking up a copy.

Moreno, Richard. *Nevada Curiosities: Quirky Characters, Roadside Oddities & Other Offbeat Stuff.* Guilford, CT: Globe Pequot Press, 2009. Moreno takes you inside some of the state's lesser-known and not-so-obvious tourist stops.

Tingley, Joseph V., and Kris Ann Pizarro. *Traveling America's Loneliest Road: A Geologic and Natural History Tour through Nevada along U.S. Highway 50.* Reno: University of Nevada Press, 2000. A guide to geologic features and other points of interest along U.S. 50 between Lake Tahoe and Great Basin National Park.

Toll, David W. *The Complete Nevada Traveler: The Affectionate and Intimately Detailed Guidebook to the Most Interesting State in America.* Virginia City, NV: Gold Hill Publications, 2008. Short histories and quick stops on a voyage around the Silver State.

Wheeler, Sessions. *The Black Rock Desert.* Caldwell, ID: Caxton Printers, 1978. Classic travelogue about the Black Rock Desert.

GEOLOGY AND ENVIRONMENT

Floyd, Ted, et al. *Atlas of the Breeding Birds of Nevada.* Reno: University of Nevada Press, 2007. Nevada is an important winter home and migratory rest stop for raptors, songbirds, and waterfowl. Birders will appreciate this indispensable guide.

Ingram, Stephen. *Cacti, Agaves, and Yuccas of California and Nevada.* Los Olivos, CA: Cachuma Press, 2008. Identification guide to the succulents of the Nevada deserts.

Jackson, Louise A. *Sierra Nevada Before History.* Missoula, MT: Mountain Press Publishing, 2010. The story of the southern Sierra Nevada's birth, geologic and natural history, and prehistoric cultures.

Kavanaugh, James J. *Nevada Trees & Wildflowers: An Introduction to Familiar Species.* Chandler, AZ: Waterford Press,

2008. A companion for photographers and horticulturists.

RECREATION

Dickerson, Richard. *Nevada Angler's Guide—Fish Tails in the Sagebrush.* Portland, OR: Frank Amato Publications, 1997. A handy, useful, and authoritative guide to 116 of the most accessible fishing spots in Nevada.

Gibson, Elizabeth. *Hiking Nevada.* Helena, MT: Falcon Press, 2006. Find the trails to fit your interests and ability level.

Glass, Mary Ellen, and Al Glass. *Touring Nevada: A Historic and Scenic Guide.* Reno: University of Nevada Press, 1983. An excellent guide, well organized into specific "circle tours" for those interested in the historical significance of the sights of Nevada.

Grubbs, Bruce. *Hiking Nevada.* Helena, MT: Falcon Publishing, 1994. A good guidebook for hikes all around Nevada that includes maps.

Hart, John. *Hiking the Great Basin.* San Francisco: Sierra Club Books, 1980. An indispensable guidebook for anyone wanting to explore the backcountry of Nevada. Wonderfully written, accurate, and detailed, with a superb attitude.

Hauserman, Tim. *Cross-country Skiing in the Sierra Nevada: The Best Resorts & Touring Centers in California & Nevada.* Woodstock, VT: Countryman Press, 2007. Say "Nevada skiing" and most people think of rushing down pristine powder. Hauserman gives Nordic fans their own reason for embracing the state.

Kelsey, Michael. *Hiking and Climbing in Great Basin National Park.* Provo, UT: Kelsey Publishing, 1988. The best book available on hiking Great Basin Park includes nearly 50 hikes with maps and photos for each.

Nemec, Jan. *Flyfisher's Guide to Nevada.* Belgrade, MT: Wilderness Adventures Press, 2010. Your battlefield plan for stalking and landing the state's legendary rainbows and elusive cutthroats.

Smith, Julie. *50 Hikes in the Sierra Nevada: Hikes and Backpacks from Lake Tahoe to Sequoia National Park.* Woodstock, VT: Countryman Press, 2009. With all that wilderness out there, you need this guide to get you to that perfectly challenging and scenic spot for your commune with nature.

White, Michael. *Nevada Wilderness Areas and Great Basin National Park—A Hiking and Backpacking Guide.* Berkeley, CA: Wilderness Press, 1997. Covers a dozen wilderness areas plus Great Basin with a total of 56 trips. Indispensable for anyone wanting to explore the highest peaks and most remote ranges as well as some of the most popular and accessible wilderness areas in Nevada.

HISTORY

Cahlan, Florence Lee, and John F. Cahlan. *Water—A History of Las Vegas.* Las Vegas: Las Vegas Water District, 1975. Written by the longtime publisher of the *Las Vegas Review-Journal* and his reporter wife, this is a sprawling two-volume history of Las Vegas that "shows how its evolution as a city closely paralleled the development of its water."

Convis, Charles L. *Outlaw Tales of Nevada: True Stories of Nevada's Most Famous Robbers, Rustlers, and Bandits.* Guilford, CT: TwoDot, 2006. Jailbreaks, train robberies, gentlemen bandits, and cold-blooded killers, they're all here in chilling exquisite detail.

De Quille, Dan. *History of the Big Bonanza: An Authentic Account of the Discovery, History, and Working of the World-renowned Comstock Lode of Nevada.* New York: Crowell, 1947. Effectively combines scholarly history, personality sketches, and the humor for which De Quille became legendary.

Ford, Jean, Betty Glass, and Martha Gould. *Women in Nevada History: An Annotated Bibliography of Published Sources.* Reno: Nevada Women's History Project, 2000. An excellent resource for finding out everything you ever wanted to know about women in the Silver State's history.

Grubbs, Bruce. *It Happened in Nevada: Remarkable Events That Shaped History.* Guilford, CT: Globe Pequot Press, 2010. Little-known details enliven Gibson's lively retelling of familiar events in Nevada's history.

Hall, Shawn. *Connecting the West: Historic Railroad Stops and Stage Stations in Elko County, Nevada.* Reno: University of Nevada Press, 2002. Informative guide to historic railroad and stage stations in northeastern Nevada. As in his earlier volumes, Hall includes a history of each site along with historic and contemporary photos, directions, and maps.

Hall, Shawn. *Old Heart of Nevada: Ghost Towns and Mining Camps of Elko County.* Reno: University of Nevada Press, 1998. Identifies and locates the ghost towns and old mining camps of Elko County and recounts their colorful histories. Divides Elko County into five easily accessible regions, lists the historic sites within each region, and provides directions to reach them.

Hall, Shawn. *Preserving the Glory Days: Ghost Towns and Mining Camps of Nye County, Nevada.* Reno: University of Nevada Press, 1999. Nevada's largest and least-populated county is also the site of many of the state's most colorful ghost towns and mining camps. A lively, informative record of Nevada's isolated interior, this book provides historical information on nearly 200 sites and a current assessment of each one, with clear directions for locating each site.

Hall, Shawn. *Romancing Nevada's Past: Ghost Towns and Historic Sites of Eureka, Lander,* *and White Pine Counties.* Reno: University of Nevada Press, 1994. A history of 175 significant sites, with historic photos and an update on the present condition of each ghost town or landmark along with easy-to-follow directions to each one.

Harpster, Jack. *100 Years in the Nevada Governor's Mansion.* Las Vegas: Stephens Press, 2009. Personal and journalistic accounts along with historic photographs tell the stories of Nevada's governors, first ladies, and children who called the mansion home.

Hulse, James W. *The Silver State.* Reno: University of Nevada Press, 1998. This cohesive and readable history provides students and general readers with an accessible account of Nevada's colorful history, exploring many dimensions of Nevada's experience and its people.

James, Ronald M. *The Roar and the Silence: A History of Virginia City and the Comstock Lode.* Reno: University of Nevada Press, 1998. This lively, thoughtful book chronicles the area's history from its earliest days through the early 20th century, when the lode finally gave out and the Comstock sank into silent decay, up to the present, when Virginia City and its environs found new life, first as a community of bohemians and artists and more recently as a tourist attraction.

Kasindorf, Jeanie. *The Nye County Brothel Wars.* New York: Linden Press, 1985. Spellbinding account of how an "outsider," who tried to open and run a brothel in Pahrump, ran afoul of the Nye County Sheriff's Department, district attorney, established whorehouse owners, and their henchmen, and how his battle against harassment, arrest, attempted murder, low-level and high-level corruption, slavery, and racketeering eventually was taken up by the FBI and U.S. attorney and tried in federal court.

Kling, Dwayne. *The Rise of the Biggest Little City: An Encyclopedic History of Reno Gaming,*

1931–1981. Reno: University of Nevada Press, 1999. The first 50 years of Reno's gaming and gambling industry, written by a long-time gaming executive and illustrated with historic photos.

Land, Barbara, and Myrick Land. *A Short History of Las Vegas.* Reno: University of Nevada Press, 2004. A lively history, illustrated with historic and recent photographs, telling the story of the Las Vegas area from the earliest visitors 11,000 years ago up to the present.

Land, Barbara, and Myrick Land. *A Short History of Reno.* Reno: University of Nevada Press, 1995. An entertaining and anecdotal history of Reno's colorful past and the larger-than-life characters who left their mark on the city, illustrated with dozens of black-and-white photos.

Laxalt, Robert. *Nevada—A History.* New York: W. W. Norton, 1977. A very personal, lyrical, and selective account of the history and shape of the state by one of Nevada's best-known and best-loved writers.

Lewis, Oscar. *The Town That Died Laughing.* Reno: University of Nevada Press, 1986. The story of Austin, Nevada—rambunctious early-day mining camp—and its renowned newspaper, the *Reese River Reveille.*

Marschall, John P. *Jews in Nevada.* Reno: University of Nevada Press, 2008. Meticulous research and attention to detail result in an engaging account of the role of Jewish people in settling Nevada, their role in crime and crime prevention, and their struggle against anti-Semitism to establish thriving communities.

Moreno, Richard. *Mysteries and Legends of Nevada: True Stories of the Unsolved and Unexplained.* Guilford, CT: Globe Pequot Press, 2010. The facts and the postulates behind Nevada's historical mysteries: Who killed Bugsy Siegel? Do relatives of Bigfoot and the Loch Ness Monster reside in Nevada?

Moreno, Richard. *Roadside History of Nevada.* Missoula, MT: Mountain Press Publishing, 2000. Memorable tales of Nevada's places and people, written with a historian's nose for details and a traveler's sense of fun, with 140 photos and detailed maps showing how to get to every place described.

Paher, Stanley W. *Nevada Ghost Towns & Desert Atlas.* Las Vegas: Nevada Publications, 2009. The definitive guide to boomtown ruins, historically significant towns, and the rich history of the Comstock Lode.

Pileggi, Nicholas. *Casino: Love and Honor in Las Vegas.* New York: Simon & Schuster, 1995. The basis for the film *Goodfellas* is a gripping account of how the mob ran and eventually lost control of Las Vegas.

Reid, Ed, and Ovid Demaris. *The Green Felt Jungle.* New York: Pocket Books, 1964. The classic book in the diatribe style describing Las Vegas as "a corrupt jungle of iniquity."

Reid, John B., and Ronald M. James, eds. *Uncovering Nevada's Past: A Primary Source History of the Silver State.* Reno: University of Nevada Press, 2004. In the words of luminaries such as Sarah Winnemucca and Mark Twain, this history uses dozens of original documents and eyewitness accounts to chart Nevada's progression from gold rush to outdoor and gambling mecca.

Sloan, Jim. *Nevada—True Tales from the Neon Wilderness.* Salt Lake City, UT: University of Utah Press, 1993. Sloan uses a reporter's eye, a novelist's pacing and plot, and a Nevadan's sensitivity to shed light on the people and atmosphere that make the Silver State unique.

GAMBLING

Anderson, Ian. *Turning The Tables on Las Vegas.* New York: Vintage Books, 1976. Ian Anderson was a pseudonym for R. Kent London, a highly successful and anonymous card counter, who goes into extraordinary detail about playing and betting strategies, camouflage, interaction with the pit personnel, and maintaining a winning attitude. Required reading for aspiring counters.

Bass, Thomas. *Eudaemonic Pie.* Lincoln, NE: IUniverse, 2000. A true hippie adventure story about a group of physicists at the University of California, Santa Cruz, who invented a computer that fit in a shoe to beat the casino at roulette.

Castleman, Deke. *Whale Hunt in the Desert: The Secret Las Vegas of Superhost Steve Cyr.* Las Vegas: Huntington Press, 2004. Inside story on casino hosts who cater to high-stakes gamblers, known in the business as "whales."

Ortiz, Darwin. *On Casino Gambling.* New York: Dodd, Mead & Company, 1986. One of the best-written and most useful how-to books for playing casino games.

Rubin, Max. *Comp City—A Guide to Free Las Vegas Vacations.* Las Vegas: Huntington Press, 2001. A former casino executive, Rubin quit his job to write this book, revealing the best-kept secrets in the casino industry about comps—free rooms, food, beverages, and shows.

Scott, Jean. *The Frugal Gambler.* Las Vegas: Huntington Press, 1998. The world's preeminent low-rolling casino buster reveals her secrets for staying free at hotel-casinos, beating casino promotions, eating and drinking on the house, and getting bumped from airplanes and flying free.

Solkey, Lee. *Dummy Up and Deal.* Las Vegas: GBC Press, 1980. Written by a Las Vegan who earned a degree in urban ethnology and dealt blackjack for seven years as part of her "field study," the book discusses with great authority the dealer culture, language, and territorial domains as well as the dealer relationship with the casino.

BIOGRAPHY

Canfield, Gae Whitney. *Sarah Winnemucca of the Northern Paiutes.* Norman, OK: University of Oklahoma Press, 1983. Biography of the daughter of Chief Winnemucca, whose book *Life Among the Piutes* became a classic.

Garrison, Omar. *Howard Hughes in Las Vegas.* Secaucus, NJ: Lyle Stuart, 1970. Everything about this troubled, mysterious billionaire is gripping, but this book, centered around the four years Hughes spent sequestered on the ninth floor of the Desert Inn, is especially eye-opening, shedding light on the public events and private life of the recluse as he set about to buy and redesign the city that may well have been "his true spiritual home."

Hillyer, Katharine. *Mark Twain: Young Reporter in Virginia City.* Reno: Nevada Publications, 1997. Tells the story of Twain's life as a young reporter in Virginia City, which was the beginning of his literary career.

Hopkins, A. D., and K. J. Evans. *The First 100: Portraits of the Men and Women Who Shaped Las Vegas.* Las Vegas: Huntington Press, 1999. One hundred in-depth profiles of the men and women who helped transform Las Vegas from a desert watering hole into the city it is today. Produced by two staff writers of the *Las Vegas Review-Journal.*

Hopkins, Sarah Winnemucca. *Life Among the Piutes: Their Wrongs and Claims.* Reno: University of Nevada Press, 1994. Daughter of Chief Winnemucca, born around 1844, writes the story of her life and her people.

Seagraves, Anne. *High-spirited Women of the West.* Hayden, ID: Wesanne Publications, 1992. Includes stories about the lives of several women important in Nevada's history, including Sarah Winnemucca, Jeanne Elizabeth Wier, and Helen Jane Wiser Stewart. Seagraves has written several good books about women in the West, all published by Wesanne Publications, including *Women of the Sierra* (1990),

Women Who Charmed the West (1991), *Soiled Doves: Prostitution in the Early West* (1994), and *Daughters of the West* (1996).

LITERATURE

Glotfelty, Cheryll, ed. *Literary Nevada: Writings from the Silver State.* Reno: University of Nevada Press, 2008. A variety of styles and voices capture the quintessential Nevada viewpoint, with all its complexities and contradictions.

McLaughlin, Mark. *Sierra Stories: True Tales of Tahoe* Volumes 1 and 2. Carnelian Bay, CA: Mic Mac Publishing. 1997–1998. Stories about Lake Tahoe and the Tahoe area.

McMurtry, Larry. *The Desert Rose.* New York: Simon & Schuster, 1983. An affectionate and poignant little character study of an aging showgirl and her ties—men, daughter, neighbors, friends, and coworkers—that McMurtry wrote over a three-week period during a lull in the writing of his epic *Lonesome Dove.*

Moore, Roberta, and Scott Slovic, eds. *Wild Nevada: Testimonies on Behalf of the Desert.*

Reno: University of Nevada Press, 2005. A tome that looks beyond the neon and under the mushroom cloud to uncover Nevada's rich, rugged, delicate beauty. Far from a manifesto on preserving nature, this book brings two diverse authors together to produce an ode to their beloved state.

Thompson, Hunter S. *Fear and Loathing in Las Vegas.* New York: Random House, 1998. Thompson's classic drug-addled novel.

Tronnes, Mike, ed. *Literary Las Vegas: The Best Writing about America's Most Fabulous City.* New York: Henry Holt & Company, 1995. A collection of previously published articles about Sin City by two dozen top wordsmiths: Tom Wolfe, Hunter S. Thompson, John Gregory Dunne, Joan Didion, Noël Coward, Michael Herr, and many more.

Twain, Mark. *Roughing It.* New York: Oxford University Press, 1996. Twain self-deprecatingly illustrates the foibles and failings of life in Nevada mining country through long narrative, wide exaggeration, and tall tales.

Internet Resources

VISITOR INFORMATION

Nevada's cities and regions maintain visitor information sites with links to area hotels, amusements, and recreational facilities. Many also produce online or print visitors guides. See these sites for specific information about the happenings during your visit:

- **Las Vegas:** www.visitlasvegas.com, www.vegas.com
- **Laughlin:** www.visitlaughlin.com
- **Reno and Lake Tahoe:** www.visitrenotahoe.com, www.gotorenotahoe.com
- **Carson City:** www.visitcarsoncity.com
- **Virginia City:** www.virginiacity-nv.org

- **Humboldt Valley:** www.cowboycountry.org
- **Great Basin:** http://ponyexpressnevada.com

Travel Nevada
http://travelnevada.com

The official site of the Nevada Commission on Tourism, with hotel deals, travel packages, and tourist attractions listed by town.

Nevada Tourism Alliance
www.nevadatourismalliance.com

Coordinates Nevada's regional tourism offices to promote the state's qualities in order to attract business and leisure travelers as well as the businesses that cater to them.

Las Vegas Convention and Visitors Authority
www.lvcva.com
The authority works to fill southern Nevada's 150,000 hotel rooms with vacationers, conventioneers, and business travelers. It runs the massive and technologically advanced Las Vegas Convention Center.

Nevada Department of Transportation
www.nevadadot.com
The site has traveler information, speed limits, weather conditions, maps, and highway safety information.

RECREATION
Nevada Division of State Parks
http://parks.nv.gov
A wealth of information on state parks, including fee schedules, hunting, fishing, camping, day-use facilities, special events, and conservation efforts.

Bureau of Land Management
www.blm.gov/nv/st/en.html
The state field office for the Bureau of Land Management has a nifty brochure on conservation efforts and the bountiful opportunities that public lands provide, as well as information on hunting, camping, and off-roading on federal land.

CULTURE
Indian Territory
http://nevadaindianterritory.com
Works to advance the political and economic causes of Nevada's Native Americans and to foster understanding of Indian ways by presenting cultural and artistic displays of their lifestyles and history. Download the beautiful brochure from the site.

University of Nevada
www.unlv.edu and www.unr.edu
The sites have enrollment statistics, applications, and sporting event schedules for Nevada's four-year universities. In addition, you'll find links to the university libraries and on-campus museums, art galleries, and gardens.

NEWSPAPERS
Las Vegas Review-Journal
www.lvrj.com
Las Vegas's major newspaper, its "Neon" section profiles the weekend's hottest events and lists the entertainment options for the coming week. Margo Bartlett Pesek's Sunday "Trip of the Week" chronicles interesting places to visit and day trips from Las Vegas.

Las Vegas Sun
www.lasvegassun.com
The other, smaller, and more liberal Vegas daily, it reports on big issue events, with less focus on day-to-day news and events.

Reno Gazette-Journal
www.rgj.com
Click the "Metromix" tab on the home page for information on restaurants, nightclubs, bars, and concerts.

Index

List of Maps

www.moon.com

DESTINATIONS | ACTIVITIES | BLOGS | MAPS | BOOKS

MOON.COM is ready to help plan your next trip! Filled with fresh trip ideas and strategies, author interviews, informative travel blogs, a detailed map library, and descriptions of all the Moon guidebooks, Moon.com is all you need to get out and explore the world—or even places in your own backyard. While at Moon.com, sign up for our monthly e-newsletter for updates on new releases, travel tips, and expert advice from our on-the-go Moon authors. As always, when you travel with Moon, expect an experience that is uncommon and truly unique.

MOON IS ON FACEBOOK—BECOME A FAN!
JOIN THE MOON PHOTO GROUP ON FLICKR